THE UNIVERSI.
WINCHI

*International Perspectives and Empirical
Findings on Child Participation*

International Perspectives and Empirical Findings on Child Participation

From Social Exclusion to Child-Inclusive Policies

Edited by Tali Gal

and

Benedetta Faedi Duramy

OXFORD
UNIVERSITY PRESS

OXFORD
UNIVERSITY PRESS

Oxford University Press is a department of the University of
Oxford. It furthers the University's objective of excellence in research,
scholarship, and education by publishing worldwide.

Oxford   New York
Auckland   Cape Town   Dar es Salaam   Hong Kong   Karachi
Kuala Lumpur   Madrid   Melbourne   Mexico City   Nairobi
New Delhi   Shanghai   Taipei   Toronto

With offices in
Argentina   Austria   Brazil   Chile   Czech Republic   France   Greece
Guatemala   Hungary   Italy   Japan   Poland   Portugal   Singapore
South Korea   Switzerland   Thailand   Turkey   Ukraine   Vietnam

Oxford is a registered trademark of Oxford University Press
in the UK and certain other countries.

Published in the United States of America by
Oxford University Press
198 Madison Avenue, New York, NY 10016

© Oxford University Press 2015

Library of Congress Cataloging-in-Publication Data
Gal, Tali.
International perspectives and empirical findings on child participation :
from social exclusion to child-inclusive policies / Tali Gal, Benedetta Faedi Duramy.
    pages cm
Includes index.
ISBN 978–0–19–936698–9 (hardback)
1. Children—Political activity.   2. Children's rights.   I. Faedi Duramy, Benedetta.   II. Title.
HQ784.P5G35 2015
323.3′52—dc23
2014037066

9 8 7 6 5 4 3 2 1
Printed in the United States of America
on acid-free paper

To our children Guy, Maya, and Leonardo

CONTENTS

ACKNOWLEDGMENTS

This book is the product of a 2013 workshop hosted by the University of Haifa School of Criminology and Haruv Institute at the Hebrew University, with additional financial assistance from Aminut Foundation for the Treatment of Violence in the Family and in Society.

We are deeply thankful to the participants of the workshop – most of the authors of this book's chapters – for sharing their extensive knowledge and promoting the overall coherence of the book.

We are also extremely grateful to OUP's staff who helped deliver this book in its final form, and in particular to Dana Bliss and Brianna Marron for their patience and professional assistance throughout the production process. In the spirit of child participation, our children (those who were interested) were involved in the process too. We are very thankful to Guy Guttman (aged 11) for contributing the concept for the book's cover, and to Leonardo Duramy (aged 2) for posing. Special thanks to Barron Bixler as a photographer. Finally, we are both very grateful for having such wonderful and supporting partners – Omri Guttman and Johan Duramy – without whom editing this book would have not been possible.

ABOUT THE EDITORS

Tali Gal

Tali Gal is an Assistant Professor and Head of the MA Program at the University of Haifa School of Criminology. Dr. Gal's research interests, teaching, and publications involve children's rights, restorative justice, victims' rights, and therapeutic jurisprudence. Her book *Child Victims and Restorative Justice—A Needs–Rights Model* was published by Oxford University Press in 2011. Prior to her academic career she practiced law as a children's rights advocate and Legal Advisor at the Israeli National Council for the Child.

Benedetta Faedi Duramy

Benedetta Faedi Duramy is an Associate Professor at Golden Gate University School of Law in San Francisco. She obtained her doctoral degree from Stanford Law School, Stanford University, where she received numerous awards for her extensive research and scholarship on gender-based violence, with a special focus on Haiti. She is the author of several book chapters and articles on human rights, gender, and children's rights. Her book *Gender and Violence in Haiti: Women's Path from Victims to Agents* was published by Rutgers University Press in 2014.

ABOUT THE CONTRIBUTORS

Nicholas Bala has been a Law Professor at Queen's University in Kingston, Canada, since 1980. He is an internationally recognized expert on legal issues related to children, families, and the justice system, focusing on such issues as parental rights and responsibilities after divorce, including alienation, young offenders, child witnesses and child abuse, spousal abuse and its effects on children. Much of his research is interdisciplinary.

Sharon Bessell holds a PhD in Politics from Monash University. She is a senior lecturer in the Crawford School of Public Policy at the Australian National University and Director of the Children's Policy Centre. Sharon's research focuses on social policy for children, with a focus on human rights, citizenship, and inclusive policy and practice. She has a keen interest in research methodology and has published widely on undertaking research with children. Sharon has worked in Australia, Southeast Asia, and the Pacific as a researcher with nongovernment organizations, and as a consultant.

Rachel Birnbaum is an Associate Professor, cross-appointed with Childhood Studies (Interdisciplinary Programs) & Social Work at King's University College–Western University in London, Ontario, Canada. She presents, publishes and conducts research related to children's participation and families involved in separation and divorce, child legal representation, and access to family justice.

Gale Burford is Emeritus Professor of Social Work and past Director of the Child Welfare Training Partnership at the University of Vermont. His research and training, and continued involvement in semi-retirement as an independent contractor, has focused mainly on child, youth, and family interventions and organizational change in statutory settings. Gale came to his first university appointment after a decade of direct social work practice and senior management experience in services for children, young people, and their families. He has provided consultation, training, and program evaluation with a wide range of services internationally. Gale is a graduate of St. Martin's University (BA), the University of Washington (MSW), and the University of Stirling (PhD).

Emily Buss is a Professor of Law at University of Chicago Law School. Her research interests include children's and parents' rights and the legal system's allocation of authority and responsibility for children's development among parent, child, and state. She has worked with students to propose court reform in the foster care system. She is currently developing a pilot program to implement and evaluate reforms in the delinquency division of the juvenile court designed to foster meaningful youth participation.

Bronagh Byrne is a Lecturer in Social Policy in the School of Sociology, Social Policy and Social Work at Queen's University Belfast. Bronagh's background is in the area of young people, disability, and education, in which she attained her doctorate. She also has expertise on children's rights, with a focus on the application of children's rights standards to local practice. Her most recent publications have included an examination of the rights of children with disabilities, and, along with Laura Lundy and Lesley Emerson, of working with young children as co-researchers.

Judith Cashmore is Professor of Socio-legal Research and Policy, Faculty of Law, University of Sydney, as well as Adjunct Professor at Southern Cross University. Her research concerns children's involvement in legal proceedings related to child protection, out-of-home care, child sexual assault, and family law. Much of Judy's research has focused on children's perceptions of legal and other processes that affect their lives and the implications for policy and practice.

Tara M. Collins is Assistant Professor, School of Child and Youth Care, at Ryerson University. She holds a PhD in law, focusing on international child rights, from the University of London. Her professional experiences include work for University College Dublin as the Marie Curie Transfer-of-Knowledge Fellow in Child Rights; University of Ottawa; a national-level nongovernmental organization; and the Canadian federal government and Parliament. In addition to participation and monitoring, her research considers rights-based approaches; the United Nations Convention on the Rights of the Child's general principles and general measures of implementation, the role and efforts of civil society, including business; and responses to violence.

Francine Cyr has been a Professor of Psychology at the Université de Montréal since 1992. Her research interests and clinical practice focus on the effects of separation and divorce on children, family mediation, parental alienation, assessment and management of high-conflict cases, and children's participation in parental separation. Much of her work relates to children and families involved in the family justice system.

Robyn Fitzgerald is a researcher with the Centre for Children & Young People (CCYP) at Southern Cross University. Her main area of research interest is the participation of children in family law. Robyn has undertaken research projects through the CCYP that seek to better understand the views and perspectives of children across the many settings of their lives.

Sarah Gallagher is an independent consultant and trainer in child welfare, youth justice, organizational development and change management. She managed the Child Welfare Training Partnership in Vermont for the past ten years. Prior to that she worked in child protection and youth justice as a social worker, trainer and regional manager for fifteen years. Her BA is from Harvard University and her MSW from the University of Vermont.

Anne Graham is Professor of Childhood Studies and Director of the Centre for Children and Young People at Southern Cross University, Australia. Anne's background is in education, sociology, and social policy. Her research and professional interests include children's social and emotional well-being, participation and engagement in schools, ethical issues in researching with children and young people, and teacher learning.

Jodi Hall, MSW, EdD, is an Assistant Professor at North Carolina State University. Her professional experiences include child welfare, social work administration, staff development, and teaching at community college and university levels. Her areas of interest are low-wealth families, child welfare, and social work field education. Her current and past publications focus on African American families and older adults. Her research is framed around critical race theory and social justice. She is the Director of MSW Field Education. Dr. Hall is currently co-principal investigator on a grant from the National Institute of Health to reduce the incidence of suicide among college students and principal investigator on a Health Resources and Services Administration (*HRSA*) of the U.S. Department of Health and Human Services (HHS) grant to increase the behavioral health care workforce serving 16–25 year olds. She is actively involved in the Council on Social Work Education and serves as accreditation site visitor.

Lynne Marie Kohm is a Professor of Family Law at Regent University School of Law in Virginia Beach. She is licensed to practice law in five jurisdictions and teaches family and juvenile law. She has written fifty-six articles on children and families. Her seminal book is *Family Manifesto: What Went Wrong with the Moral Basis to the Family and How to Restore It* (W.S. Hein Com. 2007).

Laura Lundy is a Professor of Education Law and Children's Rights in the School of Education, Queen's University Belfast, and a Barrister at Law. She is the Director of the Centre for Children's Rights and has published widely on education law and children's rights. She has particular expertise in relation to participatory research with children and young people and, along with colleague Lesley Emerson, has developed a children's rights-based approach to research that has been applied in several research projects.

Diana McKibben earned her PhD in Political Science from Claremont Graduate University and wrote her PhD dissertation on restorative justice. She currently serves on the Community Restorative Justice Commission for Monterey County, and resides in Berkeley, California.

Chelsea Marshall is a researcher in the Centre for Children's Rights at Queen's University Belfast. Her background is in rights-based approaches to the participation of marginalized groups including work with the Participation and Practice of Rights and Save the Children NI. Through her master's and doctoral research, she also has expertise in the exclusion and gendered marginalization of young people from transitional justice processes intended to help societies transition from armed conflict.

Tamar Morag is Associate Professor (Senior Lecturer) at the Stricks Law School of COLMAN (College of Management, Academic Studies) in Rishon-Lezion, Israel, and Adjunct Professor at the Faculty of Law, Hebrew University of Jerusalem. Dr. Morag, an SJD graduate of the University of Michigan Law School, focuses her research and teaching on family law, child law, and law and social change. She was the legal director of the Israeli National Council for the Child and served as vice-chair of the Israeli CRC legislative committee.

Mona Paré is Assistant Professor at the University of Ottawa, Faculty of Law, and a founding member of the Interdisciplinary Research Laboratory on the Rights of the Child. She holds a PhD in Law from the University of London, Queen Mary College. She worked previously at the United Nations on the Convention on the Rights of Persons with Disabilities. Her main research interests pertain to education rights, participation rights, and rights of vulnerable groups.

Aisling Parkes is a Lecturer in Child, Family and Disability Law at University College Cork, Ireland. She received her PhD in Law in 2007. Her research interests lie in the area of international children's rights. She has done in-depth research on Article 12 of the UN Convention on the Rights of the Child 1989 on an international scale.

Joan Pennell, MSW, PhD, is a Professor of Social Work and Director of the Center for Family and Community Engagement at North Carolina State University. The Center emphasizes youth and family leadership in decision-making, creating cultural safe forums, and involving all family members, including fathers and paternal relatives. She has conducted research on family engagement in child welfare, domestic violence, youth justice, and schools. She is frequently consulted on implementing and evaluating family group conferencing in safe, culturally respectful, and effective ways and has presented on family engagement and family violence across the United States and Canada as well as in Australia, Guatemala, the Netherlands, New Zealand, and the United Kingdom.

R. V. Rikard is a Postdoctoral Research Associate in the Department of Media and Information at Michigan State University. Dr. Rikard's research interests include health disparities, health literacy, the social impact of technology on health, and quantitative methodology. He has co-authored published research in the *Journal of Health Communication, Women & Criminal Justice, Journal of Aging & Social Policy,* and *Correctional Health Care.*

Laura A. Rosenbury is Professor of Law at Washington University Law School (St. Louis) and a co-author of the *Feminist Jurisprudence* casebook. She has also written extensively on how law influences private relationships and conduct between adults, between adults and children, and between children. Throughout her work, she considers the multiple ways that law and relationships influence the construction of gender.

Yoa Sorek has earned her BA and MA in education from the Hebrew University in Jerusalem. Since 1999 she has worked as a researcher in the Engleberg Center for Children and Youth at Risk in the Myers-JDC-Brookdale Institute. She has conducted research on a variety of topics in the field of children and youth at risk, such as evaluations of projects for Ethiopian and Caucasian children and of projects relating to children whose parents are going through divorce proceedings and children who suffer from neglect and abuse.

Cheri Tarutani, MSW, LCSW, is an Instructor and Practicum Coordinator with the University of Hawai'i School of Social Work Distance Education program. She was formerly a State of Hawai'i Child and Adult Protection Specialist for Child Welfare Services for six years. During that time, she was the designated Family Drug Court social worker and was part of the Family Drug Court team that was awarded the Natural Collaborative Leader Award in 2004 from the Mediation Center of the Pacific. Ms. Tarutani is a Board Member for Hawai'i Friends of Justice and Civic Education, whose efforts focus on solution-focused restorative justice practices. She is a restorative facilitator and earned her Bachelor of Arts in Women's Studies from the University of California, Los Angeles, and a Masters in Social Work from the University of Hawai'i, Manoa.

Nigel Thomas (PhD, University of Wales) is a Professor of Childhood and Youth Research at the University of Central Lancashire and Director of the Centre for Children and Young People's Participation. He has taught and researched in many aspects of childhood, children's rights, and child welfare, with a focus on the participation of marginalized children. He is co-editor of *A Handbook of Children and Young People's Participation*, a former co-editor of the journal *Children & Society*, and an editorial board member of the *International Journal of Children's Rights.*

E. Kay M. Tisdall is Professor of Childhood Policy and the Programme Director of the MSc in Childhood Studies at the University of Edinburgh. She is

Co-Director of the Centre for Research on Families and Relationships. She has a PhD (University of Edinburgh) and an LLB (University of Strathclyde). Her current research interests revolve around children's rights and research methods.

Eran Uziely is a special education expert and has held numerous positions in this area as a tutor, teacher, and headmaster in various institutions. He is the Head of Special Education Dept. at Achva Academic College in Israel as well as an inclusion instructor in several elementary schools. His MA thesis, entitled "Fairness in Selection to High Schools in Israel," won an award for outstanding research paper from the Israeli Council for Higher Education. Eran holds a PhD in social work from the Hebrew University of Jerusalem. His research examines the implementation of child participation in special education placement committees in Israel.

Lorenn Walker, JD, MPH, is a public health educator and restorative lawyer assisting people and organizations to deal with conflict and wrongdoing. She has developed, implemented, and researched numerous cooperative learning interventions using restorative justice and solution-focused approaches. She collaborates with a variety of individuals and organizations, including schools, prisons, courts, law enforcement, and nonprofits/nongovernmental organizations. She has written over forty published papers and three books and has been an instructor for the University of Hawai'i Honolulu Community College since 1994. She earned a master's degree in health education from the University of Hawai'i School of Public Health, Manoa in 1996, a juris doctorate degree from Northeastern University School of Law, Boston, Massachusetts in 1983, and a Montessori teacher certification from the St. Nicholas Montessori Teacher Training program, London, England (by correspondence) in 1971.

Enhancing Capacities for Child Participation: Introduction

TALI GAL AND BENEDETTA FAEDI DURAMY

INTRODUCTION

The children's rights discourse has conquered the democratic world over the past three decades. Until two centuries ago children were perceived as the property of their parents (mainly fathers); a century ago they were viewed as an endangered species in need of protection; and during some parts of the twentieth century they were often considered a public nuisance requiring behavioral regulation through labor and education laws. However, the 1989 United Nations Convention on the Rights of the Child (CRC), with its nearly universal acceptance, has had a dramatic effect on the social construction of children and childhood. For the first time, children were portrayed as separate human beings with individual needs, wishes, and feelings deserving societal recognition. In accordance with this new holistic perception of children, the CRC offered a complex mix of protective, social, and liberal rights to children. It highlighted the importance of the family and community for children as well as their need for growing independence and autonomy. Among the wide range of rights, children's right to participate in decision-making processes affecting their lives is considered the acme of the CRC and its central contribution to the children's rights discourse. If children are separate human beings with individual feelings, views, and perspectives worthy of consideration, then they must have the right to freely express them and to have them taken seriously in accordance with their age and level of development.

Since the adoption of the CRC by all the world's nations with the exception of Somalia and the United States, the concept of child participation penetrated into laws, practices, and public discussions as well as the lives of families around the globe. At the same time, the implementation of the participation right presents both theoretical and practical challenges. This edited collection brings together prominent scholars from Canada, the United States, Australia, Britain, Scotland, Ireland, and Israel to present empirical findings regarding the implementation of children's right to participation in different contexts and jurisdictions. This distinguished group of scholars met at the University of Haifa and the Hebrew University, where participants presented their respective studies and exchanged feedback and insights.[1] The presentations, brought together and edited in this book, provide a kaleidoscope of child-inclusive processes in various areas such as schooling, child protection, restorative justice, family disputes, and courts, as well as public policy and research. The chapters consider both the *ways* children are included in dialogues and the *levels of success* of these processes.

THE RIGHT TO PARTICIPATION: OBJECTIONS AND CHALLENGES

The right of children to participate in decision-making processes affecting their lives, provided by the CRC, marked a change in the perception of children from objects of protection to subjects of their own rights. Although the participation right is the symbol of the CRC, or perhaps because of it, it also raises numerous objections and challenges from different directions.

The first is the *capability* argument: At what age can children make rational choices? Can children make rational decisions at all? Those raising this concern question both the ability of children to take *any* part in decision-making processes and the *weight* their views should receive in the final decision. The younger the child, the more fiercely is the capability question raised. However, the capability obstacle is overrated. Adults who are still developing their decision-making capacities are not required to demonstrate their rationality or capacity before fulfilling their right to participation. Moreover, capability is acquired gradually, through practice; only by regular involvement in decision-making processes can children develop their decision-making skills. The argument that children lack the relevant capacities to take part in deliberative processes is, from this perspective, a social construction that sustains itself by preventing children from proving otherwise, somewhat similar to the arguments that were raised against women and people of color in previous eras.

But even if we accept that at certain developmental stages children do lack sufficient capacity to make a rational decision regarding certain matters, they still

1. The meeting took place in October 2013 and was hosted and funded by the University of Haifa School of Criminology and the Haruv Institute at the Hebrew University. We are thankful for their support and extend our gratitude to the University of Haifa and Aminut Foundation for the Treatment of Violence in the Family and in Society for additional financial assistance.

have valid views, feelings, hopes, and perceptions that adults need to take into consideration before making decisions that may affect their lives. Raising the capability objection, therefore, is not a valid justification for excluding children and young people from such decision-making processes. However, it is important to note that adults, ultimately, bear the duty to decipher and understand children's views and opinions as well as to overcome the differences in style, language, and thinking patterns between children of various ages and adults.

The best interest consideration is another concern often raised to exclude children from decision-making fora. Very often, professionals, parents, and others worry that taking part in decision-making processes would hurt children, exposing them to stress, inappropriate information, intrafamilial conflicts, and other damaging or traumatic situations. Admittedly, there are instances in which exposing children to decision-making processes might be challenging for them. A guiding principle of the CRC is that children's best interest should be a primary consideration in all matters concerning their lives; therefore, this is a valid concern when implementing the participation right. But, generally speaking, when examining this issue empirically, we find that it is more about professionals' concerns and fears than the children's own wishes and ability. When asked about their participation in decision-making processes concerning their lives, children are clear about their wishes to be listened to and be taken seriously (Graham & Fitzgerald, 2005; Marshall, 1997), declaring that it is not possible to "wrap people up in cotton wool" (Marshall, 1997, p. 74). This finding, echoed in many of this book's chapters, suggests that professionals are perhaps too often willing to give up children's "participation" for the sake of their "best interests," even though the latter might not necessarily be in conflict with the former. Perhaps a helpful insight in this context is that experiencing *difficulty* is substantively different from experiencing *harm.* While it is natural to expect that some decision-making processes may be painful or difficult for children—for example, discussions on their out-of-home placement or their parents' divorce—it would be wrong to assume that these difficulties will necessarily cause a harm greater than nonparticipation in such fora. In other words, professionals as well as parents need sometimes to use the "let-go" heuristic approach suggested elsewhere (Gal, 2011). Just as parents eventually allow their children to cross the street, go out at night, drive, and spend unsupervised time with their peers—always at a time that seems a little too early for parents and yet ripe for their children—professionals need to trust children's judgments when they say that they are ready to take the risk of participation. Naturally, "letting go" should be supported with the appropriate guidance and precautionary steps. Some of the chapters in this book demonstrate how participation may be possible even in the most painful contexts, such as divorce and out-of-home placements, with appropriate protections and support (see Chapters 7, 9, 10, and 11).

The *confrontational nature of participation is* also often raised as a reason for objecting to children's participation. The concern is that if children are provided with opportunities to state their opinions, and particularly if their opinions oppose those of their parents or other caretakers, then their participation may create conflicts and lead to exclusion from their own families and circles of support. But, as Martha Minow (1990) argued, conflict already exists when legal remedy is sought, and thus legal-rights language translates, rather than initiates, conflict. Moreover, the participation right cannot exist without a community of listeners around children. Participation is substantively different from the right to make autonomous decisions: it assumes a dialogue, a deliberative process where children become part of a community whose members jointly discuss the matter at hand. By implementing the participation right, community members negotiate the relationships between them—such as between children and adults. Children's participation right therefore is not inflammatory, as some of its objectors think, but rather enhances equality among the community members, urging the powerful/ older to listen to the weak/younger while acknowledging the centrality of social and family ties.

Finally, *cost-effectiveness* is a practical argument against child participation. Since the meaningful participation of children, in particular young ones, requires intense preparation and substantial adjustments, policymakers and practitioners are reluctant to embark on child-inclusive projects. The chapters presented in this book provide inspiration to those who are committed to children's rights in general and child participation in particular. Furthermore, by implementing the lessons learned in the projects presented here, new participatory programs may use resources more efficiently in the course of fulfilling meaningful involvement of children.

THE VIRTUES OF CHILD PARTICIPATION

Despite the arguments against child participation, there is sufficient evidence today showing that child participation is not only a universal human right of children but is also a need, a coping mechanism, and a developmental milestone that benefits children of all ages (Gal, 2011).

First, child participation addresses children's natural need for a sense of control, especially in situations of stress and crisis (Lazarus & Folkman, 1984; Weisz, 1986). Control is a powerful coping mechanism that helps children to better deal with the stressors around them (Langer, Chen, & Luhmann, 2005; Thurber & Weisz, 1997). Allowing children to have an impact on decision-making processes and their outcomes promotes their sense of control and thus helps them to cope with stressful situations.

Second, in "normal" as well as in difficult situations, when children are provided with opportunities to participate in decision-making processes, they develop their trust in others, their self-esteem, and a sense of being respected.

Having a voice is an empowering experience for everyone, but perhaps even more profoundly for those who are routinely muted or simply disregarded. Participation is also considered to have strong educational and developmental components and, accordingly, may be regarded as another basic need in a child's development (Ochaíta & Espinosa, 1997).

Third, and more broadly, children's participation is beneficial from a democratic perspective. Practice in shared decision-making processes helps children become future competent participants who are tolerant of other people's views and who respect themselves and others. These traits cannot be taught theoretically; they need to be gradually acquired through experiencing shared decision-making and problem-solving processes. More specifically, involving children in decision-making processes benefits their immediate surroundings—the family, the school, and the community—through gaining more knowledge on children's perspectives and strengthening their democratic values (Flekkøy & Kaufman, 1997). Some of the chapters in this book (see, for instance, Chapters 4, 15, and 17) demonstrate in very concrete ways the societal benefits of involving children in policymaking and research.

Involving children in decision-making processes may also lead to better decisions. Children may have valid views about their best interests that differ from those of adults. They are typically less cynical, more optimistic, and more flexible in their approach to the future and, therefore, might offer fresh ideas and creative solutions (Lansdown, 2001). Furthermore, adult-based decisions that are aimed at promoting children's welfare based on assumptions rather than on actual children's views often turn out to be mistaken or, at a minimum, insensitive toward their specific preferences (Chapters 7 and 8).

Finally, involving children in decision-making processes enhances their perception of the process as fair (Hicks & Lawrence, 1993; Lawrence, 2003; Melton & Limber, 1992). Procedural fairness is known to increase people's satisfaction with the process itself and their willingness to follow the decision that was made (Lind & Tyler, 1988; Tyler, 1990). Some of the chapters in this book echo this finding (Chapters 9 and 12).

FROM "WHY" TO "HOW": THE NEW DISCOURSE ON CHILD PARTICIPATION

It seems, then, that the question is not *whether* children should participate in decision-making processes affecting their lives because, as mentioned above, child participation often promotes the child's best interests, development, resilience, and sense of fairness. It also contributes to our society as a whole. Rather, the emerging question is *how* children should take effectively part in such processes. This is the central question that the chapters in this book aim to address. While the different arenas of child participation require individual attention and inquiry, some theoretical as well as practical generalizations can provide baseline assumptions for any child-participation practice.

Interpretation Within the Framework of the Convention's Guiding Principles

Taking children's rights seriously means that the participation right needs to be implemented in accordance with the three other basic principles of the CRC: the principle of nondiscrimination, the best interest, and the right to life, survival, and development. According to the nondiscrimination principle provided in Article 2, all children must receive equal opportunities to participate (and, therefore, the weakest children must get the most support in fulfilling their right). According to the right to life, survival, and development provided in Article 6, participation should be understood and applied in accordance with children's development and evolving capacities. And finally, following the best interests principle set out in Article 3, participation should always be implemented with children's best interests being a paramount consideration. While participation might have an empowering and therapeutic role for some children, it is important to remember, on the other hand, that forcing them to take control may be sometimes experienced as dominating them again. Therefore, participation should always be considered together with children's well-being. Whichever form of participation is chosen, children should be treated as partners during the process and should receive ongoing information about its progress in a way that is suitable for their level of development and understanding (Gal, 2011).

Participation as a Relational Process

While the CRC does not suggest that children should make their own decisions in all matters concerning their lives, it would be too narrow to interpret the participation right as consultation only. As Nigel Thomas commented (2007), true participation that follows the words and spirit of the CRC means that children take part in the actual decision-making. In other words, the participation right grants children more than a right to be heard, but less than a right to independent decision-making. This makes sense in light of the CRC's emphasis on the importance of the family and the community for children. Under the CRC, children are perceived as relational human beings and, as such, their rights are imbedded within a relational approach (Nedelsky, 2011). Therefore, adults should be sure to engage in a dialogue with the children involved in the process to allow mutual exchanges of feelings and viewpoints (Gal, 2011).

Understanding Participation Within Existing Typologies

Roger Hart's "ladder of participation" of 1992 was the first model conceptualizing the ways child's participation may be implemented. Inspired by Sherry Arnstein's "ladder of citizen participation" (1969), Hart developed an eight-rung ladder, beginning from nonparticipatory practices to child-managed projects. While Hart's ladder faced some criticism, his contribution to the children's rights discourse is unquestionable. Two of his major conceptual contributions are worth mentioning here. first, by identifying manipulative methods of "involving" children in processes that use them as decorations or through tokenism, his ladder highlights what is needed to make participation "real." Second, the ladder differentiates between processes that merely offer consultation with children (rung 5) and processes that engage children in a proper dialogue (rung 6). This differentiation moved the debate on child participation forward by acknowledging that inviting children and youth to speak out is insufficient for those striving to fulfill the spirit of the CRC. Rather, dialogue means a mutual willingness to convince and be convinced, to be changed, and to give away one's control over the decision. In what circumstances genuine dialogue is possible (and desired) and when consultation is in fact preferable from a children's rights perspective remains an empirical query that some of the chapters here try to address. Influenced by Hart's model, Harry Shier's typology (2001) went further to propose a five-level model that does not include nonparticipatory encounters. Shier's model, however, added an additional layer reflecting the various levels of the state's commitment to participation.

Other models have aimed at identifying the elements that are required to achieve meaningful participation of children, such as Laura Lundy's (2007) in the context of education, and Joan Pennell and Gale Burford's (2000, 2002) hands-on experience with the involvement of child victims of family violence in family group decision-making processes in Canada. Nigel Thomas (2007), on the other hand, has theorized a model that comprises both a politics and a sociology of children's participation to ensure their active involvement in democracy. Nicholas Bala and Rachel Birnbaum have, instead, explored avenues for children's representation and their active participation in family disputes (see Chapter 6).

Implementing Participation Within the Committee's General Comment

With the growing use of participatory experiences on the one hand, and the divergence in levels of success of such experiences on the other, the United Nations Committee on the Rights of the Child published its General Comment No. 12 in 2009. The General Comment provides the UN's formal interpretation of the participation right as well as guidance for its implementation. It also provides a list of nine basic requirements for the implementation of the right to participation: All participatory processes should be transparent and informative; voluntary; respectful; relevant; child-friendly; inclusive; supported by training; safe and sensitive to risk; and accountable (UN Committee, 2009, pp. 29–31). Many of the chapters in the book address the requirements set out by this committee and provide empirical evidence as to the ways these requirements are implemented in specific settings.

With these theoretical and practical generalizations in the background, the chapters presented in this book may provide useful guidance to how effectively children should participate in the decision-making processes affecting their lives. More specifically, they address the following questions:

1. What are the main impediments in fulfilling children's participation right?
2. What are the available instruments that can be used to overcome these obstacles and make decision-making processes more child-inclusive?
3. Where are we most successful in achieving child participation, and can we identify the reasons for such success?
4. Are there any clear criteria, such as age or developmental stage, that can be used to identify effective measures to involve children in decision-making processes?
5. What are children's own perspectives on the matter? How do children experience various fora of decision-making processes? To what extent do children feel that they can express their views freely and that their viewpoints are given due weight? How important for them is their ability to influence the outcome of the process?
6. What are the opinions of parents, professionals, and family members regarding the different ways decision-making processes may involve children?

OUTLINE OF THE BOOK

The chapters of the book discuss the participation right of children in various decision-making processes affecting their education, protection, relationship with justice, and involvement in family disputes as well as in public policy and research.

Laura Rosenbury's insightful opening for the book provides a sociohistorical perspective for child participation, echoing developments in the feminist discourse. Feminism uncovers that the legal constructions of children as incapable of making decisions regarding their health, political affiliation, sexual relationships, and more derive from political reasons rather than from developmental and biological differences.

Moreover, the construction of children as incapable and powerless constructs adults—professionals as well as parents—as capable and powerful. Granting

children decision-making power may therefore require a change in the very definitions of the roles of parents and professionals. Rosenbury's chapter provides
a valuable framework for exploring various ways of children's participation. It
demonstrates how children's incapacity is constructed by laws, and how uncovering these constructions opens the door for a different approach, one that considers children's perspectives as relevant even when they are dependent, young,
and "incapable," according to formal laws, of making their own decisions. The
individual perspectives of children, we learn from feminism, are legitimate and
important no matter what we think about their intrinsic value.

Following Rosenbury's background chapter, the book is divided into five
parts based on subject matter, providing opportunities to compare and review
various participatory mechanisms in different jurisdictions on similar subjects.
In **Part I** we bring together chapters relating to the participation of children in
education and research settings. Mona Paré explores children's participation in
the context of special education in the Canadian school system. The chapter suggests that children's participation is essential in the decision-making processes
related to special education to ensure their inclusion in regular classrooms and
curriculum activities as well as to give them adequate support with appropriate
programs and services. Her interviews with students with disabilities, parents,
and education advocates and mediators reveal that "children understood the
concept of participation and were generally happy with their level of participation in school." However, according to parents and representatives of the various organizations, the great majority of children do not participate in special
education–related processes because the younger children are not invited and
the older ones are not encouraged to attend or are not interested in coming. Her
archival analysis of laws, policies, and court decisions reveals that "children's
participation in the school system is dependent on parent–child relationships,
since the law and procedures in place do not emphasize this participation." When
parents participate in decision-making processes, she argues, their participation
typically does not reflect child representation but rather their own perceptions
of their child's best interests. Paré's chapter includes a helpful discussion on the
accommodations needed to make participation accessible and effective for children with disabilities.

Still in the area of special education, Eran Uziely examines the right of
children to participate in decision-making processes regarding their enrollment in the Israeli special education system. The chapter investigates the attitudes as well as the desired and actual level of participation experienced by
students with disabilities, parents, and professionals in the meetings held by
placement committees and its implementations. The findings reveal that students are interested in and capable of participating in the discussions related
to their educational future, and that shared information provides children with
the opportunity to better cope with and contribute to the decision. Similar to
Canada, the Israeli study finds that the participation of students with special

needs depends largely on their parents' decision. Professionals were found less eager to allow child participation, especially with regard to young pupils, compared to both parents and pupils. They were also less supportive of meaningful participation and considered lower levels of participation as desirable. Uziely's study also found that pupils who had prior experience attending a committee meeting or who had preparatory meetings participated more actively, highlighting the desirability of holding two or more meetings rather than a single decision-making encounter.

In terms of children and young people's participation in research, Nigel Thomas discusses the challenges faced in helping children to carry out their own research projects with adults' support, or to work in partnership with adults to plan and conduct research. Drawing from two specific projects (a university-based project supporting children in local schools to do their own research and a partnership project between a group of young people in public care and university researchers), the chapter provides insights into the factors that may contribute to successful child participation in research and reflects on the limitations of current inclusive practices.

Part II discusses child participation in family disputes. Aisling Parkes addresses the implementation of Article 12 in family law proceedings and the different approaches adopted by Ireland and New Zealand before and after the adoption of the General Comment to Article 12 in 2009. Parkes' comparison between Ireland and New Zealand demonstrates the importance of legislation in securing the implementation of child participation. Lacking a mandatory provision, adults in Ireland decide when, how, and where children will participate in family law proceedings. In New Zealand, where judicial interviews with children are regulated through legislation and national guidelines, judges, as well as children themselves, are supportive of direct judicial interview of children.

Bala, Birnbaum, and Cyr examine the various methods employed in Canada for children's participation in family proceedings, with a focus on judicial interviews with children. Drawing from empirical data from judges, children's legal representatives, and children themselves, the chapter reports that, for the most part, informants find judicial interviewing a useful practice. Similar to children in other studies, interviewed children clearly stated that they wanted to be involved in the decision-making process regarding their parents' dispute rather than dictate the decision—having a "voice, not a choice." Bala and colleagues capture judicial interviews as an important complementary tool that may add a new angle or confirm earlier information brought before judges. While the chapter identifies a trend toward more frequent use of judicial interviewing of children, it also suggests that more efforts should be made to educate and guide judges and lawyers about judicial meetings with children as an important opportunity for them to actively participate in the proceedings affecting their family situations.

Morag and Sorek present an evidence-based, structured child participation model in family law proceedings in Israel. The model involves the establishment of a new child participation unit in the family court and training for specialized child participation social workers. The analysis of the relevant findings shows that allowing children the opportunity to participate in family conflicts has a positive impact on the legal decisions reached by the court and contributes to children's well-being and satisfaction with the process. Considering the tension between confidentiality and children's rights, their study found that most children wanted to preserve full or partial confidentiality and wanted to maintain control over who has access to their statements. Their recorded judicial interviews were kept in a safe for appeal purposes only. Information was disclosed to their parents only with their consent. Considering the gradual growth in child participation encounters during the study, the authors highlight the importance of training, exposure, and experience in engaging parents, judges, and children themselves in child participatory processes.

Part III considers participatory mechanisms for children at risk: those who are out of home, those receiving family services, and those involved in child protection proceedings. Sharon Bessell highlights in her qualitative studies the importance of relationships as a crucial foundation for meaningful participation of out-of-home children in Australia. Without an ongoing relationship with their caseworkers, children do not feel respected, listened to, and included in decisions made about their placement. The chapter acknowledges also that interpersonal relations are often shaped by intergenerational structures as well as socioeconomic and situational power imbalances. Being a child acts as a barrier to meaningful participation; participation is regulated, monitored, and implemented by adults. When children in care were not heard by the social workers with whom they expected to have an ongoing relationship—and this was routine—they felt lonely, powerless, and sad.

In conversation with Sharon Bessell's chapter, Jodi Hall, Joan Pennell, and R. V. Rikard explore the model of child and family team (CFT) meetings that allow youth in foster care to participate in the decision-making process with their families as well as service providers and other community resources. CFT meetings are positioned in the restorative justice arena that constructs the participation of family members, including children. Unlike family group conferences, the most widely used restorative justice model in child protection, CFTs involve professionals throughout the process, with no family private time, and they meet multiple times. Drawing from a North Carolina empirical study, the chapter reveals that participating in the CFT meetings made foster children feel "important." Particularly for those who are used to being muted, participation is important in itself and, thus, represents a restorative experience for those who have suffered trauma and separation. At the same time, administrative data collected in the study showed low rates of actual youth participation in these meetings. Children were more likely to participate when there were educational or safety concerns.

Providing additional empirical evidence on a restorative justice model in child protection, Gale Burford and Sarah Gallagher report on the experiences of thirty-two foster care teenagers who were involved in either family safety plan meetings or family group conferencing designed by Vermont's Family Services Division. Their interviews reveal that adequate preparation, consistent communication, and efforts to support children's goals and to strengthen their skills enhance youth experience of inclusion.

Finally, moving back to Australia, Anne Graham, Robyn Fitzgerald, and Judith Cashmore present findings from a large-scale action research project examining how professionals working for the family relationship services sector conceptualize, practice, and advance child participation across the various Australian states. The findings uncover the importance of professionals' perceptions of childhood and children in implementing children's participation. Since child participation is adult-constructed, this action research demonstrates how educating professionals about childhood, agency, and vulnerability may enhance child participation. As the project progressed, adults' perceptions of children's vulnerability and agency as competing shifted to an understanding of these concepts as complementary. While many professionals considered "participation" to be dichotomous to "protection" in the earlier stages of the study, many of them gradually adopted more complex notions of participation. Professionals understood that "not having a say" may be harmful to children at least as much as, or more than, "having a say," and consequently began to identify creative ways of involving children in decision-making processes even in sensitive situations. The chapter, thus, suggests a set of recommendations aimed at reviewing the current policies, programs, and interventions to improve children's participation in family relationship services.

Part IV gathers contributions considering the involvement of children in the criminal process in the United States. Lynne Marie Kohm discusses teen courts, where children actively participate in the decision-making processes that deal with their peers' or their own involvement in crime. Kohm's analysis stresses the central role of families in ensuring the effective empowerment of children throughout the process and its restorative outcome. She concludes that the active involvement of children and youth in the justice process following a crime committed by themselves or their peers promotes their self-respect, satisfaction with the process, and ideally their desistance from crime. Kohm's analysis of teen courts demonstrates the practical implementation of a participatory process within a best interest paradigm.

Emily Buss denounces the antisocial developmental trajectory of the American juvenile system and the risks for children in juvenile courts of developing an unhealthy relationship with the law and legal authority. She provides a vivid look into one arena where child participation occurs regularly—and meaninglessly. The typical American youth court is described as applying child participation as procedure, at best, rather than as a relational, substantive state of mind. Her chapter draws from observations in juvenile courts and sociological and developmental psychological literature to suggest reforms aimed at involving juvenile offenders in the discussions, planning, and determination of their adjudication by fostering a healthy relationship between them and legal authority. Buss highlights that children learn best how to participate in decision-making processes when they are supported by adults. This support may be achieved either through their natural environment or, when absent, by professionals. One inspiring example is the Benchmark Hearing Program at the Cook County Circuit Court Child Protection Division. The judge develops a relationship with the youth (foster children aged 16 and over), aiming to "address the relationship void" experienced by foster children. While such a relationship cannot be as intimate as family or peer relationships, the judge strives to develop it to the maximum extent possible. To make juvenile adjudication processes more appropriate for youth's healthy development, Buss suggests two main goals for reform. First, all discussions regarding the youth's disposition should be held in court and not "behind the scenes." Second, the dialogue should be held mainly between the youth and the judge rather than among professionals.

Lorenn Walker, Cheri Tarutani, and Diana McKibben examine Hawai'i's model of reentry and transition planning circles for incarcerated people who want to restore their relationships with their children, family, and communities. Reflecting another restorative justice model, the reentry circles explicitly use a strengths-based approach to foster hope and resilience. The strengths of each participant are stated, followed by a discussion on a "good life" plan described by the incarcerated person. The chapter demonstrates how a restorative justice approach may provide an effective platform for child participation. The findings show that children's participation in the reentry circles increases their ability to cope with the trauma and suffering caused by the incarceration of a parent and helps them initiate family healing.

Finally, **Part V** discusses child participation in the public sphere. Chelsea MarshallBronagh Byrne, and Laura Lundy explore children's participation in public decision-making from the perspective of the staff members of youth participation nongovernmental organizations and young people themselves. Drawing on empirical studies conducted with a range of stakeholders in Northern Ireland, the chapter argues that the participative method of face-to-face engagement between children and duty bearers can be particularly useful in providing children and young people with the opportunity to express their views and participate in making decisions together with policymakers and other stakeholders. Such direct contact with children has a "humanizing effect" on policymakers, promoting youth's ability to influence policy. In accordance with other chapters, the authors find that "the extent to which duty bearers possess, or perceive themselves as possessing, the relevant skills, can be a key challenge" to participation. The chapter helpfully provides evidence-based insights as to the way the nine requirements for meaningful participation set out by the UN Committee (2009) may be implemented in face-to-face encounters with policymakers. Marshall and colleagues recognize four requirements—that face-to-face encounters be transparent, respectful, relevant, and accountable—as crucial, and suggest that if policymakers cannot ensure their adherence they should avoid direct interaction and use instead indirect consultations.

Kay Tisdall presents empirical evidence from two projects, a research project on school councils and a collaborative initiative with nongovernmental organizations in Scotland. Her chapter analyzes participatory institutions through a human-geography perspective, in particular through their provision of "time" and "space." Tisdall criticizes current participatory mechanisms for failing to provide children and youth a sense of citizenship. Their participation is separated from adult-led decision-making processes and they are typically unable to set new agendas. The chapter suggests ways to assist organizations, government institutions, schools, and policymakers as well as parents, children, and communities at large in making child participation a meaningful, flexible, and inclusive practice. The Scottish Youth Parliament is a prominent example of an on-going platform for youth participation in decision-making. The challenge is to allow for sufficient time and space for such standing groups not only to act reactively but also to initiate their own agendas.

Moving to the international arena, Tara Collins explores the role of child participation in international monitoring under CRC Articles 44 and 45, requiring member states to report regularly about their situation of children's rights to the United Nations Committee on the Rights of the Child. Informed by consultations with children and young people who have been involved in international monitoring, the chapter reveals that, despite being currently inadequately considered, child participation can improve monitoring results, providing a fuller picture to adults because children may know more about their situation than adults. Similar to previous discussion, Collins identifies the central role played by nongovernmental organization in executing child participation in public policy.

In the closing chapter of this part, Benedetta Faedi Duramy sketches an alarming portrayal of the experiences of Haitian girls. Facing extreme poverty, sexual abuse, violence, neglect, and slavery, many girls express their wishes to be included in decision-making processes that relate to their own lives as well as those relating to the future of their country. Faedi Duramy's chapter comes full circle with Rosenbury's. It presents a striking example of how the social constructions of children directly affect the way they are treated as well as the level of their participation in civil life. Haiti is a tragic reminder of the historical perceptions of children as their parents' property and a family commodity; this view was prevalent in many parts of the world until only more than a century ago. In Haiti, a patriarchal and hierarchical culture intersects with extreme poverty and natural disasters, leading to gross violations of the full scope of children's rights, participation being only one of them. In particular, the dual vulnerability of girls results from the combination of gender and generational inequalities, amplified by poverty and national instability.

In the concluding chapter of the book, Tali Gal identifies five general themes emerging from the various chapters: the need for *legislation*, the importance of *promoting participation among professionals*; the challenge of shifting from *token to inclusive participation*, the need for *managing expectations*, and an understanding of participation as *relational*. She further proposes an ecological model mapping the multiple layers of variables—personal, familial, professional, organizational, cultural, national, and international—affecting the level, effectiveness, and prevalence of child participation. This model can ideally be used by those committed to promote the implementation of the participation right of children across the different arenas affecting children's lives.

REFERENCES

Flekkøy, M. G., & Kaufman, N. H. (1997). *The participation rights of the child: rights and responsibilities in family and society*. London, UK, & Bristol, PA: Jessica Kingsley.

Gal, T. (2011). *Child victims and restorative justice: a needs-rights model*. New York, NY: Oxford University Press.

Graham, A., & Fitzgerald, R. (2005). *Taking account of the "to and fro" of children's experiences in family law*. Presented at Childhoods 2005 Conference, available at ePublications@SCU.

Hicks, A. J., & Lawrence, J. A. (1993). Children's criteria for procedural justice: developing a young people's procedural justice scale. *Social Justice Research, 6*(2), 163–182.

Langer, D. A., Chen, E., & Luhmann, J. D. (2005). Attributions and coping in children's pain experiences. *Journal of Pediatric Psychology, 30*(7), 615–622.

Lansdown, G, 2001. *Promoting children's participation in democratic decision-making, technical report*. UNICEF Innocenti Insight.

Lawrence, J. A. (2003). *Safeguarding fairness for children in interactions with adults in authority: computer-based investigations of the judgments of secondary school students*. School of Behavioural Science, University of Melbourne.

Lazarus, R. S., & Folkman, S. (1984). *Stress, appraisal and coping*. New York: Springer.

Lind, E. A., & Tyler, T. R. (1988). *The social psychology of procedural justice*. New York: Plenum.

Lundy, L. (2007). "Voice" is not enough: Conceptualising Article 12 of the United Nations Convention on the Rights of the Child. *British Educational Research Journal, 33*(6), 927–942.

Marshall, K. (1997). *Children's rights in the balance: the participation–protection debate*. Edinburgh: The Stationery Office.

Melton, G. B., & Limber, S. P. (1992). What children's rights mean to children: children's own views. In M. Freeman & P. Veerman (Eds.), *The ideologies of children's rights* (pp. 167–187). Dordrecht, The Netherlands: Kluwer Academic Publishers.

Minow, M. (1990). *Making all the difference: inclusion, exclusion and American law*. Ithaca, NY: Cornell University Press.

Nedelsky, J. (2011). *Law's relations: a relational theory of self, autonomy, and law*. New York, NY: Oxford University Press.

Ochaíta, E., & Espinosa, M. A. (1997). Children's participation in family and school life: a psychological and development approach. *International Journal of Children's Rights, 5*, 179–297.

Pennell, J., & Burford, G. (2000). Family group decision-making: protecting children and women. *Child Welfare, 79*(2), 131–158.

Pennell, J., & Burford, G. (2002). Feminist praxis: making family group conferencing work. In H. Strang & J. Braithwaite (Eds.), *Restorative justice and family violence* (pp. 108–127). Cambridge: Cambridge University Press.

Shier, H. (2001). Pathways to participation: openings, opportunities and obligations. *Children & Society, 15*(2), 107–117.

Tyler, T. R. (1990). *Why people obey the law.* New Haven, CT: Yale University Press.

Thomas, N. (2007). Towards a theory of children's participation. *International Journal of Children's Rights, 15*(2), 199.

Thurber, C. A., & Weisz, J. R. (1997). "You can try or you can just give up": the impact of perceived control and coping style on childhood homesickness. *Developmental Psychology, 33*(3), 508–517.

United Nations Committee on the Rights of the Child (2009). General Comment No. 12 The right of the child to be heard. UN Doc. CRC/C/GC/12, adopted July 20, 2009.

Weisz, J. R. (1986). Contingency and control beliefs as predictors of psychotherapy outcomes among children and adolescents. *Journal of Consulting and Clinical Psychology, 54*(6), 789–795.

CHAPTER 1

A Feminist Perspective
on Children and Law

From Objectification to Relational Subjectivities

LAURA A. ROSENBURY

The relationship between feminism, children, and law is varied and complex. Feminists have long sought to improve children's lives, including their treatment in law, and advocates for children have long built upon feminist arguments to argue for changes in law's approach to children, with much success. At the same time, women's rights have not generated a comparable regime of children's rights. The difference is, in part, intentional: Some feminists argue for new understandings of rights tailored to children's needs, whereas others argue that rights are not appropriate tools for addressing children's dependencies. Yet critics also question whether conflicts of interest inevitably arise when feminists purport to address the interests of both women and children.

This chapter presents a new framework for thinking about feminism and children, a framework rooted in children's participation in multiple relationships mediated by law. As such, the framework focuses on children's subjectivities rather than their rights. The framework grows out of concerns about the demise of children's rights discourse in the United States, but the framework offers insights for legal reform even in those countries that have embraced more robust approaches to children's rights.

The chapter begins by chronicling feminist challenges to law's objectification of children, highlighting the many ways that children remain the objects of adult and state authority despite the demise of the patriarchal family. Children's dependencies are thought to justify such treatment, yet feminist analysis exposes the ways in which law constructs aspects of that dependency. Law's role in constructing children's dependency in turn provides a basis to question law's continued treatment of children as objects rather than subjects.

The second part of the chapter proceeds to articulate a relational approach to children's subjectivity. Building on the work of Martha Minow, this approach highlights children's experiences as active participants in multiple relationships directly and indirectly mediated by law. Children's relationships are not confined to the family, nor do they solely involve hierarchal dynamics of development and control. Children instead experience a broad range of interactions as children, separate from or in addition to their interests in becoming adults, even as they remain dependent on adults for many aspects of their lives. Children's relationships therefore blur the traditional distinction between subjects and objects, providing a foundation for law to acknowledge and foster children's intrinsic interests as children.

Law never simply reflects reality, however, but also always has regulatory effects. The final part of the chapter analyzes the ways in which law constructs subjectivity by relying on the category of "child". The child is the empty space against which the category of the adult subject comes into being. Attempts to recognize children's subjectivity therefore challenge the very meaning of subjectivity in law. This constitutive relationship between children and adults may create conflicts of interest for feminists, and otherwise make change difficult, but it also highlights another way that adults and children are interdependent. Subjectivity therefore need not hinge on autonomy or a lack of dependency. Instead, law might recognize children as subjects even amidst their dependency, thereby constructing children as participants in multiple relationships and settings mediated by law.

CHALLENGING OBJECTIFICATION, RETHINKING DEPENDENCY

Feminism has long critiqued the traditional, patriarchal family, seeking change for both women and children. Indeed, a primary target of feminism's concern—patriarchy—boils down to male control over women and children. Beginning in the late 1800s, feminist reformers successfully challenged many of the social and legal structures that have sustained patriarchy, including the doctrine of coverture, which recognized only one legal actor per nuclear family—the husband. In addition to empowering women to act on behalf of themselves and their children, this challenge to coverture attacked the notion that wives and children were their husbands' and fathers' property. Feminism therefore played a large role in the demise of the property metaphor to describe family relationships.

These early feminist gains accrued to both women and children, but children often benefited only derivatively. All women, including wives, gained the ability to enter binding contracts, but children did not. Countries gave women the right to vote, but children remain disenfranchised. Changes in family law permitted women to divorce and maintain custody of their children, but children gained no voice about where they would live or with whom. Commentators often assumed that women, especially mothers, would exercise these new rights in ways that would take children's interests into account, but nothing required women to do so. Children were no longer their fathers' property, but they remained subject to the decisions of their fathers *and* mothers.

Beginning in the 1960s, some feminists, along with other advocates for children, began to question this state of affairs. Law continued to view children as the objects of either parental or state authority. Beyond mandating school attendance, the state generally concerned itself with children's lives only when parents failed to provide a minimal degree of care or did not prevent their children from engaging in misconduct. These interventions substituted state authority for parental authority; they did not empower children to act for themselves or otherwise position children as legal subjects. Children therefore remained objects in need of adult protection. Women's rights had not led to children's rights.

A robust discourse of children's rights emerged from this concern about the objectification of children (Minow, 1986). The U.S. Supreme Court, in *In re Gault*, 387 U.S. 1 (1967), extended many adult-like procedural rights to children in juvenile delinquency proceedings, limiting the previously unfettered discretion of juvenile court judges. The decision provided an opening for activists and scholars to call for children to be treated as legal subjects in other legal domains as well (Guggenheim, 2005; Wald, 1979). Many of these calls were successful in the United States, particularly with respect to children's claims against the state. The Supreme Court recognized children's speech rights in public schools in *Tinker v. Des Moines Independent Community Sch. Dist.*, 393 U.S. 503 (1969); extended due process protections to public school students facing expulsion in *Goss v. Lopez*, 419 U.S. 565 (1975); invalidated laws denying children access to contraception in *Carey v. Population Services, Int'l*, 431 U.S. 678 (1976) (plurality opinion); and extended abortion rights to minors without parental consent upon a judicial finding of sufficient maturity in *Belotti v. Baird*, 443 U.S. 643 (1979).

Internationally, such children's rights advocacy led to the adoption of the Convention on the Rights of the Child by the United Nations General Assembly in 1989. Every jurisdiction except the United States and Somalia is now a party to the Convention. The Convention goes beyond the negative rights conveyed by the U.S. Supreme Court in the 1960s and 1970s, calling on parties to provide children with affirmative rights to education, health care, and adequate standards of living, among other things. In addition, the Convention mandates that children be given a right, in accordance with their age and maturity, to express their views about decisions affecting their lives and to have those views respected. These dual rights to assistance and participation potentially situate children as legal subjects even as their needs differ from those of adults.

Yet this discourse of children's rights has not fundamentally altered children's position as the objects of parental or state authority (Oakley, 1994). Parties to the Convention on the Rights of the Child have not robustly implemented children's right to participation. Although children's views may now be solicited in family court and juvenile proceedings as a result of the right, state officials ultimately determine how to take such views into account. Moreover, the right to participation has not been broadly interpreted to include children's right to vote or to otherwise participate in decisions affecting their communities. In the United States, many scholars and activists have abandoned children's rights projects altogether, primarily in acknowledgment of the tensions between such rights and traditional notions of parental rights (Guggenheim, 2005; Hafen & Hafen, 1996; Minow, 1995). Lawmakers invoke such tensions to justify the refusal by the United States to ratify the Convention to this day (Bartholet, 2011; Woodhouse, 1998).

Children therefore largely remain subject to the decisions of either their parents or the state despite the Convention and other children's rights victories (Buss, 2004; Guggenheim, 2006). Children may now enjoy more protections from harm in their relationships with parents and state actors, but they remain the objects of adult authority, particularly in the United States. Existing law thus may best be described by invoking the image of an inverted triangle, with parents and the state at the top two points exerting power over children at the bottom (Rosenbury, 2007).

This legal framework responds, in part, to the fact that children are born completely dependent on adults and only over time develop the mental and physical capabilities needed to pursue more independent courses of action. Children have developmental needs, capacities, interests, and experiences often very different from those of adults. Law's existing approach ensures that parents and the state share the duty of caring for children as vulnerable individuals in need of protection, support, and guidance (Dailey, 2006). Instead of abandoning children "to their rights" (Hafen, 1976), this approach focuses on the care and socialization children need, encouraging parents to invest in and provide for their children, developing the close relationships necessary for making nuanced decisions about each child's unique circumstances (Buss, 2002).

Despite these strengths, many feminists continue to question law's approach to allocating authority over children. Law's focus on adult responsibility for children's welfare posits a world in which children are always dependent on adults, whether parents or state actors. Instead of challenging traditional perceptions of children as property, this focus may reinforce them (Hasday, 2004; Woodhouse, 1992). Indeed, children also live active lives in the here and now, pursuing unique pleasures and purposes outside of their relationships with adults. By focusing on children's dependency and developmental needs to the exclusion of other aspects of their lives, law perpetuates a particular vision or construction of childhood, one in which children are always dependent on adults, able to escape that dependency only by developing into adults (Bridgeman & Monk, 2000). Law therefore may be doing more than responding to children's dependency; it may also be perpetuating aspects of that dependency (Alanen, 1994).

Returning to the example of coverture may help illustrate this concern. Marital status traditionally conveyed virtually all legal rights on the husband, purportedly for the benefit and protection of married women. Although this legal regime responded to dependencies arising from childbearing and childrearing, the legal disabilities accompanying that response shaped perceptions of women's abilities both in and out of the home. Women were thought to lack the constitution to work long hours in factories or the capacity to vote, among other things. It took centuries to change those perceptions, but now it seems obvious that most, if not all, of them were created by law rather than a reflection of innate differences between men and women. Today, the law of marriage and divorce continues to respond to the dependencies of childbearing and childrearing but in a way that better reflects the autonomy of both spouses even amidst dependency.

Children's dependencies, of course, are much more a function of biology or maturity than are the dependencies of spouses. Yet the insights of feminism reveal that current legal approaches to children do more than reflect periods of reduced capacity due to chronological age. Instead, law may also create some of that incapacity. For example, laws in the United States and most other countries specify different ages for when children become legal adults for purposes of marriage, sexual activity, employment, driving, drinking, voting, and criminal prosecution, among other activities (Cunningham, 2006). Individuals therefore may be legal adults for some purposes and legal children for others.

These diverse legal definitions of childhood and adulthood at times reflect the relative nature of maturity, as individuals of a certain age may be mature enough to make decisions in some contexts but not others (Todres, 2012). At other times, however, the shifting age cutoffs reflect considerations other than, or in addition to, understandings of capacity and maturity (Appleton, 2014; Minow, 1986). The United States, for example, reduced the voting age to the draft age during the Vietnam War era largely for political reasons (Minow, 1995), and many states prosecute children as adults based on the severity of their crimes alone (Feld, 1993). In addition, when making individual determinations of children's capacity and maturity, in the context of delinquency or abortion bypass proceedings, for example, judges' assessments of children's development may be influenced by the race, class, or gender of the child in question.

Moreover, some forms of children's dependency and incapacity are explicit consequences of law. Because law generally does not permit children to engage in wage labor, enter into enforceable contracts, or consent to medical care, for example, children must rely on adults to perform those functions for them. In this respect, the age and maturity of children often do not matter; instead, the relevant factor is the legal status of "child" attaching to the individual in question (Appell, 2013). Law thus makes children "doubly dependent," with some aspects of their dependency "constructed by legal rules" and other aspects "in their lives as lived" (Minow, 1986).

Feminist analysis thereby unearths the constructed aspects of children's dependency, providing a basis to question law's continued treatment of children as the objects of parental or state authority. Unlike some earlier forms of children's rights discourse, however, this analysis does not focus solely on the contexts in which law might treat children like autonomous adults. An exclusive focus on the contexts in which children might be autonomous subjects fails to capture the ways in which all children, including adolescents, have interests and needs that are unique from adults. Instead, as set forth in the next two parts, this feminist analysis provides an opportunity to rethink children's subjectivity even amidst their dependency.

EMBRACING RELATIONAL SUBJECTIVITY

The concept of relational subjectivity provides one avenue to reconceptualize children's subjectivity. Martha Minow (1986) has most famously argued that children's rights must be considered alongside children's relationships with parents and the state. Instead of embracing a binary understanding of autonomy and dependency, this relational approach examines the multiple ways legal subjectivity actually comes into being through relationships with others. Children's legal subjectivity therefore need not hinge on their potential autonomy or a denial of their dependency. Instead, law can, and should, recognize children's subjectivity even as they remain dependent on adults (Freeman, 1998).

Relational subjectivity therefore hinges on two feminist insights. First, not even adults are completely autonomous (Minow, 1986). Instead, adults rely on others in various ways to provide the care and support that make seemingly autonomous action possible (Fineman, 2004; Nedelsky, 2011). Law thus grants rights to individuals even as they remain dependent in many ways. Second, law facilitates these relationships of interdependence, even in liberal states (Minow & Shanley, 1996). Law therefore does more than promote individual liberty or preserve distance between autonomous individuals; it also fosters the interconnectedness out of which both autonomy and dependency arise.

Parental rights, often viewed as the most fundamental of individual liberties, provide a compelling illustration of the ways legal subjectivity comes into being through relationships, not autonomy. Although parents generally make decisions on behalf of their children, law grants parents that authority. It does so by recognizing parent–child relationships, granting and protecting parental rights, and specifying that children lack the legal capacity to make most decisions on their own. In these ways, law places children in the private sphere of the family, inserting parents between children and the state (Minow, 1986).

In some situations, however, law carves out exceptions to parental authority, creating a direct relationship between children and the state despite children's dependency. Law more directly governs children's lives through compulsory education regimes, child protection systems, child labor restrictions, and laws responding to children's misconduct, among other means. In each of these contexts, the state has obligations that can be invoked by, or on behalf of, children even as they are otherwise dependent on their parents (Minow, 1986). As discussed in the part above, children rarely get to make their own decisions in these contexts, but the state limits parental rights, replacing parental prerogatives with the judgments of state actors.

In this way, law both facilitates the relationships that make parental rights possible and defines the scope of parental authority in light of children's interests. As such, parental rights concern much more than adults' choices about how to live their lives free from governmental control. The decision to have children initially implicates autonomy interests, but once a child is born, autonomy no longer suffices to explain parents' right to custody and control.

Instead of flowing from autonomy, parental rights flow from the unique nature of the parent–child relationship and state judgments about how to best respond to that uniqueness (Minow & Shanley, 1996). The parent–child relationship is unlike any other because children are born completely dependent on adults. Someone must be charged with children's care at birth; children cannot be left alone to make their own choices, including associational choices. Law grants parents custody and rights over children but also assigns parents the duty to provide children with life necessities, including food, clothing, shelter, and medical care. Parental rights and duties are thus intertwined. Parental rights exist to facilitate parents' responsibilities to children (Buss, 2002; Woodhouse, 1993).

In other words, the state grants rights to parents to ensure that many of children's needs are met through relationships with caring and responsible parents. Rights reinforce and protect the attachment bonds that arise as parents care for children. Of course, law does not produce such attachments. Most parents experience a degree of emotional attachment to children that independently motivates them to fulfill—and usually exceed—their legal duties. Yet parental rights do derive from the hope of such positive relationships (Dailey, 2014).

Parents' rights therefore come into being through the relationships they have with their children and the state's interests in facilitating those relationships. Parents carry the affirmative obligation to raise their children, and are protected while doing so, because law recognizes the close affective bonds that naturally often develop between parents and children and seeks to encourage them in many, but not all, contexts (Huntington, 2006). To conceive of parental rights in terms of individual autonomy is a denial of the dynamic nature of these relationships, thereby reducing children to objects or mere property interests, as discussed above. The concept of relational subjectivity instead supports an understanding of parental rights emerging from children's needs and the state's view about how parents may best fulfill many of these needs.

Applying the insights of relational subjectivity to children's lives yields an even greater payoff. Indeed, new understandings of children's legal subjectivity emerge from a focus on children's relationships, as opposed to their autonomy or lack thereof (Smart & Neale, 1999). Of course, existing law already considers children's relationships, but it focuses primarily on hierarchical relationships between adults and children, as discussed in the part above. The concept of relational subjectivity takes these relationships of guidance and control into account, but it also invites an examination of a broader range of children's relationships. Minow (1986) emphasized the diverse nature of children's relationships with parents and state actors, but a relational approach to subjectivity could also encompass children's relationships with other adult caregivers, siblings, peers, and even market actors.

Such consideration of the diverse nature of children's relationships both better elucidates law's current treatment of children and provides a foundation for new understandings of children and law rooted in feminist insights. Descriptively, a relationship-oriented approach reveals that children are not always on the receiving end of hierarchical relationships until they develop into adults. Instead, law mediates a range of children's experiences and interactions beyond submission to parental and state authority. This diversity in turn supports new normative understandings of children and law, including understandings that value and protect a fuller range of children's experiences and interests as legal subjects as opposed to objects.

Indeed, children interact with many individuals before becoming adults, and law mediates those relationships in multiple ways. As discussed above, law begins by recognizing the parent–child relationship and granting parental rights, which generally include directing young children's relationships with other children and adults. As children age, law more directly mediates children's relationships. At times, this regulation creates the conditions for new relationships. Compulsory education regimes and approaches to juvenile delinquency, for example, create opportunities for children to interact with other children and nonparental adults at school or in rehabilitative settings. At other times, law restricts children's relationships. For example, child labor restrictions limit children's ability to become employees and to interact with coworkers and customers.

Children themselves also begin to initiate new relationships as they age, irrespective of parental wishes or state mandates, and law addresses some aspects of those relationships while ignoring others. Antibullying statutes, for example, regulate the harmful aspects of children's peer relationships, whereas law is generally silent about the potentially positive aspects of children's friendships. Similarly, some statutory rape laws criminalize all teenage sex irrespective of the quality of those relationships and children's desire to be in them.

A nuanced examination of the existing regulation of children therefore reveals that children are active participants in multiple relationships directly and indirectly mediated by law. Children are not merely passive objects of adult or state authority until they become adults. Children instead experience a broad range of interactions as children, separate from or in addition to their interests in becoming adults, even as they are dependent on adults for many aspects of their lives. These interactions challenge the assumption that law regulates childhood only by allocating authority over children to parents or state actors. Although law does address children's dependency and promotes their development and emerging capacities, law also does, and could do, much more.

In this way, a relational approach lays the groundwork for new approaches to children's legal subjectivity, approaches that move beyond autonomy-based justifications for children's rights (Gal, 2011; Zafran, 2010). Although older children may benefit from autonomy-based arguments, such claims risk reinforcing the objectification of children by focusing on contexts in which children might be permitted to occupy the category of adults or engage in adult-like reasoning. Some children may thus be permitted to escape objectification, but most children remain subsumed by their presumed incapacity. Moreover, most autonomy-based approaches to children's rights rely on judges, prosecutors, doctors, or lawyers to determine whether children have the capacity to exercise autonomy, once again emphasizing children's position at the bottom of hierarchical relationships with adults.

One particularly promising alternative to autonomy-based approaches is an approach to legal subjectivity rooted in children's experiences as children (Lim & Roche, 2000). Rather than comparing children to adults, this alternative would focus on children's experiences and capacities in the here and now (Dailey, 2014; Hearst, 1997). Children are already active participants in multiple relationships mediated by law, but law almost exclusively focuses on the ways such relationships help, or thwart, children's development into adults. This development is vital, but it does not reflect the entirety of children's interests. Indeed, an almost exclusive focus on children's future development creates an overly narrow conception of children's lives and well-being. Children become pre-adults, always in the act of becoming people instead of people in the here and now (Jenks, 1996).

By analyzing the diverse dynamics of children's relationships, a relational approach better brings children's experiences and capacities as children into view. Children's relationships do foster their development, but they also permit children to experience pleasures and purposes in the here and now. Indeed, children likely have interests in all of their relationships that exceed their interests as future adults. Scholars in the fields of child sociology and psychology, for example, have long emphasized that children, from a relatively young age, are capable of creating rich social worlds, often structuring those relations with minimal assistance from adults (Alanen, 1988; de Winter, 1997; Lareau, 2003; Thorne, 1993).

These interests in the here and now might best be conceptualized as children's intrinsic interests, in contrast to children's instrumental interests in developing into adult citizens. As such, this approach borrows from strands of feminist legal theory that attempt to value activities traditionally assigned to women instead of, or in addition to, creating opportunities for women to enter traditionally male domains (Olsen, 1992). Rather than adapting to male norms, these strands of cultural or difference feminism seek to embrace and elevate norms rooted in women's experiences. Similarly, an attention to children's intrinsic interests resists the notion that children's experiences should always be evaluated in comparison to adult experiences and valued accordingly. Instead of focusing on what children lack, or what they will become, this approach focuses on what children already are. Children are much more than objects of adult authority even as they remain dependent on adults for many purposes.

In this manner, a relational approach better acknowledges and fosters children's experiences as active participants in multiple relationships directly and indirectly mediated by law. These intrinsic experiences blur the traditional distinction between subjects and objects. Children may transcend their dependency to be active participants in relationships, experiencing unique emotions and purposes, even as they have yet to attain the autonomy attributed to adults (Bessell & Gal, 2008). Children's intrinsic interests in their relationships therefore provide a strong foundation for new understandings of children's legal subjectivity.

EXPOSING CONSTRUCTIONS OF SUBJECTIVITY

Other approaches to feminism emphasize, however, that law never simply recognizes or values preexisting realities. Instead, law always has regulatory effects, subjecting people to identities instead of merely reflecting them (Butler, 2004; Foucault, 1978). This insight, informed by queer theory, illuminates how law produces the categories of adult and child and the very notion of subjectivity (Bridgeman & Monk, 2000; Diduck, 2000). Reformers might expose these constructions, identify who benefits and who is harmed, and propose alternative constructions, but reformers can never free children or adults from law's effects.

This regulatory focus provides additional insight about the interdependence of adults and children. Most saliently, it surfaces the role of the child in constituting the category of autonomous adult within legal discourse. The category of adult is simply presumed in most legal analysis, particularly when that analysis hinges on the existence of an autonomous agent, governed by his or her own will, capable of exerting power over himself or herself and others. Adult identity need not be emphasized because adults are viewed as the universal legal subject (Fineman, 2008). In this way, adult status operates in much the same way whiteness operates: as the invisible norm against which race comes into being (Flagg,

1998). In this case, adulthood is the invisible, naturalized baseline against which the category of childhood emerges (Bridgeman, 2000; Grahn-Farley, 2003).

But just as childhood gains meaning in relation to the invisible norm of adulthood, so does the norm of adulthood gain meaning in relation to childhood. Indeed, the concept of the autonomous adult agent relies on the category of child for its content. The autonomous adult agent is what the child is not: independent and capable of free will. Children's dependency thereby brings adult autonomy into relief; the child provides an empty space against which to define adulthood (Alanen, 1988). Childhood is not simply a social construction; it is the construction that makes the category of adult possible.

The concepts of child and adult are thus mutually dependent. An example of this dynamic can be found in a story told by Patricia Williams (1992) in her book *The Alchemy of Race and Rights*:

> Walking down Fifth Avenue in New York not long ago, I came up behind a couple and their young son. The child, about four or five years old, had evidently been complaining about big dogs. The mother was saying, "But why are you afraid of big dogs?" "Because they're big," he responded with eminent good sense. "But what's the difference between a big dog and a little dog?" the father persisted. "They're *big*," said the child. "But there's really no difference," said the mother, pointing to a large slathering wolfhound with narrow eyes and the calculated amble of a gangster, and then to a beribboned Pekinese the size of a roller skate, who was flouncing along just ahead of us all, in that little fox-trotty step that keep Pekinese from ever being taken seriously. "See?" said the father. "If you look really closely you'll see there's no difference at all. They're all just dogs."

Williams tells the story primarily to emphasize the ways that subject position matters to lived experience, despite universalizing impulses in legal discourse. Williams concludes that "These people must be lawyers," because, among other things, "How else do grown-ups sink so deeply into the authoritarianism of their own world view that they can universalize their relative bigness so completely that they obliterate the subject positioning of their child's relative smallness?" (Williams, 1992). Williams thereby highlights the ways that children become subject to adult reality, limiting children's opportunities to assert their own subject positions. As Williams writes, the story "illustrates a paradigm of thought by which children are taught not to see what they see" (Williams, 1992).

The story can be read to reveal even more, however. It illustrates the manner in which subject positions are necessarily defined in relation to one another. The parents in the story are not simply imposing their realities onto their child. Instead, the parents' perspectives are made possible in large part because their reality is constructed through the distinctions between adults and children and humans and "just dogs." Pursuant to this view, the concept of human agency comes into being, and is continually reconstituted, by contrasting human capabilities against those of animals. Similarly, the concept of the autonomous subject comes into being, and is continually reconstituted, by contrasting adult maturity against children's dependency. Here, the parents perform, and thereby reinforce, their positions as autonomous subjects by, first, educating their son in the distinction between human and animal and, then, asserting their power to define what relationships and fears should matter to the child as he prepares to enter the world of adult maturity. The parents thereby exist as subjects by subjecting their son to their will.

In this way, the categories of adult and child constitute one another. Even adults who are not parents depend on the relation between adult and child to give content to the concepts of autonomy and agency that constitute the legal subject. Three influential scholars of children's lives acknowledged these dynamics while arguing for expanded parental control over children, declaring

> To be a *child* is to be at risk, dependent, and without capacity to decide what is "best" for oneself.

> To be an *adult* is to be a risktaker, independent, and with capacity and authority to decide and to do what is "best" for oneself.

> To be an *adult who is a parent* is to be presumed in law to have the capacity, authority, and responsibility to determine and to do what is good for one's children. (Goldstein, Freud, & Solnit, 1979)

The categories of adult and child thereby come into being again each other. The category of parent in turn ensures that law appropriately manages, and maintains, the distinction.

Attempts to reconceptualize children as subjects, as opposed to objects, thus threaten much more than patriarchal authority. They also challenge the very conceptions of adults and parents currently embraced, and constructed, by law. If adults are defined against children's lack of subjectivity, then concepts of children's subjectivity disrupt the very distinction between adult and child.

This broader threat could explain why feminists have not done more to alter law's current treatment of children. Feminists, too, are dependent on the relation between adult and child to constitute the subject of much feminist concern: women (Castaneda, 2001). Like the category of adult, the category of woman comes into being in contrast to the category of child. The dynamic may be even more salient in this context, however, as "repronormativity" often conflates womanhood with motherhood (Franke, 2001), and women are more likely than men to provide daily care to children as an empirical matter.

Indeed, women—more so than men—may rely on children to perform their own adult subjectivity. Just as adulthood serves as the invisible baseline against which childhood emerges, so too did men traditionally serve as the invisible baseline against which gender emerged. As such, only women had a gender and, as described above, that gender was used to justify law's preferential treatment of men and subordination of women. Although the relationship between women and men is now much more egalitarian, remnants of separate spheres ideologies persist. The parent–child relationship may thus remain an attractive avenue for women to perform their subjectivity. As Mary Joe Frug wrote: "The maternalized female body triangulates the relationship between law and the meanings of the female body. It proposes a choice of roles for women" between legal and illegal sex (Frug, 1992).

A focus on the ways subjectivity comes into being therefore calls into question feminism's ability to promote the interests of both women and children. Even a relational approach may mask the power women exercise over children (Federle, 1993), including the ways women may use children to perform their own subjectivities. Such power dynamics in other contexts have prompted a call for reformers and theorists "to take a break from feminism" (Halley, 2006).

Yet feminism alone is not responsible for law's construction of subjectivity, and feminist insights have laid a strong foundation for challenging it. In fact, feminist analysis unearths the role of the child in constituting the adult legal subject. Such exposure is the first step toward altering what appears to be natural and fixed. Feminism also has long sought to identify who benefits and who is harmed by seemingly neutral legal rules, and there is no reason that feminists cannot be trusted to do so in this context. Feminists might do more to acknowledge "the blood on their hands" (Halley, 2006), but feminism remains an important tool for dissecting and reallocating power and privilege.

Importantly, feminist analyses of the construction of subjectivity provide additional insight about the interdependence between adults and children, further challenging the binary between autonomy and dependency. Autonomy is not just a myth (Fineman, 2004); it is a myth that is perpetuated through law's deployment of the category of child. As a theoretical matter, then, adults use children to assert autonomy. Autonomy is not innate or the natural byproduct of chronological age and development. Instead, autonomy must be constantly established against the child to give the concept any content. Without children, autonomy as we know it has no meaning.

This insight is similar to those underlying the relational approach to subjectivity, discussed above, but also different. The relational approach blurs the distinction between autonomy and dependency as an empirical matter, highlighting the ways adults rely on care and relationships and the ways children have interests in their relationships that exceed their dependency. In contrast, a focus on the ways subjectivity is constructed blurs the distinction between autonomy and dependency as a conceptual or theoretical matter. Adult autonomy comes into being only through children's dependency; the categories of adult and child depend on one other even as law attempts to maintain the categories as distinct. Law's denial of this conceptual interdependence may, in turn, affect the lived experiences of both children and adults, as they attempt to conform to legal expectations regarding both adult autonomy and children's development and dependency (Alanen, 1994).

By exposing and analyzing these forms of interdependence, feminism lays a foundation for new conceptions of subjectivity that transcend the binaries of autonomy and dependency and even adult and child (Diduck, 2000). The fluidity between autonomy and dependency reveals that legal subjectivity need not hinge on autonomy or a lack of dependency. Law could instead construct subjectivity differently. Drawing upon relational approaches to subjectivity, law might better acknowledge and foster children's diverse experiences as active participants within relationships. Or law might go even farther to solicit children's views on a range of issues affecting their lives and communities (Lim & Roche, 2000), taking care "to ensure that analysis of what they have to say is not framed by understandings and expectations of children held by adults" (Bridgeman & Monk, 2000).

Under either approach, children's intrinsic experiences as children would better come into view, inviting considerations of their perspectives alongside those of adults (Minow, 1990). In turn, these child-centered approaches to subjectivity would likely permit more fluid and individualized understandings of children and their capacities than the status quo currently permits. Most saliently, such approaches would challenge law's construction of children as vulnerable beings consistently in need of adult guidance, protection, and control until they develop into adults.

But such approaches would not free children, or adults, from law's effects. Reform could take multiple paths, making it difficult to predict all the ways it would affect children, adults, and the state. Yet it is certain that law would continue to have regulatory effects, producing experiences as well as reflecting them. Law and legal actors would thus continue to construct children, albeit as participants rather than objects (Diduck, 2000). Understandings of adult capacities and prerogatives would also likely shift as participation became untethered from adult status or autonomy. Feminism therefore cannot liberate children or adults from law, but feminist analysis can expose existing constructions of children and subjectivity, propose alternative constructions, and ultimately analyze who benefits and who loses under both old and new approaches.

This new framework for considering the relationship between children, feminism, and law does not provide easy answers, but it does provide a structure for challenging law's ongoing treatment of children as the objects of parental and state authority. By focusing on children's participation in multiple relationships mediated by law, the framework offers both descriptive and normative arguments for altering the status quo. Women's rights have not led to a robust regime of children's rights, but a feminist focus on children's subjectivities might finally forge a path toward better recognizing children's personhood even amidst their dependency.

REFERENCES

Alanen, L. (1988). Rethinking childhood. *Acta Sociologica*, *31*(1), 53–67.

Alanen, L. (1994). Gender and generation: feminism and the "child question." In J. Qvortrup, M. Bardy, G. Sgritta, & H. Wintersberger (Eds.), *Childhood matters: social theory, practice and politics* (pp. 27–42). Avebury: Aldershot.

Appell, A. R. (2013). Accommodating childhood. *Cardozo Journal of Law & Gender*, *19*(3), 715–779.

Appleton, S. (2014). Restating childhood. *Brooklyn Law Review*, *79*(2), 525–549.

Bartholet, E. (2011). Ratification by the United States of the Convention on the Rights of the Child: pros and cons from a child's rights perspective. *Annals of American Academy of Political and Social Science*, *633*(1), 80–101.

Belotti v. Baird, 443 U.S. 643 (1979).

Bessell, S., & Gal, T. (2008). Forming partnerships: the human rights of children in need of care and protection. *International Journal of Children's Rights*, *17*(2), 283–298.

Bridgeman, J. (2000). Embodying our hopes and fears. In J. Bridgeman & D. Monk (Eds.), *Feminist perspectives on child law* (pp. 207–226). London: Cavendish Publishing.

Bridgeman, J., & Monk, D. (2000). Introduction: reflections on the relationship between feminism and child law. In J. Bridgeman & D. Monk (Eds.), *Feminist perspectives on child law* (pp. 1–18). London: Cavendish Publishing.

Buss, E. (2002). "Parental" rights. *Virginia Law Review*, *88*(3), 635–683.

Buss, E. (2004). Allocating development control among parent, child and the state. *University of Chicago Legal Forum*, *2004*(1), 27–55.

Butler, J. (2004). *Undoing gender.* New York: Routledge.

Carey v. Population Services, Int'l, 431 U.S. 678 (1976).

Castaneda, C. (2001). The child as feminist figuration: toward a politics of privilege. *Feminist Theory*, *2*(1), 29–53.

Cunningham, L. (2006). A question of capacity: towards a comprehensive and consistent vision of children and their status under law. *UC Davis Journal of Juvenile Law & Policy*, *10*(2), 275–378.

Dailey, A. C. (2006). Developing citizens. *Iowa Law Review*, *91*(2), 431–503.

Dailey, A. C. (2014). Children's transitional rights. *Law, Culture and the Humanities.*

de Winter, M. (1997). *Children as fellow citizens: participation and commitment.* Cambridge: Radcliffe Publishing.

Diduck, A. (2000). Solicitors and legal subjects. In J. Bridgeman & D. Monk (Eds.), *Feminist perspectives on child law* (pp. 251–270). London: Cavendish Publishing.

Federle, K. H. (1993). On the road to reconceiving rights for children: a postfeminist analysis of the capacity principle. *DePaul Law Review*, *42*(3), 983–1028.

Feld, B. C. (1993). Criminalizing the American juvenile court. *Crime & Justice*, *17*(1), 197–280.

Fineman, M. A. (2004). *The autonomy myth: a theory of dependency.* New York: New Press.

Fineman, M. A. (2008). The vulnerable subject: anchoring equality in the human condition. *Yale Journal of Law & Feminism*, *20*(1), 1–23.

Flagg, B. (1998). *Was blind, but now I see: white race consciousness and the law.* New York: New York University Press.

Foucault, M. (1978). *The history of sexuality: an introduction* (Robert Hurley trans., 1990). New York: Vintage Books.

Franke, K. (2001). Theorizing yes: an essay on feminism, law, and desire. *Columbia Law Review*, *101*(1), 181–208.

Freeman, M. D. A. (1998). The sociology of childhood and children's rights. *International Journal of Children's Rights, 6*(4), 433–444.

Frug, M. J. (1992). A postmodern feminist legal manifesto (an unfinished draft). *Harvard Law Review, 105*(5), 1045–1075.

Gal, T. (2011). *Child victims and restorative justice: a needs-rights model.* New York: Oxford University Press.

Goldstein, J., Freud, A., & Solnit, A. (1979). *Before the best interests of the child.* New York: Simon & Schuster.

Goss v. Lopez, 419 U.S. 565 (1975).

Grahn-Farley, M. (2003). A theory of child rights. *University of Miami Law Review, 57*(3), 867–937.

Guggenheim, M. (2005). *What's wrong with children's rights.* Cambridge, MA: Harvard University Press.

Guggenheim, M. (2006). Ratify the U.N. Convention on the Rights of the Child, but don't expect any miracles. *Emory International Law Review, 20*(1), 43–68.

Hafen, B. C. (1976). Children's liberation and the new egalitarianism: some reservations about abandoning children to their rights. *Brigham Young University Law Review, 1976*(3), 605–658.

Hafen, B. C., & Hafen, J. O. (1996). Abandoning children to their autonomy: the United Nations Convention on the Rights of the Child. *Harvard International Law Journal, 37*(2), 449–484.

Halley, J. (2006). *Split decisions: how and why to take a break from feminism.* Princeton, NJ: Princeton University Press.

Hasday, J. E. (2004). The canon of family law. *Stanford Law Review, 57*(3), 825–900.

Hearst, A. (1997). Domesticating reason: children, families and good citizenship. In A. McGillivray (Ed.), *Governing childhood* (pp. 200–224). Aldershot: Dartmouth Publishing Group.

Huntington, C. (2006). Rights myopia in child welfare. *UCLA Law Review, 53*(3), 637–699.

In re Gault, 387 U.S. 1 (1967).

Jenks, C. C. (1996). *Childhood.* London: Routledge and Kegan Paul.

Lareau, A. (2003). *Unequal childhoods: class, race, and family life.* Berkeley: University of California Press.

Lim, H., & Roche, J. (2000). Feminism and children rights. In J. Bridgeman & D. Monk (Eds.), *Feminist perspectives on child law* (pp. 227–249). London: Cavendish Publishing.

Minow, M. (1986). Rights for the next generation: a feminist approach to children's rights. *Harvard Women's Law Journal, 9*(1), 1–24.

Minow, M. (1990). *Making all the difference: inclusion, exclusion, and American law.* Ithaca, NY: Cornell University Press.

Minow, M. (1995). Whatever happened to children's rights? *Minnesota Law Review, 80*(2), 267–298.

Minow, M., & Shanley, M. L. (1996). Relational rights and responsibilities: revisioning the family in liberal political theory and law. *Hypatia, 11*(1), 4–29.

Nedelsky, J. (2011). *Law's relations: a relational theory of self, autonomy, and law.* New York: Oxford University Press.

Oakley, A. (1994). Women and children first and last: parallels and differences between children's and women's studies. In B. Mayall (Ed.), *Children's childhoods: observed and experienced* (pp. 13–32). London: Falmer Press.

Olsen, F. (1992). Children's rights: some feminist approaches to the United Nations Convention on the Rights of the Child. *International Journal of Law and the Family, 6*(1), 192–220.

Rosenbury, L. A. (2007). Between home and school. *University of Pennsylvania Law Review, 155*(4), 833–898.

Smart, C., & Neale, B. (1999). *Family fragments.* Cambridge: Polity Press.

Thorne, B. (1993). *Gender play: girls and boys in school.* New Brunswick, NJ: Rutgers University Press.

Tinker v. Des Moines Independent Community Sch. Dist., 393 U.S. 503 (1969).

Todres, J. (2012). Maturity. *Houston Law Review, 48*(5), 1107–1165.

United Nations General Assembly, Convention on the Rights of the Child, 1989.

Wald, M. S. (1979). Children's rights: a framework for analysis. *U.C. Davis Law Review, 12*(2), 255–282.

Williams, P. J. (1992). *The alchemy of race and rights: diary of a law professor.* Cambridge, MA: Harvard University Press.

Woodhouse, B. B. (1992). "Who owns the child?": Meyer and Pierce and the child as property. William and Mary Law Review, 33(4), 995–1122.

Woodhouse, B. B. (1993). Hatching the egg: a child-centered perspective on parents' rights. Cardozo Law Review, 14(6), 1747–1865.

Woodhouse, B. B. (1998). From property to personhood: a child-centered perspective on parents' rights. *Georgetown Journal on Fighting Poverty, 5,* 313–319.

Zafran, R. (2010). Children's rights as relational rights: the case of relocation. *Journal of Gender, Social Policy & the Law, 18*(2), 163–217.

PART I

Child Participation in Education and Research Settings

CHAPTER 2

Inclusion and Participation in Special Education Processes in Ontario, Canada

MONA PARÉ

INTRODUCTION

Inclusion and *participation* are buzzwords that have been heard in different domains, mostly in relation to groups that have traditionally been at the margins of society. The use of these words is related to concerns about poverty, multiculturalism, and women's rights, for example; they are embedded in aspirations for a society that is inclusive of all and where all participate actively in political decision-making or economic production. Inclusion and participation have a more specific meaning in relation to the education of children with disabilities, where they are related to children's rights and the rights of persons with disabilities. While participation and inclusion are two different concepts, they are intrinsically linked through their connections to the concepts of equality and nondiscrimination. Traditionally, inclusion may refer to the inclusion of children with disabilities in regular schools and classrooms, or, in a wider sense, it may refer to the application of inclusive philosophies related to teaching methods, and to the accommodation of special needs. Participation can be multiform, but in law it requires hearing the voice of children with disabilities. Meaningful inclusion can only be achieved with the participation of children with disabilities both in the process that leads to inclusion and in experiencing inclusive education.

With this theoretical and philosophical framework as a backdrop, this chapter examines more specifically the participation of children with disabilities in special education procedures in Ontario. The findings are based on research conducted for the Law Commission of Ontario in 2010 (Paré, 2010), as well as ongoing research on the special education procedures and inclusive education in Canada (Paré & Bélanger, 2014). The chapter describes the existing procedures that are used to determine children's special education needs, as well as their placement. It also looks at available remedies when families disagree with decisions made by the school. In the second half, the chapter examines and evaluates children's participation in these procedures, taking into account direct and indirect forms of participation. The level and style of participation are discussed based on legal provisions, policy documents, and case law, as well as interviews with children, parents, and other stakeholders. The findings are discussed in light of the provisions of the Convention on the Rights of the Child (CRC), as well as the Convention on the Rights of Persons with Disabilities (CRPD), which specifically applies to children with disabilities. These two instruments offer valuable information as to what inclusion and participation ought to mean for children with disabilities in the school context.

PARTICIPATION AND INCLUSION

Inclusion and participation are practices that have special meaning in the context of disability movements and children's rights. They are both essential to the education of children with disabilities, marking a move away from segregation and from a type of integration that simply tolerates children with special needs in the classroom. Moreover, participation entails hearing directly from children with disabilities on matters that concern them.

The Philosophy of Inclusion and the Education System

The concept of inclusion is one that carries special meaning to persons with disabilities, and it is instrumental in the movement recognizing their rights. In the context of education, the concept of inclusive education has been promoted as a reaction to policies and practices of exclusion and segregation. For example, in Canada, until the 1960s, children with disabilities were mostly excluded from the school system (Bachor, 2007). The 1960s saw the development of special education in the form of segregated schooling. Human rights and nondiscrimination movements became increasingly popular through the 1970s and 1980s, affecting law and policy. These years saw the drafting of the CRC, and the UN Decade of Disabled Persons. In Canada, these movements started translating into inclusive policies in the 1980s and 1990s with the adoption of legislation providing for the education of children in regular schools (Education Amendment Act, 1980). In addition, a charter of rights and freedoms was added to the Canadian constitution in 1982 (Canadian Charter, 1982). The philosophy of inclusion was fully developed in the 1990s, as evidenced by the Salamanca Statement and

Framework of Action adopted at the end of the World Conference on Special Needs Education in 1994. This statement calls for inclusion to be the norm in the education of children with disabilities (Salamanca Statement, 1994). Now, the philosophy of inclusion is further strengthened in the CRPD adopted in 2006 (United Nations, 2006).

Ontario's approach to inclusive education has moved from recognition of rights to "integration" of children with disabilities into mainstream education, to the extent that it is in the child's best interest, to an understanding of inclusion as a wide concept in a multicultural society. Currently, the Ministry of Education (2009) defines inclusive education as "Education that is based on the principles of acceptance and inclusion of all students. Students see themselves reflected in their curriculum, their physical surroundings, and the broader environment, in which diversity is honoured and all individuals are respected." This is a positive step, as it depicts an inclusive philosophy that entails society being inclusive of all, as opposed to children with disabilities being "integrated" into a system that is not adapted to them. However, such a statement is meaningless if it is not followed by the adoption of programs and services that meet the special needs of children with disabilities.

Incorporating the needs of children with disabilities in a statement about inclusive classrooms would facilitate the move away from "integration" that simply tolerates the presence of children with disabilities in a regular classroom setting, and toward "inclusion" of children with disabilities in a setting that addresses the needs of all.

Participation: A Component of Inclusion and a Legal Right

Participation, like inclusion, is used in many contexts as a catch-all concept from the civil rights movements to good governance and development. As it generally implies being involved in matters affecting oneself and society, participation is also present in the discourse on persons with disabilities, where it is linked to social inclusion. In general usage, participation refers to the actual participation of persons with disabilities in everyday activities in society. It is referred to in this way in Article 23 of the CRC dealing with the rights of children with disabilities (United Nations, 1989). This article requires the existence of conditions that "facilitate the child's active participation in the community" and links it to social integration, access to education, training services, preparation for employment, and recreation opportunities. In the same vein, the World Health Organization's (2001) International Classification of Functioning defines participation as a person's involvement in a life situation. Participation in the context of disability rights is therefore linked to inclusion as opposed to segregation.

In the context of children's rights, participation has taken a more precise legal meaning, as it refers to Article 12 of the CRC, and the right of children to be heard on matters affecting them. While this article does not mention "participation," its contents, which deal with respect for the views of the child, are now commonly referred to as children's participation rights. Accordingly, UNICEF (2003) describes child participation as "adults listening to children—to all their multiple and varied ways of communicating. It ensures their freedom to express themselves and takes their views into account when coming to decisions that affect them."

Article 12 creates a two-step legal obligation for states and a procedural right for children (Paré, 2012). First, children should be able to express their views in all matters concerning them, and second, their views should be given a certain degree of weight by the decision makers. This obligation concerns all decisions affecting children individually or children as a general population group. With reference specifically to judicial and administrative procedures affecting children, the article states that children should be heard either directly or through a representative. I will refer to these as *direct* and *indirect* participation. Article 12 reads as a solid procedural right that can be claimed by children or on their behalf. Adding to CRC's Article 12, CRPD specifies in Article 7 that children with disabilities should be given disability- and age-appropriate assistance to realize their right to express their views on an equal basis with others.

SPECIAL EDUCATION PROCEDURES AND OTHER RELEVANT PROCESSES

Having examined the concepts of inclusion and participation from philosophical and legal perspectives, particularly in the context of education, this chapter will now turn to specific matters that concern children with disabilities in the area of education, outlining decision-making procedures that affect these children particularly.

Decision-Making Processes Affecting Children with Disabilities

All school systems include certain decision-making processes that are not necessarily linked to the special education context but that can affect children with disabilities. In Ontario, studies about the disproportionate impact of disciplinary measures on children with disabilities (in addition to racial minorities) have led to policy changes. As a reaction to the Ontario Safe Schools Act of 2000, which was considered to encourage a "zero tolerance" approach by school boards, the Ontario Human Rights Commission published a report on the impact of the law on certain groups of children and launched complaints against the Ministry of Education and the Toronto District School Board (Bhattacharjee, 2003). As a result, the law was revised in 2007, making it mandatory to consider mitigating factors before imposing penalties and providing flexibility for dealing with discipline on a case-by-case basis (Education Amendment Act, 1980).

This change is significant for children with disabilities, as the report by the Ontario Human Rights Commission demonstrated that the lack of adequate accommodations for students with special needs in the school system led to misunderstanding about the behavior of some students with disabilities and therefore to misguided responses, including suspension and expulsion. Children with certain types of disabilities were more affected than others; in particular the report identified intellectual and learning disabilities, autism, Tourette syndrome, and behavioral disorders as being related to disciplinary measures.

Suspension is the temporary removal of a child from school, for a maximum of 20 days, while expulsion means removing a child from a school or from all the schools of a school district for an indefinite time. There is thus an important difference of gravity between these two measures, which means that the procedures are different as well. While suspensions are decided by a school's principal, only school boards can make decisions about expulsions based on the principal's recommendation. Currently the procedure for suspensions is the following in Ontario: The principal will consider whether to suspend a pupil if he or she believes that the pupil has engaged in an activity that will have a negative impact on the school climate (Education Amendment Act, 1980). The principal must consider mitigating factors, including whether the behavior was a manifestation of a disability identified in the student's Individual Education Plan (IEP), and whether appropriate accommodation has been provided. This requires the prior accurate identification of a student's disabilities. The principal will have to notify the parents/guardians of the suspended pupil, including information about the right to appeal a suspension. Parents will need to notify of their intention to appeal, and the appeal process will happen at the board level. After the hearing, the board's decision is final. A student cannot be expelled before being suspended first. Certain activities, such as possessing a weapon, will lead to immediate suspension, during which expulsion will be considered. The same mitigating factors will be considered here. The expulsion recommendation will be sent to the parents and an expulsion hearing will be heard by the school board. Students expelled from their own school will be assigned to another school, while students expelled from all schools of the district will be offered supports in a program for expelled students. Expulsion decisions can be appealed by the parents at the school board level.

It is important also to mention "exclusions," as a type of decision that mostly concerns children with disabilities. Children with disabilities may be excluded from school without this being a disciplinary measure. The Education Act allows the principal "to refuse to admit to the school or classroom a person whose presence in the school or classroom would in the principal's judgment be detrimental to the physical or mental well-being of the pupils." This provision is routinely used to ask parents to pick up their child if the child's needs are not being met and the child's behavior is considered unsafe. Unlike suspensions and expulsions, there is no formal procedure that leads to exclusions, which may be for an indeterminate time and which give no appeal rights to parents. It can therefore lead to discriminatory use of the measure.

Special Education Procedures and Remedies

In some provinces, there are only general procedures that are applied to all decisions concerning children at school, whether they are disciplinary measures or decisions relating to their special needs. In contrast, Ontario has adopted the most detailed legislation concerning procedures that specifically deal with special education: the identification of students with special needs, and their placement and programming.

A number of law and policy documents govern special education in Ontario. The most important ones are the Education Act, more specifically Regulation 181/98 on Identification and Placement of Exceptional Pupils. According to the act, "exceptional pupil" means a pupil whose behavioral, communicational, intellectual, physical, or multiple exceptionalities are such that he or she is considered to need placement in a special education program. The Ministry of Education (2001) has adopted policies that further define and categorize these exceptionalities that are used for identification purposes.

Formal and informal processes are involved. The informal procedure involves the elaboration of an IEP by the school principal in consultation with school staff and parents. It does not necessarily lead to formal identification procedures, and it is the main avenue for receiving services and programming matching the student's special needs. An IEP identifies a student's learning expectations and outlines the special education program and services for the pupil, as well as methods of evaluation. The main difference between a formal and an informal procedure is that the IEP process does not formally identify and place a student with exceptionalities and does not give any right to contest the contents of the IEP or its poor application. Also, an IEP is mandatory for all formally identified students, while it is optional for others.

The formal process is carefully described in Regulation 181/98. Central to this process is the Identification, Placement and Review Committee (IPRC), whose role is to decide whether the student should be identified as exceptional; to identify the areas of the student's exceptionality, according to the categories of exceptionalities provided by the Ministry of Education (e.g., autism, learning disability, mild intellectual disability, low vision, speech impairment); to decide about an appropriate placement for the student (regular or special classroom, or partial integration into regular classroom); and to review the identification and placement regularly.

If parents contest the IPRC's decision concerning a specific identification or placement, they may request a second meeting of the IPRC. If this fails, they may file an appeal to the board, and the board will establish a Special Education Appeal Board (SEAB). As a last resort, the parents may go to the Ontario Special Education Tribunal (OSET), which is set up to hear appeals concerning identification and placement. The tribunal's decisions are final.

Separately from the IPRC placement process, parents may apply for their child to attend a provincial school for the deaf, blind, or deaf-blind, or for those who have severe learning disabilities. Admission is determined by an admission committee and the superintendent. Refusals are subject to appeal, and the Ministry of Education (1990) will set up a committee to decide on questions of eligibility for admission of a student.

CHILDREN'S PARTICIPATION IN PROCEDURES: THEORETICAL AND LEGISLATIVE CONSIDERATIONS

As inclusive education involves participation of children with disabilities, and as participation entails hearing children on matters affecting them, it is important to now examine the participation of children with disabilities in the education-related procedures outlined above. Both direct and indirect participation are of interest to this study, and the legislative and policy frameworks have been analyzed in light of both types of participation.

Direct and Indirect Participation

Direct participation is the most effective form of participation, as it allows children to participate in procedures that concern them by having a direct voice, feeling part of the process, and witnessing and understanding proceedings that concern them. In the context of special education, direct participation entails, for example, that children be given the opportunity to express themselves on matters that concern them directly, for example at the level of identification and placement procedures or the development of their IEP. Given their impact on children with disabilities, I will also include decisions concerning suspensions and expulsions.

Direct participation requires that children are given relevant information in a format they understand, and that they may express themselves in a way that works for them, not necessarily according to the modalities developed for and by adults. Participation rights guaranteed by the CRC and the CRPD also require that the views of children be not only heard but also taken into consideration.

Therefore, when children participate directly, it is important to make sure that procedures are adapted for their participation to be effective and not simply *pro forma*. It would be important, for example, that adults be prepared for children's participation, that children understand the procedure, that they are actively included, and that the procedure is based on dialogue rather than a confrontational model. This is especially important for more formal procedures, such as the meetings of the IPRC or SEAB.

Difficulties that are related to full participation naturally differ from one child to another, and from one context to the next (Paré, 2010). Therefore, participation has to be dealt with on a case-by-case basis. For example, in rural areas, the lack of services and the need for transportation may be obstacles to children's participation. Given the great diversity of disabilities, it is clear also that the type and degree of exceptionality must be taken into consideration. However, for all, accessibility of information and communication is crucial, and it is linked to a correct diagnosis of exceptionalities, the availability of services, and the training of involved adults. For example, a deaf child may need the services of a sign language interpreter, or a hearing aid and/or the presence of adults who are trained in the oralist method. A child with learning difficulties may need oral and/or visual information. With its detailed definitions of "communication" and "language," the CRPD gives an indication of the scope of accommodations needed to achieve accessibility of communication for all.

The child's age, level of development, and maturity must also be taken into account to ensure that all have the chance to participate in a meaningful way. Research indicates that there is no minimum age to express an opinion (Covell, 2010; Lansdown, 2001). However, adjustments must be made to allow children of different ages to participate (Committee on the Rights of the Child, 2009). For example, the participation of high school students may resemble that of adults, with some vocabulary adjustments, while a child in kindergarten may participate through drawing.

Obstacles related to age and disability are also often related to prejudices that adults may have. Adults tend to protect children and may therefore restrict their access to information that is crucial for effective participation. Awareness raising and training for adults are therefore important components of a strategy to ensure children's direct participation in administrative procedures.

While direct participation may be the form of participation to strive for, it is not always realistic. This form of participation requires many conditions to be met, including a child's willingness and capacity to participate directly, as well as procedures that are adapted so that they are accessible and child-friendly. The CRC recognizes that direct participation may not always be a feasible or desirable option for administrative and judicial proceedings, as it provides for the possibility for children to participate directly or through a representative. The more formal the procedure, the more likely it is that we resort to indirect participation through a representative. However, if a child participates through a representative, it is important that this representative transfers the child's viewpoints and does not only represent his or her own understanding of the child's best interests. While the child's representatives are usually his or her parents, and while it is understood that parents know best what is in the interest of their child, one should not forget that parents' interests do not always coincide with the child's best interests, and that parents' viewpoints will often be tainted by their own interests. At the same time, one also needs to be aware of the fact that the child's opinion does not always coincide with the child's best interests. Participation is an empowering experience in itself and has individual and social benefits that positively affect the child's development and relationships (Campbell & Rose-Krasnor, 2007). Therefore, children's participation should not be about putting forward the child's best interests, but about letting the child express his or her opinion and have the opportunity to participate, even indirectly, in a procedure that concerns him or her.

Parents should be made aware that they have an obligation to help their child exercise his or her participation rights in a way that respects the child's evolving capacities (Grover, 2008). This does not mean that parents can't represent and defend their own point of view, but if they represent their child and help the child exercise his or her participation rights, they must know their child's opinion and relay it to the decision makers. This also applies to other people who may represent children, such as lawyers, guardians *ad litem*, child advocates, education advocates, and others.

Participation in the Ontario Legislative and Policy Framework

How does the Ontario legislative framework take into account direct and indirect participation of children in the education system and particularly in relation to special education? There are very few provisions that deal with children's participation, which is a blatant omission, especially considering that education is mandatory in Ontario until the age of 18. A few provisions deal with participation at the policy level, for example providing for the election of student trustees to represent the interests of pupils on school boards. Even fewer provisions deal with students' participation in decision-making processes that concern them individually. Regarding disciplinary measures, students have a certain, albeit small, place in suspension and expulsion procedures. They do not receive notice and are not parties to hearings and appeals unless they have reached the age of majority. However, they can make a statement at suspension appeal hearings and expulsion hearings, both of which happen at the school board level. For expulsions, the law simply states that the principal, when examining the possibility of expulsion during the pupil's suspension, should endeavor to speak with the pupil. Concerning special education procedures more specifically, the Education Act is silent on student participation, while Regulation 181/98 determines that students will participate in special education procedures from the age of 16. If they are at least 16 years of age, students will be consulted in relation to the development of their IEP, and they will be invited to participate in IPRC and SEAB meetings. However, students cannot be parties to an OSET hearing. Students who are younger than 16 may participate in IPRC meetings only if requested by the IPRC and with their parents' consent. No provision deals with the participation of children under the age of 16 in the development of the IEP, and none provides for the participation of children in the development of the student transition plan. This plan, which is mandatory for children aged 14 and up, concerns their options and orientation after leaving high school.

The policy documents of the Ministry of Education do not give further details concerning the participation of students with disabilities. This contrasts with the approach of the Ontario Human Rights Commission, which has adopted policy documents concerning accessibility to education. The Commission links respect for dignity and provision of accommodation with the student's participation in the accommodation process (Ontario Human Rights Commission, 2004). The Commission also recognizes that many students have become experts in their own accommodation needs and have the ensuing responsibilities to, among others, make their needs known and participate in discussions regarding accommodation solutions.

While the Ministry of Education's policy documents have been disappointing, some nonbinding guides and reports published by the Ministry point in the right direction. A guide on conflict resolution emphasizes the importance of self-advocacy for students and discusses the desirability of having students attend conflict resolution meetings between parents and school. In the context of special education, an example would be a SEAB meeting. To decide whether a student should participate, the guide suggests examining if the student has (Ontario Ministry of Education, 2007)

- The ability to understand the procedures and content of the meeting (cognitive functioning)
- The ability to behave appropriately during the meeting (behavioral functioning)
- The ability to identify, express, and cope adequately with feelings in a meeting (emotional maturity)
- Specific needs (e.g., physical, language) that require accommodations at the meeting

In a more specific context, OSET has issued information sheets and guidelines on children's participation in the tribunal's hearings. While children cannot be parties to the hearing, they can be called as witnesses, or the parents may wish their child to attend so that he or she can observe the hearing or so that the tribunal may meet the student. However, OSET is very cautious in its approach: It exhorts parents to consider carefully whether to involve children, given that hearings may be long, complicated, and stressful. If parents decide to bring their child to the audience, and especially if the child is to testify, OSET (2014) suggests that the parents prepare the child for this by explaining the procedure and having the child visit the hearing room beforehand. OSET (2009) does recognize that allowing students to testify "gives them a voice within the process and allows them to talk about issues that affect their learning at school." Special accommodations may be provided, considering the child's physical, intellectual, or communicational disabilities; the hearing may be closed to the public on request; and the presence of a support person for the student is suggested.

Concerning indirect participation, the legislation does not address children's representation specifically, but Regulation 181/91 gives an important role to parents in discussions concerning their child. For example, parental preferences are considered when deciding on a child's placement in a special education class or in a regular class with supports. Moreover, parents will be consulted in relation to their child's IEP, they are entitled to attend IPRC meetings, and they can appeal decisions. One may therefore imagine that this could open the door to children's indirect participation in special education procedures in practice.

ASSESSING CHILDREN'S PARTICIPATION IN PRACTICE

Legislative and policy documents do not offer an adequate picture of children's participation in procedures that concern them. It is difficult to know whether children under the age of 16 are invited to participate and to what extent those who are 16 and over actually participate. The Auditor General of Ontario has noted that it is difficult to have information on the conduct of IPRC meetings because of lack of documentation. The documentation available makes it impossible to determine, for example, whether members of the IPRC had encouraged parents and students to participate in the discussions at the meeting, as only decisions are recorded, not the process and discussions that led to them (Office of the Auditor General of Ontario, 2008). Information on children's participation thus has to be obtained through other means.

Examining Case Law

Since documentation held by schools does not give enough indications about children's participation in special education procedures, one could get a better idea by examining case law concerning students with disabilities. *Eaton*, which dealt with the issue of integration of a child with disabilities in a regular classroom, is an important decision concerning the place of children's opinion in decisions that concern them. In this case, the Supreme Court of Canada recognized that indirect participation is well suited for younger children and those who do not communicate well: "for a child who is young or unable to communicate his or her needs or wishes, equality rights are being exercised on his or her behalf, usually by the child's parents . . . For older children and those who are able to communicate their wishes and needs, their own views will play an important role in the determination of best interests" (*Eaton*, 1995). The judgment by the Court of Appeal of Ontario in the same case dealt with children's participation differently (*Eaton*, 1995). Justice Arbour distinguished between parents who represent their children in processes that are linked to special education, such as the IPRC, and parents who assert their child's constitutional rights in court. In the former case parents may represent their own views, while in the latter they represent their child and make submissions on their child's behalf. The wishes of the child are therefore expressed by the parents as legal representatives.

After examining these two judgments and reading the legislation and policy documents, one can contend that the primary reason for parents' participation in the education system is to give room to parents' preferences. In all special education procedures, such as the IPRC, parents express their own preference based on what they believe is in the best interests of their child. It is therefore not an example of children's indirect participation through their parents, except perhaps in cases where the parents have actually had a discussion with their child beforehand, and they have agreed as a family on a course of action, or if they have decided to put forward their child's viewpoint instead of or in addition to their own. Therefore, some individual cases may allow for children's indirect participation, but this is not the intention of the legislation in place. Children's participation in the school system is dependent on parent–child relationships, since the law and procedures in place do not emphasize this participation.

This contrasts with the human rights system, as exemplified by the *Eaton* case and the position taken by the Ontario Human Rights Commission. When parents bring a claim to court concerning a human rights violation in the context of their child's education, there is a presumption that they are actually representing their child, since their child does not have the legal capacity to file a legal action. In this case, parents speak in the name of their child and exercise rights on behalf of their child. Only in case of a conflict of interest between the child and the parents will the parents not be allowed to represent their child and a litigation guardian may be appointed (*Arzem*, 2005). It is especially important that parents exercise rights on their child's behalf if the child is young and incapable of expressing his or her desires. As the child gains age and maturity, the court is more likely to want to hear the child's voice directly, and that voice will be important in determining his or her best interests.

Hence, there are significant differences between the education and the human rights sectors, which both deal with special education issues. The human rights sector in Canada is restricted in scope and not mainstreamed; violations of human rights, generally limited to discrimination cases, are dealt with separately by a human rights tribunal. One of the differences between the two sectors lies in the use of the best interests principle. This concept is completely absent from the education legislation in Ontario. Nonetheless, according to the Supreme Court of Canada, a child's placement has to be in the best interests of the child. This has also been the practice of OSET, which applies this criterion in its decisions, especially since the Supreme Court's ruling in the *Eaton* case.

While the concepts of the best interests of the child and child participation rights could seem contradictory given the presence of different interests and competing definitions of the best interests of a child, these concepts are intimately linked. Case law in many areas of law concerning children has determined the opinion of the child to be an important factor when determining the child's best interests (Paré, 2012). Therefore, applying the concept of best interests in the education system would probably foster children's participation and encourage decision makers to listen to children. However, it would be best to include the child's opinion as a consideration of his or her best interests in the law, as only relying on the best interests principle may exacerbate parent–school conflicts, given that school officials are the experts on children's interests in the school system and parents consider themselves to be the experts on their child's best interests generally (Bennett, Dworet, & Zhaos, 2008; Jory, 2001). Without a clear link to children's participation rights, the best interests principle can also become an instrument in a philosophical debate between inclusion advocates and those who prefer special education in a segregated setting.

Very few decisions by the OSET deal with children's participation in special education procedures. One, however, is noteworthy in this regard: *S & Peel District School Board*, which deals primarily with the identification of a child who has learning disabilities, and incidentally with the child's participation. In this case the school board wished to have the child participate, insisting on the importance of the views of the child, while the parents were opposed to it. Given this opposition, the parties agreed that the tribunal would meet privately with the child in a familiar environment: his school (*S & Peel District School Board*, 2007). OSET recognized that meeting the child was useful and productive. The parents wanted more services for their child, while the child wanted fewer and wished not to be labeled as a pupil with exceptionalities. The tribunal recommended that the parties meet with the child present to try to resolve communication problems. The tribunal emphasized the importance of considering the child's views, especially since the child was a secondary school student. In an *obiter dictum*, the tribunal thanked the child for meeting with the panel and encouraged him to continue to self-advocate.

This case was clearly a positive step toward recognizing the importance of children's participation in special education procedures. Yet it also shows how child participation can be instrumentalized by parties. Here the school board clearly wanted the child to participate, as his views were opposed to those of the parents, who were appealing the school board's decision concerning their child's identification and placement. One can easily imagine the opposite scenario where parents would want their child to testify if it reinforced their argument, while the school board would perhaps discourage it. If child participation was more systematic, it would less likely be instrumentalized by one of the parties. It would also ensure that the child's participation rights are respected and that the decision maker gets to hear the child's voice before deciding on the child's best interests.

Hearing the Voices of Stakeholders

Examination of participation through judgments does not provide an accurate picture of practice, as the cases before tribunals represent a tiny fraction of parent–school conflicts related to special education. One also has to recognize that not all special education procedures end up being confrontational. Short of a large and representative survey, some indication can be drawn from interviews with a variety of stakeholders that were held in Ontario in 2010 (Paré, 2010). The main objective of the research was to collect the viewpoints of children with special needs on the special education processes and to learn about their participation in them. However, given the difficulties in finding enough children for the interviews, more interviews were conducted with parents as well as other actors, such as education activists and representatives of a variety of organizations involved in these procedures. As a result, discussions were held with forty-eight children and youth, aged between 9 and 21 years, which is the end of school age for children with disabilities in Ontario. These children were all schooled in Francophone or Anglophone schools in the Ottawa region. Most of them participated in group discussions organized by Centre Jules-Léger, a Francophone special education school that has programs for the deaf and blind, as well as for children with severe learning disabilities. Some participated through an organization for children with intellectual and developmental disabilities, LiveWorkPlay, and only two children participated through direct contact with their parents. Three of the interviewees were not children with disabilities but rather students who have roles as student representatives at different levels. Issues discussed with the students included the significance of participation and their participation in decision-making procedures in school. A total of thirty-five parents participated in interviews, which were organized through parent associations representing different exceptionalities. Questions discussed with parents concerned their experience of participation in the education system, and more specifically in the special education procedures, their capacity to represent their child, and their child's participation in these procedures. In addition, interviews were conducted with representatives of over twenty governmental and nongovernmental organizations, associations, and committees.[1] Most of the people representing these organizations were parents of children with special needs. Only fourteen representatives did not self-identify as a parent. Questions asked concerned these people's and organizations' roles as representatives of children with disabilities.

While these research results are not in any way representative of the population with special needs and the interested stakeholders, interesting elements can be drawn from discussions with children and adults. Concerning children's points of view, discussions indicated that children understood the concept of participation and were generally happy with their level of participation in school. They also identified being heard as a right. Their participation is often limited to making choices between options that are presented to them, but they seemed not to question this. Examples of participation included choices of extracurricular activities, food choices, or co-op placement in high school. Those who participate more, such as student trustees, members of the Minister's Student Advisory Council, school councils, student councils, and student senates, recognize that they do not represent the student body as a whole and that such participation is a choice that only some students make. Most students are not interested in increasing their level of participation and seem to enjoy the optional nature of participation. Those who want to participate have the opportunity to do so. However, it seems like it is the same youth who get to participate in every realm, and these "leader" types are less likely to be children with disabilities. Nonetheless, the student representatives identified surveys as an opportunity for all students to participate.

It was also clear from interviews that children do not participate in special education–related procedures, but they were aware of these procedures and their parents' implication in them. The level of participation seemed to be greater in the provincial residential schools for the deaf, the blind, and children with severe learning disabilities that do not depend on school boards. Children from the Francophone provincial school talked about their student government, which is involved in decisions concerning activities. However, they also talked about participation in meetings and interviews leading to their enrolment in the school. They all felt that they were part of the discussions and they were asked

---

1. Association francophone de parents d'enfants dyslexiques, Ottawa-Carleton Association for Persons with Developmental Disabilities, Autism Ontario, Office of the Provincial Advocate for Children and Youth, Centre Jules-Léger, Ontario Early Years Centres (Ontario Ministry of Children and Youth Servics), Child Advocacy Project (Pro Bono Law Ontario), special advisory committees of school boards, Minister's Advisory Council on Special Education (Ontario Ministry of Education), school boards (trustees and personnel), Easter Seals, Edu-advocates, Learning Disabilities Association of Ontario, LiveWorkPlay, Ontario Association for Families of Children with Communication Disorders, Ontario Association of the Deaf, Société franco-ontarienne de l'autisme, Voice for hearing impaired children.

whether they wanted to join the school.[2] The Office of the Provincial Advocate for Children and Youth confirmed that youth are also included in discussions about appeals when their application to join such a school is refused, while this participation is not provided for in the law.

Interesting details concerning children's participation were gathered from interviews with adults. According to parents and representatives of the various organizations, the great majority of children do not participate in special education–related processes: The younger ones are not invited, and the older ones are not encouraged to attend or are not interested in coming. Only six of the adults (two parents and four organization representatives) gave evidence of their efforts to include children in these processes. Many pointed to the fact that children's participation hinges on the attitudes of schools, parents, and the children themselves. Because of lack of encouragement by schools and parents, even students who are over 16 years old tend not to participate. According to some of the adult interviewees, students' self-advocacy efforts were sometimes even discouraged or penalized by teachers or principals. When self-advocacy was encouraged, it was not so that the student could advocate for his or her rights, but so that he or she could ask for assistance to the extent that this was already offered in the school.

What was also mentioned as an obstacle to child participation was the formality of the procedures in place, especially the IPRC. These procedures are intimidating for parents, and all the more so for children. As a school board trustee stated: "I wouldn't wish any child to have to go through that. The setting is not good. Everyone talks about their disabilities, test results, weaknesses, etc." An education advocate further noted that when children participate, "professionals focus more on the wheelchair than the person in it. When kids are 16, they are encouraged to come to their own IPRC. But the majority don't, and if they come, they are talked about in the third person."

Concerning indirect participation through representatives, parents felt that the system was not adapted for them to speak on behalf of their children and to advocate for their children's needs. First of all, there is a power balance that is not favorable to parents, as they are usually alone facing a group of professionals and experts in the IPRC meetings. It was felt that the education system is based on an expert model, which is an important obstacle to parents' effective participation. Because parents are in this weak position, schools have been able to impose decisions on them. Some reported that they had even been discouraged from starting an IPRC procedure, which is the only procedure that allows parents to challenge decisions concerning their child's identification and placement. Parents reported various ways in which they were discouraged from using official recourses, ranging from misinformation to threats. The fact that 40 percent of children receiving

2. Focus group discussion with children aged 10 to 16 from Centre Jules-Léger, May 26 and 27, 2010.

special education services have not been formally identified through the IPRC process speaks to this preference by schools to avoid formalizing the process and opening the door to parent complaints.[3] All participants agreed that schools do not offer adequate information on the different procedures and that parents have to seek information outside school to be able to defend their children's rights. This is where the different associations have a crucial role. Associations that represent different exceptionalities, such as learning disabilities, autism, developmental disabilities, or hearing impairment, help parents to know their rights, to navigate the education system, and to get support during the various procedures. Despite the important support role that these associations provide for parents of children with special needs, some were critical, pointing to their weaknesses. For example, it was stated that each of these associations follows its own philosophy and values, which do not correspond to those of all the families (e.g., along the lines of the inclusion-vs.-segregation debate). Moreover, it was noted that some of these organizations are better financed and organized than others, and as a consequence some groups of children with disabilities are better represented than others.

Some people involved in the system become education advocates and offer their services to parents to help them resolve their conflicts with the school or the school board. The advocates act usually as mediators and bring a certain equilibrium to the power balance. Some of them also offer direct legal representation. All of the education advocates spoke of the importance of including children in the discussions and the procedures related to special education. One advocate elaborated on this:

> Children should be encouraged to participate in the process. I didn't do it with my daughter. Then after school she didn't know how to advocate for her rights in university. Parents must sit down with their child and explain what is [an IEP]. Have them be able to tell the teacher what works and what doesn't, know how to ask for examples, etc., say how they understand better. Parents should fill in forms with their child. It's important to start when they are very young . . . After a certain age, children should participate in the IPRC meetings. For [the IEP], parents and teachers should sit down with the child, first the parents, and then the teacher after the teacher has met with the parents.

Another advocate recognized that when children do participate in meetings, adults listen to them: "Usually kids know what they need to succeed, like extra time, a different space for quiet, a calculator. When kids come to a meeting and stand up, ask for something, usually they get it."

---

3. According to information for the 2010-11 school year, 127,000 students in Ontario were receiving special education services without being formally identified, while 191,600 were identified (Ontario Ministry of Education, 2014).

While schools and school boards were clearly avoiding the IPRC route because of its formality and appeals process, many parents also stated their avoidance of such procedures out of fear that the situation would escalate and that this would have a negative effect on their child at school. Many confirmed that these fears were justified and that parents advocating for rights and citing laws were labeled as troublemakers, which was then counterproductive for their child. Some people noted that parents' fear of confrontation and its consequences can be founded: When parents choose legal recourses they often find themselves alone defending their child, facing the school board's lawyers. These attitudes came out clearly in the OSET's *obiter dictum* in the *Eaton* case that later went all the way to the Supreme Court of Canada. The tribunal chastised the parents for having resorted to judicial and quasijudicial avenues of redress, compromising the student's well-being (*E & Brant County Board of Education*, 1993). The Ontario Court of Appeal rightly stated that the parents had simply availed themselves of the only procedures available to them by legislation in pursuit of their child's legal right to equality (*Eaton*, 1995).

CONCLUSION

Inclusion and participation are related concepts and are central to the education of children with disabilities. Inclusive education has come to mean education that is inclusive of all, in which all children feel like they belong, and in which they can actively participate. Participation in the context of children's rights means not only being socially included but also having one's voice heard in matters concerning oneself. Particularly in the context of administrative and judicial procedures, participation can be direct or indirect through a representative. To assess the participation of children with disabilities in the education context, it is therefore essential to examine decision-making processes related to special education, which may determine, for example, children's inclusion in a regular classroom or the offer of appropriate programs and services, and to examine children's participation in these procedures.

As is evident from the analysis of policy and legislative documents, as well as case law and interviews with children and other stakeholders, Ontario currently does not allow for children's participation in an inclusive education context. Not only are the special education procedures not specifically geared toward inclusion, but also children's views are not being sought, especially if they are under 16 years of age. Obstacles to children's participation include the lack of legislative provisions and policy statements. More significantly, obstacles are related to the attitudes of adults and the nondisabled toward the capacities and interest of those who are perceived as vulnerable. There is some support for participation, for example through the positions taken by the Ontario Human Rights Commission. However, applying the documents and principles that support participation takes will and the understanding that including children in decision-making procedures that concern them is part of their participation rights and contributes to inclusive education.

In this context, it would be preferable to take concrete steps to improve the participation of children with disabilities in education processes that concern them and to ensure that participation is not entirely dependent on attitudes. The following is a nonexhaustive list of recommendations:

- Monitor the application of guidelines adopted by the Ontario Ministry of Education and the Human Rights Commission that promote student participation and that give clear guidance on how to include students.
- Create directives on the participation of students, over and under the age of 16, in IPRC meetings and other special education processes, to ensure that all actors comply with a participatory process.
- Ensure that students are informed of their participation rights in the special education context, and prepare them for participation in formal processes.
- Create campaigns to educate parents on the importance of student participation and about their role in encouraging their child to participate and preparing their child for participation.
- Change the law to allow students who are 14 to participate in special education processes, and include them in the development of their transition plan.
- Ensure that student governance systems are transparent, and encourage students with disabilities to participate in policy discussions.
- Include human rights language in education legislation and policies.

REFERENCES

Arzem v. Ontario (Community and Social Services), 2005 HRTO 11 (CanLII), para. 233.

Bachor, D. (2007). Special education in Canada. In C. Reynolds & E. Fletcher-Janzen (Eds.), *Encyclopedia of special education* (3rd ed., vol. 1, p. 351). Hoboken, NJ: Wiley.

Bennett, S., Dworet, D., & Zhaos, M. (2008). Special education rights: services for children with special needs in Ontario schools. In T. O'Neill & D. Zwinga (Eds.), *Children's rights: multidisciplinary approaches to participation and protection* (p. 283). Toronto: University of Toronto Press.

Bhattacharjee, K. (2003). The Ontario Safe Schools Act: school discipline and discrimination. Ontario Human Rights Commission. Available at http://www.ohrc.on.ca/en/ontario-safe-schools-act-school-discipline-and-discrimination.

Bill 212, the Education Amendment Act (Progressive Discipline and School Safety Act), S.O. 2007, c. 14.

Campbell, K., & Rose-Krasnor, L. (2007). The participation rights of the child. In K. Covell & B. Howe (Eds.), *A question of commitment: children's rights in Canada* (p. 209). Waterloo: Wilfrid Laurier University Press.

Canadian Charter of Rights and Freedoms, Part I of the Constitution Act, 1982, being Schedule B to the Canada Act 1982 (UK), 1982, c 11.

Committee on the Rights of the Child (2009). General Comment no. 12, "The Right of the Child to be Heard," UN Doc. CRC/C/GC/12.

Covell, K. (2010). School engagement and rights-respecting schools. *Cambridge Journal of Education*, 40(1), 39–51.

E & Brant County Board of Education, Ontario Special Education (English) Tribunal, file #19, 19.11.1993.

Eaton v. Brant County Board of Education, [1995] Ontario Court of Appeal, O.J. No. 315.

Education Amendment Act (1980), S.O. 1980, c. 61.

Grover, S. (2008). Comments on *Eaton*. In S. Grover, *The child's right to legal standing* (p. 180). LexisNexis.

Jory, D. (2001). Problems with the Supreme Court's *Eaton* decision. Ontario Coalition for Inclusive Education. Available at http://www.inclusive-education.ca/resources/documents/eaton_decision.pdf

Lansdown, G. (2001). *Promoting children's participation in democratic decision-making.* Innocenti Insight. Florence: UNICEF.

Ministry of Education (1990). *Policy/Program Memorandum No. 89: The residential demonstration schools for students with learning disabilities: general information and details of the referral process.* Ontario.

Ministry of Education (2001). Special education. A guide for educators. Ontario. Available at http://www.edu.gov.on.ca/eng/general/elemsec/speced/guide.html

Ministry of Education (2009). *Realizing the promise of diversity: Ontario's equity and inclusive education strategy* (p. 4). Ontario.

Office of the Auditor General of Ontario (2008). Annual report (Chapter 3.14, Special Education). Available at http://www.auditor.on.ca/en/reports_2008_en.htm

Ontario Human Rights Commission (2004). Guidelines on accessible education. Available at http://www.ohrc.on.ca/en/guidelines-accessible-education, referring to the Commission's 2000 policy document: *Policy and guidelines on disability and the duty to accommodate.*

Ontario Human Rights Commission (2004). The opportunity to succeed: Achieving barrier-free education for students with disabilities. Available at http://www.ohrc.on.ca/en/opportunity-succeed-achieving-barrier-free-education-students-disabilities/roles-and-responsibilities

Ontario Ministry of Education (2007). Shared solutions—A guide to preventing and resolving conflicts regarding programs and services for students with special education needs. Available at http://www.edu.gov.on.ca/eng/general/elemsec/speced/shared.html: 27

Ontario Ministry of Education (2014). An introduction to special education in Ontario. Available at http://www.edu.gov.on.ca/eng/general/elemsec/speced/ontario.html

Ontario Special Education Tribunal (2009). Practice direction—Student as witness. Available at http://www.oset-tedo.ca/eng/directions.html

Ontario Special Education Tribunal (2014). Information for parties, Information Sheet no. 3. Available at http://www.oset-tedo.ca/eng/pdfs/Information.pdf

Paré, M. (2010). The participation of persons with disabilities in the decisions that concern them: the example of education. Law Commission of Ontario. Available at http://www.lco-cdo.org/en/disabilities-call-for-papers-pare [in French].

Paré, M. (2012). Exploring children's participation as a right protected under Canadian law. In E. Murray (Ed.), *Children matter—Exploring child and youth human rights issues in Canada* (Chapter VII). Mount Royal University [e-book].

Paré, M., & Bélanger, N. (2014). La recherche de l'inclusion scolaire à travers les recours offerts aux familles: perspective comparative canadienne dans un contexte franco-phone minoritaire. *Canadian Journal of Law and Society, 29*(3), 327–344.

S & Peel District School Board, Ontario Special Education (English) Tribunal, file #58b, 12.02.2007.

Salamanca Statement on Principles, Policy and Practice in Special Education (1994). World Conference on Special Needs Education, Salamanca, Spain, June 10, 1994, UNESCO.

UNICEF (2003). Child participation. In *The state of the world's children 2003*. Available at http://www.unicef.org/sowc03/contents/childparticipation.html

United Nations (1989). Convention on the Rights of the Child, A/RES/44/25.

United Nations (2006). Convention on the Rights of Persons with Disabilities, A/RES/61/106.

World Health Organization (2001). The International Classification of Functioning, Disability and Health, http://www.who.int/classifications/icf/en/

CHAPTER 3

Implementing the Principle of Child Participation

Pupils' Participation in Placement Committees in Israel

ERAN UZIELY[1]

INTRODUCTION

Children's Rights and the Right to Participate

In 1991, Israel joined other countries in ratifying the United Nations Convention on the Rights of the Child (CRC), which in turn required the government to advance both legislation and practice of issues pertaining to the rights of children. In addition to reiterating the commitment to ensure children's nurturance rights, which appeared in previous international documents, the convention also referred to civic and political rights, which had never before been granted to children: freedom of expression, the right to privacy, and the right to participate in decisions that pertain to their own lives (Melton, 2005a). While children's nurturance rights are fairly obvious, as they depend on adults to access basic needs and to obtain protection, the right to self-determination is not self-evident and has been the source of numerous disputes (Bohrnstedt, Freeman, & Smith, 1981; Ruck, Keating, Abramovitch, & Koegl, 1998).

Since its ratification, the convention has functioned as a legal, moral, and judicial source influencing legislation, policymaking, and the delivery of social

1. This research was partly funded by the Minerva Center for Human Rights at the Hebrew University of Jerusalem.

services in Israel (Dolev & Ben Rabi, 2002). Nonetheless, the issue of the right to self-determination for children continues to arouse discussion to this day, and practical as well as theoretical debates regarding children's ability to participate in decision-making processes are still common. Various opinions can be found among parents, professionals, and members of academe, ranging from a conservative approach that views the child as the parents' property, to the inverse approach, which claims that children should enjoy the same rights as adults do. This chapter considers the fulfillment of the participation right of children in educational settings in the context of placement decisions in Israel. Its findings, however, may be relevant to other topics as well as to other jurisdictions.

Pupils' Participation in Placement Processes in Israel

According to the Special Education Law 5748 (1988), the placement committee is the professional body that decides whether a pupil is eligible to receive special education services. It also determines which educational framework is most suitable for the child: a mainstream framework, a special education classroom within a mainstream school, or a special education school. The decision is based on the child's educational needs and the obligation to place children in the least restrictive environment possible.

The committee is headed by a representative of the local authority and includes a psychologist, a special education supervisor, and a representative of the Parents Council. For every pupil, an invitation is issued to include two representatives from the child's current school (homeroom teacher and either school counselor, psychologist, or principal) and the child's parents.

Prior to its amendment, the law stated that the committee is obligated to hear the parents and their claims; it did not state that the pupil's voice should be heard as well (Special Education Law 5748, 1988). There are no precise data available regarding the rate of pupil participation at that time. An earlier study that analyzed placement committee decision-making processes reported that of the sixty observations conducted, a pupil was present in only one discussion (Igell, 2006). Following an educational intervention initiated by Igell, the rates of participation rose to 16.7 percent.

As mentioned, Israel ratified the CRC in 1991. The convention obligates signing countries to present a report once every five years to enable the international community and the general public to critique the progress of CRC implementation (CRC Article 44). In 2001, the first report examining CRC implementation in Israel was issued. The authors of the report found that within the special education placement process, children—unlike their parents—had no say in the committee's review process (Dolev & Ben Rabi, 2002).

As a result, in 2005, Special Education Law (Amendment 8) was issued— "Right to a Hearing for the Pupil in Placement and Appeals Committees." It stated the following: "The placement committee will issue an invitation to the parents of the child with special needs and to the child, and will enable them—or a representative on their behalf—to state their claims." In addition, the amendment stipulates that in the decision-making process, the committee should take into consideration the pupil's preferences. It is important to note that the law posed no conditions regarding the child's participation (such as age or severity of the disability). The regulations for the implementation of this law were detailed about a year later, in the Ministry of Education's Director General's Circular 66/8(B) 2006. The authors of the regulatory document noted the fact that the moral rationale for the procedure was grounded in the CRC.

Issues Related to Regulation Implementation

The terms dictated by the law are clear: The placement committee must include the pupil and hear the pupil's perspective before reaching a decision. Nevertheless, several issues remain unresolved.

1. Pupils' opinions regarding their own participation in the committee were never sought, whether they were interested in participating, and if so in what fashion, since even the very issue of children's participation was initiated and monitored by adults (May, 2005).
2. According to Kozminsky (2004), special education children fare worse than other children in terms of educating for participation and independence. More specifically, teachers of children with special needs tend to let them participate less, allow them fewer opportunities to make choices in the course of their studies, and assign them fewer responsibilities. The pupils, for their part, demonstrate a greater dependency on their teachers, avoid taking responsibility for decisions, and refrain from participation. Therefore, to ensure that children with special needs participate in the placement committee's meeting in a significant manner, a professional and ongoing process should be established to prepare and accompany them. Such processes have been devised in Israel and throughout the world in an attempt to strengthen the self-representation skills among pupils with special needs (Kozminsky, 2004; Mason, Field, & Sawilowsky, 2004; Test & Neale, 2004). Circular 66/8(B) 2006 requires the school staff to conduct a broad and comprehensive preparation process with the child prior to the committee's meeting; however, it is unknown whether or to what extent this regulation is implemented.
3. The law enables parents to decide regarding the presence of their child at the committee and mentions that the parents' decision should be based on considerations pertaining solely to the child's well-being (Special Education Law, Amendment 8, 24/1/2005). Clearly, parents have their own interests that do not always match those of their child (Matthews, Limb, & Taylor, 1999).

4. In the spirit of the CRC, the Israeli law instructs the placement committee to take the pupil's position into consideration when making the decision regarding the pupil's future (Special Education Law, Amendment 8, 24/1/2005). There are many participants in the placement committee, all of whom wish to have their own opinion prevail. How will the pupil's opinion be weighted relative to the opinions of the parents, the school representatives, or any other committee members?

Clearly the pupil's opinion is based on neither expertise nor experience in the realm of education. In addition, the child is the object of negative stereotyping and prejudices directed at people with special needs (Leake & Cholymay, 2004). A relatively large proportion of the pupils in special education also belongs to ethnic or cultural minorities and thus are the target of prejudices and stereotypes reserved for minorities (Bevan-Brown, 2006; Geenen, Powers, & Lopez-Vasquez, 2001). On top of all of these difficulties, and in contrast to all other committee participants, the pupil belongs to a segment of the population whose opinion is routinely ignored, namely children (Matthews et al., 1999). Taking all of these aspects into consideration, it is not likely that the committee will give much consideration to the opinion of the pupil.

Melton (2005b) refers to this issue and suggests that the interactions in the committee should not be perceived as a zero–sum game, in which each participant aims to enforce his or her viewpoint on the other participants. Instead, Melton claims, the committee's deliberations should be treated as a process in which all participants share one goal: to think about and determine the best option for the child. Unfortunately, this is not the atmosphere that consistently characterizes the committee's deliberations. The Margalit Report (2000), which reviewed the implementation of the Special Education Law, including the work of the placement committees, describes a culture of suspicion, offense, and anger as characteristic of some of the committees. The interactions in similar committees in other countries have also been described in terms of a power struggle, marked by victories and losses (Harry, 1992).

Summary and the Goal of the Study

The current study analyzes actual discussions in placement committees, in which both adults and youths experienced child participation, in order to examine the fulfilment of the legal participation right stated in the Israeli Special Education Law and its regulations.

Two measures were used to determine whether pupils' participation in the placement committee coincided with the vision intended by the law. The first measure was the extent to which pupils participated in the discussion. Given that not all pupils are interested in participating in the discussion to the same extent, and maybe some would have preferred not to participate at all, the other major indicator of the process of participation was the pupils' overall satisfaction with the process, in the sense that the discussion was conducted fairly and that the committee enabled them to voice their opinions.

Based on the findings, a picture emerges. The discussion focuses on factors that may advance or limit participation, and on possible ways of promoting pupil participation in the placement committee.

METHODS

Study Population and Sample

The study referred to three population groups: pupils who were the focus of placement committee discussions, their parents, and professionals who participate in the decision-making process of the placement committees.

The pupil questionnaire was distributed to nine special education classes of seventh-grade pupils attending public schools in the cities of Jerusalem, Modi'in, and Ramle during the months of October and November 2009. The questionnaires were filled by a total of seventy-two pupils, constituting 86 percent of all the pupils in these classes. All of the cases of these pupils were reviewed in placement committees that were convened just before they were to enter middle school (seventh grade in Israel), and about four months before the questionnaires were filled out. When they attended the placement committee meeting, these pupils were between the ages of 12 and 14—that is, young people whose opinion is typically sought in the culture in which they live.

The parent sample consisted of the parents of the pupil sample participants (one parent for each child) and included a total of forty-seven parents (56 percent of the sample), among them eleven participants whose child did not complete the pupil questionnaire.

The sample of professionals included 115 participants from all over Israel who participate in placement committees, among them committee chairs, regional supervisors of special education, inclusion teachers, homeroom teachers, and school psychologists. The professionals reported on their experience in placement committees in general, whereas pupils and their parents reported on the specific placement committee meeting they attended.

Variables and Measures

Data were collected using three questionnaires: one for pupils, one for parents, and one for professionals. The questionnaires were similar (with the necessary adjustments made) and gathered information on three groups of variables.

Variables Related to the Pupil's Background and Family

The pupil questionnaire referred to the following background variables: participants' gender and religion, number of siblings, parents' education level and occupation, year of immigration, and country of origin. Adults were asked to provide additional information: their age, personal status, and family income.

The questionnaire for the professionals gathered in addition the following information: number of years in the profession, role in the committee, and age and type of the population with which the professional works routinely (mainstream or special education). Professionals were divided into three groups according to their specific roles: professionals who work in the field (e.g., homeroom teacher), professionals who do not interact intensively with pupils on a daily basis (e.g., school principal), and professionals whose educational work does not involve interaction with pupils (regional educational supervisor).

Dependent Variables

Level of Pupil Participation

For the purposes of the study, an eight-point linear scale was developed to describe various levels of pupil participation in the discussion. This scale was based on a scale for evaluating civic participation in political decision-making (Arnstein, 1969). Arnstein constructed a linear scale to describe the degree of influence civilians have on decision-making processes compared to the influence of politicians and bureaucrats. At the low end of the scale, citizens are invited to participate in the process, yet the intention is not sincere; rather, the government seeks to impose its preference on the participants or to educate them. In the middle range of the scale (in a gesture of tokenism, or false participation), citizens are asked to present their perspective; however, there is no mechanism that ensures that the decision makers will take their perspective into consideration. At the high end of the scale, the citizens' influence comes into play, either through civic representation among the decision makers, or, at the highest end of the scale, where citizens have complete control over the project.

Other theoreticians have outlined various models to describe different levels of participation and the relations between them; some, like Hart's ladder of young people's participation (1992), are even specifically children-oriented. However, none describes the shift from child neglecting to child control in such a simple yet accurate manner as this version of Arnstein's ladder. This is a linear scale, so each stage includes the ones that preceded it and adds a step toward pupil control:

1. The committee convenes without informing the pupil.
2. The pupil is informed of the committee meeting but is not asked to attend.
3. The pupil is asked to attend as an observer.

4. During the discussion, the pupil is offered an explanation of what is taking place in the committee.
5. The pupil is present and expresses an opinion before the committee members.
6. The pupil expresses an opinion, asks questions, and answers others' questions.
7. The pupil has a vote just like any other member of the committee.
8. The pupil alone decides which school to attend.

On this scale, participants were asked to mark two levels: first, the level that represented their perception of the optimal (desired) level of pupil participation, and second, the actual level of pupil participation during the committee meeting.

Satisfaction of Pupils and Parents Regarding the Placement Committee Meeting

Pupils' satisfaction regarding the committee meeting was assessed using four different statements such as "participants let me express my opinion" and "I was treated fairly." The participants ranked each statement on a four-point scale ("agree completely" to "do not agree at all"). Parents and professionals were asked also about the parents' satisfaction regarding the committee meeting. As internal consistency between the statements was high, the average ranking of items was considered a reliable measure of the pupils' and the parents' satisfaction regarding the meeting.

Independent Variables

Preparation for Participating in the Committee's Discussion

Using a dichotomous item, pupils were asked whether they had been prepared for the meeting; if the answer was positive, pupils were asked who helped them prepare.

Participants' Attitudes to Unconditional Participation

Using a dichotomous item, participants were asked to indicate whether in their opinion each pupil should have the right to participate in his or her own placement committee. If the answer was negative, participants were asked to define which populations should not participate in the discussion.

Participants' Attitudes Regarding the Best Representatives of the Pupils' Interests

Participants were asked who, in their opinion, best represents the pupils' interests in the committee. Instructions were to choose only one representative;

nevertheless, some of the parents (who had filled in the questionnaires at home) chose more than one figure.

Participants' Support for Rights in Different Contexts

This measure was based on a questionnaire used in the study of Khoury-Kassabri, Haj-Yahia, and Ben-Arieh (2006). Statements from the original questionnaire were rewritten to coincide with the pupils' reading level. Participants were asked to mark on a scale from 1 to 4 the extent to which they supported each of the nine statements, which represented different facets of children's rights. Cronbach's alpha for internal consistency was not high (.681 for pupils, .626 for parents, and .557 for professionals). Factor analysis recognized three content areas: children's rights as pupils at school (four items, α = .516), children's rights as members of the community (two items, α = .595), and children's rights in the family (three items, α = .473). For each content area, the average of items was calculated. The first category explained 49.4 percent of the variability among participants; the remaining categories did not fit the model (Table 3.1).

Table 3.1. FACTOR ANALYSIS OF STATEMENTS RELATED TO CHILDREN'S RIGHTS

Items: Every Student has the Right to:	Factor Loadings		
	Rights as a School Student	Rights as a Member of the Community	Rights Within the Family
Learn at school	**.795**	.104	
Express an opinion in class discussion	**.629**		.213
Not be abused physically or verbally	**.577**	.347	−.120
Explain his or her perspective before being penalized	**.540**		.159
Attend a school demonstration		**.832**	.226
Participate in the neighborhood's costume parade	.232	**.790**	
Express a preference regarding his or her place of residence when parents divorce		.245	**.700**
Not let others handle his or her private belongings			**.687**
Decide which extracurricular activities to pursue	.422		**.629**

Numbers in bold letters indicates that items share mutual factor

Participants' Reports on the Level of Children's Participation
Within the Participant's Family

Based on the questionnaire used in the study of Khoury-Kassabri and colleagues (2006), twelve statements were formulated that describe various situations of children's participation within the family (e.g., participating in family decisions and expressing an opinion during an argument). On a four-point scale, participants indicated the degree to which each statement described the situation in their family.

Following the factor analysis, three statements were excluded. Due to the relatively high level of internal consistency between the remaining statements (α = .696, .694, and .741, for pupils, parents, and professionals, respectively), the average score for the nine remaining items was considered a reliable measure of children's level of participation within the family, as experienced by the participants.

Pupils' Reports Regarding Participation at School

All pupils assessed the level of pupil participation in their school. To this end, the study relied on the questionnaire used in the study of Khoury-Kassabri and colleagues (2006); however, the number of statements was reduced and the language was adapted to match the participant population. The outcome was a section on the questionnaire that consisted of eight statements, describing situations in which pupils may participate within the educational framework (e.g., expressing an opinion during class discussion and disagreeing with the teacher's decision). On a four-point scale, participants indicated the degree to which each statement reflected the situation at their school.

Internal consistency was found to be .505 Cronbach's alpha, which is not high. A factor analysis identified two major factors: pupils' freedom of expression (four items, α = .645) and teachers' receptivity (two items, α = .388). The first category was found to explain 58.9 percent of the variability among participants; no other factors were included in the model (Table 3.2).

Average item rankings were calculated for each content area, and the two additional statements were used separately.

Procedure

The research procedure met four ethical standards: (1) the research rationale was presented to the participants in full transparency; (2) members of the sample were given the opportunity to refuse to participate; (3) the questionnaires contained no hurtful statements; and (4) the participants would remain completely anonymous.

Table 3.2. FACTOR ANALYSIS OF STATEMENTS RELATED TO
STUDENTS' PARTICIPATION AT SCHOOL

Items	Factor Loadings		
	Freedom to Express an Opinion	School's Receptivity	Non Categorized Statements
1. Students are encouraged to express their opinions in the classroom	**.794**	.138	
2. Teachers wants to know what students think of their school	**.771**	−.309	
3. Students feel free to express their opinions	**.512**	.472	.379
4. Teachers explain their decisions	**.472**	.255	.452
5. Students are not afraid to express a critical opinion about their school		**.769**	
6. Students feel free to disagree with teachers' decisions		**.748**	.222
7. The school administration involves the students in setting regulations	.156	.112	**−.854**
8. Teachers respect the rules of the school	.234	.182	**.628**

Numbers in bold letters indicates that items share mutual factor

The study used a self-reporting, structured questionnaire, prepared in three versions: for pupils, for parents, and for professionals. Questionnaires were approved by the Ministry of Education and by the Ethics Committee of the Hebrew University. Questionnaires were distributed in special education classes in the presence of the researcher, who explained the context to pupils and made it clear that the questionnaires would remain anonymous and that pupils were not obligated to participate in the study. One pupil opted out after hearing the subject of the research.

The adults in the classroom helped pupils read the questionnaire and encouraged them to relate to each of the items and to complete the entire questionnaire. Pupil questionnaires were numerically coded so that each one could be matched with the questionnaire of the pupil's parent at a later stage.

Pupils were asked to deliver a numerically coded questionnaire to their parents; parents were to complete the questionnaire at home and return it to the homeroom teacher in a sealed envelope. Later, the researcher collected the sealed envelopes, matched each pupil's questionnaire with that of his or her parent, and sent the questionnaires for transcription.

The professionals were contacted by an emailed letter, which included a link to an online questionnaire. Obviously, data collected online did not require transcription.

Data Analysis

The data were first analyzed descriptively: The distribution of variables was examined and averages and standard deviations were calculated. Next, internal reliability (Cronbach's alpha) was examined for variables containing several items. Factor analysis was conducted for variables with a low rate of internal reliability, and content areas were defined. Factor analysis included the entire sample of pupils, parents, and professionals to enable a group comparison to be made at a later stage. The groups' averages for each statement were then used as the study variables.

Finally, correlations between the study variables were calculated to find significant relationships. A stepwise multiple regression analysis was conducted for each of the main variables. T-tests for independent samples and paired samples (pupils and their parents) were used to test the statistical significance of the differences found between the study populations. Differences between various types of professionals were examined in a one-way ANOVA.

FINDINGS

Sample Characteristics

The pupils who participated in the study were 12 to 14 years old; 62.5 percent were male and 37.5 percent were female. Approximately half of the pupils (48.6 percent) reported that this was the first time they had been present at a placement committee meeting, and 11.4 percent reported never having attended a meeting. Only 45 percent of the pupils reported that the school staff had prepared them for the committee meeting.

Among the 115 professionals who completed the questionnaire were committee chairs, regional supervisors of special education divisions and their representatives, teachers with expertise in inclusion, homeroom teachers, school psychologists, and others. With the exception of five professionals, all other respondents (110) were female. Of the professionals, 41 percent had daily interactions with pupils who were the subject of committee deliberations, 25 percent interacted with them infrequently, and 33 percent had no prior interaction with these pupils.

The distribution of income per family and the level of education in the parents' group were similar to those of the general population. The socioeconomic characteristics of the professionals were very different: All of them held academic degrees, 60 percent had a postgraduate degree, and 61 percent earned an income higher than the national average.

Distribution of the Main Study Variables

Denial of the Right to Participate

The right to participate unconditionally in the placement committee meeting is supported by 75 percent of the pupils and by 80 percent of the parents, in contrast to 54 percent of the professionals, who are in fact responsible for implementing the law.

According to 13 percent of the pupils, the right to participate could be denied due to behavioral difficulties, whereas 6.5 percent of pupils indicated both young age and learning difficulties as a sufficient justification for denying a pupil's right to participate. According to parents, the only legitimate reason for denying a pupil the right to participate in the placement committee meeting was young age (16 percent), with the exception of one parent who indicated extreme disability as a justification, and another parent who indicated that pupils should not be allowed to participate at all. The main justifications for denying participation according to the professionals were young age (28 percent) and extreme cognitive disability (10 percent). Three percent of the professionals indicated that pupils should not be allowed to participate at all.

The Desired Level of Participation

The distribution of the three groups regarding this variable is described in Figure 3.1.

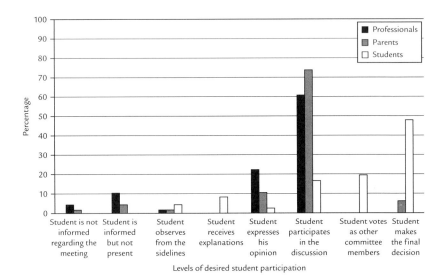

Figure 3.1:
Levels of desired student participation indicated by the population groups.

Of the professionals, 60.7 percent agreed with the spirit of the Special Education Law, indicating the sixth level of participation as the desirable level. None of the professionals indicated that pupils should be allowed to participate in the decision-making process itself, and 15.2 percent indicated that pupil participation was unnecessary. The average distribution for professionals was $M = 5.07, SD = 1.541$.

The parents in general favored higher levels of pupil participation in the placement committee meetings $(M = 5.71, SD = 1.363)$; 6.5 percent indicated that the pupil should decide which school to attend, and only 6.5 percent indicated that pupil participation was unnecessary.

In the pupil group, the distribution regarding the desired level of participation was completely different $(M = 6.71, SD = 1.655)$. Not a single pupil indicated that the pupil's presence in the committee meeting was unnecessary, and only 8.5 percent indicated that passive participation was sufficient. Furthermore, 47.9 percent indicated that the pupil alone should decide which school to attend and 19.7 percent indicated that he or she should be allowed to vote like a committee member.

All differences between the groups' averages regarding the desired level of participation were found to be statistically significant.

Actual Levels of Participation

The distribution in the three population groups regarding actual levels of pupil participation in placement committee meetings is described in Figure 3.2.

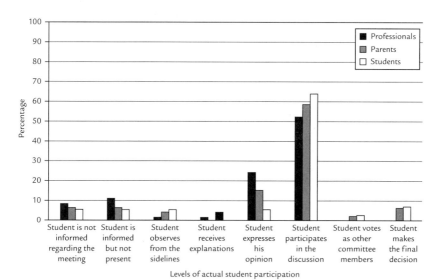

Figure 3.2:
Levels of actual student participation indicated by the population groups.

There is relatively high agreement among participants regarding actual pupil participation, not only between the parent and pupil who attended the same meetings ($M = 5.28$, $SD = 1.747$; $M = 5.36$, $SD = 1.714$ for parents and pupils, respectively) but also including the professionals, who reported on placement committee meetings in general ($M = 4.79$, $SD = 1.720$). The correlation coefficient between parents and pupils was significant and quite strong ($r = .627$, $p < .01$), and t-tests for dependent variables indicated that the difference between the distribution of parents and pupils on this issue was not statistically significant ($t(35) = -0.384$, $p > .05$). Likewise, the difference between parents' and professionals' distribution was not statistically significant ($t(151) = -1.603$). Only between the pupils and the professionals was the difference statistically significant ($t(177) = -2.165$, $p < .05$).

More than half of the participants reported that in the committee meetings they attended the law was fully implemented; 19.6 percent of the professionals and 13 percent of parents and children reported that the child was absent from the meetings. Approximately 7 percent of parents and children indicated that the pupil decided which school to attend.

Comparing Actual and Desired Levels of Participation

As can be seen in the figures, both parents and professionals indicated that the actual level of participation approximates the desired level of participation; however, in the pupil group, there is a large gap between the two. This conclusion is supported by the findings of t-tests: No significant difference was found between the professionals' estimation of pupils' actual and desired levels of participation ($t(45) = 1.738$, $p > .05$). The same goes for the parents ($t(105) = 1.927$, $p > .05$); however, in the pupil group, there was a significant difference in the ranking of these two variables ($t(70) = 6.302$, $p < .05$).

The Best Representatives of Pupils' Interests

Almost 80 percent of the parents indicated themselves as the people best suited to represent the pupil's interests before the committee. A high percent of the parents favored the homeroom teacher (44 percent) as well as the pupil (44 percent), whereas only 30 percent and 9 percent considered the school psychologist and social worker, respectively, to be the best choice for representing the pupil's interest. It should be noted that many of the parent participants marked more than one answer on the questionnaire.

Among the pupils, 51 percent indicated the parent as best representing their interests. The homeroom teacher was favored among 25 percent and the school psychologist was indicated by 7 percent. Only 14 percent of the pupils indicated themselves as their best representatives.

Among the professionals, 30 percent indicated the parents as the pupil's best representatives, 25 percent indicated the school psychologist, and 24 percent favored the homeroom teacher for this role. Only 16 percent indicated that the pupils are their own best representatives.

Satisfaction of the Parents and the Pupils Regarding the Committee Meeting

Table 3.3 features the averages and standard deviations of the levels of satisfaction of the parents and pupils regarding the meeting in the different participant groups.

All groups broadly agreed that parents and pupils alike were treated respectfully and fairly during the committee meeting. Statistical analysis indicated that distribution differences were not significant.

Gaps were found between the professional subgroups' assessments of pupils' satisfaction: Committee chairs and regional special education supervisors' assessment of pupils' satisfaction was higher than that indicated by the remaining committee members. A one-way ANOVA found that the difference between the subgroups was significant ($F(6,91) = 2.634, p <.05$).

Correlations Between the Main Research Variables

Correlations Pertaining to the Pupil Group

Relationships between main variables found in the pupil group are presented in Table 3.4.

On the measure of pupils' overall satisfaction, girls indicated a slightly higher degree of satisfaction than did boys ($r = .235$). With the exception of this finding, no other correlation was found between gender and other research variables.

Table 3.3. STUDENTS' AND PARENTS' SATISFACTION REGARDING THE COMMITTEE MEETING (ON A SCALE OF 1–4)

	Students' Satisfaction	Parents' Satisfaction
Professionals' average	**3.523**	**3.717**
(N = 112) SD	0.629	0.383
Parents' average	**3.494**	**3.524**
(N = 44) SD	0.728	0.706
Students' average	**3.426**	–
(N = 64) SD	0.647	–

SD = standard deviation

Table 3.4. CORRELATIONS (PEARSON'S R) BETWEEN DEPENDENT AND INDEPENDENT VARIABLES PERTAINING TO THE STUDENT GROUP

		Desired Level of Participation	Actual Level of Participation	Student's Satisfaction During the Committee Meeting
Desired Level of Participation	Pearson's r	–	.247*	.119
	Significance	–	.038	.354
Degree of Support for Children's Rights (in General)	Pearson's r	.246*	.139	.389**
	Significance	.038	.245	.001
Rights as Students at School	Pearson's r	.204	.135	.461**
	Significance	.088	.259	.000
Rights as Members of the Community	Pearson's r	.165	.054	.214
	Significance	.170	.654	.090
Rights in the Family	Pearson's r	.221	.131	.205
	Significance	.064	.273	.104
Freedom of Expression at School	Pearson's r	−.107	.003	.371**
	Significance	.376	.977	.003
School's Receptivity	Pearson's r	.128	−.143	.081
	Significance	.287	.230	.526
Degree of Participation in the Family	Pearson's r	−.074	.038	.315*
	Significance	.541	.753	.011
Preparing for the Meeting	Pearson's r	−.008	.387**	.093
	Significance	.947	.001	.465
Number of Placement Committee Meetings Attended	Pearson's r	−.004	.437**	.050
	Significance	.976	.000	.698
Mother's Level of Education	Pearson's r	−.315*	.274	−.243
	Significance	.040	.072	.148
Gender	Pearson's r	−.107	.173	.108
	Significance	.374	.147	.395

*Level of (two-way) significance—0.05
**Level of (two-way) significance—0.01
Numbers in bold letters indicates that items share mutual factor

A multiple stepwise regression analysis of the desired degree of participation among pupils found four variables that had a significant effect $(F(4,37) = 7.6, p < .01)$: rights as a pupil at school, level of actual participation, the mother's level of education, and the child's level of participation within the family. These variables explained 45.1 percent of the variance.

The analysis of actual level of participation among pupils found that two variables had a significant effect $(F(2,39) = 29.6; p < .01)$: preparation prior to the meeting and the desired level of participation. These variables explained 60.3 percent of the variance.

Finally, a multiple regression analysis of pupils' satisfaction regarding the meeting found only one variable that fit the model $(F(1,33) = 12.9; p <.01)$: the child's rights as a pupil at school. The model explained only 28.1 percent of the variance.

Correlations Pertaining the Parent Group

Table 3.5 presents relationships between dependent and independent variables pertaining to the parent group.

Similar to the finding in the pupil group, a correlation was found between the desired and the actual levels of participation, although this correlation was much stronger $(r = .533)$. Parents' assessment of pupils' satisfaction regarding the meeting and parents' satisfaction themselves did not correlate significantly with any of the variables tested.

A multiple stepwise regression analysis of actual level of pupil participation as indicated by the parents found three variables with a significant effect $(F(3,36) = 14.05, p <.01)$: the desired level of participation, the level of income, and the number of children in the family. These variables explained 53.9 percent of the variance.

Correlations Pertaining to the Professional Group

Relationships between the main variables pertaining to a professional group are presented in Table 3.6.

Table 3.5. CORRELATIONS (PEARSON'S *R*) BETWEEN DEPENDENT AND INDEPENDENT VARIABLES PERTAINING TO THE PARENT GROUP

		Desired Level of Participation	Actual Level of Participation	Parent's Satisfaction During the Committee Meeting	Student's Satisfaction During the Committee Meeting
Desired Level of Participation	Pearson's *r*	–	**.533****	−.039	**.167**
	Significance	–	.000	.795	.279
Income Level	Pearson's *r*	−.303	**−.508****	**.305**	**.080**
	Significance	.054	.001	.052	.628
Number of Children in the Family	Pearson's *r*	−.218	**−.441****	−.022	−.190
	Significance	.145	.002	.883	.217

**Level of (two-way) significance—0.01
Numbers in bold letters indicates that items share mutual factor

Table 3.6. CORRELATIONS (PEARSON'S *R*) BETWEEN DEPENDENT AND INDEPENDENT VARIABLES PERTAINING TO THE PROFESSIONAL GROUP

		Desired Level of Participation	Actual Level of Participation	Parent's Satisfaction During the Committee Meeting	Student's Satisfaction During the Committee Meeting
Desired Level of Participation	Pearson's r	–	.377**	−.035	.070
	Significance	–	.000	.715	.483
Actual Level of Participation	Pearson's r	.377**	–	.018	.483**
	Significance	.000	–	.858	.000
Attitude Toward the Child's Right to Participate	Pearson's r	.289**	.144	.161	.029
	Significance	.002	.138	.089	.764
Degree of Participation in the Family	Pearson's r	−.033	.156	.135	.253**
	Significance	.734	.110	.158	.009
Proximity to the Field	Pearson's r	.087	.047	.048	.249*
	Significance	.369	.640	.623	.011

*Level of (two-way) significance—0.05
**Level of (two-way) significance—0.01
Numbers in bold letters indicates that items share mutual factor

A multiple stepwise regression analysis of the desired degree of participation as indicated by the professionals found a significant correlation with two variables ($F(2,96) = 11.74, p < .01$): the actual degree of participation and the attitude toward pupils' right to participate. These variables explained 19.6 percent of the variance.

A regression analysis of pupils' actual degree of participation as indicated by the professionals correlated significantly with only one variable ($F(1,97) = 16.09$, $p < .01$): the desired degree of participation. This model explained 14.2 percent of the variance.

Finally, a regression analysis of pupils' satisfaction regarding the meeting as perceived by the professionals found a significant correlation with two variables ($F(2,90) = 28.28, p < .01$): actual level of participation and the interaction level with pupils. These variables explained 38.6 percent of the variance.

DISCUSSION

The right of participation heralds a revolution in society's perception of children. This right confirms our recognition of children's ability to represent their own interests and validates their status as citizens with rights in general (Earls, 2011). Based on this conception, Israeli legislators determined that any pupil whose case is discussed in a placement committee has the right to participate in the discussion, express an opinion, and share in the decision-making process (Amendment 8 to the Special Education Law, January 2005). This law is a direct expression of Paragraph 12 of the CRC, which determines that every child has the right to participate in decision-making processes related to his or her own life.

The following section presents the current state of affairs regarding pupils' participation in the placement committee, the factors that affect it, and possible ways to promote participation.

Actual Pupil Participation

Current State of Affairs

In the current study, 89 percent of the pupils reported being present at the placement committee meeting; the rate reported by the professionals was slightly lower, at 80.4 percent, probably because their reports related to all age groups, including pupils much younger. In any case, this is a respectable rate of presence, which demonstrates the ability of the law to change social norms.

The rate of attendance has risen; however, the purpose of the law is to promote active participation in the discussion. Indeed, the study found that the level of pupil participation among those who attended the placement committee meeting was very high: 89.1 percent of these pupils indicated taking an active role in the discussion, and 95.3 percent of the professionals also reported that pupils participated actively. Thus, given the chance, pupils are able to make good use of the opportunity to participate. This is evidence that despite their many difficulties and the excitement of the moment, pupils have a message to deliver and feel that it is important for them to take part in the decision-making process.

Interestingly, several pupils left the meeting feeling that the decision taken was left up to them. It appears that this was not merely a figment of their imagination, since identical reports were provided by the parents who were present at those meetings. This may be a result of the committee chairs' efforts to give the pupils the sense that they had the freedom to choose, whereas, in effect, the decision was made for them and they were merely manipulated toward it. Another possible explanation may be that a true dilemma arose during the discussion and, unable to resolve it, members of the committee left the decision up to the pupil. This scenario as well does not reflect a progressive liberal ideology but rather a pragmatic solution to a problem that emerged. There is nothing wrong with adopting the pupils' preferences; however, it is important to make it clear to the young pupils that their decision is supported by the adults, who are prepared to share in the responsibility (Westman, 1999).

Explanatory Factors

Explanatory Factors in the Pupil Sample

Other than the attitude toward participation, the pupil sample contained two variables that correlated with a high level of participation in discussion: prior preparation for the meeting and prior experience attending a placement committee meeting.

Pupils who had not been prepared for the discussion participated at a relatively low level (4.3 average) compared to pupils who were prepared by their parents (5.6) or by the homeroom teacher (5.8). Despite the clear instructions in the regulations (Circular 66/8(B) 2006), more than half of the pupil participants (55 percent) attended the committee meeting without having received any significant kind of preparation from the educational staff. This sad state of affairs creates a negative, self-perpetuating circle, since improper preparation results in poor participation, which in turn justifies the resistance to pupils' participation and to the dismissal of the importance of prior preparation.

It was also found that pupils who attended the committee meeting for the first time participated at a lower level than did pupils who had previously attended such meetings. This strengthens the claim that pupils should participate in different settings starting at a young age, since this would enable them to develop the necessary skill, which requires training and experience (Melton, 2005b).

Explanatory Factors in the Parent Sample

The study found that parents with a higher income reported a lower level of their child's participation in the discussion. A possible explanation is that when parents from a stronger segment of the population are present at the committee meeting, the child's role becomes secondary, as these children can rely on their parents to adequately represent their interests. In contrast, when parents from a less advantaged segment of the population attend the committee meeting, the pupils are less confident in their parents' ability to adequately represent their interests and, consequently, they feel compelled to represent themselves.

Another factor that was found to be related to the level of pupil participation in the parent sample was the number of children in the family: Parents of small nuclear families reported a higher level of pupil participation. A similar finding was reported in a study by Ben-Arieh and Attar-Schwartz (2013). It is important to note that the phenomenon is not a reflection of other social variables as income levels, education levels, family status, or commitment to religion. It is possible that in smaller families, the struggle for resources is less intensive and family members have more time to invest in listening, sharing, and offering guidance.

Attitudes Regarding Pupil Participation

Findings of the study indicated a significant correlation between the attitude toward participation rights and the actual level of participation in each of the sample groups. Two measures were used to assess attitudes toward participation. The first was the participants' attitude toward the full-fledged wording of the law, which grants each pupil the unconditional right to participate (although in accordance with the individual's abilities). The second measure was the subjects' indication of the desired level of pupil participation.

State of Affairs

The study found that 80 percent of the parents supported the extensive version of the law, according to which each pupil has the right to participate in the placement committee's discussion; 75 percent of the pupils held the same opinion. Among the professionals, the rate of support of the law was only 54 percent. This finding pertains mainly to the participation of young pupils, since 28 percent of the professionals (mostly school psychologists) in principle were against the participation of young pupils in the discussion.

This study also found that 13 percent of the pupils were opposed to the participation of pupils with behavioral difficulties, indicating that they perceive the right to participation as conditional and reserved only for pupils who are "well-behaved." This finding is not unique: A Canadian study found that a significant rate of adolescents (as high as 42 percent) believed that the denial of their rights could be used as a penalty for inappropriate behavior (Ruck et al., 1998). Such findings are worrisome, since young adults might consider themselves unworthy of their rights, liable to represent themselves poorly or even relinquish their rights completely.

Also on the measure of the desired level of participation, this study found that professionals supported lower levels of participation than did either the parents or the pupils. This too indicates that many professionals are opposed to the spirit of the law, even though they are the ones responsible for its implementation. Given this state of affairs, it is difficult to find viable ways to promote pupil participation, given that the pupils depend on adults to enable and assist their participation (Matthews et al., 1999; May, 2005).

It was surprising to find that the professionals were less supportive of pupil participation than the parents, since previous studies found that adults from a secure social background were more likely to have positive attitudes regarding children's rights (Bohrnstedt et al., 1981; Wong, Zimmerman, & Parker, 2010). This finding appears to be the joint outcome of two factors. The first is that parents of children with special needs tend to have a heightened awareness of social issues and children's rights (Harry, 1992). The second is that professionals refrain from empowering the pupils in the discussion because they fear this will detract from their own power of influence (Kozminsky, 2004; Melton, 2005b).

Even more surprising was finding that among the pupils, approximately half indicated their belief that they alone should decide which school to attend, and another fifth believed that their vote should be counted alongside those of the committee members. Such a radical attitude, which essentially calls for nullifying the adult voice, is difficult to accept, as it negates the potential contribution of adults' experience and worldview (Wong et al., 2010).

This finding may signal that the pupils are hesitant to rely on the adults, most likely because they fear that the adults might not understand their needs and priorities (Fattore, Mason, & Watson 2009) or that interests other than their own might come into play in the decision-making process. It is also possible that young pupils have learned that the power imbalance between children and adults is so immense that the only way for a child's opinion to count is by completely removing the adults from the process (Camino, 2005). In such a scenario, the pupils' radical attitude constitutes a reaction to the helplessness they experience in everyday life. And yet, it is unusual for pupils to act out during the discussion. It appears that the pupils capitulate to the adults' authority and accept the process as is.

More than half of the pupils indicated that the parents are those most capable of representing their cause. Approximately 25 percent of them indicated the homeroom teacher as the person who best represents their interests, a finding that reflects their confidence in the teachers' good will. Only 14 percent indicated that self-representation was the optimal choice. It would seem that this finding contradicts the previous one, namely that pupils aim to actively influence the decision of the committee. I suggest that pupils differentiated between two different skills: their ability to persuade and their ability to make decisions. The first requires representativeness, the ability to speak clearly before an audience, and high verbal skills, which children with special needs rarely possess. Pupils were uncertain of their ability to represent themselves in the best manner possible and saw the adults accompanying them (parents or homeroom teacher) as a better option. However, when it came to decision-making, they would have preferred to be the ones in control to ensure that ultimately the decision would not be affected by considerations other than their own.

Also among the parents, a high rate of responders considered themselves to be the best representatives of their children's interests. Both the children and their teachers were ranked second, and the school psychologist was ranked fourth. This too indicates recognition of the homeroom teachers' professional abilities as well as approval of the children's ability to represent themselves.

The only group that did not give parents a high ranking as representatives of the child's interests was that of the professionals; their preference was divided among the parents, the homeroom teacher, and the psychologist. It would appear that the majority of the professionals perceive the parents as lacking the proper knowledge and consider their perspective to be subjective and biased. Apparently, professionals convey this attitude, either implicitly or explicitly, to the parents during the committee meeting, and it becomes the source of a great deal of tension (Margalit Report, 2000).

Explanatory Factors

Only in the pupil group was there a correlation between pupil participation and attitudes regarding children's rights in general; however, this correlation was weak ($r = .246$). This may be due to the weak internal consistency of the concept of "children's rights" (Peterson-Badali, Morine, Ruck, & Slonim, 2004), which encompasses the right to protection, sustenance, and self-determination.

There was a relatively strong correlation between the right to participate in the committee discussion and the child's right to self-expression in the classroom ($r = .471$). This finding supports the claim that education toward participation should not begin with major decisions, but rather with the handling everyday decisions in a democratic environment (Melton, 2005b; Wong et al., 2010).

Children of mothers with a relatively high level of education were less determined to participate actively in the discussion. It is possible that pupils who rely on the parent accompanying them to the committee meeting feel well represented and, hence, make do with a lower level of participation. By contrast, the parents of pupils from disadvantaged backgrounds were less inclined to participate in the discussions (Geenen et al., 2001; Harry, 1992; Sharpe, 1997); consequently, the representation of pupils' interests was left to the pupils themselves.

Satisfaction of the Parents and Pupils Regarding the Placement Committee Meeting

State of Affairs

A majority of participants from all of the study groups reported that pupils were treated fairly and respectfully (3.49 on average, out of 4). Only 10 percent of the parents ranked the committee's attitude toward them as lower than 3 on average, and more than 50 percent gave the highest ranking to each of the components of this variable. These findings are important, as they refute the generally accepted view of the meeting as a hostile battleground in which the parents are either helpless or unwittingly deceived (in Israel: Dorner Report, 2009; Margalit Report, 2000; elsewhere: Harry, 1992; Yssel, Engelbrecht, Oswald, Eloff, & Swart, 2007).

Explanatory Factors in the Pupil Sample

Due to the noticeable gap between pupils' desired level of participation and their actual level of participation, I suspected that this gap might have left them feeling that they had not been treated respectfully or fairly during the meeting. To address this concern, the gap between the desired and the actual level of participation was calculated per pupil. No correlation was found between this gap and the individual pupil's satisfaction regarding the committee meeting. Pupils accepted the participation regulations that were dictated by the adults and acknowledged that they were treated respectfully and fairly, even when they were dissatisfied with their own (low) level of participation.

The study found three variables that had a positive effect on the pupils' satisfaction regarding the meeting: an atmosphere of participation at home, an atmosphere of participation at school, and the pupils' level of support of children's rights. It seems that there is a two-way relationship between these variables, such that living in an accepting environment shapes children's consciousness (awareness of and support for children's rights) and vice versa (i.e., this consciousness affects the way of life).

Hence, participation in the placement committee's discussion should not be treated as a single or unique event; the message of the child's empowerment should be delivered constantly from innumerable sources, including home, community, and school.

Pupils who experience their environment as uninterested in their views in everyday life are not in the habit of expressing their opinions. These pupils might feel uncomfortable when invited to participate or experience it as tokenism—that is, a cynical attempt at feigning a positive attitude toward pupil participation (Wong et al., 2010).

Explanatory Factors in the Professional Sample

According to I findings, professionals treated two concepts, pupils' actual level of participation and pupils' satisfaction about the meeting, as related and thus interpreted a low level of participation as reflecting pupils' negative feelings about the meeting. As previously noted, the pupils—in contrast to what the professionals assumed—differentiated between these two concepts.

As in the pupil sample, a correlation was found between professionals' assessment of pupils' satisfaction about the meeting and their assessment of their own children's participation within their personal family framework. Thus, professionals who created a democratic climate at home were apt to demonstrate the same approach in the relationships they created in the context of the committee.

Findings indicate that the committee chairs and supervisors tended to assess the atmosphere as more pleasant and respectful than did the other professionals.

Two explanations are suggested. First, high-ranking professionals who are removed from fieldwork tend to overestimate the effect of programs that promote pupil participation, compared to their colleagues who struggle with the pupils' everyday challenges (Mason et al., 2004). Second, committee chairs and supervisors are the ones responsible for conducting the meeting, including creating a pleasant and respectful atmosphere. Thus, by ranking pupils' feelings as positive, they in fact declared that they fulfilled their role properly. Other committee members were more likely to admit that the meeting was less pleasant than they might have wished.

Study Limitations

There were a few limitations to this study. First, it assumed that several variables were constant, such as the age of the child and, to a certain extent, the severity of the disability. As a result, the effect of these two variables on the remaining dependent variables could not to be examined.

With a pupil response rate of 86 percent, the findings of this study can be considered representative of the population of pupils in Israel's public middle-school special education classes. However, neither pupils with relatively mild disabilities who were not eligible for studying in these classes nor pupils with complex disabilities who were placed in special education schools were represented in this study. Furthermore, the parents' questionnaire required reading comprehension skills and the ability to follow instructions at a level that may not have been appropriate for all of the parents sampled. Thus, for example, pupils of Ethiopian descent and their parents are conspicuously missing from the sample.

Finally, as in any research of this type, data were collected only from those who chose to participate and cooperated with the authors of the study. It is probable that the decision to exclude oneself from the study might not have been incidental, thus indicating the individual's attitude regarding participation rights.

Summary and Recommendations for Research, Practice, and Policymaking

This study can serve as the foundation for a research-based body of knowledge on the topic of pupils' participation in the decision-making processes that are relevant to their lives. Here, for the first time, the pupils themselves—along with their parents and professionals—were asked about their attitude regarding participation in the placement committee meeting and its implementation.

For the purpose of this study, a precise scale was constructed, which is user-friendly for participants and researchers alike. The linear structure of the scale enabled participants, both children and adults, to precisely describe the level of participation they experienced and the level of participation they would desire. Likewise, the ordinal structure of the variable presented researchers with the opportunity to statistically measure the distribution of responses within each group of participants, to compare between the groups, and to calculate the gap between desired and actual levels of participation for each individual participant. This research tool can be used in other studies, as well as by education policy-makers, assessing the degree of children's involvement in a given situation, or measuring and comparing pre- and post-intervention responses.

The study found that pupils are interested in and able to be present at the committee's discussion, express their opinions, and participate in a process that determines their educational future. These findings refute claims suggesting that pupils are either unwilling or unable to participate in a significant manner in important discussions about their future (Helwig & Turiel, 2002; Matthews et al., 1999).

Another issue typically raised in opposition to pupils' participation deals with the supposed trauma that the child experiences at being exposed to the information reviewed in the committee's discussion. All of the pupils in the current study demonstrated an interest in being present during the committee's discussion, including the few pupils who preferred not to take an active role in the discussion. In effect, hiding information from the child essentially deprives the child not only of the right to participate but also of the opportunity to cope in a normative and desired manner. Sharing the information with the child can actually help rather than harm the child's coping abilities (Weithorn, 1998).

In each of the participant groups, a clear and consistent relationship was found between attitudes toward pupil participation and the indicated levels of actual participation. Thus, one can promote children's participation by changing the relevant parties' attitudes toward children's rights in general and the right to participate in particular. This can be done through class activities, workshops for teachers, parents, and professionals, as well as promotion in the public media.

It was found that the level of participation of pupils who underwent a preparatory process was higher than that of the remaining pupils. This finding is in line with studies that found that preparation improved self-representation in committee meetings (Kozminsky, 2004; Test & Neale, 2004). In fact, the Margalit Report (2000) recommended conducting preparatory workshops for pupils, and Circular 66/8(B) 2006 made it a regulatory requirement. Nonetheless, according to pupils' reports, a large proportion of the pupils did not benefit from in-school organized preparation.

The study found that pupils who had prior experience attending a committee meeting participated in the discussion in a more active manner. Such experience can be acquired in preliminary procedures at school. Nevertheless, and despite the regulations published by the Ministry of Education stipulating pupil participation in these discussions (Circular 66/8(B) 2006), many pupils are absent from schools' internal committee meetings. Here again, the Ministry of

Education relied on legislature and regulations, ignoring the resistance emanating from the field, responses that ought to be addressed. A true change can take place only if such legislation is accompanied by efforts to promote the issue in the public media, as well as in the teachers' room (Igell, 2006; Mason et al., 2004).

In recent years, Western society has become increasingly aware of the importance of children's rights in various fields (Mason et al., 2004; May, 2005); however, the changes that are taking place are not always for the better. The Dorner Report (2009), which aims to reconstruct the process of educational placement in Israel, recommended leaving the placement decision "in the hands of the pupils and their parents," yet it does not suggest any mechanism for ensuring the pupils' participation. Consequently, for all practical purposes, the recommendation denies pupils the opportunity to participate and effectively leaves the decision to the parents. Clearly, although there have been many positive developments, vigilance is still necessary to ensure that pupils can practice their right to participate and that their voices are heard.

REFERENCES

Arnstein, S. R. (1969). A ladder of citizen participation. *Journal of the American Institute of Planners, 35*(4), 216–224.

Ben-Arieh, A., & Attar-Schwartz, S. (2013). An ecological approach to children's rights and participation: inter-relationships and correlates of rights in different ecological systems. *American Journal of Orthopsychiatry, 83*, 94–106.

Ben-Arieh, A., Khoury-Kassabri, M., & Haj-Yahia, M. M. (2006). Generational, ethnic, and national differences in attitudes toward the rights of children in Israel and Palestine. *American Journal of Orthopsychiatry, 76*, 381–388.

Bevan-Brown, J. (2006). Beyond policy and good intentions. *International Journal of Inclusive Education, 10*(2-3), 221–234.

Bohrnstedt, G. W., Freeman, H. E., & Smith, T. (1981). Adult perspectives on children's autonomy. *Public Opinion Quarterly, 45*, 443–462.

Camino, L. A. (2005). Pitfalls and promising practices of youth–adult partnerships: An evaluator's reflections. *Journal of Community Psychology, 33*, 75–85.

Dolev, T., & Ben Rabi, D. (2002). The convention on the rights of the child: General principles and their implementation in Israel. *Social Security, 63*, 131–153 [in Hebrew].

Dorner, D. (2009). *Report of the Committee for Examination of the Special Education System in Israel headed by former Supreme Court justice Dalia Dorner.* Submitted on 29/1/2009 to the ministry of education, Jerusalem [in Hebrew].

Earls, F. (2011). Children: from rights to citizenship. *Annals of the American Academy of Political and Social Science, 633*, 6–16.

Fattore, T., Mason, J., & Watson, E. (2009). When children are asked about their well-being: towards a framework for guiding policy. *Child Indicators Research, 2*, 57–77.

Geenen, S., Powers, L. E., & Lopez-Vasquez A. (2001). Multicultural aspects of parent involvement in transition planning. *Exceptional Children, 67*(2), 265–282.

Harry, B. (1992). Restructuring the participation of African-American parents in special education. *Exceptional Children, 59*(2), 123–131.

Hart, R. (1992). *Children's participation: From tokenism to citizenship.* Florence: UNICEF International Child Development Centre.

Helwig, C. C., & Turiel, E. (2002). Civil liberties, autonomy, and democracy: Children's perspective. *International Journal of Law and Psychiatry, 25,* 253–270.

Igell, C. (2006). *Decision making in interdisciplinary educational team—A research of decision making processes in "placement committees" mandated by the Special Education Law.* Thesis submitted for Doctor of Philosophy degree, University of Haifa, School of Education, Israel [in Hebrew].

Khoury-Kassabri, M., Haj-Yahia, M. M., & Ben-Arieh, A. (2006). Adolescents approach toward children's rights: Comparison between Jewish and Palestinian children from Israel and the Palestinian Authority. *Children and Youth Services Review, 28,* 1060–1073.

Kozminsky, L. (2004). *Talking for themselves: Self-advocacy of learners with learning disabilities.* Tel Aviv: Yessod Publishers & MOFET Institute [in Hebrew].

Leake, D., & Cholymay, M. (2004). *Addressing the needs of culturally and linguistically diverse students with disabilities in postsecondary education.* Information Brief, National Center on Secondary Education and Transition, University of Minnesota (NCSET). Volume 3, Issue 1.

Margalit, M. (2000). *Report of the committee for examination of the implementation of the Special Education Law.* Unpublished manuscript, Israel Ministry of Education.

Mason C., Field S., & Sawilowsky, S. (2004). Implementation of self-determination activities and student participation in IEPs. *Exceptional Children, 70*(4), 441–451.

Matthews, H., Limb, M., & Taylor, M. (1999). Young people's participation and representation in society. *Geoforum, 30*(2), 135–144.

May, H. (2005). Whose participation is it anyway? Examining the context of pupil participation in the UK. *British Journal of Special Education, 32*(1), 29–34.

Melton, G. B. (2005a). Treating children like people: a framework for research and advocacy. *Journal of Clinical Child and Adolescent Psychology, 34,* 646–657.

Melton, G. B. (2005b). Building Humane Communities Respectful of Children: The Significance of the Convention on the Rights of the Child. *American Psychologist, 60*(8), 918–926.

Ministry of Education (2006). Director General's Circular 66/8(B).

Peterson-Badali, M., Morine, S. L., Ruck, M. D., & Slonim, N. (2004). Predictors of maternal and early adolescent attitudes toward children's nurturance and self-determination rights. *Journal of Early Adolescence, 24,* 159–179.

Ruck, M. D., Keating, D. P., Abramovitch, R., & Koegl, C. J. (1998). Adolescents' and children's knowledge about rights: some evidence for how young people view rights in their own lives. *Journal of Adolescence, 21,* 275–289.

Sharpe, M. (1997). Disproportionate representation of minorities in special education: a focus group study of parent perspectives. *Final Report Phase II: Minority Parents.* ERIC (ED429409).

Special Education Law 5748 (1988).

Special Education Law (Amendment 8), 24/1/2005: Right to a hearing for the student in placement and appeals committees.

Test, D., & Neale, M. (2004). Using "the self-advocacy strategy" to increase middle graders' IEP participation. *Journal of Behavioral Education, 13*(2), 135–145.

Weithorn, L. A. (1998). Youth participation in family and community decision making. *Family Futures, 2,* 6–9.

Westman, J. C. (1999). Children's rights, parents' prerogatives, and society's obligations. *Child Psychiatry and Human Development, 29,* 315–328.

Wong, N. T., Zimmerman, M. A., & Parker, E. A. (2010). A typology of youth participation and empowerment for child and adolescent health promotion. *American Journal of Community Psychology, 46*, 100–114.

Yssel, N., Engelbrecht, P., Oswald, M. M., Eloff, I., & Swart, E. (2007). Views of inclusion: a comparative study of parents' perceptions in South Africa and the United States. *Remedial and Special Education, 28*, 356–365.

CHAPTER 4

Children and Young People's Participation in Research

NIGEL THOMAS

INTRODUCTION

Children and young people's participation in research can mean anything from taking part in adults' research projects, to working in partnership with adults to plan and conduct research, to carrying out their own research projects with support from adults. This chapter focuses on the second and third of these.

Children and young people's participation in research is an area of practice that has developed significantly in the past decade, throwing up both practical challenges in terms of how to make children and young people's participation real and theoretical/methodological questions about the value of their research and how it differs from research by adults. This chapter will focus mainly on the practical challenges but in the process will also consider some of the theoretical and methodological questions. It begins with a brief review of recent developments in the field and key texts before moving into a presentation and deeper exploration of two projects that I conducted with colleagues The first was a university-based project to support a small group of children in two primary schools to plan and carry out their own research projects. The second was a partnership project, the original idea for which came from a group of young people in public care, who were supported by university researchers to submit a funding bid and conduct a research project together. In what follows I review the factors that contributed to the success of the two projects, reflect on the shortfalls and disappointments, and consider what these experiences can tell us about the limitations of current practice in including children as active participants in research. I argue that this is partly a question of researcher skills and knowledge but is also related to a wider context in which children's participation rights are seen as problematic.

BACKGROUND

Recent innovations in research involving children and young people are mainly a product of three factors: a greater emphasis in the social sciences on children and young people's agency; an increasingly powerful global discourse of children's rights; and a wider concern to bring service user perspectives into research and evaluation (Alderson, 2001; Beazley, Bessell, Ennew, & Waterson, 2009; Grover, 2004; Kellett, 2010). The innovations to which I refer include not only bringing children's voices into adult research by using more "participatory" methods but also enabling children and young people to take an active part in research themselves (Boeck & Sharpe, 2009; Kirby, 1999, 2001; Liebel, 2008). This may mean (i) contributing to adult projects, for example by helping to gather data; (ii) directing their own research with support from adults; or (iii) working together with adults on joint research. The two research projects discussed in this chapter fall into the second and third categories, but we should also consider the wider context.

Since the earliest research where young people took an active role (for example West, 1995), a growing number of projects have been led or co-led by young people. Many have focused on particular issues and problems in schools, communities, or service settings. Frequently these problems are identified by adults, and the research is initiated as part of a strategy to improve service provision.

Petrie, Fiorelli, and O'Donnell (2006) report on a qualitative study on teenage pregnancy and young parenthood in northern England that included young people as research participants. Young people (aged 16–20) advised on the project, conducted most of the interviews, and contributed to data analysis and to dissemination—two of them co-authored the article. The authors conclude that involving young people in research in a meaningful way is possible and enhances the research process, but that it carries risks for the young people (in this case, media exposure in the community).

> It would not have been possible for the researcher to understand the culture and socio-economic context of young people without the help of the Young People's Advisory Group. Also, the group interviews in and outside the school setting would have been more difficult without their contributions at the pilot stage. (2006, p. 44)

Kilpatrick, McCartan, McAlister, and McKeown (2007) describe the use of a peer research methodology to explore disaffected young people's views on alternative education. The aim was "to ensure an equilibrium of power between interviewer and interviewee, allow marginalised young people's voices to be heard and help generate social action" (p. 351). A team of peer researchers (age range 15–27) were formally employed on the project, a government-funded study of provision for disengaged or disaffected 14- to 16-year-olds in Northern Ireland. Although the team experienced significant difficulties in communication and commitment (the project lasted thirty months), both adult and young researchers concluded that their involvement had real value for themselves and for the research.

> The peer research team who were recruited reflected a much broader understanding of young people than the adult team. This included shared experience, similar demographic and socio-economic profile, regional identity, language, physical appearance and importantly the very recent experience of being a young person. (2007, p. 356)

A related conclusion is drawn by Thomson and Gunter (2007) regarding student-led research in schools, where under the umbrella of "pupil voice" students are involved in research into teaching and learning, curriculum, and school policies and practices. The authors suggest that this may be seen as "standpoint research," exemplified through a project in which photo-elicitation and verbal scenarios based in students' understandings of their school produced not a homogenous "voice" but multiple perspectives on the school and the classroom.

Burns and Schubotz (2009) also consider the benefits and challenges of involving peer researchers in social research projects, again in Northern Ireland. A study of pupil participation in policymaking on school bullying was commissioned by the Commissioner for Children and Young People. The research used a mixed methods approach, including questionnaires, focus group discussions, and one-to-one interviews. The team trained and employed nine 15- to 18-year-old peer researchers. Six peer researchers were interviewed after the project about their experiences, which appear to have been largely positive: They were involved at a level where they were comfortable; their involvement added reliability to the results; they were able to contribute to antibullying policies in their own school and more widely; they felt that their work and efforts were valued; and they achieved a sense of empowerment.

Fleming, Goodman Chong, and Skinner (2009) were commissioned by Leicester City Council to evaluate its Teenage Pregnancy Prevention Strategy. The team recruited, trained, and supported young people as peer researchers. They conclude that

> the experience of being a peer evaluator was valuable and beneficial to those who took part. It allowed young participants in the evaluation to talk with young people that they could relate to. The peer evaluators described the extent to which they had personally gained from the experience . . . Their involvement strengthened the research in terms of the development of information collection tools, their rapport with young participants and the insights they gave to the data analysis. All this contributed to a high quality report for the commissioner which she reports is likely to have a far-reaching impact on the funding and strategic development of teenage sexual health services in the city. (2009, pp. 288–289)

On occasion similar projects have involved younger children; for example, Butler (2005) worked with 6- to 11-year-olds in a Welsh primary school to explore ways in which they could have more influence in their school and neighborhood. Another strand has been where children and young people have been encouraged to identify themselves as potential researchers and choose topics based on their own interests, for example through the work of the Children's Research Centre at the Open University (Aoslin, Baines, Clancy, Jewiss-Hayden, Singh, & Strudwick, 2008; Bucknall, 2010; Frost, 2007; Kellett, Forrest, Dent, & Ward, 2004).

The types of research that children and young people can undertake range from projects such as these, whose primary purpose is to articulate young people's views or to make a particular case, or fact-finding, evaluative, exploratory, or interpretive research, to participatory action research (PAR), where change is not merely an outcome but intentionally part of the process. Clark (2005) focuses on the involvement of children and young people in PAR, including issues of power alongside the methodological, practical, and ethical considerations in involving young participants (particularly school pupils) as researchers. Projects and case studies are used to highlight the potential benefits. Clark concludes that

> Previous research indicates that it is important to go beyond the tokenistic involvement of young people, to as full a model of participation as possible, whilst not compromising the quality of the data collected, nor the experiences of the young people concerned. The role of the young person as researcher should not be an abusive, exploitative one, nor should it be regarded as collecting data "on the cheap." Participatory research involving children and young people should be ethically sound, training and development should be offered and provided, alongside continual support throughout the process, as by engaging young people as researchers of other young people, we will change their role from "peer" to researcher. (2005, p. 14)

Bland and Atweh (2007, p. 337) evaluated a students-as-researchers project in Brisbane (Student Action Research for University Access [SARUA]) and found that PAR "offers a means by which marginalised students, teachers, and university researchers can work collaboratively towards positive outcomes for the participants and their schools." They conclude that

> Students as researchers projects, such as SARUA, provide a means for marginalised students to re-engage with their education. Through involvement in the PAR process, students can find ways of contributing their voices to the educational issues affecting their own lives and opportunities and those of their peers. The SARUA project scaffolds student voice through, firstly, positioning the students as the principal researchers in the PAR collaboration and creating an environment in which they feel comfortable expressing their ideas and opinions. Secondly, the project presents challenges to the student researchers, such as presenting and discussing their findings at

conferences and through publication. The increased confidence experienced by the students helps to re-engage them with their own education and expand their educational opportunities. Further, where schools are open to the voices of such students, they have access to insider knowledge that can assist the schools to improve student retention and to provide more relevant and engaging curriculum. (2007, p. 346)

A more radical approach is taken by Cahill (2007), who offers a broad overview of the principles of participatory research and reflects on her own experience of doing a PAR project with young people. She discusses a "collective praxis approach" (a set of rituals and practices for sharing power within the research process), the role of the facilitator, and the processes of collective data analysis. She concludes that

Committed to bringing new and underrepresented voices into the academy, PAR acknowledges the intellectual power of what Gramsci identifies as "organic intellectuals" whose critical perspectives are developed from everyday experiences. Starting with the understanding that all people, including young people, develop social theory in their course of their life experiences, PAR foregrounds the perspectives of marginalized groups, opens up critique and troubles the status quo. While certainly not all young people are marginalized, as a group their voices are not often taken seriously and they are excluded from many decisions that affect their lives. (2007, p. 308)

Lind (2007) describes a PAR project undertaken as a partnership between student, teacher, and nurse co-researchers at an "alternative" high school in western Canada. Students ranged in age from 14 to 19 years. The research design was "hermeneutically-inspired PAR with an appreciative inquiry lens" (p. 373). The research question was: What is the meaning of adolescent involvement in mental health promotion through their participation as partners in, rather than solely as objects of, a project? The student researchers were encouraged to take part in interpretation and analysis and found this to be a transformative experience.

O'Brien and Moules (2007) reflect on a research project commissioned by the Children's Fund in England, investigating use and nonuse of services within a local area. The involvement of children was a key element of the project, and nine young researchers aged 7 to 13 were recruited. The article focuses on two cycles of PAR involving recruiting the researcher and training young researchers. The authors conclude that "without children's perspectives there cannot be a complete account as to why services are not being used, therefore involving them as co-researchers has helped us as adult researchers to understand this problem from children's perspectives" (p. 399).

The contributions young people can make to projects may include data collection, planning and design, data analysis and final presentation, or combinations of these. Data analysis has often been seen as a particularly challenging aspect for young people, although there have been interesting attempts to overcome this (Coad & Coad, 2008; Coad & Evans, 2008).

Some of the issues and challenges that have arisen for children and young people as active researchers and for adults supporting them include perceptions of competence, particularly in relation to younger children; the reception given to research that has been designed and/or led by children and young people; ethical concerns and governance problems; and the sustainability of young people's involvement. My own research with the Children's Commissioner for Wales was unusual in that it continued for three years with substantially the same group of young people involved (Thomas, 2012; Thomas, Cook, Cook, France, Hillman, Jenkins, Pearson, Pugh-Dungey, Sawyers, Taylor, & Crowley, 2010). In terms of the categories outlined above, it was evaluative research where practical outcomes were intended to follow on completion of the research. The research was commissioned by Peter Clarke, the first Children's Commissioner in the United Kingdom, who was eager for young people to participate as much as possible in the evaluation of his office. The research was largely planned and conducted by a group of young people, working together with two professional researchers. The young people were involved from the outset of the project, and the majority remained involved throughout the three years of the evaluation. They were recruited from young people's networks across South Wales and included care leavers (young people with personal experience of out-of-home care) and members of local youth councils. At the start of the research there were fifteen young researchers aged 12 to 20 (average age 16), ten of whom remained with the project at the end of the three years. The young researchers took an active part in every stage from design to dissemination, including analysis and interpretation.

The new Commissioner took office as we were completing the evaluation and asked us to provide a set of recommendations from our research. All these recommendations were accepted in principle by the Commissioner, the majority for immediate action and others for consideration in the future. In a newspaper column on New Year's Day 2009, largely devoted to the impact of the evaluation on his work, the Commissioner suggested that our report had enabled him to "hit the deck running" by highlighting the office's strengths and indicating areas that needed development. Our research demonstrated that it is possible to involve children and young people directly in evaluating the effectiveness of such a public office. Working together as a group with a wide range of skills, knowledge, and life experience, we were able to sustain our inquiry over a period of three years and to examine different aspects of the Commissioner's work using a range of methods. Because it was important to make sure that all members of the group fully understood what we were doing, we had to use methods that were relatively simple and straightforward but that in combination gave us a well-grounded and rounded view of the Commissioner's Office, from the perspective of the young people whom the Commissioner is there to serve.

THE "YOUNG RESEARCHERS" PROJECT

This project supported children in primary school to design and carry out their own research studies. It was conceived as a pilot project, initially inspired by the experience of the Open University Children's Research Centre (Kellett 2005a, 2005b; Kellett, Forrest, Dent, & Ward, 2004). Personal contacts were used to recruit two local primary schools in disadvantaged areas of the city, where the head teachers had experience of research and were willing to be innovative. An initial planning meeting with the two head teachers clarified the objectives of the project, which were (a) to offer a challenging and positive experience for children and (b) to produce research of real value. It was agreed to offer the opportunity to Year 5 pupils (aged 9 and 10) in the first instance, four in each school.

The local education authority were briefed on the project and were fully in support. The two schools identified the eight children for the pilot project. The head teachers approached individuals who they thought would enjoy the project and benefit from it, and two boys and two girls in each school agreed to take part. Although the university researchers encouraged the schools to select less advantaged children rather than the most academically successful, only one of the two schools fully followed this advice.

The project began in November, two months into the new school year, with an initial meeting at one of the schools for the children, their two class teachers, the head teachers, and the two academic staff who would lead the project (Nigel Thomas and Alex Morgan). This meeting started with a couple of introductory exercises, which led to a discussion of research. Alex and Nigel described the work of the Open University Children's Research Centre and talked about their own enthusiasm to do something similar. They explained that they needed the children's help to learn how this could work, about the sort of research that it is practical to do in terms of time and resources, and how social research is different from other types of research. Four Digital Blue video cameras had been bought for the project, and the children had a chance to play with them and begin to think about how they might use them in doing research. The children then divided into four pairs (same-sex, same-school pairs, by their own choice) to explore issues that they might find interesting to research. Each group came up with a list of possible topics. It was agreed that next time we would be meeting at the university, where they would meet other academic colleagues and carry out a short piece of research in real time to find out more about the process. The children all confirmed that they wanted to continue with the project, and the teachers confirmed that consent had been obtained from their parents.

There followed a series of three sessions with the children in the university. This provided an introduction to principles and methods of social research and gave the children an opportunity to choose their own research projects. The learning process was an interactive rather than a didactic one; there was a minimal amount of formal instruction, and the emphasis was on exploring the topic together through conversation and games and "learning through doing." For example, the children were invited to learn something about what it was like to do research by planning and conducting a mini-research project where they interviewed members of academic staff about their experience of research. The aim was to introduce a few basic concepts: quantitative and qualitative methods, open and closed questions, and the guiding principle that research should be "systematic, sceptical and ethical" (Kellett, 2005a). The aim was then to build on this learning through supported work on the children's individual projects.

The second phase of the research involved the young researchers in engaging with their own research projects. They were offered the option to work individually but chose to work in pairs and grouped naturally into their same-sex, same-school pairs. A member of staff was allocated to support each pair (Alex Morgan, Nigel Thomas, Tim Waller and Jane Waters). The pattern was for the academic supporter to meet the young researchers every two or three weeks in their school to offer guidance and assistance in the detailed planning and execution of their projects.

The projects selected by the children were

- "Golden time"—pupil and teacher perceptions of a school good behavior scheme
- "Star of the week"—ditto
- Learning and enjoyment—do pupils learn more from lessons they enjoy?
- Healthy eating—children's beliefs and attitudes

The projects were largely complete by the following Easter or shortly afterward, and in June the young researchers spent a day in the university sharing their findings with each other and working with academic staff on polishing their presentations. In the following autumn term, when the young researchers had commenced their final year of primary school, a further session in the university was held where the children presented their work to the class and head teachers, and discussion took place about the future direction of the project. Everyone agreed that it had been worthwhile and everyone wanted to continue with the project if possible, although this was dependent on academic staff time and funding.

During the project the young researchers were regularly invited to reflect on how they thought the project was going. In addition they were asked to complete feedback questionnaires at the conclusion of each phase of the project (i.e., in December and again in June/July). The December evaluations were extremely positive, especially about the interviewing practice and the use of video cameras. A couple of children commented that more examples would have been helpful. The June evaluations elicited the following comments from children:

> "I liked the part when we went to the university and interviewing Tim, Trisha and Jane."

"I liked making the PowerPoint presentations."

"I have learned the three words ethical, scepticle (sic) and systematic."

In June the teachers were also invited to give feedback:

"The children were given a lot of responsibility during the project. They dealt with this with great maturity at times and demonstrated they were capable of things beyond my imagination."

"They were motivated all times and seemed to enjoy the challenge of being stretched in their thinking."

When asked what could have been done better, teachers responded

"More time for the university staff to work with the children. The children were not used to working independently."

"Opportunities to publish their work on the Web would give the children an extended audience."

Children responded

"More time to do our work . . . More time to sort out the data"

It was clear that the young researchers enjoyed the project and believed they had learned useful skills. Some of them indicated that they had gained confidence in themselves and their abilities as a result of their participation in the research. Head teachers and class teachers valued the opportunity given to the individual children and also noticed an impact on other pupils of the approach to learning that the young researchers brought back with them.

For their part, the academic staff began to learn about how to support children in undertaking research. A number of issues were identified during the project:

1. Practical issues in enabling young researchers to have easy access to various kinds of resources. For example, although the schools were well provided with computers, which the children used relatively freely, websites and email accounts were restricted, as was the use of devices to transfer files between school and home. Time and space that had been booked for research support might be commandeered at the last minute by a teacher for some other purpose.
2. Arrangements for contact—the way these were set up left the initiative with the academic staff, not with the children. Although we gave them our business cards with email addresses, they did not use these to contact us and we could not contact them directly, only through school staff.

3. Internalized models of learning and perceptions of appropriate teacher–pupil interaction were an issue; children had to adjust to different expectations of how they might relate to adults. A good example was the use of first names. The children quickly learned to use our first names but were then unsure how to address the teachers who accompanied them. Throughout the project we could see them trying to make sense of the different relationships that were possible under the general headings of "teaching and learning" and "child and adult."

To the academic staff the following questions were also relevant:

1. How far are these children really in charge of their own research? On the one hand, they chose their own projects, and in supporting them we made every effort to let them take the lead. On the other hand, they were dependent on us for the tools to carry it out, and on the school to make the time available to them. The school setting is a very powerful structuring and may have influenced both what research they chose and how they were able to carry it out.
2. Do they have the knowledge and skills to decide what they want to research? It was the task of the academic staff to make their specialist knowledge and skills available to the children to the extent that they could benefit from this. On the other hand, the children had their own expert knowledge of the school setting and the people who inhabit it. As Kellett, Forrest, Dent & Ward (2004) point out, what is distinctive in child-led research is precisely that children have their own particular angle, based on standpoint and experience.
3. Do they have the access to resources they need? As indicated above, this was at times a significant drawback in doing school-based research.
4. Do they feel sufficiently in control? Only they could answer this, and we did not ask directly. It is possible that if the project had been repeated then the children would have been more assertive in this respect.

More broadly, the project raised questions about children's agency in research: What is the scope for agency, and what are the factors that affect their agency? Key factors here appeared to be

1. Context—what kind of project and how it is set up. Who takes the initiative, and on whose "territory" is it initiated? How are children selected, and to what extent are they truly volunteers? What is the overall purpose, from the perspective of the various "players"—children, teachers, academic researchers?
2. Time and space—is there enough of both for the research to be done properly? How much control do children have over their use of time and space?
3. Curriculum in school—does this allow space for independent research? Is the research seen to "fit" with the standard curriculum, or is it an "optional extra"?
4. Resources available to children and young people—see above.

5. Commitment of adult researchers—this project was able to proceed because staff were able and willing to make time for it. It did not continue into a second phase because that no longer applied.

6. Skills of adult researchers—we were learning "on the job," but all had experience of teaching various age groups, including young children, and of doing research with children. We also shared a bias toward interactive and child-led approaches to learning, which were congruent with the objectives of the project.

7. Skills of young researchers—the children were all bright and interested. Although they had no direct experience of this kind of research, they were able to pick things up quickly. Others have worked with groups who are challenged in various ways, or on the other hand with groups already experienced in research, and this must make a difference.

8. Level of interest of young researchers—the project could not have worked if the young researchers had not been genuinely interested, curious, and willing to make time in school—including giving up breaks on more than one occasion.

This whole question of agency can also be looked at in terms of *dispositions*—how disposed adults are to cede power to children, and how disposed children are to take it when offered. In reflecting on the experience of the research (Waller, Morgan, Thomas & Waters, 2006), we drew on the related concept of "affordances" (Greeno, 1994) to ask questions about the sort of space (e.g., geographic, interactive) available for the research to develop in, what affordances the space offers for particular kinds of activity, and what constraints the space imposes on that activity. In some respects the space in the university offered affordances—in terms of physical resources, but also in ways of being in the space and relating to each other and to adults—that the school setting did not offer. At the university the academic staff had access to and control over classrooms, equipment and materials, and were able to extend this to the child researchers in ways that enabled them to extend their thinking and behavior beyond what they would have done in the school. When the project work continued in the school, meetings often took place in confined or unsuitable spaces because of the need to fit in with timetables and other requirements of the setting, and computer access was often difficult too. The fact that the children felt comfortable in being on first-name terms with the academic staff also gave a different flavor to the interaction.

In terms of the value of the research, it is not claimed that the children's individual research projects made a significant contribution to academic knowledge. That may be the case with other child-led research, but these projects were too basic to add anything of substance. They did, however, add to situated knowledge and understanding in the school, among pupils and teachers, in relation to disciplinary regimes, learning styles, and healthy eating. However, the principal value of this research was in what the children learned about their own capacities, the consequential effects of that learning in the school community, and what we as academic researchers learned about supporting child-led research.

"HOW'S MY WORKER DOING?" THE YOUNG PEOPLE'S APPRAISAL AND ASSESSMENT PROJECT

The Centre for Children and Young People's Participation was created in 2008 to research and promote participation of children and young people. One of the principal aims is to support children and young people to do their own research. In the early stages of establishing The Centre, young people in care supported by Lancashire Children's Rights Service (a service commissioned by the local authority from The Children's Society), together with members of local Youth Councils, attended meetings with academic staff and discussed aspects of their lives and interests where they might like to do some research. The young people in care talked about their dissatisfaction with some social workers who, for example, didn't visit them when they promised to, or didn't return calls. They thought this was sometimes due to lack of understanding of the situation of children and young people in care, and sometimes to lack of motivation. They had some experience of being involved in training but wondered if there were also ways in which they could be involved in assessment of students and regular appraisal of staff, to help ensure that those employed to work with children and young people understood and followed certain basic standards.

The Children's Workforce Development Council (CWDC) was at the time advertising for the second round of its Participation Fund projects, with one project in each region of England, so we decided to apply for the regional project in the North-West, as a combined team of adult and young researchers. The main aims of the project would be to find out how children and young people could be involved in staff appraisal and student assessment, and to produce materials that would help organizations to implement this. We wrote the application together: All the content was discussed systematically with the young people, and then the academic researchers completed the forms.

We asked for £30,000, which was the amount allocated by CWDC for each project; £5,000 of this was to be set aside for dissemination. Most of the money was budgeted to pay for the time spent on the project, both by the academic researchers and by the young people. It was agreed from the start that the young people would work on every part of the project, leading it as much as possible, and would be paid a proper wage for their time. This was done through a scheme called LACES operated by Lancashire Children's Rights. We submitted the application in July 2008, and in September we heard that we had been successful. Work started in October.

The project had six steps:

1. Recruit and train researchers and design the research.
2. Carry out research into staff appraisal and student assessment.
3. Produce materials for involving young people in appraisal and assessment.
4. Pilot use of the materials.
5. Redraft the materials to reflect learning from pilots.
6. Wider circulation of the materials.

Young people were invited to apply to work on the project and were selected by a panel that included young people. We worked together to develop the skills and knowledge we needed to do the project and to plan the research in more detail. Some of this happened at a series of evening meetings, and it was completed at a residential meeting in the Lake District at the end of October. The first day included workshops on research methods and on ethics and safety, and people's rights in research. The second day was mainly devoted to planning how we would do the research, in particular the focus groups. Between these formal sessions, we played a lot of games and had a Halloween walkabout.

Afterwards the academic researchers used the work done at the residential session to produce information sheets and consent forms for research participants and submitted an application for ethical approval to the Faculty of Health Ethics Committee.

We decided to do a survey to find out what, if anything, was happening currently to involve young people in assessment and appraisal. We sent a questionnaire to all twenty-three local authorities delivering social services in the North-West (via the Regional Government office). Seven local authorities replied. None of them was currently involving children and young people in staff appraisal or student assessment. We also circulated social work courses in the region, and the response to this was also negative.

We ran focus groups with young people (six), students (six), and staff (nine). All the focus groups were led by the young researchers, with adults helping for example with note-taking. The key questions for all the focus groups were

- What do you know about staff appraisals and student assessment?
- What would help involve children and young people in appraisals and assessment?
- Do you know of any examples of good practice?
- Are there any problems in involving children and young people?
- What safeguards are needed?

We analyzed the records of the focus groups together, reading through the notes of the three groups carefully and discussing the messages that came out of them. One of the key points that came out of the groups was the view that children and young people ought to have a choice of different ways to participate, for example attending a meeting or completing a form online. Another point was that safeguards were needed to ensure that staff and students did not feel threatened by the process, because their willingness to cooperate would be very important.

We used the results of our analysis to produce detailed guidance on how best to involve children and young people in appraisals and assessment. We also drafted a questionnaire that children and young people could use to give their views on their social or children's worker.

We sent the draft materials to nine agencies, including the local authorities that had responded to our survey, and asked them to try them out for a short period. Four agencies replied. Because the time was so short they had little opportunity to use the materials in "live" appraisal, but they had discussed them with groups of young people, and some young people had completed the questionnaire and commented on it. Following this we made minor changes to the materials.

We uploaded all the materials onto our project website at http://www.the-centre.org.uk/appraisal. We also sent the materials to all Directors of Children's Services in North-West England and to The Children's Society, NCH Action for Children, and the CWDC. We used the dissemination allocation in the budget to hold a free conference for agencies in the region; forty-three people attended. Here the young people talked about why and how we had done the research and presented the results.

Ten young people worked on the research, at different stages. Some took part in the initial planning and others in actually carrying out the research; only two were involved throughout. This was a reflection of the unstable lives of many children in care, with placement moves and other changes, often unexpected, making it difficult to achieve continuity. Although levels of commitment varied, all those who took part indicated that they found it a valuable and enjoyable experience, and the four young people who were involved in the final conference were extremely enthusiastic and appreciative of the opportunity. Ages ranged from 15 to 20.

From the point of view of the academic researchers, there was no doubt that it was as much the young people's project as ours. Not only was it their own idea in the first place, but they took an active part in every stage, from the initial planning and training through the reporting and dissemination.

The project was labor-intensive, as agency policies and transport logistics required that the young people were accompanied by agency workers in pretty much a one-to-one ratio. Although the agency was strongly committed to the research and to working collaboratively with The Centre, and relationships among the academic researchers, the agency workers, and the young people were extremely positive, the written and unwritten rules under which agency workers operated were experienced as an inhibiting factor on young people's full and free engagement with the research. On the other hand, the fact that young people were paid properly for their time was an important factor in ensuring their commitment to the work and in creating relationships of relative equality in the research team as a whole.

DISCUSSION

In their own terms both projects were successful. All participants—children and young people, teachers and agency workers, academic staff—expressed satisfaction and pleasure both with the processes and with the outcomes. In the school project, each pair of child researchers produced a final report, which they were able to present at a seminar and to take home to their families. I met three of the children three years later and they still had very positive memories of the project, and the research itself was of value. It is not known whether the school built on the children's research, although in the absence of continued input from the university it appears unlikely. In the second project, the materials were presented at a large conference and distributed to social work agencies and courses, as well as being available on a continuing basis on the Internet. Again, I have since been in contact with two members of the group as well as with agency workers, and all have continued to talk very positively about the experience. They were eager to continue with similar work, and the same team worked together to submit another bid to CWDC the following year, but this was unsuccessful. (After that the program was discontinued.)

One set of questions that can be asked about research conducted by children and young people has to do with the quality of the research and how it differs from research conducted by adult professional researchers. The first thing to be said, based on the experience of these and other projects, is that the questions asked are often different when they are partly or wholly framed by children or young people. Partly this is a matter of methodological naïveté (not necessarily a bad thing), but largely it is a matter of perspective and standpoint. Children literally see the world differently, from a different angle or angles. In my experience it is not a question of research questions and approaches being better or worse, but different. As for competence, children's capacity to learn, and to move into new territory with guidance and scaffolding from others, is well established. The fact that professional researchers have years of training does not mean that nothing of value can be done by beginners and is not a reason for denying beginners the opportunity to try things out for themselves, with those others' years of training as a resource supporting them.

Another, perhaps related, problem that often arises with research led by children and young people is a tendency for it not to be taken seriously—for example by adult policymakers. This was the experience of Glenn Miles working with children to present research outcomes to government in Cambodia, and of Vicky Johnson doing similar work with health service providers in southern England (Johnson, 2009; Miles & Thomas, 2007). It was not the experience of the Young People's Appraisal and Assessment Project described above, where we found social work agencies to be highly receptive to learning from work carried out by young people with relevant life expertise. However, there is no doubt a tendency in many parts of society to regard research done by children as inherently being of limited value.

There is a wider problem to do with children and young people's ability—or lack of ability—to operate as free agents. In Western or minority world societies, this tends to be constrained by their lack of physical freedom of movement in a car-dominated environment, and even more by the expectation that they will be accompanied, supervised, and chaperoned every step of the way, so that even when a child is very eager and committed to a project, her or his effective participation is limited to the extent to which adults and their organizations are able or willing to contribute the necessary time and resources.

Finally, there are issues of ethics and more particularly of ethical governance, when children and young people are involved as researchers rather than research participants. In each of these two projects, the relevant ethics committee was persuaded that its scrutiny was only required at the point when the research team (including children and young people) was ready to seek approval for a research plan. The initial planning with the children and young people was not regarded as research with them as participants but as research planning with them as researchers; although appropriate safeguards had to be in place, this was not managed under a heading of research ethics but rather of professional practice. However, there remains ambiguity here, and some would argue that because the adult researchers are learning from the experience of working with the young people, this does constitute research with them as participants. The argument that the young people are researchers, and not participants requiring ethical protection, is perhaps more convincing in projects such as the second one reported here, where the main objective was to make an impact on social work knowledge and practice, than in the first project, where the more important findings were those relating to the process itself rather than those emerging from the individual pieces of research.

CONCLUSION

Fleming and Hudson (2009), quoted in Fleming and Boeck (2012), distinguish between tokenism, consultation, collaboration, and control in young people's involvement in research projects. Boeck & Sharpe (2009), also quoted in Fleming and Boeck (2012), propose the following criteria for participatory research practice: the project is as far as possible defined by the young people; all work is carried out in equal partnership; everyone has a unique contribution to make; and everyone is able to learn from everyone else. In the conclusion to their recent edited collection, Boeck and Fleming (2012) consider the gains from children and young people's research projects in terms of (i) working with and enhancing the critical and creative capacities of young people in the research process; (ii) enhancing power and control; and (iii) research leading to change. These two examples—of projects that, I would suggest, involve a mixture of collaboration and control—may serve to illustrate some of the changes, for themselves and in the wider world, that can be achieved by children and young people participating through the medium of research, and also some of the obstacles that lie in the way of such outcomes.

The two projects may be taken to illustrate two different directions in work with children and young people as researchers. In the first case, learning was a central consideration, because of the school setting (and the orientation of some of the academic researchers). There was a focus throughout the project on learning styles and skills, and methods of working with the children to support them in taking initiative. The benefits were read by all participants in terms of the impact on learning and relationships in the school—although the children were also extremely proud of their individual project reports. In the second case, the main focus for all was on the value of the research in itself, and on strategies for maximizing its impact on practice. In comparing such diverse projects it is important to be clear about the objectives in each case, and to recognize that these may be very different. In both cases, however, the aim was also to explore the possibilities for working with children and young people as researchers, and that exploration continues.

REFERENCES

Alderson, P. (2001). Research by children. *International Journal of Social Research Methodology, 4*(2), 139–158.

Aoslin, A., Baines, R., Clancy, A., Jewiss-Hayden, L., Singh, R., & Strudwick, J. (2008). *WeCan2 Research*, http://wecan2.open.ac.uk/

Beazley, H., Bessell, S., Ennew, J., & Waterson, R. (2009). The right to be properly researched: research with children in a messy, real world. *Children's Geographies, 7*(4), 365–378.

Bland, D., & Atweh, B. (2007). Students as researchers: engaging students' voices in PAR. *Educational Action Research, 15*(3), 337–349.

Boeck, T., & Fleming, J. (2012). Conclusion: Emerging processes to maximize the involvement of children and young people in research. In J. Fleming & T. Boeck (Eds.), *Involving children and young people in health and social care research*. Abingdon: Routledge.

Boeck, T., & Sharpe, D. (2009). An exploration of participatory research with young people. *Coyote, 14*, 14–17.

Bucknall, S. (2010). *Children as researchers: Exploring issues and barriers in English primary schools*. PhD thesis, The Open University.

Burns, S., & Schubotz, D. (2009). Demonstrating the Merits of the Peer Research Process: A Northern Ireland Case Study. *Field Methods, 21*(3), 309–326.

Butler, V. (2005). *Research Report of Phase One of the Generation 2020 Project*. Cardiff: Barnardo's Cymru.

Cahill, C. (2007). Doing research with young people: participatory research and the rituals of collective work. *Children's Geographies, 5*(3), 297–312.

Clark, J. (2005). Participatory research with children and young people: philosophy, possibilities and perils. *Action Research Expeditions* 4.1.

Coad, J., & Coad, N. (2008). Children and young people's preference of thematic design and colour for their hospital environment. *Journal of Child Health Care, 12*(1), 33–48.

Coad, J., & Evans, R. (2008). Reflections on practical approaches to involving children and young people in the data analysis process. *Children & Society, 22*(1), 41–52.

Fleming, J., & Boeck, T. (Eds.) (2012). *Involving children and young people in health and social care research.* Abingdon: Routledge.

Fleming, J., Goodman Chong, H., & Skinner, A. (2009). Experiences of peer evaluation of the Leicester Teenage Pregnancy Prevention Strategy. *Children & Society, 23*(4), 279–290.

Frost, R. (2007). Developing the skills of seven- and eight-year-old researchers: a whole class approach. *Educational Action Research, 15*(3), 441–458.

Greeno, J. (1994). Gibson's affordances. *Psychological Review, 101*(2), 336–342.

Grover, S. (2004). Why won't they listen to us? On giving power and voice to children participating in social research. *Childhood, 11*(1), 81–93.

Johnson, V. (2009). Children's autonomous organization—reflections from the ground. In N. Thomas (Ed.), *Children, Politics and Communication: Participation at the Margins.* Bristol: Policy Press.

Kellett, M. (2005a). *How to Develop Children as Researchers: A Step by Step Guide to Teaching the Research Process.* London: Paul Chapman.

Kellett, M. (2005b). Children as active researchers: a new research paradigm for the 21st century? Published online by ESRC National Centre for Research Methods, NCRM/003 www.ncrm.ac.uk/publications

Kellett, M. (2010). *Rethinking children and research.* London: Continuum.

Kellett, M. Forrest, R. Dent, N., & Ward, S. (2004). Just teach us the skills, we'll do the rest: empowering ten-year-olds as active researchers. *Children & Society, 18*(5), 329–343.

Kilpatrick, R., McCartan, C., McAlister, S., & McKeown, P. (2007). "If I am brutally honest, research has never appealed to me . . ." The problems and successes of a peer research project. *Educational Action Research, 15*(3), 351–369.

Kirby, P. (1999). *Involving young researchers: How to enable young people to design and conduct research.* York: Joseph Rowntree Foundation.

Kirby, P. (2001). Participatory research in schools. *Forum: Journal for Promoting 3-19 Comprehensive Education, 43*(2), 74–77.

Liebel, M. (2008). *Child-led research with working children.* First International Conference of International Childhood and Youth Research Network, Nicosia, 28–29 May.

Lind, C. (2007). The power of adolescent voices: co-researchers in mental health promotion. *Educational Action Research, 15*(3), 371–383.

Miles, G., & Thomas, N. (2007). "Don't grind an egg against a stone"—Children's rights and violence in Cambodian history and culture. *Child Abuse Review, 16*(6), 383–400.

O'Brien, N., & Moules, T. (2007). So round the spiral again: a reflective participatory research project with children and young people. *Educational Action Research, 15*(3), 385–402.

Petrie, S., Fiorelli, L., & O'Donnell, K. (2006). "If we help you what will change?" Participatory research with young people. *Journal of Social Welfare & Family Law, 28*(1), 31–45.

Thomas, N. (2012). A long-term partnership—adult and young researchers working together on the evaluation of the Children's Commissioner for Wales. In J. Fleming

& T. Boeck (Eds.), *Involving Children and Young People in Health and Social Care Research*. Abingdon: Routledge.

Thomas, N., Cook, M., Cook, J., France, H., Hillman, J., Jenkins, C., Pearson, T., Pugh-Dungey, R., Sawyers, B., Taylor, M., & Crowley, A. (2010). Evaluating the Children's Commissioner for Wales: report of a participatory research study. *International Journal of Children's Rights, 18*(1), 19–52.

Thomson, P., & Gunter, H. (2007). The methodology of students-as-researchers: Valuing and using experience and expertise to develop methods. *Discourse: Studies in the Cultural Politics of Education, 28*(3), 327–342.

Waller, T., Morgan, A., Thomas, N., & Waters, J. (2006). *Children as researchers: affordances and constraints*. British Psychological Society Education Conference.

West, A. (1995). *You're on Your Own: young people's research on leaving care*. London: Save the Children.

PART II

Child Participation in Family Disputes

CHAPTER 5

Implementation of Article 12 in Family Law Proceedings in Ireland and New Zealand

Lessons Learned and Messages for Going Forward

AISLING PARKES

INTRODUCTION

Over the past few decades, there has been a heightened awareness globally around the need to include the views of children in family law decision-making processes. In effect this means that children are being recognized as key stakeholders in family law cases, with potentially important information to contribute. This relatively new focal point of attention is in large part owing to the existence of Article 12 of the United Nations (UN) Convention on the Rights of the Child 1989 (CRC), an international legal standard that, at a minimum, specifically requires that all children have a voice in all matters affecting them once they are capable of forming views. Thus, this extends to all decisions made within a family court setting.

In many common law jurisdictions across the world, such as Ireland and New Zealand, family law proceedings take place in an adversarial setting—a system designed by adults for adults. Yet, decisions are being made in family law courtrooms on a daily basis that may have a direct impact on the life of a child. Indeed, in this context, the UN Committee on the Rights of the Child, the international monitoring body for the CRC, has highlighted the fact that "[i]n cases of separation and divorce, the children of the relationship are unequivocally affected by decisions of the courts" (UN Committee, 2009, para. 51) and thus it is imperative that they have some involvement in the decision-making process.

While Article 12(1) sets out a general requirement that children have an opportunity to contribute to the decision-making process, Article 12(2) is more specific in that it requires that children have the opportunity to be heard directly or indirectly in judicial (and administrative) proceedings. The UN Committee has interpreted this provision to require that children be duly informed about their options concerning direct and indirect participation, to be allowed to decide whether they would like to contribute, and if so, to choose the most appropriate method of participation for them (UN Committee, 2009).

In 2009, the UN Committee issued a General Comment on Article 12 detailing the specific requirements of effective implementation (UN Committee, 2009). Prior to this, in the absence of specific guidance from the UN Committee concerning Article 12, states approached the obligation to involve children in family law cases concerning them in a myriad of ways. While some countries embraced the idea of facilitating children's expression in such cases, others have been less active in the area. At a minimum, however, and despite the lack of consensus concerning the most appropriate means of doing so, there is a general acknowledgment of the need to involve children who are affected by family breakdown.

This chapter highlights the importance of listening to children in family law proceedings. In particular, it tracks the progress of family law reform with an emphasis on the implementation of Article 12 in two comparatively similar common law jurisdictions—Ireland and New Zealand—both before and after the adoption of the General Comment on Article 12 in 2009. The extent to which the General Comment on Article 12 has had any measurable impact on state constitutional and legislative reform in the context of family law proceedings is explored and discussed. This chapter highlights what are perceived to be the most prevalent barriers to the implementation of Article 12 in practice. Furthermore, suggestions and recommendations for reform in terms of implementation are made for State Parties law reform going forward.

IMPORTANCE OF LISTENING TO CHILDREN IN FAMILY LAW CASES

Traditionally, the family courtroom has been an adult-centered sphere where "children's futures have been decided upon the views of adults" (Lowe, 2001, p. 137). This is despite the fact that children have been identified as the main victims of marital breakdown (Freeman, 1983). Indeed, given the fact that children's lives are almost always directly affected by family breakdown, nowadays it seems unimaginable that they would be denied a say in the decision-making process both during and after parental separation. Yet, some legal systems worldwide have been reluctant to include children in court proceedings for a variety of reasons, many of which have centered on the fact that it may not be in the best interests of the child. As acknowledged by Cashmore and Parkinson (2009), traditionally children were excluded from the family courtroom for their own protection and due to their limited capacity to make reasoned choices about such matters. Ultimately, this discomfort has been fueled by the argument that it is very easy for children to be subject to manipulation or indeed for their views to be tampered with in contested proceedings. As a result, it essentially becomes a conversation shaped and edited by parents, counselors, and legal representatives (Fitzgerald, 2002). As a result of this reasoning, the views of children have in many jurisdictions been ascertained, interpreted, and presented through the medium of an adult professional before the court. This is despite the fact that children have a right to have their views represented accurately under international law in such cases.

Child Participation—Not Always a Good Thing?

It would be naïve to assume that involving children in decision-making processes after separation cannot harm them. In fact, Kirby and Laws (2010) point out that where decisions are being made about a child's life, the consequences of the child's actively taking part in the decision-making process can prove serious for the child. However, the risks arise not from facilitating the expression of the child's views *per se*, but from an incorrect approach to the process of participation, one out of line with Article 12 (Parkes, 2013). Inevitably, involving children in family law proceedings can result in some harm to children through anxiety, loyalty conflicts, or damage to family relationships if the right to participation is applied without limits (Tapp, 2006). However, failing to involve children in these decision-making processes may cause them more harm—both psychologically and developmentally in the long term.

The Overarching Goal

New Zealand's former Principal Family Court Judge, Peter Boshier (2006), has appropriately pointed out that the goal of any family law proceedings "must be to involve children to the greatest degree possible, while making sure that they are not overly exposed to these potential ill effects." Thus, vigilance concerning the effective implementation of this right in practice must be observed. Indeed, at a European level, it has been acknowledged that "[w]hen promoting a meaningful participation by children, special attention should be paid to avoid putting them at risk in any way, and to avoid harming, pressurizing, coercing or manipulating them; children should have access to child-friendly information, appropriate to their age and to their situation" (Council of Europe, 2013). However, as acknowledged by Marshall (1997), adults cannot deny children the fundamental right of participating on the basis that it may prove damaging to the child.

OBLIGATIONS ON STATES PARTIES IN TERMS OF IMPLEMENTATION

The CRC establishes grounds for comprehensive and holistic law reform that require states parties to examine the whole spectrum of family laws and policies that affect children and their rights, in particular Article 12 and the principle of respect for the views of the child. In 2009, the UN Committee, specifically in the context of Article 12, stated that "[t]he child's right to be heard imposes the obligation on states parties to review or amend their legislation in order to introduce mechanisms providing children with access to appropriate information, adequate support, if necessary, feedback on the weight given to their views, and procedures for complaints, remedies or redress" (UN Committee, 2009, para. 48).

Thus, reform involves reviewing not only the family laws themselves but also the measures necessary to effectively implement them, including regulations, institutions, policies, budget allocations, and the overall process of reform in a country in general (UNICEF, 2008). Unfortunately, in many jurisdictions, Ireland being one example, the process of reform is not systematic; indeed, it is more *ad hoc* and reactive in nature, with changes to the law occurring in response to a gap highlighted by a high-profile court case or the media. In the context of children's rights specifically, this is despite the set of obligations enshrined within Article 4 of the CRC. Since Article 4 places a positive obligation on states parties to implement the civil and political rights of the child under the CRC, jurisdictions worldwide are under an immediate obligation to establish a framework for ensuring that children's views are part of the family law reform process. To date, there is little evidence of this occurring in Ireland and New Zealand.

According to UNICEF, states parties must ensure that existing and new legislation as well as judicial practices are compatible with CRC provisions. This can best be achieved by undertaking a number of basic steps: making a comprehensive review of existing laws and policies; considering measures such as the incorporation of children's rights into the constitution; developing specific laws to reflect the CRC principles and provisions; and adopting remedies for children and their representatives if children's rights are breached (UNICEF, 2004).

ARTICLE 12 IN FAMILY LAW PROCEEDINGS— HOW, WHEN, AND WHERE?

While it is now well accepted that children must be allowed to participate in family law proceedings (Paetsch, Bertrand, Walker, MacRae, & Bala, 2009) the question remains as to how this can be done most effectively, when is it necessary, and in what context it should be done. As Birnbaum and Bala (2010) acknowledged, generally there is not as much consensus regarding how and when children's voices should be heard following marital breakdown. The reality is that decision-making within the confines of the traditional adversarial framework can, in and of itself, serve as a barrier to effective and meaningful child participation in family law proceedings. Moreover, the nature and extent to which children participate in this "adult-centric" environment are largely decided on and determined by adults.

Form and Method of Child Participation in Family Law Proceedings

Article 12 has served as a major catalyst for change in the context of including children in family law decisions affecting them. Article 12 requires that all children who are capable of forming views have the opportunity to express them, with due weight being afforded to those views in accordance with the child's age and maturity. Thus, the child must be provided with a space for expressing his or her views in the first instance, and then the weight attributed to such views is assessed on a case-by-case basis in accordance with the child's age and maturity. While the child's views must be seriously considered, they are not determinative or exclusive.

Further detail for the inclusion of the views of children in family law proceedings is provided under Article 12(2), together with Article 9(2) of the CRC (Parkes, 2013). Article 12(2) provides that the child shall be provided with the opportunity to be heard in any judicial and administrative proceedings affecting him or her either directly or through a representative or an appropriate body in a manner consistent with the procedural rules of national law. Article 9(2) provides that the child must be provided with the opportunity to participate in any proceedings that occur as a result of the child's being separated from one or both parents so that the child may make his or her views known.

Methods of Direct Participation

In the case of direct participation in family law proceedings, the UN Committee has interpreted Article 12 to mean that in each case, once a child is deemed capable of forming views, he or she should have the option of being heard directly by the judge. There are two main ways this could happen: in open court or in a private discussion in chambers. Hearing the child in open court has been strongly discouraged by the UN Committee, which has emphasized confidentiality issues in such cases (UN Committee, 2009, para. 43). Hearing a child in open court in family law cases is very rare in Ireland and is not an accepted practice in New Zealand.

Judicial Discussions with Children

In both New Zealand and Ireland, judicial discussions with children are recognized as one method of ensuring that a child's views are heard in family law proceedings. However, the approaches adopted by each jurisdiction vary greatly. In New Zealand, where there are special family courts and well-trained judges, this is a right of the child incorporated into domestic law through legislation. In particular, Section 6 of the Care of Children Act 2004 requires that the child must be given reasonable opportunities to express views either directly or through a representative and such views must be taken into account. While there is still an element of judicial discretion in these cases, according to Fernando, "Judges in New Zealand meet with children reasonably frequently when compared to other jurisdictions" (Fernando, 2013, p. 387). Indeed, the well-established practice of judges having discussions with children in family law cases in New Zealand is evidenced by the fact that guidelines were drafted for this purpose.

The 2007 "Judicial Guidelines—Decisions with Children" (www.justice.govt.nz) were intended to serve as a guide to the procedures and recommended standards of judicial practice for judges engaging in discussions with children in New Zealand. While the extent to which the guidelines are adhered to is at the discretion of each judge, it seems that these have proved very effective. In all cases, the judge expects the lawyer for the child to indicate whether the child would like to meet with him or her and, if so, the proposed purpose of that meeting. The judge must record the reasons why he or she did or did not meet with the child. If the judge decides to meet with the child, he or she must decide when and where the meeting will take place, whether the meeting will be recorded, and how such a record is to be conveyed to the adult parties involved. The lawyer for the child will be present at the meeting as well as anyone else the judge deems important. The meeting will be confidential if this is deemed to be in the child's best interests. The parties will be able to respond to the content of the meeting when it is conveyed to them, and the judge will decide whether to tell the child the outcome of the hearing.

Cashmore and Parkinson have asserted that most common law jurisdictions adopt a protective approach toward children, meaning that they are reluctant to allow children to enter the court environment (2007). This has traditionally been the case in Ireland. Unlike New Zealand, there are no special family courts in Ireland, and judges are not obliged to undergo any training if they were appointed before 1996. Direct contact with the judge is not a systematic right of the child in Ireland, partly because it is not specifically enshrined in legislation. Furthermore, judicial discretion forms an important element of family law proceedings in Ireland. Under Irish law, Section 17(2) of the Guardianship of Infants Act 1964 (as amended) provides in a general sense that the child's wishes must be taken into consideration by the court in custody and access proceedings.

However, the form and method of participation are not set out under the legislation. The judge may conduct an informal interview with the child in his or her chambers to ascertain these wishes, but this is at the judge's discretion. The judicial practice of listening to the views of the child directly in family law proceedings and the exercise of judicial discretion in such cases are well illustrated by Keane CJ in *RB v AS* [2002] 2 IR 428:

> It has long been recognised that trial judges have a discretion as to whether they will interview children who are the subject of custody or access disputes in their chambers, since to invite them to give evidence in court in the presence of the parties or their legal representative would involve them in an unacceptable manner in the marital disputes of their parents. Depending on the age of the children concerned, such interviews may be of assistance to the trial judge in ascertaining where their own wishes lie.

More recently, Abbott J noted the following in *O'D v. O'D* (2008) IEHC 468:

10. Talking with the Children

10.1 It is important to explain the approach of the court as regards talking with children in these cases. The Brussels II bis Regulation requires that judges are trained in the work of hearing cases regarding parental control, and I am fortunate that since my appointment as judge, I have had the opportunity of training relating to this area through networking and conferencing with judicial peers, lawyers, academics and professional experts, both nationally and internationally. I have taken a number of guidelines from such training when speaking with children, which are as follows:

1. The judge shall be clear about the legislative or forensic framework in which he is embarking on the role of talking to the children as different codes may require or only permit different approaches.
2. The judge should never seek to act as an expert and should reach such conclusions from the process as may be justified by common sense only, and the judge's own experience.
3. The principles of a fair trial and natural justice should be observed by agreeing terms of reference with the parties prior to relying on the record of the meeting with children.
4. The judge should explain to the children the fact that the judge is charged with resolving issues between the parents of the child and should reassure the child that in speaking to the judge the child is not taking on the onus of judging the case itself and should assure the child that while the wishes of children may be taken into consideration by the court, their wishes will not be solely (or necessarily at all) determinative of the ultimate decision of the court.
5. The judge should explain the development of the convention and legislative background relating to the courts in more recent times actively seeking out the voice of the child in such simple terms as the child may understand.

6. The court should, at an early stage ascertain whether the age and maturity of the child is such as to necessitate hearing the voice of the child. In most cases the parents in dispute in the litigation are likely to assist and agree on this aspect. In the absence of such agreement then it is advisable for the court to seek expert advice from the s. 47 procedure [court report], unless of course such qualification is patently obvious.

7. The court should avoid a situation where the children speak in confidence to the court unless of course the parents agree. In this case the children sought such confidence and I agreed to give it them subject to the stenographer and registrar recording same. Such a course, while very desirable from the child's point of view is generally not consistent with the proper forensic progression of a case unless the parents in the litigation are informed and do not object, as was the situation in this case.

. . . There is no formal training programme in place to enable judges to fulfill the task of interviewing children, although proposals are being considered by the Committee for Judicial Studies.

The latter guidelines are not wholly compliant with Article 12. For example, the reference to the requirement that the "court should, at an early stage ascertain whether the age and maturity of the child is such as to necessitate hearing the voice of the child" is completely contrary to the requirement that the child must have the opportunity to express his or her views and then due weight should be applied based on his or her age and maturity. Moreover, it is well accepted that the inclusion of the views of children in family law cases is not for forensic purposes (Taylor & Caldwell, 2013), and so the reluctance to hear children in confidence due to the fact that it is "not consistent with the proper forensic progression of a case" is also not consistent with Article 12. The extent to which judges in Ireland hear the views of children directly is evidenced by a relatively recent study of family law cases in the Circuit Court in Ireland, where the inconsistent approach adopted by judges was made very clear (Coulter, 2009). The guidelines set out in *O'D v. O'D* are the only ones in existence to date in Ireland, unlike the comprehensive guidance provided by and for the judiciary in New Zealand Judicial Guidelines as issued by the Family Court of New Zealand (2007).

Judicial Experiences of Listening to Children

The Family Justice Council in the UK has set down guidelines for judges meeting with children who are subject to family proceedings. These guidelines aim

to encourage Judges to enable children to feel more involved and connected with proceedings in which important decisions are made in their lives and to give them an opportunity to satisfy themselves that the Judge has understood their wishes and feelings and to understand the nature of the Judge's task . . . The primary purpose of the meeting is to benefit the child.

Much has been written about the extent to which judges have engaged with listening to children directly and the positives and negatives associated with the process. In New Zealand, where this is a well-established and well-accepted practice, much empirical research has been carried out documenting multiple perspectives on the process (Taylor & Caldwell, 2013). As acknowledged by Taylor and Caldwell, the empirical research conducted in New Zealand to date confirms that "there is a trend of increasingly positive attitudes towards, and greater use of, judicial interviewing" (2013, p. 446). The use of the judicial interview assumes all the more importance because there is evidence that children are not uniformly happy with the manner in which their views are presented indirectly through a representative. Thus, in this context, judicial interviews with children have become an invaluable tool for family court judges in New Zealand (Parkes, 2013, 94).

Moreover, New Zealand judges themselves have observed the value of judicial interviews. They believe that it is important when making a decision for them to have a personality in mind rather than working in a vacuum and relying on evidence alone. Sometimes a judge will request a lawyer for the child to be present, or the judge may consider it inappropriate that the child be interviewed again. There are also natural justice concerns that are addressed through the recording of interviews. By way of comparison, in Ireland there has been very little done in terms of empirical research concerning the nature and scope of judicial interviews with children in family law proceedings. Thus, the only insight we have is provided through judicial statements delivered through case law and other fora. Sir Mark Potter, former President of the Family Division in the UK, has suggested four strong and convincing reasons why judges should be less reluctant to meet with children in both public and private family law cases:

1. To enable the child to have a picture of the judge in their mind as the decision-maker in their case where they have decided not to, or it has been deemed inappropriate for them, to attend the hearing.
2. To enable the child, when they wish to do so, to tell the judge directly of his or her wishes and feelings in respect any issues arising in the case.
3. To reassure the child that they are, or have been, at the centre of the decision-making process and that the judge has wholly understood and taken into account what they have said.
4. Following the judgment, to enable the judge to explain his or her decision to the child, thus helping the child to understand the process and assisting the child in accepting the outcome. (2008, pp. 146–147)

Are Judicial Discussions with Children Always a Good Thing?

Raitt (2004) has noted that while some judges like to interview children, since it allows them to form their own opinion of the child, this is not every judge's practice. Indeed, many reasons have been put forward against this practice by judges and academics alike (Parkes, 2013):

- It may place undue pressure on the child.
- The judge's chambers may represent an intimidating environment for the child.
- Children's views may change over time due to a minor change in circumstances (Hunter, 2007).
- By interviewing the child, the judge is no longer capable of being a neutral decision maker, assessing all the evidence presented, but instead becomes a participant in the process (Parkinson & Cashmore, 2007).
- The child may be coached by either or both parents (Hunter, 2007).
- The interview represents a departure from the normal adversarial process in that the views expressed by the child to the judge in chambers are not subject to cross-examination, as a result of the child's desire for confidentiality (even though the child's views are not supposed to be obtained for forensic purposes).
- The judge may lack the skills and training for dealing with children under such circumstances, so indirect methods are far superior to the judge interviewing children directly (Cashmore & Parkinson, 2007).

Asking the Experts: What Do Children Think?

Children have pointed out many reasons why they wanted their views to be heard by the principal decision maker. For example, children interviewed by Cashmore and Parkinson stated that judges should know the person they are making the decision about; they wanted to say things to the judge without one or both parents knowing what they said; they feared hurting their parents if their views were known; and it was important for the judge to know exactly how they were feeling, without any mixed messages or misinterpretations of their views (Cashmore & Parkinson, 2007).

Characteristics of the Judicial Discussion with the Child

At a minimum, the judge should ensure that the child understands the circumstances of the case. The child should be provided with an explanation of the judge's role in the proceedings in a manner appropriate to the age and maturity of the child. Members of the judiciary presiding over cases involving children must undergo training that details the nature and scope of Article 12 of the CRC in the context of family law proceedings. Byrnes (2011) points out that training of judges to consider the process through the eyes of a child needs to continue, as well as training in appropriate interviewing techniques and the various stages of child development. Indeed, the UN Committee (2003, para. 53) has emphasized "[s]tates' obligations to develop training and capacity-building for all those involved in the implementation process—government officials, parliamentarians and members of the judiciary."

INDIRECT METHODS OF INCLUDING THE CHILD'S VOICE

The reference under Article 12(2) to the child's right to be heard indirectly in judicial and administrative proceedings implies the use of alternative mechanisms. Mechanisms have been adopted in Ireland and New Zealand to facilitate indirect participation of children in family law proceedings. These include the use of court/expert/social reports, the guardian *ad litem* service, and separate legal representatives.

Court Reports

A prevalent means through which the children's views are presented indirectly to the judge is via a court report. In New Zealand, reports are generally compiled by a psychologist or a psychiatrist (Fernando, 2013). The lawyer for the child must discuss the contents of the report with the child.

In Ireland, the court may appoint a probation and welfare officer or a qualified social worker, psychologist, or psychiatrist to write the report. The court may then use the report during the proceedings, and the author of the report may be called as a witness. The cost of the report (and any subsequent appearance in court) must be met by such party or parties as decided by the court. The content of the report is rarely discussed with the child.

In both jurisdictions, while these reports may reveal the views of the child, this is not their sole focus (Fernando, 2013). Furthermore, they are quite expensive and can result in long delays in the proceedings (Clissmann & Hutchinson, 2006). Indeed, as acknowledged by Clissmann and Hutchinson, in the case of *McD v. L* [2008] IEHC 96, Justice Hedigan asserted that a court report should be treated with the same status as a medical report, and

> because the expert producing a s47 report does so on the instructions of the court rather than either party, the report should be accorded great weight. Save for grave

reasons against, which I think the court should set out clearly; the s47 report ought to be accepted in its recommendations.

This is particularly worrying, especially where the report is the only mechanism used to present the child's views before the court. Moreover, there is no guarantee that the child's views will be accurately represented in the report. Indeed, it has been acknowledged that children are "unhappy about a process that requires them to express their views to a person who subsequently includes those views amongst other matters in a report to the court" (Fernando, 2013, p. 392).

Guardian *Ad Litem*

The guardian *ad litem* (GAL) is another common method of providing children with the opportunity to be heard indirectly in accordance with Article 12(2) in family law proceedings. However, in the absence of guidance from the UN Committee, there is currently no universally accepted definition of what constitutes a GAL or indeed what functions he or she should have. It has been suggested that a GAL is someone who is appointed as "a guardian for a law suit" (Guardian Ad Litem Group, 2001, p. 4). Moreover, it would seem that the GAL should have a dual function: to elicit and represent the child's wishes and feelings in court proceedings and to determine and present to the court what he or she considers to be in the child's best interests. Despite the fact that these appear to be two conflicting roles, it is possible to reconcile the two since it is in the best interests of the child that his or her views are presented to the court, regardless of whether they conflict with the GAL's opinion as to what is in the child's best interests. Indeed, the GAL must be clear as to the child's wishes.

In Ireland, section 28 of the Guardianship of Infants Act 1964 provides that a GAL may be appointed in custody and access proceedings "if in special circumstances" it appears to the court "necessary in the interests of the child to do so." However, as pointed out by an Non-Governmental Organisation (NGO) report in 2006, the provisions of the Children Act 1997 have not yet come into force (Children's Rights Alliance, 2006, para. 135), and this remains the case today. As a result, in private law proceedings, currently there is no provision for the appointment of a GAL to report on the child's articulated views and independently to assess the child's best interests as part of the court's deliberations. Indeed, the NGO report has recommended that an independent, national GAL service, encompassing both private and public law, be established. In May 2009, the Children's Acts Advisory Board in Ireland issued "Guidance on the Role, Criteria for Appointment, Qualifications and Training of Guardians *ad litem* for Children in Proceedings under the Child Care Act, 1991." According to the guidelines, the role of the GAL should be to "independently establish the wishes, feelings and interests of the child and present them to the court with recommendations."

Indeed, the GAL must undertake a dual role—to inform the court of the child's wishes and feelings and to advise the court as to the child's best interests. In New Zealand, the role of the GAL is less important because there is a requirement for separate legal representation in all cases involving children.

SEPARATE LEGAL REPRESENTATION

Currently in Ireland, despite the existence of an adversarial framework in Irish family law proceedings, there is no provision or systematic use of separate legal representation for children in these cases. Even solely from a due process perspective, this is highly problematic. In New Zealand's system, the notion of separate or independent legal representation for children in family law proceedings has long been used to represent the child's voice in accordance with Article 12.

The Law Society of New Zealand (2000) issued a set of best practice guidelines as a result of the research. They state that

> children have the right to be given the opportunity to be heard in any judicial and administrative proceedings affecting them in line with the UN Convention on the Rights of the Child; child clients have the right to be treated with the same respect as clients who are adults; children have the right to information about the case in which they are involved including information on the progress and outcome of the case; children have the right to the highest quality representation from experienced and skilled practitioners.

New Zealand has since provided for the appointment of a separate legal representative for the child in family law proceedings under the Care of Children Act 2004. According to the Third and Fourth Periodic Report of New Zealand (2011, para. 131):

> Under the Act, the Family Court continues to appoint an independent lawyer to act for a child if a dispute affecting them seems likely to go to a Court hearing. The role of the lawyer is to:

- Represent the child through the Court process and in any negotiations between the parents or other parties to the case
- Find out the child's views and make the Judge aware of them
- Make sure the child's best interests and all issues affecting their welfare are put before the Court for it to consider
- Explain the Court process to the child and, at the end of the process, explain the Judge's decision.

Thus, New Zealand "employs a direct representation model but the lawyer must also ensure that the child's best interests are protected" (Fernando, 2013, p. 394). Interestingly, in recent times, the guarantee of the child's right to be heard has been extended to include mediation proceedings. The Family Court Matters Act 2008 amends the Care of Children Act 2004 to provide for family mediation processes to take better account of children's views. Where such proceedings have been filed, a lawyer for the child may be appointed to take part in the mediation. Furthermore, the existence of the Practice Note for Lawyers for Children makes the possibility of attaining genuine child participation more of a reality.

The New Zealand Practice Note, "Lawyer for the Child: Code of Conduct," was issued by Judge Boshier on March 8, 2007. According to the practice note, children have the right to information about the case in which they are involved, including information on the progress and outcome of the case and, if relevant, information on any reports the court has ordered concerning the child. Indeed, the right of the child to be fully informed before, during, and after the decision-making process is emphasized throughout the General Comment. Furthermore, the child's lawyer must provide independent representation and advice to the child. The UN Committee has stated that the representative must represent only the views of the child, not those of any other party, and the best way to ensure this is by developing a code of conduct (UN Committee, 2009, para. 37) The lawyer must put the child's views before the court but cannot force the child to express a view if he or she does not wish to do so. If the child tells the lawyer something in confidence, the lawyer will not be ordered to disclose this information to the court.

Boshier asserts that the role of the lawyer is always to represent the child's views to the court, regardless of whether the lawyer believes they are in the child's best interests. He asserts that "any deviation from this role would negate the child's right to participate" (Boshier, 2008, p. 153). The lawyer could subsequently inform the court of his or her opinion as to whether such views are contrary to the child's interests and welfare. However, Heneghan argues that while the child's independent voice is recognized by imposing a duty on the lawyer to put the child's wishes and views before the court, this is "watered down and potentially drowned" by a further duty to put other factors that influence the child's welfare before the court (2008, p. 117).

In Ireland there is no provision for separate legal representation for children in family law proceedings. However, given recent developments at the constitutional level, in its most recent Third and Fourth Periodic Report, published in July 2013, Ireland has noted that

> The procedures for obtaining the views of children in Court proceedings, both child care and family law related, will be subject to further examination having regard to the specific reference to this objective proposed for insertion into the Constitution in accordance with the Thirty-first Amendment of the Constitution (Children) Bill 2012.
>
> (Third and Fourth Periodic Report: Ireland, July 2013, p. 237)

DEVELOPMENTS AFTER GENERAL COMMENT 12

The General Comment issued by the UN Committee on Article 12 in 2009 shed some light on states' obligations under Article 12 in the context of family law proceedings. The extent to which the General Comment has had any meaningful influence on child and family law reform in both Ireland and New Zealand since 2009 is unclear since neither jurisdiction has specifically referred to the contents of the General Comment in the family law reform process.

In New Zealand, partly because the child's right to be heard is already well established in legislation, there has been no significant law reform in this context since 2009. Indeed, the need to recognize that law reform is an ongoing process was something that was highlighted by the UN Committee when it was considering the Third and Fourth Periodic Report of New Zealand in 2011. Unexpectedly, the UN Committee highlighted shortcomings in New Zealand's approach toward listening to children in family law cases. This may perhaps be in part due to the fact that in its Alternative Periodic Report, Children and Youth in Aotearoa highlighted the fact that the child's right to be heard in family law proceedings "is constrained by complex procedural formalities which require the child to have a litigation guardian" (para. 3.26). While it is unclear from the Concluding Observations alone why the UN Committee is not content with the approach adopted in New Zealand to date, it is nonetheless worth highlighting its comments in this regard:

> The Committee ... regrets ... that the State party does not systematically take into consideration children's views when formulating laws and policies that may affect them and that their right to be heard in judicial and administrative proceedings is not sufficiently respected. (Concluding Observations, New Zealand, 2011, para. 26)

The Committee further recommended that New Zealand:

> in accordance with article 12 of the Convention, and taking into account ... its general comment No. 12 (2009) on the right of the child to be heard:
>
> (a) Promote, facilitate and implement, in legislation as well as in practice ... in administrative and judicial proceedings, the principle of respect for the views of the child; and
>
> (b) Systematically consider the views of the child in formulating laws and policies.

On the other hand, in the Irish context, Article 12 and the interpretation given to it by the UN Committee appear to have had some influence on the child law reform process. Following a review of the Second Periodic Report of Ireland in

2006, the UN Committee made a number of suggestions for child and family law reform. It encouraged Ireland to

> Strengthen its efforts to ensure, including through Constitutional provisions, that children have the right to express their views in all matters affecting them and to have those views given due weight . . .
>
> Ensure that children be provided with the opportunity to be heard in any judicial and administrative proceedings affecting them, and that due weight be given to those views in accordance with the age and maturity of the child . . .
>
> Take into account the recommendations adopted on the Committee's day of general discussion on the right of the child to be heard in September 2006. (Concluding Observations: Ireland, 2006, para. 25)

In November 2012, after many promises to incorporate children's rights into the Irish Constitution (which currently contains no reference to children's rights), a national referendum was held to amend the Irish Constitution 1937 to include a new provision on children's rights—Article 42A. This provision, partly mirroring Article 12(2), contains a specific reference to the right of children capable of forming views to have their views considered and given due weight in all guardianship, custody, and access cases concerning them. While the thirty-first amendment of the Constitution was passed on November 10, 2012 (by a majority of 58.01 percent, with a voter turnout of 33.5 percent) at the time of writing, this amendment has not yet been inserted into the Constitution. The constitutionality of this provision was challenged unsuccessfully before the High Court of Ireland, and this judgment is now subject to appeal before the Irish Supreme Court. The relevant part of the proposed Article 42A4 states that

> Provision shall be made by law for securing, as far as practicable, that in all proceedings referred to in subsection 1° of this section in respect of any child who is capable of forming his or her own views, the views of the child shall be ascertained and given due weight having regard to the age and maturity of the child.

If this provision is inserted into the highest source of Irish domestic law, it will be complemented by legislation that, it is anticipated, will set out the legal detail required for the effective implementation of the child's right to be heard in family law cases affecting him or her.

MOVING FORWARD

Despite the many positive initiatives that have been adopted to facilitate children's voices being heard in family law cases concerning them in New Zealand, particularly over the past decade, the UN Committee has reinforced the need for New Zealand to pay particular attention to General Comment No. 12 (2009) on the right of the child to be heard and in particular to

> ... (a) Promote, facilitate and implement, in legislation as well as in practice, within the family, schools and the community as well as in institutions and in administrative and judicial proceedings, the principle of respect for the views of the child ... (2011, para. 27)

It would appear that New Zealand, having taken the lead until recently in terms of listening to children in family law cases, has regressed somewhat in recent times if one is to pay attention to the feedback of the Committee and the Alternative NGO report. Furthermore, since there is now more concrete guidance from the UN Committee on the minimum requirements of implementation, arguably this raises the bar for all countries in their quest to adhere to Article 12. On the other hand, while Ireland has yet to appear before the UN Committee since the 2009 General Comment, there has been a great deal happening in the field of law reform, which provides a strong basis for receiving constructive feedback from the UN Committee on the efforts it has taken to implement Article 12 in family law proceedings.

REQUIREMENTS OF ARTICLE 12

As part of the recently adopted General Comment on Article 12, the UN Committee has set out five steps that must be taken by states parties to ensure the effective implementation of the child's right to be heard. These five steps apply not only to family law proceedings but to all types of decisions concerning children.

First, for the purposes of preparation, children must be kept informed throughout the process. Children not only must be informed of their right to express their opinions on all matters affecting them but must also be made aware of the option of communicating those views directly or indirectly and about the consequences that their views will have on the outcome of the process. The decision maker must explain in child-appropriate language the details concerning how, when, and where the hearing will take place and who the participants will be.

Second, in relation to the proceedings themselves, the circumstances in which the child exercises his or her right to be heard must be such that the child is encouraged and facilitated in expressing his or her views. While the adult decision maker must provide children with the opportunity to be heard, he or she must also be adequately equipped to listen to the child's views. Heneghan believes that the main concern is not the child's competence to express views but the adult's competence to elicit them (2005, p. 22).

Third, once the child is capable of forming views, he or she must be allowed to express them. Determination of the child's capacity will essentially involve a case-by-case assessment of each child.

Fourth, the decision maker must inform the child of the outcome of the process and the extent to which the child's views were taken into consideration. This must also be carried out in a child-appropriate manner.

Finally, if the child's right to be heard is not respected in circumstances where he or she is capable of forming views, legislation must be put in place that provides some redress to the child in the form of an appeals or complaints procedure. These processes must be accessible to the child.

COMMON BARRIERS TO IMPLEMENTATION OF ARTICLE 12

In addition to the fact that the family law systems in both jurisdictions are adversarial in nature and more suited to the needs of adults, there are a number of challenges as well as opportunities for both jurisdictions, albeit to differing extents.

Adult Gatekeepers—Challenging Attitudes

While generally it is well accepted in both countries that children should have a voice in matters affecting them, there remains debate around the extent to which this may be done while safeguarding the best interests of the child. Since adults are in control of the family law proceedings system and all the elements thereof, in light of Article 12, it is important that they ensure that the child's voice is always accurately represented irrespective of whether they agree with the child's views. While children are entitled to have a voice in the process and an accurate representation of that voice, their views are never conclusive and are only one small piece of the jigsaw.

The child's right to be heard has been enshrined in the legislative framework in New Zealand for some time, so there is less room for adults working in this context (e.g., lawyers and Judges) to act as gatekeepers for any children affected exercising their fundamental right to be heard in family law proceedings. Moreover, children will always have a right to separate legal representation, owing to a legislative guarantee to that effect. In contrast, in Ireland, in the absence of any specific legal obligation to hear children in family law cases, key professionals working in the area tend to restrict the extent to which children have an input in such cases, based on the traditional argument that it will cause them more harm than good. Moreover, the judge, as the final decision maker, exercises his or her discretion when deciding whether a child will be heard, and in many cases they rely on the practitioners or expert for such input. To compound this, there is no separate legal representation for children in Ireland. Thus, it is clear that when there is legal protection of the fundamental right of the child to be heard in family law proceedings, there is less room for this right to be denied or restricted to children by adults working on the case in question.

Lack of Professional Training

The UN Committee places a heavy emphasis on the obligation of states parties "to develop training and capacity-building . . . for all those working for and with children" (UN Committee, 2003, para. 53). Indeed, the absence of a training program aimed at equipping professionals who are representing children in family law proceedings has the potential to seriously limit the extent of their participation (Parkes, 2013). As pointed out by Taylor, Tapp and Heneghan (2007), in the context of family law proceedings specifically, a multidisciplinary approach must be adopted and professional training must be provided to support this approach. Thus, all professionals working for and with children must receive sufficient training to prepare them to effectively elicit the views of such children. Thus, it should be a legal requirement that all judges, lawyers, and GALs who wish to represent children in family law proceedings should receive special professional training to help them to deal most effectively with the sensitive nature of such proceedings and the effects that such proceedings can have on children.

A flaw apparent in the legal systems of some jurisdictions is that there is no requirement for the judiciary to undergo any special training for dealing with children in cases of such a sensitive nature. For example, in Ireland members of the judiciary who were appointed prior to the Courts and Courts Officers Act 1996 are not obliged to undergo any training. Even though some judges undertake continuing professional development willingly, there is no statutory duty to receive training, notwithstanding the clear need for it in family cases especially involving children. Similarly, in New Zealand, it was highlighted in the NGO alternative report that some legal counsel acting for children have little or no empathy with their clients, as they have no training in child development, and only recently has the law society's training program addressed the issue of children's rights. As a result of the lack of training, many counsel for children put forward what they perceive to be in the child's best interests, which defeats the purpose of having a separate legal representative for children. Indeed, children regularly complain about the issue, and many matters are settled without regard to the child's views.

Thus, even though there is a legal framework for children to be heard in family law proceedings in New Zealand, this may be limited in terms of its effect in cases where the legal representatives are not adequately trained. In Ireland, the absence of compulsory legal training for the judiciary and the complete absence of legal representation for children, not to mention trained separate legal representatives, leaves Irish law falling far short of international standards.

Skills of the Listener

One of the more challenging aspects of Article 12 is the obligation to give due weight to the child's views in accordance with both age and maturity. Thus, the question remains as to who is responsible for determining the child's age and maturity. Moreover, as Moloney (2005) points out, listening to children requires an ability to be open, it demands skills on the part of the adult listener, and it brings with it a heavy degree of adult responsibility. Indeed, the overall quality of the information obtained by interviewing the child regarding his or her views is wholly dependent on the skills of the interviewer (Donnelly, 2010). Thus, specifically designed programs must be developed that ensure that those responsible for hearing children are well equipped to do so and become well skilled in their craft (Moloney, 2005). Judge Van Doogue (2006) in New Zealand has outlined a number of characteristics that the adult listener must possess. He or she must have the ability and training to understand that children and adults view the world very differently and that children use different language to portray their experiences. The adult listener must be able to create surroundings that will facilitate and encourage the expression of views freely in terms of the types of questions that are asked and how they are asked. The hearing should be more of a talk rather than an interrogation of the child (UN Committee, 2009, para. 43).

Resources

The lack of financial resources and the lack of persons who are adequately trained and qualified to represent children in family law proceedings also constitute obstacles to the effective involvement of children. The UN Committee needs to strongly encourage states parties to set aside adequate resources for the representation of children in all private family law proceedings and give some clear guidance as to what type of training should be provided for professionals working for and with children in this area.

CONCLUSION

The adversarial family court system, one adopted by many common law jurisdictions, was a system designed by adults for adults in a time when children's rights were unheard of. The reality of the adversarial system, which currently frames family law proceedings in both Ireland and New Zealand, has meant that the true implementation of Article 12 has proved very challenging in practice. This, in and of itself, strengthens the argument for further measures to be taken to protect the rights of children where a decision is being made that can potentially have a lifelong impact on them. That said, we are living in a children's rights era where international law requires that children have a voice in family law proceedings affecting them. As this chapter has shown, countries that have agreed to be legally bound by the same legally binding international standard as set out under Article 12 have attempted to implement that standard in very different ways.

For example, in recent times, New Zealand, which has a special family law court system, has for the most part led the way by legally incorporating specific mechanisms for children to be heard in family law cases affecting them. Such mechanisms include a right of separate legal representation for children as well as the possibility of speaking directly with the decision maker. On the other hand, in Ireland, there is no special family court system, and children in such cases have no right to be heard directly or indirectly. Furthermore, there is no provision for separate legal representation for children. Recent times, however, have seen not only an attempt to constitutionally incorporate children's rights (and part of Article 12) into the fundamental law of the Irish state but also the emergence of a new debate concerning the possibility of a special family court system. It is hoped that these developments will pay particular attention to the best practice guidance set out by the UN Committee in its General Comment on Article 12.

New Zealand's family court system has for a long time dominated discussions concerning how and when to listen to children, but in recent times, the discussion has been less than positive. While Ireland is striving to make improvements in this area, New Zealand appears to have taken its foot off the pedal. Both jurisdictions have the potential to lead the way in terms of listening to children, but they must adhere to the good practice guidance set out in the General Comment, which has been made available by the UN Committee.

Moreover, the UN Committee, as the CRC monitoring body, also has a role to play in this movement toward better protection of children who are directly affected by the breakup of their parents. Rather than generally pointing states in the direction of the General Comment No. 12, it would no doubt be more difficult for states parties to ignore calls by the UN Committee for specific measures to be taken (or no longer taken, as the case may be) in the context of listening to children in family law cases, by the next reporting date. This could include a reference to a compulsory training program for all legal professionals, including members of the judiciary, for example.

There is still much work to be done in terms of facilitating the transition from a paternalistic way of thinking about children to a children's rights–based approach in family law proceedings. Article 12 and the interpretation given to it under the General Comment offer much flexibility in terms of how children can be encouraged to express their views on issues affecting them in family law cases. However, it is clear that many common law legal systems are seeking to incorporate Article 12 through their existing legal and practical frameworks, which may not necessarily be conducive to listening to children. If we are truly committed to implementing children's rights, we need to see the process through the lens of children and amend the system to reflect their needs rather than the wants of adults.

REFERENCES

Birnbaum, R., & Bala, N. (2010). Judicial interviews with children in custody and access cases: comparing experiences in Ontario and Ohio. *International Journal of Law, Policy and the Family, 24*(2), 398–422.

Boshier, P. (2006). Contact and relocation: focussing on children, involving children in decision-making: lessons from New Zealand. Available at http://www.justice.govt. nz/courts/family-court/publications/speeches-and-papers/contact-and-relocation.

Boshier, P. (2008). International family justice from a New Zealand perspective. *International Family Law,* 149–154.

Byrnes, P. (2011). Voices of children in the legal process. *Journal of Family Studies, 17,* 44–58.

Cashmore, J., & Parkinson, P. (2007). What responsibility do courts have to hear children's voices? *International Journal of Children's Rights, 15,* 43–60.

Cashmore, J., & Parkinson, P. (2009). Children's participation in family law disputes—The views of children, parents, lawyers and counsellors. *Family Matters, 82,* 15–21.

Children and Youth in Aotearoa. (2010). New Zealand Non-Governmental Organisations Alternative Periodic Report to the United Nations Committee on the Rights of the Child www.acya.nz

Children's Rights Alliance (2006). From Rhetoric to Rights: Children's Rights Alliance Second Shadow Report to the United Nations Committee on the Rights of the Child, Dublin.

Clissmann, I., & Hutchinson, P. (2006). The right of the child to be heard in guardianship, custody and access cases (II). *Irish Journal of Family Law, 9*(2).

Coulter, C. (2009). *Family law in practice: a study of cases in the circuit court* (p. 128). Dublin, Clarus Press.

Council of Europe (2013). Promoting the participation by children in decisions affecting them, Recommendation 1864 (2009)1.

Donnelly, C. (2010). Reflections of a guardian ad litem on the participation of looked-after children in public law proceedings. *Child Care in Practice, 16*(2), 181–193.

Family Court of New Zealand (2007). Judges' guidelines: decisions with children. Available at http://www.justice.govt.nz/courts/family-court/practice-and-procedure/guidelines/judges-guidelines-decisions-with-children

Family Court of New Zealand (2007). New Zealand Practice Note, "—Lawyer for the Child: Code of Conduct, http://www.justice.govt.nz/family-justice/about-us/info-for-providers/documents/practice-notes/lawyer-for-the-child-coc.pdf.

Family Justice Council Briefing. (2013). Child participation in family proceedings. Available at www.family-justice-council.org.uk

Fernando, M. (2013). How can we best listen to children in family law proceedings? *New Zealand Law Review,21*(3), 387–407.

Fitzgerald, R. (2002). How are children heard in family law proceedings in Australia? *Southern Cross University Law Review, 6.*

Freeman, M. D. A. (1983). *The rights and wrongs of children* (p. 192). Great Britain: Frances Pinter Publishers.

Guardian Ad Litem Group (2001). *Giving Children a Voice: The Case for the Independent Representation of Children*, Dublin.

Heneghan, M. (2005). *Children and lawyers acting for children in legal proceedings: what does a child's right to be heard in legal proceedings really mean?* Paper presented at the 4th World Congress on Family Law and Children's Rights, March 2005, Cape Town, South Africa.

Heneghan, M. (2008). What does a child's right to be heard in legal proceedings really mean? ABA custody standards do not go far enough. *Family Law Quarterly, 42*(1), 117–129.

Hunter, R. (2007). Close encounters of a judicial kind: "hearing" children's "voices" in family law proceedings. *Child and Family Law Quarterly, 19*(3), 283–303.

Initial State Party Report: Ireland, UN Doc. CRC/C/11/Add.12, para.120,17/06/1996.

Kirby, P., & Laws, S. (2010). Advocacy for children in family group conferences: reflections on personal and public decision-making. In B. Percy-Smith & N. Thomas (Eds.), *A handbook of children and young people's participation: perspectives from theory and practice*, 113–120. UK: Routledge.

Law Society of New Zealand (2000). New Zealand best practice guidelines. Available at http://www.law.yale.edu/rcw/rcw/jurisdictions/oceania/australianewzealand/newzealand/NZ_Best_Prac_Guidelines.pdf

Lowe, N. (2001). Children's participation in the family justice system—Translating principles into practice. *Child and Family Law Quarterly, 13*(2), 137–158.

Marshall, K. (1997). *Children's rights in the balance: the participation–protection debate* (p. 103). Edinburgh: The Stationary Office.

Moloney, L. (2005). Children's voices: reflections on the telling and listening. *Journal of Family Studies, 11*(2), 216–226.

O'D v. O'D (2008). IEHC 468.

Paetsch, J. J., Bertrand, L. D., Walker, J., MacRae, L. D., & Bala, N. (2009). Consultation on the Voice of the Child at the 5th World Congress on Family Law and Children's Rights, Canada: Justice Canada.

Parkes, A. (2013). *Children and international human rights law: the right of the child to be heard*. UK/New York: Routledge.

Parkinson, P., & Cashmore, J. (2007). Judicial conversations with children in parenting disputes: the views of Australian judges. *International Journal of Law, Policy and the Family, 21,* 160–189.

Parliamentary Assembly of the Council of Europe, Recommendation 1864 (2009). Promoting the participation of children in decisions affecting them. Available at www.coe.int.

Potter, M. (2008). The voice of the child: children's rights in family law proceedings. International Family Law 140–148, September.

Raitt, F. (2004). Judicial discretion and methods of ascertaining the views of the child. *Child and Family Law Quarterly, 16*(2), 151–164.

RB v. AS (2002). 2 IR 428.

Second Periodic Report: Ireland, UN Doc CRC/C/83/Add.16, para. 333, 07/11/2005.

Tapp, P. (2006). Judges are human too: conversation between the judge and the child as a means of giving effect to section 6 of the Care of Children Act 2004. *New Zealand Law Review*, 35–74.

Taylor, N., Tapp, P., & Heneghan, M. (2007). Respecting children's participation in family law proceedings. *International Journal of Children's Rights, 15,* 61–82.

Taylor, N., & Caldwell, J. (2013). Judicial meetings with children: documenting practice within the New Zealand Family Court. *New Zealand Law Review, 19*(4), 445–463.

Third and Fourth Periodic Report: New Zealand, UN Doc. CRC/C/NZL/3-4 at para. 131.

Third and Fourth Periodic Report: Ireland, July 2013, www.dcya.gov.ie/documents/publications/UNCRC_2013.pdf

UN Committee on the Rights of the Child, General Comment No. 12: The Right of the Child to be Heard, UN Doc. CRC/C/GC/12 at para. 48, 20/07/2009.

UN Committee on the Rights of the Child, General Comment No.5: General measures of Implementation for the Convention on the Rights of the Child, UN Doc. CRC/GC/2003/5, para. 53, 19/09-03/10/2003.

UNICEF (2004). *Summary report of the study of the impact of the implementation of the Convention on the Rights of the Child.* Florence, Italy: UNICEF.

UNICEF (2008). *Handbook on legislative reform: Realising children's rights.* New York: UNICEF.

Van Doogue, J (2006). A view from the bench on ascertaining children's views. *New Zealand Family Law Journal, 12,* 198–220.

CHAPTER 6

Judicial Interviews of Children in Canada's Family Courts

Growing Acceptance but Still Controversial

NICHOLAS BALA, RACHEL BIRNBAUM,
AND FRANCINE CYR

INTRODUCTION

As in most countries, it is accepted in Canada that in family proceedings the courts must take into account the child's "views and preferences" in making a determination about the child's "best interests" and deciding on post-separation parenting arrangements for the child. A decision that will best address the needs of the child must take into account information about the child's perceptions of his or her interests, needs, preferences, and relationships with parents. Further, there is a strong argument that both the promotion of the interests of children and the protection of their rights require that children should be afforded the opportunity to meet with the person making a critical decision about the child's future. Therefore, judicial meetings with children can help both children and the courts.

This chapter reviews the various methods used to allow children to participate in legal disputes between separated parents, and then focuses on the law and empirical research on experiences in Canada regarding children meeting with judges.[1] As part of a broader agenda of research into children's

---

1. In this chapter, the terms judicial "meeting" and "interview" with children are used interchangeably. The word "meeting" has a more informal sound and is more appropriate for use in conversation with children, while the term "interview" is more commonly used in legislation, jurisprudence, and legal literature. While judges meet with children at different

involvement in the family justice process, the authors have undertaken a number of studies of the attitudes and experiences of judges, lawyers and children concerning judicial interviewing of children in family cases. In this chapter, we briefly review the literature, legislation, and jurisprudence on judicial interviewing of children, with a focus on legal practices in Canada, and then present and discuss key findings from our empirical research.

Our central argument is that children should be offered the opportunity to express their views directly to decision makers in a manner that is sensitive to their needs and circumstances. Children should never be required to speak to a judge if they do not wish to, but they should have the opportunity to do so.

THE PERSPECTIVES OF CHILDREN IN MAKING PARENTING PLANS

Many family cases are resolved by negotiation between parents, by mediation, or through the use of collaborative family law, while only a relatively small portion of cases are resolved by judges through litigation. Children's views are more likely to be canvassed in a high-conflict case before the court by an assessment report prepared by a mental health professional than in low-conflict cases where the parents make their own arrangements about the children without the courts or involvement of professionals. A common reason for not consulting with children in lower-conflict cases where parents make their own arrangements for their children is that there is "no real decision" being made (Walker, McCarthy, Stark, & Laing, 2004). It is, however, important that children's views and perspectives are taken into account by parents and professionals when parents are using consensual dispute resolution processes. It is, for example, valuable for mediators to meet with children and if appropriate, to involve children in some mediation sessions, or for a mental health professional involved in a post-separation parental dispute to meet with the child and share the child's perspectives with the mediator and the parents (McIntosh, Wells, Smyth, & Long., 2008). Consideration of how children should participate in these consensual dispute resolution processes is important, but it is beyond the scope of this chapter.

The focus of this chapter is whether and how judges should meet children in high-conflict cases that are resolved in family courts. While this practice is now an accepted part of the family justice process in some jurisdictions, it is still controversial, occurring rarely or not all in other jurisdictions. This chapter explores

stages of proceedings and with different intended purposes, in our view it is artificial and potentially confusing to distinguish between "meetings" and "interviews." Meetings with a child may have more than one purpose before they begin, or their nature may change once the meeting starts.

this controversy, in particular in the Canadian context, and suggests how these meetings should be conducted in the family courts.[2]

Why Children's Voices Are Important in Family Proceedings
Wishes and Preferences: Canadian Law

Justice R. James Williams (1999) of the Nova Scotia Supreme Court provides a list of factors that judges should consider when assessing the significance of the wishes of a child in a family case:

(a) Whether both parents are able to provide adequate care [i.e., if there is no real choice about care arrangements, the child's wishes may not be that significant];
(b) How clear and unambivalent the wishes are;
(c) How informed the expression is;
(d) The age of the child;
(e) The maturity level;
(f) The strength of the wishes;
(g) The length of time the preference has been expressed for;
(h) Practicalities of the child's preferred plan;
(i) The influence of the parent(s) on the expressed wish or preference;
(j) The overall context; and
(k) The circumstances of the preference from the child's point of view.

Despite the importance of children's wishes, it is their best interests and not their wishes that judges use to determine custody and access arrangements. A child may be unduly influenced into rejecting one parent due to the alienating conduct of the other parent. Or a child may be manipulative, or simply want to live with the parent who is most indulgent, while the court must determine which placement is "best" for the child. So the views of a younger child should never be determinative, but in parental separation cases involving teenagers, judges tend to take a different approach. Even if the judge believes that a teenager's preferences reflect a desire to live with the parent who has the fewest rules, and that this placement may not be in the child's long-term interests, a judge may nevertheless make an order based on those preferences, recognizing that with older children (especially 14 years and older) there may be little utility in doing anything else (*Ladisa v. Ladisa*, 2005).

---

2. In this chapter, the term "family court" is used to refer to the court where family cases are resolved. In many places in Canada there are courts that specialize in dealing with family cases, although in much of the country, family cases are not dealt with by special judges and there is not a true "family court."

THE CHILD'S RIGHT TO BE HEARD

Although still considered controversial by some, there is growing acceptance of the principle that children who are capable of articulating views have the right to have those views considered by a court making a decision about their future. This type of rights-based claim to participation (but not decision-making) is most likely to be influential in a child protection case, where a state-sponsored child welfare agency may be threatening the child's relationship with parents and siblings, but it is also very relevant for private litigation between separated parents.

The United Nations (UN) Convention on the Rights of the Child (CRC) requires decision makers to receive and consider the "views" of children, although it does not specify the manner in which children's views are to be heard:

Article 12

1. States Parties shall assure to the child who is capable of forming his or her own views the right to express those views freely in all matters affecting the child, the views of the child being given due weight in accordance with the age and maturity of the child.
2. For this purpose, the child shall in particular be provided the opportunity to be heard in any judicial and administrative proceedings affecting the child, either directly, or through a representative or an appropriate body, in a manner consistent with the procedural rules of national law.

There is some disagreement about the proper interpretation of Article 12 and what is required for compliance. The UN Committee on the Rights of the Child, which provides advisory opinions about the proper interpretation of the CRC, has suggested that this provision requires that "all children involved in judicial and administrative proceedings must be informed in a child friendly manner about their right to be heard, modalities of doing so and other aspects of the proceedings" (Fernando, 2013, p. 96). The UN Committee has characterized Article 12 as creating the right for children "To speak, to participate, to have their views taken into account." The UN Committee (2009) has also observed that the right to be heard in proceedings is a right of children, not an obligation, and children are entitled to choose not to be heard or involved in proceedings.

The words of Article 12 allow for children to be heard indirectly, and it can be argued that this requirement is satisfied when children are heard through a "representative . . . even if the child wants to be heard directly." However, the UN Committee (2009) has expressed the view that wherever possible, children should be given the choice about whether to be heard directly or through a representative, after being informed about the different ways that they can share their views with the court.

Only a relatively small number of jurisdictions have enacted legislation providing that children who are the subject of family proceedings have the right, to the extent consistent with their communication capacity, to be heard by the judge. In most jurisdictions it is a matter of judicial discretion whether a judge will meet a child. However, some jurists are starting to accept that, even without explicit legislation, children have the right to meet with the judge making a decision about their future. This trend is reflected in the Canadian decision in *B.J.G. v. D.L.G* (2010), which is discussed below.

In some jurisdictions, children with the capacity and willingness to articulate their views may even have a constitutional right to participate in certain types of family proceedings. Although the courts are generally reluctant to grant children constitutional rights when separated parents are litigating over their custody or care, Canadian courts have accepted that children may have independent constitutional rights in child protection cases, where the state is a party.[3] Canadian courts have also held that children's constitutional rights of participation may arise in Hague Child Abduction Convention cases, which may result in state enforcement of an order removing a child from one country and returning her or him to another country.[4]

THE VALUE FOR CHILDREN OF BEING HEARD

There is a large body of social science literature on the effects of divorce on children and a growing body of qualitative research focused on children's participation in post-separation decision-making. Studies reveal that children are rarely asked about their views about parenting arrangements, their adjustment to their parents' separation, or whether they want to be involved with the different family justice professionals, including speaking to a judge (Birnbaum, Bala, & Cyr, 2011; Birnbaum & Saini, 2012; Cashmore & Parkinson, 2008). While many children do not want to "take sides" between their parents, most children whose parents are involved in a dispute would at least like to be asked by justice system professionals, in a nonthreatening way, if they have views (Tisdall, Bray, Marshall, & Cleland, 2004). These studies also suggest that older children are more likely to be consulted in some way than younger children.

While there is a need for much more research on children's experiences and perspectives on family litigation and on the effect of different types of involvement on their long-term outcomes, the existing literature clearly suggests that ensuring that children's views are appropriately canvassed is very likely to promote their well-being and interests, and doing so will clearly promote their rights.

A German study, one of the few longitudinal studies of the family justice process, followed children through an assessment during the litigation process

---

3. For a Canadian case recognizing the constitutional rights of children in child protection cases, see *A.C. v. Manitoba (Director of Child and Family Services)* (2009).

4. See, e.g., *A.M.R.I. v. K.E.R.* (2011), recognizing that a Hague Convention application threatened the "liberty" of a 13-year-old child, and accordingly under Canada's Charter of Rights s. 7, she had the right to notice of the application and a right of participation.

(including both settled and tried cases) and then into adulthood (Kaltenborn, 2001). This study suggests that if a court order about parenting arrangements fails to take into account children's relationships with their parents and their residence preferences, there is a significant likelihood that the child will suffer psychological problems and that the order will have to be varied.

The few studies about the experiences of children with parental litigation raise concerns about how effectively lawyers and custody evaluators interview children and communicate their wishes to the courts (Australian Law Reform Commission, 1997; Birnbaum & Bala, 2009; Sawyer, 2000). Those interviewing a child about the sensitive issues that arise in the context of a family case need to have the training and time to establish rapport with the child.

Another related concern, especially in high-conflict cases, is that one or both parents may create feelings of guilt or fear in children, which may result in children masking their true feelings. Not only are these cases difficult for the courts, but they can cause considerable anguish to children as well (Wolman & Taylor, 1991). Some mental health professionals have concerns that asking children about their views about parenting arrangements can be emotionally destructive, especially for pre-adolescents, as children may fear being disloyal to one or both parents if they are forced to express their views (Warshak, 2003). A sensitive interviewer, whether a lawyer, a social worker or a judge, should not confront a child, especially a younger child, with direct questions about "choosing" which parent to live with, but rather should allow views and preferences to be revealed more indirectly by asking children questions about their activities with each parent. Children with strong and clear preferences will inevitably make them known, even if questioning is indirect, while children with loyalty conflicts may be distressed by direct questions and may not provide answers that accurately reflect their true feelings.

How Children Can Participate in Family Proceedings

While it is now accepted that the views of a child should be considered by the judge in a family case, there is considerable variation and controversy about how this is to be done. A number of different methods can be used to bring evidence of a child's views, preferences, observations, and perspectives before a court (Bala, Talwar, & Harris, 2005):

- Hearsay evidence,[5] related by a witness, such as a parent or social worker;
- A video-recording or audiotape of an interview with the child;

5. The term "hearsay" evidence refers to testimony by a person relating statements made by another person who is not a witness. While hearsay evidence is presumptively inadmissible in common law courts, there are some important exceptions to the hearsay rule that allow witnesses, in some circumstances, to testify about a child's statements to them.

- Written statements from a child such as a letter or affidavit;
- A report or the testimony of a mental health professional as part of a custody or access assessment;
- A report from a lawyer or social worker who has conducted an interview and prepared a Voice of the Child Report;
- Counsel for a child presenting the child's views to the court;
- Testimony by the child in court; and
- A meeting with the child in the judge's chambers.

There are advantages and disadvantages to each of these methods of bringing the child's "voice" into family proceedings. Which method is used in a particular case will depend on a number of factors, including the resources available for a particular case.

THE VOICE OF THE CHILD IN CANADIAN FAMILY PROCEEDINGS

There is great variability across Canada in the extent to which professional services are available to facilitate a child's views being shared with the family courts. For parents who have the financial resources, the court has the authority to order them to pay for an assessment of the case by a psychologist or social worker. This assessment will report on interviews with the parents and other significant figures, as well as interviews with the child, and will usually include recommendations about the case. However, these private assessments are expensive, and many parents cannot afford them. In Canada there are limited government-funded programs to allow for an assessment report by a social worker or psychologist, and in many parts of the country these programs are unavailable or available only to service a small portion of the families before the courts.

In some Canadian jurisdictions, including Ontario, Quebec, and Alberta, there is the possibility that a government-paid lawyer may be appointed to represent the child whose parents are litigating about parenting arrangements. There is variation in the extent to which lawyers are obliged to advocate a position based on the child's wishes. Many of these lawyers advocate for an outcome based on their own assessment of the child's best interests, although ensuring that the court and parents are aware of the child's views (Bala, Birnbaum, & Bertrand, 2013).

Further, the hearsay rule is usually somewhat relaxed in family proceedings. However, judges in family cases may discount hearsay evidence from parents and other interested parties about what they say a child told them; the concern is not just about the reliability or honesty of parents or other interested parties, but also about the influence that they may have had on the child (Bala, Talwar, & Harris, 2005).

There is also a growing use in some parts of Canada, including British Columbia, Saskatchewan, Manitoba, Ontario, and New Brunswick, of Voice of the Child Reports. These are short, focused reports. While the parents are usually required to pay for them, they are much less expensive than a full assessment, as only a few hours of professional time is required. A lawyer or social worker with some training interviews the child and prepares a report for the court about what the child said. The interviews will take from 30 minutes to a couple of hours, and a report can be prepared quickly. There is generally only one interview, although sometimes two or three interviews will occur to ensure that a child is expressing consistent views and preferences. No other information is provided in the report about the child, and there is no recommendation about parenting arrangements (*O.(B.T.) v A. (A.)*, 2013).

In deciding how the court should receive evidence of the views of children, judges and lawyers should consider a number of competing objectives:

- Providing the court with as much accurate information as possible;
- Minimizing trauma or distress to the child;
- Ensuring a fair process for the parents;
- Ensuring a fair process for the child; and
- Resolving disputes in a way that is as cost effective as possible for the parties and the court.

There are differences of opinion among judges, lawyers, mental health professionals, and scholars about how to balance these different objectives. For example, some place a greater emphasis on minimizing distress to the child and obtaining as much information as possible for the court, while others may place a greater emphasis on fairness to the parents or the efficiency of the court process.

Further, there is an important distinction between evidence about the perceptions and preferences of children, in particular about where they want to live and how often they will visit a parent (the legal issues of custody, access, and adoption), and evidence about their experiences, especially relating to allegations of child abuse or spousal violence. Although these are not completely mutually exclusive categories, there are significant differences between these two types of evidence, and the family courts deal with them in different ways.

It is generally accepted in Canada that judicial interviews with children should not be "forensic"; in particular, they should not be intended to ascertain the truth of a child's allegations of abuse or violence. While children's testimony in court about abuse is common in criminal cases in Canada, in family cases, evidence of the child's reports about abuse or neglect is rarely if ever introduced by having the child testify, and never by having a child meet with the judge. This type of evidence of a child's disclosure or report of abuse is generally introduced in family cases by having hearsay evidence admitted, meaning that an adult, perhaps the parent but often a social worker or child protection worker, testifies about the child's disclosures of abuse.

In our research, we found a few judges who reported that in rare family cases during a judicial interview a child made statements about abuse that had not previously been disclosed; these cases were all reported by the judges involved to child welfare authorities to allow for a proper, neutral investigation (Birnbaum & Bala, 2010).

Canadian Law on Judicial Interviews with Children

In civilian Quebec, consistent with the approach to judicial interviews with children in some other civilian jurisdictions like Germany, Article 34 of the Civil Code establishes that children in family cases have the right to an "opportunity to be heard" by the court, provided their "maturity and discernment" warrant this.

In the other jurisdictions in Canada, all of which have common law legal systems, case law or legislation establishes that it is a matter of judicial discretion whether a judge interviews a child; until recently there has been no suggestion that children might have the "right" to meet with a judge. For example, in Ontario, the Children's Law Reform Act Section 64 creates a discretionary regime, providing that judges in family cases "may" interview children to learn their "views and preferences." In other provinces, case law has accepted that even without explicit legislative provisions, judges have the discretion to meet children to ascertain their wishes, without the consent of the parties (*Jandrisch v. Jandrisch*, 1980).

Except for in Quebec, with its presumptive statutory provision, until recently Canadian judges were very reluctant to exercise their jurisdiction to meet children. The frequently cited 2004 Ontario case of *Stefureak v. Chambers* reviewed the various methods of bringing a child's views before the court, and after analyzing the problems associated with judges interviewing children, the judge stated this should be "only as a last resort." The judge in that case suggested that it was normally preferable that a mental health professional interview the child and testify about the child's views and preferences. In refusing to interview a 7-year-old child, the judge stated that "a chambers interview is not feasible . . . as I have no training or known skill in interviewing children."

Canadian judges have also expressed concern that an interview might traumatize a child. For example, in the Ontario case of *S.E.C. v. G.P.* (2003), where the father was claiming alienation of the child by the mother and the mother was alleging serious claims of domestic abuse against the father, Justice Perkins decided not to interview the child or permit her to testify in court. The judge observed (at para. 32) that

> It would be ironic in the extreme on a custody and access issue, where the only factor is what is in the best interests of the child, if the litigation process were used so as to cause harm to the child for the ostensible purpose of ascertaining her wishes or even shedding light on her best interests.

Another reason that Canadian judges provide for refusing to use their discretion to interview children is that such action might undermine the "appearance of justice." (*Ali v. Williams*, 2008).

In a significant departure from previous Canadian common law cases, the 2010 Yukon decision of Justice Martinson in *B.J.G. v. D.L.G* expressed strong support for the right of children to meet the judge deciding a case, as well as emphasizing the potential value of the practice for the court. The judge cited CRC Article 12, which is considered an "interpretative tool" for applying legislation and common law by Canadian courts, and concluded that (2010, at para. 6 & 21)

> The *Convention* is very clear; children have legal rights to be heard during all parts of the judicial process, including judicial family case conferences, settlement conferences, and court hearings or trials. An inquiry should be made in each case, and at the start of the process, to determine whether the child is capable of forming his or her own views, and if so, whether the child wishes to participate. If the child does wish to participate then there must be a determination of the method by which the child will participate ... Obtaining information of all sorts from children, including younger children, on a wide range of topics relevant to the dispute, can lead to better decisions for children that have a greater chance of working successfully.

While cited a number of times since being rendered, this decision still does not represent the dominant legal approach in Canada's common law provinces.

Canadian Research on Children's Meeting Judges

As part of a broader agenda of research into children's involvement in the family justice process, the authors have undertaken a number of studies of justice system professionals and children that address the issue of judicial meetings with children, including the following:[6]

- A Web-based survey of judges from across Canada who attended a 2013 National Judicial Institute family law education program for judges. Sixty-two of the ninety-six judges attending the program responded.

---

6. This chapter is the first publication to synthesize and summarize all of our data on judicial interviewing of children, although some of the material in this chapter has been published before in the context of reports on individual studies: see Bala, Birnbaum, & Bertrand, 2013; Birnbaum & Bala, 2009, 2010, 2014; Birnbaum, Bala, & Cyr, 2011.

- Interviews in person and by telephone with judges in Ontario in 2009 by Birnbaum and in Quebec in 2013 by Cyr. Thirty judges were interviewed in Ontario (seventeen women, thirteen men) and thirty judges in Quebec (eighteen women, twelve men).
- Web-based surveys of lawyers attending family law continuing education programs in Ontario and Alberta in 2012. Seventy-one lawyers in Alberta and seventy-nine in Ontario responded.
- Interviews with children and young adults whose parents litigated over custody or access when they were children. A total of twenty-one children were interviewed by a judge. Birnbaum interviewed thirty-two children and youth in 2009, of whom sixteen had been interviewed by a judge, and the rest were represented by a lawyer or had an assessment by a mental health professional. Cyr interviewed forty children (up to 17 years of age), of whom five met a judge.

JUDICIAL VIEWS AND PRACTICES

In the national survey of judges, just over half (52 percent) of the respondents reported that they had some experience as a judge in meeting with a child in a family law case. In some measure, the variation in their practices reflects differences in the law, with judges from Quebec, with its statutory presumption of a child's right to be heard, all reporting that they had experience with meeting children. Differences in the availability of professional resources are also a factor, with a number of judges commenting that they do not feel that they need to meet with children because where they preside there is good access to lawyers or mental health professionals who can interview children and present their views in court. However, it is also clear that there are differences of judicial opinion and practice regarding meeting with children, even within jurisdictions.

Although there is a division of opinion within the Canadian judiciary about the appropriateness and utility of meeting with children, the survey revealed that more judges are now interviewing children than a few years ago. About one third of all judicial respondents indicated that their practice had changed in the past couple of years, with almost all of those who reported a change stating that that they had started or increased the extent to which they engaged in the practice; only a few indicated that they were less inclined in recent years to meet with children because there was an increase in the availability of access to counsel for children in their jurisdiction.

Judicial meetings with children occur at all stages of proceedings, including at motions, at pretrial settlement-oriented conferences, and at trial. A number of judges also reported that, in selected cases, they meet with children after they have rendered a judgment to explain their decision, or write a letter to the child for this purpose (with copies to the parties).

Judges who meet with children generally expect to gain a sense of the child's personality and views from such meetings, and want to give the child an opportunity to ask questions. Most judges also want to make clear to children that it is they, not children, who must take responsibility for the decision. There are Canadian decisions that emphasize that judges should avoid using interviews with a child to resolve factual matters in dispute between the parents (e.g., *Ward v. Swan,* 2009). Most judges avoid using these meetings to "ascertain facts," although in our survey a few respondents indicated that they sometimes use judicial meetings to question children about factual matters that may be in dispute between the parents.

While there is a growing tendency for Canadian judges to meet with children, judges do not consider it appropriate to meet with a child in every case where there is a dispute over their care. Judges report that they are more likely to meet with children who are older. These children are more mature and better able to communicate with judges, making judges more comfortable in meeting them. The frequency of such interviews increases with the age of children involved, but quite a few judges are prepared to meet with children aged 6 to 9 years.

Judges are also more likely to meet with children if there is no assessment or legal representation for the child, especially if there is urgency for a decision. This reflects the reality that in some places, especially where parents lack resources, a judicial meeting with a child may be the only way to have the child's views heard by the court. Some judges will meet with a child even if there is counsel for a child or an assessment. For many judges a request from the parents or the child for a meeting is a significant factor in deciding whether to meet the child. In Quebec, around a quarter of the judges interviewed reported that they would occasionally tell the parents that they want to meet with a child despite the parental failure to raise the issue.

A few judges meet alone with a child, even outside the courthouse, for example taking the child to a fast-food restaurant. The vast majority of judges, however, always have someone else present, such as a court clerk. If the child has counsel, that lawyer is invariably asked to be present.

About half the judges who meet with children do this in their chambers or in a conference room in the courthouse. Some judges, notably in Quebec, are likely to meet the child in the courtroom with counsel for the parents present but the parents absent. Counsel for the parents sit at the back of the courtroom and listen as the judge talks to the child. In our interviews with Quebec judges, only a few reported that that they regularly meet with children in their offices without counsel for the parents present rather than in the courtroom.

About two thirds of the judges who meet with children reported that they ensure that a record is made of the interview, usually by having a court reporter present. In Ontario, legislation requires judges to record interviews with children, at least when they are held during a motion or trial (but a recording is not required if the meeting is part of a settlement conference or if it is for the purpose of telling the child about the court's decision). In other jurisdictions, concerns about a possible appeal prompt most judges to ensure that there is a record of the interview.

Some judges provide the parents with a full transcript of the interview, usually informing the child that this will be done (*McAlister v. Jenkins,* 2008). This ensures that parents can fully respond to any comments of the child. However, a majority of the judges who meet children do not provide parents with a transcript or allow their lawyers to attend. Many judges have concerns about embarrassing children or potentially damaging their future relationships with a parent, and accordingly provide the parties with only a summary of the statements of the children, softening any negative comments that children may have made about their parents.

In Quebec, it is common practice to have lawyers for parents attend the judge's meeting with the child, addressing due process concerns, but judges often ask parents to waive their right to hear a recording of the interview. Judges in Quebec seem somewhat less likely than judges in other jurisdictions to explicitly discuss the issues of confidentiality or disclosure of a recording with the child. In Quebec, more than one third of the judges interviewed reported that they do not tell the child anything about the confidentiality of the meeting, and about a third tell the child that they will give only a summary to the parents.

The national survey reveals that most Canadian judges who interview children reported that they find it helpful (82 percent). Significantly, in the study of Quebec judges, who are obliged by legislation to interview children who request it, a substantial majority (77 percent) believe that it is very useful or generally useful to meet children, while 18 percent of judges report that it is sometimes useful, and only 5 percent of the judges believe that these meetings have limited or no utility. The value of meetings with children is illustrated by the comments of judges:

> "Very favorable results and very positive feedback."

> "Great tool, when used with wisdom and discretion."

> "Permits me to confirm impressions from other sources."

> "Allows me to assess when a child is being manipulated by a parent."

> "Permits the court to respond to the child's desire to be heard and to be part of the process."

A Quebec judge, who is statutorily required to meet children, commented that[7]

> "Coming from another area of practice [than family law], I had a real apprehension about meeting with children at the start ... However, those apprehensions receded

---

7. All interviews with judges and children in Quebec that are reported in this chapter were conducted in French and translated by the authors.

and I find the practice most interesting. I now like to meet children. I have seen children who gave me much, which I found very useful."

It should be noted that in the national study those judges who do not interview children have generally considered the issue and articulated clear reasons for not doing this, including noting their lack of expertise and training, and the better qualifications of lawyers or mental health professionals for ascertaining the child's views and bringing them before the court. There is also a concern expressed by some judges that meeting with a child is inconsistent with the traditional judicial role and, in the words of one respondent, places the "judge ... in the position of being a witness." Another judge expressed concern that "untrained and inexperienced judges will grab on to [the growing] ... support for judicial interviews and do real harm."

FAMILY LAWYERS

Only about a third of the lawyers who responded to our national survey had ever had a family case where a child had met with a judge. Although those who had cases where children met the judge generally seemed positive about this, many lawyers expressed concern about the practice, especially from the perspective of representing parents, even though they had no experience with this process.

Of those lawyers who represent children, most reported that they never encourage their child clients to meet with a judge for an interview. There are a range of reasons for the reluctance of lawyers for children to ask children whether they want to meet the judge, including a concern that this might be distressing for children and a belief that their role is to communicate with the court on behalf of the child. However, as discussed below, since the study was done in 2012, there has been more education and discussion within the legal profession about the value of judicial interviews with children, and attitudes and practices of lawyers may be changing.

REPORTS OF CHILDREN

We interviewed a total of seventy-two children and young adults whose parents had litigated about custody or access, of whom twenty-one met a judge; the others were interviewed by a mental health professional about their views and preferences or were interviewed by a lawyer appointed to represent them. Most of the children (thirteen) who had judicial interviews were actually in the American state of Ohio, where the practice is much more common as legislation requires an interview if requested by a parent, or it may occur on the court's own motion; three were from Ontario and five were in Quebec.

Regardless of which family justice professional the children spoke to, they unanimously reported that they wanted to be involved in the decision-making process in some way, but most did not want to decide. Indeed, only one stated that at the time of the proceedings he felt that he wanted to make the decision, but when interviewed as a young adult, he reported that he had been manipulated by one parent into rejecting the other parent. None reported negative effects as a result of their interviews with judges or other professionals. However, virtually all of them expressed profound sadness and distress over their parents' separation, and some felt traumatized years later. The majority reported that they had not been consulted by their parents about their living arrangements after the separation, although those 10 years of age and older at the time of separation generally said they had some input into the decision.

The children who were interviewed by a judge acknowledged that they were initially anxious about this meeting. However, these children reported that the judge made them feel comfortable and less anxious. They all reported that they appreciated having had an opportunity to be heard by the judge, even those who did not get the outcome they wanted. Some of the comments of the children who were interviewed by a judge included the following:

"It was stressful before talking to the judge. When the judge arrived, he said to me: 'Don't worry, I am going to make the decision, and it's going to go fine. Don't worry.' It was a load off my shoulders [to know that the judge would decide]."

"I saw the judge, twice I think. I wanted to and felt good about it."

"Not great about going to see the judge [before I got there], but the [judge] made me feel comfortable."

"Judge told me the decision and I was not happy about the decision, but felt it was good for the judge to see who I was . . . I knew the judge was struggling with the decision."

A significant portion of those children who had been interviewed by a custody assessor or were represented by a lawyer reported that if they had a choice, they would have also liked to have had the opportunity to meet with the judge. Some of the comments of those who did not have an opportunity to meet with the judge included the following:

"That would be good to speak to a judge, but I did not get that chance . . . my mother did and my lawyer did."

"Want a say and not a report on me . . . would like to have met the judge for sure."

"I would have asked to see a judge [if I had known that I could]."

Conducting Judicial Interviews with Children
Guidelines

In some jurisdictions, including England and Wales,[8] New Zealand,[9] and California,[10] guidelines have been introduced to help judges to exercise their discretion whether and how to meet with children. The Office of the Chief Justice of the Ontario Court of Justice has prepared a document for judges of that court considering interviewing a child (August 2012); it is widely available to lawyers in the province but is not published or easily accessible to the public. Many of the judges and lawyers who participated in our research indicated that it would be desirable for their jurisdictions to adopt legally mandated guidelines for judicial interviewing of children. As a result of our empirical research, we have developed some principles and suggestions for inclusion in guidelines for judicial interviews of children (Bala, Birnbaum, Cyr, & McColley, 2013). While guidelines should reflect the resources, law, and culture of a particular jurisdiction, it is our view that they should always include provisions that address the purpose of the interviews, the duty of professionals, the absence of parents, and disclosure of information.

PURPOSE OF JUDICIAL INTERVIEWS

Judicial meetings with children may occur at any stage of a family proceeding, including at an interim motion, a pretrial settlement conference, and at trial, and the purpose and conduct of the meeting should reflect the stage of the proceedings at which it occurs.

A child meeting with a judge is generally *not* the best source of information for courts or parents about the views, feelings, and preferences of children. Where available, evidence about a child's needs, wishes, and feelings is usually best ascertained and presented to the court by means of an assessment report prepared by a mental health professional appointed by the court, or by representations from a guardian *ad litem* or counsel appointed for the child. Such information can be obtained from a series of meetings with the child that can occur as part of a broader inquiry into the child's circumstances. Some children are ambivalent or change their minds, perhaps heavily influenced by their most recent experiences or even which parent brought them to an interview, so having

8. England & Wales: Family Justice Council, *Guidelines for Judges Meeting Children who are Subject to Family Proceedings* (2010), available at http://www.fnf.org.uk/downloads/ Guidelines_for_Judges_Meeting_Children.pdf.
9. New Zealand: Family Court of New Zealand, *Judges' Guidelines—Decisions with Children* (2007), available at http://www.justice.govt.nz/courts/family-court/practice-and-procedure/guidelines
10. In 2012 the state adopted the California Rules of Court 5.250.

a number of meetings with a lawyer, guardian, or mental health professional may help to reveal this.

Despite the involvement of an assessor, or a guardian *ad litem* or lawyer for the child, there is a complementary role for a judicial interview with a child. There may be value for the child, judge, and parents in having such a meeting, even if it only confirms information already provided. There may also be cases where, despite or perhaps because of earlier meetings with other professionals, a child will reveal additional information to a judge.

A primary purpose of a judicial interview should be to help children to feel involved in the process in which important decisions are made about their lives, and to give them the opportunity to meet the judge and to understand the nature of the judge's task. A judge who meets a child should emphasize to the child that while the child has a right to be heard, it is the judge, not the child, who has the responsibility for making the decision about the child's future: "Children have a voice, but not a choice."

While there is a growing trend of judges meeting with children, it is not appropriate for a judge to meet with a child in every case where there is a dispute over his or her care. These interviews may be more appropriate for older children, although there may be value for the judge and child meeting even if the child is as young as 4 or 5 years of age.

Although judicial interviews should not be viewed as replacements for legal representation for the child or an assessment, they may be more likely to occur if there is no assessment or representation for the child. This reflects the reality that in some places, especially where parents lack resources, a judicial meeting with a child may be the only way to have the child's views heard by the court. Even and perhaps especially in this context, judges should avoid using interviews with a child to resolve factual matters in dispute between the parents. Evidence about contested factual matters should always be presented in a way that parents can directly understand and challenge it.

DUTY OF PROFESSIONALS

In our view, it should be an ethical duty and practice of lawyers or guardians *ad litem* appointed to represent children and mental health professionals undertaking a custody and access assessment to discuss with children, in a manner appropriate to their developmental understanding, whether they want to meet the judge. If the child does not wish to meet the judge, then the lawyer, guardian *ad litem,* or assessor should ask the child whether there are other ways of enabling the child to feel a part of the process. The parents should be told not to try to persuade the child to change his or her mind about how to be involved. If children tell an independent professional that they wish to meet the judge, that wish should be conveyed to the judge and should normally result in a meeting with the judge.

A primary purpose of a meeting with the judge is to benefit the child. However, a meeting between the child and the judge may also serve to provide important insights to the court and promote sound decision-making. Parents may also learn more about their children as a result of hearing about the outcome of such a meeting. Giving the parents a better understanding of their child's views and needs may facilitate settlement by the parents or result in greater acceptance of the judge's decision by them.

ABSENCE OF PARENTS AND DISCLOSURE OF INFORMATION TO THEM

One of the more contentious issues for lawyers and judges about judicial interviews is whether parents should be present or provided with a transcript of the interview. Some argue that parents should have complete information about the interview, both to satisfy due process requirements and to allow a full testing of the accuracy of any statements made by the child. Accordingly, some judges provide parents with a transcript of the interview, informing the child at the start of the interview that they will do so (*McAlister v. Jenkins*, 2008). Other judges have the parents' lawyers present during the interview. The most common judicial approach, however, is to exclude parents and their counsel from any judicial interview with the child. Many judges record their interviews with children in some way, in the event of an appeal, but provide only a summary to parents and their lawyers of what the child said, in a way that will avoid embarrassing the child or potentially poisoning the child's relationship with a parent, and generally without any quotes. An example of a court taking this approach is the 1969 New York decision in *Lincoln v. Lincoln*, where the Court of Appeals wrote the following:[11]

> The trial court here concluded that the only method by which it might avoid placing an unjustifiable emotional burden on the three children and, at the same time, enable them to speak freely and candidly concerning their preferences was to assure them that their confidences would be respected. This could only be done in the absence of counsel, and we see no error or abuse of discretion in the procedure followed by the trial court.

This approach recognizes that judicial interviewing is a practice unique to family cases; while the judge may rely on the information and insights obtained to formulate a decision, the evidence obtained is different from other types of evidence used in the justice system. The practice of providing parents with only

---

11. For a Canadian case taking this approach, see *Demeter v. Demeter* (1996).

a summary of the child's statements, while keeping a full record for the appeal court, seems to adequately balance concerns about fairness to the parents and reliability against protection of the welfare of children who are the subject of litigation.

The Right of Children to Be Heard

Many Canadian judges continue to be reluctant to meet with children as there is a concern that meeting with a child is inconsistent with the traditional judicial role. Increasingly, however, Canadian judges are willing to meet with children to directly learn their views and to give children an opportunity to ask questions and feel part of the process. The change in attitudes and practices is in significant measure a result of ongoing dialogue and education about this issue among Canadian judges and lawyers. A number of professional education programs in different parts of the country have addressed this issue. These educational programs and ongoing research have led to changes in Canada. The ongoing discussion and education within Canada also reflects the influence of Canadian judges engaging in discussion with judges in jurisdictions where the practice is more common. In particular, the experiences of judges from Quebec have been shared with judges in the rest of Canada at judicial meetings, which has influenced the practice of judges outside of that province.

A judicial interview with a child in the absence of the parties is a unique process, reflecting the special nature of proceedings where the future of a child is being decided. Allowing children to express their views in a safe, neutral, nonjudgmental way to a family justice professional, including a judge, can assist children's adjustment after separation. Although children should never be pressured to express their preferences, they should always be afforded the opportunity to share their perspectives. This is not to suggest that it is always valuable for a child to meet the judge, or to have a lawyer, or to participate in an assessment by a mental health professional. In some cases, children's interests may be served by having an opportunity to meet with a range of different professionals at different points during the process.

No professional, whether a judge, mediator, lawyer, or assessor, should rely on just one interview to establish a child's views and preferences, as the expressed views of a child may change and be affected by such factors as who brought the child to the meeting, as well as the child's feelings of comfort and trust with the interviewer. It is for this reason, among others, that the most reliable information about a child's views and preferences is likely to be obtained by a trained mental health professional who has had the opportunity to meet the child on a number of occasions in the course of an assessment. However, even a single meeting with a judge or mediator can be useful for giving the professional some insights about the child, and it can be valuable for the child. Such a meeting can also signal to parents that their child's views are important.

It is important for parents, lawyers, and judges who are making decisions about the care of children, to fully understand the perspectives and experiences of those who are most affected—the children involved. In jurisdictions where judicial meetings with children are not common, this practice should be encouraged. Judicial meetings with children will be facilitated if there are systemic changes. This will require professional bodies, legislatures, or judicial councils to formulate guidelines for judicial interviewing with children. It is preferable for each jurisdiction to develop guidelines using a multidisciplinary, collaborative effort, informed by the research and experience discussed in this chapter, as well as its relevant legislation and the resources and culture of the jurisdiction.

There is also a need for interdisciplinary education and training in issues related to judicial interviewing of children and more generally children's involvement in the family dispute resolution process. However, even without training, most adults have the capacity to meaningfully communicate with children in a way that does not traumatize them. It is not expected that judges or lawyers should have the knowledge or skill of custody assessors. Rather, the purpose of such education and training is to prepare judges and lawyers for the particular issues that may arise in a judicial meeting with a child who is the subject of litigation between parents. Such education can prepare judges for the experience; role-playing exercises or videos may help judges prepare for cases where children may express powerful emotional reactions.

As noted in this chapter, there is a growing body of research on children's experiences with being interviewed by judges. However, more research should be done on the experiences of children, parents, judges, lawyers, and other professionals, not only with judicial interviewing but with all aspects of the separation and dispute resolution process. In what situations are different ways of engaging children most helpful, in the short and the long term? To the extent that different jurisdictions adopt different practices and processes, there will be real value to comparative research as well, to learn what practices are most effective. While we are advocates of judicial interviewing of children who want to be interviewed, judicial meetings are only one, relatively small part of the typical family dispute resolution process, and more needs to be known about all aspects of this process and their effects on children. Although there is a clear need for further research, in our view there is by now sufficient knowledge about the rights, needs, and interests of children to make judicial interviewing an encouraged practice.

REFERENCES

A.C. v. Manitoba (Director of Child and Family Services), 2009 SCC 30.
Ali v. Williams, [2008] CarswellOnt 1757 (Ont. S.C.J.).

A.M.R.I. v. K.E.R., [2011] ONCA 417.

Australian Law Reform Commission (1997). *Seen and heard: priority for children in the legal process.* Report No. 84.

Bala, N., Birnbaum, R., & Bertrand, L. (2013). Controversy about the role children's lawyers: advocate or best interests guardian? Comparing attitudes & practices in Alberta & Ontario—two provinces with different policies. *Family Court Review, 51,* 681–697.

Bala, N., Birnbaum, R., Cyr, F., & McColley, D. (2013). Children's voices in family court: guidelines for judges meeting children. *Family Law Quarterly, 47,* 381–419.

Bala, N., Talwar, V., & Harris, J. (2005). The voice of the children in family law cases. *Canadian Family Law Quarterly, 24,* 221–274.

Birnbaum, R., & Bala, N. (2009). The child's perspective on legal representation: Young people report on their experiences with child lawyers. *Canadian Journal of Family Law, 25*(1), 11–71.

Birnbaum, R., & Bala, N. (2010). Judicial interviews with children in custody and access cases: Comparing experiences in Ontario and Ohio. *International Journal of Law, Policy and the Family, 24,* 300–337.

Birnbaum, R., & Bala, N. (2014). A survey of Canadian judges about their meetings with children: becoming more common but still contentious. *Canadian Bar Review, 91,* 637–655.

Birnbaum, R., Bala, N., & Cyr, F. (2011). Children's experiences with family justice professionals and judges in Ontario and Ohio. *International Journal of Law, Policy and the Family, 25,* 398–422.

Birnbaum, R., & Saini, M. (2012). A scoping review of qualitative studies on the voice of the child in child custody disputes. *Childhood, 20*(2), 260–282.

B.J.G. v D.L.G., [2010] YKSC 44, 324 DLR (4th) 376.

Cashmore, J., & Parkinson, P. (2008). Children's and parents' perceptions on children's participation in decision making after parental separation and divorce. *Family Court Review, 46,* 91–104.

Children's Law Reform Act, RSO 1990, c. C-12. S. 64 [Ontario].

Civil Code, S.Q. 1991, chap. 64, Art. 34 [Quebec].

Demeter v. Demeter, [1996] O.J. 1470 (Ont. Sup. Ct.).

Fernando, M. (2013). Express recognition of the un convention on the rights of the child in the Family Law Act: what impact on children's participation. *University of New South Wales Law Review, 56,* 88–106.

Jandrisch v. Jandrisch, [1980] M.J. 6 (C.A.).

Kaltenborn, K. F. (2001). Children's and young people's experiences in various residential arrangements: A longitudinal study to evaluate criteria for custody and residence decision-making. *British Journal of Social Work, 31,* 81–117.

Ladisa v. Ladisa, [2005] O.J. 276, 11 R.F.L. (6th) 50 (C.A.).

Lincoln v. Lincoln, (1969), 24 NY 2d 270.

McAlister v. Jenkins, [2008] CarswellOnt 4266 (Ont. S.C.J.).

McIntosh, J. E., Wells, Y. D., Smyth, B. M., & Long, C. M. et al. (2008). Child-focused and child-inclusive divorce mediation: comparative outcomes from a prospective study of post-separation adjustment. *Family Court Review, 46,* 105–124.

O.(B.T.) v A, (A.), [2013] ONCJ 708.

Sawyer, C. (2000). Ascertaining the child's wishes and feelings. *Family Law, 30,* 170–174.

S.E.C. v. G.P., [2003] O.J. No. 2744 (Ont. S.C.J.).

Stefureak v. Chambers, [2004] CarswellOnt 4244, 6 R.F.L. (6th) 212 (Ont. S.C.J.).

Tisdall, K. M. E., Bray, R., Marshall, K., & Cleland, A. (2004). Children's participation in family law proceedings: a small step or a step too small? *Journal of Social Welfare & Family Law, 26,* 17–33.

United Nations Committee on the Rights of the Child (2009). *General comment no. 12: the right of the child to be heard.* CRC/C/GC/12.

Walker, J., McCarthy, P., Stark, C., & Laing, K. (2004). *Picking up the pieces: marriage and divorce two years after information provision* (Centre for Family Studies, University of Newcastle Upon Tyne). London: Department of Constitutional Affairs.

Ward v. Swan, [2009] O.J. 2107 (Ont. Sup. Ct).

Warshak, R. (2003). Payoffs and pitfalls of listening to children. *Family Relations, 52,* 373–384.

Williams, R. J. (1999). *If wishes were horses then beggars would ride.* Paper presented at the National Judicial Institute, Family Law Program, Halifax, February 1999.

Williams, S. (2010). *Listening to children directly in separation and divorce proceedings: individual, institutional and international guidelines.* National Judicial Institute, Family Law Program, Toronto.

Wolman, R., & Taylor, K. (1991). Psychological effects of custody disputes on children. *Behavioural Sciences and Law, 9,* 399–417.

CHAPTER 7

Children's Participation in Israeli Family Courts

An Account of an Ongoing Learning Process

TAMAR MORAG AND YOA SOREK

INTRODUCTION

The importance of children's participation in family conflicts has gained increasing recognition in recent years. This recognition rests on the International Convention on the Rights of the Child (CRC) and its interpretation,[1] and on the growing body of studies pointing to the significance of this participation for both the children and the decision-making process (Bala, Birnbaum, Cyr, &

---

1. The principle of participation is set out in Article 12 of the UN Convention on the Rights of the Child, which states:

   1. States Parties shall assure to the child who is capable of forming his or her own views the right to express those views freely in all matters affecting the child, the views of the child being given due weight in accordance with the age and maturity of the child.
   2. For this purpose, the child shall in particular be provided the opportunity to be heard in any judicial and administrative proceedings affecting the child, either directly, or through a representative or an appropriate body, in a manner consistent with the procedural rules of national law.

   Recognition of the obligation to implement the right of participation in the context of divorce proceedings is expressed in Section 52 of the General Comment of the UN Committee, stating that "all legislation on separation and divorce has to include the right of the child to be heard by decision makers and in mediation processes" (Committee on the Rights of the Child, General Comment No. 12). On the right of the child to be heard, see http://tbinternet.ohchr.org/_layouts/treatybodyexternal/Download.aspx?symbolno=CRC%2fC%2fGC%2f12&Lang=en

McColley, 2013; Birnbaum & Bala, 2010; Cashmore & Smart, 2002; Taylor, Smith, & Tapp, 1999).

In many countries, this process has been accompanied by changes in practice. Whereas in the past children had largely been excluded from legal proceedings touching on family conflicts (Smith, Taylor, & Tapp, 2003; Taylor, 2006), many countries have now expanded the scope of children's participation in these proceedings (Taylor, Fitzgerald, Morag, Bajpai, & Graham, 2012). Various experts still differ, in principle, on the advantages and disadvantages of children's participation in family conflicts (Smith et al., 2003; Warshak, 2003).[2] Nevertheless, as Birnbaum and Bala (2010) have noted, the focus of the discussion has shifted in recent years from the question of whether children should participate in legal proceedings involving family conflicts to the question of when and how they should be involved.

This chapter aims to contribute to the developing knowledge on the importance of child participation in court proceedings relating to family conflicts, as well as to the research findings concerning the best models for child participation in such proceedings. We examine a unique model of children's participation that was implemented in a pilot project in family courts in Israel, the findings of a study evaluating this pilot project, and a follow-up study. The article examines the implications of both studies on the formulation of policy and legislation in this area. The Israeli pilot project is one of the first attempts in the world to regulate the legal details of children's participation in family court proceedings.

The child participation model was established by the Israeli CRC legislative committee. It was first applied as part of a pilot project operated by the Israeli government in 2006–2009 in two family courts in Israel (in Jerusalem and Haifa) and was accompanied by an evaluation study. In October 2011, the Israeli Minister of Justice issued regulations prescribing the permanent implementation of this model in these two family courts and the gradual implementation of the model in all Israeli family courts over a period of three years. The expansion of these regulations to additional courts has been delayed and is planned for the beginning of 2014.

The implementation of the pilot project was accompanied by two studies—a formative evaluation and a follow-up study. The formative evaluation was designed to evaluate the model implemented in the pilot study and make the necessary adjustments on an ongoing basis. Three years after the conclusion of

2. The prime claims raised against children's participation include the possibility of children's exposure to parental manipulation; the potentially harmful effects to parent–child relationships; increasing children's tension; concern about children's increasing alienation against one of the parents; doubts about the children's ability to formulate positions on these matters; judges' lack of expertise on children's participation patterns; and concern about compromising the fairness of proceedings due to the need to ensure the confidentiality of the children's views.

the pilot and toward its expansion to all family courts in Israel on a permanent basis, a follow-up study examined the operation of the model in the Jerusalem and Haifa courts. In addition to the implementation of the model in these two courts, the follow-up study also considered changes in the patterns of inviting children to participate and in the modalities of hearing children in family courts where the regulations were not yet applied.

The detailed findings of the evaluative study appeared in a previous publication (Morag, Rivkin, & Sorek, 2012). The present chapter seeks to derive the cumulative insights emerging from these two studies, with the findings from the follow-up study appearing here for the first time. These insights can serve as a foundation for the continued development and implementation of the model in Israel toward its application in all family courts, as well as for the development of similar models in other countries, relying on the Israeli experience.

The article comprises three parts. The first part presents the model of children's participation that was developed in the CRC legislative committee and the pilot project that applied the committee's recommendations. The second part presents key findings from the evaluative study and from the follow-up study, focusing on the following issues: patterns of children's participation during and after the pilot project; children's satisfaction and insights about the participation process; contents of the involvement; protecting the confidentiality of children's statements; participation of alienated children; attitudes of parents, professionals, and judges; and the legal and emotional contributions of the participation. The third part presents the main conclusions drawn from a joint examination of these two studies.

THE CRC LEGISLATIVE COMMITTEE ON CHILD PARTICIPATION

Recommendations and Their Implementation in the Pilot Project

CRC Legislative Subcommittee

In 1998, the Minister of Justice appointed the CRC legislative committee. This committee was asked to examine the entire corpus of Israeli child law in view of the CRC principles[3] and to devise mechanisms for implementing them in domestic legislation. The committee submitted a report to the Minister of Justice in 2004, including specific recommendations on children's participation

---

3. For a discussion of this committee's aims, see the 2003 *Report of the Committee for the Examination of Basic Principles in the Area of the Child and the Law* by the Israeli Ministry of Justice, "General Part," p. 32. Available online at http://www.justice.gov.il/MOJHeb/ HavaadLeZhuyot DochKliali/

in family courts formulated by a subcommittee on children and their families.[4] The subcommittee developed an extensive legislative model for child participation in family courts. The basis for the subcommittee's work was the recognition of children as rights bearers, which endorsed children's right to be heard as its ideological starting point. This view was specifically noted in the first article of its proposal, which stated: "All children have the right to express their feelings, views, and positions and to be heard freely in every matter affecting them that arises in the family court."

Israeli Family Courts

The Family Courts Law was enacted in Israel in 1995. Family courts are magistrate civil courts dealing with all family-related matters, with one judge presiding. Adjunct to the family courts, the Ministry of Social Affairs and Social Services operates social services units (SSUs) staffed by social workers and psychologists. Their function is to assist the court in reaching decisions on matters involving family disputes, including assistance in clarifying expert opinions submitted to the court. The unit provides counseling to the parties and holds mediation proceedings.[5]

Model for Child Participation Proposed by the Committee

The CRC legislative committee recommended establishing a Child Participation Department (CPD) attached to the family courts' SSUs, to be staffed by social workers who specialize in work with children and youth (participation social workers [PSWs]).

The subcommittee recommended adopting the following model of children's participation:

1) Following a judicial decision that the PSW will relay to the parents, the court will invite the child to a meeting at the CPD. Information on the proceedings will be provided to parents and children and, if the parents have legal representation, to their lawyers as well.
2) Children will attend a preliminary meeting at the CPD, where their right to be heard in the proceedings will be explained in terms appropriate to their age and level of maturity. The PSW will clarify the purpose of the hearing, the

4. The Committee for the Examination of the Basic Principles in the Area of the Child and the Law, Report of the Sub-Committee on Children and their Families, the Israeli Ministry of Justice. Available online at http://index.justice.gov.il/Units/YeutzVehakika/NosimMishpatim/HavaadLeZhuyot/Pages/HayeledVemishphto.aspx
5. The operation of the welfare units is regulated by the Family Courts (Establishment of Welfare Units, Modes of Operation, and Working Arrangements) Order, 5756-1996.

technical aspects, and the rules of confidentiality and disclosure that apply to all the proceedings. Children will be offered the option of meeting with the judge hearing the case or conveying their wishes to the court via a PSW. Children will also be told they are entitled to waive their right to be heard.

3) Should the child choose to be heard by the judge, a meeting will be set up to be attended by the child, the judge, and the PSW.

4) Should the child choose to be heard by the PSW, the PSW will provide a written record of what the child wished to convey to the court, together with a review of the child's behavior and state at the time of the hearing.

5) Records of the PSW reports and of the court protocol will be kept in the court's safe and will be confidential, available only to the court of appeal. A court hearing a child will not relay the child's statements in its decision, but may decide to disclose some or all of them if the child consented and if the court decided that the disclosure would advance the child's best interests.

6) Should the court be asked to ratify an agreement between the parents on matters that concern their children, the court secretariat will provide the parents information on the importance of hearing the children on matters that affect them before submitting the agreement to the court for ratification.

7) When ratifying the agreement, the judge will establish whether the parents had heard the child. The judge may refer the parents to the SSU for information and guidance about children's hearings and the relevant proceedings.

8) Following a hearing by a judge or by a PSW, the judge will explain to the child when issuing the decision or soon thereafter, directly or through the PSW, the main points in it relevant to him or her in a way suited to the child's age and level of maturity, unless the court decides that, in the circumstances of the case, it does not need to invite the child to hear the decision.

9) Following the meeting with the child and if the child consents, PSWs may establish contact with the parents and inform them of all or part of the contents of their child's statements.

Pilot Project on Child Participation

Given the complexity of the issues involved in devising an appropriate model for the participation of children, the legislative subcommittee recommended conducting a pilot project accompanied by a formative evaluation study to test the application of the model developed by the committee. Special family court regulations were enacted, providing for the pilot's implementation in two family courts—Jerusalem and Haifa—between June 2006 and March 2009.[6] The pilot was to be confined to cases of custody, visitation rights, immigration, and education (without including

---

6. Chapter 20.2 (Participation of Children) in Civil Procedure Regulations 1984, KT 5744, 2220 (Isr.).

adoption and abduction cases), to children aged 6 and up. Nevertheless, when a child who was at least 6 years old had a younger sibling, regulations permitted the court to allow the younger sibling to be heard as well.

A steering committee[7] appointed by the Ministry of Justice supervised the pilot project through the evaluative study. Members of the committee also met regularly with judges and with PSWs in both family courts to discuss the project's implementation and to introduce changes. The steering committee also sponsored seminars and ongoing training for family court judges, lawyers, and social service workers (SSWs) in the geographic areas of the pilot and in the country as a whole.

RESEARCH FINDINGS

This section presents the methodology and the findings of the formative evaluation and the follow-up study. It presents the main insights emerging from them and the changes in the functioning of the children's participation model from the beginning of the pilot until three years after the end of the formative evaluation.

The Formative Evaluation: Aims and Structure

The evaluation study examined the model's judicial applicability and the warranted changes. It related to the following aspects: the patterns of child participation, the factors promoting or impeding participation, the professional practice of the various parties involved, and the perceived impact of child participation.

The formative evaluation was conducted in two stages. The first stage proceeded during November 2006 to February 2008. After the findings were presented to the steering committee in March 2008, the committee initiated several changes in the pilot program. The second stage extended from March 2008 to March 2009.

Data collection relied on the following tools:

1) Forms documenting contacts were completed for all the children who were invited to participate: 448 children.[8]

---

7. The public committee for the implementation of the pilot was chaired by Judge (ret.) Saviona Rotlevy. Committee members include Dr. Tamar Morag, chair of the committee; Judge Shlomo Elbaz, from the Jerusalem Family Court; Anat Inbar, National Commissioner for Welfare Units in the Ministry of Social Affairs and Social Services; Dr. Peretz Segal, Ministry of Justice; Adv. Moriah Bakshi, Ministry of Justice; Shachar Schumann, Head of the Children and Youth Unit in Ashalim; and Adv. Efrat Wenkart, director of the pilot. The pilot ran as a joint project of the Ministry of Justice, the Ministry of Social Affairs and Social Services, and Joint-Ashalim, a nongovernmental organization working together with government offices to develop models for intervention in areas affecting children at risk.

8. PSWs completed forms for every child invited to participate, of whom 216 were heard by the PSW and 232 were not.

2) Judges' feedback forms, filled out by the judge after meeting with the child, were completed for fifty-one children.[9]
3) Telephone interviews with parents of children invited to participate were conducted with 103 parents.[10]
4) Telephone interviews with children who were invited to participate, aged 10 and up, were conducted with ninety-nine children.[11]
5) In-depth interviews with children[12] (five); parents[13] (six); PSWs (eight); psychologists working with the CPD (two); directors of SSUs (four); judges (seven); lawyers[14] (seven); and court-appointed social workers (four).

The Formative Evaluation: Main Findings

Age of the children: 37 percent of the children were aged 10 to 13, 31 percent were 14 to 18 years old, 29 percent were 6 to 9 years old, and 3 percent were 3 to 5 years old.

Judges' referrals to the CPD: Child participation regulations prescribed that judges must refer all relevant cases to the CPD for the purpose of inviting children to participate, unless they hold that participation would be more harmful to the child than nonparticipation. In practice, judges referred to the CPD about 40 percent of the files. In the in-depth interviews, judges said that some of the reasons for not referring children were technical—unmarked pilot cases or parents reaching agreement—and others reflected the court's concern that participation, rather than being in the best interests of the child, would overburden the children or place undue pressure on him or her. Other reasons for nonreferral claimed

9. Fifty-four children met with judges in the course of the study, which means that judges completed feedback forms for an absolute majority of the children they met with.
10. The telephone interviews with parents were planned and conducted only at the second stage of the study, from July 2008, applying insights derived from the implementation of the pilot project. Interviews were sought with 119 parents whose children were invited to participate, and only sixteen refused. In all, interviews were conducted with seventy-three parents of children who were heard by a PSW or by the court, and thirty parents of children who were not heard.
11. These interviews too were conducted only at the second stage of the study. From July 2008 until the end of data collection, interviews were sought with 155 children aged 10 to 18. The children were approached only with the consent of both parents and, therefore, forty-seven of the children were not interviewed after one or both parents refused. The children were then asked if they agreed to be interviewed, and nine refused. Of those interviewed, eighty-four children had actually participated in the pilot. The other fifteen, although invited, did not come to the meeting set up with the PSW.
12. Ten of the ninety-nine children interviewed by phone and holding a range of views on the pilot were selected for in-depth, semistructured interviews. Five of the ten agreed to be interviewed.
13. Nine of the 103 parents interviewed by phone were selected for semistructured in-depth interviews, and six agreed.
14. Interviews were conducted with lawyers dealing with proceedings at the courts where the pilot was implemented—Jerusalem and Haifa.

by judges were overload and the concern that participation would not assist the court's decision in a specific case.

Participation rates: Significant differences in participation rates were recorded between the first and second stages of the pilot. At the end of the first stage, only 35 percent of the children who had been invited to participate had attended the meeting. The main reason for children's low participation rates was parental opposition. To increase child participation, PSWs adopted steps aimed at explaining to all parents whose children were invited to participate in the pilot study the program's aims and operating methods. Given that parents tend to follow their lawyer's advice, the latter's stance may influence the parents' position concerning their children's involvement in legal proceedings. To enlist the lawyers' cooperation and reduce parental opposition, several seminars for lawyers in the field of family law were held in the areas where the pilot was operating. The wording of the judges' invitation to the participation process was changed, from a formulation stating, "The child is invited to the CPD" to "I order the child to come to the CPD." These steps led to a significant rise in the children's participation rates, from 35 percent in the first stage to 60 percent in the second.

Children's requests to meet with the judge: During the first stage of the pilot, only 15 percent of the children who met with the PSW chose to meet with the judge. The implementation committee thought these meetings were important and instructed the PSWs to encourage children to take advantage of this option. The PSWs proceeded to explain to children the nature of these meetings and showed them photographs of the court in an attempt to reduce their anxiety about the setting. These efforts proved effective and, at the second stage of the pilot, the percentage of children asking to meet with the judge rose to 32 percent.

In-depth interviews with the PSWs showed that changes in the children's rates of participation in general and in the rates of meetings with judges in particular followed not only from changes in the format of the pilot but also, and perhaps mainly, from ongoing changes in the attitudes of the PSWs themselves. As the pilot progressed, the PSWs became increasingly convinced of the project's benefits and were therefore more successful in persuading the parents to allow their children to participate. These changes were evident, *inter alia*, in the following statement of a PSW: "We too changed our views. Our voices became more confident. We are convinced of the importance of the project, and we have no doubt that we must continue with it."

Children's satisfaction and the content of participation: Participating children were asked whether they thought it was a good idea to give children in general the chance to express themselves on the subject of their parents' conflict. Ninety-three percent answered in the affirmative. The children were also asked whether they would recommend participation to friends, and 92 percent said yes. To the question of whether participation had helped them, 62 percent of the children said it had. When asked how, they mostly reported that they felt their opinions and feelings had been respected, that the conversation had helped them decide what they really wanted, and that the involvement with the PSWs had contributed to improved relationships with one of the parents. Children who said that participation had not helped them were asked why not. The most frequent response was that participation had changed nothing or that it had not swayed the judicial decision in the direction they would have liked.

Most children shared with the CPD's social workers and with the judges their thoughts and feelings on the effects of their parents' litigation on them, as well as information on such topics as their hobbies and their schools. CPD social workers reported that most children (71 percent) conveyed their views on visitation and custody arrangements, and that most children had felt comfortable at meetings with them and with the judge—70 percent had expressed themselves easily and 69 percent had seemed relaxed.

Confidentiality: One issue that proved controversial when developing the model, due to the adversarial character of litigation in the Israeli system, was the confidentiality to be granted to the child's statements. The legislative committee recommended granting broad confidentiality to children's statements. The recommendation was made part of the children's participation model and formulated as follows:

> The record of the court or of the social worker, or what the child sought to tell the court, as pertinent [. . .] will be kept in the court's safe and will be confidential vis-à-vis every person, except the court of appeal. A court that heard a child will not relay the child's statements in its decisions, but the court may decide to disclose all or some of them if the child agreed to the disclosure and if the court found that disclosure would advance the child's best interests.[15]

This arrangement is compatible with the view of the UN Committee on the Rights of the Child, asserting that statements by children who are heard in the course of custody proceedings should be confidential. Section 43 of the General Comment on child participation relates to forms of hearing children in legal proceedings and states as follows: "Experience indicates that the situation should have the format of a talk rather than a one-sided examination. Preferably, a child should not be heard in open court, but under conditions of confidentiality."[16]

The study examined the children's views on confidentiality. Interviews with the children showed that 77 percent of them sought to preserve full or partial confidentiality vis-à-vis their parents: 50 percent requested full confidentiality, 27 percent wanted partial confidentiality, and 23 percent asked to waive confidentiality altogether vis-à-vis their parents. Findings regarding the significance that children ascribed to

15. Regulation 258 (33) 9.
16. Committee on the Rights of the Child, General Comment No. 12, The Right of the Child to be Heard (2009), UN Doc. CRC/C/GC/12, available at http://www2.ohchr.org/english/bodies/crc/comments.htm

retaining control of the use to be made of what they said supported the committee's decision to grant children the right to decide whether to waive confidentiality.

Participation of alienated alienated children: A concern raised by various professionals before and during the pilot was that children's attitudes might be the result of parental alienation and manipulation. When asked for their impressions in this regard, PSWs reported that, in their view, most (86 percent) of the children who had chosen to participate in the court proceedings had expressed their own opinions, and about one fifth (19 percent) had expressed opinions dictated to them by one of their parents.

Two questions were examined in the context of alienation: 1) To what extent can the invitation *per se* exacerbate alienation? and 2) Should alienated children be heard? On the first question, some PSWs objected to involving alienated children, claiming that the very act of stating words of incitement before authority figures could deepen the abuse of the children. One PSW said: "I'm concerned about alienated children. The parents want to throw them into yet another arena and aggravate the conflict." Other PSWs, however, said that the very act of inviting children to participate neither causes nor intensifies alienation, which is a process that began long before the child was invited: "Alienated children are alienated children and nothing can be done about it. They are exploited all along and not just for this pilot. Children who are alienated, even where no pilot exists, embark on a crusade in order to meet with the judge."

On the question of hearing alienated children, judges, lawyers, and CPD staff held a range of views. Some claimed that hearing alienated children is superfluous for legal proceedings. One judge argued: "When I hear a child in cases of parental alienation, I do not give any weight to what the child said, and meeting such children is therefore redundant." By contrast, other interviewees held that there are advantages to hearing children expressing views dictated to them by others. According to one judge: "Meeting the child allows me to identify the alienation and its depth . . . This is crucial when making judicial decisions."

Contributions and benefits of participation: Two potential types of benefits to the children were examined in the study: the contribution of participation to the judicial decision and to emotional well-being and family relations.

Concerning the contribution to the judicial decision, judges were asked whether meeting the child had contributed to their understanding of the case or shed different light on it. Six percent of the judges reported that the meeting had contributed "to a very large degree" and 48 percent responded it had contributed "to a large degree." In-depth interviews with judges and with SSWs revealed that judges felt that the meeting had contributed by strengthening their own impressions or contributing another perspective. Only toward the end of the formative evaluation study did judges point to a few isolated cases where the meeting had led to a significant change in the judicial decision.

For example, a judge described a case where an 11-year old girl expressed her wish that her father rather than her mother be her custodial parent: "Her voice was so authentic, and her will so clear and sharp . . . I myself went through a process after my encounter with her. In the end, I ruled that custody for the girl be transferred to her father. Her wishes were given very significant weight in the decision."

Considering emotional well-being and family relations, PSWs reported that their impression had been that the children they had met had had no one to talk about the conflict. Their parents had not been emotionally available and had faced difficulties in attempting to cope with their children's problems in the midst of the conflict. PSWs estimated that 88 percent of the children had benefited from this opportunity to express their feelings. Children also reported this contribution in their interviews: "It was good to let go of things that were weighing down on me and not keep everything inside. I felt good that it was with a professional."

A significant finding of the evaluation research was that realizing their right of participation in custody decisions enabled the children to disclose their views not only to the judges but also to their parents. In-depth interviews with PSWs revealed that parents are frequently unaware of the wishes, emotional state, distress, and needs of their children. One PSW reported: "I often surprise the parents with the things their children say. The intensity of the children's pain really shocks the parents and we also found things that disturbed the children which the parents had not even imagined."

In accordance with the regulations, PSWs are authorized to disclose the child's statements to the parents, with the child's consent. PSWs can also invite parents and children to three or four short-term intervention sessions, with them and/or with the CPD psychologist. PSWs reported that they had relayed their impressions of the children's emotional state and needs in 63 percent of the cases. Concerning 25 percent of the children, PSWs reported that, following the participation meeting, one or both parents had adapted their conduct to the needs of the child, as shown in the in-depth interviews with parents and children. For example, one of the children attested: "Participation creates a bridge between children and parents. Following the participation meeting, I have better conditions at home."

According to one of the mothers:

> My daughter told a CPD worker something I had not known. She said it bothered her that I'm not always home on the evenings of my days with her and her older brothers sometimes took care of her if I went out. Ever since, every evening she is with me I'm home from seven, I serve her a hot meal, we read books together, and I put her to bed. It has given greater stability to my days with her.

The Follow-Up Study: Aims and Structure

The aim of the follow-up study was to examine the developments in the application of the model after the conclusion of the pilot in the Jerusalem and Haifa courts, where the model continued to function in accordance with the regulations, as well as the changes in the patterns of children's hearings in courts where the regulations had not yet been put into effect.

A qualitative study was conducted for this purpose in January through March 2013, which included fourteen in-depth interviews with the following professionals: the national supervisor of SSUs (one); SSU directors in the Jerusalem and Haifa courts (two); CPD directors (three); PSWs in Jerusalem and Haifa (two); lawyers working in the Jerusalem and Haifa courts (two), and judges from the Jerusalem and Haifa Courts (four).[17] In addition to the in-depth interviews with two directors of SSU, questionnaires were sent to directors of fourteen SSUs in courts where the project was not yet implemented.

The Follow-up Study: Main Findings
In Courts Where Regulations Apply

Children's participation. In the Jerusalem and Haifa courts where the model was still implemented in accordance with the regulations after the conclusion of the pilot, PSWs and judges reported that, since the end of the pilot, changes had been recorded in the scope and type of cases that judges refer to the CPD. Interviewees reported a rise in the scope of complex and difficult referrals where parents are involved in an intense conflict and a decline in referrals of easier cases. One of the judges conveyed this view as follows: "I invite children when disputes are deep and genuine, for example, when children wish to move from one parent to another and are unhappy with the current arrangements."

From interviews with PSWs and SSWs, we also learned about another interesting development in this period. SSWs launched a new initiative and referred to the CPD children whose parents took part in mediation proceedings at the SSUs. In these cases, the child is heard at the CPD and the PSW presents to the mediation forum whatever the child agreed to disclose. Children's participation in mediation proceedings had been included in the model formulated by the legislative committee and in the regulations but was not implemented in the pilot project. After the pilot, the regulations were applied to children's participation in mediation proceedings. Unlike the judges' referrals to the CPD, however, which focus on the more complex cases, cases referred in the context of mediation proceedings also include low- to medium-intensity conflicts.

Ongoing participation. One innovation introduced in these courts after the end of the pilot was to hear children more than once over a period of time, as reported by both PSWs and by judges. As one judge stated: "Sometimes I hear children more than once, particularly when serious problems are involved, and every time I refer

---

17. In Israel, interviewing judges requires authorization from the Chief Justice.

the children to the CDP." Ongoing participation is sometimes prompted by the court and sometimes initiated by the children, who turn to the CPD.

Professionals' views on model for child participation. Findings pointed to growing acceptance of the model among PSWs, lawyers, and parents. One PSW commented: "Before the pilot, I opposed children's hearings on professional grounds. Now it's reversed." SSWs and SSU directors reported increasing backing of lawyers and parents: "We have successfully influenced lawyers. At first, they were strongly opposed, and today they are extremely supportive. They themselves propose children's participation to the court" (PSW). "Far less parental opposition. It's become something natural, probably influenced by lawyers' support" (PSW).

Judges' views on the participation model. Judges' attitudes proved more complex. Interviews with judges and with PSWs revealed that, together with their growing support for participation in difficult, complex cases, judges at this stage had greater reservations than at the time of the formative evaluation regarding implementation of a universal right to child participation in all cases. One judge summed up this attitude as follows: "The issue is to identify the proper case, that's the main problem, not to invite children to participate as a set ritual in all cases. Proportions, that's the key."

Judges pointed mainly to issues of workload and efficiency as grounds for this position and for the decline in their referrals of less complex cases that, as noted, had been reported by SSU staff and by PSWs. However, they also pointed to the emotional strains evoked by the hearings, where they faced the children's distress without any tools to help them. These strains come to the fore in the following statement of a family court judge:

> I feel deeply frustrated because we lack genuine power to deal with these cases. When a minor and his father do not meet and the boy says: "I am 14 years old, I do not want to see him. I'll call him if I want to," there's nothing I can do . . . It's painful, because you know that, in a few years, he'll be an injured person, and I feel impotent. There are emotional aspects and our toolkit is truly poor. I feel pain as a person, not as a judge. . . . There are visitation arrangements. The father comes to fetch the child and the mother disappears. The wars between the parents are fatal, and I believe that the children experience all this. Has anyone ever thought of what the child is going through? What tools do I have for coping with this? Discuss visitation rights for each holiday separately? Judicial involvement in every detail? I cannot do this and that is the frustrating part of the work as a family court judge. All of this has become clearer to me since the meetings with the children.

SSU staff members have suggested a broader spectrum of possible explanations for the judges' opposition to the recognizing and implementing of a universal participation right:

- *Fear of the increasing workload resulting from universal hearings*: "We know that, except for the judges who very much wanted this and did it, other judges are afraid of anything that imposes further tasks on them."

- *A perception of children's participation as a therapeutic function:* Judges see hearings as a tool intended to improve the children's well-being rather than as part of the legal proceedings:

> Many judges think of the system as dealing with problems in legal, authoritative terms and as concerned with justice. Emotional issues of well-being should be left to the ministry of social services. They see participation as almost illegitimate in the legal world. They have not yet related to the child's rights. They think of it as promoting the child's well-being. (PSW)

- *Concern about the limitation of judicial discretion:* SSU staff members noted that delaying the application of the regulations to all family courts lowered the motivation of the Jerusalem and Haifa court's judges to fully implement the model in general, and specifically its provisions regarding the right of every child to be heard, which significantly limited judicial discretion.
- *Judges' emotional difficulties:* SSU staff also noted the emotional difficulties attendant on hearing children as one reason for the judges' recoil from children's universal participation: "Unconsciously, judges may avoid referring children to participation hearings due to the difficulties they experienced in their meetings with children" (PSW). According to the PSWs, one motivation of the judges' emphasis on inviting children in complex cases was to obtain additional information that they required for making a decision rather than the recognition of a right to participate as an independent right of children. One PSW commented: "We draw a distinction between interviewing children and participation. An interview is a meeting between the judge and the child, when the judge wishes to interview the child out of his or her own interest. Many judges invite children to `testify,' and this is not participation" (PSW).
- *Reduced follow-up on the judges' work:* One aspect of the pilot had been to follow up on the work of all the professionals involved. Judges participating in the pilot were required to fill out forms every time they conducted a hearing. They also took part in set meetings with steering committee members and participated in seminars. These activities were discontinued at the end of the pilot. PSWs noted that they were less active in the projects' maintenance and in encouraging judges to refer cases to the CPD: "In the past, I had set up a system to encourage referrals—I built tables to report data, organized the data at various levels, and gave it to the judges. I also discussed with them the prevalent trends and defined aims for encouraging participation" (PSW). After the pilot ended, the PSWs' activities designed to encourage the scope of judges' referrals to the CPD also declined somewhat, partly because they no longer needed to fill out the follow-up forms that had been required during the formative evaluation and partly due to burnout.

The follow-up study, then, revealed that judges have difficulties recognizing participation as a universal right of children. Note that we only interviewed judges who had already been in office at the time of the formative evaluation. The implications of this conclusion should nevertheless be qualified in light of the SSWs' impressions pointing out that, unlike senior judges, new judges are more willing to have children participate: "New judges accept participation as part of the process" (SSW).

Confidentiality. Confidentiality, as noted, had been a controversial issue in the development of the model. The formative evaluation explored the children's attitudes on this topic and the follow-up study examined the cumulative experience. One interesting finding was that the unusual arrangement of granting children's views absolute confidentiality was accepted unquestionably in both the Jerusalem and Haifa courts. Judges reported no significant problem in implementing this regulation: "We have had no problems regarding confidentiality. The recording is made by a legal aide, typed, and stored in an envelope in the safe. We have a private file closed to the parties. We write up a summary for ourselves and the full record is placed in the safe" (judge). "What the child says is recorded and placed in a safe, and I know how to relay messages to the parents indirectly, without revealing the child's views" (judge). Lawyers did not challenge this regulation: "We feared lawyers would complain about granting confidentiality to children, but it hasn't happened. The idea of participation and the idea of confidentiality have both been accepted" (SSU director).

Alienated children. The follow-up study, like the formative evaluation, approached the participation of alienated children by asking whether participation would exacerbate or hinder alienation. Views ranged from judges and CPD staff who argued that participation does not encourage alienation to others who argued that, in some cases, it might. CPD staff and judges, however, still claimed that alienated children should be heard, and some even noted that, if parental alienation is presumed, participation entails several advantages:

- *Opportunity to encourage expression of genuine feelings*: The alienation of children in the course of a prolonged parental conflict and the children's feeling that they are "caught in the middle" (Afifi, 2003; Buchanan, alienated children, forced to cope with the need to meet the expectations of the alienating parent, run the risk of "erasing" parts of their personality and harming their development in the long range. Emotional ventilation at the participation meeting could thus prove crucial. According to a CPD staff member, meeting alienated children is at times positive in that it provides them a space for emotional ventilation:

  At times, children try to hold on to what they were told to say and recite. But sometimes, when we promise children protection, what's underneath begins to surface . . . The children find place for expressing anger or a very helpful to the children. (PSW)

- *Meeting the judge may reduce parental alienation*: Judges believe they can use their authority vis-à-vis the parents beyond the judicial decision, when providing feedback to the parents after meeting with the children. They can reflect to the parents the depth of the alienation and warn against its negative effects on the child: "Sometimes I tell the parents, you have a great kid and look at what this is doing to him. This definitely affects the parents" (judge). Some judges also noted that they clarify to the children that decisions are ultimately made by the judge, releasing the children from responsibility for acting as their parents' spokespersons in an attempt to affect results.
- *Participation strengthens the judges' understanding of alienation:* As was found in the formative evaluation, some interviewees in the follow-up study also believed that hearing alienated children may help judges in their decision-making process by giving them a deeper understanding of the parent–child relationships. "When I face a child's refusal to see a parent, I feel I must see the child, and even when I fail to persuade . . . the decision comes from a deeper understanding of the relationship and the parental alienation" (judge).

Contributions and benefits of participation. A prominent finding of the follow-up study was the growing influence of the children's participation on judicial decisions. In the formative evaluation, the judges had noted that children's hearings had provided additional insights and perspectives. Toward the end of the pilot, they pointed out that, in isolated and relatively rare cases, participation led to changes in the judicial decision. By contrast, in the follow-up study, both the judges and the PSWs cited many examples where participation not only had contributed to the proceedings but had also played a decisive role in the decision-making process and, at times, had even led to changes in a judicial ruling. In one instance a ruling was changed after a meeting of two boys with a judge and a PSW:

> In a case where parents shared custody, a judge ratified an agreement between the parents stating that, were one parent to move to the United States, the children would spend two years in the United States and two years in Israel. After the children had spent two years in the United States with the mother, she requested sole custody of the children. An expert's opinion recommended that the children should spend a year in Israel with the father and then reopen the case. The children, who were eleven and thirteen, met with the judge and expressed their strong will to stay there. The judge felt that they had become Americans—the younger child mixed in English words, the older one spoke of college plans. The judge assigned significant weight to the children's wishes and granted custody to the mother. (PSW)

The other side of the judges' focus on hard and complex cases is that the judges hear children when they hold this to be important and when the children's views could affect the ruling. The children's influence on the judicial decision, then, became stronger at the time of the follow-up study.

SSWs and judges pointed to the significant emotional contribution of participation, resembling the picture that emerged during the formative evaluation. The main issues they pointed to were opportunities for expressing feelings and sharing distress, the empowerment of children, identifying problems and referring for therapy in suitable cases, and the parents' involvement in issues raised by the child so as to improve their relationships with their children. For example: "One child spoke of his relationship with the mother's partner. The children had told the mother about their problems with him, but the mother had ignored the issue, thinking this was natural and the children's attitude would change. The participation meeting led to a serious talk on the subject and to improved relationships with the mother's partner" (PSW).

One issue emphasized in the follow-up study was the potential contribution of children's participation to the renewal of the child–parent relationship: "Sometimes, usually at the participation meeting, we find that the parent and the child are not in contact. We would never have known about it otherwise, and we refer these cases to a special service in the SSU for the renewal of the child–parent relationship" (PSW).

In Courts Where Regulations Do Not Yet Apply

Concerning most family courts where the regulations do not yet apply, SSU directors reported that the number of children invited to participate had increased and, in some, the increase had even been significant. In most cases, the judge and the PSW hear the child together. In the Kiriyat Bialik family court, the model is almost fully implemented. Cases are referred for participation to the court's SSU and the judges apply most regulations. The expansion of the project to these courts is evident in the willingness of the staff at SSUs to engage in tasks involved in children's participation. Staff members from SSUs at all family courts participated in a comprehensive training program on issues of child participation, and most SSUs in Israel have appointed social workers responsible for children's participation.

Although the regulations have not yet been expanded to additional courts, then, the influence of the model based on the regulations is growing in these settings and the right to participation is increasingly exercised in these courts as well.

CENTRAL INSIGHTS EMERGING FROM A JOINT APPRAISAL OF THE FORMATIVE EVALUATION AND THE FOLLOW-UP STUDY

The operation of the children's participation model during and after the pilot project has been the subject of a prolonged appraisal. Several key conclusions can be drawn about the model that was formulated by the legislative committee and about the success of its implementation.

Children are comfortable and satisfied with the participation process. The findings of the formative evaluation show that most of the children felt comfortable during the participation process, expressed satisfaction with it, and felt it had made a significant contribution to them. Later, the in-depth interviews in the follow-up study showed no change in this regard. This finding strengthens recognition of the need to grant children the right to participate. The children's satisfaction and good feeling with the participation process can largely diminish concerns that the process could be harmful to them. Some of the children, however, did feel tension during the meetings with PSWs and judges and expressed discomfort. Although they were a minority, attention should be paid to the practices applied in meetings with parents and children so as to limit such phenomena.

Participation makes a significant contribution to the legal proceedings. The studies showed that the children's participation in general contributes to the legal proceedings and influences the pertinent judicial ruling. The formative evaluation revealed that, in 54 percent of the cases, the child's participation contributed new information or shed different light on the case. And yet, when judges were asked to cite instances of cases where participation had changed their decision, they could only find isolated examples. By contrast, in the follow-up study, judges easily found many concrete examples of participation significantly influencing their decision. In this context, however, it deserves mention that, at the follow-up stage, judges *a priori* tended to refer to the CPD cases where participation could potentially contribute to their decision.

Participation made a significant emotional contribution to the children. Both studies showed that one of the most significant contributions of children's participation is that it provides the children an opportunity for containment and emotional expression. Findings indicated that participation empowered the children and enabled identification of their anxieties and referral to therapy in the appropriate cases. These findings point to the importance of working with an interdisciplinary model, which integrates judges and social workers.

Participation strengthened parent–children bonds. Both studies showed that participation often exposes children's feelings and worries of which parents had been unaware. Following their involvement in the participation process, parents often changed their conduct. Another aspect connected to better parent–child relationships that emerged from the follow-up study is that, in some cases, participation can lessen the depth of parental alienation and even renew contacts between parents and children.

Confidentiality is vital to the children and doesn't raise significant difficulties. When developing the model, the matter of granting confidentiality to the child's statement proved controversial. The starting assumption was that confidentiality would be a critical issue for the children and would enable truer and fuller participation, but opposition was feared on the part of parents and lawyers. According to the model, as noted, children were assured that their statements would remain entirely private. The findings of the formative study clarified that confidentiality is indeed a foremost concern for the children. The follow-up study indicated that, contrary to the fears of some of the pilot designers, the arrangement faced no serious opposition—it was generally acceptable to judges, lawyers, and parents and had been fully implemented throughout.

Judges and PSWs support hearings of alienated children. Another issue that proved controversial when designing the model concerned participation of children alienated by their parents. Even though some judges and some PSWs had believed that the very act of inviting alienated children could exacerbate alienation, most professionals supported these children's participation. Their general support was already evident at the time of the formative evaluation and became very prominent in the findings of the follow-up study. By this stage, judges and PSWs came to believe that child participation in these cases could actually be helpful to the location of the alienation and to its moderation. Some of the judges, as noted, believed that a direct meeting with the child in these cases is of special significance.

The idea of children's participation according to the model took root in courts even without formal implementation. The follow-up study showed that, over time, the possibility of hearing children in decisions bearing on family conflicts was also implemented in courts where the model was not formally in operation. SSWs reported increased rates of children's participation in some courts where the project was not implemented, and the adoption of the model's work patterns. Most SSUs in Israel's family courts had appointed a person responsible for children's participation, the model had been fully implemented in the Kiryat Bialik court, and joint hearings by judges and SSWs had become routine. The model's voluntary endorsement by courts to which the regulations did not yet apply denotes its persuasive power.

PSWs play a major role in the promotion and operation of the project. The formative evaluation revealed that, prior to the pilot, SSU staff had not met with children and had reservations about such meetings. Yet, despite their professional opinion that children should not be involved in the conflict, they did perform the role assigned to them. Through the actual experience of hearing children, they underwent a significant change of views and began to support children's participation. Already at the formative evaluation, the link between the PSWs' growing support for the project and their ability to promote it became explicit. Thus, for example, the more PSWs supported the project, the more they succeeded in persuading parents and lawyers to agree to their children's participation and in persuading children to meet with judges, thereby lowering the parental opposition blocking the children's realization of their right to participate. The follow-up study revealed strengthening support for the project among PSWs and SSU directors, leading them to encourage children's participation in places where the project had not yet been officially implemented. One sign of this development can be found, for example, in the appointment of a person responsible for children's participation in courts where the project was not yet operational and in the significant development of children's participation in mediation proceedings. Furthermore, according to the PSWs' impressions, they also played a major role in driving judges to refer relevant cases for children's hearings to the CPD.

Ambivalent judicial views. Judges have shown increasing support for children's participation in complex cases, together with reservations about recognizing the children's right to participate in the legal proceedings conducted in family courts as a universal right. These "mixed" feelings were already manifested at the formative evaluation stage, in findings showing that the scope of the cases that judges were referring to the CPD was limited. The follow-up study, however, pointed to a strengthening of this trend, leading to referrals for participation mainly of children who were involved in complex cases, where parents are strongly antagonistic. The judges' reservations about recognizing the right to participate as a universal right were in tension with the model's starting point, which acknowledged participation as a right of children without considering the intensity of the parents' conflict. This was also the approach largely endorsed by the PSWs. Together with these reservations, evidence showed that judges did support participation in the more complex cases and definitely acknowledged that, in those cases, hearing children can make a vital contribution to the legal proceedings.

Children's participation poses emotional difficulties for some judges. A significant finding of the study touched on the judges' emotional strains when faced with hearings involving children trapped in a prolonged and vicious parental conflict. Some of the judges pointed to the meager toolbox at their disposal, which does not provide them with sufficient means to help the children in any significant way.

CONCLUSIONS—IMPLICATIONS FOR PRACTICE, POLICY, AND RESEARCH

This chapter reviewed the formative evaluation study and the follow-up study on the model of children's participation in legal proceedings conducted in family courts in Israel. First, it is important to note that these studies differed in their character and, therefore, the possibility of comparative cross-sections between them was limited. The scope of the formative evaluation study was far broader than that of the follow-up study and some of the issues examined in the former could not be addressed in the latter. Thus, for instance, the follow-up study did not examine the children's or the parents' levels of satisfaction. Second, the formative study used quantitative methods for examining children's participation patterns and satisfaction levels with them, whereas the follow-up study relied solely on qualitative methods. Hence, we could not analyze changes and trends in these areas and relied only on the interviewees' impressions.

Despite these limitations, we can learn from these studies about the importance of hearing children in family conflicts and on the proper ways of doing so. Generally, findings support the research corpus pointing to the importance of hearing children in family conflicts and to its contribution at the legal, emotional, and family levels. The studies revealed the advantages of having social workers accompany children throughout the participation process—children felt comfortable talking to them, and social workers took initiatives for further involvement in improving parent–child relationships. As for judges hearing children, findings showed that children felt comfortable in these situations and judges were influenced by the children's participation.

The studies also revealed the potential of the Israeli model for developing a mechanism for children's hearings in both adversarial and nonadversarial proceedings. The main barrier to the implementation of children's right to participate as a universal right emerging from the studies seems to be the reservations of some of the judges regarding broad recognition of this right. These reservations come to the fore in the spreading practice of limiting children's participation mainly to hard and complex cases.

Findings revealed the judges' ambivalent attitudes during the implementation of the pilot project, an ambivalence that became even more acute after its conclusion. On the one hand, as noted, findings exposed the judges' growing reservations about recognition of participation as a universal children's right. On the other, we found that judges significantly supported children's participation in complex cases, including cases of alienation. They showed readiness to genuinely listen to children and to be affected by them in the decision-making process.

The key to the fuller implementation of the child participation model developed by the subcommittee, then, seems to lie in the success of enlisting judges more fully in support of recognizing children's participation as an independent right rather than as a tool that may assist them in deciding complex cases. Promoting this change in the judges' attitudes requires, as a first step, clearly anchoring in the legislation the child's right to participate as a universal right. A significant move in this direction will be the extension of the regulations to all family courts. Moreover, appropriate ways should be found to respond to the difficulties that judges conveyed regarding their limited toolbox and the emotional strains they confront when hearing children.

POSTSCRIPT

In September 2014, after the completion of this article, the regulations regarding child participation in family courts were extended to all Israeli family

courts.[18] This represents a significant milestone in promoting child participation in Israeli family courts. Implementation will require, however, significant effort related to the training of judges and social workers and developing,
improving and reevaluating the model for participation applied under the regulations. We hope that the findings of the studies discussed in this article will
contribute to the implementation and development of this model in a manner
that would enhance meaningful and effective participation of children.

REFERENCES

Afifi, T. D. (2003). Feeling caught in stepfamilies: Managing boundary turbulence through
    appropriate communication privacy rules. *Journal of Social and Personal Relationships*,
    20, 729–756.
Birnbaum, R., & Bala, N. (2010). Judicial interviews with children in custody and access
    cases: Comparing experience in Ontario and Ohio. *International Journal of Law,
    Policy, and the Family*, *24*, 300.
Bala, N., Birnbaum, R., Cyr, F., & McColley, D. (2013). Children's voices in family
    court: Guidelines for judges meeting children. *Family Law Quarterly*, *47*(3), 381–410.
Buchanan, C. M., Maccoby, E. E., & Dornbisch, S. M. (1991). Caught between par-
    ents: Adolescents' experience in divorced homes. *Child Development*, *62*, 1008–1029.
Cashmore, J., & Parkinson P. (2007). What responsibility do courts have to hear children's
    voices? *International Journal of Children's Rights*, *15*, 43.
Kelly, J. B. (2002). Psychological and legal interventions for parents and children in custody
    and access disputes: current research and practice. *Virginia Journal of Social Policy
    and the Law*, *10*, 129–163.
Morag, T., Rivkin, D. & Sorek, Y. (2012). Child participation in the family courts—Lessons
    from the Israeli pilot project. *International Journal of Law, Policy and the Family*,
    26(1), 1–30.
Neale, B., & Smart, C. (1998). Agents or dependents? Struggling to listen to children in
    family law and family research. Centre for Research on Family. *Kinship & Childhood,
    Working Paper*, *3*.
Parkinson, P., & Cashmore, J. (2008). *The voice of the child in family law disputes*.
    Oxford: Oxford University Press.
Parkinson, P., Cashmore, J., & Single, J. (2007). Parents' and children's views on talking to
    judges in parenting disputes in Australia. *International Journal of Law*, *21*(1), 84–107.
Israeli Ministry of Justice. (2003). *Report of the Committee for the Examination of Basic
    Principles in the Area of the Child and the Law*. General Part, p. 32.
Smart, C. (2002). From children's shoes to children's voices. *Family Court Review*, *40*(3),
    307–319.
Smith, A. B., Taylor, N. J., & Tapp, P. (2003). Rethinking children's involvement in
    decision-making after parental separation. *Childhood*, *10*(2), 201.
Taylor, N. (2006). What do we know about involving children and young people in family
    law decision making? A research update. *Australian Journal of Family Law*, *20*, 154.

18. *Yalkut HaPirsumim* (the official publication of the government of Israel), 2014 July 2nd.

Taylor, N., Fitzgerald, R. M., Tamar, M., Bajpai, A., & Graham, A. (2012). International models of child participation in family law proceedings following parental separation/divorce., *International Journal of Children's Rights, 20*(4), 645–673.

Taylor, N., Smith, A. & Tapp, P. (1999). Children, family law and family conflict: subdued voices. Available online at http://www.lawyers.org.nz/conference/pdf%20files/ S13%20papers.pdf (accessed July 1, 2012).

Warshak, R. A. (2003). Payoffs and pitfalls of listening to children. *Family Relations, 52*(4), 373–384.

PART III

Participatory Mechanisms
for Children at Risk

CHAPTER 8

Inclusive and Respectful Relationships as the Basis for Child Inclusive Policies and Practice

The Experience of Children in Out-of-Home Care in Australia

SHARON BESSELL

INTRODUCTION

Over the past two decades, protecting the human rights of children in alternative or out-of-home care has been an increasing social policy concern both globally and within countries—often against a backdrop of serious rights violations. The United Nations Convention on the Rights of the Child (CRC) and the United Nations Guidelines for the Alternative Care of Children provide an international framework for the care, protection, and treatment of children. Each includes the right of a child to express his or her views and to have those views taken into account. This is often described as the right to participate.

At the domestic level within Australia there have been important developments. In recent years state governments have paid increasing attention to the rights of children and young people in out-of-home care. Seven of Australia's eight state jurisdictions have adopted Charters of Rights for Children and Young People in Care. In July 2011 the Commonwealth, State, and Territory Governments agreed to National Standards for Out-of-Home Care, building on the 2010 National Framework for Child Protection. In each of these documents, and in related discourse, rights have been taken seriously. The right of children to participate in decisions made about their lives is a central principle.

Yet, despite the existence of policy frameworks globally and nationally, the extent to which children without parental care can appropriately and meaningfully participate in decisions made about their lives is limited. There is evidence, in Australia and elsewhere, to suggest that many children in out-of-home care feel excluded from decisions made about their lives. There remains a chasm between the vision of participation proclaimed in policy documents and the reality experienced by many children.

This chapter is based on research undertaken with children and young people in Australia about their experiences of out-of-home care, including whether and how they have been involved—or would like to be involved—in decisions made about their lives. I argue that while participation is an important principle in policies around out-of-home care in Australia, it has become a bureaucratic process rather than one that has meaning for most children experiencing out-of-home care. To make participation meaningful for children and young people in out-of-home care, it is necessary to reconceptualize it not as a process but as grounded in inclusive and respectful relationships.

OUT-OF-HOME CARE IN AUSTRALIA

In the Australian context, out-of-home care is defined as "alternative accommodation for children under 18 years of age who are unable to live with their parents, where the State or Territory makes a financial payment or where a financial payment has been offered but declined" (FaCHSIA, 2010, p. 2). Out-of-home care is generally taken to refer to children who have been removed from their parents as a result of abuse or neglect. Out-of-home care takes five primary forms in Australia: foster care, kinship care, residential care, family group homes, and independent living. The most common forms of care are foster care, where care is provided in a private home by a family not related to the children, and kinship care, where the caregiver is a family member or person with whom the child has an existing relationship. Foster care and kinship care are collectively described as home-based care, with 93.6 percent of children in this form of care (49.2 percent in foster care and 48.5 percent in kinship care) (Australian Institute of Health and Welfare, 2011). The relatively small percentage of children not in family-based care live in residential care,[1] in family group homes,[2] or independently.

---

1. Residential care is within a residential building with paid staff (rostered staff, live-in caregivers, or off-site staff).
2. Family group homes are residential buildings run like family homes with a limited number of children and twenty-four-hour care by paid carers or substitute parents.

According to Australian Institute of Health and Welfare statistics (2013), there were 39,621 children living in out-of-home care as of June 30, 2012. The number of children in out-of-home care has risen each year since the late 1990s. In the decade from 1997 to 2006, the number of children in out-of-home care doubled (Bromfield & Osborn, 2007).

Under Australia's federal system, responsibility for child protection, education, health and welfare lies with each of the eight state and territory governments (see Bromfield, Higgins, Osborn, Panozzo, & Richardson, 2005). Consequently, each jurisdiction has its own legislative framework and department to deal with out-of-home care. Nongovernmental organizations (NGOs) are involved in the delivery of services for children and young people in out-of-home care, with the precise nature of nongovernmental services varying across states and territories. This creates a complex and differentiated system across the country, whereby the role of the federal government has been limited. In recent years there has, however, been a trend toward national frameworks, but not national legislation, with the adoption of the National Framework for Child Protection in 2009 and the National Standards for Out-of-Home Care in 2011. Each of these documents draws on the language of human rights. The National Framework for Child Protection draws explicitly on the United Nations Convention on the Rights of the Child, noting Australia's obligations as a signatory. The first paragraph of the Framework draws on a generalized notion of rights: "All children have the right to be safe and to receive loving care and support. Children also have a right to receive the services they need to enable them to succeed in life." The first overarching principle of the National Standards for Out-of-Home Care is that "Children and young people in out-of-home care have their rights respected and are treated in accordance with the United Nations Convention on the Rights of the Child" (FaHCSIA, 2011). Article 12 of the CRC is evoked in Standard 2, whereby "Children and young people participate in decisions that have an impact on their lives." The National Framework for Child Protection and the National Standards for Out-of-Home Care are indicative of a shift that has occurred over the past decade, whereby ideas of children's rights have become a feature of policies around child protection and out-of-home care (see Bessell, 2010). The recognition of children's rights in out-of-home care policies began not with these recent developments at the national level but by the adoption of Charters of Rights among states and territories, commencing with the inclusion of a charter of rights in the Queensland Child Protection Act 1999. Currently, seven[3] of Australia's eight state and territory jurisdictions have Charters of Rights for Children and Young People in Out-of-Home Care.

---

3. The Northern Territory has standards for out-of-home care, which refer to the rights of children, but does not have a Charter of Rights.

THE RIGHT OF CHILDREN IN OUT-OF-HOME CARE TO PARTICIPATE

Australia ratified the CRC in 1990 but was slow to incorporate its principles into domestic law and policy (see Bessell, 2010). From the late 1990s, the principle that children have the right to express views on matters affecting them began to influence policy relating to out-of-home care for two broad reasons. First, the adoption of charters of rights reflects a tentative but increasing normative commitment to the idea that children are the bearers of human rights. Second, a series of inquiries or audits into out-of-home care and child protection systems across Australia revealed serious shortcomings that resulted in violations of children's rights, ranging from poor educational outcomes for children in care to physical, sexual, and emotional abuse (see Tilbury, 2007). In 1997, a report undertaken by the Australian Law Reform Commission and the Human Rights and Equal Opportunity Commission found that many children in out-of-home care were not placed in safe environments (1997). Two years later, the Government of Queensland established a commission of inquiry to examine whether there had been any abuse, mistreatment, or neglect of children in Queensland institutions between 1911 and 1999 (Forde, 1999). More than 150 orphanages and detention centers were investigated, with over 300 individuals providing information. This inquiry found that a range of abuse had occurred, from physical, psychological, and sexual abuse and excessive use of corporal punishment to inadequate provision of food and clothing and failure to provide adequate education (Forde, 1999). The resulting report described a social and political context within which abuse of children in institutions could occur with impunity. The report used the language of children's rights in seeking ways of guarding against violations. Adopted in the same year as the release of this report, the Queensland Child Protection Act 1999 established the rights to which all children in care in that state are entitled (under Section 74, Schedule 1). Among the rights guaranteed to children in care are the right to be consulted about and to take part in making decisions affecting their lives and the right to be given information about decisions and plans concerning their future and personal history. Specific reference is made to the right of children to take part in decisions about their living arrangements, contact with family, health, and schooling. This act states that children's right to participate in decisions and to have information about decisions made on their behalf should take into account their age or ability to understand the relevant issues. As in many similar policy documents, how age and ability should be taken into account is not clearly articulated.

From the late 1990s, other jurisdictions adopted Charters of Rights for Children in Out-of-Home Care. Each of these charters includes participation rights in some form. On the surface, this may be seen as broadly reflecting Article 12 of the CRC, which requires states parties to provide children with the opportunity to express their views on all matters affecting them and to be taken seriously.

However, within each charter, the right to participate is framed differently and is variously presented as children and young people's right to be consulted, have a say, or take part in decisions. There are important distinctions between these different concepts underpinning the various charters. Being consulted or having a say may be forms of participation but do not equate to having one's views taken seriously, nor do they necessarily result in any form of shared decision-making (see Hart, 1997; Shier, 2001). In several charters, the right to participate is stated in rather vague terms. For example, the Victorian charter entitles children to the right to "have a say and be heard," while the South Australian charter tells children that their thoughts and opinions are to be asked for and considered. Interestingly, the Western Australian charter states that children have the right to be heard, but adds in parentheses "and to show the same [respect] to other people's views and opinions."

As discussed, Australia introduced National Standards for Out-of-Home Care in 2011. Standard 2 calls for children and young people to "participate in decisions that have an impact on their lives." The National Standards go on to explain that

> Children and young people in out-of-home care are actively involved in decision-making about their lives. This is critical to emotional development and self-esteem and is a key provision within the United Nations Convention on the Rights of the Child.
>
> Children and young people are to be provided with objective advice, able to ask for help, have their concerns heard and given information about, and access to, review mechanisms. In all these areas, the level of active involvement will be appropriate to the young person's age and developmental stage.

The implementation of the standard is to be measured by "The proportion of children and young people who report that they have opportunities to have a say in relation to decisions that have an impact on their lives and that they feel listened to" (FaHCSIA, 2011, p. 8). These standards provide no detail on how children should be asked to report on their participation. Moreover, the proposed monitoring of whether a child's view has been taken into account in case planning and details of how a child's view was sought were postponed until after 2015.

MOVING TOWARD GENUINE PARTICIPATION?

It appears that Australia has moved steadily toward a commitment to the participatory rights of children and young people in care in decisions made about their lives. This commitment is part of a strengthening of the regulatory regime around out-of-home care, whereby procedures of accountability are "administered and imposed by the State" (Tilbury, 2007, p. 216). Tilbury (2007, p. 215) has observed that government regulation of out-of-home care has become "more formal, detailed and rigorous." Relationships between children and the state, and the services and treatment to which children are entitled, have become codified and are no longer subject to the determination of individuals or institutions charged with their care. Participation in decision-making has been conceptualized as both a right and as a procedure within the regulatory regime of out-of-home care, enshrined in either law or policy across Australian states. This formal commitment to the participation of children and young people in decisions made about their lives would appear to represent an important move forward. Yet, as the next section of this chapter discusses, there is a gap between formal commitment to the process of participation and the creation of safe, supportive spaces within which children can meaningfully express their views and be part of decisions about deeply personal and often troubled aspects of their lives. Children and young people who participated in the research discussed below described the extent to which they are excluded from decisions made about their lives; many described having little control over their lives and not knowing why situations change (or do not change).

There has been relatively little research in Australia with children, particularly younger children, about their experiences of out-of-home care generally or their participation in decision-making specifically. In large part, this is the result of longstanding structural obstacles to children's participation in research and the difficulties researchers face in gaining access to children in care (see Gilbertson & Barber, 2002; Mason, Urquhart, & Bolzan, 2003). Recent studies have tended to focus on important issues of stability in care, contact with birth families, and reunification (Delfabbro, Fernandez, McCormick, & Kettler, 2013; Kiraly & Humphreys, 2013; Tregeagle & Hamil, 2011) and transitioning from care (Natalier & Johnson, 2012; Mendes, Johnson, & Moslehuddin, 2011). In one of the few studies focusing explicitly on children's views on how they might be involved in decision-making while in out-of-homecare, children and young people identified their need to have a "voice," to be heard, and to exercise choice (Mason & Gibson, 2004, p. 36). Mason and Gibson (2004, p. 71) described children as "feeling trapped by powerlessness" when they are not listened to or are excluded from decision-making processes. While not all children described such experiences, nonparticipation or not being heard was a strong theme of Mason and Gibson's findings. CREATE Foundation, a not-for-profit organization dedicated to representing children and young people in care, produces an annual report card based on a survey of children and young people in care. The 2013 report card identified several key themes, including the importance children and young people placed on being involved in decisions made about their lives (McDowall, 2013). The report card found that 62.9 percent of children and young people surveyed said they were able to have a say "reasonably often," with older respondents (aged 15–17) more likely to feel able to have a say than those in younger age groups. Interestingly, an open-ended question found that

13.9 percent of respondents indicated they could have a say on "most things," while 10.3 percent said they were "never consulted on anything" (McDowall, 2013, p. 67). Existing studies indicate that children in out-of-home care want to be involved in decisions made about their lives. However, the limited research available on the extent to which that wish is fulfilled presents—at best—a mixed picture, with a significant proportion of children feeling they do not have a say and are not listened to.

To explore further children's experiences of participation in out-of-home care, I will now draw on two qualitative studies undertaken with children and young people. The first study sought to understand children's views on the issues they face in out-of-home care. This study was facilitated by the relevant government department, which managed the process of seeking informed consent from the children's guardian or parent as appropriate. Informed consent was sought from children and young people prior to the research and again at the beginning of each research session. Thirty-six children and young people between the ages of 8 and 24 participated in this study, twenty-five of whom were in out-of-home care at the time of the study. The second study involved twenty-eight young people aged between 16 and 21 years who had experienced out-of-home care but were no longer in the system. This study was part of a broader research project on children and young people's views and experiences of participation (see Bessell, 2011). The methodology that underpinned each study was informed by rights-based and participatory principles (see Bessell, 2009; Bessell, 2013), whereby children and young people were able to engage on their own terms to the greatest extent possible. A range of participatory methods were used, including interviews, group discussions, brainstorming sessions, and visual methods, such as dialogue boxes and problem trees, with children and young people able to choose the methods with which they were most comfortable. Participation in both studies was entirely voluntary, even when adult carers/guardians had provided consent, and children and young people were reassured that they could withdraw from the research at any time if they wished.

The studies discussed here do not claim to be representative of the views or experiences of all children and young people in care. Rather, they aim to make three contributions to understanding the barriers to and opportunities for greater participation among children in out-of-home care. First, the qualitative, in-depth design of the research provides insight into the priorities of children and young people; second, the findings help us to understand the experience of out-of-home care from the perspective of children and young people; and third, the research sought to co-construct knowledge of out-of-home care with children and young people who have direct experience of the system.

The remainder of this chapter draws on the insights provided by the children and young people involved in my studies in an attempt to understand "participation" from the perspective of children and young people in out-of-home care. Two questions are central. First, what did children and young people say about their experiences of participating in decisions made about their lives? Second, how can participation be made real and genuine for children and young people in out-of-home care?

WHAT CHILDREN AND YOUNG PEOPLE SAID ABOUT PARTICIPATION AND NONPARTICIPATION

Echoing the findings of other studies (Mason & Gibson, 2004; McDowall, 2013), my research found that being involved in decision-making was extremely important to children and young people. Significantly, very few children and young people who participated in these studies indicated that they wanted to make all decisions themselves. Rather, they wanted to be *included* in decisions; they wanted their dreams, wishes, hopes, and fears to be listened to, respected, and taken seriously when decisions were being made about their lives. They wanted to talk about options with people they knew and trusted, to seek advice, and to share ideas. Children and young people described feeling valued when someone listened, took their concerns seriously, and provided real options. When children and young people discussed situations in which their views, priorities, and concerns had been taken seriously, the intrinsic value of participation to their sense of self was clearly evident. Matt (aged 16) summed up the views of most children and young people who participated in the research:

> You should have a say, it's your life. And when someone listens to you and says "yeah, that's important," you feel like you're worth something. When they just ignore you and don't care what you think then you just feel like shit.

The children and young people who participated in my research said very clearly that there are serious problems in the "participation process" for children and young people. Children described complete "nonparticipation" when they entered care, and for the majority nonparticipation continued to shape their out-of-home care experiences.

CHILDREN AND YOUNG PEOPLE'S REFLECTIONS ON ENTERING CARE

Several children and young people reflected on their experience of entering out-of-home care. A crucial aspect of the care and protection system in Australia, as elsewhere around the world, is that children and young people very rarely have any control over whether they are taken into care or over where they are placed. While removal from birth parents may be a process that unfolds over time, the moment of removal is often triggered by one incident and is generally surrounded by trauma. Folman (1998, p. 11) provides a succinct and powerful description:

> The events of the day of placement constitute a crisis for children because everything in their lives changes and the children are overwhelmed with feelings of abandonment, rejection, worthlessness, guilt, and helplessness. Moreover, the children's old ways of perceiving the world and of coping with challenges no longer work.

The fact and the nature of the removal of children from birth parents mean that children's entry into the care system is characterized by exclusion from what is likely to have been the most significant decision made about their lives. As Delfabbro, Barber, and Bentham (2002, p. 531) clearly articulate, the impact of being taken into care continues to shape children's lives:

> Prolonged abuse, disillusionment, and frustration in not being able to see siblings or parents, are only some of the factors contributing to ongoing feelings of unhappiness in foster children, which can persist even in the most stable placements. For children, it is not necessarily the qualities of individual placements, but the very fact that one is in care, separated from one's family, perhaps in a community area in which they do not want to live.

The views and experiences of the young people in my studies suggest that to the factors identified by Delfabbro, Barber, and Bentham we should add the disillusionment and frustration of having no say and no control over one's life. Children and young people's lack of control was particularly acute when they were initially taken into care. Brady (aged 15) explained his experience:

> I was thirteen when I went into care. I was left in a room alone and not told what was happening. I was left alone in the room for five or six hours. I didn't know what was going to happen—it was scary.

Brady's experience of not knowing what was happening and being intensely afraid was echoed by other young people who participated in my study. Jo (aged 15) described her experience in very similar terms:

> My little brother and I were taken from home, it was the middle of the night, you know, and there was yelling and screaming. We didn't know what was going on. We were taken away and then left in a room. It was like hours, and we didn't know what was going on, or when we'd go home, or where mum was. My brother was like crying and I was trying to calm him down, but you know I was really scared.

Neither Brady nor Jo was sure precisely where he or she was while alone, or which agencies or government departments were involved. This uncertainty itself highlights the confusion and lack of control children feel when taken into care. It is important to note that it is not possible to verify whether the children were actually left alone for several hours. However, the veracity of those claims is not particularly important; what is important in the context of this chapter is that they *felt* that they had been abandoned at a time in their lives when they most needed support. Children and young people described their fear and sense of helplessness being exacerbated by the absence of information provided to them as they entered care. It is also important to note that all states and territories have clear processes designed to support and safeguard children as they enter care. In some cases, children and young people's descriptions of their experience suggested that workers had done their best to provide explanation and support in a situation of chaos and crisis. Some children and young people said they had been provided with written material as they entered care. From a child's standpoint, however, adherence to processes and provision of carefully worded information helped little as they dealt with the pain, fear, and confusion of their lives being turned upside down. When children and young people spoke of their entry into care, a strong and highly significant theme emerged: There were many people involved in the first traumatic hours and days, but not one consistent person to provide ongoing support, information, and reassurance. For the most part, children and young people described an overwhelming sense of being entirely alone.

BEING "A KID IN CARE"

"Who doesn't listen when you're a kid in care? Everybody!" (Sam, aged 16)

Sam articulated succinctly the views of many children and young people who participated in my research when he explained the failure of adults to listen to children in out-of-home care. While entry to care is characterized by nonparticipation, the majority of children and young people involved in my studies said that they rarely felt involved in, or even informed about, decisions made about their lives while in care. Disturbingly, a significant minority of the young people participating in my study had felt on at least one occasion that their only "choice" was to run away or find a means of exiting the system.

> I had to run away before anyone would listen to me. Then I just got a letter saying I was grounded for two weeks. But no-one really listened or did anything. Everyone in care is running away—there is nothing else you can do. (Jen, aged 15)
>
> When you are a kid in care, the only choice you have is homelessness. (Matt, aged 16)

More than half the children and young people who participated in my research said they usually felt they had no one to turn to when things went wrong. In an especially disturbing comment, a young woman in her early twenties, when reflecting on who she had turned to in difficult times while in out-of-home care, said, "The Rape Crisis Centre helped me."

Significantly, several children and young people indicated that they had been in what they described as good foster care placements at times, where their experience had been largely positive. Even in such situations, however, there was a general feeling that ultimately they were alone. As Emma (aged 19) explained:

> I had mainly positive experiences, not all but mostly. I was with one family for a long time, and they are like my family. But I always knew that if things went wrong, there was nowhere to turn.

Fiona (aged 17) described feeling similarly alone:

> I'm in a good placement now, you know they are like, you know like my family. But I always know that if anything goes wrong, I'm on my own. No one is going to listen [referring to the government department and nongovernmental agency responsible for placement], and there is no one to turn to or complain to. You know, you're on your own.

A common theme in each of my studies was the important role played by children's caseworkers and people within the out-of-home care bureaucracy. Children and young people were acutely aware of the power these people held over their lives. A significant number of children and young people who participated in my studies felt that their caseworker(s) did not know them well and were often unresponsive to their wishes and concerns. And yet, children and young people also described the myriad ways in which the decisions of their caseworkers shaped their lives. Most children and young people were very conscious that their relationship with their caseworker played out within a system, which they often struggled to make sense of. Two factors were particularly important in explaining why many children and young people felt disconnected from their caseworkers and powerless within the system. First, regular changes of caseworkers meant that the opportunity to develop a meaningful relationship with a caseworker was often limited. As Katie (aged 14) put it:

> You know, they [caseworkers] change a lot. Sometimes I don't even know the old one's gone 'til the new one turns up. And then you have to start all over again, you know, this is what happened, this is what I do. I just get sick of it, you know, saying the same stuff again and again. Sometimes I just can't be bothered. They ask questions and I just say "dunno."

Katie, like other children and young people involved in my studies, described adopting a form of passive resistance toward individual workers and toward the out-of-home care system. Her refusal to engage seemed to her to be her only viable means of responding to a situation beyond her control. Frustrated by the turnover of caseworkers and the expectation that she would continually have to retell her story to strangers, Katie purposefully distanced herself from her caseworkers. As a result many decisions were made about her life with no or little input from her.

The second issue that young people raised was the ways in which "the system" governed their lives. Some children and young people expressed great frustration because their caseworkers and foster carers had to seek approval for a range of activities and decisions. For example, children and young people explained they were not allowed to go to friends' houses for sleepovers or attend school excursions unless there was formal approval from the department or agency managing their care. Here, a decision about everyday life was subject to bureaucratic processes, over which children had no control and very little influence. Similarly, young people described having to engage with an often lengthy bureaucratic process to gain approval for day-to-day items such as clothes. Gem (aged 16) described her experience as follows:

> You have to ask for clothing vouchers and the workers can't give them straightaway. The big boss has to sign off. I have to wait three weeks for a $50 clothing voucher—and I sometimes really need it.

The bureaucracy surrounding day-to-day decisions, such as sleeping over at a friend's house or buying a T-shirt, was a source of extreme aggravation for many children and young people in an immediate sense. More broadly, the result was a sense of disempowerment, whereby children and young people were well aware of their position as a very small part of a very large and bureaucratic system. The environment created is characterized by exclusion, nonparticipation, and powerlessness. Such an environment is hardly conducive to children and young people's meaningful participation in decisions about their lives.

Despite the rhetoric of participation, the majority of children and young people described being excluded from important decisions. All described at least one situation whereby an important decision was made without their involvement or, in some cases, knowledge. Several children and young people described placements coming to an abrupt and unanticipated end. Jess described having been in a placement that she knew was short term, but not being told exactly when she would move to a new placement. Instead, her caseworker arrived unexpectedly to take her to her "new family." Jess (aged 15) said she had no time to prepare, or to let her friends know she would be moving; moreover, she had no input into her new placement.

> They shoved me with a family [on the other side of the city]. I'd never been there before and I didn't know anyone there. I phoned my friends and I was just crying and crying . . . I didn't want to be there, away from everyone and everything I knew. The

family had younger kids—around 10 and 12. I had no say in it at all. I said, "I don't want to go there" and Family Services said "You have to." I didn't even meet them [the family] before, I was just dropped at the door.

Jess' situation illustrates how exclusion from what may appear to be a single decision (in her case, a new placement) prevented her from having a say on a range of important issues: where she lived, with whom she lived, the option to say no, the opportunity to meet the family with whom she would live, the choice of staying close to her friends, and the option of continuing at her current school.

The out-of-home care system in Australia is under severe pressure. As discussed earlier, the number of children and young people in out-of-home care has increased markedly since the mid-1990s, with the number doubling between 1997 and 2006 (Bromfield & Osborn, 2007). The number of available foster carers has not kept pace with the number of children in the out-of-home care system. While an increasing proportion of children are placed in kinship care, there remains a serious shortage of foster care placements. In such a situation, the possibility of children and young people being involved in decisions about their care placement is negligible. Given the limited placement options for most children, it is not surprising that the National Standards on Out-of-Home Care and state-based Charters of Rights are silent on children's involvement in decisions about where they live. Yet, for children and young people, this is likely to be the most significant decision made about their lives—and a decision that shapes many other aspects of life, as Jess' case indicates. Interestingly, the children and young people who participated in my research did not argue that they should be able to choose their foster carers, although full participation might arguably require this. Most did, however, suggest improvements on current practice. Three changes were repeatedly raised. First, most (although not all) children and young people wanted to be placed with their brothers and sisters. The decision of whether siblings should stay together was one in which all children and young people wanted to be involved. Second, children and young people wanted the opportunity to meet and get to know their foster carers before being placed with them for any significant period of time. As Jess said:

It would be good to just meet them, and you know, get to know them a bit. Maybe have a coffee or dinner, or go to a movie, anything really, just talk . . . so you feel you know them a bit . . .

Third, children and young people wanted to be placed with people with whom they were likely to have some connection or common interest. Sophie (aged 13) described feeling very uncomfortable when placed with a religious family who regularly attended church and practiced their religion in an everyday manner. Sophie understood that religion was very important to the family, but she said her own beliefs were different. She explained the breakdown of that placement as resulting from irreconcilable beliefs. In contrast, Lee (aged 12) explained a good placement, where his connection with his foster family arose from a shared love of football. Lee and his foster mother both explained that their common interest was a matter of luck rather than design. Lee said no one had asked him very much about his interests before his current placement. He explained he knew his caseworkers were very busy and went on to say

> The workers don't usually talk to us [Lee and his younger brother]. They might just say "how are you" or "how's school?" but they don't talk or ask more … and I don't say much. I don't really know them much.

MAKING PARTICIPATION REAL FOR CHILDREN AND YOUNG PEOPLE IN OUT-OF-HOME CARE

There remains, as Badham pointed out in the context of the United Kingdom a decade ago, a "gap between the high tide of the rhetoric of participation and the low tide of effective delivery of improved services for those most socially excluded" (2004, p. 153). What, then, might help to bridge this gap and make participation real and meaningful for children in out-of-home care? Throughout my research, children and young people repeatedly identified strong and supportive relationships as making a positive difference in their lives. Moreover, those who described having strong, supportive relationships with caseworkers and/or carers were more likely to describe being able to participate in decision-making. The message was clear and simple: relationships matter.

Several children and young people spoke of individual caseworkers in very positive terms and identified ways in which these people had supported them, listened to them, and acted on their behalf. In each of these cases, children and young people spoke of some form of positive relationship. Importantly, they consistently said that "good workers" knew them and cared about them. In several cases, children and young people described some caseworkers as supportive and inclusive even when decisions were made that they did not like or did not agree with. In most cases, they said that good caseworkers, with whom they had positive relationships, included them in conversations about what might happen. These conversations were not one-off meetings, held in formal settings. Rather, conversations—sharing thoughts, feelings, and concerns—occurred over time and often in informal settings. Several children and young people described sharing issues with good caseworkers in a coffee shop or in the park. In several cases, the same children and young people described refusing to share their concerns or preferences at case review meetings, which were often dominated by adults and held in formal and unfamiliar environments. Several key words emerged as important when children and young people described situations in which they had felt included in decisions: "relationships," "conversations," "support," "know me," and "care about me." Fiona (aged 16), for example, described one highly supportive caseworker:

> Kay, well, she's special. She talks to me and she remembers my birthday. Even now she's not my worker anymore she remembers! Look, here's a text . . . And I could tell her stuff and she'd listen.

Fiona felt strongly that Kay cared about her as a person, not only as a case. As a result, Fiona described being able to tell Kay how she was feeling and also said she knew Kay would listen and would always take her concerns and wishes seriously. Similarly, Jen (aged 15) said

> I had one great caseworker. She took me shopping, we went for coffee. We did the things that mums and daughters do—you need to do that. She came to visit me. We talked, we talked lots. You know, she really cared.

Jen said not only that this caseworker cared, but also that she knew her. As a result, when decisions were made, Jen felt her caseworker had a clear idea of what she wanted. Unlike other situations she had experienced, Jen explained that this caseworker never "put her on the spot" and asked for an instant decision. Both Fiona and Jen said they felt involved in decisions because they could talk the issues through with these caseworkers. Importantly, issues were not discussed in the context of a formal meeting at a single point in time, but over time in a range of contexts. Both Jen and Fiona described the loss they felt when their caseworker moved on—and neither was able to re-establish an equally supportive relationship with future caseworkers.

Of the children and young people who participated in my studies, Jen and Fiona spoke most positively about their relationship with a particular caseworker. Other children also spoke of the importance of having a strong and supportive relationship with their caseworker, and many explained the difficulty of forming such a relationship within what is often a very bureaucratic process. Three issues were particularly significant, from the perspective of children and young people, in obstructing the development of positive relationships. The first issue relates to adult attitudes and the nature of child–adult relationships. Children and young people described many of the caseworkers involved in the out-of-home care system as more likely to discuss both everyday matters and life-changing decisions with adults (often their foster carers) rather than with them. The majority of children and young people said that most caseworkers usually asked them how school was going, but little else. Sarah (aged 13) described an experience that she found more marginalizing:

> I had one worker who always called me by another name. My foster mum would say, "her name is Sarah," and she'd say "oh sorry" and then the next time call me the wrong name.

Sarah explained that this particular caseworker rarely spoke to her beyond saying hello, but instead discussed her behavior and progress with her foster mother.

The second obstacle identified by children and young people is the formalized and bureaucratic nature of their relationship with most caseworkers. While some caseworkers, such as those Jen and Fiona described, were clearly able to create spaces for genuine and supportive relationships, many children felt their caseworkers engaged with them only because they were required to as part of their job. Many children described a lack of trust, not so much in individuals but in the system itself.

The third issue raised by children and young people as an obstacle to the development of positive relationships was the amount of time available to caseworkers. Most children said that in general their caseworkers seemed to have very little time to get to know them or to "hang out" with them. Several children and young people attributed the problem to caseworkers having too many children with whom to deal. For example, Amy (aged 15) argued as follows:

> There need to be more workers. It is stupid to have too many kids—two or three kids per worker should be it. It needs to be so Family Services workers can be there for the child they are dealing with. The Family Services worker needs to be there for that certain kid.

Amy argued that unless caseworkers looked after only a small number of children, it was impossible for children and caseworkers to get to know one another and for a child to feel both supported and listened to. The importance of a caseworker "being there" for an individual child was raised by children and young people repeatedly, suggesting a gap between what children want from the system and what is provided under current arrangements in most (perhaps all) jurisdictions in Australia.

The aim of this chapter is not to criticize social workers, caseworkers, or others employed in the out-of-home care system. Rather, it is to raise the issues children and young people identified as problematic—and as restricting their ability or preparedness to participate in decisions made about their lives. At the heart of the problem—from the standpoint of children and young people—is the fact their engagement with caseworkers and their participation in decisions occurs within a system that is ill equipped to foster the relationships that were identified as so important by children and young people. This mismatch between the system and children and young people's priorities was clearly articulated by Cass (aged 14):

> Family Services doesn't really act as your parent—even though they act as your parental guardian. They should be there 24/7. Who are you meant to talk to when your caseworker goes on holidays? It's not like your parent just leaves you for a day off or a holiday. Why do they say they are your parental guardian when they are not?

For Cass, the concept of "guardianship" or "parental responsibility" was not a legal construct; it was based on her understanding of human relationships. She described feeling excluded by a system in which she was primarily positioned not as a person but as a case. The sense of exclusion described by Cass made it difficult for her to take part in decision-making. Rather than feeling able to reveal and talk through her concerns, problems, and preferences to trusted people, Cass described keeping quiet about personal issues. Her reluctance to share her experiences or views was heightened in meetings that she described as formal and involving "a bunch of people" she barely knew. In Australia as elsewhere, the participation of children in out-of-home care is often translated in practice as their taking part in or being present at meetings—either case review meetings involving several people or one-on-one meetings with caseworkers. Like Cass, many of the children and young people involved in my studies described being present at case meetings but feeling excluded from the discussions and often bewildered by the process. Many described their experiences of having adults talk about them, but feeling unable to participate themselves. Many described feeling uncomfortable and often confronted when asked for their views at meetings. Like Cass, many described remaining silent at such meetings.

Children and young people were generally critical of formal meetings. In contrast, the majority emphasized the importance of relationships in which they are respected, listened to, involved in discussions, able to negotiate, and able to disagree. Several children and young people described positively situations in which their views were not ultimately acted upon. What was important in these situations was that their views were not simply dismissed or ignored, but that they were listened to, taken seriously, and part of the ultimate decision. In essence, children and young people were describing relationships within which respect and inclusive decision-making are everyday practice. For them, it is supportive, inclusive relationships that form the basis for participation, not the periodic, formal meetings or reviews that represent efforts to operationalize policy commitments to children and young people's right to participate.

UNDERSTANDING NONPARTICIPATION

The empirical studies discussed in this chapter highlight the chasm between the rhetoric of participation that has been adopted within child protection and out-of-home care policy in Australia and the experiences of at least some children and young people. How can we understand this gap? Why is it that the children and young people who participated in these studies described experiencing exclusion and nonparticipation when policies entitle them to the right to participate? Much can be said about the gap between vision and reality in issues of social policy, social justice, and human rights generally. In this case, however, understanding the gap between stated vision and lived reality must begin with an interrogation of generational relations and the social status of children generally and of those in out-of-home care in particular. There exists a significant body of literature focusing on models of participation and the processes that might best foster children's genuine involvement in decision-making (Hart, 1997; Lansdowne, 2001; Shier, 2001). What is lacking is a deeper understanding of the relational context, both interpersonal and intergenerational, within which participation occurs or does not occur. Indeed, it was relationships that the children and young people who participated in my studies consistently identified as being of greatest importance.

"Children," as an analytic and social category, have long been the focus of research. Since the 1980s, research has increasingly focused on children as social actors. There is now a well-developed and ever-growing body of literature that identifies children as research subjects, participants, or partners. As a result, knowledge of children's lives is perhaps greater now than at any other point in history. "Childhood," as an analytic and social category, has also received attention, but arguably less than children. The distinction between "children" and "childhood" as the focus of analytic attention is important in understanding why children and young people in out-of-home care feel so little control over decisions made about their lives despite the rhetoric of participation.

In the spirit of qualitative research that places the standpoint of participants at the center, I have in this chapter—so far—sought to ensure children and young people's perspectives, priorities, and experiences dominate. Empirical studies of this kind give us crucial insights into children's lives and to the barriers to genuine participation that are regularly encountered, but they do not sufficiently explain the structural contexts that create such barriers. Rather, as Alanen (2005, p. 288) reminds us, we need to "link empirical manifestations on the level of children's childhoods with their macro-level contexts, social structures and mechanisms which 'determine' those manifestations." If we are to understand nonparticipation, and foster genuine participation, we need deeper conceptual insights not only into the interpersonal relations that are so important to children but also into the intergenerational relations within which they play out. I now turn to consideration of childhood as a social category crucial to understanding the nonparticipation children and young people described.

Qvortrup (1994) has argued that childhood and adulthood must be understood in a relational sense, whereby intergenerational relations occur within a structured and stratified social system. From this perspective childhood is not only, or primarily, a phase of life through which human beings transition to reach adulthood, but a social category that bestows social status. The concept of intergenerational relations has been further developed by Alanen (2005, p. 287), who argues that "childhood is an essentially generationally defined social condition." For Alanen (2009, p. 162), youth is the defining marker of children's social status: "children's lives and experiences are, in addition to being gendered, classed, raced, and so on, also—and first of all—generationed." For Alanen, children's experiences of their worlds is shaped by their social status as children; however, she emphasizes that not all that is known or observed about children's lives and experiences can or should be attributed to their "childness."

The experiences of Lee and Katie, discussed earlier, serve to illustrate Alanen's point. Both Lee and Katie described having little communication or interaction with their caseworkers. Lee described being "quiet" when his caseworker was around, while Katie described responding with "dunno" when new caseworkers asked her questions that she preferred not to answer. Both Lee and Katie had little power within their situations; indeed, the only power they could exercise was to withdraw or refuse to answer questions. Lee and Katie may have appeared to many of their caseworkers, and to other adults in their lives, to be unresponsive or unable to communicate effectively—to be essentially "childish." Yet, for Lee and Katie, withdrawal and unresponsiveness resulted not from their childishness but from their social status and their efforts to maintain a small degree of control over their lives in a situation controlled almost entirely by the adults around them.

For children in out-of-home care, intergenerational relations are played out in multiple ways. Here, I briefly consider three aspects of intergenerational relations that shape participation and nonparticipation for children in out-of-home care. First, the macro-social context, within which the out-of-home care system is situated, is shaped by intergenerational relations whereby adults are able to determine the conditions under which children's participation in decision-making occurs. Whether the social status of "child" is the most significant marker of identity for all children, as Alanen suggests, is open to debate. In some social and cultural contexts, ethnicity, religion, class, or gender may be as significant, or more significant, than youth. Yet, youth intersects with all other social categorizations and is thus essential to social analysis. In understanding barriers to children's participation, generation is a crucial analytic concept. Despite the influence of the CRC, the decision of who participates and how participation occurs remains the preserve of adults. Wyness (2013, p. 342) argues that Article 12 of the CRC "gives adults, professionals and organisations a framework within which they can closely monitor and structure children's participation." Wyness' point is well made, and while it is relevant across Australian society, it is especially relevant in the context of out-of-home care. In out-of-home care, the forms that participation will take are designed and implemented by adults, ostensibly for the benefit of children, and are always subject to adult regulation. This is particularly so in a context where children's participation has been adopted as a normative value at precisely the same time as the regulation of out-of-home care has become more "formal, detailed and rigorous" (Tilbury, 2007, discussed earlier in this chapter). Moreover, in policies providing for the participation of children and young people in out-of-home care in decisions made about their lives, the "right" to participate is qualified by the child's capacity. As Wyness notes, the assessment of capacity—like decisions about the nature of participation—is the preserve of adults.

Second, for children in out-of-home care, intergenerational relations are over-laid with their economic and social status. Generally, children in out-of-home care are from economically disadvantaged and socially marginalized backgrounds. Socioeconomic status combines not only with youth but also with the categories of "vulnerable child" and "disadvantaged child" to further subordinate children within intergenerational relations. Adult professionals' assessments of children's capacity to participate are often heavily influenced by assumptions about "vulner-ability" and "disadvantage," which are generally seen as limiting factors. While Alanen's argument that children's lives are first and foremost "generationed" is of fundamental importance, we must also pay heed to other characteristics that are ascribed to children in out-of-home care, for these intersect powerfully with youth to determine the intergenerational hierarchies and relations within which participation (or nonparticipation) plays out.

Third, the out-of-home care system is characterized by the binary position-ings of "professional workers" and "developing (or incompetent) children" or "adult protectors" and "vulnerable children." While the rhetoric of participation has infiltrated policy, protection remains the dominant discourse and often plays out as protecting children and young people from information about their lives. While the participatory turn in policy may partially disrupt generational hier-archies and dominant attitudes, it is unlikely to dislodge them (see Tregeagle & Mason, 2008). Thus, to move the participation agenda forward, we need greater analysis of intergenerational relations, both at the societal level and within out-of-home care specifically, to understand the deeply entrenched structural and atti-tudinal barriers to genuine participation.

The importance of intergenerational relations, at the sociostructural level, is however only one dimension of the insights that emerge from children and young people's accounts. Also important are the human relationships that structure children's day-to-day lives. If we are to learn anything from the empirical studies discussed here, it is that children and young people want respectful, supportive, and—crucially—ongoing relationships with the adults in their lives, including adult professionals. Without such relationships, participation is likely to remain little more than window dressing in policy documents. Without such relation-ships, efforts to promote participation are likely to remain "tick-a-box" exercises that fail to genuinely engage with children and young people. If we are to gain only one insight from the empirical studies discussed here, it must be the impor-tance of human relationships. Feeling a connection to and trust in the adults who hold ultimate decision-making power over their lives is crucial if children and young people in care are to feel respected and valued. It is on this foundation of strong personal relations that genuine participation can be built.

Yet, while understanding the importance of interpersonal relations is essen-tial, it is not sufficient. Day-to-day human relationships and intergenerational relations, as structuring forces in society, are intrinsically connected. In fostering interpersonal relations, we must not neglect intergenerational relations and their role in structuring the systems and processes of out-of-home care. As Jen and Fiona's experiences demonstrate, caring, supportive individuals make a positive difference in the lives of children and young people in care. Such individuals can foster the kinds of relationships that are essential to children and young people's participation in decision-making. Yet, we must remember that these individual relationships take place within a broader context of intergenerational relations and within a bureaucratic system. As several children and young people pointed out, even when they had a strong, supportive relationship with a caseworker or carers, they knew—ultimately—that they were at the mercy of a bureaucratic system.

BRINGING RELATIONSHIPS TO THE FOREGROUND

"Participation" has been accepted as a normative principle within policies and standards around out-of-home care in Australia. Significantly, there have been concerted efforts to build participation into systems and processes, as exemplified by Charters of Rights and the National Standards. The studies that underpin this chapter indicate that there is a considerable distance to travel before the rhetoric of policy becomes the reality of children's and young people's lives.

Each of the qualitative studies discussed here was relatively small, with thirty-six children and young people participating in the first and twenty-eight in the second. As such, they do not claim to be representative of all children and young people in out-of-home care. Like many small-scale, qualitative studies, however, they do provide considerable insight into children's lives, experiences, and priorities. A clear finding emerged: If the participation agenda for children and young people in out-of-home care is to be advanced, relationships must be given far greater analytic and practical importance. The genuine participation of children is dependent on many factors. The studies discussed here suggest that of these, the most important may well be inclusive, respectful relationships. Building such relationships is extremely difficult in a system characterized by bureaucratic processes and rigorous, formal regulation. It is further complicated by the nature of intergenerational relations, as a structuring force within society more broadly. Prioritizing inclusive, respectful relationships—both interpersonal and intergenerational—is one crucial means of advancing genuine participation. The challenge this finding presents is, however, substantial. It implies challenging the assumptions and attitudes on which age-based social hierarchies are based and reconceptualizing the very nature of existing systems, whereby children and their relationships with adults—not processes and upward accountability—are at the center.

REFERENCES

AIHW (Australian Institute of Health and Welfare) (2011). *Child Protection Australian 2009–2010*. Canberra: Australian Institute of Health and Welfare.

AIHW (Australian Institute of Health and Welfare) (2013). *Child Protection Australian 2011–2012*. Canberra: Australian Institute of Health and Welfare.

Alanen, L. (2005). Women's Studies/Childhood Studies: Parallels, Links and Perspectives. In J. Mason & T. Fattore (Eds.), *Children taken seriously*. London: Jessica Kingsley Publishers.

Alanen, L. (2009). Generational order. In J. Qvortrup, W. A. Corsaro, and M. Honig (Eds.), *Handbook in Childhood Studies*. Houndsmill, Basingstoke: Palgrave Macmillan.

Australian Law Reform Commission and Human Rights and Equal Opportunity Commission (1997). *Seen and Heard: Priority for children in the legal process*, Canberra: Australian Government Publishing Service.

Badham, B. (2004). Participation—for a change: Disabled young people lead the way. *Children & Society*, 18(2), 143–154.

Bessell, S. (2009). Research with children: thinking about method and methodology. In Sue Dockett (ed.), *Involving children in research*. Sydney: ARACY and the NSW Commission for Children.

Bessell, S. (2010). Do rights make a difference? The evolution of policy for children in out-of-home care in Australia. In A. Nevile (Ed.), *Human rights and social policy*. Edward Elgar, Cheltenham, UK.

Bessell, S. (2011). Participation in decision making in out-of-home care in Australia: What do young people say? *Children and Youth Services Review*, 33(4), 496–501.

Bessell, S. (2013). Child-centred research workshops: a model for participatory, rights-based engagement with children. *Developing Practice*, 37, 11–20.

Bromfield, L., Higgins, D., Osborn, A., Panozzo, S., & Richardson, N. (2005). *Out-of-home care in Australia: messages from research*. A report to the Community Services Ministers Advisory Council commissioned by the Australian Government.

Bromfield, L., & Osborn, A. (2007). Getting the big picture: A synopsis and critique of Australian out-of-home care research, *Child Abuse Prevention Issues*, 26. Available at http://www.aifs.gov.au/nch/pubs/issues/issues26/issues26.html#introduction

Delfabbro, P., Fernandez, E., McCormick, J., & Kettler, L. (2013). Reunification in a complete entry cohort: A longitudinal study of children entering out-of-home care in Tasmania, Australia. *Children and Youth Services Review*, 35(9), 1592–1600.

Delfabbro, P. H., Barber, J. G., & Bentham, Y. (2002). Children's satisfaction with out-of-home care in South Australia. *Journal of Adolescence*, 25(5), 523–533.

FaHCSIA (Department of Families, Housing, Community Services and Indigenous affairs together with the national Framework Implementation Working Group) (2010). National Standards for Out-of-Home Care consultation paper. Available at http://www.dss.gov.au/sites/default/files/documents/facs_37724_out_home_care.pdf

FaHCSIA (Department of Families, Housing, Community Services and Indigenous Affairs together with the National Framework Implementation Working Group) (2011). An outline of National Standards for Out-of-Home Care: A priority project under the National Framework for Protecting Australia's Children 2009–2020. Available at http://www.dss.gov.au/sites/default/files/documents/pac_national_standard.pdf

Folman, R. (1998). I was token. *Adoption Quarterly*, 2(2), 7–35.

Forde, L. (1999). *Commissions of Inquiry Order (No. 1) 1998*. Brisbane: Government of Queensland.

Gilbertson, R., & Barber, J. G. (2002). Obstacles to involving children and young people in foster care research. *Child and Family Social Work, 7*(4), 253–258.

Hart, R. (1997). *Children's participation: the theory and practice of involving young citizens in community development and environmental care*. London: Earthscan and UNICEF.

Kiraly, M., & Humphreys, C. (2013). Perspectives From young people about family contact in kinship care: "don't push us—listen more." *Australian Social Work, 66*(3), 314–327.

Lansdown, G. (2001). *Promoting Children's Participation in Democratic Decision-Making*. Florence: UNICEF Innocenti Research Centre.

Mason, J., Urquhart, R., & Bolzan, N. (2003). Defining children's needs in out-of-home care: Methods and challenges of a collaborative research project. *Children Australia, 28*(2), 32–37.

Mason, J., & Gibson, C. (2004). *The needs of children in care: A report on a research project: Developing a model of out-of-home care to meet the needs of individual children, through participatory research which includes children*. Sydney: Burnside Uniting Care.

McDowall, J. (2013). *Experiencing out-of-home care in Australia: The views of children and young people* (CREATE Report Card 2013). Sydney: CREATE Foundation.

Mendes, P., Johnson, G., & Moslehuddin, B (2011). Effectively preparing young people to transition from out-of-home care: An examination of three recent Australian studies. *Family Matters, 89*, 61–70.

Natalier, K., & Johnson, G. (2012). Housing Pathways of Young People Who Have Left Out-of-Home State Care. *Housing, Theory and Society, 29*(1), 75–91.

Qvortrup, J. (1994). Introduction. In J. Qvortrup, M. Bardy, G. Sgritta, and H. Wintersberger (Eds.), *Childhood Matters: Social Theory, Practice and Politics*. Public Policy and Social Welfare 14. Aldershot, UK: Avebury.

Shier, H. (2001). Pathways to participation: openings, opportunities and obligations. *Children & Society, 15*(2), 107–117.

Tilbury, C. (2007). The regulation of out-of-home care. *British Journal of Social Work, 37*, 209–224.

Tregeagle, S., & Hamil, R. (2011). Can stability in out-of-home care be improved? An analysis of unplanned and planned placement changes in foster care. *Children Australia, 36*(3), 74–80.

Tregeagle, S., & Mason, J. (2008). Service user experience of participation in child welfare case management. *Child and Family Social Work, 13*, 391–401.

Wyness, M. (2013). Global standards and deficit childhoods: the contested meaning of children's participation. *Children's Geographies, 11*(3), 340–353.

CHAPTER 9

Child and Family Team Meetings

The Need for Youth Participation in Educational Success

JODI HALL, JOAN PENNELL, AND R. V. RIKARD[1]

CHILD AND FAMILY TEAM MEETINGS AND RESTORATIVE JUSTICE FOR FOSTER YOUTH

Globally, restorative justice proponents are urging far greater inclusion in decision-making of children and adults who have suffered trauma and separation. In child welfare, emergency placements of children usually take place without the prior consent of the parents or caregivers, making it all the more crucial to engage family members in restorative processes after the fact. Even when the placement is voluntary and collaboratively decided, the removal of children from their homes has a profound impact on family members of all ages.

The participation of child and adult family members is viewed as a human right and as a means of respecting diverse cultures, building trust, supporting healing, and cultivating peaceful relationships (Zinsstag & Vanfraechem,

1. This research was made possible by Grant Number 90CO1075/01 from the U.S. Department of Health & Human Services, Administration for Children and Families, Children's Bureau though the Child Welfare–Education System Collaborations to Increase Education Stability. Its contents are solely the responsibility of the authors and do not necessarily represent the official views of the U.S. Department of Health and Human Services. We wish to acknowledge the contributions of the following individuals: Kara Allen-Eckard, Karen Bullock, Sarah Guill, Irwin Kelley, Denis Pelletier, Claudia Phillips, Heather Skeens, Al Spain, Chaney Stokes, Jasmin Volkel, and Barbara Williams-Gray. For further information, please contact Dr. Jodi Hall, Department of Social Work, North Carolina State University, C.B. 7639, Raleigh, NC 27695-7639, jkhall@ncsu.edu.

2013). The paradigm shift to attend to the rights of children to participate in decision-making was affirmed by the United Nations Convention on the Rights of the Child. A restorative justice framework shapes the context in which child welfare systems seek to engage young people as active participants to achieve collaborative planning and successful outcomes. Although not usually referencing restorative justice, child welfare systems more and more often are mandating family engagement in decision-making, and for good reason. Studies report that involving the family group—that is, the immediate and extended family—in decisions increases the likelihood that children will be reunified with their parents or placed with relatives (Ottolini, 2011; Pennell, Edwards, & Burford, 2010; Wang, Lambert, Johnson, Boudreau, Breidenbach, & Baumann, 2012).

As Sharon Bessell points out in Chapter 8 of this volume, young people in care yearn most of all for close and lasting relationships and want planning processes that strengthen their connections to family and other supports. This means that a stronger emphasis needs to be placed on the importance of including youth and their support persons in planning meetings and decision-making. Youth who participate in planning meetings report greater contact with family and better quality of relationships with family, even for those who cannot return home (Dawson & Yancey, 2006). At these conferences, youth want to be heard and want to exert influence over the plans (Holland & O'Neill, 2006). Youth in out-of-home placement are more comfortable expressing their views when they are accompanied by people whom they trust to lend support (Dalrymple, 2002). The plans better reflect their interests when key service providers, such as school and mental health personnel, are in attendance (Holton & Marsh, 2007; Pennell & Anderson, 2005).

In the United States, family engagement practices in child welfare are called by various names, including family group conferencing, family group decision-making, and family team meetings. North Carolina, a southeastern state, adopted the term "child and family team" (CFT) meetings to refer to a joint planning process of the family, community supports, and child welfare. In keeping with restorative tenets, state policy (NC DHHS, 2009, p. 2) mandates that "at all times, Child and Family Teams shall be a family led, youth guided, and agency supported process." The policy further stipulates regular intervals at which CFT meetings are to be held, whether children live in their homes or are placed in care.

In North Carolina, CFTs were adopted by other systems, including child welfare, to support a unified service approach. The CFT model emerged out of the mental health movement called "system of care" to place children and their families at the center of planning and wrap services around families rather than fitting them into preexisting services (Burns & Goldman, 1999; Stroul & Friedman, 1986). CFT meetings and conferencing share in common restorative principles of partnership but diverge in processes. CFT meetings include professionals throughout the planning process and typically have recurring meetings, while conferencing supports family alone time to make plans, and meetings are less frequent (Burchard & Burchard, 2000).

Drawing on data from one county in North Carolina, this chapter addresses four questions using youth-reported data and data gathered by agency administrators. Did the youth participate in a CFT meeting? Does the youth feel important at his or her CFT meetings? How often are youth present at their CFT meetings? What factors predict youth's attendance at their CFT meetings? The chapter begins by examining why foster youth, in particular, need a greater voice in decision-making to achieve successful launches into adulthood. Gaining a sense of self-efficacy and the necessary supports may help to counteract the all-too-common patterns, in the United States, of foster youth struggling with poverty, homelessness, early parenthood, incarceration, and emotional and behavioral issues later in life (Barth, Duncan, Hodorowicz, Kum, Buchanan, & Macomber, 2010; Dworsky, Dillman, Dion, Coffee-Borden, & Rosenau, 2012; Koball, Dworsky, & Korom-Djakovic, 2011).

FOSTER YOUTH AND DECISION-MAKING

When children are removed from their homes, they are thrust into situations that are often unfamiliar and anxiety-provoking. They have little, if any, input into where they will be placed or where they will attend school. They struggle in an unfamiliar environment to make sense of what is happening to them. These are children who have already experienced abuse, neglect, and/or abandonment. Consequently, foster care alumni suffer from posttraumatic stress disorder at a rate twice that of veterans of the Iraq and Afghanistan wars (Pecora, Kessler, Williams, O'Brien, Downs, English, White, Hiripi, White, Wiggins, & Holmes, 2005). Sheets, Wittenstrom, Fong, James, Tecci, Baumann, & Rodriguez (2009) found that children who participated in family group decision-making were less anxious and that parents and extended family were more satisfied with services than those who did not have a conference. Similarly, a study in North Carolina reported that adhering to system-of-care tenets was associated with increased caregiver satisfaction and decreases in children's behavioral problems (Graves, 2005).

Connolly and Ward (2008) examined child welfare as a justice matter with family group conferences as a restorative practice. This practice, Connolly and Ward found, provides opportunities for youth to gain a sense of control in their lives and perhaps offer action steps that will reduce some of the negative effects of out-of-home placements. Participation in conferencing can permit foster youth to have contact with their family. Youth who have contact with their family during out-of-home placement are less likely to be involved with juvenile justice and more likely to graduate from high school (Charles & Nelson, 2000).

In different countries, conferencing is seen as a culturally responsive process for affirming children's rights to take part in administrative decisions (Rotabi, Pennell, Roby, & Bunkers, 2012). Attention, though, needs to be paid to the experience of diverse cultural groups within agency contexts. For example, McRae and Fusco (2010), in a study of the impact of conferencing specifically on African American children, found that 70 to 90 percent of family participants reported satisfaction with the process. Receipt of a conference, however, increased for African American children if they had African American child welfare workers—yet only 20 percent of these children had an African American social worker. McRae and Fusco (2010), while uncovering information relevant for minority children, did not include feedback from foster youth themselves.

Few studies are mindful of the role that youth can play not only in creating plans but also in identifying agency and interorganizational processes that affect their lives. The foster youth themselves are able to bring attention to agency-specific or interagency barriers. The problems that families in the child welfare system experience co-occur with poverty, mental health or addiction issues, and inadequate support systems (Ehrle, Andrews Scarcella, & Geen, 2004; Hutson, 2003); thus, families with complex needs require services from multiple agencies. All agencies that serve families to address these issues need to work in concert to surmount the barriers.

When an out-of-home placement is called for, a restorative justice model can help in identifying and taking steps to repair the damage, emotional and social, resulting from these often abrupt transitions. Joint deliberations can transform or restore the relationships among the youth, family members, community groups, and any other involved system. Often, though, there are gaps in the flow of information, exchange of information, and service delivery. Fearing privacy concerns, agencies are often reluctant to share information (Andrews, Bess, Jantz, & Russell, 2002) or may lack the structure to do so. As a result, the interests of youth and families are lost and service delivery is disjointed in a system unprepared to manage such complexities. It is particularly difficult to bring youth views into the decision-making process if the agency systems and family systems do not have a process for doing so.

The partnerships that families form with agencies and that agencies form with each other may lack the clarity and cohesiveness necessary to provide services that are client-centered. These fractured partnerships in child welfare are those to which families are loosely connected, often involuntarily, and those in which organizations loosely work together to serve families while being hampered by limited resources and agency policies. The youth and families receiving child welfare services are not included in decision-making unless concerted efforts are made to do so. For children removed from the home, these fractured partnerships make finding solutions even more difficult. Separation from family, community, and culture and a pervasive sense of losing control are at the center of experiences for youth in out-of-home placement. Yet, at the same time, the child welfare system and its collaborative partners are themselves victims of under-funding, political infighting, and budget cuts (Connolly & Ward, 2008). The foster youth quickly become part of a system with many moving parts that do not communicate with each other and especially do not communicate with the child.

Restorative approaches in child welfare offer new ways to view and address issues faced by youth in care and as they transition out of care. The process can empower youth by encouraging them to take an active role in deliberations in a manner that includes them without overloading them to make decisions on their own. The forums can create safe contexts in which youth and their families can express their views and map out action steps and in which agency representatives can come together in support of these plans.

Studies of youth engagement in decision-making are strengthened by looking at the process from different points of view. To understand this process, the study asked foster youth about their experiences in care and with CFT meetings, and the researchers analyzed administrative data on CFT meetings and child placement and removals. Integrating the two sets of information provided a fuller picture of efforts to involve youth in decision-making forums. Because child welfare policy mandated CFT meetings for foster children, North Carolina offered a setting in which to examine implementation of this approach.

STATE AND COUNTY CONTEXT

A North Carolina collaborative with representation from family and youth advocates and different human services, including the North Carolina Division of Social Services, endorsed the following definition of CFTs:

> Family members and their community supports that come together to **create, implement and update** a plan **with** the child, youth/student and family. The plan builds on the strengths of the child, youth and family and addresses their needs, desires and dreams. (emphasis in original, North Carolina Collaborative, 2007, p. 1)

The North Carolina Division of Social Services (NC DHHS, 2009) included this definition in its policy manual and required the use of CFT meetings for children receiving child welfare services both in their homes and in out-of-home placements. In regards to children's participation, the manual stated, "Involving children/youth in the CFT meeting is a critical and complicated issue." However, "it is not a question about whether the children/youth should be involved in the process, but rather how they should be involved in the process" (p. 13). To engage families in making permanent plans for their children in care, the policy specified that the CFT meetings were to be scheduled within 30 days, 60 days, and 90 days of entry into care and then subsequently every 6 months or when there was a change in the family's circumstances or plan.

To support CFT meetings, the North Carolina Division of Social Services funded statewide training by the Center for Family and Community Engagement at North Carolina State University. Some of these trainings focused on strategies for workers' including children and youth in CFT meetings, and more recently a curriculum was developed specifically for foster youth so that they would understand how to make use of CFT meetings. Co-training with a youth partner helped to increase foster youth's comfort at the well-received workshops (Pennell, 2013). Recognizing that CFT meetings were one strategy for increasing foster youth's stability in where they lived and went to school, the Center for Family and Community Engagement reached out to Cumberland County to partner on a federally funded project.

Cumberland County was among the earliest North Carolina counties to adopt CFT meetings, which fit with its vision of wrapping a set of unified services around children and their families. Partnering with Cumberland County also made sense because of its relatively transient population resulting from poverty, homelessness, or military affiliations. The county accounts for a signification percentage of active-duty U.S. military personnel across three branches of the military—the Army (n = 53,231), the Navy/Marine Corps (n = 254,942), and the Air Force (n = 7,900), according to 2009 U.S. Census data. From July 2012 to June 2013, there were 861 children in custody of child welfare: 33 percent were white, 57 percent were African American, and 7 percent were Hispanic (Duncan, Kum, Flair, Stewart, Vaughn, Bauer, & Reese, 2013).

As reported elsewhere (Pennell & Rikard, 2013), the project succeeded in putting into effect its three primary strategies: enhancing the leadership of foster youth, formulating data-driven policies and procedures, and providing training to foster youth, caregivers, university students, and service providers. The study reported in this chapter draws upon the results from the first two strategies.

METHODOLOGY

The study, as noted previously, addressed four research questions. The first two asked, from the youth's perspective, Have you participated in a CFT meeting? and Do you feel important at your CFT meeting? In answering these questions, the study used a three-staged process: (1) consulting with a youth advisory council on the research foci and approach, (2) conducting focus groups on youth's experience of care, and (3) surveying youth about their CFT meetings and needed adult supports and agency resources. This staged approach made it possible to encourage and respect youth leadership in the conduct of the research and to consider the experience of CFT meetings within the wider context of the youth's lives. In addition, the earlier phases served as a platform from which to construct the next steps in the research process.

The second set of research questions asked: How often are youth present at their CFT meetings? What factors predict youth's attendance at their CFT meetings? Answers to these questions was made possible because the Cumberland County Department of Social Services (DSS) during the project period created an automated system and transferred the deidentified data to the Center for Family and Community Engagement for analysis. For the purpose of gathering these data, two administrative files from the DSS automated system were merged to create dyads of files for each youth receiving services. Initially, one file had data on CFT meetings and the other had data on children's different placements in care. The merger of the files made it possible to have two sources of data on the same youth so that the analysis could consider a range of predictors of youth participation in CFT meetings.

The description of the research procedures and the summary of their results are detailed first for the youth perspectives and then for the administrative records. The research protocols were approved by the university's Institutional Review Board for the Protection of Human Subjects in Research. ATLAS.ti, version 6.2, was used to analyze the qualitative data, and SAS, version 9.2, was used to analyze the quantitative data.

YOUTH PERSPECTIVES ON CHILD AND FAMILY TEAM PARTICIPATION

Stage 1: Youth Advisory Council

Project staff, including a foster alumna, worked with the county's LINKS (independent living preparation) coordinator to organize a youth advisory council. This council was established to advise the project, including its research with foster youth. The council met six times over the 17-month project. Members were between 13 and 18 years old and received a gift certificate for their participation on the council. In an iterative process, the councilors were consulted about how to involve youth in the research and what questions to ask them. The results of the data collection were shared with councilors for their ideas on necessary action steps. The recommendations of the youth council were then presented at the cross-agency project advisory council. A foster youth participated in later meetings of the project advisory council.

Stage 2: Youth Focus Groups

Participants and Procedures

The purpose of the youth focus groups was to gather information on the perceived and needed supports available to youth residing primarily in Cumberland

County. The answers were qualitatively analyzed for themes about the participants' experiences in care and their recommendations on how to improve their experience. Three focus groups were held in spring 2012. The fifteen focus group participants (seven female, eight male) ranged in age from 13 to 17 years. The youth were recruited through the LINKS coordinator. Each focus group occurred just before the regular LINKS meeting held in the county Social Services building. This arrangement ensured that social work staff were available to the youth if the need arose. Participation was voluntary; dinner was provided; and youth received a gift card for taking part.

Themes

Among the youth's responses, three themes stood out. The first was that foster youth who often arrived after the start of the academic year were not permitted to join extracurricular activities such as sports. As a result, they did not have this motivation to improve their grades To stay on the teams. One youth explained, "Everybody in here likes sports. Most of the time, sports help keep your grades up." A related frustration was that their social workers were not always on top of matters and did not sign permission forms for activities in a timely manner.

Another concern was that they felt singled out at school and picked on by peers because they were in care. As one youth shared, "Kids think you are some reject kid that no one wants." Riding to school in a van with the agency's name especially made them feel conspicuous. Third, youth experienced so many moves that they felt disconnected from their families. A young mother noted, "My baby doesn't know who my family is anymore because she is little and we have been in [placement name] and out of [placement name]."

In general, the youth felt that they lacked adequate supports and were ill prepared for college or independent living. Speaking at length, one youth pointed out, "I don't know anything about college except what TV tells me. I don't know anything about a bank account . . .. My mom didn't really talk to me about these things. It goes beyond school—I need to know how to set up a bank account and how to get a job." Reflecting on solutions, one youth volunteered, "I wish the school would have a meeting to share with the teachers how it is different for us and so they could support us better." What was learned from the youth focus groups served as the platform from which to construct the youth surveys.

Stage 3: Youth Surveys
Participants and Procedures

The purpose of the youth surveys was to learn from the youth about their experiences of CFT meetings, adult support, and school needs. From October to December 2012, the project administered surveys to foster youth or former foster youth. In total, forty participants completed the survey, thirty-three in an electronic format and, because of computer difficulties at one location, seven in a paper-based format. The respondents ranged in age from 12 to 24.

Data collection occurred in conjunction with meetings held by the Cumberland County LINKS program or by SaySo, a statewide association for youth in substitute care. These venues ensured access to supportive adults if needed, and the statewide association permitted expanding participants beyond one county. The survey respondents received a gift certificate for their participation.

The survey had sixteen items: Thirteen questions were closed-ended (fixed choices) and three open-ended questions provided space for comments. The questions asked about the participants' experience of CFT meetings, the availability of supportive adults, and facilitators of school success.

Findings

Three quarters of the youth (thirty) reported that they were currently in foster care. Somewhat less than half (seventeen) of the youth said that they had signed a voluntary agreement to continue in foster care after they turned 18 years. A supportive adult was involved in thirty-nine of the youth's lives, and thirty youth reported that their social worker paid attention to their school progress. Of those thirty youth, six reported that some attention was being paid to their progress and twenty-four reported that a lot of attention was being paid to their progress. Ten said that their social worker paid no or little attention to their progress.

Three questions specifically referenced CFT meetings. The first asked, "Do you attend Child and Family Team meetings?" Twenty-six (65 percent) said yes and fourteen (35 percent) said no. A second question asked, "Do you feel important at your Child and Family Team meetings?" Twenty-five of the youth (63 percent) said yes; two said no. With one exception, all the youth who attended a CFT meeting said that they felt important at the meeting. A remaining thirteen youth did not respond, all of whom had previously stated that they had not attended a CFT meeting. A third open-ended question asked, "What might help you feel more important at your Child and Family Team meeting?" Four youth responded: Two wanted "more listening," a third wanted "to finally have one [a CFT meeting]," and a fourth noted, "Never had one."

YOUTH PRESENCE AT CHILD AND FAMILY TEAM MEETINGS

Datasets and Analytic Procedures

Data for the analyses came from four administrative databases for children in Cumberland County DSS custody at some point between March and June 2013. The unit of analysis across the four datasets was the CFT meeting. The first, second, and third datasets contained information related to the CFT meeting participants, type of meeting, and family and/or agency concerns. The three datasets also included a unique child identifier created from the first three letters of the child's last name, four-digit year of birth, two-digit day of birth, and two-digit month of birth as well as a sequential numeric identifier for the CFT meeting. The three datasets were merged using the CFT identifier with a total of 1,215 CFT meetings. Because CFT meetings are held across different types of child welfare involvement, this dataset included children receiving services in their family home and in care.

The fourth dataset was restricted to children in care. This set contained information regarding a child's placement in and removal from foster care, the child's demographic information (i.e., age, race/ethnicity, and sex), and the type of foster placement. There were a total of 234 placement and removal records in the fourth dataset. In addition, the placement/removal dataset included the unique child identifier described above. The CFT and placement/removal datasets were merged using the unique child identifier, thus providing a complete dataset for a total of 218 CFT meetings. Thus, of the 234 cases, the records indicated that only sixteen did not have a CFT meeting during the study period but might have had one previously or subsequently. With a description of the dataset, the next section specifies the variables in the analyses.

Dependent Variable

For a CFT meeting, participants received a numeric value ranging from one to nine (i.e., Mother = 1, Father = 2, School = 3, Support = 4 [someone whom the family invites], Service Provider = 5, Guardian *ad litem* Officer = 6, Placement = 7, Relative = 8, and Child = 9). Thus, one CFT meeting might have up to nine entries if all nine types of participants were present. Therefore, the values for the participants were arrayed to create the unique participant combination or composition and nine separate variables containing the participant's numeric value for the specific CFT meeting. The ninth value (9) was recoded into a dichotomous dummy variable indicating child attendance (i.e., Absent = 0, Present = 1).

Independent Variables
Participant Composition

As described directly above, participant composition was the unique numeric value assigned to a CFT participant. The first through eighth values (1–8) were recoded into dichotomous dummy variables indicating (i.e., Absent = 0, Present = 1) *Mother, Father, School, Support, Service Provider, GAL Officer,*

Placement, and *Relative.* In the multivariate analyses (i.e., Tobit regression models), the exclude or comparison participant was the Support personnel.

Child's Demographics

Age was computed as the number of years between the child's year of birth to the present. The child's sex was entered as F or f for Female or M for Male (U for Unknown in one observation). The single Unknown observation was deleted and the F and f entries were recoded into a single Female group. Female and Male children were recoded into a dichotomous dummy (i.e., Female = 1, Male = 0), and male children were the comparison group in the multivariate analyses. Children were initially categorized into eleven racial/ethnic groups; these were collapsed into four groups: whites, Hispanic or Latino, African American, and Other. These four groups were recoded into dichotomous dummy variables and the Other racial/ethnic group was the comparison category.

Type of CFT Meeting

Child welfare classified CFT meetings into three categories according to the stage of work: initial, review, and case closure (i.e., Initial = 1, Review = 2, and Case Closure = 3). The three types were recoded into dichotomous dummy variables and Case Closure meetings were the comparison category in the analyses.

Family/Agency Concerns

Child welfare categorized the CFT meetings by the type of the concern or issue raised at the meeting. Family and/or agency concerns expressed at a CFT meeting included Placement Change/Move, Petition, Parent Concerns, PPAT/Service Agreement Update, Child/Family Services Needs, Parent Noncompliance, Safety Issue, and Other, with each receiving a numeric value ranging from one to eight (i.e., Placement Change/Move = 1, Petition = 2, Parent Concerns = 3, PPAT/Service Agreement Update = 4, Child/Family Services Needs = 5, Parent Noncompliance = 6, Safety Issue = 7, and Other = 8). PPAT stands for permanency planning action team, and these teams have to be convened to consider long-term arrangements for children in care. Sometimes CFT and PPAT meetings are combined. Parent Concerns are identified by the family as a reason for holding a CFT meeting. Safety Issues includes concerns such as domestic violence, volatile emotions among family members, and hostility against workers. The eight family and/or agency concern categories were recoded into dichotomous dummy variables and Other concerns served as the comparison category in the analyses.

Foster Placement Type

Initially, there were eleven types of foster placements for children in Cumberland County Social Services custody. The three types for which CFT meetings were most frequently held were Unlicensed Relative Home, Family Foster Care Home, and Small Group Home (Residential). The remaining eight foster placement types were collapsed into a single Other Type of Placement group. The four types were recoded into dichotomous dummy variables and Other Type of Placement served as the comparison category in the analyses.

Results

Two analytic techniques were employed to answer the research questions on the children's presence at their CFT meetings. First, descriptive statistics were computed for all variables in the analyses. We reiterated that the unit of analysis is the CFT meeting. For example, in Table 9.1, the Type of CFT Meeting includes Initial, Review, and Meeting to Close Case. The mean or average values for each category are the percentage of Initial, Review, and Meetings to Close Case. Second, a series of Tobit regression models estimate the likelihood that a child was present at his or her CFT meeting. Tobit regression, rather than logistic regression, is the appropriate estimation technique given that the observations on the dependent variable are censored or limited but not the data on the predictor (independent) variables. In general, logistic regression, as opposed to Tobit regression, is applied as the estimation technique when the dependent variable is binary (i.e., two available categories), in this case child presence or absence. Logistic regression, however, is an appropriate analytic technique only when the binary categories are relatively proportionate. In the present analysis as reported below, there were relatively few children attending the CFT meetings.

Table 9.1 presents the descriptive statistics for all the variables in the analyses. The percentages for the variables under participant composition, type of meeting, placement type, and family/agency concerns do not total to 100 percent because there were missing data and in some cases the numeric value did not correspond to a valid response category and were recoded and collapsed.

Children were, on average, 10 years of age, and 42 percent were female. Fifty-four percent of the CFT meetings were held for children who were African American and 27 percent were held for children who were white. Thus, the CFT racial distribution was relatively comparable to that for the foster children as a whole (57 percent African American and 33 percent white) in Cumberland County (Duncan et al., 2013).

Approximately 6 percent of the CFT meetings had a child or children in attendance. The child's mother and the GAL officer attended 18 and 14 percent of the CFT meetings, respectively. The greatest number of CFT meetings were the

Table 9.1. DESCRIPTIVE STATISTICS (N = 218)

	Mean	Std Dev	Minimum	Maximum
Child Demographics				
Age	10.57	5.73	0.00	21.00
Female	0.42	0.49	0.00	1.00
Male	0.58	0.49	0.00	1.00
White	0.27	0.44	0.00	1.00
Hispanic or Latino	0.04	0.19	0.00	1.00
African American	0.54	0.50	0.00	1.00
Other Race/Ethnicity	0.16	0.21	0.00	1.00
Participant Composition				
Child at CFT Meeting	0.06	0.25	0.00	1.00
Father at CFT Meeting	0.06	0.25	0.00	1.00
Mother at CFT Meeting	0.18	0.38	0.00	1.00
Placement at CFT Meeting	0.08	0.27	0.00	1.00
GAL at CFT Meeting	0.14	0.35	0.00	1.00
Relative at CFT Meeting	0.07	0.25	0.00	1.00
School Official at CFT Meeting	0.01	0.12	0.00	1.00
Service Provider at CFT Meeting	0.06	0.25	0.00	1.00
Support at CFT Meeting	0.04	0.19	0.00	1.00
Type of Meeting				
Initial Meeting	0.19	0.40	0.00	1.00
Review Meeting	0.15	0.36	0.00	1.00
Meeting to Close Case	0.00	0.00	0.00	0.00
Placement Type				
Unlicensed Home of Relative	0.23	0.42	0.00	1.00
Family Foster Care Home	0.22	0.42	0.00	1.00
Small Group Home (Residential)	0.10	0.30	0.00	1.00
Other Type Placement	0.16	0.36	0.00	1.00
Family/Agency Concerns				
Placement Change/Move	0.11	0.31	0.00	1.00
Petition	0.11	0.31	0.00	1.00
Parent Concerns	0.08	0.28	0.00	1.00
PPAT/Service Agreement	0.05	0.22	0.00	1.00
Child/Family Services	0.22	0.42	0.00	1.00
Parent Noncompliance	0.05	0.21	0.00	1.00
Safety Issue	0.06	0.25	0.00	1.00
Other	0.04	0.19	0.00	1.00

initial ones (19 percent), and the greatest number of placements at the time of the CFT meeting occurred in the unlicensed home of a relative (23 percent). A need for Child/Family Services was the most frequently cited family/agency concern at the CFT meeting (22 percent).

Table 9.2 presents a series of Tobit regression models in which the dependent variable is the child's attendance at the CFT meeting. The child's demographic characteristics were entered into Model 1. For every additional year of age, a child is approximately 1 percent more likely to attend the CFT meeting. Model 2 includes the composition of participants at the CFT meeting. Net of the child's demographic characteristics, compared to support personnel, fathers' attendance at the CFT meetings reduces the likelihood of child attendance by 18 percent, but mothers' attendance increases the likelihood by 11 percent. GAL attendance increases the likelihood that a child attends by 31 percent compared to support personnel attendance. When a relative attends the CFT meeting, the likelihood of child attendance decreases 26 percent, but if a representative from the child's school attends, the likelihood of child attendance increases 111 percent compared to support personnel attendance. The two types of meetings were entered into Model 3 and showed that the type of meeting has no effect on child attendance.

Model 4 includes the placement type and family and/or agency concern variables. The placement type variables do not have an effect on child attendance. Four of the family and/or agency concerns recorded at the CFT meeting, however, do have an effect. First, a petition concern where a case will be brought to court decreases the likelihood of child attendance by 14 percent, parental concerns increase the likelihood of child attendance by 24 percent, PPAT/service agreement concerns increase the likelihood of child attendance by 19 percent, and safety issues increase the likelihood of child attendance by 43 percent, compared to some other concern expressed in the CFT meeting. The coding of safety issues is used when there is concern that a CFT meeting attendee poses a safety risk. A more in-depth analysis is needed to determine why a safety concern would increase the likelihood of child attendance at a CFT meeting.

FOSTER YOUTH AND RESTORATIVE JUSTICE

Youth Presence and Participation Findings

The administrative data showed that CFT meetings were held for most children in care but that children attended only 6 percent of their meetings during the three-month study period. Not only the children but other key participants such as parents, relatives, and community supports were frequently absent from the meetings. The findings on child presence cannot be explained simply on the basis of the children's age. In the first model of the Tobit regression analysis, older

Table 9.2. TOBIT REGRESSION ANALYSIS—LIKELIHOOD OF CHILD IN CFT MEETING (N = 218)

	Model 1	Model 2	Model 3	Model 4
Child Demographics				
Age	0.007*	0.005	0.005	0.005
Female	−0.006	0.040	0.036	0.002
White	−0.088	0.007	0.006	0.030
Hispanic or Latino	−0.077	0.058	0.066	0.066
African American	−0.001	0.024	0.031	0.051
Participant Composition				
Father at CFT Meeting		−0.183**	−0.157	−0.057
Mother at CFT Meeting		0.113**	0.094	0.153**
Placement at CFT Meeting		0.057	0.009	−0.011
GAL at CFT Meeting		0.318***	0.260***	0.180**
Relative at CFT Meeting		−0.265***	−0.262***	−0.237***
School Official at CFT Meeting		1.112***	1.107***	0.798***
Service Provider at CFT Meeting		0.085	0.070	−0.046
Type of Meeting				
Initial Meeting			0.005	0.020
Review Meeting			0.125	0.037
Placement Type				
Unlicensed Relative Home				0.019
Family Foster Care Home				0.012
Small Group Home (Residential)				0.045
Family/Agency Concerns				
Placement Change/Move				−0.040
Petition				−0.140**
Parent Concerns				0.241***
PPAT/Service Agreement				0.190**
Child/Family Services				−0.094
Parent Noncompliance				0.060
Safety Issue				0.436***
Neg-2 Log Likelihood	−5.80	−154.64	−161.85	−250.21

*p >.05; **p >.001; ***p >.0001

age increased the likelihood of child attendance by less than 1 percent. In the later models, this predictor of children's attendance no longer was statistically significant.

Overall, the analyses indicate that children's demographic characteristics, type of meeting, and placement type did not affect the likelihood of meeting participation. Meeting composition and topics of concern, however, had a significant impact on the likelihood of participation. In particular, the presence of a school official and safety concerns expressed by staff or family greatly elevated the likelihood that the child would be present, respectively by 111 and 43 percent. It does make sense that the attendance of a school official would probably be precipitated by a student issue whose resolution required the youth's participation in the planning and implementation of the plan. There is not an intuitive explanation for child's attendance when there is a safety concern related to violence, volatility, and/or hostitlity. One could speculate, however, that hostility may increase when there is a close bond between an adult and child.

Compared to the agency data, the youth survey results reveal far higher youth attendance at CFT meetings, with 65 percent of the forty participants stating that they attended a meeting. These survey results yielded a striking finding: All but one of the youth who attended a CFT meeting stated that they felt "important" at their meeting. This near-unanimity reflects well on the CFT meeting process and indicates that the youth were more than physically present—they were genuine participants. Moreover, the findings provide strong support for all efforts to ensure that youth are consistently at their CFT meetings.

The focus groups and survey results suggest many areas in which youth wanted more support and would have welcomed a CFT meeting. Youth had a positive regard for their social workers but wanted assistance in a timelier manner. Further, the youth highlighted the need for social workers and teachers to understand and aid with the prejudices and biases that the youth faced daily. The youth identified the lack of money and the skills necessary to manage their finances once they aged out of care. Relatedly, youth reported that they felt unprepared academically and socially for college. Youth expressed a need for their social workers to understand that they wanted to maintain contact with their families. Maintaining family connections is something that CFT meetings could encourage.

Study Limitations

A limitation of the study is the differential findings of youth CFT attendance between the youth surveys and the administrative data. The respondent selection process for the youth survey is not representative of Cumberland County youth and, in fact, included respondents from outside Cumberland County and participants who were no longer in care. In contrast, the administrative dataset is a census of the CFTs from March through May 2013 for Cumberland County foster children.

The youth survey responses, however, may better indicate the cumulative rate of child presence at CFT meetings. The time-limited Cumberland County data could not examine whether children were present before March 2013. Given state-specified intervals to hold CFT meetings for children in foster care, it is likely that older children and youth took part in CFT meetings before the start of the three-month period. Therefore, expanding the time period would assist with determining the rate of youth presence in their CFT meetings over time. In addition, youth may not have realized that they had attended a CFT meeting, pointing to the need for far more training directed to foster youth on these meetings. In the workshops conducted by the Center for Family and Community Engagement, foster youth needed training on how to ask for a CFT meeting and how to identify support persons to be with them at the meetings.

Restorative Process

Communication and decision-making for youth who have experienced the trauma of separation due to out-of-home placement can be intimidating. Finding a mechanism and venue for listening and hearing their voices can be a form of restorative justice. While they may not have any decision-making authority in the removal action, hope can be restored as they engage in the planning of their placement and as meaningful connections are made among the youth, their peers, informal support members, and formal providers. In this project, the inclusion of youth was not limited to the case level. By invoking the restorative process, it was possible to cultivate youth leadership through supporting the youth advisory council and participation in LINKS events. The county child welfare and school systems were quick to take part in training on CFT meetings directed both to its staff and foster youth and generally worked to coordinate their efforts.

The youth advisory council offered sound guidance on what to ask the survey participants. In particular, the question about whether youth felt "important" at their CFT meeting tapped into deep-seated sentiments about foster children feeling devalued in their homes and schools. The resounding "yes" from those who had taken part in CFT meetings bodes well for CFT meetings as a restorative process that heals and transforms relationships. Youth participation is not simply a tool for planning. For foster youth, participation in itself can rebuild connections and a sense of worth. The restorative justice model provides a theoretical framework to practitioners for conducting meetings, combining information about structural components for conference planning and process components for allowing optimal experiences. The distinction for people to be present at the meeting to experience the same communication was noted as essential. Many involved in the project felt that this restorative approach created the context for making meaning of the trauma, separation, and placement experiences that could not have been comprehended without this level of youth engagement.

Further research on the application of restorative approaches in child welfare is warranted. Process evaluation is needed to further understand what enhances CFT meetings to influence restoration, especially as it relates to creating a forum for making meaning of placement experiences for foster youth. Finally, the approach of engaging youth as leaders and decision makers challenges the conventional models of child welfare, in which the children are passive recipients of information. The restorative justice model gives us hope that the call made by the United Nations Convention on the Rights of the Child for the care, protection, and treatment of children will be answered by a proliferation of new and innovative approaches to child welfare locally, regionally, and globally.

REFERENCES

Andrews, C., Bess, R., Jantz, A., & Russell, V. (2002). *Collaboration between state welfare and child welfare agencies.* Assessing the New Federalism Policy Brief. Washington, DC: The Urban Institute.

Barth, R., Duncan, D., Hodorowicz, M., Kum, C-H., Buchanan, R., & Macomber, J. (2010). Felonious arrests of former foster care and TANF-involved youth. *Journal of the Society for Social Work and Research,* 1, 104–123. doi:10.5243/jsswr.2010.9.

Burchard, J. D., & Burchard, S. N. (2000). The wraparound process with children and families. In G. Burford & J. Hudson (Eds.), *Family group conferencing: New directions in community-centered child and family practice* (pp. 140–152). Hawthorne, NY: Aldine de Gruyter.

Burns, B. J., & Goldman, S. K. (Eds.) (1999). Promising practices in wraparound for children with serious emotional disturbance and their families. *Systems of Care: Promising Practices in Children's Mental Health,* 1998 Series (Vol. IV). Washington, DC: Center for Effective Collaboration and Practice, American Institutes for Research.

Charles, K., & Nelson, J. (2000). *Permanency planning: Creating lifelong connections. What does it mean for adolescents?* The University of Oklahoma, National Resource Center for Youth Development.

Connolly, M., & Ward, T. (2008). *Morals, rights and practice in the human services: Effective and fair decision-making in health, social care and criminal justice.* Philadelphia: Jessica Kingsley.

Dalrymple, J. (2002). Family group conferences and youth advocacy: The participation of children and young people in family decision making. *European Journal of Social Work,* 5(3), 287–299.

Dawson, A., & Yancey, B. (2006). Youth participants speak about their family group conference. *American Human FGDM Issues in Brief,* 1–4.

Duncan, D. F., Kum, H. C., Flair, K. A., Stewart, C. J., Vaughn, J., Bauer, R., & Reese, J. (2013). *Management assistance for child welfare, Work First, and food & nutrition services in North Carolina* (v3.1). Retrieved October 26, 2013, from University of North Carolina at Chapel Hill Jordan Institute for Families website, http://ssw.unc.edu/ma/

Dworsky, A., Dillman, K.-N., Dion, M. R., Coffee-Borden, B., & Rosenau, M. (2012). *Housing for youth aging out of foster care: A review of the literature and program typology.* Washington, DC: Mathematica Policy Research.

Ehrle, J., Andrews Scarcella, C., & Geen, R. (2004). Teaming up: Collaboration between welfare and child welfare agencies since welfare reform. *Children and Youth Services Review, 26*(3), 265–285. dx.doi.org/10.1016/j.childyouth.2004.01.001

Font, S. A. (2014), Kinship and nonrelative foster care: The effect of placement type on child well-being. *Child Development, 85,* 2074–2090. doi:10.1111/cdev.12241

Graves, K. N. (2005). The links among perceived adherence to the system of care philosophy, consumer satisfaction, and improvements in child functioning. *Journal of Child and Family Studies, 14*(3), 403–415.

Holland, S., & Rivett, M. (2008). 'Everyone started shouting': Making connections between the process of family group conferences and family therapy practice. *British Journal of Social Work, 38,* 21–38.

Holton, L., & Marsh, P. (2007). Education family group conferences: 'Before I try to teach you I must first reach you... '.C. Ashley & P. Nixon (Eds.), *Family group conferencing - Where next? Policies and practices for the future* (pp. 131–156). London, United Kingdom: Family Rights Group.

Hutson, R. Q. (2003). *A vision for eliminating poverty and family violence: Transforming child welfare and TANF in El Paso County, Colorado.* Washington, DC: Center for Law and Social Policy. Retrieved from www.clas.org/admin/site/publications/files/0108.pdf

Koball, H., Dworsky, A., & Korom-Djakovic, D. (2011). *Synthesis of research and resources to support at-risk youth* (OPRE Report #2011-22). Washington, DC: Office of Planning, Research and Evaluation. Retrieved from http://www.acf.hhs.gov/sites/default/files/opre/Synthesis youth.pdf

McCrae, J. S., & Fusco, R. A. (2010) A racial comparison of family group decision making in the USA. *Child & Family Social Work, 15*(1), 41–55. dx.doi.org/ 10.1111/j.1365-2 206.2009.00636.x

North Carolina Collaborative for Children, Youth and Families (2007). Child and family teams. Retrieved from http://www.nccollaborative.org/content/what+is+system+of+care/9651

North Carolina Department of Health and Human Services, Division of Social Services [NC DHHS] (2009). *Family services manual, Vol. I: Children's services, Chapter VII: Child and family team meetings.* Raleigh, NC: Author. Retrieved from http://info.dhhs.state.nc.us/olm/manuals/dss/csm-55/man/CSVII.pdf

Ottolini, D. (2011). *The family conferencing: a ground-breaking practice for community based child protection in Kenya.* Limuru, Kenya: Franciscan Kolbe Press.

Pecora, P. J., Kessler, R. C., Williams, J., O'Brien, K., Downs, A. C., English, D., White, J., Hiripi, E., White, C. R., Wiggins, T., & Holmes, K. E. (2005). *Improving family foster care: Findings from the Northwest Foster Care Alumni Study.* Seattle, WA: Casey Family Programs. Available at http://www.casey.org.

Pennell, J. (with Allen-Eckard, K., King, J., & Latz, M.) (2013, September). *Family-centered practice project: Annual report to the North Carolina Division of Social Services, fiscal year 2012–2013: Summary report.* Raleigh, NC: North Carolina State University, Center for Family & Community Engagement.

Pennell, J., & Anderson, G. (Eds.). (2005). *Widening the circle: The practice and evaluation of family group conferencing with children, youths, and their families.* Washington, DC: NASW Press.

Pennell, J., Edwards, M., & Burford, G. (2010). Expedited family group engagement and child permanency. *Children and Youth Services Review, 32,* 1012–1019. doi:10.1016/j.childyouth.2010.03.029

Pennell, J., & Rikard, R. V. (2013, June). *Fostering youth educational success: Final evaluation report* (Grant # 90CO1075/01). Washington, DC: U.S. Department of

Health and Human Services. Retrieved from http://www.cfface.org/documents/
Fostering_YES_Final_Report_June_2013_edited_v3.pdf

Rotabi, K. S., Pennell, J., Roby, J. L., & Bunkers, K. M. (2012). Family group conferencing as
a culturally adaptable intervention: Reforming intercountry adoption in Guatemala.
International Social Work, 55(3), 402–416. doi:10.1177/0020872812437229

Sheets, J., Wittenstrom, K., Fong, R., James, J., Tecci, M., Baumann, D. J., & Rodriguez, C.
(2009). Evidence-based practice in family group decision-making for Anglo, African
American and Hispanic families. *Children and Youth Services Review, 31,* 1187–1191.
doi:10.1016/j.childyouth.2009.08.003

Stroul, B. A., & Friedman, R. M. (1986). *A system of care for severely emotionally disturbed
children and youth.* Washington, DC: Georgetown University Child Development
Center, CASSP Technical Assistance Center.

U.S. Census Bureau (2012). Statistical abstract of the United States: 2012. National Security
and Veteran Affairs. Retrieved on April 10, 2014, from http://www.census.gov/com-
pendia/statab/2012/tables/12s0509.pdf

Wang, E. W., Lambert, M. C., Johnson, L. E., Boudreau, B., Breidenbach, R., & Baumann, D.
(2012). Expediting permanent placement from foster care systems: The role of family
group decision-making. *Children and Youth Services Review, 34,* 845–850.

Zinsstag, E., & Vanfraechem, I. (Eds.). (2013). *Conferencing* and *restorative justice: International practices and perspectives.* Oxford, United Kingdom: Oxford
University Press.

CHAPTER 10

Teen Experiences of Exclusion, Inclusion, and Participation in Child Protection and Youth Justice in Vermont

GALE BURFORD AND SARAH GALLAGHER

INTRODUCTION

Youth: Yeah, the outcome was good. Um, there at the meeting I felt like it was kind of embarrassing a little bit, because some of the negative choices I made were presented to my entire family. And they weren't really supposed to know about that, but other than that I felt pretty supported and happy with the outcome. My life is just falling back together, so it's nice, and this was, like, the first step.

Interviewer: Do you feel like you were prepared for what was going to happen at the meeting?

Youth: Um, no. I had no idea, um, I felt really unprepared. I didn't really go in at first because it was a little awkward for me, just because of my family that was there. I hadn't seen them in a long time and I knew what was going to happen because she [the meeting coordinator] did prepare me really well. She told me what they were going to talk about, and who was going to be there. It was just a little of my [things I considered personal], so other than that, she definitely did a good job of doing that.

Interviewer: And what was it like once you were actually in there?

Youth: Um, I don't know, I could barely breathe!

We ask the reader: Was the above young person prepared to fully participate in the meeting? Was she able to understand and assert her rights? Was her right to privacy violated? Were her rights to express herself and to have her views taken into account honored? Was she truly included and engaged? We hope to shed light on those questions in this chapter. We begin by acknowledging the myriad of challenges faced by young people in having a say, that is participating, in important decisions in child welfare and youth justice processes where competition for air time with adults (pun intended) reigns supreme. The rules for who can speak, when they can speak, the language they must use, and the decorum they must display must seem to young people like deliberate attempts to frustrate them. Yet, young people risk peril if they ignore or treat the adult processes with disrespect or disdain, as their behavior may be taken as evidence of their incapacity to make decisions and understand consequences. Frequently their mere presence in meetings, especially if their family is also present, raises concerns that they could be traumatized, or retraumatized, and hence should be excluded from participation "for their own good." Even youth advocates, who would normally include young people as a matter of course, face systemic reminders that youth participation is seen as an add-on, a privilege rather than a right.

THE NUANCE OF INCLUSION, EXCLUSION, ENGAGEMENT

Interviewer: If you weren't here with me right now, where would you be?
Youth: Probably playing with my dog and everything, not really my dog.
Interviewer: So there's a dog at your foster home?
Youth: I have six of them.
Interviewer: Is there one that you like in particular?
Youth: I have my dog. She's mine. I call her mine. She thinks she's mine. They call her mine too. Her name is [name deleted]. She's a [color and breed] mix.

The young person above is acutely aware of the tentative relationship he has with the "family" pet and clearly aware that he can be removed at any time without regard to his preferences. For any young person, but especially for one who has become a "state's child," simply granting rights to participate is insufficient to achieve social inclusion or to achieve any semblance of meaningful participation. We argue that the experience of inclusion and exclusion is multifaceted and cannot be understood in wholly objective terms.

Huntington (2006) warns that focusing solely on rights-based models in child participation research fails to protect the interests of either parents or children by obscuring the pervasive effects of poverty and fosters adversarial, competitive relations between the state and the family. She says of the tension between law and relationships that "The structure and practice of traditional family law … stands strikingly at odds with the fundamental cycle that underlies the nature of familial relationships" (Huntington, 2008, pp. 147–148). Braithwaite argues that the very structure and organization of regulatory services in child welfare defy the known psychology of what is best for children and the meaningful development of a shared vision of hope (Braithwaite, 2004, 2009). Both make the case that the use of "reparative" approaches that reduce adversarial decision-making and motivate more persistent and long-lasting relationships than those altered or created in the eyes of the law are essential to promote participation.

Barnes and Morris (2008) go farther and challenge the conservatism behind most definitions of social inclusion. They argue that advocates of social inclusion too often focus on technical dimensions such as risk assessment, or on cosmetic or tokenistic aspects of inclusion that do not take into account intergenerational, social, and economic barriers. These barriers are seen to foster more state intervention at the expense of capacity building and support for sustaining permanent connections in familial, community, and social networks and education. Similarly, Sen (2009) argues that rights need to be understood in a context of capabilities and "social choice" that is dependent on a person making a reasonable assessment of the interests of others in considering his or her own rights. Participation, in this sense, is closely tied to a young person's own developing capacity for empathy and growing understanding of the impact of his or her own behavior. It is often said that democracy is best learned through discussion coupled with the experience of procedural fairness (Tyler, 2011) rather than simply following or learning procedures or complying with requirements. Braithwaite's recent work (2013) on motivational postures sheds light on dimensions of engagement in the ways people position themselves in relation to authorities, and it has important implications for the ways in which responses to these postures can foster further reactivity and exclusion or enlist cooperation. In his study of youth explanations for placement disruptions in care, Jakobsen (2013) points to the stark damage done by systematized failure to take matters of importance to young people into account when making care decisions. Failure to listen and understand the young person provokes reactance.

While there is considerable consensus that the benefits of including young people outweigh the costs of alienation and disaffection (Bell, 2011; Hart, 1992; Jim Casey Youth Opportunities, 2012; Oswell, 2014; Thomas, 2013), there is less agreement about how to offset the forces that work to exclude them (Heino, 2009). Morton and Montgomery's (2013) systematic review of research finds little evidence of a relationship between youth empowerment and outcomes, but the research reviewed emphasized finding "proof" that youth engagement gets better treatment outcomes and masked studies that emphasize youth involvement as a right. Checkoway and Aldana (2013) shed light on issues of young people having a say when they are both the subjects and objects of intervention, and Daniel and Bowes (2011) point to the very structures in the system of services that privilege adult and especially professional voices and fail to take into account growth and development over the lifespan. Caught between roles of being a child or youth living in a family, especially for youth in foster care (Munson, Lee, Miller, Cole, & Nedelcu, 2013), and the challenges of emancipation, young people find themselves in decision-making fora with little preparation to be there and often react in ways that make things worse—that invite escalation to manage their behavior or slip into over-conformity.

Pennell, Burford, Connolly, and Morris (2011) argue that family engagement approaches to including young people and families can be used to simultaneously uphold both child and family rights. Such approaches recast young people to the role of full participants as citizens in their families and communities rather than labeling them and their families as dysfunctional clients (Burford, 2005; Burford & Pennell, 2004; Connolly & Ward, 2008; Gal, 2011; Pennell et al., 2011) subject to being immersed in plans that incorporate available or off-the-shelf services as opposed to ones developed through their participation. Such plans risk, as one senior administrator in Vermont said, "wrapping them so tightly with services that they are strangled off from their families and communities." Service-driven plans that measure young people's progress through compliance are seen as the antithesis to participation and inclusion.

BACKGROUND TO STUDY IN VERMONT

Like most jurisdictions in the United States and internationally, Vermont has committed to a multiyear transformation of its system of child welfare and youth justice in the direction of increased engagement with the wider family, youth engagement in their own plans, and the use of more responsive casework processes (Burford, 2013; Burford with Barron, 2013; Vermont Department for Children and Families, n.d.). As one of the smallest states in the United States (9,216 square miles, 2013 population of 626,630), it is also one of the least diverse states in the nation, with 94 percent of the population identifying as white alone (not Hispanic or Latino). Child and family welfare in the state is administered through the Family Services Division (FSD) of the Agency of Human Services. Notably, both child protection and youth justice are administered under the same umbrella. This means that children in need of protection and young people who have come in conflict with the law are often found in the same worker's caseloads. In 2009, legislation was passed requiring the department to "actively engage families, and solicit and integrate into the case plan the input of the child, the child's family, relatives, and other persons with a significant relationship to the child" (Added 2007, No. 185 (Adj. Sess.), § 1, eff. Jan. 1, 2009). The FSD developed a practice model that aims to include young people and their families in shaping their future and to use strategies that aim for more precision in the assessment and planning process. Efforts have been made to realign policy, finance, legislation, training, outside contracts, and interagency agreements with engagement practice (Burford with Barron, 2013). To promote the principles associated with youth engagement, a variety of work groups and activities have been designed and implemented to increase youth participation.

STUDY DESIGN, METHODOLOGY, AND SAMPLE

Interviewer: DCF has been trying to change the ways they work with families and be more inclusive of young people and their families in terms of decision-making and that kind of stuff. Is that something you're aware of?

Youth: A little bit. I was working with a program through [one of a number of youth development committees in the state] which is for foster youth in DCF custody, who had once been or are still, and it was designed to give direct feedback from youth to DCF. It didn't work as well because the youth weren't very self-motivated and they'd get excited on one thing and then since everyone was changing homes they would always drop out. They were dealing with, like, "If we wanted to change X, how would we do that sort of thing?" I haven't seen any direct changes made.

This study of a sample of young people's experiences in a changing system is one part of a larger evaluation of those changes. We have tried to weave in the young people's voices as faithfully as possible and also to map the main themes and subthemes that came up in the interviews. To give additional context to the interviews, we note that survey data gathered at the end of family safety plan meetings and family group conferences, which were both introduced as part of practice reforms, indicate high levels of teen satisfaction with these meetings. In particular, the family group conferences (N = 132) have received significantly higher ratings by teens on items such as "Other people at the meeting really listened to what I had to say"; "I liked where the meeting was held"; and "I think the right people helped make the plan." These meetings almost always have a higher proportion of family members and people of the family's, including the teen's, choosing and fewer professionals in attendance. Importantly, the family group conferences are designed to be more democratic fora in that family and youth are meant to be given considerable say in the planning of the meeting and more time is invested in bringing the extended family to the table. While this indicates the potential for these fora to be good vehicles for the engagement and participation of youth in decision-making, the meetings are offered on a wholly discretionary basis in the state. Few families have access to them, as compared to the family safety plan meetings and to individualized casework and traditional treatment team meetings typically attended mainly by professionals.

To date, thirty-two young people have been interviewed (sixteen were male and sixteen female). Twelve were living in foster homes at the time they were interviewed, two were living with a relative not their parent, and a third was in transition from living in foster care to a kin placement. Eight were living at home with a parent or parents and nine were living in residential congregate care facilities. Importantly, some of the young people interviewed entered the system prior to the state's systematic efforts to emphasize youth participation, and practices vary considerably between districts (Burford with Barron, 2013).

The interviews were carried out in two stages. In the first stage, we recruited young people who had been involved with one of the two fora for family engagement: family safety plan meetings or family group conferences. Hence, our sample may be somewhat biased knowing retrospectively that teens give these meetings, especially the family group meetings, very high satisfaction ratings. More recently, young people who represented "success stories" were invited from each of the twelve FSD districts; these were young people whom the district staff felt had not only been exposed to their efforts to partner with them but who also might be able to assess how well the department's efforts were accomplishing the aims associated with partnership practice. Some of the young people interviewed in the second stage did not have a family meeting of any kind and a few were unsure whether they had one or not. We could not check the files of these young people. Young people who had not had a meeting were those most clearly estranged from their families.

Recruitment for all thirty-two interviews was done through third parties. In the case of young people who were in custody at the time they were recruited, referrals were vetted by the Vermont Juvenile Defender's Office. A change was made in the human subjects protocol during the study that allowed us to begin offering a $25 bank card to the young person at the completion of the interview. Half the interviews were done before this change. Twenty-six of the interviews were carried out by a research assistant working with the ongoing evaluation, four by student interviewers, and two by the principal investigator. All but one of the interviews were tape-recorded; in that instance the young person preferred that the interviewer took hand-written notes. All the tape-recorded interviews were transcribed. Interviews lasted from thirty to ninety minutes. The first seventeen young people were asked to fill out a fidelity checklist relative to the family meeting they had attended, while the final fifteen were asked to fill out a survey that was more generic.

Both authors are involved throughout the state in training that involves hands-on case consultations to give training in vivo. In this analysis, we have held to the views of the teens as rigorously as possible, even in situations when we knew the views of other family members and professionals, including when those views diverged. To hold ourselves to account to the teen's voices, we employed comparative memo writing, close reading and rereading, coding, displays, data matrices, and diagrams borrowing from Glaser and Strauss (1967), Strauss (1987), and Glaser (1992). We drew on Boeije (2002) to make the approach to constant comparison systematic and thereby increase the traceability and verification of our analyses. This involved being clear about our activities, aims, and results and the questions we were shaping at each step to move back and forth from the transcripts to the literature using discussion and comparisons to refine our categories. Our analysis aimed to map the major themes and subthemes as they could be understood through the lenses of participation, inclusion, exclusion, and engagement (Novak, 1998; Novak & Cañas, 2008; Novak & Gowan, 1997).

Instead of asking the young people directly about their feelings of being included or excluded, we tried to get them to describe their experiences through the use of open-ended questions. The interview was constructed to give the young people the opportunity to reveal what they observe or notice in their everyday lives, how they typify their experiences with the state's services, and how they coordinate the meaning they make of their experiences into agendas or hopes for the future. Interviewers were asked to begin, as much as was possible, by asking the young people about their present situation, transition into events of the past in such a way that invited them to present a coherent narrative of themselves, and ask questions that would help reveal through their descriptions and accounts the extent to which they viewed themselves as having agency, including enough support to regulate their own behavior and to exercise power and influence in their lives. The open-ended probes generally included starting questions like "What would you be doing today if you weren't meeting with me?" and proceeded with "How much do you know about what DCF has been doing to change the way they work with young people?" and "What has been your experience with DCF?" with possible prompts about whether they had a family meeting, what placements they had, what schools they attended, and what those experiences were like to set a context for asking further open-ended probes. We also asked what had been helpful about their experience with DCF and what things had been unhelpful, allowing as much as possible for them to take the lead. We asked how they had managed to have a "normal" adolescence while they were involved with DCF and included questions about their hopes and plans for the future. Interviewers were instructed to ask what the young people would change about the educational experience for young people in custody and whether they had close ties with adults or peers in the long run if those two issues had not been addressed in the interview. The final question in the interview was typically what advice they might give to another young person coming into the system.

It is unlikely that our sample of young people is representative of all young people who come into contact with the FSD through either the child welfare or youth justice gateway, especially since we deliberately invited referrals of young people who were thought to have been exposed to the "new" practices in the state.

THE INTERVIEWS AND ANALYSIS

Six major themes relating to participation emerged from our analysis of the interviews: External Views and Influences on Participation; Youth Voice; Relationships as Sources of Power, Influence, and Perceived Social Location; Interaction of Time and Access to Information; Plans and the Sense of Moving Ahead and Purpose; and Personal Agency. These are clearly interrelated and overlapping, reflecting the complexities for both youth and professionals in attempting to provide meaningful participation of youth in crucial decision-making processes. What follows is a summary of each theme and illustrative quotes from interviews.

EXTERNAL VIEWS AND INFLUENCES ON PARTICIPATION

These young people tended to be highly aware that they were the "subjects" of prefigured views of them imposed in various ways but all clearly influencing the choices being made by/for them, the opportunities available to them, and the extent to which they could meaningfully participate in decisions affecting their lives. While their knowledge of these views varied considerably, awareness was revealed in the language they used to describe and to refer to the legal, medical, psychiatric, mental health, educational, child protection, and family views of them. Those views include their "statutory" status as being "in custody" or as being "neglected," "abused," or "delinquent" and their normative developmental statuses as "teens," "family" or "not-family," a "foster child," and "nobody's child" in one instance. They were also aware of medical assessments and diagnoses such as Attention Deficit Hyperactivity Disorder, Attention Deficit Disorder, bipolar, traumatized, substance abusers, and sexually reactive. Young people aligned with or resisted these views. In some instances the views were "totalizing" parts of the way they saw themselves (e.g., "I'm bipolar") but in all instances they were ones that youth saw as needing to be negotiated.

The status and culture of their family of origin deeply permeated their voiced experience. Poverty, addiction, family criminality, delinquency, neglect, and illness (whether physical or mental) were cited variously, and in combination, as reasons they entered state custody in the first place, as reasons they could or could not return to their family, and as barriers they have had to overcome. Importantly, the young people were not asked directly for these reasons.

These external views invariably surfaced in descriptions of how their lives were organized around legal, professional, medical, and family meetings and visits that typically were scheduled for the convenience of professionals. Many youth decried the impact of these fora on their ability to lead a "normal" life and participate in activities they enjoyed.

> **Interviewer:** What's a normal day like in your life?
> **Young Person:** Well it's pretty chaotic right now, 'cause of everything going on. So I have a lot of appointments.
> **Interviewer:** Oh, what's going on?
> **Young Person:** Um, well, I have court all the time and medical appointments because I was medically neglected. So I missed, like, three months of school because I had so many appointments every single day and I had surgeries and, um, we have court at

least every other two weeks. I have court next Thursday. So it's not like a normal day where I just get to sit home and relax like a normal teenager.

Awareness of these external views was often longstanding and associated with stressful events.

"Like, we were sitting there having a normal day, and I hear this knock on the door. I go to open the door and it's a DCF worker with two state troopers sitting at the door waiting to snatch me away, so . . . I thought maybe my mom had done something, but I didn't know that they would, like I thought it was just gonna be like a call for maybe like a detective or something. Um, but no, I didn't know it was gonna be a DCF worker. I thought maybe it was a detective with two cops coming to deal with something my mom might have done. But when I heard the words 'Coming to take your son,' I was, like, 'Oh shit.' I was, like, 'No, I'm going to be taken in right now.' So, yeah, it was hell to go through right off the bat. I couldn't deal with it piece by piece, I had to deal with it all at once."

When young people felt that the system made unreasonable, one-sided demands, they frequently took matters into their own hands. Generally, the avenues available to them to "participate," in the absence of legitimate ways to object, landed them in hot water, leading to more restrictions on future participation.

"It wasn't like I didn't talk to her [mother] for, like, two years. The longest time I didn't go, that I went without talking to her, was, like, four months. And that was, like, from November all the way up until when I came here. That was the same time they took my visit, there was no communication. I had to figure out ways to break the rules to be able to talk to her . . . um, which in the end succeeded in being able to talk to her, but um . . . I did get in trouble for it. But I wasn't really scared for the trouble. I was, like, 'Well, I'm not gonna sit here and not talk to my mom. You guys can say that I'm not allowed to talk to her, doesn't mean that I'm not gonna find a way to do so.'"

Important to young people were whether the views and processes represented were seen as fair and the extent to which they fit with the young person's own views of what was "right." Whether they were known first hand or vaguely from second-hand sources, each of these views figured into the youth's understanding of where they stood and how they positioned their own voice. Having extended family members come together for meetings with the professionals invariably had a dynamic effect on the way the young person felt he or she was viewed by the professionals.

YOUTH VOICE

Frequently, young people who had been to family meetings said they felt the professionals had listened to them because they had a credible group of adults showing interest in them. Understanding the young person's voice necessitated taking into account his or her often complex and contradictory understandings of other's preferences for him or her. Young people were influenced by their relationships, positively and negatively, with their parents and other family members, siblings, substitute caretakers, social workers, mental health therapists and other counselors, the court, and school personnel and also by their perception of the relationships these people had with one another. In this way, the young person's voice could be understood as a synthesis of his or her own wants and of what the young person believed others expected of or preferred for him or her. Sometimes these came out in what sounded, even to themselves, like contradictions, typical for most adolescents who simultaneously want immediate gratification (soccer shoes, partying with friends) and trustworthy guidance to help them navigate the challenging shoals of reaching adulthood. They also want close connections with trusted adults and family members, while also desiring space to explore their growing independence. What they say in any given moment may reflect one more than the other, but the contradictions they voice reflect the contradictions they feel. The youth's voices could be understood as shaped by how they perceived all these important relationships and the levels of tension or collaboration between them, and their posture toward each of those relationships. Hence, participation in a particular decision-making forum on a particular day may be influenced by the mood of the young person and what is happening for him or her on that day, showing the crucial importance of maintaining ongoing relationships between young people and their families, workers, and caregivers to ensure meaningful participation (Osborn & Bromfield, 2007).

One young woman explained particularly well how it is that trusted adults in her life helped her to navigate these complexities and how much she appreciated being taken seriously in negotiations.

> "Well, like, if they're talking about me or [foster mother] disagrees with my future plans, then that's a huge, like, 'I don't want to disappoint her,' and when there were big things happening, like, 'I'm going to go to [community college] for the next 2 years and then I'll transfer to [state university]' and everyone was, like, 'That's a horrible idea' and I was, like, 'No, it's not!' and they kind of talked over my head about that, like, 'OK, so we both agree that this is a bad idea and this is the message we need to send to [youth] that this is a bad idea and there are better choices' and they were able to say '[youth name], this is a horrible idea' and I was, like, 'No, it's not!' and then finally I was, like, 'OK, yeah, I guess it was.' You know, they still understand I'm only 17 and while I still act, talk, and dress like an adult I'm stupider . . . I just make bad decisions sometimes and they get that and they're OK with it. And [social worker] is almost like a whole part of the family at this point."

The following young man voiced distance from his worker after a family meeting that was described by his extended family and the professionals present as a great success for getting this young man back in touch with family after a long estrangement:

> **Interviewer:** To get back to the meeting, was there anything about it that was helpful?
>
> **Young Person:** Not really. It was nice seeing all my family in one room for once, though. That rarely ever happens.
>
> **Interviewer**: And why do you think they were there?
>
> **Young Person:** They were there for me. They love me. At least I think they do. I know they do. I know my sister does. My sister would cut off her left hand for me.
>
> **Interviewer:** So it meant something to you that they all showed up.
>
> **Young Person:** Yeah. My gram couldn't make it, though, 'cause she was working. She has one of those jobs where she doesn't get days off much . . . If they don't make it, they always have a good reason. They wouldn't just dump me for nothing. I don't feel like she did dump me.
>
> **Interviewer:** So there was no plan. You ended up with no plan.
>
> **Young Person:** No plan. No conclusion to the meeting. Just whatever. Accomplished nothing. We all walked out, smoked a cigarette. That was the end of it. My social worker is, like, "I can't believe you're smoking in front of me." I said, "What are you gonna do? It's not like you bought them for me."

Similarly, this young person's preferences at one level seem contradictory. Importantly, he had many meetings over the years but this was the first attempt to engage him in the "newer" practices.

> **Interviewer:** So what were they hoping to accomplish by this [family] meeting?
>
> **Young Person:** I don't think it accomplished much besides a lot of talking and writing things down. I mean, I can see how it would be helpful for a lot of kids. It's just I've been through it enough. I've done enough of these type of plans, and out of all the plans I did it was the most helpful. It actually got to the point of things. It wasn't all, like, "Oh, you're feeling angry; name ten things you are going to do to deal with it" and that's, like, bull.
>
> As the interview progressed:
>
> **Interviewer:** What do you think they should have done [years earlier]?
>
> **Young Person:** I have no idea. I really don't know. I don't know what there was they could have done. I wouldn't have listened. I still don't listen to what people tell me to do now. The only thing the whole two years really taught me is patience. You know you go to [residential program], and you have to sit in twelve-hour power struggles with ten adolescent boys who all have anger management problems and all don't want to be living [there]. Basically they get you to your lowest point and when you have finally given up, they let you out. That's what I think. It's just a lot of stuff.
>
> **Interviewer**: So, OK, you are at the meeting. How did you feel sitting there with all those people?
>
> **Young Person:** The meeting was productive. It got to a lot of stuff. I told them a lot of the story. I just felt the only thing being a teenager sitting in a room for two hours is

a bit much . . . But that's probably the only thing that was negative at all about it was just sitting in there for that long. It was productive. I mean, we got a lot of solid stuff set out. Like, it showed that there is a lot of support there.

Young people typically understood, or thought they understood, the views of others, including those of their parents, siblings, state social worker, therapist, or substitute caregiver and sometimes conflated the views of people most important to them with their own.

> **Young Person:** With me and my mom it's very hard to get along with the DCF workers, and faculty, and case managers, and policemen, the foster care program. Um, we've always had an issue with every one of our DCF workers. We've only had three of 'em and we've had issues with all three; we still have issues with our current DCF worker. We just don't get along with them, I guess; there's not really much to say about it, we just don't get along with them.
> **Interviewer:** OK, so you and your mom?
> **Young Person:** Yeah, I mean, like, with me and my mom, if one of us doesn't like them, then that gives several reasons why the other shouldn't like them. Um, so, it's like if I didn't like my case manager, she and my mom would already have the possibilities, because it's what they expect . . . We connect on; we're like that, like if one of us doesn't like something to do with this, the other doesn't almost directly off the bat.

Like most teens, these young people had an eye for what they perceived to be unhelpful bureaucracy, especially those who felt captive and voiceless:

> "I think, like, 'hold' placement is very unhelpful. Like when I got up here, they didn't want to take the time to search for a foster home that I could be in. They put me in [program], which is like lockdown, so I had to spend a month in lockdown until the program here came to be, and then I am pretty sure my DCF worker felt a little stupid being, like, 'Wow, he's so successful here! Like, we would have just found a foster home and we wouldn't have had to put a second step in the way.'"

When the behavior of young people escalates, the system most often responds with coercive tactics to contain the situation and keep the young person (and community) "safe." Not uncommonly, the capacity for meaningful connection and inclusion is reduced as escalation increases. In this young man's view, disagreement over the nature of his treatment needs and hypocritical behavior on the part of the adults led to what he felt were unnecessary, coerced decisions in which he had no say:

> "I've actually had a couple social workers. My first social worker, she just didn't know what she was doing, right out of college. So she quit. That was kind of why she quit. 'Cause they didn't have a place for me after [residential placement]. 'Cause I—they

tried to make me do this therapy thing. They made me go to therapy like a bunch of times a week. I said I was only going to go once a week. That was as much as I was going to give it and as much as I was going to meet them. And so my social worker was, like, 'All right, well, if you don't want to be there, then here you go, you can go the juvenile detention thing.' It's kind of like halfway between [secure residential placement] and [less secure residential placement]. So they put me in the halfway house for three weeks just because, because they had nowhere else for me to go. They wanted me to take space, but I think it was a little traumatic."

RELATIONSHIPS AS SOURCES OF POWER, INFLUENCE, AND PERCEIVED SOCIAL LOCATION

The perceptions of the young people about where they stand in terms of their capacity to influence and the extent to which they felt anyone cared were deeply felt experiences of inclusion and exclusion. For most, the experience of removal from their primary caregivers was traumatic and most often disruptive to their relationships with their parents, other significant relatives, peers, schools, and communities and disruptive to their very identity. This was especially the case for young people who had been in the system the longest. For these young people, few efforts had been made to keep them connected to family beyond their parent. Exceptions were noted where efforts had been made to minimize placement changes and/or keep a young person in the same school district. The experience of being in custody without ongoing contact with their social networks left young people wondering whether people in those networks still cared about them.

Involving the extended family in meetings in child welfare brings in a dynamic that has been largely invisible to child welfare and youth justice personnel and young people, especially in relation to fathers and other paternal relatives who have been historically excluded. In these interviews, the youth who had family meetings and youth who did not had, for the most part, starkly different "maps" of who their family was and who they expected to be connected with in the future. Having a meeting of their family typically shifted power (including their own,) especially in those cases when their extended family came together around them. In other cases the meeting resulted in a clear message for the young person that he or she could not count on any family members at all.

In this way, engagement helped young people refresh, or in some cases create, their knowledge of who is in their family and community network and the potential for future connections of those relationships. These meetings with their entire network of formal and informal helpers were usually the first time professionals ever saw the young person's family beyond the parent. Young people reported these encounters in emotional terms and often viewed them as turning points in the direction things had been going with their case.

We understood the maps of their networks of relationships as revealed in their descriptions as a reflection of both their "normal" life stage and their reaction to the complexity of being "in the system." The latter requires them to make nuanced distinctions between themselves and who they perceive as their "normal" peers or families, and often led to descriptions of their time in custody as reminiscent of incarceration. Indeed, young people experience the state, the courts, out-of-home care providers, and treatment programs as overwhelmingly powerful, and many young people learn that compliance is the way to survive and get a bit more of what is important to them at the cost of being engaged with those around them and hoping things will change.

> "I'm 17 and I can be treated like a 12-year-old in DCF . . . I'm the kid who can't go hang out with his friends, can't go to parties. I'm the kid that does his thing during the day and then comes home, goes to bed and does it all over again. I'm just trying to get through it."

The complex positioning of themselves in these relationships had implications for bodily feeling, understanding of social rules and interactions, and the extent of their power and influence. For young people, it's not just participation in the big decisions affecting their lives that is important, but also having a say over how they spend their time in day-to-day life (Osborn & Bromfield, 2007). Neither of the following young people felt that they could be full participants in the life of their host family. Sadly, their experiences of exclusion are so private that they probably escape detection by some well-meaning substitute caregivers:

> "I just think that children develop so much stress being able to live in a home, because when someone first moves into a home, a foster home, you just feel really weird. Like, you always have to keep things really clean and pick up after yourself all the time, and ask to get into the fridge or take a shower or ask to do those things. I mean, really, when you are at a home that you call home, you don't have to ask for any of those things."

> "It was just, you kinda play by their rules. Like, I wasn't allowed [to do the activities] . . . They were, like, 'If you get hurt that's our ass so . . .' . . . It was always play by their rules—like, if they went to church, you went to church. Like, if they had no TV after 3 a.m. or in the afternoon, that's what you did. I didn't really like that you couldn't be yourself. You had to be their child."

At the same time, having someone in the system—a worker, a foster parent, and in one case an administrator—who can cut through what the young person perceives as unnecessary regulation is a signal that they are valued and have relationships with influence (Soenen, D'Oosterlinck, & Broekaert, 2013). In the words of one young person: "She [the social worker] agreed that it [what was being required] was stupid."

After detailing a long history of out-of-home placements that included multiple stays in residential group care, multiple hospitalizations, and foster placements, one young person said of his current foster placement that had lasted just under two years that "It's, like, the one good house I have had ever." The interviewer asked him to elaborate:

> "Finding I guess, myself. Like determination, like being determined to not be what my parents think I am going to be . . . [and] find[ing] out that pretty much what I had been told from when I was four [years old] down was a lie. Everything that happened as to why I was with DCF and everything was a lie."

Asked how he found out "the truth," he explained that he had briefly reconnected with extended family members in another part of the country who gave a different version of how he had come into care. Upon returning home he took initiative through his social worker to see his case file:

> **Young Person:** I had [social worker] pull my old file.
> **Interviewer:** Any problem with looking at your file?
> **Young Person:** They did for like half a second. She [social worker] was like, "I'm not sure, but I'll check" and [DCF administrator] was, like, "Absolutely."

The combination of a foster parent who stuck with him and an agency administrator who understood the importance of his quest and responded positively to his initiative made a big difference for him.

Similar themes in interviews revealed that most young people, no matter how things have gone with their families, are preoccupied with these relationships:

- "My Dad left me before I could meet him. I've asked about my father . . . I've wanted him to come back into my life, but she's done several tests, DNA tests, with several men to find him, and he's not on the radar."
- "Technically it was probably healthier for me that she [mother] just dropped out, but it didn't feel very good for me to be abandoned again and again . . . We're not really talking, but I expect to see her at my graduation in 2 weeks."

Young people's descriptions reveal that they view the system as set up for the convenience and power of professionals and not for young people. Despite the more favorable ratings of both family meeting types by young people, concerns about all encounters with the state being stacked in the direction of professionals and the sense that any opportunity to have a say is a privilege, versus the way things work, were paramount:

- "I couldn't start therapy with my parents until we finished the court process because anything that was used in therapy could be used against me in the criminal court process."

- "It's like torture. It's like straight-up torture, it makes you go crazy, being in your room." [youth talking about a rule in his congregate care setting that young people stay in their room for 11.5 straight hours on weekend nights]
- "Foster youth court happens Wed. mornings. And for someone who is struggling in school . . . if a court hearing is at 10 you might as well not go the whole day because it happens at noon and then I'm not going back to school for 2 hours after my mom just dragged me through hell and back."

Communication, or lack thereof, was a consistent theme in young people's calculus of who cared about them, whether they were included in meaningful ways, and whether they had sufficient contact with family members. They especially rebelled at having contact with their family rigorously limited (see quotes above) and at a perceived lack of responsiveness of social workers. When they talked about "bad" social workers, the evidence cited was almost always about lack of competence, lack of responsive communication and contact, or arbitrary decisions.

This young man was caught between the views of his parent and the department and felt he could not bring the differing views together:

> **Interviewer:** So you felt like the communication wasn't there between DCF and your mom and that maybe they weren't supporting her?
> **Young Person:** Yes, and they kept on saying that, like, "Oh, we did give her information," but I can tell when my mom is kind of lying or not but she . . . like, they didn't really give her any information; they just said, like, "Oh, there's a meeting" and when my mom would ask when, they just wouldn't give her a date or a time. But now they do, like since last year they have been, but in the past they just didn't do anything. Like, if I had a meeting they wouldn't give her any paperwork on me, she couldn't go to any of the TPR [termination of parental rights] meetings because I guess she was flipping out. Yeah, I think they should change their communications. They should go tell the actual foster parent or guardian first and then, like, right after they get off the phone with the foster parents they should go to the actual parents and tell them, but they don't.

Having a worker who listened and gave support reinforced this young person's resilience in feeling that his goals were valued:

> **Interviewer:** So this is a big question: What things have been helpful to you during your time you've been involved with DCF? I mean, you've said that it was your own . . .
> **Young Person:** Yeah, pretty much it's just me having resilience and being, like, "it wasn't me, it was mainly my family, so I can still be successful"—like, that kinda thing, and the one good thing, like when I had my last DCF worker [name], she was a real Debbie Downer if you will. That was up until I was 11 and I was, like, I've always been set on the goal of being a [career goal], and whenever I'd come up with

something as a plan, like, I'd be, like, "I want [to take steps in that direction], it was, like . . . "Are you sure that you'll be successful?" . . . and my new DCF worker has been, like, behind me. Like, when I went to [do an activity] . . . he signed for me. He was, like, "Yeah, you can go . . . do the things you love" . . . He's always, like, if I, in treatment team meetings we get a certain amount of money a month for clothes, and I've always been kinda set on clothes, like, umm . . . and he was always behind me if I needed [special clothes and equipment] and I didn't really have the money, um, he would be, like, "Well, if that's something you love, I don't see what's wrong with that." He's been more supportive of my goals than any other DCF worker.

THE INTERACTION OF TIME AND ACCESS TO INFORMATION

Young people's experiences of participation were deeply intertwined with their experience of time and having information they needed to participate: time present, as is the case for most adolescents, and developmental time, as was the case for young people who felt they had "lost their childhood" or had to "become adults" or simply could not have a "normal" adolescence. The ability to self-regulate in the moment was intimately tied to the extent to which things they thought were important were happening at all, and to how that pace fit with their own sense of urgency. When things were not moving, emotions were highest. Their experiences were tied up with their perception of whether they could influence things within what they thought was an acceptable time frame, the sense that things of importance to them were moving forward, and whether the people around them were responding to what they thought was important with the proper sense of urgency. Like many adolescents, when they did not feel they could participate constructively in the moment, they turned up the heat on people around them to take action.

- "If there was, like, a four-month period where I was getting nowhere with them, I would eventually either get kicked out of the program or just get a new case manager. Most of the time it was getting kicked out, because I would just let my anger out."
- "I never got below a 95, straight A student, high honors. Every class. Soon as I was taken into state's custody, I said, screw it. So I'm failing every single class."

For the young people who found themselves suspended, or paralyzed, the sense of anxiety and tension according to them takes over everything and their only choices seem to be to engage in what often turns out to be self-defeating behavior or to completely give in and dissociate. Not knowing in advance what they might expect next from the system significantly exacerbated their feelings of not being important or included and hence not being able participants in the planning.

> **Young Person:** Yeah, um, just, I guess, the lack of communication. Um, and by lack of communication I mean, like, when I have a meeting that important they won't sit here and tell me about it until the day that it happens. Like, I won't know about it until someone says, "Oh, there's someone here to pick you up for this meeting." I'm, like, "What meeting." They're, like, "You didn't know you had a meeting today?" "No, not at all." Um, but it's not something that's been happening recently; it's happened through my entire seven years.
> **Interviewer:** OK, that's something that was, you didn't like.
> **Young Person:** It started from the get-go, yeah, and I haven't liked it at all because I'll sit here and have plans for the time period that I'm gone for the meeting if it's an after-school type deal. I'll be, like, "What the hell. I already had these plans. I guaranteed people I'd be there to do this with them and now I have to sit here in a meeting?"

Young people rightly associated access to decision makers with their own ability to influence decisions:

> "[Social worker] was also really accessible to me. There was never a point where I felt like she hasn't gotten back to me in a proper amount of time, which I know a lot of foster kids feel because there's urgency around everything. Even when I was feeling something needed to be addressed right then, it was addressed in a timely enough manner where I wasn't like scratching at the walls. She was very timely and thoughtful about arranging the meetings. If we knew I was going to have a busy month and I would need two meetings, she would purposely arrange for there to be two. So even if I knew I needed something really badly, I knew I could wait another week and a half at most before I saw her again or contacted her. She was very good at communicating. Still is."

Some young people linked their sense of urgency around moment-to-moment negotiations for their needs in what could become a contest of wills or what Braithwaite (2013) calls resistant defiance based on perceived unfairness:

> **Young Person:** Just a lack of being able to listen to what I'm saying and what I need, and actually using what I said that I needed. 'Cause I can say that "I need this," and they'll give me something that is similar to it but not directly what I said. Um, but if they tell me that they literally cannot get what exactly what I needed, then I'll be, like, "Alright, this will do." But, like, if they told me that they couldn't get it, but I know deep down that they are just lying to me, then I'll sit there and be like, "No, I know that you can get what I need because other people have gotten it before." Um, so, just a lack of getting me something similar when I know that they can get me exactly what I want.

Interviewer: OK, can you give me an example?

Young Person: So, if I needed, um, like a plan to sit here and even if I may not be a person who needs, like, a direct one-to-one ratio with a staff member, um, if I'm not a person who is not already on that list, and they make it, and I need a one-to-one for a certain period of time. They can sit there and be, like, "Well, if you need someone to talk to or go with you somewhere, we can have you go for thirty minutes with someone, but no longer." But I know they can get me a one-to-one for that time period, I'll sit there and be, like, "Alright, I know that you can get me a one-to-one. Why don't you go ahead and try instead of sitting here and just getting me it for thirty minutes?"

PLANS AND THE SENSE OF PURPOSE

Not having a plan or knowing what was happening was associated with lost freedom and autonomy. Being "out of the loop" registered as painful the longer it had been going on—that is, for the young people who were in the system the longest and did not know what the plan was:

- "I feel like it has set me back. I feel like . . . I've wasted two years of my life, of my teenage years where I can be crazy and get away with it but I can't because I'm here. So I miss it. I miss what I did have."
- "They've taken away a lot of my privileges because of, like, things that I've done that every teenager tends to do."
- "I want to get back into school and go every day. I want to actually be able to go to my senior year and do school and not go like an hour a day or once a week. So I just want to be back in, like, a normal day."

It was also associated with losing touch with sources of identity and influence through multiple moves or moves to placements out of their home area:

- "All my friends that I know are down in Vermont right now. They probably won't even remember me anymore, I've been gone out of Vermont so long."
- "It was very gruesome. Just a lot of traumatic stages that I went through, anywhere from places like this [congregate care], to foster care, mental hospitals . . ."
- "I have been in DCF custody my whole life. Since I was like 5, I think. So I just kinda bounced around."
- "[I wanted] to get in contact with my family because they felt as though they couldn't get in contact with me because I was so far away and they didn't know, like, what they could do or anything."

These young people's sense of being able to engage constructively as a way of attaining or sustaining the experience of "being included," and to exercise control and choice, was closely tied in with the extent to which they had knowledge of and a sense of control in regard to next steps. Young people described those times when they didn't know what was happening and couldn't get workers or family to respond to them with information they thought was necessary as among their worst experiences.

Furthermore, the extent to which young people felt the plan addressed issues of particular importance to them made a big difference in their feelings of inclusion and their ability to make meaning of the events of daily life and to have hope for future. This was true in regard to a range of issues, from family contact to whether the youth felt the plan acknowledged and built on his or her interests and strengths instead of focusing relentlessly on what went wrong in the past.

- "My social worker's name is [name] and she is absolutely wonderful. I was fortunate enough to get a really young social worker willing to kind of not, like, break the rules but bend them so they would function for me."
- "Like, some of the other programs, some kids say they are gonna be this and that and they just start. Just other programs kinda hold you up more, I think, like they are not with you in your goals. They're not. They're just there to make you believe that whatever your problem is needs to be fixed so you need to do this and that, which if you just be yourself and start doing what you want and like, what you dreamt of being . . ."
- "Like, they tried to make me sound like a bad kid in front of my family. Like, like why? They made me sound so much worse than I am. You know what I mean? They didn't say how good I'm doing here or say how good I've been these last two years. They didn't say anything like that."

YOUTH PERSONAL AGENCY

The capacity of young people to tolerate the many frustrations of being in the system and to regulate their behavior and comply with rules and regulations seems in large part to determine the extent to which they feel their voice is truly heard. Young people described the strategies used by caregivers and residential treatment programs in draconian terms, while acknowledging ways they were helped to learn skills that have led to gaining a greater measure of what they feel is important. Education and training and support to pursue "normal" hobbies and youth activities were important sources of agency and were viewed as places where they could exercise developmentally congruent choices. They were often seen as more important than meetings that were necessary only because they were in the system. Importantly, young people frequently identified their own resilience and determination as the primary causes of their success while mourning the loss of childhood innocence occasioned by their time in custody, which was most often seen as a hurdle they had to overcome to get on with their lives.

The following young woman illustrated for us, among several other themes, the difference between young people who were seen as being cooperative, comparatively speaking, and who were in their own views seen by the professionals as "low risk." This was one key indicator for youth of how much autonomy or freedom they believed they could expect:

> "I was very adamant that I wanted to be included in absolutely everything. I never wanted there to be a meeting without me . . . and they kind of said, 'Well, in order to gain that, you kind of need to speak for yourself' and be able to keep my temper because I have a temper and really be able to advocate, and once I learned that's what was expected, then I'd be able to advocate like I am. They listened to what I said and it was kind of like, 'If you respect us then we'll respect you' and it worked. It really did."

Her posture with her worker is one of basic belief that the state wants to be helpful and she wants to appear to be cooperating and undefiant. Similarly, the following young person does not want to appear defiant but wants "out" from a system he came into for his own protection but that increasingly focused on his behavior as he started to resist:

> **Interviewer:** [So] you knew they were trying to be helpful, but it was more than you wanted?
> **Young Person:** I think they, like, . . . one of the ladies who was there, X. Don't get me wrong: She's a great lady. She is one of the most on-the-job people who works with children I have ever seen. Like, she has got everything down to a tee. She's got a million ideas of every single thing possibly that could help you. Ever. And it's just overwhelming to listen to her talk. I mean this . . . she's too helpful. But she has some great ideas. It's just—I kind of want to be done with it. I don't want to get the follow-up help. I didn't even want the help to begin with. Like, what I said for that two years is that you are hurting me more by trying to help me than if you had just left me alone. I don't know how many times I said that, in court, case plan reviews, phone calls to social workers, lawyers, GALs, you know, it's just . . . DCF is good for a lot of things it does, like child abuse, adoptions, foster homes, you know, all kind of stuff, but their juvenile delinquency branch or whatever they want to call it, that's where they don't have—I don't want to say experience, but they don't have the knowledge of what goes on in their county today to know how to deal with it.

Young people who had a family meeting reported increased personal agency:

- "But it [family meeting] was also a reconnection with me and my family. I think that was the biggest impact. Actually my dad ended up getting sick back in February and I went to [another state] for ten days. And I stayed with my aunt who had come up here and it took, believe it or not, the group conference for our family to get back together."

- "My parents and I are getting along better than we were before this [family meeting] came along. We're working stuff out still and it's getting better."
- "I was kind of surprised at all of the people that came because the people that came don't exactly like me in my family. Um, my grandmother and my uncle came and then it was my dad and my mom too, and that went well."

Importantly, many of the young people had been diagnosed with single or more often multiple labels and many had long histories of taking behavioral medications. Their assessment of whether they could effectively stand up for themselves and voice their views was clearly related to these diagnoses and the extent to which they were viewed as competent by professionals. We wondered how this might connect to the research findings that young people in foster care are prescribed much higher rates of psychotropic medications than children not in foster care (US Government Accountability Office, 2013). These young people's assessments were both acute and deeply motivated by the question of what rights they could assert in the moment, including in the face of professional assessments. For the following young person, the construction of the problem as a medical one contributed to his being without voice:

> **Young Person:** I'm just trying to do my stuff to get out of here.
> **Interviewer:** . . . What do you have to do to get out of here?
> **Young Person:** Well, it's—everyone is based differently. It all depends on what you got in here for. I'm in here mainly for anger management.

And later in the interview, the young person elaborated:

> "It was based off of me and the anger and then also medication stability, um, trying to figure out my meds, what I should be on and what I shouldn't . . . because that was after they had started putting me on meds. They didn't know what exactly to put me on at the time. So they put me in there to try to make sure I had structure so that way they could figure out what I needed."

Young people who had been in the care system longer had emotional experiences of connecting with extended family who had not been invited to be part of decision-making at the time the young person came into care. The "new" family meetings had been used to connect them with or without parental involvement. One of the young women had two family meetings that were aimed at reconnecting her with her parents, siblings, and other extended family. She had experienced a lengthy period of thinking they did not want anything to do with her due to lack of any contact. Simultaneously, as she learned, they believed it was she who did not want anything to do with them. She was aging out of the system and wishing she had connections with family, a somewhat typical reason for referral for family meetings when they are discretionary. One of the young men thought the biggest problem he faced in the future was that his mother would find a way to have contact with him. He felt vulnerable, for what sounded like good reason, but no connections had been made with other family members, who also wanted nothing to do with his mother, to help him buffer such contact in the future. Young people who were most estranged from their families were counting highly on their education and the close relationships they had developed with temporary caregivers and prosocial friends to suffice in the future.

Young people described differences between their families and what they perceived as middle-class norms and tended to be protective of and/or silent about those differences. The exceptions were the few youth who actively sought state protection from a very unsafe home environment, and those young people settled into middle-class norms in foster care with some relief.

Especially for those young people whose abuse histories left them estranged from their parents and family, the idea of having to skip childhood, adolescence, and any hope of a "normal" life while being confronted with taking on adult responsibilities was a predominant theme of repositioning their identity.

> I don't know. I think DCF should take into account what each kid's like. I know when I first got there, like, my goal was to be back with my family when, really, I'll be the first to admit my family is pretty shitty. They'll drag me down in a second—like, even the other day, like, when I went to spend a weekend with my brother and mom and my other brother, it's, like, they still do what they would always do—like, they are still going to be drug addicts and, like, I don't smoke weed anymore because that's just, like, an instant loss of any drive you have. Like, I won't go work out every day, I won't ride my dirt bike, I'll just be like, 'Oh, I'll just stay here and eat potato chips' . . . I can't stress that enough. It's within yourself. You can't rely on anybody else to change you, and I think what a kid needs to realize is that he needs to help himself. I know little kids can't really do that, and he is going to need help from other people, but I don't really. Like, when I look back, DCF kinda helped me see that, but then again they didn't because it was me—but I mean, I think what helps is they're more supportive than your family and [in] that aspect they are, like, not really family but then again family when you don't have your family.

Subthemes of youth voice emerged in examples of young people saying "no" to things they did not want to happen and their abilities to self-regulate in the moment when they were experiencing the force of the others' power. Some of the young people clearly had honed skills in negotiation, and the extent to which they perceived their needs or demands were being accepted as legitimate by others was a mark of their feeling included and engaged rather than having to "dig a deeper hole" to stand up for themselves.

CONCLUSION

In part to meet the obligations to protect dependent children and to safeguard against discrimination in the way services are provided, many jurisdictions in the United States have embraced youth participation. While a number of justifications have been offered, and criticized, for embracing participatory practices (Farthing, 2012), there is widespread agreement that children and young people who come into the care of the state are placed at higher risk for unemployment, poor educational outcomes, negative health behaviors, incarceration, homelessness, and more.

Particularly for the age group of young people we interviewed, concerns about the transition to adulthood, family connections and identity, and independence permeate all their thinking. Even for those young people whose estrangement from family sounded permanent, family relationships continued to figure centrally, as was the case for the young woman who took the strongest of measures to get out from under her mother's control but still hoped her mother would show up at her high school graduation. We learned that the meaning of participation, while unique to each of the young people, was in large measure about wanting to feel that they could have a meaningful say in setting the terms of their relationships.

These young people were at very different stages of engagement in planning for their eventual transition, ranging from young people whose energies were wholly taken up with getting through daily routines and thinking about the security of their immediate connections to young people who were achieving independence. As mentioned, participation had very different and contextualized meanings and helped us understand the connections between participation and a sense of belonging. Young people shared concerns about trying to figure out in what sounded at times like excruciating detail how to participate in the physical space of a foster home, having learned from previous experiences that the rules of how to sit, stand, be close, and be separate, even down to what could be assumed about access to food, television and attachments with the family pet, vary from home to home. We contrast that with a young woman whose motives for participating in the interview for this study were about "giving back" in gratitude for the support she had received from the system.

We conclude too that youth participation must ensure that young people are aware of their rights and actively engaged in planning for their future. This includes ensuring that young people are supported at least until they succeed in postsecondary education or career training. At the heart of these young people's concerns are questions about where they stand with family connections. We conclude that an investment in young people's family, meaning the people they consider family, is an investment in the young person.

The expectation that young people will be given opportunities and preparation to play age-appropriate and developmentally appropriate roles in their daily lives and in all assessment and planning activities is clearly set in policy in Vermont. Yet, as we see from the interviews, not all these young people are full participants. Some have had experiences where they felt coerced and without voice and either reacted or simply gave in. Clearly there is no across-the-board or one-size way to craft participation. We have emphasized the importance of young people being knowledgeable about the external factors that determine and shape the parameters of their participation; the primary importance of lasting relationships in which they feel understood and experience the power of connections; the importance of young people having timely access to information and other resources that support their capacities to engage with educational, leisure, and employment pursuits; the crucial role of ensuring they have opportunities to take initiative and voice their frustrations, ideas, and hopes; and support to build self-efficacy through taking risks and learning from their successes and errors.

As for the main questions about how these young people experience the various fora for decision-making, we see that this is an easier question to answer based on some of the interviews than it is for others. For those young people who had participated in either of the family meetings on offer, they experienced them as different from other meetings they had attended. Importantly, the family meetings have been initiated in the state both to reduce the need for formal court hearings and to increase the ratio of informal supports and family participants in planning meetings as compared with the more traditional "treatment team" meetings, which tend to include many professionals and often a lone teen. Clearly, these teens experienced their family meetings as nonadversarial; even the two young people who said the meetings accomplished nothing ended up describing results that were perfectly in line with the stated purposes: greater participation of young people and their families. These meetings have high potential for reducing the tensions among the state authorities, the family, and the young person by attempting to reconcile the rights of the family with the rights of the young person to participate in decisions that affect him or her (Huntington, 2008; Pennell et al., 2011).

For young people who had not been involved in the "engagement" meetings, the experiences were highly variable. Some teens sounded as if they were treated with great respect and were given considerable opportunities to negotiate, to identify their needs, and to get timely and clear responses and had access to information when they needed it. Others described being placed in restrictive settings that they believed even their worker thought were too restrictive but had nowhere else to place the young person. Most teens described living in worlds where the professional systems of court, medical, and counseling sessions and time structuring took complete priority over daily life and what they considered to be "normal" teen, family, and school routine. The message is that most young people see the system as being organized around the needs of the system and the professionals rather than their needs.

We conclude that even though participation is complex and requires a nuanced understanding of each young person's experience and a thorough understanding of the context in which the young person is being served, it is the immediate sense of having someone the youth sees as both a legitimate source of power and unambiguously aligned with him or her that makes the biggest difference. These young people play many roles in their daily lives. They are invited, or not, to participate in legal processes as children whose responsibility for their actions and for what has happened to them is diminished in the eyes of the law by virtue of their age. They are patients, clients, delinquents, addicts, students, future workers, and children who have rights to full participation and to assert claims to due process, evidence-based therapeutic services, and quality educational and living environments. They have rights to be connected to family and to informal helping networks that go beyond the beneficence of the state. They have rights to enjoy a normative childhood and to learn the skills that will help them emancipate into productive work and civic lives. It is generally the expectation that parents and other significant people will help children and young people prepare for the future and will support them through these complex roles. A young person's or a family's confidence in the integrity of the public agency and their willingness and ability to participate can be undermined and shaped from many directions. Ensuring that the young person's voice is heard and understood and that he or she is given support for enactment often has much to do with who sticks with the young person and helps him or her navigate what matters to him or her in day-to-day living. In our view, these young people's expectations were quite ordinary and normative, including their wishes to have timely access to information and respectful responses from professionals (Hart, 1992). Social workers, foster parents, and family members who want to honor a young person's rights to participate often find themselves swimming against the tide of people who think they know what is best for the young person. Clearly, fora that involve young people and their families/informal supports in a respectful dialogue with the state offer more likelihood that young people will have a voice. Systematizing access to these fora may well increase the participation of young people in state custody. It is equally important, however, to ensure that authorities engage young people regularly in decisions that affect their daily lives. As Osborn and Bromfield (2007, p. 9) assert, "Even small oversights can have a lasting and negative impact on the child or young person."

We are giving the final say to a young woman struggling to put into words the themes shaping these notions of inclusion and exclusion in her life:

> **Interviewer:** And the one question I haven't asked: if you were to encounter a young teen who's just started in DCF custody, what advice would you have for them?
>
> **Young Person:** Don't make things worse! Things are usually pretty bad when they step in. They're not, like, "Wow, everything is great! Let me just insert myself in this family!" I think teens have—a lot of even young people, we just have a tendency to make things worse, either by—I usually just egg my mom on, 'cause I'd be, like, "I

could piss her off by doing this" and then, of course, she'd be all pissed off and then everyone would hear about it. You know, I was quite vicious sometimes. But that only made things worse for me, because DCF would be, like, "Nope, you're not having an adult relationship. You can't be treated like an adult." And then I'd get all frustrated because I didn't get what I wanted because I didn't deserve it. And I understand that now. But back then I was, like, "Oh, I hate my life." So I would definitely advise not to make things worse. I guess you have to rethink everything once you're put into DCF custody because a lot of things are changed. It's the whole growing-up-quick thing, which I think is difficult because it's . . . some part of me can no longer enjoy hanging out with peers without feeling superficial. I know I'll never be another person's child again, so that kind of realization was really heartbreaking.

Interviewer: No, wait. I'm not sure I understand what you mean.

Young Person: I mean, my mom will never ever be my mom. And while [foster parent] can be a perfect parent, she will never be my mom. There is no way she can have a mom relationship with my mom, so I'll never ever be someone else's child . . . That's the whole warm and fuzzy cocktail.

We borrow again from Braithwaite (2013, p. 7) to highlight the crucial assumptions about participation, inclusion, exclusion, and the young person's agency to engage the space between them: Well-being is strengthened when people are nestled in social groups that "nurture their adaptability" while supporting their interrelationships with and value to others in the group. We believe that those social groups are essential to young people's feelings of social inclusion, which are themselves essential for meaningful participation to occur.

REFERENCES

Barnes, M., & Morris, K. (2008). Strategies for the prevention of social exclusion: An analysis of the Children's Fund. *Journal of Social Policy, 37*(2), 251–270.

Bell, M. (2011). *Promoting children's rights in social work and social care: A guide to participatory practice*. London: Jessica Kingsley.

Braithwaite, V. (2004). The hope process and social inclusion. *Annals of the American Academy of Political and Social Science, 592,* 128–151.

Braithwaite, V. (2009). *Defiance in taxation and governance: Resisting and dismissing authority in a democracy.* Cheltenham, UK and Northampton, MA: Edward Elgar Publications.

Braithwaite, V. (2013). Defiance and motivational postures. In D. Weisburd & G. Bruinsma (Eds.), *Encyclopedia of criminology and criminal justice.* New York, NY: Springer Verlag.

Boeije, H. (2002). A purposeful approach to the constant comparative method in the analysis of qualitative interviews. *Quality & Quantity, 36,* 391–409.

Burford, G. (2005). Families: Their roles as architects of civil society and social inclusion. *Practice: A Journal of the British Association of Social Workers, 17*(2), 79–89.

Burford, G. (2013). Family group conferences in youth justice and child welfare in Vermont. In K. S. van Wormer & L. Walker (Eds.), *Restorative justice today: practical applications* (pp. 81–92). Thousand Oaks, CA: Sage.

Burford, G., with Barron, L. (2013). *Final report on the NCIC implementation project practice transformation: Department for Children & Families Family Services Division.* Burlington, University of Vermont, Department of Social Work.

Burford, G., & Pennell, J. (2004). From agency client to community-based consumer: The family group conference as a consumer-led group in child welfare. In C. D. Garvin, L. M. Gutierrez, and M. J. Galinsky (Eds.), *Handbook of social work with groups* (pp. 415–431). New York: The Guilford Press.

Chekoway, B. & Aldana, A. (2013). Four forms of youth civic engagement for diverse democracy. *Children and Youth Services Review, 35,* 1894–1899.

Connolly, M., & Ward, T. (2008). Navigating human rights across the life course. *Child and Family Social Work, 13,* 348–356.

Daniel, B., & Bowes, A. (2011). Re-thinking harm and abuse: Insights from a lifespan perspective. *British Journal of Social Work, 41,* 820–836.

Farthing, R. (2012). Why youth participation? Some justifications and critiques of youth participation using New Labour's youth policies as a case study. *Youth & Policy, 109,* 71–97.

Gal, T. (2011). *Child victims and restorative justice.* New York: Oxford University Press.

Glaser, B. (1992). *Basics of grounded theory analysis: Emergence vs. forcing.* California: Sociology Press.

Glaser, B., & Strauss, A. (1967). *The discovery of grounded theory: Strategies for qualitative research.* New York: Aldine de Gruyter.

Hart, R. (1992). Children's participation: From tokenism to citizenship. *Innocenti Essays #4.* Florence, IT: UNICEF International Child Development Centre. Available at: http://www.unicef-irc.org/publications/pdf/childrens_participation.pdf.

Heino, T. (2009). *Family Group Conference from a Child Perspective Nordic Research Report.* National Institute for Health and Welfare. Helsinki, Finland: Gummerus Printing. Available at: http://www.thl.fi/thl-client/pdfs/da905b95-70f6-4db8-9 d82-91b74fe55ed0.

Huntington, C. (2006). Rights myopia in child welfare. *UCLA Law Review, 53,* 637–699.

Huntington, C. (2008). Repairing family law. *Duke Law Journal, 51*(5), 1245–1319.

Jakobsen, T. B. (2013). Anti-social youth? Disruptions in care and the role of "behavioral problems." *Children and Youth Services Review, 35,* 1455–1462.

Jim Casey Youth Opportunities Initiative (2012). Resources for your work engaging young people. Accessed January 6, 2014, at: http://jimcaseyyouth.org/browse-resources/engaging-young-people.

Morton, M., & Montgomery, P. (2013). Youth empowerment programs for improving adolescents' self-efficacy and self-esteem: a systematic review. *Research on Social Work Practice, 23*(1), 22–33. doi:10.1177/1049731512459967.

Munson, M. R., Lee, B. R., Miller, D., Cole, A., & Nedelcu, C. (2013). Emerging adulthood among former system youth: The ideal versus the real. *Children and Youth Services Review, 35*(6), 923–929.

Novak, J. D. (1998). *Learning, creating, and using knowledge: Concept maps as facilitative tools in schools and corporations.* Mahwah, NJ: Lawrence Erlbaum.

Novak, J. D., & Cañas, A. J. (2008). The theory underlying concept maps and how to use them. Technical Report IHMC CmapTools. Available at: http://cmap.ihmc.us/Publications/ResearchPapers/TheoryUnderlyingConceptMapsHQ.pdf

Novak, J. D., & Gowan, D. B. (1997). *Learning how to learn.* New York: Cambridge University Press.

Osborn, A., & Bromfield, L. (2007). *Participation of children and young people in care in decisions affecting their lives. Getting the big picture.* Research Brief. Melbourne: Australian

Institute of Family Studies, National Child Protection Clearinghouse. Retrieved from: http://www.aifs.gov.au/nch/pubs/brief/rb6/rb6.html

Oswell, D. (2014). *The agency of children: From family to global human rights.* Cambridge: Cambridge University Press.

Pennell, J., Burford, G., Connolly, M., & Morris, K. (2011). Taking child and family rights seriously: Family engagement and its evidence in child welfare. *Child Welfare, 90*(4), 9–16.

Sen, A. (2009). *The idea of justice.* Cambridge, MA: The Belknap Press of Harvard University Press.

Soenen, B., D'Oosterlinck, F., & Broekaert, E. (2013). The voice of troubled youth: Children's and adolescents' ideas on helpful elements of care. *Children and Youth Services Review, 35,* 1297–1304.

Strauss, A. (1987). *Qualitative analysis for social scientists.* Cambridge: Cambridge University Press.

Thomas, N. (2013). Review of *The agency of children: From family to global human rights. British Journal of Social Work, 43*(8), 1670–1672.

Tyler, T. R. 2011. *Why people cooperate: The role of social motivations.* Princeton, NJ: Princeton University Press. Available at: http://press.princeton.edu/chapters/p8230.pdf.

U.S. Government Accountability Office (2012). Children's mental health concerns remain about appropriate services for children in Medicaid and foster care. Retrieved from http://www.gao.gov/assets/660/650716.pdf

Vermont Department for Children and Families Family Service Division (n.d.). Transforming services for families. Retrieved from http://dcf.vermont.gov/sites/dcf/files/pdf/fsd/FSD_Transformation_Plan.pdf.

CHAPTER 11

Professionals' Conceptions of "Children," "Childhood," and "Participation" in an Australian Family Relationship Services Sector Organization

ANNE GRAHAM, ROBYN FITZGERALD,
AND JUDITH CASHMORE

INTRODUCTION

In 2006, the Australian government amended the Family Law Act 1975 (Family Law Amendment [Shared Parental Responsibility] Act 2006 [Commonwealth]) to facilitate shared parenting arrangements and encourage an ongoing relationship with both parents, where possible, as the optimal postseparation arrangement for children (Australian Government, 2005). Family dispute resolution practitioners (FDRPs) at 65 community-based family relationship centers (FRCs) nationwide are required to assist parents to negotiate a mutually agreeable parenting plan as an innovative alternative and as a prerequisite to taking the matter to the Family Court (Moloney, Qu, Weston, & Hand, 2013; Parkinson, 2013; Schepard & Emery, 2013). More recent amendments, which came into force on June 6, 2012, seek to address significant community concerns around child safety arising from the 2006 reforms while "continuing to support the concept of shared parental responsibility and shared care, where this is safe for children" (Family Violence Bill, cited in Theobald, 2012). The court *must* consider options for equal shared care or for children to spend substantial time with each parent. An additional object giving specific effect to the United Nations Convention on the Rights of the Child (CRC) has also been included in the 2012 amendments (Family Law Act, section 60B(4)).

While the primary focus of the reforms is on changing the postseparation culture of parents (Cashmore, Parkinson, Weston, Patulny, Redmond, Qu, Baxter, Rajkovic, Sitek, & Katz, 2010), there is some scope for promoting the rights of children to participate, together with the critical importance of their "best interests," in family law policy and practice (Fitzgerald & Graham, 2011a). Such an emphasis is arguably reflected in the language of the Commonwealth Government's Family Support Program, whereby provision is made for FRCs to engage in "child-inclusive" and "child-focused" practice (Commonwealth of Australia, 2009). At the same time, however, the lack of clarity and agreement regarding the meaning of children's participation within Australian family law has given way to increasingly conflated interests between child and parental rights (Fitzgerald & Graham, 2011a). This is most evident in debates concerning whether it is appropriate for children to be placed center stage in their parents' conflicts, whether it is right to burden children with the responsibility of decision-making, whether involving children potentially undermines adult (particularly parental) authority, and whether parents may unduly attempt to influence children (Humphreys, Houghton, & Ellis, 2008; Lansdown, 2006).

Over the past decade, there has been increased research in Australia and internationally involving children who have experienced parental separation and divorce (Cashmore et al., 2010; Fitzgerald & Graham, 2011b; Graham & Fitzgerald, 2006, 2010; Lodge & Alexander, 2010; Maes, De Mol, & Buysse, 2012; Parkinson & Cashmore, 2008). Notwithstanding debates and concerns about children's competence to participate and placing unnecessary burden on them, much of the available research suggests that children value having their voice heard even if they don't wish to make a definitive choice (Cashmore, 2011; Cashmore & Parkinson, 2008; Fitzgerald & Graham, 2011b). Such evidence suggests that if involvement is appropriately supported, children cope better and feel happier about the new situation (Cashmore & Parkinson, 2008; Graham & Fitzgerald, 2010).

The role and potential influence of FDRPs, counselors, and educators in family relationship services are therefore quite considerable in this regard. More often than not, it is these professionals who identify whether, how, and to what extent children might be included and what impact, if any, their participation will have on decision-making. However, little is known about the assumptions, values, beliefs, and practices of such family relationship professionals regarding children, childhood, and notions of children's participation.

The research findings presented in this chapter are drawn from a large action research project, undertaken between December 2009 and December 2011, that sought to examine how children are recognized within programs and services offered by one major Australian family relationship services (FRS) provider. This research focused on understanding professionals' conceptualizations and

practices concerning children's participation in the FRS sector and on strategies for embedding the principle into service delivery within the FRCs. The
research builds on previous studies undertaken with the organization that
highlighted a gap between support for the principle of children's participation and its implementation (Graham, Fitzgerald, & Phelps, 2009; Graham &
Fitzgerald, 2010).

BACKGROUND

Theoretical Conceptualizations of Children, Childhood, and Participation

In addition to the legislative and policy context outlined above, this research was
influenced by the notions of children's rights under the CRC and the emerging
interdisciplinary understandings of children and childhood, exemplified in the
field of Childhood Studies. Such theorizing suggests that the experience of childhood is not universal but varies in its construction, interpretation, and enactment across different cultures, time, and contexts (Jenks, 2005; Percy-Smith &
Thomas, 2010; Woodhead, 2009).

   Childhood Studies conceptualizes children as active social agents, able to
contribute and already contributing to families and communities. Children
therefore are understood as having their own views and as having a developing capacity to reflect upon and articulate these (Greene & Hill, 2005; Prout &
James, 1997; Smith, 2007). Interpretations of children's abilities, competence,
views, and best interests therefore stem from adult conceptions of children and
childhood (Trinder, 1997). Such conceptions, in turn, have major implications
for how children are responded to and involved in family law settings (Gal &
Bessell, 2006), especially in relation to their participation.

Professionals' Assumptions, Attitudes, Beliefs, and Practices Regarding "Children," "Childhood," and "Participation"

Typically, practitioners in the FRS sector are well versed in research evidence concerning the impact of family transitions on children and their well-being (Amato,
2010; McIntosh, Burke, Dour, & Gridley, 2009; Rodgers, Gray, Davison, &
Butterworth, 2011). However, it seems that fundamental questions about the
nature of "children" and "childhood" (What is a "child"? How can we make sense
of "childhood"?) are often overlooked or summarily dismissed (Jenks, 2005,
p. 4). Rarely is the link explored between conceptualizations of children and
the tacit and explicit ways we engage with them. Nor is there a critical examination of how the assumptions embedded in child–adult relations reinforce and/

or challenge dominant discourses about childhood that shape our relationships with children (James, 2010).

Similarly, notions of what participation means are contested and subject to different interpretations. For example, Tully (2004) describes a range of definitions and assumptions about children's participation, including assumptions about the "space" of participation (as neutral or embedded in power relations), the role of the decision maker (as independent and unaffected or prejudiced), and outcomes (solutions handed down from on high or negotiated in dialogue).

Since children's involvement is generally at the behest of adults, adult views and concerns will significantly influence the policies and practices that "operationalize" children's participation (Kirby & Laws, 2010; Percy-Smith & Thomas, 2010). However, there are significant gaps in our knowledge regarding professionals' views, assumptions, and beliefs about their role as facilitators of children's participation, the understandings they hold, the processes they engage, and the nature of relationships between children and significant adults. The studies that have explored professionals' attitudes to children's participation in decision-making have revealed attitudes and beliefs that are diverse, polarized, ambiguous, and uncertain (see, for example, Parkinson & Cashmore, 2008; Shemmings, 2000; van Nijnatten & Jongen, 2011). The research described below sought, in part, to shed further light on why this may be the case.

METHODS

This project took a large system action research approach. Action research involves the collaboration of professional researchers with stakeholders to seek and enact solutions to real-life issues or problems in context (Greenwood & Levin, 2005). The relationship between the researcher and stakeholders is based on bringing together the researchers' knowledge and expertise in relevant methods and processes with the stakeholders' contextual knowledge and experience of the context and the particular problem at hand. The action research was firmly grounded in collaborative processes, which involved staff across the organization in cycles of planning, acting, observing and reflecting on their practice, and the implications of changed practice (Cohen, Manion, & Morrison, 2000). The aim of the collaborative research process was to explore the assumptions, attitudes, beliefs, knowledge, and practices of professionals and how these influence the participation of children in their service delivery. The project also invited and identified opportunities for staff to work closely with researchers in facilitating organizational change (Reason & Bradbury, 2008).

Twelve local action research groups were established within the organization's centers, which are located in urban, regional, and rural locations across the state of New South Wales. These groups involved most staff (approximately

220) within the organization, including counselors, FDRPs, client services staff, educators, members of the executive, and all eight directors of the board, across a two-year time frame. Each of the twelve groups participated in two action research cycles. In each cycle, researchers engaged collaboratively with staff in each location to identify the aspects of children's participation and practice they wished to focus on, the issues they wanted to inquire into, and the methods they would use to collect data. Research questions they chose to investigate included: What factors influence an FDRP's decision to engage a child's participation via the child consult process? How can we encourage the participation of children so that they are recognized in decisions regarding them or their well-being? How does/could our service provision support parents to focus on communicating with their children in ways that recognize children and promote their appropriate participation in family decisions? How can we better understand children's experience of our center, including their experience of participation and recognition in our service? What would it take to increase child participation in the context of family dispute resolution? Some centers chose to focus on research questions that required them to engage directly with the families and children already involved in their service, while others were more focused on practitioners and internal processes. The university researchers did not engage directly with families and children. Overall, twelve local action research projects consisting of 24 action research cycles were conducted by staff, collectively involving 186 children and 58 parents.

Four project facilitators (PFs), generally two managers and two FRS professionals, were appointed at each location to facilitate, guide, monitor, and support the local action research projects. The PFs attended an initial two-day workshop with the university researchers. The aim of the workshop was to explore professionals' understandings and practices in relation to children, childhood, and participation to identify strategies and initiatives that might improve the recognition of children within the organization's programs and services. The overall approach of the first day of the workshop was to take current organizational practice dealing with children's participation and participants' own experience as a foundation from which to explore how children, childhood, and participation are conceptualized at both a personal and an organizational level. From here, workshop participants were introduced to key concepts from childhood studies and recognition theory and were encouraged to reflect on how these ideas might challenge and inform their understandings and practice around children, childhood, and participation. On the second day, participants were introduced to key principles of action research before beginning to plan how to introduce the research in their own regions. This planning involved (1) identifying key learning from the workshop to be shared with staff in their centers (involving children, childhood, participation, recognition, and action research); (2) exploring the main tenets of action research (identifying an area of inquiry concerning participation, deciding what actions to take, collecting data, reflecting on what was found out and/or on any changes that occurred); and (3) discussing the best approach to facilitating the research in their centers in collaboration with the university researchers. The workshop processes were designed to ensure that the PFs reflected on their own personal assumptions, values, beliefs, and practices so they could facilitate deeper learning regarding children's participation back in their centers as the action research was implemented.

Upon returning to their region, the PFs facilitated an abridged version of the workshop for the remainder of the staff at their center, and the focus of the local research project was identified during this process. As part of the collaborative approach to undertaking the research, the university researchers met monthly with project facilitators and managers from every region via an on-line Elluminate session or by teleconference. Meetings usually lasted an hour and were designed to support PFs through every stage of the project, including creating professional development sessions for staff based on workshop ideas, identifying problems, planning and implementing initiatives in their centers, collecting and analyzing data, and writing reports. In addition, PFs were in regular and ongoing communication with the researchers via email and telephone, and a regional midcycle visit by researchers took place to ensure the action research was understood and well supported in each center. These midcycle visits also provided an important face-to-face opportunity to clarify any issues or concerns, solve problems involving time constraints and staff changes, discuss any data already collected, share what was happening at other centers, and generally affirm and invigorate the action research activities at each site. Consistent with core tenets of action research, any issues raised by professionals in their particular communities of inquiry were not predetermined nor pushed prematurely toward an outcome (Burns, 2007).

To support local action research cycles, a mixed-method approach was adopted by the research team to track assumptions, attitudes, beliefs, and knowledge of the professionals and the implications for organizational change. These data were derived largely from five surveys delivered at key junctures throughout the two-year project: before the project, after the initial two-day workshop (PFs only), after the midcycle visit by university researchers to each location, after the final workshop (PFs, board, and executive only), and after the project. Data were also drawn from the evaluation forms completed by the PFs during the initial and final workshops and from the action research reports written by each Centre. Figure 11.1 shows how these various points of inquiry are overlaid across the local action research cycles.

Most of the data reported in this chapter come from the surveys taken before and after the project, which sought the professionals' personal views about children, childhood, and social inclusion, their professional relationships with children, and their views on children's participation within their organization. In addition to gathering written qualitative responses, the surveys asked

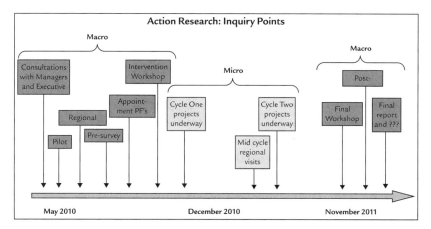

Figure 11.1:
Overview of the inquiry points within the large scale action research project. The question marks in the final box signify the various ways in which the study may have an impact on individuals and the organization.

respondents to indicate on a 5-point Likert scale their agreement ("strongly agree" to "not agree at all") with a range of statements about children, childhood, and participation, with some of these repeated to ask respondents about their views about "young people."[1]

Upon completion of the regional action research projects, a final workshop was held and attended by the PFs from all regions and members of the executive, including the chief executive officer. The aim of the workshop was to identify key learnings emerging from the project and to explore whether and how these might influence policy and practice across the organization. The workshop opened with a series of presentations from PFs who shared their action research initiatives, discussed their findings, and outlined their recommendations to the executive. Once the findings from all twelve regions had been presented, workshop participants were guided through a process designed to identify how each of the regional projects addressed the research questions for the overall action research project. The workshop also included PFs' feedback on the various inquiry points, including discussion about what aspects of these produced changes in learning and practice and the challenges experienced in relation to this.

1. The terms "children" and "young people" were not explicitly defined in the survey. Instead, participants were asked whether they engaged with children in their work, and separately whether they engaged with young people. This encouraged them to consider their own delineations of these terms rather than influencing them with a rigid age-related definition in the subsequent questions. While this aligned with our aim to explore assumptions and beliefs, it may present a slight limitation to the absolute comparability of the survey data.

RESULTS

Overall, the findings indicate four main themes in the conceptualization of "children's participation" among professionals within the organization. The first is that these professionals' conceptualizations of children, childhood, and young people are dominated by two specific constructs: children's need for protection and their agency. Second, over the duration of the study, professionals' engagement with these constructs shifted from an "either/or" emphasis to a "both/and" understanding, in that both children's vulnerability *and* their agency needed to be taken into account when considering their participation. However, a third key finding suggests some ambivalence for professionals in relation to childhood agency, most evident in tensions between acknowledging children's right to participate while still questioning their capacity to do so. Finally, the study reveals some lack of clarity about what these professionals see as constituting "children's participation." Given that the aim of this research was to examine professionals' conceptualizations and practices concerning children's participation in the FRS sector, and the role that the workshop intervention played in intentionally provoking critical thinking in relation to constructions of children, childhood, and participation, these four themes offer rich insights into the complexities of translating the principle of participation into practice.

Professionals' Conceptions of Children and Childhood

The survey asked participants to indicate their level of agreement with eleven statements relating to constructs of children and childhood (e.g., "children are innocent," "they depend on adults for protection," "they are not capable of knowing their best interests," "they need to express their views," "they have a right to express their views"). The data from the surveys taken before and after the project indicate that professionals perceived "children," "childhood," and "young people" both in terms of their vulnerability and their agency. In relation to vulnerability, there was very strong support for the view that children "depend on adults for protection," with 97 per cent of respondents in both surveys agreeing "strongly" or "mostly" with this statement. Respondents also agreed "strongly" or "mostly" with statements that "children are innocent" (first survey, 80 per cent; second survey, 81 per cent) and "vulnerable" (96 per cent vs. 87 per cent). Notably, the percentage of respondents framing children as vulnerable decreased in the second survey, a finding discussed in detail below.

Most survey respondents also strongly supported statements affirming children's agency: "children have the right to express their views to be heard" (97 per cent vs. 94 per cent); "children need to express their views" (94 per cent vs. 93 per cent); and, to a lesser extent, "children have a right to be involved in decisions that affect them" (77 per cent vs. 81 per cent).[2]

A Shift in Conceptualization to Accommodate Both Agency and Vulnerability

Both quantitative and qualitative data suggest that the perceived relationship between children's agency and vulnerability began to change through the study. For example, in the quantitative data, professionals reporting constructions of children and young people as "vulnerable" noticeably decreased (from 96 per cent to 87 per cent). While this may partly be attributed to a small drop in the proportion of staff completing the second survey, when interpreted alongside other qualitative data derived from interim staff feedback and the final workshop, the findings suggests a shift in some professionals' understandings. This shift is from more polarized notions of children's vulnerability as precluding children's participation to a more nuanced understanding of children's agency *and* their need for protection as the basis for their participation. For example, at the beginning of the study, children's dependence on adults was typically conceptualized as precluding opportunities for the expression of their agency (i.e., protection or agency):

> "[The organization's] construct of children appears to see them as vulnerable and in need of protection." [first survey]

> "The most dominant view [in the organization] is the desire to protect children from parental conflict." [first survey]

As the study progressed, however, professionals began to articulate an understanding of participation that could accommodate children's agency as well as their protection. For example, following the midcycle visits, several PFs reported they were questioning how best to balance children's protection and their agency:

> "It has made me challenge my thinking about 'how do I know what children want' and 'what is it that they actually need protection from'. It has also helped me to see the fears that influence my and other staff's thinking and practice with children." [PF, midcycle visit]

2. Responses to the term "young people" were very similar to those concerning "children," the only exception being that respondents were less likely to "strongly" or "mostly" agree with the statement that "young people are innocent" (first survey, 51 per cent; second survey, 5 per cent) and more likely to "strongly" or "mostly" agree with the statement that young people have a right to be involved in decisions that affect them (94 per cent for both surveys). Not surprisingly, this indicates some expected different age-related conceptualizations of capacity.

"I am thinking more about weighing up the benefits of participation compared to the potential safety risks associated with participation. I am also still wrapping my head around the definition of participation . . ." [PF, midcycle visit]

By the final workshop, PFs reported that, as a result of the project, they were asking how children's participation could be facilitated *while* keeping them safe:

"My belief that childhood should be a place where children are protected from difficulties (difficult conversations, positions, situations) has changed. Now, I see childhood as the place where we learn how to 'deal' with difficulty. FDRPs can help kids in that process." [PF, final workshop]

"The challenge has been balancing protection of children and allowing them to have choice." [PF, final workshop]

"However, [the study] has challenged my arrogance in simply saying children need to be protected, and not embracing child participation could place children in a position of not having the support they need." [PF, final workshop]

The following comments from respondents in the survey taken after the project provide further evidence of the shift in recognizing how children's agency might be able to co-exist alongside their protection. Here, respondents describe safety in participation:

"Children being given the opportunity to express their feelings, thoughts and to be supported with their emotions and behaviours. I think children should have a safe place where they can have their experiences clarified, normalised and affirmed. Also where they can be given some strategies that they can use to cope. Young people should also be allowed to voice their opinions on what they want safely without fear."

"Children and young people are dependent on adults to provide for their basic needs and vulnerable to reactive parental relationships and lack of parental reflective capacity. There is no question that children and young people have a right to participation. The challenge is, how can they participate? How can professionals support their participation so that it 'does no harm'?"

Similarly, staff began to consider more creative and innovative ways to approach children's participation, demonstrating a shift away from thinking about childhood in oppositional terms:

"I have become passionate about the establishment of a YAP [Youth Advisory Panel] and can visualise possible changes which may occur for [the organisation] and for members of the YAP." [PF, final workshop]

"We are now having regular staff discussions regarding the children and how we can best provide them with support, ongoing discussions with the children—not

just about them, but with them, including regarding about our services to them."
[Regional Center 10, final report]

"I think the learnings will translate into practice as almost 'permission' to involve, consult and prioritise children and their needs. The findings of the project will encourage more conversations and "noticings" which may have been seen as 'risky' or 'inappropriate' in the past. Creating the AND not the OR of protection and participation." [PF, final workshop]

"Many different ways and approaches—however, the main learning is to NOTICE children. By 'joining' with them, making a special space for them, not only in your facility, but in yourself." [second survey]

A similar shift in thinking is emphasized by the recommendations from the regional action research projects, which include establishing a YAP, consulting with children and young people about existing policies and processes, and seeking feedback and input directly from children and young people on an ongoing basis.

Likewise, in commenting on the tendency to keep children "out of the picture" where there are child protection concerns or when parents are assessed as not competent to hear the views of their children, one project facilitator observed: "Hippocrates said, 'Do no harm'. He didn't say, 'Do nothing'!" This awareness of the scope of participation as also encompassing nonparticipation is evident in respondents' comments that they are thinking much more critically about the impact that "not having a say" can have on children:

"I also understand the impact of not having a say—the powerlessness, the sadness and the loneliness that can result." [PF, final workshop]

This changing picture suggests that the professionals began to think in less polarized terms about children's vulnerability and agency (i.e., their "participation or protection") and embraced more nuanced and inclusive approaches ("participation and protection"). Notwithstanding such insights, some data from the survey taken after the project points to resistance within the organization to furthering the recognition of children's agency, particularly in the context of family dispute resolution processes:

"The FRC and the work of the FRC is not a place to bring children except in some specific instances. I believe the emphasis of our work needs to be to support and assist parents to develop . . . the 'scaffolding' around their children, to protect them and keep them safe to do the work of childhood, while the parents focus on building a strong parental alliance and capacity to help each other to be the best parent they can be. Other parts of [the organization's] services are better positioned to work with and include children."

Ambivalence Concerning Children's Agency

The third main finding of the study concerns some ambivalence in professionals' understanding of children's agency. This ambivalence is most evident in the tension between strong support for children's participation rights, on the one hand, and little support, on the other, for the idea that children are competent to participate. The survey data reported above indicate strong support for children's participation rights. In addition, the majority of respondents reported that children and young people should "usually" or "always" be encouraged to express their views (87 per cent in both the first and second surveys). When asked how much influence the views of children should have in decision-making, the majority of respondents reported that they should have "moderate" influence (62 per cent vs. 59 per cent). No respondent thought the views of children should have no influence. The influence that young people (vs. children) should have was deemed to be higher, with two thirds reporting that they young people should have a "major" influence on decision-making processes (67 per cent vs. 63 per cent).

Despite this strong consensus on children's participation rights, there was incongruity concerning their competence to participate. In the first survey respondents were split in relation to the statement "Children are not capable of knowing their best interests" (26 per cent "mostly agree/strongly agree," 36 per cent "mixed feelings," 38 per cent "not at all/a bit"). In the second survey this ambiguity remained, with a greater proportion of respondents indicating "mixed feelings" (44 per cent) versus "mostly agree/strongly agree" (22 per cent) "and "not at all/a bit" (34 per cent).

Adding to this uncertainty was the suggestion that professionals perceive adults' competence (on the part of both parents and professionals) rather than children's competence as barriers to children being able to express their views. As Figure 11.2 shows, professionals identified four factors as "usually" or "always" restricting children's participation: perceptions that parents know best (first survey 55 per cent, second survey 53 per cent); adults' reluctance to involve them (52 per cent vs. 50 per cent); adults' ability to listen to children (49 per cent vs. 42 per cent); and not thinking to include children (41 per cent vs. 43 per cent). Notably, the same four factors were identified by professionals as restricting the participation of young people (vs. children), albeit with slightly lower levels of support.

Lack of Clarity About What Constitutes "Participation"

Data presented in the local action research reports indicated that child consultations take place in less than 5 per cent of the organization's family dispute resolution processes. Therefore, as noted above, while professionals reported that the principle of children's participation was widely supported in the organization, at the same time they felt considerable uncertainty about its practice:

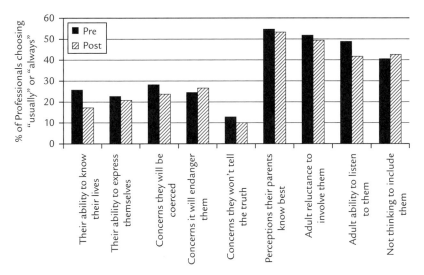

Figure 11.2:
Professionals' thoughts on factors restricting children's participation.

"Prior to the research project, there was not an aligned position from the organisation and FDRPs about what sort of participation is appropriate for children and
young people. There were barriers to participation that were limiting children's recognition, mainly in the form of competing values and beliefs amongst [the organiza-
tion], FDRPs, parents and even possibly children." [PF, final workshop]

Similarly, the board and executive noted:

"We were concerned because the values and mission of [the organization] referred to
'families' and not specifically 'children'."

Conceptualizations of the practice of children's participation tended to be
divided between professionals who understood participation to be a particular
model for working with children and young people (specifically "child-inclusive"
and "child-focused" family dispute resolution models) and those who conceptualized a broader "rights-based approach" to the practice of children's participation.
These two different understandings of children's participation appear to contribute to uncertainty about what children's participation "looks like" in practice.

The coupling of "children's participation" with "child-inclusive" and
"child-focused" practice models is evident in the following comments:

"In FDR present professional practice, 'participation' involves child consultation—
where the views of the child are directly sought by a child consultant who feeds back
to the parents appropriately those views which become part of the FDR process."
[first survey]

"Participation can be direct or indirect. At the FRC, if we see [only a few] children, we are STILL engaging with their parents to ensure that their participation is included even if they are not present." [second survey]

"Giving children the right to express their view either directly or indirectly." [second survey]

Children's participation as a "rights-based" practice, however, is equally prominent in the data:

"Children have the right to express how they are feeling about their family situation and gain support during separation. This support or their participation can occur formally—counselling or groups or informally—child-friendly place." [first survey]

"Ensuring children and young people have the opportunity and right to participate in decisions that impact on them in whatever way is relevant to them and conveying to them in attitudes and actions that they are valued as persons in their own right." [first survey]

"Participation is taking part, being actively involved, having a say and being heard. It's about respect. Children and young people have the same rights as adults and should feel that their participation is welcomed and valued." [second survey]

"Children and young people have a right to say how it is for them when their parents live apart. They should be assisted not to choose alliances but to give their parents an insight into their world and seek their response to address what is troubling them." [second survey]

Therefore, as the project progressed there was increasing general support for children's participation:

"It nagged me in critical reflection around how we conceptualise the status of children and the ways in which we engage them based on these understandings. [I now bring] a more intentional focus on children as service users in their own rights which has fostered thinking about our strengths and gaps as an organisation in terms of engaging children." [PF, midcycle visit]

"Several staff commented that the learnings from the project, including feedback from the children, have generated 'leverage' for practitioners when working with parents or considering a child consult intervention. This suggests that in one sense, the project has had an empowerment effect for practitioners, through the generation of knowledge that enables them to develop their capacity to facilitate child participation in different therapeutic contexts." [Regional Center 1, final report]

The uncertainty about the practice of children's participation was noted by some PFs as needing to be addressed if the organization is to make a cultural shift that accommodates the participation *and* protection rights of all children:

> "The idea that above all children need protection rather than rights is culturally so dominant that an organisation would have to be willing to take significant risks and be a real leader if they were to make any real change." [PF, midcycle visit]

However, the following comment highlights the complexity of promoting children's participation in the current "protectionist" legal and policy climate, whereby the speedy resolution of the dispute and the safety of children continue to limit conceptualizations of children's participation:

> "The research highlights discrepancies between the messages [the organization] is sending to both parents and FDRPs. [The organization] currently promotes the protection of children *from* conflict. If [the organization] is to promote children's participation *in* conflict, it will need to ensure that as an organisation, this will not be done at the expense of children's safety, is in alignment with the broad range of practitioner, parental and societal discourses currently in place, and does not disrupt power balances that assist FDR to be successful for families." [Regional Center 1, final report]

Despite this, PFs overwhelmingly reported that their own participation in the project had changed their practice through challenging their assumptions, attitudes, and values or by affirming their existing practice. For example, following midcycle visits, 87 per cent reported that facilitating the research project had already changed their practice in relation to children and young people. At the final workshop, in reflections on the research questions, all but one PF reported that their practice had changed in their work with children and families:

> "I find the broad construction of children's participation more congruent with my values than the narrow focus on direct participation through such mechanisms as child consultation in FDR. A broader approach is consistent with a family systems perspective for recognition of children." [PF, final workshop]

> "Made me think about what is 'true participation' and the importance putting into action any feed-back that children give us, not just getting their feedback." [PF, final workshop]

> "I have a stronger sense of their resilience and need to be included—sometimes even in the ugly stuff." [PF, final workshop]

"My practice as a child consultant has been influenced by having a greater awareness of the power difference between the child and myself, and my tendency to want to protect rather than empower a child." [Regional Center 2, PF, final report]

"To truly value them I must be prepared to hear them as thoroughly and deeply as I would an adult even when this challenges and confronts my previously held values." [PF, final workshop]

"Understanding this project has often been a humbling exercise for a former early childhood practitioner. It has been, at times, confronting to recognise that my former practice has been tokenistic. I can reflect that although these practices have encouraged children to participate, engage and have a voice, it was not often followed through with evaluation nor change. I am grateful for the learnings of this research, causing me to reflect deeply around walking the talk of advocating for children." [PF, final workshop]

The participants reflected on these changes as indicative of wider organizational change, resulting from direct engagement in the action research approach:

"To say that we were challenged through this research is an understatement. Initially there was a high level of dissonance from practitioners. While this can be explained by many things, including research fatigue and other environmental issues, however, much of this dissonance was a result of staff not being comfortable or believing in the engagement of children and young people at [the organization]. This feeling shifted immensely as a result of this research. Practitioners clearly stated that they now see giving children a voice, and more, giving them a service is vitally important." [Regional Center 3, final report]

"Instead of being told we were asked to 'discover.' This reduced resistance in our team. We were the drivers of the research and came up with questions and implemented data collection on our own terms—in this way it was relevant to our practices." [PF, final workshop]

"I really believe that it is very effective in changing both culture and practice. I am surprised how it brings on change in very subtle ways (rather than sudden and 'conscious'). As a process that unfolds and moves freely, it does not stay in the head only. It is transformative because it is not forceful." [PF, final workshop]

DISCUSSION

The ways in which professionals conceptualize children, childhood, and participation have major implications for how we come to know, respond to, and support children (Gal & Bessell, 2006). Deeply embedded assumptions, values, and beliefs about children, childhood, and participation have a direct impact on how children's views, experiences, needs, and wishes will be heard and responded to.

Organizations such as the family service provider in this study play an important role in shaping the conditions of childhood through the work they do with parents to reconstruct family life following parental separation and divorce. It is therefore critical that attention is given to the tacit and explicit ways in which the organization appropriates, reinforces, and/or challenges prevailing discourses about childhood and children's participation.

This study represents a significant development within the organization in acknowledging that any claims it makes in relation to the practice of children's participation are inextricably linked with a complex amalgam of assumptions, attitudes, values, and beliefs that professionals bring to their work. The findings point to this complexity and delineate some particular understandings about children, childhood, and participation that are potentially influential in shaping practice. As other studies have also shown, the influence of conceptualizations of childhood on practice is by no means unique to this group of professionals (Archard & Skivenes, 2009; Graham & Fitzgerald, 2010; Parkinson & Cashmore, 2008; Shemmings, 2000; Trinder, 1997). Indeed, as Jenks (2005, p. 2) reminds us, "despite a long cultural commitment to the good of the child … what remains perpetually diffuse and ambiguous is the basic conceptualisation of childhood as social practice".

This study reveals that underpinning the work of the professionals in this organization are two dominant images of childhood: children as in need of protection, and children as social agents. These prevailing images are somewhat contradictory constructs that are likely to be immensely influential in shaping children's relationships with significant adults (Dewar, 1998; Taylor, 2006). What is particularly salient in the FRS context are the ways in which these two constructs interact with each other. A key finding is that professionals' understandings about children and childhood, and the impact of these on their views and practices about children's participation, changed over the period of the action research.

At the beginning of the study, it was evident that professionals assumed that children's right to be heard existed unless there are concerns for their safety and well-being. Conceptually, the constructs of children's agency and children's vulnerability were seen as largely mutually exclusive. Further, the desire to protect children includes protection from the perceived burdens of decision-making, with the main threat to children not the divorce or their parents but inappropriate involvement in adult issues and having to deal with the aftermath of recriminations and guilt (Trinder, 1997). While consistent with the literature, which emphasizes that contemporary Western childhoods remain "an essentially protectionist experience" (Jenks, 2005, p. 122), such a polarization of images (children's agency vs. vulnerability) hides a paradox: that precluding children from expressing their views and perspectives when family violence or abuse is involved constitutes a form of protection.

However, across a wide range of studies, children have advocated for the importance of having their views heard, particularly in relation to new living arrangements (Backhouse & Graham, 2010; Cashmore & Parkinson, 2008; Dunn & Deater-Deckard, 2001; Hewitt, 2008). This has been particularly emphasized by children who have experienced high levels of conflict, violence, and abuse; for them, being able to choose the parent they preferred was important in terms of safety (Cashmore & Parkinson, 2008). Of course, children can feel torn between a desire to participate and anxiety about having to choose one parent over another (Backhouse & Graham, 2010; Cashmore & Parkinson, 2008; Cashmore et al., 2010). On balance, the evidence suggests that children are eager to have their views heard in a safe environment, but not to have overall autonomy and responsibility for the decisions (Backhouse & Graham, 2010; Cashmore, 2011; Cashmore & Parkinson, 2008).

The challenge, identified by many professionals in this study, is to identify approaches to the delivery of programs and services that acknowledge that safety and vulnerability do not necessarily preclude the agency and participation rights of all children, regardless of their circumstances. This was particularly noted in the final workshop, where PFs discussed how children's participation could be facilitated while keeping them safe. By the time this study was drawing to a close, there was evidence to suggest that many of the organization's professionals were engaging much more critically with such tensions. In doing so, they began to consider more creative and innovative ways to approach children's participation and protection rights such that these were not intractable in practice settings. For example, the recommendation for the establishment of a YAP is particularly significant in that it signals that children and young people have a valuable contribution to make to the development, implementation, and evaluation of programs and services (Lansdown, 2006). This was also evident in discussions about "noticing" children and young people, which is a good early step toward participation in the organization.

While acknowledging and engaging more critically with the tensions between children's protection and participation, there nevertheless remained quite evident uncertainty concerning children's agency. For example, while there was almost universal support among professionals for children having the right and the need to express their views and to be heard, approximately two thirds of these professionals continued to lack confidence in, or felt uncertain about, children's capacity to know their own best interests. In other words, children may have the right to participate in decisions that affect them, but they may not have the requisite capacity to do so. This finding is also consistent with the literature and reveals one of the most persistent and prejudicial images of childhood in family law settings: that children lack the capacity of adults and that it is "right and proper" they are not treated as full citizens (Bessant & Watts, 2008, p. 19; Lister, 2007). Consequently, children are largely excluded from contributing their views and experiences to decision-making processes that profoundly shape their lives—despite evidence that children have a valuable contribution to make (Butler, Scanlan, Robinson, Douglas, & Murch, 2002; Cashmore et al.,

2010; Graham & Fitzgerald, 2010; James, 2008; Parkinson & Cashmore, 2008; Smart, Neale, & Wade, 2001).

Paradoxically, professionals' views about their own capacity to assess the competence of children appeared to be inextricably linked with their decisions about whether or not to involve them. This finding points to the importance of understanding not only how these professionals construct children but also how they know and construct themselves and their engagement with children. As Kogler and Stueber (1999, p. 146) suggest, "we understand another person . . . by putting ourselves in the shoes of the other person, imagining the world as it would appear from his [sic] point of view" and "then deliberate, reason and see what decision emerges." At the risk of oversimplifying this much more sophisticated philosophical position of Kogler and Stueber (1999), it may be useful in the context of this research to help deepen understanding of what shapes and influences our encounters with others, including with children, in making decisions about their capacity and competence to participate in decision-making processes (Smart, 2002).

Overall, the uncertainty that existed among the professionals about children's participation was reflected in the fact that children were directly involved (i.e., in a child consultation) in only 5 per cent of the organization's cases.[3] This figure might be partly explained by the evident uncertainty about professionals' conceptions of children, childhood, and participation. While professionals offered a range of conceptualizations of children's participation, from child-inclusive approaches to family dispute resolution to more generalized principles aligned with CRC and the Childhood Studies literature, a degree of uncertainty persisted. By engaging through this action research project with interdisciplinary knowledge about children and childhood, and trying new initiatives in different centers, substantial and productive dialogue was generated between researchers and the executive and staff within the organization. This enabled the development of a shared language around the theory and practice of children's participation that will undoubtedly inform further organizational change (Mullen, Greenlee, & Bruner, 2005).

Importantly, the dialogue generated through the project provided a space for professionals to "risk" their views because of a perceived sense of shared purpose. While discussion and debate in many of the centers was reportedly robust, the data suggest that professionals' thinking and practice were examined and refined through the process. This is consistent with the principles and intent of action research, which emphasize the importance of creating spaces for inquiry where people feel able to tell their stories; these stories, in turn, enable emergent

---

3. As one of the action research reports from Regional Center 1 noted, there were two major factors in explaining this low figure of only 5 per cent: (1) the organizational policy of not providing a child consultation until at least the first mediation had been undertaken and (2) the significant number of children who are under the age of 5.

understandings to be supported and to trigger further inquiry (Burns, 2007). Rather than "stall" due to resistance in some centers (both to the research and to change), professionals were able to engage with such resistance "on their own terms". At times, the discussion within centers required the active facilitation of PFs to ensure all staff were able to participate as well as to actively challenge those who sought to undermine the research process. Ultimately, however, the research proved a valuable way of opening up taken-for-granted assumptions about children, childhood, and participation and any disconnect between existing child-inclusive approaches and the broader participation of children.

LIMITATIONS

While the scope of the study was a strength in terms of organization-wide change, it also brought some challenges and limitations. Action research can be unwieldy to manage given its collaborative nature, practitioner-led emphasis, diverse options for data collection, and difficulty in maintaining momentum with multiple cycles amid competing priorities. Given the number of sites, staff, parents, and children involved in this project, it was, at times, a challenge for the university-based researchers to provide the level of close mentoring and support required to sustain the project over the two years.

A second related limitation was the resource-intensive nature of the project. The study required, for much of the period it was under way, an equivalent full-time researcher working closely with the PFs across the centers. Allocations of time had to be found for PFs, and center staff members were required, in many instances, to invest time beyond that which could be made available given caseloads, funding constraints, and so forth. The project required the university researchers to travel to regional centers on two occasions, and these visits were found to be integral to the success of the project. The costs associated with such activities may limit opportunities for further action research of this nature.

A third limitation relates to the relationship between individual center projects and the overall action research. PFs played a critical role as conduits between the two layers of research (the overall project and site-specific initiatives). Considerable focus needed to be given to aligning the twelve site-specific initiatives with the overall aim and research questions of the larger project. The PFs worked closely with the university researchers to ensure that the initiatives being implemented reflected the broader interests of the project. In doing so, it is possible they may have filtered in or out some of the issues, questions, concerns, and findings arising at particular sites as they endeavored to ensure projects stayed on track.

Finally, there was considerable staff movement (resignations, role changes) within the organization over the course of the project. This had a considerable impact on the value of the two surveys since it was not possible to match staff responses. Staff changes also had an adverse effect on project facilitation and on the sustainability and/or momentum of some project initiatives when key staff associated with these resigned or moved to other positions within the organization.

CONCLUSION

This action research was an ambitious two-year project that sought to improve how children are recognized within programs and services offered by a major Australian provider of family relationship services following parental separation and divorce. The focus was on the ways in which children's participation is conceptualized and practiced. The method involved challenging and extending these conceptualizations through professional development, and by developing initiatives that reflected revised understandings of participation and collecting data about these. The findings revealed some promising shifts in understanding and practice while also highlighting the complexity of the work of professionals in the family relationships sector as they seek to balance the rights, interests, and well-being of children with those of the adults involved.

REFERENCES

Amato, P. R. (2010). Research on divorce: continuing trends and developments. *Journal of Family, 72,* 650–666.

Archard, D., & Skivenes, M. (2009). Hearing the child. *Child & Family Social Work, 14*(4), 391–399.

Australian Government (2005). *A new family law system: A government response.* Canberra: Commonwealth of Australia.

Backhouse, J., & Graham, A. (2010). Grandparents raising their grandchildren: An uneasy position. *Elder Law Review, 6*(1), 1–9.

Bessant, J., & Watts, R. (2008). Children and the law: an historical overview. In G. Monahan & L. Young (Eds.), *Children and the law in Australia* (pp. 3–22). Chatswood: LexisNexis Butterworths.

Burns, D. (2007). *Systemic action research: A strategy for whole system change.* Bristol: Policy Press.

Butler, I. Scanlan, L., Robinson, M., Douglas, G., & Murch, M. (2002). Children's involvement in their parents' divorce: implications for practice. *Children & Society, 16*(2), 89–102.

Cashmore, J. (2011). Children's participation in family law decision-making: theoretical approaches to understanding children's views. *Children and Youth Services Review, 33*(4), 515–520.

Cashmore, J., & Parkinson, P. (2008). Children's and parent's perceptions on children's participation in decision making after parental separation and divorce. *Family Court Review, 46*(1), 91–104.

Cashmore, J., Parkinson, P., Weston, R., Patulny, R., Redmond, G., Qu, L., Baxter, J., Rajkovic, M., Sitek, T., & Katz, I. (2010). *Shared care parenting arrangements since the 2006 family law reforms: report to the Australian Government Attorney-General's Department*. Sydney: Social Policy Research Centre, University of New South Wales.

Cohen, L., Manion, L., & Morrison, K. (2000). *Research methods in education*. London: Routledge.

Commonwealth of Australia (2009). *Developing a family support program*. Canberra: Attorney-General's Department.

Dewar, J. (1998). The normal chaos of family law. *Modern Law Review, 61*(4), 467–485.

Dunn, J., & Deater-Deckard, K. (2001). *Children's views of their changing families*. York: Joseph Rowntree Foundation.

Fitzgerald, R., & Graham, A. (2011a). The changing status of children within family law: from vision to reality? *Griffith Law Review: Law Theory Society, 20*(2), 421–448.

Fitzgerald, R., & Graham, A. (2011b). Something amazing I guess: children's views about having a say about supervised contact. *Australian Social Work, 64*(4), 487–501.

Gal, T., & Bessell, S. (2006). *Forming partnerships: the human rights of children in need of care and protection*. RegNet Seminar Series, The Australian National University.

Graham, A., & Fitzgerald, R. (2006). Taking account of the 'to and fro' of children's experiences in family law. *Children Australia, 31*(2), 30–36.

Graham, A., & Fitzgerald, R. (2010). Exploring the promises and possibilities for children's participation in family relationship centres. *Family Matters, 84*, 53–60.

Graham, A., Fitzgerald, R., & Phelps, R. (2009). *The changing landscape of family law: exploring the promises and possibilities for children's participation in Australian family relationship centres: final report*. Lismore: Southern Cross University.

Greene, S., & Hill, M. (2005). Researching children's experience: methods and methodological issues. In D. Hogan & S. Greene (Eds.), *Researching children's experience: methods and approaches* (pp. 1–21). London: Sage.

Greenwood, D. J., & Levin, M. (2005). Reform of the social sciences and of universities through action research. In N. Denzin & Y. Lincoln (Eds.), *The Sage handbook of qualitative research* (3rd ed., pp. 43–64). London: Sage.

Hewitt, B. (2008). *Marriage breakdown in Australia: social correlates, gender and initiator status*. Canberra: Department of Families, Housing, Community Services and Indigenous Affairs.

Humphreys, C., Houghton, C., & Ellis, J. (2008). *Literature review: better outcomes for children and young people experiencing domestic abuse: directions for good practice*. Edinburgh: The Scottish Government.

James, A. L. (2008). Children, the UNCRC, & family law in England and Wales. *Family Court Review, 46*(1), 53–64.

James, A. L. (2010). Competition or integration? The next step in Childhood Studies. *Childhood, 17*(4), 485–499.

Jenks, C. (2005). *Childhood* (2nd ed.). London: Routledge.

Kirby, P., & Laws, S. (2010). Advocacy for children in family group conferences: reflections on personal and public decision making. In B. Percy-Smith & N. Thomas (Eds.), *A handbook of children and young people's participation: perspectives from theory and practice* (pp. 113–120). London: Routledge.

Kogler, H. H., & Stueber, K. (1999). *Empathy and agency: the problem of understanding in human sciences*. Boulder, CO: Westview Press.

Lansdown, G. (2006). International developments in children's participation: lessons and challenges. In K. M. Tisdall, J. M. Davis, M. Hill, & A. Prout (Eds.), *Children, young people and social inclusion: participation for what?* (pp. 139–156). Bristol: Policy Press.

Lister, R. (2007). Why citizenship: where, when and how children? *Theoretical Inquiries in Law, 8,* 693–718.

Lodge, J., & Alexander, M. (2010). *Views of adolescents in separated families: a study of adolescents' experience after the 2006 reforms to the family law system.* Barton, ACT: Australian Institute of Families.

Maes, S. D. J., De Mol, J., & Buysse, A. (2012). Children's experiences and meaning construction on parental divorce: a focus group study. *Childhood, 19*(2), 266–279.

McIntosh, J., Burke, S., Dour, N., & Gridley, H. (2009). *Parenting after separation: a position statement prepared for the Australian Psychological Society.* Melbourne: Australian Psychological Society.

Moloney, L., Qu, L., Weston, R., & Hand, K. (2013). Evaluating the work of Australia's family relationship centres: evidence from the first 5 years. *Family Court Review, 51*(2), 234–249.

Mullen, C. A., Greenlee, B. J., & Bruner, D. Y. (2005). Exploring the theory-practice relationship in educational leadership curriculum through metaphor. *International Journal of Teaching and Learning in Higher Education, 17*(1), 1–14.

Parkinson, P. (2013. The idea of family relationship centres in Australia. *Family Court Review, 51*(2), 195–213.

Parkinson, P., & Cashmore, J. (2008). *The voice of a child in family law disputes.* London: Oxford University Press.

Percy-Smith, B., & Thomas, N. (2010). *A handbook of children and young people's participation: perspectives from theory and practice.* London: Routledge.

Prout, A., & James, A. (1997). A new paradigm for the sociology of childhood? Provenance, promise and problems. In A. James & A. Prout (Eds.), *Constructing and reconstructing childhood: contemporary issues in the sociological study of childhood* (pp. 7–33). London: Falmer Press.

Reason, P., & Bradbury, H. (2008). *The Sage handbook of action research: participatory inquiry and practice* (2nd ed.). London: Sage.

Rodgers, B., Gray, P., Davidson, T., & Butterworth, P. (2011). *Parental divorce and adult family, social and psychological outcomes: the contribution of childhood family adversity.* Social Policy Research Paper No. 42. Canberra: Commonwealth of Australia.

Schepard, A., & Emery, R. E. (2013). The Australian family relationship centres and the future of services for separating and divorcing families. *Family Court Review, 51*(2), 179–183.

Shemmings, D. (2000). Professionals' attitudes to children's participation in decision-making: dichotomous accounts and doctrinal contests. *Child and Family Social Work, 5*(3), 235–243.

Smart, C. (2002. From children's shoes to children's voices. *Family Court Review, 40*(2), 307–319.

Smart, C., Neale, B., & Wade, A. (2001). *The changing experience of childhood: families and divorce.* Cambridge: Polity Press.

Smith, A. B. (2007. Children as social actors: an introduction. *International Journal of Children's Rights, 15,* 1–4.

Taylor, N. (2006). What do we know about involving children and young people in family law decision making? A research update. *Australian Journal of Family Law, 20*(2), 154–178.

Theobald, P. (2012). *Supporting children when families separate*. Paper read at Family Law Pathways, May 18, 2012, at Coffs Harbour, Australia.

Trinder, L. (1997). Competing constructions of childhood: children's rights and children's wishes in divorce. *Journal of Social Welfare & Family Law, 19*(3), 291–305.

Tully, J. (2004). Recognition and dialogue: the emergence of a new field. *Critical Review of International Social and Political Philosophy, 7*(3), 84–106.

van Nijnatten, C., & Jongen, E. (2011). Professional conversations with children in divorce-related child welfare inquiries. *Childhood, 18*(4), 540–555.

Woodhead, M. (2009). Childhood studies: past, present and future. In M. J. Kehily (Ed.), *An introduction to childhood studies* (pp. 17–34). London: Open University Press.

PART IV

Child Participation in the Criminal Process

CHAPTER 12

Teen Courts

Children Participating in Justice

LYNNE MARIE KOHM

Participating in justice is uncommon for children, even when the process is about their own actions. A new juvenile diversion program in the United States, however, not only relies on a child's participation in his or her own justice but also creates a construct of shared decision-making that presents a broader sense of active citizenship for children. Resting on a best interests approach to participation, and in the context of positive peer influence, the teen court process serves as an alternative disposition program for children as young as age 9 and as old as age 17 who have committed nonviolent minor offenses (National Association of Youth Courts [NAYC], 2013; Regent Study, 2012).

A child's participation in the teen court process empowers him or her through offender rehabilitation and provides a meaningful and life-changing participation opportunity for the child, both during sentencing and afterward as a juror or other teen court actor. The teen court method offers an opportunity for a child offender to move away from a potential life of crime toward a healthy and thriving adulthood. It also offers rich participation opportunities for children in the judicial process of a peer offender.

The central advantage of teen courts is that through participation in a teen court program, teens develop citizenship abilities and civic skills and generally enhance their decision-making processes by participating as jurors in the program (Hirschinger-Blank, Simons, Volz, Thompson, Finely, & Cleary, 2009). This active participation fosters a sense of being vested with rights, privileges, and duties among the juveniles who are involved and is reflected not only in their own procedures as offenders but later when they take part in peers' trials. Through their participation, youth jurors, advocates, and prosecutors gain practical knowledge about and respect for the judicial system, which in turn validates sentencing and enforces the effectiveness of peer support in the context of the rule of law (Forgays, Kirby, DeMilio, & Schuster, 2004).

This chapter discusses how teen courts advance child participation in justice. It also examines the research and methodology of this new program of teen courts to determine whether and how a teen court forum can enhance and develop a child's decision-making process in the context of a reliable rule of law based on a jury of peers. The objective is to evaluate how teens can also develop their verbal and communication skills by serving as prosecutors or defense counsel, and how teen courts allow children to gain knowledge of decorum and protocol by serving as bailiffs, among other benefits.

These wonderfully rich opportunities for child offenders and other child participants are unique to the teen court process of juvenile justice and may provide an alternative that can positively contribute to the administration of justice to juvenile offenders.

JUVENILE JUSTICE IN AMERICA

The juvenile justice system in America, rather than circumscribing the best interests of the child, essentially rests on the tradition of the best interest standard and is applied to the extent that the child is not transferred to adult criminal courts but sought to be rehabilitated in a court designed to meet the needs of children (Mack 1909-10). Current juvenile justice systems, however, are in somewhat of a crisis (Public News Service, 2012). For four decades the U.S. government has increased funding for incarcerating American youth, who are otherwise not a danger to public safety, in adult-like prisons. This trend has perpetuated juvenile crime into a lifestyle and placed juvenile offenders at grave risk for abuse and a criminal future. "Juvenile delinquency is of perpetual concern in the United States. In 2007, law enforcement agencies reported 2.18 million arrests of juveniles. . . It is estimated that $14.4 billion is spent annually on the federal, state and local juvenile justice systems" (Alfrey, 2009, p. 5). Juvenile courts do not appear to be adequately handling juvenile crime, nor are they necessarily leaders in helping children in rehabilitation away from crime (Sickmund, 2009). In fact, the focus of the system is retributive, whether by intent or by caveat.

Combating this problem, a fascinating trend is emerging in juvenile justice—teen courts. As peer-based fora appearing in pockets throughout the United States, teen courts are designed to actively draw the child into his or her own criminal process. While garnering the attention of researchers for some time (Williamson, Chalk, & Knepper, 1993), much is still unknown about these teen disposition forums. Also sometimes referred to as a youth court, these courts are specialized community programs that accept, hear, try, and sentence mostly first-time misdemeanor offense cases when the defendant is a child, most often between the ages of 12 and 17. With professional guidance from adults, these diversion fora are quasicourts organized by children, for children, with children acting as prosecutor, defense attorney, juror, bailiff, and in some cases even judge. Supported by the local community in schools, churches, treatment centers, or law schools, youth courts offer an alternative to traditional juvenile justice based on the notion that a jury of peers may more adequately administer justice in a way best for a child (Singer, 1998). They seem to work because children operate largely in a framework of peer influence, and this chapter examines that further. When that influence is positive, the result is positive as well. These programs are generally focused on providing community, peer, and family support for the child offender, involving that child centrally in his or her own justice, fostering the child's best interests, and including that child later in the justice process of peers. When children participate in their own justice and the justice of their peers the experience seems to create a natural pathway to building a broader sense of active citizenship. This chapter explores these notions in depth.

RIGHTS OR BEST INTERESTS?

Although largely an American concept, the best interest of the child doctrine has had a global impact, culminating in various United Nations conventions regarding children, most particularly the Convention on the Rights of the Child, which established a rights framework to protect children participating in their own life decision-making (Kohm, 2008). Tension has developed, however, between notions of protectionism and autonomy for children (Aguirre & Wolfgram, 2002). A jurisprudence of children's rights is based in the best interests of the child standard but can serve to place children in an adversarial relationship with the adults around them (Bix, 2013; Mason, 1994). Child participation in justice is fostered by the best interest framework of the teen court model, where a child offender can participate in the process only after assuming culpability for his or her actions. The child must lay aside procedural rights to participate in the process.

These specialized courts encourage teen respect through program participation with the support of family, peers, and community while strengthening and restabilizing even the most fragmented families with that child's participation in justice. Being a teen is a time of great risk but also a time of great opportunity (Giedd, 2008). When children are viewed as rights holders, they are recognized as entitled to be engaged in the process of justice (Lundy & McEvoy, 2011). The teen court diversion program, however, illustrates how a teen offender who understands his or her procedural rights in the juvenile justice system, but who chooses to forego those rights in return for true and active participation in his or her own justice in a diversion setting, can develop self-respect, peer respect, and a better future by participating in a teen court.

WHAT IS A TEEN COURT?

A teen court, also sometimes referred to as a youth court, peer court, or student court, is a public or private program in which youth who acknowledge minor, nonviolent delinquent and status offenses and other behavioral problems are represented and sentenced by their peers. These courts produce children who more clearly understand the impact of their actions by participating in their own justice. There are currently over one thousand youth courts around the United States, and that number appears to be increasing (NAYC Map, 2013). These courts can be based in the juvenile justice system, the community, or the school, and their primary function is to determine a fair and rehabilitative disposition for a child offender. Each type of teen court arranges for an appropriate disposition with the participation of a jury of teen peers.

Possibly because the concept of teen courts is a relatively new one, the literature is slim. Publications produced by the U.S. Department of Justice (Butts & Buck, 2000), the NAYC network, established only as recently as 2007 (NAYC, 2013), and a 2012 independent survey of teen courts performed by Regent University School of Law's Center for Global Justice (Regent Study, 2012) provide the foundational literature. These sources join a few implementation guides (Godwin, Steinhart, & Fulton, 1998; Godwin Mullins, 2004). Several law and criminal justice journal articles have researched the teen court phenomenon, and others have addressed that research. Some are supportive of the trend and its positive effects, while others are not.

Norris, Twill, and Kim (2011) found positive trends and outcomes in a Midwestern teen court where child criminals benefitted from the participation with lower recidivism rates compared to those resulting from traditional juvenile justice courts. Harrison, Maupin, and Mays (2001) examined the teen court process and the outcomes and saw similar positive results. Others, however, have been critical of the process. Stickel, Connell, Wilson, and Gottfredson (2008) question whether teen courts reduce recidivism and whether they actually enhance the rule of law for children. Methods often seem unclear, creating possibilities for abuse of authority (Stickel et al., 2008). A team of researchers from New Zealand reviewed and summarized the studies available on teen courts and concluded that there is a lack of good research in that most studies of teen courts had mixed outcomes and methodological problems (Madell, Thom, & McKenna, 2013). Other data on teen courts reflect self-promoting material for particular fora and will be discussed in this chapter.

HOW DOES A TEEN COURT WORK?

A teen court works by referrals from several points of contact, such as school disciplinary or diversion programs, juvenile courts, authorized law enforcement,

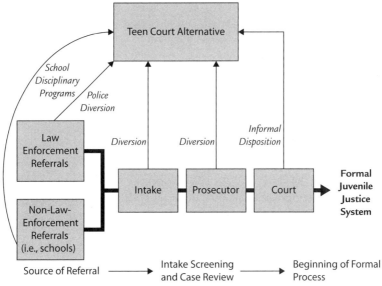

Figure 12.1:
Points at Which Juvenile offenders Can Be Diverted to Teen Court.
Source: Butts & Buck 2000, at p. 2.

prosecutors, or judges, to divert a child offender into a teen court alternative
(Fig. 12.1).

When a child commits a crime, if a teen court program is operational in that
locale he or she may be referred to this diversion alternative by a school, teacher,
or administrator, or by a law enforcement official, such as an arresting police officer or a probation officer. The child might also be referred to a teen court program
from an intake office, or from a prosecutor, or even directly from a judge or court.
Once the child's case is reviewed by the court administrator, the formal process
of sentencing begins (Butts & Buck, 2000).

Teen courts operate with various methods and results. Of the four primary
program models the most common is the adult judge model, which is used in
approximately half of all teen courts, where children run every aspect of the
court except the final judicial decision-making. The peer jury model, where teen
jurors question offenders, is used in almost one third of all teen court programs.
Discussion ensues between the jurors and the offender, and they all agree to a
fair sentence. This model is similar to the youth tribunal model, which is used
in 10 percent of the programs and works with a panel of teen judges. Finally,
the youth judge model is used in less than 20 percent of the teen courts and is
dependent on a teen judge (Godwin et al., 1998; NAYC, 2013; Regent Study,
2012). Most youth courts accept teen offender cases with misdemeanor nonviolent offenses, such as petty theft, vandalism, alcohol and tobacco use, assault, dis-
orderly conduct, possession of marijuana, and curfew violations. Violent crimes
are never accepted for the teen court process. Approximately half of all youth

courts also accept traffic offenses, truancy violations, trespassing, criminal mis-
chief, possession of drug paraphernalia, drug-related offenses, harassment, and
fraud (NAYC, 2013). The reasons for these differences are not apparent from
the literature and vary from court to court. Sentences also vary from court to
court, ranging from community service as the most popular rehabilitative measure along with oral and/or written apologies, to jury duty, restitution, and alcohol and drug assessments where appropriate. Other sentences include curfews,
tutoring, counseling, victim awareness classes and victim/offender mediation,
jail tours, teen court observation, and mentoring (NAYC, 2013; Regent Study,
2012). These hearings generally require confidential and closed communications, preserving the child's privacy and ensuring personal security (Godwin et
al., 1998). Furthermore, these courts are economically efficient, run largely by
volunteer adults and youth, operating at a cost of approximately $32,000 annu-
ally (NAYC, 2013).

The central means of participation for children in the teen court model takes
two forms. The first is in the participation of the child offender, and the second
form is manifested in the operation of the court by other children to carry out justice for child offenders. The first form of participation begins with the offending
child coming to terms with his or her own crime in a courtroom-style context in
the presence of peers. He or she must admit to the crime as charged to participate
in the process. Thus, participation begins first with the child offender himself or
herself choosing the process and "owning" the offense. Whether he or she does so
because of incentives, or to avert the juvenile justice process, or because of peer
pressure, he or she still must make the choice to participate in a teen court as an
alternative to the traditional justice process. From that point, the child offender
has acknowledged responsibility for his or her action, knowing that his or her
destiny in regard to the penalty for the crime lies at the feet of his or her peers.
Thereafter, the child offender participates in his or her own justice by conferring
with the teen court about the act, discussing an appropriate sentence or even several sentences, and then fulfilling that sentence in a timely manner as directed by
the teen court.

The second form of child participation in teen courts is as role players in other
teens' processes. Here, children serve as advocates for the offender and as prosecutors of the offense. They gather evidence, discuss the matter with the offender,
interview witnesses, and learn what factors may have mitigated or aggravated
the crime. They put on the sentencing case for the teen court jury. Children also
take on administrative roles such as bailiff. Most significantly, children participate in the deliberations of the court as jury members. The teen court program is
different from what happens, for example, in a restorative justice process, where
the process itself constructs shared decision-making. With a teen court, a child
offender participates by submitting himself or herself to the court of peers and
trusts their participation in carrying out justice for him or her. This presents an
interesting idea of the broader sense of community living under the rule of law

carried out by peers. The child offender learns the consequences of living under the rules of a society by submitting himself or herself to that society. This process also presents for the teen participants who operate the court a sense of active citizenship in carrying out the rule of law on behalf of other children. Their involvement in "making justice" in other people's justice processes can prove very useful. That process builds in each participant a sense of a community of peers being responsible to and for each other. It is significant in developing civic responsibility for children because it helps children learn and use methods for treating each other with civility but also accountability.

Critics of teen courts see how these qualities of the process can be abused or manipulated by the teens who direct the process. Stickel, Connell, Wilson, and Gottfredson (2008) argue that placing the rule of law in the hands of children can be extremely dangerous, and rightly so, because they lack the training, knowledge, and experience to meet out justice. A teen court could easily become a tyranny of intimidation for a child offender. For the process to work, proper adult supervision is important. A teen court, however, can build understanding among children in the treatment of peer offenders in the justice process.

WHY DO TEEN COURTS WORK?

Programs in which youth are heard and sentenced by their peers for minor nonviolent delinquent and status offenses and other behavioral problems seem to have positive effects for a few targeted reasons. They create a powerful environment of informed respect and active participation (Barrett, 2012), which begins to come more into focus when looking back at the beginnings of teen courts and what caused their rise.

The U.S. Congress established the Juvenile Justice and Delinquency Prevention Act of 1974 on the premise that "young people who understand the Nation's laws are less likely to violate them" (Williamson et al., 1993, p. 54). Although historical details are scant, apparently teen court–style fora began independently in the United States sometime in the 1970s when individuals and communities around the nation separately and distinctly began to realize that children respond better to changing their behavior when surrounded by peer support and decision-making (NAYC, 2013). In January 1983 the American Bar Association's Special Committee on Youth Education devoted a distinct section to teen courts at the Fifteenth Annual National Law-Related Education Seminar, bringing together founders of teen courts across the country, somewhat representing first steps toward nationalization of the teen court approach to juvenile justice (Williamson et al., 1993). In 1994 there were seventy-eight programs in just a few states; by 2010 there were over one thousand in operation in nearly every state (NAYC, 2013).

These courts seem to produce a generally good result for the teens who participate in them. When the child defendant successfully completes his or her participation in the teen court process, his or her charges are dismissed at a rate of 63 percent, and youthful offender records are immediately expunged at a 27 percent rate (NAYC, 2013). One study of four teen courts revealed six-month recidivism rates of 6 percent to 9 percent (Butts, Buck, & Cogeshall, 2002), while traditional juvenile justice courts carry a recidivism rate of 55 percent based on a one-year time frame (Office of Juvenile Justice and Delinquency, 2004). While the results are difficult to compare fairly, teen courts present an attractive diversion option for minor offenses and seem, at the very least, not to increase recidivism rates.

The interplay between teen offenders and their peers seems to be the essence of teen court success. Several sociological theories are useful in explaining this influence on adolescents. Classical conceptions of control theory and interactional theory are frequently used to explain delinquency (Thornberry, Lizotte, Krohn, & Farnworth, 1991). Peers influence a child's choice to adopt society's standards or to deviate from those standards. Social learning theory emphasizes the importance of observational learning and posits that people learn from observation, imitation, and modeling (Bandura, 1977). Peers who operate the teen court present the model for behavioral expectations of the child offender. By participating with his or her peers in the justice process, the child offender learns by observation, interaction, and joint decision-making. Furthermore, empowerment theory considers psychological empowerment through community-based research and intervention (Perkins & Zimmerman, 1995; Rappaport, 1984). By linking individual strengths and competencies, natural helping systems, and proactive behaviors to social policy and social change, various theories (particularly social learning theory and empowerment theory), research, and intervention attach individual well-being to the larger social and political environment (Perkins & Zimmerman, 1995). In the context of juvenile justice, this conjecture might suggest that with regard to conduct commonly associated with the onset of delinquent behavior, pressure from prosocial peers may strongly influence youth toward law-abiding behavior, especially when those involved participate in an integrated fashion such as that offered by a teen court program. While peer pressure is extremely effective in the lives of teens, it can also be negative, a factor that could be unhelpful to teen court effectiveness (Stickel et al., 2008). Experienced trial court judges and attorneys sometimes have authoritative trouble with juvenile offenders despite their position, influence, experience, and wisdom. A valid concern may be that a teen judge would not be able to bear the weight and authority vested in him or her by the teen court equitably. Participation with peers, nonetheless, creates the unique environment of the teen court.

Some scholars posit that more research and theory are necessary to adequately evaluate teen courts and their use of peer influence (Dick, Pence, Jones, & Geertsen, 2004). The growth of teen courts and the development of various juvenile justice initiatives across the United States, however, seem to reveal positively correlated trends between peer influence and juvenile cooperation with justice alternatives that promote the participation of children in their own justice process. While the peer operation of the court levels the playing field for child offenders, the child's participation in the process supports a personal accountability to that peer community from which the child offender benefits in generally better future behavior. This process builds mutual respect and can encourage troubled teens to move successfully through adolescence and into adulthood.

HOW TEEN COURTS ADVANCE PARTICIPATION

An examination of a few of these nearly one thousand courts around the United States (NAYC, 2013) brings the participation process and its effects into better focus. One of the most renowned teen courts in the country is the Time Dollar Youth Court (TDYC, 2013) in Washington, DC. In a city known around the world for crime (Urbina, 2008), child offenders learn by observation and therefore are not unlikely to turn to crime. The TDYC seems to be making a difference to some teens in this high-crime scenario, proving to be not only effective but also inspiring and healing to children from fragmented or never-formed families (TDYC, 2013). A juvenile diversion program for first-time offenders, TDYC provides an alternative method for juvenile criminal dispositions. Placing responsibility on the child offender to participate in the justice process, the key component of the program is a peer jury, where an adjudicated defender may later serve as a juror as well. "The philosophical underpinning of TDYC is that the process of performing jury duty service leads to the development of enhanced self-efficacy and civic engagement" (Flowers, 2013, p. 4).

Handling nearly nine hundred juvenile cases in a one-year period, this court's goal is to "create a change in the outlook of the juveniles that progress through its program. . . [to] focus on changes in life-skills, community involvement and future aspirations" (Flowers, 2013, p. 11). Referred to the court from metropolitan police forces or by juvenile court order, the child participants self-reported a 3 percent recidivism rate, with problem solving being a critical advantage gained by participants (Flowers, 2013). One teen offender rejoiced that because of the Youth Court he had a community service résumé rather than a criminal record (TDYC, 2013). Many of the teen participants in this program have minimal family stability and associate the program itself with their closest circle of support. In their interviews they claim that their lives have been directly changed for the better because of their participation in this court. They seem to say that the opportunity to participate in justice, both their own and that of others, is the most significant component of the court (TDYC, 2013).

On the other side of the country, the Calabasas Teen Court (CTC) in the small town of Calabasas, California, meets in the Calabasas Library. This program provides an alternative for child offenders from a more small-town population and gives a different picture of how a teen court operates and assists children in participation of justice (CTC, 2013). The program provides a simple model that functions with the assistance of a local volunteer judge or attorney and teen peer prosecutors and defense attorneys for teen offenders between the ages of 13 and 17 who have committed a misdemeanor-type crime, with the objective of "interrupt[ing] the developing pattern of criminal behavior in juveniles by promoting self-esteem, motivation for self-improvement and forming a healthy attitude toward authority" (CTC, 2013). The offenders assume responsibility for their behavior and accept the consequences of their actions through community service work, serving on the teen court jury, and serving any punishment sanctioned by the jury of their peers. Most significantly, the CTC gives children a unique "challenge and opportunity to demonstrate to adults and themselves their capacity for self-government and responsible citizenship" (CTC, 2013). This occurs through the process of requiring the child offender to own up to his or her actions by admission, an initial act of self-government, followed by submitting to a jury of child peers for sentencing. Referred to the court by the State Attorney's Office, local law enforcement, or the local department of juvenile justice, the teen offender comes before the court generally with family support and having acknowledged his or her guilt. "The offender and their parent/guardian meet with the Teen Court Coordinator for a pretrial interview to go over the rules and guidelines of the program. Once the teen has been accepted into the program, a Waiver of Speedy Trial is signed" (CTC, 2013). The children who operate the court's procedures are trained in advance. "The teens are given `hands-on' experience with the legal process, become familiar with the Court system and learn about various career opportunities the Court system has to offer. The offenders also learn about various career opportunities through the community service they perform" (CTC, 2013). A forward-looking perspective presents the context for current sentencing: "In the Court session, after the teen clerk calls the case, the Judge explains the offense committed. The teen defense and prosecution attorneys then present the case to the teen jury through the testimony of the offender, the incident report and a pretrial information sheet compiled by the Coordinator. After carefully listening to the facts, the teen jury deliberates the case and decides a constructive sentence for the offender. . . The offender and their parent/guardian then meet with the Coordinator to sign a contract to complete the sentence received from the teen jury" (CTC, 2013). Family members and other citizens of the local community can be admitted to the courtroom venue upon agreement of the parties to the proceeding. Parents and guardians can see their children taking responsibility for their actions. The court involves the child's family at the initial program entry, throughout the process, and in the final outcome. The larger community of Calabasas might also witness the children taking an active role in the trials of other children through the teen court. This can foster a sense of respect and pride toward the children who participate in the teen court process.

In an American town along the porous Mexican border, a teen court in Doña Ana County, New Mexico, was the subject of an empirical study to identify its successes and failures for youths charged with relatively minor offenses. Child offenders were given the teen court option as an alternative to the traditional juvenile court procedures, and those who made the choice for the teen court made up the pool of participants. Examining 478 randomly selected teen court participants over a four-year period (1994–1998) researchers found a 25 percent recidivism rate, which was affected by youth's gender and age, the presence of a prior referral, and the person with whom the juvenile resided (Harrison, 2001). Referral to the teen court tended to achieve more comprehensive family support for the child than would a traditional juvenile court experience, and therefore a more efficacious result for the child. But even with the teen court, residential circumstances were a significant factor in recidivism. Teen court participants who were supported by family or parental involvement had lower recidivism rates than those without stable family residences (Harrison, 2001), a factor that is not dissimilar to positive outcomes for traditional juvenile justice fora.

Teen courts researched in the Midwestern United States show varying results. A study of 648 youths in an Illinois teen court over an eight-year period found that sentencing and referral-based models supported an interpretation in which development of the offender's character in the teen court process was central to the outcomes (Rasmussen, 2004). How the child responds to the teen court process based on his or her support structure seems to be significant. Another study evaluating a Midwestern teen court, however, found that in a survival analysis of 186 regular diversion participants, no significant differences in recidivism rates were apparent, although teens who completed the program were half as likely to reoffend as those who did not complete the program (Norris et al., 2011). Another study that focused on sentence completion and recidivism of juveniles referred to teen court for a disposition by their peers as an alternative to judicial sentencing found that more than 70 percent of the teens completed their sentence; less than a third of those teens recidivated over a one-year period of follow-up (Minor, Wells, Soderstrom, Bingham, & Williamson, 1999). Their findings implied the need for teen courts to be guided by sound program-development efforts that are based on research to circumvent the panacea phenomenon. Two other studies did not discuss child participation as an asset of teen courts but rather focused on the teen court as an asset to the community as stakeholders in future citizenship by providing a forum more suitable for child offenders (Gilbert & Settles, 2007; Payne & Button, 2009). Another study showed a lower recidivism rate in teen court effectiveness, however, for second-time offenders (Forgays & DeMilio, 2005).

A study of an urban Pennsylvania teen court in an African American community just outside of Philadelphia expressly illustrates the significance of child participation. Survey evaluations completed by parents revealed the satisfaction levels of both children and parents in terms of fairness of treatment, the helpfulness of the process, and the respect both parent and child gleaned from the court for themselves, each other, and the process because of the child's participation in the program. The results illustrated high to very high satisfaction levels, particularly among parents (Hirschinger-Blank et al., 2009). Teens seem to hold high value for the program. "Research indicates that jurors enjoy the responsibility of sentencing their peers and take pride in assuming adult roles and contribution to the community" (Hirschinger et al., 2009, p. 38, citing Forgays, DeMilio, & Schuster, 2004, and Mahdavi & Smith, 2002).

Importing a popular innovation from adult courts, state and local governments have started hundreds of specialized teen drug courts to provide judicial supervision and coordinate family involvement in substance abuse treatment for drug-involved juvenile offenders. The number of children affected by these new courts is relatively small, but the programs are spreading rapidly and their presence is changing how practitioners and policymakers think about adolescent drug use. They also seem to add evidence to the significance of the drug-abusing child's participation in the process. In these specialized courts, child drug offenders are actively involved with a team of adult professionals with whom the child must work in monitoring his or her substance abuse behavior. Probably one of the most profound and insightful pieces of evidence for how child participation and peer respect create good responses from youthful offenders is found in the teen court model of the Daniel Bryant Youth and Family Treatment Center. That program illustrates the impact a youth drug court diversion program has on teens and their parents alike in diverting the teen from substance abuse behavior through program participation and the positive peer influences the child encounters in that process (Daniel Bryant, 2013).

Like traditional youth courts, the popularity of juvenile drug courts is increasing significantly, yet researchers have only begun to test whether they stop or reduce teen substance abuse more effectively than other programs (Butts & Roman, 2004). These specialized drug courts serve juvenile offenders in a rehabilitative capacity and are focused on empowering the child. They aim to implement justice through alternative forms such as dispute resolution and treatment options, all of which require the child's participation (Geraghty & Mlyniec, 2002). These courts and programs focus on minimizing harm to the children involved, even as youthful offenders, and seek to foster the best interest of the child paradigm, viewing the child's participation as critical to achieving that outcome. Although these specialized courts vary in methodology (Butts, Roman, & Lynn-Whaley, 2011), they all focus on increasing family involvement to accomplish what is best for the child substance abuser to achieve his or her best outcome by participating in the justice process.

WHY PARTICIPATION MATTERS

In a four-decade review by American social service researchers, a formidable connection was established between child welfare and juvenile justice involvement

(Benda & Corwyn, 2002). Although a legal process is at its core, the entry, exit, and prolonged involvement of any child in the juvenile justice system are influenced by a host of factors that include social aspects, cultural factors, and individual characteristics (Maschi, Hatcher, Schwalbe, & Scotto Rosato, 2008). The objective for juvenile courts is generally to make positive use of these factors in the process, and teen court allows for the consideration of these factors. The juvenile justice system has three major objectives: protection of public safety, holding juvenile offenders accountable for their behavior, and providing treatment and rehabilitation services for juveniles (Maschi et al., 2008). Rehabilitation is most likely to be successful when the child is empowered with the inimitable combination of participation and peer involvement in the process. The trends visible with teen courts bear out this notion and point to some additional positive indicators for the benefits to families, communities, societies, and nations of empowerment through child participation in justice.

A majority of adolescents enter the juvenile court system between the ages of 13 and 16 (Henning, 2006). During these years, youth naturally rely on their parents, a fact that should be anticipated during juvenile delinquency proceedings (Edwards, 1993; Henning, 2006). Family support is significant to a child. (Waldfogel, Craigie, & Brooks-Gunn, 2010). The importance of a father connection became particularly clear in a study of African American adolescent marijuana use by Mandara, Rogers, and Zinbarg (2011), where boys were significantly deterred from drug use when living with a biological father. The study by Burton and Jarrett (2000) demonstrated that even in a fractured family structure, families can mitigate harmful neighborhood influences to minimize juvenile crime. Family structure matters, and whether due to unformed families, family fragmentation, or divorce, children pay the price for lost parental support on numerous levels (Blankenhorn, 1996; Muehlenberg, 2002). The teen court experience can provide structure for a delinquent child from a broken or unstable family and can also help build respect and esteem for and in the child through the process, as other adults and peers provide support to him or her. Furthermore, teen courts can encourage open communication and foster a continuing healthy relationship between the child and an available parent (Henning, 2006). Family fragmentation, however, may be both an indicator and a result of poor application of juvenile justice. While a teen court program cannot be the panacea, communities where law enforcement works together with peers and family members to develop adolescent accountability appear to enhance diversion from a formal and intimidating process to a respectable peer form that promotes participation and community support. "Tightly coupling" or closely connecting juvenile justice with family and community, both at the stage of deciding when to divert a juvenile from the formal court process and during the process itself, seems to be more effective (Singer, 1998). All these outcomes seem to rest on the opportunity for the child to actively participate in his or her own justice and reap the benefits accordingly.

Moreover, and most significantly, the teen court model provides for personal and civic development on many levels for the teens who operate the court. The central virtue of teen courts is the involvement of juveniles in justice processes of others like them. Becoming a jury member, particularly after being the subject of sentencing previously, can work to rehabilitate a child socially among his or her peers, personally in renewed self-esteem, and civically in trust and responsibility. Mutual peer respect is a significantly positive factor for teens because they seem to highly value the contributions of each other. Community respect for the process and the teens involved grows and improves, particularly as teen courts receive community support across a wide spectrum, from the legal community to business partners (Butts & Buck, fig. 8 at p. 7, 2000). These circles make up the teen's society and can also become important factors for predicting social outcomes. The child who participates in justice receives a considerable additional benefit of understanding and respecting the rule of law. These elements are significant benefits of a teen's participation in justice.

There is growing recognition that antisocial behaviors are produced by a combination of environmental and genetic factors, with research revealing that those specific factors work interactively and often moderate the effects of each other. One study examining how neighborhood disadvantage interacted with certain genomes predicted three different antisocial measures: adolescent victimization, contact with delinquent peers, and involvement in violent delinquency (Beaver, Gibson, DeLisi, Vaughn, & Wright, 2011). An analysis of male respondents drawn from the National Longitudinal Study of Adolescent Health revealed that the association between the targeted genes and the measures of antisocial outcomes tended to be stronger in disadvantaged neighborhoods (Beaver et al., 2011). Involving those same children in positive alternative sentencing in youth courts significantly changes results. For example, one teen offender participating in the TDYC stated that she was at ease and felt self-esteem in the teen court process (TDYC, 2013). A reporter observed the process:

> Geraldine Martin, a teenage judge in the D.C. Youth Court, said that sometimes she and a juror will sit for 15 or 20 minutes after a case, talking to the defendant. "We'll ask: 'do you think what you did is right? Disrespecting your mother, yelling, cursing—your younger brother or sister would see you doing it and think it's O.K.' A juror who is free to tell a defendant he is out of line would never say the same thing in school or on the street corner. (Rosenberg, 2011a, p. 4)

Participation with peers is vital:

> "The most powerful factor is peer support for pro-social behavior," said Jeffrey Butts, one of the authors of the Urban Institute study,. . . now the director of the Research and Evaluation Center at John Jay College of Criminal Justice in New York. (Rosenberg, 2011b, p. 3)

Teen courts seem to illustrate that children do better when they contribute to the solution to their problems, especially when the children interact with peers who have experienced similar hardship. Even though a teen understands that he or she is in trouble, attitudes are altered by the peer review circumstances presented in the teen court setting. This setting sends a message of respect that is critically significant. An extraordinary situation occurs when teen offenders find that the adjudicators consist of a jury of their peers, children like them, instead of adults (Rosenberg, 2011a). The teen experiences, possibly for the first time in his or her life, a sense of respect and regard, that somehow his or her position and plight might just be understood and even empathized with, producing an atmosphere ripe with the potential for extremely positive results. "Youth court is one of the few places where teenagers hear disapproval of their behavior from people whose respect they crave the most: their peers" (Rosenberg, 2011b, p. 1). This peer respect is important to the teen offender and motivates a response of involvement. The process is also beneficial because it gives the offender the opportunity to observe directly how his or her behavior has affected the victim or victims and his or her community of peers. Victims write impact statements and the judge and jury address the offender directly, reinforcing the teen court philosophy. The process is seen as beneficial because the sanctions are handed down by the offender's peers rather than an intake officer or another adult; the child is receiving judgment from his or her peers, a right typically not extended to juveniles in the juvenile justice system (Butts & Buck, 2000; Rosenberg, 2011a).

When a child participates in his or her own justice, many facets of his or her life are developed and strengthened. These include the child's sense of personal responsibility, confidence, self-esteem, public and community awareness, and appreciation for the trust placed in him or her by family and community members and the state inherent in the process. There is evidence, however, that youth courts do more than simply divert teenagers from juvenile justice: they actively create pro-social behavior. (Butts & Ortiz, 2011). The Urban Institute study found a major clue: The courts that give the most autonomy to the teens themselves work best. The process is more effective because the teen defendants see their peers as speaking to them personally, rather than conveying a message from adults (Butts & Buck, 2000). It may be argued that the important feature is non-hierarchical, peer feedback, rather than active engagement of the juvenile. Yet without the offending child's choice to participate in the teen court, this peer criticism and response might not be as effective, or even as possible. Furthermore, the more courts are run by teenagers, the more authority and respect they enjoy. "In the roughest neighborhoods, respect goes to those who are most feared. For some teenagers it is probably eye-opening to see their peers commanding respect for good behavior" (Butts & Ortiz, 2011). That command of respect, in turn, works to afford the child self-respect.

Teen court participants also gain a respect for the rule of law. In teen court a system of universal principles of individual and government accountability operates under clear, stable, and just laws to protect fundamental rights and personal and property security. The legal process that is administered and enforced is accessible, fair, and efficient, reflecting the community being served (World Justice Project, 2008–2014). To participate in most teen court programs, a child must take responsibility for his or her involvement in the offense, accepting the charges against him or her as a violation of the law. This requires agreement of culpability at the outset. "Youth courts allow teens to hold each other accountable for their illegal actions" (Youth Courts, at p. 1, 2011). When children participate in their own justice and the justice process of their peers, they come away with a greater respect for the law and local law enforcement (Office of Juvenile Justice and Delinquency, 2004).

A central advantage of teen courts is that teens develop citizenship abilities and civic skills and generally enhance their decision-making process by participation as jurors (Hirschinger-Blank et al., 2009). This active participation and sense of citizenship are reflected not only in their own procedures as offenders, but later when they serve in peers' trials. Through their participation, youth jurors gain practical knowledge about and respect for the judicial system as well, which in turn validates sentencing and enforces the effectiveness of peer support in the context of the rule of law (Forgays et al., 2004). Teen courts enhance and develop a child's decision-making process in the context of a reliable rule of law based on a jury of peers. Teens are also able to develop their verbal and communication skills by serving as prosecutors or defense counsel. They gain knowledge of decorum and protocol by serving as bailiffs. These wonderfully rich opportunities for child offenders are unique to the teen court process.

The evidence surrounding risk factors for juvenile delinquency "suggests that youth who encounter the juvenile justice system have a history of concurrent and/or sequential service needs and prior human service involvement." (Maschi et al., 2008). These factors, easily visible in a teen court program, can be considered by peers in a subsequent determination, just as they can by a judge in a juvenile court. But the teen court provides a diversion from that system. In light of collective responsibility norms, the diversion offered by a teen court makes children accountable to themselves, their family, their community, and the victim (if there is one) rather than solely to the criminal justice system itself. In communal cultures such as the Middle East, South America, Africa, and Asia, where it is important for the victim and the local community to feel that the child has repaid the individuals affected, a teen court could be extremely helpful because the teen takes public responsibility for his or her actions by accepting culpability, and his or her peers confer together on his or her recompense, and how the punishment can bring healing to the victim and rehabilitation to the child offender. This method provides the child offender with tools that may work to ensure that he or she will not repeat the offense, but that he or she can also move beyond this and positively contribute to the development of the local community.

Respect is a formidable key to explaining the success of the teen court process. With parental involvement, that respect also converts to loving support for the youthful offender. Teen courts provide the right peer-supportive environment for positive and healthy diversion of child offenders where they participate in the justice process.

CONCLUSION

The growth of teen courts across the United States is fostering significant and meaningful child participation. There remains, however, significant room for further study of this phenomenon. The facts thus far seem to strongly indicate that teen courts work because they involve a peer process that relies on active and meaningful participation of children in justice.

Teen courts have the potential to be part of the solution to the problems facing the American juvenile justice system. The concept set forth in this chapter is that teen courts foster esteem and empowerment in children by their integrated participation in the justice process. The direct goal of this process is to alter and improve justice for juveniles, but the indirect result can be a simultaneous strengthening and stabilization for a child through his or her meaningful participation in justice. Teen courts are an alternative to traditional juvenile justice that provides an authentic opportunity to participate in justice. These programs can also be a helpful tool in creating a better future for a child. Although they are not the solution to family fragmentation or the crisis in juvenile justice, teen courts can be a first step in allowing a child's crime to help move him or her toward personal, family, and community stabilization. Most significantly, teen courts allow for children to participate in the justice of their peers. Teen courts take a negative—a child's initial involvement with the criminal justice system—and invert it into a potentially positive life-altering experience by making children central actors in the process.

When a child's participation in justice is respected and trusted by his or her immediate peers, family, and community and by the judicial system, that child is empowered. The teen court process, where children participate in justice, culminates in a stronger, safer, and more sustainable community because children become stakeholders and participants rather than outsiders caught up in a system of reprisal. The teen court trend in participatory justice may be an effective avenue to empowering children in the criminal justice process.

REFERENCES

Aguirre, M. S., & Wolfgram, A. (2002). United Nations policy and the family: redefining the ties that bind. A study of history, forces and trends. *Brigham Young University Journal of Public Law, 16,* 113–178.

Alfrey, C. (2009). Juvenile delinquency and family structure: implications for marriage and relationship education. National Healthy Marriage Resource Center. Accessed Nov. 13, 2013, at www.healthymarriageinfo.org/download.aspx?id=405. Also citing

Kumpher, K. L. (2004). Strengthening America's families: Exemplary parenting and family strategies for delinquency prevention. *CASA*. Accessed Nov. 13, 2013, at http://www.strengtheningfamiles.org.

Bandura, A. A. (1977). *Social learning theory*. Englewood Cliffs, NJ: Prentice Hall.

Barrett, C. J. (2012). *Courting kids: inside an experimental youth court*. New York: NYU Press.

Beaver, K. M., Gibson, C. L., DeLisi, M., Vaughn, M. G., & Wright, J. P. (2011). The interaction between neighborhood disadvantage and genetic factors in the prediction of antisocial outcomes. *Youth Violence and Juvenile Justice, 10*, 25.

Benda, B. B., & Corwyn, R. F. (2002). The effect of abuse in childhood and adolescence on violence among adolescents. *Youth & Society, 33*(3), 339–376.

Blankenhorn, D., (1996). Fatherless America: Confronting Our Most Urgent Social Problem (HarperPerennial).

Burton, L. M., & Jarrett, R. L. (2000). In the mix, yet on the margins: the place of families in urban neighborhood and child development research. *Journal of Marriage and Family, 62*, 1114.

Butts, J. A., & Buck, J. (2000). Teen courts: a focus on research, U.S. Dept. of Justice: Office of Juvenile Justice and Delinquency Programs. Accessed Nov. 13, 2013, at http://youthcourt.net/wp-content/uploads/2010/05/183472.pdf, and http://www.youthcourt.net/wp-content/uploads/2010/05/teencourtsfocus.pdf. (which includes Fig. 1: Points at Which Juvenile Offenders Can Be Diverted to Teen Court, and also includes Urban Institute, National Survey of Youth Courts and Teen Courts, 1998, Figure 8: Perceived Levels of Support from Community Groups).

Butts, J. A., Buck, J., & Cogeshall, M. (2002). The impact of teen court on young offenders. The Urban Institute. Available at: http://www.urban.org/uploadedpdf/410457.pdf.

Butts, J. A., & Ortiz, J. (2011, Jan. 14). Teen courts—do they work and why? *New York State Bar Association Journal, Jan. 2011*, pp. 18–21. Accessed Nov. 3, 2014, at http://johnjayresearch.org/wp-content/uploads/2011/04/buttsortizjrnjan11.pdf.

Butts, J., & Roman, J. (Eds.) (2004). *Juvenile drug courts and teen substance abuse*. Urban Institute Press, Washington, D.C.

Butts, J. A., Roman, J. K., & Lynn-Whaley, J. (2011). Varieties of juvenile court: nonspecialized courts, teen courts, drug courts, and mental health courts. In B. C. Feld & D. M. Bishop (Eds.), *The Oxford handbook of juvenile crime and juvenile justice*. New York: Oxford University Press.

Calabasas Teen Court (2013). Calabasas, CA. Accessed Nov. 12, 2013, at http://www.cityofcalabasas.com/teen-court.html.

Daniel Bryant Youth and Family Treatment Center (2013). *Teen court: an innovative approach to justice*. Santa Barbara, CA. Accessed May 13, 2013 at http://cadasb.org/youth-services/daniel-bryant-treatment-center.aspx. Accessed May 22, 2013 at http://www.youtube.com/watch?v=e-_sIo5tIOA.

Dick, A. J., Pence, D. J., Jones, R. M., & Geertsen, H. R. (2004). The need for theory in assessing peer courts. *American Behavioral Scientist, 47*, 1448–1461.

Edwards, L. P. (1993). A comprehensive approach to the representation of children: the Child Advocacy Coordinating Council. *Family Law Quarterly, 27*, 417.

Flowers, A. S. (2013). Time Dollar Youth Court: 2010 evaluation final report. Global Youth Justice. Accessed Nov. 12, 2013, at http://www.globalyouthjustice.org/uploads/Washington_DC_s_Time_Dollar_Youth_Court.pdf.

Forgays, D. K., & DeMilio, L. (2005). Is teen court effective for repeat offenders? A test of the restorative justice approach. *International Journal of Offender Therapy and Comparative Criminology, 49*, 107–118.

Forgays, D. K., DeMilio, L., & Schuster, K. (2004). Teen court: what jurors can tell us about the process. *Juvenile & Family Court Journal, 55*, 25–33.

Geraghty, A. H., & Mlyniec, W. J. (2002). Unified family courts: tempering enthusiasm with caution. *Family Court Review, 40*, 435–452.

Giedd, J. (2008). The teen brain—insights from neuroimaging. *Journal of Adolescent Health, 42*, 335–343.

Gilbert, M. J., & Settles, T. L. (2007). The next step: indigenous development of neighborhood-restorative community justice. *Criminal Justice Review, 32*, 5–25.

Godwin, T. M., Steinhart, D. J., & Fulton, B. A. (1998). *Peer justice & youth empowerment: an implementation guide for teen court programs.* Accessed May 22, 2014, at http://books.google.com/books?id=Mm4rKf7FJicC&printsec=frontcover&source=gbs_ge_summary_r&cad=0#v=onepage&q&f=false.

Harrison, P., Maupin, J. R., & Mays, G. L. (2001). Teen court: an examination of processes and outcomes. *Crime & Delinquency, 47*, 243–264.

Henning, K. (2006). It takes a lawyer to raise a child? Allocating responsibilities among parents, children, and lawyers in delinquency cases. *Nevada Law Journal, 6*, 836–843.

Hirschinger-Blank, N., Simons, L., Volz, G. L., Thompson, R., Finely, L., & Cleary, J. (2009). A pilot assessment of a school-based youth court in a resource-poor African-American urban school district: lessons learned from youth court volunteers. *Juvenile & Family Court Journal, 60*, 31.

Kohm, L. M. (2008). Tracing the foundations of the best interests of the child standard in American jurisprudence. *Journal of Law & Family Studies. 10*, 337. Available at: http://papers.ssrn.com/sol3/papers.cfm?abstract_id=1957143

Lundy, L., & McEvoy, L. (2011). Children's rights and research processes: Assisting children to (in)formed views. *Childhood, 19*(1), 129–144.

Mack, J. M. (1909-10). The juvenile court. *Harvard Law Review, 23*, 120.

Madell, D., Thom, K., & McKenna, B. (2013). A systematic review of literature relating to problem-solving youth courts. *International Journal of Law and Psychiatry, 34*, 49–55.

Mahdavi, J., & Smith, P. (2002). The operation of a bully court and perceptions of its success: A case study. *School Psychology International, 23*, 327–341; Accessed Nov. 3, 2014, at http://www.bully.org/images/bullycourts.pdf.

Mandara, J., Rogers, S. H., & Zinbarg, R. E. (2011). The effects of family structure on African American adolescents' marijuana use. *Journal of Marriage and Family, 73*, 557–569.

Maschi, T., Hatcher, S. S., Schwalbe, C. S., & Scotto Rosato, N. (2008). Mapping the social service pathways of youth to and through the juvenile justice system: A comprehensive review. *Children and Youth Services Review, 30*, 1376–1385.

Mason, M. A. (1994). *From fathers' property to children's rights: The history of child custody in the United States* (pp. 121–126). New York: Columbia University Press.

Minor, K. I., Wells, J. B., Soderstrom, I. R., Bingham, R., & Williamson, D. (1999). Sentence completion and recidivism among juveniles referred to teen courts. *Crime & Delinquency, 45*, 467–480.

Muehlenberg, B. (2002). The case for two-parent family, part II. *National Observer, 53*, 49–58.

Mullins, T. G. (Ed.) (2004). *Selected topics on youth courts: A monograph.* Office of Juv. Justice & Del. Prevention, and National Highway Traffic Safety Adm. Accessed May 22, 2014, at http://www.aidainc.net/monograph.pdf.

National Association of Youth Courts (2013). Youth court functions. Accessed November 13, 2013, at http://www.youthcourt.net/?page_id=24;

NAYC. Map of Youth Courts. Accessed Nov. 12, 2013. http://www.youthcourt.net/?page_id=3.

Norris, M., Twill, S., & Kim, C. (2011). Smells like teen spirit: evaluating a Midwestern teen court. *Crime & Delinquency*, 57, 199–221.

Office of Juvenile Justice and Delinquency (2004). *Selected topics on youth courts: a monograph*. U.S. Dept. of Justice. 61.

Payne, P. K., & Button, D. M. (2009). Developing a citywide youth violence prevention plan: perceptions of various stakeholders. *International Journal of Offender Therapy and Comparative Criminology*, 53, 517–534.

Perkins, D. D., & Zimmerman, M. A. (1995). Empowerment theory, research, and application. *American Journal of Community Psychology*, 23, 569.

Public News Service (2012). Report: juvenile justice system in crisis. Accessed Oct. 13, 2013, at http://www.publicnewsservice.org/index.php?/content/article/28300-1.

Rappaport, J. (1984). Studies in empowerment: Introduction to the issue. *Prevention in Human Services*, 3, 1–7.

Rasmussen, A. (2004). Teen court referral, sentencing, and subsequent recidivism: two proportional hazards models and a little speculation. *Crime & Delinquency*, 50, 615–635.

Regent Study (2012). *State survey of United States teen courts*. Center for Global Justice, Human Rights, and the Rule of Law. Regent University School of Law. Virginia Beach, VA, 2012. Accessible at http://www.regent.edu/acad/schlaw/globaljustice/publications.cfm.

Rosenberg, T. (2011a). For young offenders, hope in a jury of their peers. *New York Times*. Accessed Oct. 13, 2011, at http://opinionator.blogs.nytimes.com/2011/10/13/for-teen-offenders-hope-in-a-jury-of-their-peers/.

Rosenberg, T. (2011b). Where teens find the jury isn't rigged against them. *New York Times*. Accessed Oct. 18, 2011, at http://opinionator.blogs.nytimes.com/2011/10/18/where-teens-find-the-jury-isnt-rigged/.

Sickmund, M. (2009). Delinquency cases in juvenile court. The Office of Juvenile Justice and Delinquency Prevention. Office of Justice Programs. Accessed Nov. 13, 2013, at http://www.ncjrs.gov/pdffiles1/ojjdp/224538.pdf.

Singer, S. I. (1998). Criminal and teen courts as loosely coupled systems of juvenile justice. *Wake Forest Law Review*, 33, 509–527.

Stickel, W. P., Connell, N. M., Wilson, D. M., & Gottfredson, D. (2008). An experimental evaluation of teen courts. *Journal of Experimental Criminology*, 4, 137–163.

Thornberry, T. P., Lizotte, A. J., Krohn, M. D., & Farnworth, M. (1991). Testing Interactional Theory: an examination of reciprocal causal relationships among family, school, and delinquency. *Journal of Criminal Law and Criminology*, 82, 3–35. Available at http://scholarlycommons.law.northwestern.edu/cgi/viewcontent.cgi?article=6689&context=jclc.

Time Dollar Youth Court (2013). Accessed Nov. 12, 2013, at http://www.youtube.com/watch?v=Hqp8MzJzm4M, and http://www.youtube.com/watch?v=bIL1Ch9OET0.

Urbina, I. (2008). Washington officials try to ease crime fear. *New York Times*. Dec. 7, 2008.

Waldfogel, J., Craigie, T., & Brooks-Gunn, J. (2010). Fragile Families and Child Wellbeing in *The Future of Children* 20, 87–112. Available at http://futureofchildren.org/futureofchildren/publications/docs/20_02_05.pdf.

Williamson, D., Chalk, M., & Knepper, P. (1993). Teen court: juvenile justice for the 21st century? *Federal Probation*, 87, 84.

World Justice Project (2008–2014). What is the rule of law. Accessed Nov. 13, 2013, at http://worldjusticeproject.org/what-rule-law.

Youth Courts (2011). Fact sheet. Administrative Office of the Courts, Judicial Council of California. Accessed Nov. 13, 2013, at http://www.courts.ca.gov/documents/Youth_Courts.pdf.

CHAPTER 13

The Developmental Stakes of Youth Participation in American Juvenile Court

EMILY BUSS

INTRODUCTION

In the United States and throughout the world, innovative responses to juvenile crime focus on the value of engaging young people directly and significantly (Dowd, 2011). But these innovations occur exclusively *outside* the courts and are expressly offered as an alternative to court involvement. Because most youth are better served by avoiding court involvement altogether, this diversionary use of youth-engaging programming is well justified. But some young people, especially the oldest, the most serious offenders, and youth of color, will go to court, and in these courts, despite broad due process protections under law, they are systematically barred from meaningful participation. It is precisely this group of young people, however, whose social development is at most serious risk, and it is precisely this group of young people who stand to gain the most from their participation in the decision-making process. If an active supported engagement in important decision-making concerning an adolescent's life can have any developmental impact, as considerable social science suggests it can, we would do well to offer this opportunity to those young people who need it the most.

This chapter applies social scientific evidence of the developmental value of meaningful participation to the special population and context of juvenile court. I argue that the juvenile court process, particularly at disposition, should be dramatically reformed to bring the young person to the center of dispositional decision-making. The American juvenile justice system targets for juvenile court involvement those deemed at serious risk of developing into adult criminals who are nevertheless entitled to an additional societal investment aimed at protecting them from that outcome. The juvenile court context constitutes official government decision-making that is required to take into account, among other things, the special needs of the accused youth and the mechanisms available for the state to help him.[1] For this target population in this context of decision-making, meaningful participation could have a special developmental value: It could nurture youths' decision-making competence in a manner that fosters an understanding of self as part of, rather than outside, the community enforcing the law.

These developmental projections are necessarily speculative, as the participatory experience advocated in this chapter has not been attempted, let alone tested. But it is speculation built on extensive developmental and social psychological research and the track record developed through numerous relevant if distinct programs and practices. After describing the juvenile court's target population and decision-making context in more detail, I turn to the developmental literature to sketch out the primary developmental projects and mechanisms of adolescence. I then consider how those projects are undermined by young people's current experience in juvenile court and draw on the social psychological literature as well as numerous experiments in distinct but relevant contexts to argue for reform. It is my hypothesis that these reforms could have an important developmental effect on youth participating in the court process, particularly on their understanding of themselves in relation to law and legal authority. I hope that the case will be strong enough to inspire judges to pilot the reforms and social scientists to study the results.

THE CONTEXT AND TARGET OF JUVENILE COURT

The Decision-Making Context of the Juvenile Court

Since their founding at the turn of the twentieth Century, juvenile courts in the United States were designed to separate children from adults in the criminal justice system. This separation had the simple value of keeping young people away from the destructive social influence of adult criminals (Zimring, 2002), but it also offered an opportunity to shape the substantive and procedural law to fit youthful offenders (Mack, 1909; Rubin, 1953). What this tailoring has meant has changed over the years, reflecting changes in crime, politics, and law. But throughout their 115-year history, juvenile courts have maintained a commitment to addressing youth needs and a process that manifests some compassion, even as other goals and processes have been added that have qualified these commitments somewhat.

---

1. Throughout this chapter, for the sake of simplicity and clarity, young people will be referred to as "he" "him" and "his," and judges and lawyers as "she" and "her."

In the early years of juvenile court, young people who were maltreated by their parents were handled in the same courts, pursuant to the same laws, as young people who had committed crimes. All of these children, the legislatures and courts reasoned, reflected some sort of deficit in their upbringing that it was the state's duty to address (Scott, 2000). These two sources of juvenile court jurisdiction were subsequently split, and in the latter part of the twentieth century perceptions of a rising tide of juvenile crime, and particularly violent crime, led states to amend their juvenile court acts to add punishment and community safety to their list of purposes guiding the imposition of sentences. In none of these states, however, did the state affirmatively disavow the goal of assisting youth, whose offending was understood as a likely indicator of some sort of unmet need for assistance. While this goal was often set out under the familiar criminological term of "rehabilitation," some more recent legislative language has better captured the development framing of the goal with language such as "equipping juvenile offenders with competencies to live responsibly and productively."[2] Young people, understood to not yet be fully formed, are to be aided in that process of formation, rather than remade after manifesting a formed character that requires rehabilitation.

Other purposes, which have been given stronger emphasis in the laws governing juvenile courts in the various states in recent years, have widely been perceived as in tension with the goal of youth assistance, but the conflict between these goals is not inevitable. Where "holding youth accountable" has generally been understood to mean the imposition of punishment suitable to fit the crime, without regard to its harmful effects on the individual child, there is no reason this accountability could not be understood as an element of a developmentally appropriate response to a youth's actions. A well-tailored sentence will be developmentally valuable in part because it gives the youth a real sense that he is being held accountable and why.

Running parallel to the juvenile court's substantive innovations were procedural ones. The vision of the creators of the first juvenile courts was to displace the harsh formality of criminal court with the avuncular attention of a juvenile judge, who would wear no robe, wrap his arm around the shoulder of the errant youth, and offer kindly advice (Mack, 1909). The terminology of the process was modified to reflect the distinctive (noncriminal) nature of the proceedings: Trials were renamed "adjudications" and sentences renamed "dispositions."

From the beginning, this procedural vision was not matched with procedural reality, and cases were rushed through the courts with neither formal protections nor avuncular attention. The lack of attention given to these cases eventually led to a series of Supreme Court decisions applying the U.S. Constitution, and particularly the due process clause, to juvenile defendants. In cases beginning with *In re Gault*,[3] the Supreme Court took the juvenile courts in a more formal

2. 705 Illinois Consolidated Statutes 405/5-101.
3. 387 U.S. 1 (1967).

direction, requiring that youth have notice of charges, lawyers, and an opportunity for compelled witness testimony and cross-examination. Understood at the most general level, these due process cases established young people's constitutional right to participation. Thus, where youth are denied an opportunity for meaningful participation in juvenile court, as I will argue they routinely are, that failure has important legal as well as developmental implications. I have addressed those legal implications elsewhere (Buss, 2003, 2005). Here I focus on the potential developmental consequences of that deprivation.

The Supreme Court's due process decisions were heavily focused on the adjudicative, or "guilt," phase of juvenile court proceedings, and the Court in *Gault* suggested that the dispositional phase of a case could continue to be treated very differently from adult sentencing, to allow the very different aims, both substantive and procedural, of the juvenile justice system to be achieved. As the juvenile court process has evolved, however, those formal procedures found by the Court to be required in the adjudicatory phase have largely carried over into the dispositional phase. From start to finish, juvenile court proceedings follow the basic form of the adult criminal process, with the same modifications throughout. In contrast, the proposal set out in this chapter takes advantage of the opportunity created by the constitutional space left open at the postadjudicatory phase of the process by *Gault* and subsequent cases. It calls for a marked change in process at the dispositional phase, during which the needs of the young person are to be addressed and the focus of the proceeding shifts from the young person's past to his future.

The Target Population of the Juvenile Court

Contrary to the original vision, juvenile courts now divide their jurisdiction between child protection, or "dependency," and criminal offending, or "delinquency." Unlike dependency jurisdiction, whose age range extends to all individuals defined as minors by law, delinquency jurisdiction generally sets narrower age limits, which roughly track adolescence. Some states set a minimum age, typically 10, with younger children suspected of criminal activity sent to child protection or mental health systems. And all states set a maximum age—often 18, but sometimes 17 or even 16.[4] Once that maximum age has been exceeded, all charges of criminal activity will be filed in "adult" court. Most states also set a second, higher, age line for court jurisdiction, as two ages are relevant: the age at which the alleged offense occurred, and the age at which an individual can no longer be supervised by the juvenile court. States commonly allow juvenile courts to keep cases open until a youth turns 21, and California allows jurisdiction to

4. OJJDP (2012b).

continue until a youth turns 25.[5] Thus, although the precise age profile for a juvenile court's delinquency jurisdiction will vary from one state to another, in general terms these courts are focused on adolescent offenders.

Laws and policies, however, further focus the target population of the juvenile court. Many young teens, minor offenders, and first offenders are screened out of the court process altogether. These individuals are sometimes simply given a serious talk and sent home to their parents, or "diverted" to programs designed to assist them outside the formal system (Office of Juvenile Justice and Delinquency Prevention [OJJDP], 1999). On the other end of the spectrum, the oldest, most serious, and repeat offenders within the juvenile court's age range are sometimes diverted to the adult criminal system, whether this transfer is mandated by law or done at the discretion of the prosecutor or the judge (OJJDP, 2012a). The focus of juvenile court, therefore, at least in principle and increasingly in fact, is on fairly serious and repeat offenders who are understood to be at substantial risk of developing into adult criminals but nevertheless merit our ongoing investment in efforts to prevent that outcome.

In a series of recent cases, the Supreme Court suggested that some measure of this investment was constitutionally required. While the Court's focus in *Roper*,[6] *Graham*,[7] and *Miller*[8] was on minors lawfully tried in adult court for their offenses, the Court's determination that juvenile offenders could not be executed for any crimes and could only be sentenced to life without parole under very narrow circumstances was supported by the Court's conclusion that juvenile offenders were still in the process of psychosocial development and therefore were entitled to a "chance to demonstrate maturity and reform."[9] While the investment mandated by the Constitution might be understood as fairly modest (the investment of keeping an individual alive and giving him an opportunity, sometime in life, to prove that he is reformed), a state's decision to go further, and keep a minor in juvenile court, reflects an additional investment in the young person's potential for a prosocial future. This is so whether the decision is made by legislators or individual prosecutors and judges.

THE DEVELOPMENT TASKS IMPLICATED IN THE JUVENILE COURT PROCESS

Young people in their middle to late adolescence have two important and interrelated developmental projects that are of considerable relevance to offenders' experience in court. The first is the development of competence in decision-making

5. Cal. Welfare and Institutions Code Sec. 607(b).
6. *Roper v. Simmons*, 543 U.S. 551 (2005).
7. *Graham v. Florida*, 560 U.S. ___ (2010).
8. *Miller v. Alabama*, 567 U.S. ___ (2012).
9. *Graham v. Florida*, at ___.

and autonomous action. The second is the development of an understanding of self, as an individual and as a member of relevant communities. Of course the two tasks are entangled, as self-discovery is enhanced through the exercise of decision-making control over one's own life, and decision-making becomes increasingly competent as an individual comes to know himself and his communities. These projects are shared by all adolescents in this age range, whether they are involved in the juvenile court or not, but juvenile court involvement poses special risks to, and offers special opportunities for, these young people's pursuit of these developmental projects. I begin this section with a discussion of the relevant aspects of normative adolescent development, for it is only with this broader understanding that the more specific issues confronting young offenders in juvenile court can be properly understood.

Developing Decision-Making Competence

By midadolescence, youth have the cognitive capacity of adults—that is, the brain power to reason through options and make decisions—but their psychosocial immaturity continues to impair their decision-making ability (Cauffman & Steinberg, 2000). This competence goes both to the substance of the decisions they make and to their psychosocial control over the decision-making process. Developing this competency is essential if they are to be prepared to assume responsibility for their own lives and to function successfully in society, and although psychosocial immaturity is understood to be linked to brain development, the maturation process is clearly aided by experience (Scott & Steinberg, 2008). To develop decision-making competence, young people need to practice every step in the process of decision-making and self-guided action, from assessing their short- and long-term interests, to developing plans that serve those interests, to acting on those interests, to taking responsibility for those actions (Zimring, 1982).

   Studies of adolescent development in more standard contexts suggest that two factors contribute significantly to the value of the practice young people gain through their decision-making experience. The first is the relevance of the context of decision-making to the lives of the juveniles (Scott & Steinberg, 2008). The more they care about the outcome, the more young people can gain from their involvement in the decision-making process. For the typical non–court-involved adolescent, such contexts are amply supplied in their school, extracurricular, and family lives (Larsen & Collins, 2009; Mahoney, Vandell, Simpkins, & Zarrett, 2009). For youth involved in the juvenile justice system, however, one of the most relevant contexts in which they have an opportunity to participate and make decisions is the juvenile court.

   The second factor that bears on the value of young people's decision-making practice is the presence of adult monitoring and support: Where adults are present to aid the teen's decision-making process, they can help the teen learn from his mistakes, take account of multiple factors he has identified as important, and distinguish short- from long-term costs and benefits (Scott & Steinberg, 2008). These caring adults can also help the teen learn to regulate his emotions in stressful decision-making contexts. Typically these adults would be family members, religious leaders, coaches, and teachers, adults with considerable involvement and a strong relationship with the teen in question. While many of those involved in the juvenile courts have such adult supports available in their lives, and an important aim of the juvenile justice system should be connecting them with these supports, some court-involved youth do not, and whether or not they do, the various court personnel, particularly the judge, can offer a source of support that is unique in its power and, relatedly, its value.

Developing an Understanding of Self

The second central developmental task of adolescence is identity formation. There is both an individual and group aspect to identity development, and social interactions play an important role in both. Adolescents use their observation of and interaction with others to help them craft their sense of who they are as individuals. Interactions with others serve as valuable points of comparison. They ask: With whom do I share what attributes? How am I different? But others also serve, importantly, as mirrors that allow adolescents to learn about themselves by asking: How do others interact with me, and what does this tell me about myself? Group interaction also offers adolescents an opportunity to try on different personalities, values, and styles (Hopkins, 2010; Scott & Steinberg, 2008).

Related, but distinct, is the adolescent's development of a social identity. Adolescents look to others not just to learn about themselves, as individuals, but also to get a sense of the meaningful affiliations in their lives. They explore the questions: With whom do I belong? Who is my community? To a large extent, we build our values and commitments around those affiliations, as we consider: Whose esteem is most important to me? How can my behavior signal these commitments and affiliations? (Ashmore, Jussim, & Wilder, 2001; Gilovich, Keltner, Chen, & Nisbett, 2013; Swanson, Edwards, & Spencer, 2010). For adolescents who are members of a racial minority group, an important piece of this social identity development focuses on race and culture, as they work through what it means to be black or Latino in the United States, and how this affects their relationships with others (Swanson et al., 2010).

Sorting between "us" and "them" is a central piece of social identity development, and individuals' motivation to paint a positive self-image inclines them to make positive associations with their identified "in-groups" and to define group identity in terms opposed to their out-groups (Brewer, 2001). This inclination to differentiate, and define oneself in positive and oppositional terms, may be exacerbated in settings that inspire frustration and anger (Gilovich et al., 2013). And it is particularly likely to occur when adolescents perceive that the "us" and the "them" divide along racial lines (Ashmore et al., 2001; Swanson, Spencer, Dell'Angelo, Harpalani, & Spencer, 2002). In this way, young people can develop a sense, even a proud sense, of self as a "deviant," one whose group is opposed to mainstream society, including its commitment to and enforcement of the law (Sherman, 1993). A court process that reinforces this deviant in-group identity development disserves the youth it is designed to support and undermines its mission of transforming these youth into law-abiding adults.

Decision-making competence and identity formation are distinct developmental ends, but they are often served by a common set of experiences and interactions. Contexts in which young people are given decision-making authority over matters of importance to them and in which adults engage them in a manner that is supportive and respectful allow young people to develop decision-making skills, learn and recover from their mistakes, and build on their successes. In the course of doing so, young people also learn about themselves both as individuals and as members of groups that include those adults with whom they have engaged. Where that interaction is positive, adolescents might be expected to maximize the value of the practice and experience an affiliation with the involved adults and the institutions they represent. Where negative, we should worry both that their learning may be undermined and that they may see themselves as opposed to, or at least disconnected from, the participating adults. This chapter suggests that the special role and powers of a judge make her a particularly valuable source of support for young people making decisions under juvenile court auspices, as the power vested in the court, and the potential for the judge to use that power to aid a young person's attainment of his goals, could foster development of the young person's decision-making competence while reinforcing his sense of affiliation with those with legal authority.

Legal Socialization

An aspect of development that shares considerable territory with social identity development, and to a lesser extent the development of decision-making competence, is legal socialization—the process by which young people develop their understanding of law and legal actors and, most important, their own relationship with the law and legal actors. We consider an individual's legal socialization to have been successful if he grows up to believe it is his obligation to obey the law and to have the competencies required to actually live as a law-abiding citizen. But behind those outcome markers is a story about social identity development: Whether and why one obeys the law is tied to one's understanding of one's relationship to society, particularly society functioning as law maker and law enforcer (Sherman, 1993).

An adolescent might develop hostility to this authority and determine that the laws are entitled to no respect or that they should only be obeyed because society has the power to impose serious costs for breaking the law. What we hope, however, is that young people will come to see themselves as an integral part of the society that makes and enforces the law. This is likely to lead to a more stable and consistent commitment to lawful behavior, but at least as important, it is likely to reflect a self-understanding that predicts for prosocial integration rather than alienated, if otherwise prosocial, detachment. If we aspire not only to a crime-free society but also to the productive engagement of all youth in that society, we must aim for a legal socialization grounded in societal connection, rather than merely pragmatic obedience (Fagan & Piquero, 2007).

While it is a secondary theme in the context of legal socialization, the development of decision-making competence—the other primary developmental task of adolescence—also plays a role in successful legal socialization. Youth desist from criminal offending in part because they develop the decision-making competence to do so. This enhanced decision-making competence has both a short-term and longer-term dimension. As young people mature, they gain the ability to control their impulses and to resist the pressures of the group. But they also gain knowledge and experience that allow them to engage in more long-term planning—to make choices about how they will behave, today, in a manner that reflects their plans and ambitions for the future. As their investment in the future goes up, their inclination to thwart the law goes down (Scott & Steinberg, 2008).

The socialization process of adolescence, however, can also lead young people away from law-abiding behavior, and where youth engage in criminal offending, they are at enhanced risk of developing social connections that encourage rather than discourage criminal offending. To be sure, some offending reflects developmentally normal adolescent experimentation with risk and rule breaking that will end with the assumption of prosocial roles in adulthood (Moffitt, 1993). This is one of the primary arguments for keeping youth out of the adult criminal justice system and even the juvenile justice system altogether (Scott & Steinberg, 2008). But if the juvenile justice system is successful in targeting young people who are at serious risk of becoming adult criminals, that system should place a high value on the effective legal socialization of the young people who end up in its courts, and at a minimum should take pains to avoid contributing to their antisocial identity development.

Perversely, the current effect of the court process on young people's legal socialization is likely negative. Their experience in juvenile court reinforces their identity as law breakers and their affiliation with other criminal offenders and visibly and forcefully keeps them outside the circle of those enforcing the law.

The following section describes the courtroom dynamics that create these effects. Based on this description, I argue that securing meaningful youth participation through a wholesale restructuring of the court process (at and beyond disposition) offers an opportunity to affect young offenders' emerging under-standings of themselves as members of a community governed by law.

THE REALITY OF YOUNG PEOPLE'S EXPERIENCE IN JUVENILE COURT

As a courtroom observer,[10] it is impossible to avoid seeing the irrelevance of the young person to the conduct of the proceedings. Indeed, the sense one gets is that the young person is affirmatively disregarded most of the time by the court per-sonnel in the room, even those who are working hard to serve the young people in their system well. But, on paper, it is difficult to capture how a system that affords young people lawyers and many of the attributes of a formal criminal process could fail so completely to engage young people in the proceeding.

In a typical American juvenile court, each judge presides over one court-room, and on any given day, a large number of cases are assigned to that judge in that courtroom. Cases have an assigned public defender, the lawyer appointed to represent the minor, and a prosecutor, who represents the state in the crimi-nal proceeding. Cases also commonly have a probation officer assigned, and, depending on the nature of the case and the location from which the juvenile is being brought, a sheriff may also be present when the case is heard. Additional witnesses and involved professionals, including caseworkers, mental health eval-uators, drug treatment counselors, and the like, may also be involved in the case and, depending on the issues to be addressed, may be expected to be present in court. In addition to the judge, who moves in and out of the court as cases are called and adjourned, there are one or more clerical employees of the court who generally stay in the courtroom throughout the day to manage the paperwork associated with the proceedings. The accused youth are commonly expected to be present, and family members are allowed, and sometimes required, to attend.

---

10. What follows is my attempt to capture what I have observed in many juvenile court-rooms in many states over many years. Three decades ago, these observations began when I was serving as a lawyer for youth in foster care. More recently, I have conducted observa-tions in connection with work with students focused on court reform. My own impressions have been reinforced by countless observations by students and conversations with lawyers and others practicing in various juvenile court jurisdictions throughout the United States. My description is not based on any formal study, although many of my observations were specifically focused on young people's experience in court. It is also consistent with studies that document the small amount of time spent on each case in juvenile court, the limited involvement and effectiveness of defense counsel, and the significant gaps in the young peo-ple's understanding of proceedings (Grisso, Steinberg, Woolard, Cauffman, Scott, Graham, Lexcen, Reppucci, & Schwartz. (2003); National Juvenile Defender Assessments). I can-not, of course, claim that what I describe is universally true, but I note that the problems I describe here occur with remarkable consistency despite the impressive efforts of some judges, lawyers, and other court personnel to serve young people better within the existing court process.

The volume of cases scheduled and the number of personnel involved make it difficult to schedule and call cases for designated times. Instead, in most jurisdictions, the various players in the courtroom wait for the full set of expected participants to arrive and then request that the case be called. This means that, for many young people and their families, they are required to wait for hours, missing work and school, until a witness or professional, very possibly one who does not have supportive things to say, finally shows up. In most jurisdictions, they are required to remain outside the courtroom, while all the professionals involved in the case wait together inside. In some, they wait inside, observing the courtroom dynamic as it proceeds with little regard for them.

The large volume of cases scheduled does not, as one might expect, produce an overly full schedule of hearings, called back to back and filling the courtroom from the opening of court to the end of the working day. Indeed, even in the busiest courtrooms the bulk of the courtroom day is commonly spent between cases, and the days tend to end early. Ironically, there is often a sleepy feel that pervades these overloaded courts. What the overload has done is shaped the process, and with it the culture, in material ways: The race to get through the pile leads to a triage-style approach to everything that gets done, and the height of the stack encourages routinization of all aspects of the process. Reports are reduced to summaries, summaries to recommendations, and recommendations to initials. Lawyers pick up one another's cases so that a single lawyer is ready to pull a file from anywhere in the pile and fill her highly routinized role. Reaching agreement is at a premium, and calling for a contested hearing the source of considerable resistance and almost certainly weeks of delay.

Another very important aspect of this downtime dynamic is social. For the bulk of a long day, all the lawyers, law enforcement agents, court personnel, and other systems professionals are hanging out together in the courtroom killing time. This time is filled with storytelling, joke cracking, teasing, flirting, and gossip. Plans for the weekend are a good topic, as are the triumphs and tribulations of the local sports teams. Intermingled with this often boisterous social talk is talk about the upcoming cases—visible to all in the room, and shared across positions with no evidence of any division in allegiance or related motivation. Much of the case-related talk is similar in tone to the gossip and joking that preceded and follow it. The only time the energy level perceptibly drops, paradoxically, is when cases are called.

Until that occurs, the young people and their families wait. A lawyer for a minor may leave the courtroom to discuss matters with her client, but those departures are rare and short. When the case is finally called, the family is ushered in, and in some cases introduced. The lawyers most committed to making a connection with their clients will give some form of acknowledgment, and occasionally exchange whispers with their clients during the proceedings. In many cases, the lawyer will give only a passing glance, and not infrequently even this most minimal of eye contact and acknowledgment is omitted. However much acknowledged the client, the proceeding takes off in a manner that reflects the fact that everyone else involved already knows what the proceeding is about, and, more to the point, how it will come out. If the client is lucky enough to get an explanation, he will be told what has already been worked out. He is being hastily brought up to speed rather than invited in to a process in which he has any hope of affecting how issues are resolved, let alone which issues are addressed.

In most circumstances, the presentation of the cases to the judge is a presentation of matters already concluded, whether simply for the judge's approval or for the making of final choices in a circumscribed and well-defined range of options. This is true both at the adjudicatory phase, when most accused youth are encouraged to plead guilty, and at the dispositional or sentencing phase, which is the focus of this chapter's call for reform. While the routine entry of guilty pleas raises issues of its own, the avoidance of comprehensive courtroom deliberations at the dispositional or sentencing phase is particularly troubling in ways that bear directly on young people's interest in participation. Young people attend dispositional hearings with their expectations well established through some combination of conventional wisdom and portrayals in the media. These hearings, they understand, are about setting their punishment for the offense done.

What will escape them, unless it is clearly and comprehensively explored in court, is that the disposition is also the opportunity to assess their circumstances and determine what aid the state can offer them in charting a promising future. Whatever assessing of circumstances and needs is required of the state is done by a probation officer in advance of the court hearing, and that investigation is generally reduced to a recommendation, which is presented in court. Even where the probation officers are required, in preparing these recommendations, to ask valuable and individualized questions about a young person—What are his ambitions? What does he see as his major obstacles? How has he done in school and what accounts for failures there?—the judge's interest in these matters, let alone the reason for the judge's interest, are largely hidden from the young person's view. The invisibility of this important, future-focused aspect of dispositional hearings would prevent even a young person intent on participating from doing so in a meaningful or effective way.

Many judges, concerned that young people be given a "voice," will pause during the brief hearing and offer an opportunity for the young person to speak. In many cases, the young person will decline the opportunity, whether because he understands such an opportunity to be risky or pointless, or whether he simply finds the setting too intimidating. If he does speak, the phrase "giving voice" is apt, as things proceed much as if the judge had invited the young person to sing an aria. Everyone pauses, some with interested looks on their faces, some showing impatience. And when the young person finishes, the judge makes some acknowledgment, sometimes even offers a response to some of the things said by the young person, but the young person's speech rarely affects the subsequent flow, pace, or progress of the case.

When the proceeding is concluded, the young person and his family get at most a cursory dismissal, and, if no other case immediately follows, the courtroom breaks back into the gossipy frivolity of the intracase interludes. It is common for this transition to occur before the family has left the room, leaving families with the distinct impression that they are the irrelevant outsiders who have stepped awkwardly and temporarily into a club whose members consist of all the professionals who remain in the courtroom, regardless of their roles.

ASPIRING TO MEANINGFUL PARTICIPATION IN JUVENILE COURT

It is clear that the current process in American juvenile courts fails to engage young people in their proceedings in any meaningful way. The process hurries young people through court, conceals from them the issues to be addressed, and ostentatiously treats them as outsiders. These barriers to participation are imposed despite a century-long commitment to addressing youths' developmental needs and a half-century–long recognition of their right to due process. At a minimum, this failure deprives young people of a special opportunity to develop a connection with the society that polices them. At worst, this failure exacerbates the developmental risks that brought them into the system.

Achieving young people's meaningful participation in dispositional decision-making in juvenile courts will require much more than affording them lawyers or offering them an opportunity to speak at proceedings. It will require an entire remaking of the hearing to ensure that decision-making is actually occurring in a manner that can be tracked by the young people and their families in the courtroom, and that makes participation comfortable and comprehensible. With this shift must come a shift in tone and attention. The behavior of all court personnel, throughout the day, should reflect the centrality of the young people to the decision-making process and the court personnel's shared obligation, in their many different roles, to facilitate young people's engagement in that decision-making process.

Contemplating reforms designed to enhance young people's engagement in the juvenile court process raises two basic questions: Is such engagement achievable? And, if so, would it have developmental value? The first question is best answered by looking to promising models in other contexts and considering the extent to which those models could apply in the juvenile court context. The second is best answered by looking to the social psychological literature that studies the correlation between individuals' experience with legal authority and their views about the law and their obligations under law. Models in child welfare, in juvenile justice outside the courts, and in courts that have experimented with a treatment-focused approach suggest that significant changes in procedures and expectations in juvenile court could have a dramatic effect on youth engagement.

Research on procedural justice and related research on legal socialization suggest that making these changes could well have a positive developmental impact on young people. After setting out the potential developmental value of engaging youth more meaningfully in the juvenile court process, this chapter looks to potential models to craft a set of proposed reforms.

The Potential Developmental Value of Meaningful Participation

At dispositional hearings and subsequent reviews, the law directs the juvenile court to take account of a young person's needs in fashioning its orders, particularly needs associated with making a successful transition to prosocial adulthood. When a young person does not participate in the hearing, however, it is unlikely that whatever plan is put together by the professionals in charge and endorsed by the judge will accurately reflect the young person's needs and related aspirations with any subtlety, or that the plan will be well designed to address those needs and aspirations. It is equally unlikely that any program of assistance designed by these professionals, however well tailored, could be implemented effectively without the young person's understanding of and commitment to the plan. Meaningful youth participation is thus, at a minimum, a practical necessity for program success (Barnum & Grisso, 1994).

There is considerable reason to expect the exclusion of young people from the dispositional planning process to have a more immediate and direct developmental impact as well. Already noted are the lost opportunity for decision-making practice and the potential reinforcement of a social identity that is antagonistic to those who follow and enforce the law. Left to explore is the potential positive developmental impact of doing things differently.

An extensive social scientific literature suggests that the nature and extent of young people's participation in their court proceedings can be expected to have a material effect on their social identity development, whether in a positive or negative direction. These hearings bring young people accused of committing crimes face to face with a judge—the personification of state legal authority charged with adjudicating guilt and then assessing the consequences that should follow. Meaningful youth participation in these hearings could materially change the relationship between these young people and the judge, with potentially positive effects on their understanding of who they are and with whom they belong.

Procedural Justice

In a wide variety of contexts, social psychologists have documented a connection between adult individuals' experience in the court process and their view of the law's legitimacy and, relatedly, their obligation to obey the law (Tyler, 1990). The term "procedural justice" has been used to capture the importance of people's perception of the court process (as well as the law enforcement process in other contexts) and the essential elements that go into their perception that the process was "fair." Chief among these elements are individuals' perceptions of how they were treated and, in particular, whether they were shown respect and given a meaningful opportunity to be heard. Also relevant are perceptions of the judge's neutrality and the trustworthiness of the decision-making process employed (Blader & Tyler, 2003; Tyler, 1990). Studies suggest that individuals' perception of procedural fairness (or the lack thereof) can matter more than substantive outcome in shaping their attitudes about the law and government authority more generally (Tyler, Casper, & Fisher, 1989). These attitudes, social scientists have found, affect not only legal compliance but also individuals' commitment to cooperation and engagement with legal authorities in their communities (Tyler & Jackson, 2013).

The relationship between court experience and children's attitudes about the law has been much less extensively studied. This is somewhat striking, as it can be expected that whatever attitudinal and developmental effects the court process has on adults would be felt even more strongly by children, who are generally understood to be more actively developing, and therefore also more subject to influence (Murphy, 2013; Piquero, Fagan, Mulvey, & Steinberg, 2005). A modest but growing body of research has focused on these procedural justice effects on adolescents, and some of this research has found the same connection between experience with courts and law enforcement and attitudes about the law among children and adolescents (Birckhead, 2009; Fagan & Tyler, 2005; Greene, Sprott, Madon, & Jung, 2010; Tatar, Kaasa, & Cauffman, 2012). Of course, the effect can only be demonstrated if some subjects experience the process as procedurally just, an experience that court observations suggest would generally be lacking among juvenile offenders (Piquero et al., 2005).

If the presence or absence of the elements of procedural justice in juvenile court is an important determinant of young people's emerging understanding of the law and its legitimacy, young people's current experience in juvenile court is troubling indeed. The description set out earlier in the chapter captures the failure of the process to satisfy any of the conditions for procedural justice. Most central to this discussion here is the manifest lack of respect for the young person shown by the process and, as part of this, the failure to include the young person meaningfully in the process. But also of concern, and related to this exclusion, is the message that the entire court-full of professionals, including the young person's own lawyer and even more significantly the judge, are on a single team that excludes the young person. Nothing about the process would inspire trust in a young person who entered with distrust, a distrust that has been shown to be particularly great among minority youth (Tyler & Huo, 2002; Woolard, Harvell, & Graham, 2008). Perhaps the court is working hard to faithfully apply the law and help the offender (this is presumably usually the case), but this is something we conclude based on our broader understanding of the law; it is not in any informative way in evidence in the courtroom. And unless the court process is retooled to effectively engage young people, there is no reason to expect the process to inspire that trust.

It might be argued that the best way to secure a young person's meaningful participation is through the active advocacy of his attorney. At least in theory, a lawyer could insist on slowing the process down, on making the issues clear to her client, and deliberating on these issues at some length in the hearing. At least in theory, the lawyer could articulate the relevant legal standards and emphasize the importance of developing a dispositional plan that adequately reflected her client's concerns and commitments. But the social and legal conventions of the courtroom constrain this zealous insistence on youth inclusion in legitimate and illegitimate ways. The illegitimate, but very real, constraint is tied to that group dynamic. The day-to-day social allegiance is not to the client, but to the other repeat players in the courtroom (Breger, 2010). When it comes down to it, few lawyers in that social setting will have the stomach to take action that their quasicolleagues will find annoying at best and perhaps even hostile. The more legitimate resistance comes from the lawyer's professional obligation to take into account the actual effects of her advocacy on her client's interests. Lawyers will worry about antagonizing the people on whose good will her clients depend. Throwing a wrench in the court process that imposes delays and challenges the work of all involved, including the judge, could easily undermine a lawyer's effectiveness, whether with the client in question or future clients. Because any effort to engage young people meaningfully in their dispositional proceedings will severely disrupt expectations and impose considerable burdens, it must come from the judge.

The question remains whether that effective engagement can be achieved in the context of juvenile court proceedings even by a judge completely convinced that such an end should be achieved and fully prepared to disrupt the conventional process. Experimentation within the delinquency division of the juvenile courts to achieve this engagement has been minimal. Experiments in other contexts, however, offer some insight about how this engagement might be accomplished.

Models

A number of models in a range of contexts suggest that changes in procedures in juvenile court could be effectively implemented that would achieve material changes in the level of youth engagement in the court process. Some of these models were designed to address youth offending outside the court process and therefore share the general aims of the juvenile court process. Other models were developed to address particular problems understood to be correlated with

criminal offending and therefore shed special light on needs-focused engagement. And one model was developed by and implemented in juvenile court in the
context of child welfare proceedings, suggesting that there is room for productive
flexibility in juvenile court proceedings themselves.

Lessons from Diversionary Programs

A wide variety of diversionary programs has been developed to address youth
offending while keeping youth out of the courts. Two in particular are worth
mentioning in the context of this discussion—restorative justice processes and
peer courts—because both have as a central aim the engagement of the youth
offender in a discussion and decision-making process concerning the appropriate consequences to be imposed in response to the offense. Both approaches have
been extensively studied and discussed; indeed, a version of each is discussed
in separate chapters of this book (Chapters 10 and 12). Here, the focus is on
the potential for youth engagement demonstrated by program successes under
both approaches, and a consideration of the distinctions between the contexts in
which those successes were demonstrated and the context of juvenile court that
might limit the models' relevance.

Restorative justice describes a range of out-of-court processes designed to
respond to criminal offending in a manner that addresses the needs of the victim, the offender, and the community. Youth offenders are invited to bring family
members and other sources of support to the process, often called a conference,
as are the victims of the offense. At the conference, victim and offender are present together, and the focus of the discussion is on the harm done to the victim and
the larger community by the youth's acts, and the appropriate steps to be taken
to address that harm. At the same time, the young offender has an opportunity
to share his own concerns and seek his community's support in addressing those
needs that bear on his offending behavior. The term "reintegrative shaming" is
sometimes used to characterize the offender's experience of the process—he is
forced to face the harm he has done and the pain he has caused in a personal and
meaningful way, while at the same time experiencing the community's ongoing
commitment to him as a community member (Braithwaite, 1989; Crawford &
Newburn, 2003).

In restorative justice conferences, the youth is expected to play a central role in
the discussion. This is achieved, in part, through the expectation itself: The conference cannot go forward without the young person's engagement. Participation
is also facilitated by the elimination of professional surrogates, lawyers or others,
speaking on the young person's behalf. Such surrogates are replaced with familiar sources of support, who enable rather than displace his participation. Run as a
discussion, the young person's understanding keeps pace with decision-making.
Numerous studies suggest that offenders are more likely to experience these

conferences as fair than traditional court proceedings (Barnes, Hyatt, Angel, & Strang, 2013; Miller & Hefner, 2013).

Two attributes of the restorative justice model might limit the applicability of this approach to dispositional decision-making in juvenile court. The first possibly significant distinction is that the conference process generally begins with an admission of guilt. It is a program offered to offenders that will keep them out of the court process altogether and begins with a recognition that the youth committed the offense. As already noted, however, in most cases assigned to juvenile court, adjudication of guilt follows a guilty plea rather than a contested hearing; even in cases where guilt is contested, the focus of the proposed reforms here is on the dispositional phase, which applies only to those who have been found guilty of the charged offense. While the difference between a free admission of guilt and a contested finding of guilt could materially affect a young person's engagement in a discussion of what should follow, the voluntariness of a young person's admission offered in exchange for staying out of court could easily be exaggerated.

The second distinction, which may be more important, applies to all diversion-based models. By definition, diversion programs do not involve a judge, let alone a judge with ultimate control over the decisions that are made and the obligations of state and youth that follow. The judge's authority in developing the dispositional order would inevitably alter the dynamic of any conferencing group, and, with that change in dynamic, we might expect the youth's participation to decline, both because it is, in fact, less essential to the process's outcome and because a young person is likely to be intimidated by the court setting and the judge's authority. But this distinction offers an insight as well: Courts will likely be most effective in engaging young people in meaningful ways if judges can succeed in bringing young people, together with their communities of support, into a discussion, and courts may be more likely to fashion dispositions that achieve their ends if the ends and means set out in their orders have been vetted in a process over which they relinquish considerable control. Sentencing circles, explored in some Native American communities, reflect an attempt to build upon this insight (Ross, 1996).

Another form of diversionary program that sheds some light on youth participation is the peer or teen court. The basic idea behind these courts is that young people who have themselves been offenders can be particularly effective in engaging young offenders and helping them take responsibility for their offending and move beyond it (Pearson & Jurich, 2005). Again, part of the design is to offer youth a means of making amends while avoiding the court process altogether, and this opportunity for diversion is itself highly valuable to young people seeking a fresh start. But the process also creates an opportunity for reflection and engagement. Overall, peer court programs receive mixed reviews (Butts, 2002; Hissong, 1991; Seyfrit, Reichel, & Stutts, 1987; Minor, Wells, Soderstrom, Bingham, & Williamson, 1999), and documented successes may say more about the minor nature of the original offending than the ability of the program to change behavior, but less contested is the fact that young people who participate in these programs often engage in meaningful discussions with their peer adjudicators (Forgays & DeMilio, 2005). Moreover, many such programs require offenders to also take a turn as adjudicators, a requirement that continues their engagement with the process even beyond their own case and reinforces the message that they are part of the community that enforces the law (Pearson, 2003; Kohm, Chapter 12 in this volume).

While it seems likely that a young person might be more effectively engaged in any number of subjects relevant to his disposition by a group of peers, particularly peers with whom the young person can relate, it is not clear whether group discussion among young people could be readily imported into the court process. That being said, a key element of the treatment court model, discussed below, is the opportunity for group engagement, and the value such engagement has for each individual's understanding of and commitment to the court-compelled treatment process.

Both restorative justice conferences and peer courts address issues that roughly track those issues to be addressed at a dispositional hearing, but they shift the participants and format of the decision-making discussion in a manner that makes that decision-making more accessible to the young person whose life will be most directly affected by it. That accessibility, in turn, makes it possible for the young person to assume a more central role in the process.

Lessons from Treatment Courts

In recent years, there has been a growing interest in, and some political support for, treatment courts, also called problem-solving courts. These courts are designed to address an underlying problem associated with criminal offending and to shift the response to this offending from incarceration to treatment. The two most prominent examples of such courts are drug courts and mental health courts, and while there is considerable diversity in how these courts are administered in various jurisdictions, there are a number of distinct features common to the most successful programs (Holst, 2010-11; Hora, Schma, & Rosenthal, 1999).

These courts cast the judge in a very different role from that of a traditional criminal court judge. After a defendant has been adjudicated, he returns frequently to the court for status hearings that assess his compliance with his mandatory treatment program and his progress in addressing his underlying drug addiction or mental illness. The judge monitors this progress directly, bestowing warnings and praise in response to what she learns. She develops a more friendly relationship with the defendants, communicating her concern and inviting their trust and commitment to the process.

The procedures followed in these status hearings also diverge significantly from traditional criminal court procedures. Status hearings consider the progress of many individuals at the same time, and the defendants are expected to be open with one another and with the judge in reporting on their progress. Defendants speak with the judge directly, sharing triumphs and setbacks, and all involved personnel, including the judge, prosecutor, defense counsel, treatment providers, and case managers, are expected to work as a team in supporting the defendant's treatment (Kaye, 2004). These procedural distinctions, however, are generally introduced only after the defendant's guilt has been adjudicated, allowing defendants to be afforded traditional due process protections in the guilt phase of the process.

While the effectiveness of these courts has only begun to be studied, programs showing the greatest success in treatment compliance and reduced recidivism appear to be those in which the defendant has frequent contact with the judge (Hora & Stalcup, 2008; Rossman, Roman, Zweig, Rempel, & Lindquist, 2013). One study concluded that the most successful programs required weekly meetings with the judge as well as weekly drug testing and case management meetings (Rossman & Zweig, 2013). This frequent contact allowed the judge to give immediate feedback, including personalized praise and chastisement, as well as the imposition of consequences, for achievements and failures. The short time between infractions and the court's awareness of infractions also allowed the court to help the defendant confront and address problems early, before they became entrenched. Defendants asked about their experience in treatment court emphasize the special relationship they had with the judge, and the greater respect and interest shown to them by the judge. This, in turn, led defendants to conclude that the treatment court process was more fair (Rossman et al., 2013).

These treatment courts offer a particularly good model for the juvenile courts in some important respects. Like the juvenile court process, these are actual courts presided over by actual judges with the full range of criminal sentencing authority. And like the juvenile court, these courts have an explicit and central goal of providing assistance to offenders. Moreover, like the juvenile court process, these treatment courts can be structured to afford defendants full criminal procedural rights at the adjudicative phase. The different approach treatment courts take after adjudication suggests that a similar radical change in process focused on assisting and supporting the offender, and achieved by establishing a more direct and meaningful relationship with the judge, might also be successfully introduced at disposition in juvenile court.

There are, however, some distinctions in these two court contexts that might limit the usefulness of the treatment court model. Although both juvenile court and treatment courts are focused, after adjudication, on helping offenders move their lives in a positive direction, treatment courts are all single-issue courts, whereas juvenile courts contemplate addressing a broad range of issues that may be putting a young person's prosocial development at risk. The single-issue focus of treatment courts allows a judge to more readily dispense individualized attention and responses in a group setting. In basic terms, the goals (e.g., avoiding drug use) and the path to those goals (e.g., drug treatment and related conditions) are the same for all offenders present. This cannot be said for the goals of juvenile offenders. Indeed, one of the ways in which a court conveys indifference to the individual child is by imposing cookie-cutter prescriptions, without regard to fit. The group approach in treatment courts presents other problems as well: The interest in protecting the privacy of young offenders and their families would clearly be undermined by the group approach, and there might also be a concern that such a group approach could reinforce young offender's emerging sense that they "belong" with other offenders.

Lessons from Benchmark Hearings

Experiments in the child welfare context suggest that judges can engage adolescents directly in an ongoing planning and decision-making process if they are willing to structure their hearings in a dramatically different way. The most notable example of this shift in approach is the Cook County Juvenile Court's Benchmark Permanency Hearings,[11] which have served as a model for a small number of other forward-thinking child welfare courts around the country (Dobbin, 2009). This approach was developed in large part by a single Cook County judge originally assigned to hear the cases of older teens in foster care.

At the Benchmark Hearings, the judge and the young person (ranging in age from 16 to 21) are the two primary participants, and they engage in a direct conversation focused on the young person's short- and long-term goals. As these goals are fleshed out, the judge can manifest the state's power and support by ordering the assistance of the state actors charged with the young person's care. The young person's lawyer is present at the hearings, but largely silent. Her work is focused, instead, on preparing her client, in advance of the hearings, to engage with the judge, and on ensuring, after the hearings, that state agency personnel comply with the judge's orders. The young person is encouraged to bring a familiar adult who can serve as a source of support at the hearings, in the spirit of the family group conferencing model. And as with that model, that individual is also asked to continue to support the young person in pursuing the goals established at the hearings.

With the young person's greater role in the proceedings comes greater responsibility and accountability as well. The young person develops a written contract with the judge that serves as the basis for services provided in support of the young person's ambitions and as a record of the commitments made by the young person. At the next hearing, which will often be scheduled within weeks or even days of the previous hearing, the judge will assess the young person's compliance

---

11. State of Illinois, Circuit Court of Cook County, http://www.cookcountycourt. org/ABOUTTHECOURT/JuvenileJusticeChildProtection/ChildProtection/Benchmark HearingProgram.aspx

with those commitments and reflect with the young person on successes and failures. This short time frame also allows the judge to assess state agency compliance with court-ordered obligations to help the young person. This visible process of enforcement increases the chance that the ordered aims will actually be achieved. At the same time, it demonstrates to the young person the judge's commitment to using her considerable power to help, at government expense.

While the relationship between judge and young person is supportive, there is also room for the judge's expression of disapproval and calls to do better. Such chastisements, and even the imposition of anticipated consequences, so common in a typical juvenile court proceeding, are far more likely to be effective when embedded in the context of a relationship and accompanied by a message of support and assistance. Such relationships and interactions between adults and adolescents are common in families, schools, neighborhoods, clubs, and religious institutions. While, again, it is preferable to nurture these relationships in such other contexts, the Benchmark proceedings were developed to address a relational void in the lives of adolescents in foster care. A relationship between judge and adolescent will necessarily be less intimate than a relationship a young person could have with a family member or close friend, but the success of the Benchmark proceedings is tied to the judge's commitment to developing her relationship with the adolescents in her courtroom to the maximum extent possible in that context.

While not yet formally studied, the Benchmark Hearing process has been praised by former participants and imitated in other jurisdictions (Dobbin, 2009; Schoenberg, 2005; Smith, 2011). The Benchmark process is frequently held up as one of the ways to improve foster youths' preparation for independence, and the emphasis on better youth participation, decision making, follow-up, and support clearly offers young people meaningful practice in decision making and related autonomous action.

Of course, the attribute of the Benchmark proceedings that might make their success less relevant in juvenile justice proceedings is that all the youth involved are foster youth, not youth who have committed crimes. But in important respects, the issues to be addressed at the dispositional phase of juvenile offenders' proceedings are strikingly similar to those addressed in these foster care reviews. And the same risks that confront youth offenders confront foster youth transitioning to adulthood: a lack of education, drug addiction, mental illness, poverty, and family instability. If the commitment to meeting the needs of juvenile offenders is tied to an interest in facilitating their successful transition to adulthood, then the dispositional goals of the two systems overlap substantially. Moreover, to the extent youth offenders have identified themselves as young people at special risk of developing a social identity that is antagonistic to the law, the opportunity to establish a strong connection with a judge and to engage collaboratively in a planning and decision-making process with that judge may have heightened value in the juvenile justice system.

Proposals for Reform

The changes suggested by these models, and by the underlying problems that demonstrate the need for reform, are simple to describe, if not to implement. In very basic terms, dispositional hearings should be changed in two respects to secure meaningful youth engagement with its likely developmental benefits. First, all decisions relevant, under law, to the court's dispositional order should be made during the hearing, with a full opportunity for deliberation at a level and in a manner understandable to the young person. Second, the primary discussion at the hearing should be directly between the young person and the judge, and the young person's role in decision-making should be clearly highlighted. What follows is additional detail designed to serve these two goals.

For young people to participate effectively, as listeners, speakers, and collaborators in decision-making, the legal questions at issue in the hearings need to be made plain. In particular, the importance of the young person's future well-being to the dispositional order and subsequent reviews, and the obligation of the judge to consider how the state can help the young person to grow up successfully, must be apparent. The relevance of these considerations cannot simply be stated, for, unless the relevance is manifest in the court's conduct of the hearings and the final orders entered, young offenders would be wise to discount the claims made. To manifest the relevance of these considerations, issues that bear on youths' needs and future life course need to be identified, in full detail, during the hearing itself. These are the sort of issues sometimes documented extensively in a probation report and then hidden in a court file.

Of course, a significant focus at disposition is backward-looking, because it is at the disposition hearing that the court imposes consequences for the young person's offense. These aspects of dispositional decision-making will also be enhanced by a young person's clearer understanding of the factors taken into account in determining those consequences, and his opportunity to engage meaningfully in a discussion of what consequences are appropriate and why.[12] But a primary thrust of the proposed reforms is to clearly define distinct, forward-looking concerns and to expressly shift greater control over that forward-looking decision-making to the young person.

To achieve this, the judge will need to develop, through ongoing conversation, an understanding of the young person's views about his needs and aspirations. A young person will not, and should not, believe a judge's claim that his needs

---

12. Supported by the Models for Change Program of the John D. and Catherine T. MacArthur Foundation, juvenile defenders involved in the Juvenile Indigent Defense Action Network developed model judicial colloquies to help ensure that young people understand the sentencing process. A pilot has been initiated to test these colloquies in Washington state juvenile courts (Models for Change, Innovation Brief, Model Juvenile Court Colloquies).

are important to the judge's development of the dispositional order if that order is developed without any significant input from the young person. Significant input, in turn, requires the substantial back and forth between judge and young offender necessary for the judge to get a clear and nuanced understanding of the young person's actual views. Indeed, no judge should have any confidence that she understands the actual views of a young person who has been offered only a brief opportunity to speak and is likely motivated by some combination of intimidation and eagerness to please.

This sort of sharing of information between judge and young person will also require development of a relationship that will best occur over time. The expectation should be that the judge will not only take considerable time at each hearing, the sort of time commonly taken in the restorative justice conferencing context, but will also revisit the relevant issues, and the young person's progress in addressing those issues, frequently, as is done in the Benchmark Hearings and the treatment court proceedings shown to be most effective. This frequent contact creates an opportunity for the development of trust and a growing understanding of the offender, both by the judge and by the offender himself. The frequent hearings will also allow dispositional planning to be responsive to the inevitable unexpected changes in a young person's circumstances and viewpoints. They will allow the judge to bring immediate support to bear when a young person encounters the sort of obstacle that could derail his progress toward dispositional goals, and to hold a young person meaningfully accountable when he falls short of his relevant commitments.

The aim, at this dispositional stage of the proceedings, should be to create a conversational atmosphere, with the primary conversants, as in the Benchmark Hearings and the treatment courts, being the young person and the judge. This would still allow participation by others, and special value would be placed on others, as in the restorative justice context, who could offer support for the young person and give him a sense of comfort in the process. The young person's lawyer would be among those who played that role, but, as with others in the role, the lawyer would not be allowed to speak for her clients, but only to support her clients in speaking for themselves. Lawyers would, as in the Benchmark proceedings, stay on the sidelines during the discussion between judge and young person. In addition to their traditional role as zealous advocates at the adjudicatory phase of proceedings, the lawyers' important work, at the dispositional phase, would be focused on prehearing preparation to ensure that their clients understood the issues to be addressed and had fully prepared to engage on those issues effectively, and monitoring after the hearing to ensure that those who were ordered to assist their clients in various ways had met their obligations.

The lawyers' lack of control of their clients' comments at the hearings could put clients at risk if the candid information produced in one hearing to aid in dispositional planning was used against the client in the prosecution of another offense. This risk could be avoided without undermining the value of an open discussion between judge and juvenile by imposing an evidentiary rule that would prevent statements made by juveniles in the course of dispositional discussions to be used against them. This is a standard evidentiary approach taken in contexts in which it is determined that the benefits of facilitating candor outweigh the potential costs to adjudicatory accuracy, such as settlement discussions and plea negotiations.[13]

None of these reforms speaks directly to the problem of the tone and clubby dynamic that sends a powerful message of exclusion to young people and their families in juvenile court. This tone must be eliminated if the proceedings are to convey respect and to succeed in engaging young people effectively. Because none of the reforms set out above could be accomplished without a change in the underlying courtroom dynamic and the tone it produces, it can be expected that the institution of these reforms, aimed most directly at engaging young people in the substance of the dispositional decision-making, would address the more atmospheric obstacles to youth participation as well. Ultimately, it would be the judge's responsibility to ensure, as an aspect of her altered role in the proceedings, that this tone and atmosphere were eradicated.

CONCLUSION

There is no magic in the detail of the reforms set out here, and some of the specific recommendations might introduce new problems along with some benefits. These details should best be understood as a starting point, an invitation to test a possible solution to an evident and intransigent problem. And it would be absurd to suggest that these changes in courtroom process could, operating in isolation, fix all the problems facing juvenile offenders and transform their lives. But it may be just as absurd to expect any dispositional programming, however well conceived, to be effective if young people are ordered to participate in that programming without having been engaged in the process of decision-making leading up to that order.

Under current procedures, young people who have been identified, by their involvement in the juvenile court, as at especially high risk for antisocial development face insurmountable obstacles to participation in hearings designed to offer them assistance in making a successful transition to adulthood. A growing understanding of adolescent development suggests that young people's participation in these hearings could have important developmental value for these at-risk youth. These reforms offer an approach to try, and then to evaluate, to further illuminate that understanding.

13. See, e.g., Federal Rules of Evidence, Rules 408 and 410.

REFERENCES

Ashmore, R. D., Jussim, L., & Wilder, D. (2001). *Social identity, intergroup conflict, and conflict reduction.* Oxford: Oxford University Press.

Barnes, G. C., Hyatt, J. M., Angel, C. M., Strang, H., & Sherman, L. W. (2013). Are restorative justice conferences more fair than criminal courts? Comparing levels of observed procedural justice in the Reintegrative Shaming Experiments (RISE). *Review,* http://www.sagepublications.com

Barnum, R., & Grisso, T. (1994). Competence to stand trial in juvenile court in Massachusetts; issues of therapeutic jurisprudence. *New England Journal on Criminal and Civil Confinement, 20,* 321–344.

Birckhead, T. R. (2009). Toward a theory of procedural justice for juveniles, *Buffalo Law Review, 57*(5), 1447–1513.

Blader, S. L., & Tyler, T. R. (2003). A four-component model of procedural justice: Defining the meaning of a "fair" process. *Personality and Social Psychology Bulletin, 29*(6), 747–758.

Braithwaite, J. (1989). *Crime, shame and reintegration.* Cambridge: Cambridge University Press.

Breger, M. (2010). Making waves or keeping the calm? Analyzing the institutional culture of family courts through the lens of social psychology groupthink theory. *Law & Psychology Review, 34,* 55–90.

Brewer, M. (2001). Ingroup identification and intergroup conflict. In R. Ashmore, L. Jussim, & D. Wilder (Eds.), *Social identity, intergroup conflict, and conflict reduction* (pp. 17–41) New York: Oxford.

Buss, E. (2003). The missed opportunity in *Gault. University of Chicago Law Review, 70,* 39–54.

Buss, E. (2005). Constitutional fidelity through children's rights. 2004 *The Supreme Court Review,* 355–407.

Butts, J. (2002). The impact of teen court on young offenders. *Urban Institute Justice Policy Center 13.*

Cauffman, E., & Steinberg, L. (2000). (Im)maturity of judgment in adolescence: Why adolescents may be less culpable than adults. *Behavioral Sciences and the Law, 18,* 741–760.

Crawford, A., & Newburn, T. (2003). *Youth offending and restorative justice.* Cullompton, Devon: Willan.

Dobbin, S. (2009). Learning from model court jurisdictions. In B. Kerman, M. Freundlich, & A. Maluccio (Eds.), *Achieving permanence for older children and youth in foster care* (pp. 210–221). New York: Columbia University Press.

Dowd, N. E. (2011). *Justice for kids, keeping kids out of the juvenile justice system.* New York: New York University Press.

Fagan, J., & Piquero, A. R. (2007). Rational choice and developmental influences on recidivism among adolescent felony offenders. *Journal of Empirical Legal Studies, 4*(4), 715–748.

Fagan, J., & Tyler, T. R. (2005). Legal socialization of children and adolescents. *Social Justice Research, 18*(3), 217–242.

Forgays, D. K., & DeMilio, L. (2005). Is teen court effective for repeat offenders? A test of the restorative justice approach. *International Journal of Offender Therapy and Comparative Criminology, 49,* 107–118.

Gilovich, T., Keltner, D., Chen, S, & Nisbett, R. (2013). *Social psychology* (3d ed.) New York: Norton.

Greene, C., Sprott, J. B., Madon, N. S., & Jung, M. (2010). Punishing processes in youth court: procedural justice, court atmosphere and youths' views of the legitimacy of the justice system. *Canadian Journal of Criminology and Criminal Justice, 52*, 527–544.

Grisso, T., Steinberg, L., Woolard, J., Cauffman, E., Scott, E., Graham, S., Lexcen, F., Reppucci, N. D., & chwartz, R. G. (2003). Juveniles' competence to stand trial: A comparison of adolescents' and adults' capacities as trial defendants. *Law and Human Behavior, 27*, 333–364.

Hissong, R. (1991). Teen court. Is it an effective alternative to traditional sanctions? *Journal of Juvenile Justice and Detention Services, 6*, 14–23.

Holst, K. Y. (2010-2011). A good score?: Examining twenty years of drug courts in the United States and abroad. *Valparaiso University Law Review, 45*, 75–106.

Hopkins, P. (2010). *Young people, place, and identity.* London: Routledge.

Hora, P. F., Schma, W. G., & Rosenthal, J. T. A. (1999). Therapeutic jurisprudence and the drug treatment court movement: Revolutionizing the criminal justice system's response to drug abuse and crime in America. *Notre Dame Law Review, 74*, 439–537.

Hora, P. F., & Stalcup, T. (2008). *Drug treatment courts in the twenty-first century: The evolution of the revolution in problem-solving courts. Georgia Law Review, 42*, 717–811.

Kaye, J. S. (2004). Delivering justice today: A problem-solving approach. *Yale Law and Policy Review, 22*(1), 125–151.

Larsen, B., & Collins, A. (2009). Parent-child relationships during adolescence. In R. Lerner & L. Steinberg (Eds.), *Handbook of adolescent psychology* (vol. 2, 3rd ed., pp. 3–42). Hoboken: John Wiley & Sons, Inc.

Mack, J. W. (1909). The juvenile court. *Harvard Law Review, 23*, 104–122.

Mahoney, J., Vandell, D., Simpkins, S., & Zarrett, N. (2009). Adolescent out-of-school activities. In R. Lerner & L. Steinberg (Eds.), *Handbook of adolescent psychology* (vol. 2, 3rd ed., pp. 228–269). Hoboken: John Wiley & Sons, Inc.

Miller, S. L., & Hefner, M. K. (2013). Procedural justice for victims and offenders? Exploring restorative justice processes in Australia and the U.S. *Justice Quarterly.* Available at: http://dx.dol.org/10.1080/07418825.2012.760643.

Minor, K. I., Wells, J. B., Soderstrom, I. R., Bingham, R., & Williamson, D. (1999). Sentence completion and recidivism among juveniles referred to teen courts. *Crime and Delinquency, 45*, 467–480.

Models for Change Innovation Brief, Model Juvenile Court Colloquies. (2013). Available at http://www.modelsforchange.net/publications/501

Moffitt, T. (1993). Adolescence-limited and life course persistent antisocial behavior: A developmental taxonomy. *Psychological Review, 100*, 674–701.

Murphy, K. (2013). Does procedural justice matter to youth? Comparing adults' and youths' willingness to collaborate with police. *Policing and Society.* Available at http://dx.doi.org/10.1080/10439463.2013.802786.

National Juvenile Defender Center, State-Based Assessments. Available at http://njdc.info/our-work/juvenile-indigent-defense-assessments/

Office of Juvenile Justice and Delinquency Prevention (1999). Diversion programs: an overview. Available at www.ncjrs.gov/html/ojjdp/9909-3/div.html.

Office of Juvenile Justice and Delinquency Prevention (2012a). Transfer of juveniles to adult court: effects of a broad policy in one court. Available at http://www.ojjdp.gov/pubs/232932.pdf

Office of Juvenile Justice and Delinquency Prevention (2012b). Statistical briefing book, juvenile justice system structure and process, jurisdictional boundaries. Available at http://www.ojjdp.gov/ojstatbb/structure_process/qa04102.asp?qaDate=2012&text=&print=yes

Pearson, S. S. (2003). *Youth court: a path to civic engagement voices and recommendations from the field*. National Youth Court Center Policy Brief. http://www.youthcourt.net/wp-content/uploads/2010/09/Policy_brief_civic_engagement.pdf

Pearson, S., & Jurich, S. (2005). Youth court: A community solution for embracing at-risk youth. *American Youth Policy Forum*. http://www.aypf.org/publications/Youth%20Court%20-%20A%20Community%20Solution.pdf

Piquero, A. R., Fagan, J., Mulvey, E. P., & Steinberg, L. (2005). Developmental trajectories of legal socialization among serious adolescent offenders. *Journal of Criminal Law and Criminology, 96*(1), 267–298.

Ross, R. (1996). *Returning to the teachings*. Toronto: Penguin Books.

Rossman, S. B., Roman, J., Zweig, J. M., Rempel, M., & Lindquist, C. (2013). *The Multisite Adult Drug Court Evaluation: executive summary*. Available at http://www.urban.org/publications/412353.html (last visited Dec. 31, 2013).

Rossman, S. B., & Zweig, J. M. (2013). *What have we learned from the Multisite Adult Drug Court Evaluation? Implications for practice and policy*. Available at http://www.nadcp.org/sites/default/files/nadcp/Multisite%20Adult%20Drug%20Court%20Evaluation%20-%20NADCP.pdf (last visited Dec. 31, 2013).

Rubin, S. (1953). Protecting the child in the juvenile court. *Journal of Criminal Law, Criminology, & the Police, 43*, 425–440.

Schoenberg, N. (2005, Dec. 30). Young woman moves on, creates new life. *Chicago Tribune*. Available at http://articles.chicagotribune.com/2005-12-30/features/0512300001_1_foster-care-system-benchmarkprogram-preschool.

Scott, E. (2000). Criminal responsibility in adolescence: lessons from developmental psychology. In T. Grisso & R. G. Schartz (Eds.), *Youth on trial: A developmental perspective on juvenile justice* (pp. 291–324). Chicago: University of Chicago Press.

Scott, E., & Steinberg, L. (2008). *Rethinking juvenile justice*. Cambridge, MA: Harvard University Press.

Seyfrit, C., Reichel, P., & Stutts, B. (1987). Peer juries as a juvenile justice diversion technique. *Youth and Society, 18*, 302–316.

Sherman, L. W. (1993). Defiance, deterrence, and irrelevance: A theory of the criminal sanction. *Journal of Research in Crime and Delinquency, 30*(4), 445–473.

Smith, C. (2011, Jan. 20). Study: Courts can do better with long-term foster care. *Texas Tribune*. Available at http://www.texastribune.org/2011/01/20/courts-can-do-better-with-long-term-foster-care/

Swanson, D., Edwards, M., & Spencer, M. (2010). *Adolescence: Development during a global era*. Boston: Academic Press.

Swanson, D. P., Spencer, M. B., Dell'Angelo, T., Harpalani, V., & Spencer, T. R. (2002). Identity processes and positive youth development of African Americans: An explanatory framework. *New Directions in Youth Development, 95*, 73–99.

Tatar, J. R., Kaasa, S. O., & Cauffman, E. (2012). Perceptions of procedural justice among female offenders. *Psychology, Public Policy, and Law, 18*(2), 268–296.

Tyler, T. R. (1990). *Why people obey the law*. New Haven, CT: Yale University Press.

Tyler, T. R., Casper, J. D., & Fisher, B. (1989). Maintaining allegiance toward political authorities: The role of prior attitudes and the use of fair procedures. *American Journal of Political Science, 33*(3), 629–652.

Tyler, T. R., & Huo, Y. J. (2002). *Trust in the law*. New York: Russell Sage Foundation.

Tyler, T. R., & Jackson, J. (2013). Popular legitimacy and the exercise of legal authority: Motivating compliance, cooperation, and engagement. *Psychology, Public Policy, and Law*. Advance online publication. doi:10.1037/a0034514.

Woolard, J. L., Harvell, S., & Graham, S. (2008). Anticipatory injustice among adolescents: age and racial/ethnic differences in perceived unfairness of the justice system. *Behavioral Sciences and the Law, 26*(2), 207–226.

Zimring, F. (1982). *The changing legal world of adolescence.* New York: The Free Press.

Zimring, F. (2002). The common thread: diversion in the jurisprudence of juvenile courts. In B. Dohrn, M. Rosenheim, D. Tanenhaus, & F. Zimring (Eds.), *A century of juvenile justice* (pp. 142–157). Chicago: University of Chicago Press.

CHAPTER 14

Benefits of Restorative Reentry Circles for Children of Incarcerated Parents in Hawai'i

LORENN WALKER, CHERI TARUTANI,
AND DIANA MCKIBBEN

REENTRY CIRCLE BACKGROUND

Fifteen-year-old Jennifer has long blonde hair and wears brown-rimmed, narrow eyeglasses. She sits in a circle with five others and is flanked by two of her older brothers, 17-year-old Alan and 18-year-old Tray. Her grandmother and father are also included in the circle, and all listen attentively to the comments being made. "She helps around the house a lot. I can always talk to her. She always listens," says Alan about Jennifer. Tray echoes Alan's sentiments: "I can count on her to listen. She's always there for me." Jennifer slightly turns in her brothers' directions and shares a small smile as they talk about her strengths. The words "Tray and Alan can talk to her" and "good listener" are added to a long list of characteristics under a heading labeled "Jennifer's Strengths." The list is hand-written with felt-tipped pen on large poster paper taped to the wall. A woman standing outside the circle writes the information as people speak for all participants to see.

It is December 26, 2008, and the circle is being held at the Waiawa Correctional Facility in Hawai'i, where the teens' father is incarcerated for substance abuse-related crimes, including car theft. The three youth, along with their grandmother, their father, and a prison substance abuse counselor, are participating in a reentry circle that the father applied for. They sit in old upholstered chairs with the stuffing bursting out of the seams in a room that needs a coat of paint and some new window screens, but no one seems to notice. One empty chair sits in the circle. That chair contains a paper with answers to questions provided by Ray, the oldest sibling, who is in the military stationed outside Hawai'i and unable to attend. The circle facilitator contacted Ray by telephone a few weeks earlier and asked him the same questions his three siblings will discuss during the circle. Ray asked that his grandmother read his answers during the circle.

Their father asked for an opportunity to apologize for the harm he has caused his children and family. For most incarcerated parents to request a circle, they must be accountable for harm they have caused their children or the request will be denied. In this case, the children's father was accountable for the harm he caused and is being provided a circle.[1] During an extensive solution-focused interview, the father stated, "I'm sorry for all the hurt I caused my children. I want them to know that." During the interview, the facilitator asked questions about the impact on his children, not the impact on him. An inmate's answers should reflect a level of empathy toward his children for what he has put them through. An inmate's ability to speak about the harm caused to his children, and not only the harm caused to him through the separation from his children, indicates empathy and remorse. During the interview, the facilitator assesses for genuineness and sincerity. The incarcerated parents cannot ask the children for anything, not even for forgiveness. The intent of the circle for imprisoned parents is for them to ask their children what they can do to repair the harm to help them heal.

The American Psychological Association (APA) suggests that adults should help children to "see that there is a future beyond the current situation and that the future can be good" (APA, 2013). Parents can encourage an optimistic and positive outlook by keeping a rational perspective and maintaining a hopeful outlook, which enables children to see the good things in life and encourages them to keep going even when things are difficult. Glaze and Maruschak, statisticians for the United States Bureau of Justice Statistics (2008), report that 1.7 million children had a parent incarcerated in 2004 and 715,600 would reach the age of 18 while their parent was incarcerated. Continued face-to-face contact with an incarcerated parent is crucial to the parent–child attachment that affords these children the best chance of long-term benefits and outcomes (Miller, 2006).

Jennifer, Alan, and Tray were prepared to participate in the circle by their grandmother, who has been their custodian for about 13 years since their parents' substance abuse disrupted their parenting. Their mother left and their father was later incarcerated. When parents are incarcerated for more than 22 months, the likelihood of children being adopted by either a relative or foster parent increases due to the Adoption and Safe Families Act of 1997, which requires termination of

---

1. Being "responsible" is a complex concept and depends on the case. We provided a reentry circle for an imprisoned mother who claimed she was innocent. She was not accountable for a crime she didn't commit, but she felt she had done other things that harmed her children, including substance abuse. A circle can help an innocent person address the harm he or she suffered from being incarcerated. People can be responsible for facing their situation and for making a plan to deal with it without being responsible for what caused them to be imprisoned and other problems they face.

parental rights if a child has been in care for 15 of those 22 months (P.L. 105-89). Children of incarcerated parents, especially incarcerated mothers, are often placed with grandmothers (Miller, 2006). Jennifer's grandmother explained to her and her brothers why they were asked to participate in the circle and how they could participate. A guide has been prepared to assist caretakers in preparing children to participate in reentry circles (Appendix A). The guide includes examples of statements and also solution-focused questions (De Jong & Berg, 2013) to ask children to encourage a positive circle experience.

During her father's circle, each person was given a chance to state Jennifer's strengths, which included "open-minded, caring, loving, forgiving" and "means the world to her grandparents." A list of Alan's strengths included "funny, very friendly, personable, charismatic, humorous and creative." Tray's list included "street smart, calm, understanding, and pragmatic."

According to the APA (2013), one of the strategies to build resilience in children is to nurture a positive self-view. The circles begin to nurture a child's positive self-view at the beginning of the process when participants list the child's accomplishments and attributes. This strengths-based approach sets the tone for the circle by reminding child participants, and their caretakers, that the children have strengths and the ability to be resilient.

After the children's strengths have been identified by all the circle participants, their father is given the opportunity to describe what he has accomplished since he has been incarcerated. This gives the family members, especially the children, a chance to see that their father is committed to making positive changes in his life. The children and other participants are also given a chance to identify their father's strengths. Once everyone's strengths have been identified, their father is asked how he wants his life to be different. Parents often describe a life that involves their children much more, activities that they want to participate in with them, and how they will commit to living a different, usually law-abiding and sober lifestyle. This vision of a better future usually prompts regret for their absence in their children's lives and is a pathway to the next step, where the father verbalizes his accountability for his past behavior and incarceration.

After their father has taken responsibility for himself and apologized, Jennifer, Alan, and Tray discuss how they were affected by his behavior and his imprisonment. Children often cite the shame they felt from having a parent in jail or prison and the parent's absence at school, sporting, and family events. The children are then given the opportunity to suggest what the parent can do to help repair the harm. Jennifer, Alan, and Tray said they want their father to be clean and sober, have a job, and spend time with them. Details are gathered from the youth about what they mean by "spend time with us." Alan wants his father to take him fishing once a week, and all the teens want him to take them surfing once a week. Ray requests that his father repair the harm he suffered by remaining "at home and involved with our family. Eat dinner with them, watch my sister's volleyball games, do whatever they need."

By identifying these specific activities for their father, the children provide a concrete way for him to start helping them heal from the trauma they incurred from his past behavior and incarceration. Imagining a positive future can assist the children in letting go of painful past memories (Furman & Ahola, 1992). This part of the circle process provides hope for a new life. Even if incarcerated parents renege on their promises, this part of the process still helps children envision a new life in which their parents play a different role.

According to the APA (2013), creating hopefulness is another strategy to help children become resilient. Allowing the children to explain how they have been affected by their parent's behavior and imprisonment, and what their parent can do to make things right, fosters hope.

A few days after the circle, a six-page typed reentry plan, based on what was discussed and developed at the circle, will be prepared and distributed to all the circle participants. What the father will need to lead a law-abiding and sober life are addressed in the reentry plan, including his housing, employment, transportation, documents (e.g., social security card, driver's license), a list of his supporters, and what he needs to do to maintain good emotional and physical health. In 2012, the need for "leisure time" was added to the model, and participants have included under this heading things like "go to the beach," "dance," and "spend time with my children" as examples of what they will do with their leisure time.

INCARCERATION EFFECTS ON YOUTH OF INCARCERATED PARENTS

Although recently declining, the United States has the highest rate of incarceration in the world (Bureau of Justice Statistics, 2013; Population Reference Bureau, 2013). There are serious detrimental effects on children when a parent is imprisoned, especially for racial minorities and educationally disadvantaged families. "[L]ongitudinal data indicate that parental imprisonment has emerged as a novel—and distinctively American—childhood risk that is concentrated among Black children and children of low-education parents" (Wildeman, 2009, p. 265). Similar to African Americans on the U.S. continent, Native Hawaiians are disproportionally represented in the Hawai'i criminal justice system and prisons (Office of Hawaiian Affairs, 2010). Hawaiians make up 24 percent of the general population in Hawai'i but almost 40 percent of the total prison population. More than half of the people interviewed for this evaluation were Native Hawaiian, and three quarters of the children interviewed were Native Hawaiian. According to the Children's Bureau of the U.S. Department of Health and Human Services (2013a), 17.6 percent of children who were adopted between October 1, 2011, and September 30, 2012 were Native Hawaiian.

According to a study of boys undertaken in the United Kingdom, "Qualitative research suggests that parental imprisonment affects children because of separation, stigma, loss of family income, reduced quality of care, poor explanations given to children, and children's modeling of their parents' behavior" (Murray & Farrington, 2005, p. 1276). Impacts of parental incarceration also include economic hardship, child placement issues, children's functioning, and the parent–child relationship (Miller, 2006). Children experience emotional and behavioral consequences, lack of contact with the parent, and involvement with the child welfare or juvenile justice system (Seymour 1998). The child-centered evaluation of the reentry circles discussed here shows that the process improves explanations given to children, and provides them with positive parental modeling. The reentry circle process helps improve overall healing for children, ideally countering the potential negative impact that parental incarceration may have.

One of the more harmful consequences of parental incarceration is disintegration of the family home. "One of the recurring findings is that the more changes in placement a child experiences, the greater the likelihood of adult criminality and violent criminal behavior [Hensey, Williams, & Rosenbloom, 1983; Lynch & Roberts, 1982; Widom, 1990]" (National Research Council, 1999, p. 243).

Hawai'i is an island state, with most of its prisons located on O'ahu. Traveling to and from the islands is costly for most families with a loved one in prison. Depending on the length of sentence, children with imprisoned parents may be permanently placed with caregivers until adulthood when their parent is released. Understandably, these displaced children face emotional and economic hardships and are under the care of adults experiencing the same hardships. Child welfare workers have been plagued with challenges to maintain visitation between children and incarcerated parents, especially if geographically distant (Seymour, 1998).

In 2004, 52 percent of inmates in American state prisons and 63 percent of inmates in federal prisons reported that they were parents (of children under 18 years of age). Between 1991 and midyear 2007 the number of incarcerated parents in state and federal prisons increased by 79 percent and the number of children of incarcerated parents increased by 80 percent (Glaze & Maruschak, 2008). While the number of children in foster care has generally declined in the United States since 2002 (U.S. Department of Health and Human Services, 2013b) some research shows that the number of foster children with incarcerated parents has increased. A study of earlier data shows that this percentage increased from 5.7 percent in 1986 to 7 percent in 1997 (Johnson & Waldfogel, 2008). The same study found that children with an incarcerated parent made up 11.8 percent of U.S. children who lived with a grandparent caregiver without a parent present in 1997 (Johnson & Waldfogel, 2008). Another study shows that between 1991 and 2007 the number of children with a mother in prison increased by 131 percent, and the number of children with a father in prison increased by 77 percent (Glaze & Maruschak, 2008).

A needs assessment conducted on the island of Hawai'i indicated that 75 percent of a sample of women in prison had at least one child (Brown & Kay, 2007). These children are placed in formal relative foster care or nonrelative foster care through the child welfare system. High costs of living in Hawai'i can add huge financial burdens on caregivers who lack resources. Although these formal caregivers are given subsidies, they are often not enough to allow children to participate in extracurricular activities or visit the incarcerated parent, especially if the parent is incarcerated on another island.

Reentry circles provide a safe place for children to vividly describe what life is like without the incarcerated parent and what they need to help them deal with that. Parents gain an acute awareness of the harm they have caused when they hear the stories through their children's voices. The circles also give the incarcerated parent an opportunity to repair damaged family relationships caused by their absence. When a reentry plan is developed, activities to promote continued communication between the incarcerated parent and the children can create a connection or relationship that mediates the physical absence of the parent.

REENTRY CIRCLE MODEL DEVELOPMENT AND DESCRIPTION

The reentry circle, which is being replicated in New York and California, is similar to a previously developed model for foster youth preparing to leave Hawai'i state custody (Walker, 2005). Hawai'i's E Makua Ana Youth Circle process was inspired by Australian peacemaker John Braithwaite, who suggested restorative interventions for youth to plan for their eventual independence (Braithwaite, 2004). In Hawai'i the youth circles have benefitted over a thousand foster children and are annually funded by the federal government (EPIC 'Ohana, 2013).

Similar to youth circles, reentry circles have several purposes. One is giving imprisoned people an opportunity to take responsibility for their lives by determining their goals and identifying their strengths, and to make amends and repair the harm their criminal behavior and imprisonment caused. This includes considering how they can repair their relationships with their children. A circle is only provided when the incarcerated parent takes responsibility for repairing the harm his or her children have suffered.

Another purpose for reentry circles is to provide an opportunity for healing for loved ones, the community, and especially children harmed by an imprisoned parent's past behavior. Many incarcerated people have said that "living a law-abiding and clean and sober life" is how they can repair things for the community at large and for their loved ones. Unrelated victims[2] do not participate in

---

2. We make every effort to not use the terms *victim, offender,* or *inmate* in this chapter and in providing the circle program. These labels are generally based on limiting deficits and can be unhelpful. In the instances we use the terms here it is only to clarify meanings.

the circles, but the group determines what the incarcerated person could do to repair harm he or she may have caused them.

The reentry circles follow carefully selected solution-focused language, which invites incarcerated people to be accountable for their behavior and their lives (De Jong & Berg, 2013). The use of solution-focused language during the circle process focuses on the future, not the past. Time is not spent on asking why crimes were committed or rationalizing past misbehavior. Solution-focused dialogues instead assist incarcerated people and their children to build a vision of what they would like their life to look like in the future. The circles also focus on how people and their children were harmed by past behavior, including the loss of a loved one to prison, and what might be done to repair that harm. This approach can help create better relationships.

Making concrete plans for repairing the harm can lead to reconciled relationships and create a positive support system for future success. Planning also inspires optimism, which is key for health and psychological well-being (Peterson, 2000). To respect each participant's cultural or religious beliefs, the circles begin with the incarcerated person opening the process in whatever way he or she chooses. This allows for individual cultural and ethnic values to be introduced. Circles have been opened with Hawaiian chants, Christian prayers, reciting poems, a moment of silence, and numerous other unique approaches. After the opening, the incarcerated person is asked "What accomplishments are you most proud of that you achieved since you've been in prison?" This solution-focused and strength-based question helps establish the positive things that the imprisoned person has done in prison despite whatever adverse behavior may have caused his or her incarceration. It is also a way to inform participants, especially children, that the incarcerated parent is accomplishing things and trying to improve his or her life in prison.

Next, the strengths of any children attending the circle are gathered from all the participants. Beginning with the children helps to identify them as positive figures and respects them as key participants. It also provides positive reinforcement and recognition for their efforts and successes.

After identifying strengths, the incarcerated person identifies the relationship that was harmed by his or her behavior and imprisonment that needs reconciliation. He or she begins by stating how any children present in the circle were affected by his or her behavior and imprisonment. This is a poignant part of the circle and healing for the children who hear their parents acknowledge some of their pain and hardship. Jennifer's father said, "I missed her volleyball games."

Next the children identify how they have been harmed. They tell their story in their own words. Telling one's story is a powerful part of the healing process, which requires validation and helps address pain (Starks, Vakalahi, Comer, & Ortiz-Hendricks, 2010). Many youth describe the embarrassment and shame they felt about having an imprisoned parent and the sadness of not having them attend school and sporting events. "I was always the only kid with no parents at the soccer games," lamented one young girl. Their stories are full of emotion, and they are personal and unique to each child. They can be very detailed and difficult to verbalize, and are often stated with tears. The children's courage is always acknowledged after their sharing. If they do not want to share, they are free not to, but to date all who were old enough to speak have said something about how they were affected by losing a parent to prison. After the children have told their stories, other participants in the circle share how they have been harmed by the imprisonment of their loved one.

When asked what their father could do to help "repair the harm," Jennifer, Alan, and Tray all said: "Spend time with us." The facilitator probed the youth further to specify exactly what "spend time" meant to them. Almost all reentry circles conducted to date have also included the request that the imprisoned person stay clean and sober.

The circles take approximately three hours to conduct. Addressing reconciliation usually takes the most time. The remaining time is used to address the other needs of the incarcerated person, as detailed earlier. The group offers suggestions and help. Timelines for carrying out intended activities are established (e.g., "write and mail letter to health department by March 1st for information on obtaining birth certificate").

Children may also have ideas for how to help. For instance, once when a circle group discussed how an incarcerated woman could deal with stress and stay clean and sober, her six-year-old daughter suggested: "She can play with me." Many youth wanted their parents to spend time with them, and their families, to repair the harm.

The circles also provide hope for the incarcerated person that he or she will have resources when transitioning back into the community, and that family members and others will assist and support a successful transition. Likewise, the children witness a concrete plan being developed for their parent that also provides hope that once he or she is released back into the community, they will experience a better life and relationship.

The circle ends with each participant complimenting the imprisoned person for being accountable, willing to reconcile, and anything else. Finally, the incarcerated person closes the circle by explaining how it was helpful for her or him. He or she thanks the participants for coming and allowing him or her a chance to make things right. Incarcerated people have often said that the circle process was also healing for them, that they had a "weight lifted" from them, and that the opportunity to reconcile helped them address their own trauma.

Such trauma may involve childhood abuse, for example, or other experiences of foster care. Although Hawai'i does not keep statistics, anecdotally it is known that many imprisoned people in Hawai'i were formerly in foster care.[3]

---

3. This chapter's lead author is a former Hawai'i state deputy attorney general who defended numerous cases resulting from prison violence, and in litigating these cases, she reviewed dozens of inmate files, noting that many of the imprisoned people were former foster children.

A California study showed that 14 percent of 2,564 incarcerated people were former foster children (California Senate, 2011). According to Nicholas Zill, with the Center on Children and Families (2011, p. 2), "Former foster youth are over-represented among inmates of state and federal prisons. In 2004 there were almost 190,000 inmates of state and federal prisons in the U.S. who had a history of foster care during their childhood or adolescence. These foster care alumni represented nearly 15% of the inmates of state prisons and almost 8% of the inmates of federal prisons. The cost of incarcerating former foster youth was approximately $5.1 billion per year." Research by the University of Chicago found that a higher level of former foster children from three Midwestern states became involved with the criminal justice system compared with children from intact homes (Courtney, Dworsky, Brown, Cary, Love, & Vorhies, 2011).

The APA suggests that looking for opportunities for self-discovery also builds children's resiliency. Participation in circles often allows children to see that they are a strength for their parents and that they can be an integral part of their parent's success. A 16-year-old New Yorker who participated in her mother's circle, which was held at a jail in that state, said: "Thank you for helping me and my mom through this and showing her that she has the power and strength to get through anything" (Davis, 2013, p. 1).

Not all circles involve children, but when they are participants, the facilitator takes a child-centered approach because the children are the most vulnerable and need attention and care. Whenever children and young people participate for a parent, their strengths are identified by the group at the beginning of the circle. Also outside a legal setting, children can see that the parents are not coerced into apologizing, being accountable, or participating, and that the circles are a voluntary and a genuine process.

In addition to focusing on how harmed people can be helped, the reentry circle model also applies basic public health learning principles. The World Health Organization articulated these principles in 1954 when it published its first report on "Health Education of the Public." Public health learning principles include using activity based and experiential processes for participants:

> The fact that learning is an active process is of particular significance to the health educationist. He cannot assume that people learn merely because he disseminates health information. . . . Learning takes place more effectively when the experience has meaning for the learner and he is able to see the full implications of the experience. (World Health Organization, 1954, p. 10)

By participating in the circle, Jennifer, Alan, and Tray got to share their stories about how they were affected by their father's past behavior and his imprisonment. They saw their father being accountable and people wanting to hear their stories. This showed them that their stories and voices have meaning. Also being able to tell their father what he could do to repair the harm they suffered helped make it more meaningful for the three youth.

Finally, the youth experienced participating in their own healing. In 2008, Jennifer said that what she liked most about the circle was "Everything, because it helped me realize what I can do to help make things better." Five years later, in 2013, her attitude reflected similar self-determination when she discussed the value of participating in the circle:

> It made me feel a lot better, especially about myself. I came to the realization it is not my fault. Things happen for a reason and I am not responsible for changing others including my dad. I can forgive, but not forget. I will keep the things that happened to me in mind. Coming from where I was, I am so much better. I appreciate what happened in how it made me grow.

In addition to providing a meaningful experience, the circles also incorporate other public health learning principles by focusing on goals, offering positive motivation, and using group process (Walker & Greening, 2013). These public health principles are consistent with restorative justice and solution-focused approaches, which also appreciate the influence of others to repair harm (Zehr, 1990), and find solutions to difficulties (De Jong & Berg, 2013).

EVALUATION METHOD

This research used a quantitative method to assess how the reentry circles influenced the children of imprisoned parents. A questionnaire was developed to probe how the circles may have increased the children's perception of their own healing after participating in a circle. A five-point scale was developed to rate healing in terms of respondents' hope about the future and letting go of the past. If the respondent answered that he or she had experienced healing after participation in the circle, a qualitative open-ended question was asked so that the respondent might describe the healing that had occurred. Fifty-six families were selected from more than one hundred records based on their having children who participated in their circles.[4] Subjects were contacted by

---

4. One youth who locked his keys in his car did not arrive at the prison in time for his father's scheduled circle, and the prison did not allow him to participate directly in the circle, but regardless his input was recorded concerning before and after the circle because he experienced differences in his father and himself as a result of the circle.

telephone. The time since their participation in the circles ranged from eight years to three weeks.

Questionnaire Development

The questionnaire was developed in an attempt to best operationalize the concept of healing. The goal was to understand whether and how much healing was experienced among children participating in and affected by the reentry circles. The questions were developed with the guidance of medical research on the measurement of healing.[5] The definition of healing used here is basically the ability to forgive according the work of Fred Luskin, which is simply no longer wishing for a different past (Luskin, 2002), and also increased optimism for the future, as developed by Martin Seligman and his work in positive psychology (Seligman, 2011).

The questions included the perceived health of the relationship between the youth and their incarcerated loved ones before and after participation in the circle. Two questions were also asked about the interviewee's ability to let go of painful memories (forgiveness) and his or her trust in the future (optimism) before and after participating in the circle. The work of researchers who developed an instrument to describe and measure the psychological and social construct of healing in clinical medicine was studied in designing the questionnaire for this study. The Self-Integration Scale, Version 2.1 (Meza & Fahoome, 2008), was reviewed as a basic guide for the questions about whether interviewees could let go of painful past memories and whether they felt they had trust in the future. Finally, the interviewees were asked whether they felt that they had personally healed from the circle experience, and they were provided an opportunity to explain how or why this healing did (or did not) occur in an open-ended statement.

Interviewees

A total of twenty-eight people were interviewed concerning the influence of the circles on children. Eleven of these interviewees were adult caretakers of the incarcerated person's children; three were aunts; and fourteen interviewees were children of an incarcerated parent. Seventeen interviewees were of Hawaiian descent, and eleven of the youth interviewees were of Hawaiian descent. The ages of the youth at the time their parent participated in a reentry circle ranged from 10 to 24 years. All but one child (see footnote 3) were able to participate in the

---

5. The questionnaire used for this study is attached as Appendix B.

circles, and all were able to speak to its influence. In 2013, when this study was conducted, the youth were between the ages of 12 and 32.

While this research focuses on youth responses, the discussion briefly alludes to interviews with other adult parents and caretakers to supplement explanations of the circles' healing effects on the broader family.

Interview Responses

The views of the fourteen children of incarcerated people trend in the positive direction before and especially after the circle. This appears to be because there was commonly an attitude of hopefulness and attachment among the children, who frequently stated that they had a positive relationship with their parents both before and after the reentry circle. There were some exceptions, however, and the complexities of these relationships are more apparent in the open-ended responses about how youth felt they had (or had not) healed.

Exceptions included instances when children believed their relationships with their incarcerated parents were positive until they participated in the circle, which exposed realities about the parent that were unknown before. In one case, two teenage sisters realized that their father was more concerned about his own interests than theirs. This realization had positive effects for the girls, nevertheless, who throughout their teenage years gauged their romantic relationships by their father's model. Their mother reported that one sister would remark to the other: "Hey, red flag, he's acting like dad" when they became involved with teenage boys who appeared selfish or self-centered. Another 20-year-old who participated in a circle for her father remarked:

> I feel like all the pain my dad put me and my family through made me stronger. I took it as a positive. Not having a father is hard. The circle was an eye-opener about who he was.

The healing experiences from the circle experience did not always include reconciliation:

> Yeah—I got some closure. . . hard to explain. It helped me more individually than our relationship. I guess the. . . closure was helpful because I got to see her sober. But she's still basically a child. Before the circle, I was done trying to have expectations of her. Y'know? But now, I expect her to stay sober, and I now realize she may not grow as a person and she may stay selfish. So even though she's sober she hasn't really changed. So I learned that and that's all I expect. I don't expect her to be the mother I missed out on in my life and I'm okay with that now.

Qualitative data collected in the open-ended responses explain the tendency of circles to promote healing in different ways. Other youth comments include this one from a 25-year-old woman. She was 17 at the time she participated in the circle for her father, who had been in and out of prison numerous times throughout her childhood:

> I was older by the time I did a circle and was able to share feelings about how it was growing up. I never really got to sit down before and say, "this sucked" to my dad. The circle set the stage for being able to do that without it being awkward. I was expected to talk about my feelings, so that was helpful. Normally I probably wouldn't have said anything at all. It's different when it's your parents, y'know, because there's a boundary between respect and honesty.

Two youth respondents felt that they had a very positive relationship with their parents before the circle. Almost half of the respondents (n = 6) felt that they had a positive relationship with their incarcerated parent before participating in the restorative justice circle, while the remaining six were divided between mixed (n = 3) and negative (n = 3) feelings about their relationship with their incarcerated parents. After the circle, youth respondents were divided almost evenly between very positive (n = 6) and positive (n = 5) about their relationship with their incarcerated parent. The remaining respondents had mixed feelings (n = 2) and negative feelings (n = 1) about their relationship.

Some children felt that they had positive relationships with their incarcerated parents and participating in the circle reinforced this. Some statements from youth were:

> "I didn't have any grudges. Things turned out alright."
>
> "I guess I felt relieved because I hadn't seen my mom in so long. When I finally got to see her, it was like she wasn't gone that long."

Before participating in the restorative reentry circle, youth respondents largely responded "yes" to the question about whether they could let go of painful or difficult past memories (n = 9) and the remainder were split between "somewhat" (n = 2) and "no" (n = 3). After participating in the circle, twelve youth respondents said "yes" to letting go of difficult past memories, while the remaining two said they were "somewhat" able to let go. Zero youth respondents said "no" to the question of whether they could let go of painful past memories after the circle. The following figure shows how youth respondents felt about painful past memories before and after participating in the reentry circles.

Letting Go of Difficult Memories: Qualitative data gathered from the youth indicate that some were able to move forward and some were not, but they appreciated the opportunity to tell their story, showing the importance of being heard and listened to at the circles.

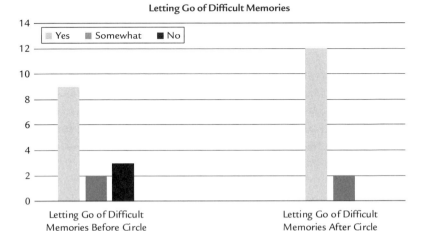

Letting Go of Difficult Memories

"My personal feeling that I'm not trying to dwell on the past, and my relationship with my mother is better than it used to be."

"It was a good feeling. I feel like I can talk with my mom more."

"When I saw my father cry, I thought he was realizing. . . but then I knew he was just putting on a show. The circle was hard because it was hard to see him that way. At the same time it gave us a chance to let him know how we're feeling."

Trusting in the Future: Seven respondents said "yes" to the question of whether they trusted that the future would be OK before participating in the restorative justice circle. The remaining respondents were divided between "somewhat" (n = 4) and "no" (n = 3). After the circle, ten respondents said "yes" to this question, while four responded "somewhat" regarding their level of trust in a positive future. Zero youth respondents said "no" to the question. The following figure shows how youth respondents felt about the future before and after participating in the reentry circles.

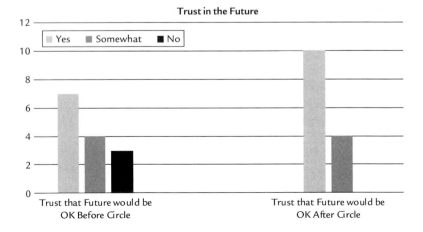

Trust in the Future

One respondent commented on how the future appears for him now that he is a father himself: "I don't have anxiety attacks anymore. Yeah, I used to have anxiety when I would get stressed out. I'm a father now, so yeah, it's all good."

The following figure illustrates whether youth felt that they had personally healed after the restorative reentry circle. Eleven responded "yes" and three said "somewhat."

Personal Healing: One respondent likened his healing to a kind of relief: "It's hard to explain. You feel like everything is lifted off of your shoulders. Things are just better between us."

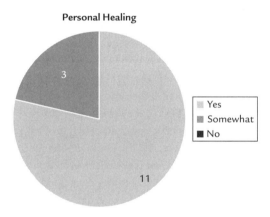

The following response came from a young person who had participated in a circle six years before. He reflected on his changed relationship with his father:

> The restorative justice circle was effective. I would say that the circle really addressed the personal effects that I've seen as his son. I don't think he was aware of it, and at the same time, in my upbringing, I thought the behavior that he had was just how it was. . . .. I didn't see it as an issue. It was only revealed later through other family members and through the restorative justice circle. I realized this does have an effect. I was only a child/adolescent, and those things do have an effect on you in your developmental stage. With the circle, a lot of emotional aspects and the emotional damage were revealed, and it made me and my father aware of the challenges I've seen which caused emotional damage. There were challenges that were met, and I don't know if that would have succeeded if the restorative justice circle had not been a part of his program. It was a program that everyone, or anyone, entering into it should follow through with. It should be completed. It was definitely something that does make a difference at any magnitude. . . provided that the individual completes the program. That's the hard part. I can tell you my father and I speak or at least text now on a regular basis. The circle was absolutely very, very effective. And I haven't turned out as a negative person at all. In fact I went the other way. My father has owned up to it, and it allowed us to heal.

DISCUSSION

The views of the youth trend in the positive direction both before, but especially after, participating in the circle. Healing was defined in various ways, which were at times captured better in open-ended responses than in the survey instrument that sought to measure the effects of the circles. Healing is personal. Sometimes it is simply the ability to move on, or let go, and this may show up on a survey as having healed only "somewhat."

Sometimes the relationship between a child and his or her incarcerated parent may become worse after experiencing a reentry circle, but this does not mean there is not important healing at work. Some young people mentioned that they had learned to adjust their expectations of their parents and accept that they would not change. In some cases, youth respondents mentioned that they had personally healed by being able to express their honest feelings without worrying about disrespecting their parents. In another case, two sisters learned from the poor behavior of their incarcerated father and applied that knowledge in their own lives to avoid men who behaved in the same negative way.

There are many other factors affecting the healing process, and one of these is timing. While a family may appreciate the circle experience, its healing effects may not be immediate. It may take time for an incarcerated person to gain insight into his or her own behaviors after hearing stories from children during the circle. Even relapse can occur from the time of a circle and an inmate's release, which certainly affects a family's healing.

Restorative justice does not claim to be an easily measured cure-all for the emotional pain and suffering caused by criminality and the loss of a loved one to prison. Reentry circles can nevertheless be an important and meaningful approach, which can offer the possibility of healing. This comes in different forms for families, and especially for children and youth.

CONCLUSION

The criminal justice system expends vast resources on incarceration for those who violate laws, but it does little in the way of assistance for their children, who are unrecognized victims of their parents' criminal behavior and imprisonment. This research shows that the restorative reentry circle model can mediate the collateral and detrimental effects that these children suffer by providing them with a powerful instrument for meaningful participation in the planning of their parent's release program.

Simply giving youth a voice to tell their story in a respectful setting, with their families who are interested and listening, can be helpful (Parkes, 2013). "Perhaps the central benefit to victims in restorative justice is the sense of empowerment they achieve through telling their stories and being listened to" (Gal, 2011, p. 125). These stories can also provide a start for the incarcerated parent to reconcile and serve as an opportunity for children and youth to move beyond the trauma and find hope for the future. As Jennifer said immediately following the circle, "[The circle] was really helpful because we talked about things, the things my dad has done, and why he's done it and his feelings on the whole subject." Tray also explained how the circle helped him: "Good to get your feelings out. The feelings were trapped in there for so long, it was really good to talk to my brother and sister, my dad, and my Grandma too, because she was there. It really helped me close the feelings that I kept inside." The circles provide a powerful arena for children to meaningfully participate, which can help them heal.

The circles also provide youth with positive role modeling. Parents who have participated in the circles are voluntarily being accountable for the harm their crimes and imprisonment have caused their children, their families, and the community at large. A parent's assumption of responsibility and efforts to address and repair the harm[6] he or she has caused others presents the children with positive role modeling, which, as Murray and Farrington (2005) suggested, is lacking when parents are imprisoned. As this research has shown too, when parents feign positive role modeling or are perhaps unaccountable during the circles, their children can still benefit from understanding this reality.

Jennifer mentioned the effects of the circle on her "brothers [Alan and Tray, who, like their father], took the wrong path too. It's helpful to see they've done the right thing, because of the circle it's helped a lot." Alan explained in more detail what that wrong path was for him:

> Before [the circle] I was hanging out with the bad kind of people because of what my dad did and I got into some bad things like *pakalolo* [Hawaiian local slang for marijuana] for instance, but that has stopped completely ever since I thought about what my dad did, and I don't want to go through that same path. The restorative circle made me realize I don't wanna do that. I saw there was a lot of pain and suffering that people went through.

Ray mirrored Alan's insight, saying that their father's criminal behavior "made me more conscious of making good choices myself. I learned from my dad's bad behavior not to do it myself."

Jennifer moved away from Hawai'i after she graduated from high school. She is currently in a work-study program in another state, becoming a certified nursing assistant, and is happy with her life. She reports that Alan and Tray are both doing well; one is in the military and the other is working full time. Ray also continues to do well in the military and is completing a special intelligence training program in another state.

---

6. During circles facilitators state the fact that the imprisoned person, by applying for and having a reentry circle, is accountable and is taking responsibility for any harm caused by his or her past behavior and imprisonment.

Further research should be undertaken to make circles more effective at addressing the serious inequities that children of incarcerated parents suffer. Funding could be provided to meet the basic social and the unique needs of individual youth whose parents are imprisoned. Many people incarcerated in the United States are poor (but because they are incarcerated, they are not counted in common measures of poverty or unemployment). Research shows that the compounded influence of a person's interaction with the penal system is intergenerational: "it affects the social and economic mobility of inmates themselves after their release, but it also affects their families and children" (Western & Pettit, 2010, p. 8). Importantly, children lack the opportunities to participate in programs that would help them develop and become more resilient despite their hardship. Circles can help here. Reentry circles also offer an alternative approach to help incarcerated adults transition back into society by providing opportunities to reconcile with those they have harmed. The input from their children can be especially important because children have been negatively affected by their parents' incarceration, often by out-of-home placement or severe economic hardship.

For Native Hawaiian families, who are disproportionately poor and underserved in areas of education, housing, and health, children placed in their care face extreme difficulties (Office of Hawaiian Affairs, 2010). Government subsidies, student scholarships, grants, loans, housing allowances, and other financial assistance, which could be arranged and provided through circles, may help address the inequities that children of incarcerated parents suffer. Funding to ensure continued relationships with the incarcerated parent, either for direct transportation costs or transportation subsidies, would assist in the healing process after a reentry circle is held. More circles should be provided and the effects on children and youth should be studied more extensively.

REFERENCES

American Psychological Association (2013). Resilience guide for parents & teachers. Retrieved October 9, 2013, from http://www.apa.org/helpcenter/resilience.aspx#

Braithwaite, J. (2004). Emancipation and hope. *Annals of the American Academy of Political and Social Science, 529,* 79–99.

Brown, M., & Kay, J. (2007). *Hawai'i County's children of incarcerated parents: A needs assessment of parents, children, and caregivers.* Honolulu: Hawai'i County Children of Incarcerated Parents Task Force.

Bureau of Justice Statistics (2013). U.S. prison population declined for third consecutive year during 2012. Retrieved July 2, 2013, from http://www.bjs.gov/content/pub/press/p12acpr.cfm

California Senate Office of Research (2011). State survey of California prisoners: what percent of the state's polled prison inmates were once foster children? Policy matters. December. Retrieved July 23, 2014 from http://www.sor.govoffice3.com/vertical/Sites/%7B3BDD1595-792B-4D20-8D44-626EF05648C7%7D/uploads/Foster_Care_PDF_12-8-11.pdf

Courtney, M., Dworsky, A., Brown, A., Cary, C., Love, K., & Vorhies, V. (2011). Midwest evaluation of the adult functioning of former foster children: outcomes at age 26. Retrieved October 10, 2013, from http://www.chapinhall.org/sites/default/files/Midwest%20Evaluation_Report_4_10_12.pdf

Davis, I. (2013). Personal correspondence to Lorenn Walker October 3, 2013.

De Jong, P., & Berg, I. K. (2013). *Interviewing for solutions* (3rd ed.). Pacific Grove, CA: Brooks/Cole.

EPIC 'Ohana (2013). E Makau Ana Youth Circle. Retrieved September 15, 2013, from http://www.epicohana.net/youthcircle.aspx

Furman, B., & Ahola, T. (1992). *Solution talk: hosting therapeutic conversations.* New York: W.W. Norton & Co.

Gal, T. (2011). *Child victims and restorative justice: a need-rights model* (p. 125). New York: Oxford University Press.

Glaze, L., & Maruschak, L. (2008). *Parents in prison and their minor children.* Washington, DC: Bureau of Justice Statistics, Special Report. Retrieved July 23, 2014 from http://www.bjs.gov/content/pub/pdf/pptmc.pdf.

Hensey, O., Williams, J., & Rosenbloom, L. (1983). Intervention in child abuse: Experiences in Liverpool. *Developmental Medicine and Child Neurology, 25,* 606–611.

Johnson, E., & Waldfogel, J. (2008). Trends in parental incarceration and implications for child welfare. CW360, Spring 2008 issue.

Luskin, F. (2002). *Forgive for good: a proven prescription for health and happiness.* New York: HarperCollins.

Lynch, M., & Roberts, J. (1982). *Consequences of child abuse.* London: Academic Press.

Meza, J., & Fahoome, G. (2008). The development of an instrument for measuring healing. *Annals of Family Medicine,* 6(4).

Miller, K. (2006). The impact of parental incarceration on children: an emerging need for effective interventions. *Child and Adolescent Social Work Journal,* 23(4).

Murray, J., & Farrington, D. (2005). Parental imprisonment: effects on boys' antisocial behavior and delinquency through the life-course," *Journal of Child Psychology and Psychiatry, 46,* 12.

National Research Council (1999). Understanding and preventing violence. Retrieved October 2, 2013, from http://www.nap.edu/openbook.php?record_id=1861&page=38

Office of Hawaiian Affairs (2010). The disparate treatment of Native Hawaiians in the criminal justice system. Executive report. Retrieved March 18, 2014, from http://www.oha.org/sites/default/files/es_final_web_0.pdf

Parkes, A. (2013). *Children and international human rights law.* New York: Routledge.

Peterson, C. (2000). The future of optimism. *American Psychologist,* 555(1), 44–55.

Population Reference Bureau (2013). http://www.prb.org/Publications/Articles/2012/us-incarceration.aspx

Seligman, M. (2011). *Flourish: a visionary new understanding of happiness and well-being.* New York: Free Press.

Seymour, C. (1998). Children with parents in prison: child welfare policy, programs and practice issues. *Child Welfare,* 77(5).

Starks, S., Vakalahi, H., Comer, M., & Ortiz-Hendricks, C. (2010). Gathering, telling, preparing the stories: a vehicle for healing. *Journal of Indigenous Voices in Social Work,* 1(1), 1–18.

U.S. Department of Health and Human Services, Administration for Children and Families, Administration on Children, Youth and Families, Children's Bureau (2013a). Race/ethnicity of public agency children adopted: October 1, 2011 to September 30, 2012 (FY 2012). Retrieved April 2, 2014, from http://www.acf.hhs.gov/sites/default/files/cb/race2012.pdf

U.S. Department of Health and Human Services, Administration for Children and Families, Administration on Children, Youth and Families, Children's Bureau (2013b). Recent demographic trends in foster care. Office of Data, Analysis, Research, and Evaluation Data Brief 2013-1. Retrieved from http://www.acf.hhs.gov/sites/default/files/cb/data_brief_foster_care_trends1.pdf

Walker, L. (2005). E makua ana youth circles: a transition planning process for youth exiting foster care. *Connections, 21*(5), 12–13.

Walker, L., & Greening, R. (2013). *Reentry & transition planning circles for incarcerated people* (3rd ed.) Honolulu: Hawai'i Friends of Justice & Civic Education.

Western, B., & Pettit, B. (2010). Incarceration and social inequality. *Daedalus, 139,* 8.

Widom, C. (1990). *Research, clinical, and policy issues: Childhood victimization, parent alcohol problems, and long-term consequences.* National Forum on the Future of Children, Workshop on Children and Parental Illegal Drug Abuse. National Research Council: Institute of Medicine, March 8, 1990.

Wildeman, C. (2009). Parental imprisonment, the prison boom, and the concentration of childhood disadvantage. *Demography, 46*(2), 265–280. Retrieved November 1, 2014 from http://www.ncbi.nlm.nih.gov/pmc/articles/PMC2831279/pdf/dem-46-0265.pdf.

World Health Organization (WHO) (1954). Expert committee on health education of the public. Technical Report Series, No. 89. Retrieved December 19, 2013 from http://apps.who.int/iris/bitstream/10665/40254/1/WHO_TRS_89.pdf.

Zehr, H. (1990). Changing lenses: a new focus for crime and justice. Scottdale, PA: Herald Press.

Zill, N. (2011). Adoption from foster care: aiding children while saving public money. Children and Families Brief #43, Retrieved August 5, 2014 from http://www.brookings.edu/~/media/research/files/reports/2011/5/adoption%20foster%20care%20zill/05_adoption_foster_care_zill.pdf

APPENDIX A

PREPARING CHILDREN FOR A REENTRY CIRCLE

The circle is ONLY conducted when the parent is accountable for helping repair the harm that has child has suffered. Please let your child know that his or her parent asked for a circle because he or she is sorry and wants to repair harm that has been caused.

Example for elementary school children:

"Your mother would like to be in a circle with you. The circle will be at the prison with you, me, your mother, and people that will help us all talk. Your mother wants a circle because she is sorry for things she has done that have hurt you."

Example for adolescents:

"Your father would like you to be in a circle with him at the prison. He wants you to know he is sorry for what he has done that has hurt you, including his being imprisoned and being unable to be a part of your life."

Let the children and youth know they will have an opportunity to speak, and say what their parent can do to help repair the harm caused to them, but they don't have to.

Example for elementary school children:

> *"You will have a turn to tell your mom how you were hurt and then you can tell her what she can do to make things better for you."*

Examples for adolescents:

> *"You will also have a chance to tell your father how the harm he's caused you has affected your life. You can tell him what the consequences have been for you of his past bad behavior and his being in prison. And you will be able to tell him what he can do to make things better for you."*

If a child does not want to speak at the circle, they can write a statement to be read by an adult, however, they may change their mind once they are in the circle or they may choose to read their statement while participating in a circle. The facilitator will give them an option to speak, read, or have someone else read any previously prepared statements during the circle.

Once a child or adolescent has have a general understanding of what will happen at the circle, you can ask questions to help them think about what they would like:

- What kinds of things are you good at/accomplishments can you share with your mom/dad when they ask how you are doing?
- How would you like things to be better between you and your mom/dad?
- What do you like best about your mom/dad?
- What would be the best thing that could come out of this circle?
- If you could close your eyes and when you opened them your mom/dad was out of prison, what would your life look like?

APPENDIX B

'Ohana Participant's Huikahi Circle Evaluation of Youth/Families Hawaii Friends of Civic & Law Related Education

Name:

Age:

Date:

Date of Circle:

Relationship to Incarcerated person: e.g. son, daughter, mother, father, auntie, friend, etc.

Phone:

Hawaiian? Yes/No

1. *Before* you participated in Huikahi Restorative Circle, your relationship with your loved one(s) was:

   1 Very Positive   2 Positive   3 Mixed   4 Negative   5 Very negative

2. *Before* you participated in the Circle:

   a. Were you able to let go of painful/difficult past memories?
      Yes   Somewhat   No

   b. Did you trust that things could turn out OK in the future? (Did you feel positive about life generally?)
      Yes   Somewhat   No

3. *After* you participated in the Circle:

   a. Were you able to let go of painful/difficult past memories?
      Yes   Somewhat   No

   b. Did you trust that things could turn out OK in the future? (Do you feel positive about life generally?)
      Yes   Somewhat   No

4. *After* you participated in Circle, your relationship with your loved one(s) was:

   1 Very Positive   2 Positive   3 Mixed   4 Negative   5 Very negative

5. Have you personally healed after participation in the Circle?
      Yes   Somewhat   No

   a. If yes or somewhat, describe the healing that you feel has occurred, including your relationship with your parent if this is relevant.

   b. If no, describe the healing you would have liked to occur.

PART V

Child Participation in
the Public Sphere

CHAPTER 15

Face to Face

Children and Young People's Right to Participate in Public Decision-Making

CHELSEA MARSHALL, BRONAGH BYRNE,
AND LAURA LUNDY

INTRODUCTION

While all human beings have a right to freedom of expression, only children have the right to have their views given due weight. Article 12(1) of the United Nations Convention on the Rights of the Child (CRC) states that

> States Parties shall assure to the child who is capable of forming his or her own views the right to express those views freely in all matters affecting the child, the views of the child being given due weight in accordance with the age and maturity of the child.

The inclusion of this additional obligation in the CRC recognizes that children often lack power and influence in the decisions that are made for them and that, as rights holders, they are entitled to be heard and to help shape the decisions that have an impact on their lives (Freeman, 2000; Lundy & Stalford, 2013). The Committee on the Rights of the Child ("the Committee"; 2009) explains that Article 12 applies to the decisions that affect individual children (e.g., decisions made about their personal health care and education) as well as groups of children (e.g., decisions made about local, national, and international laws and policies related to criminal justice or social care systems). This chapter focuses on the latter—children's participation in public decision-making.

As a signatory to the CRC, the UK government is obligated to ensure that children are given safe and inclusive opportunities to form and express their views, supported by information and guidance; children are facilitated to express themselves in a medium of their choice; participation is voluntary; and children's views are taken seriously and influence decisions as appropriate (Lundy, 2007). However, despite the significant advances in relation to the implementation of Article 12 in the UK, participation is not always routine, nor is it always meaningful (e.g., Hill, Davis, Prout, & Tisdall, 2004; Tisdall & Davis, 2004). Public consultations on local and national policies may provide space for children to engage with public decision-making. However, these processes are frequently not developed in ways that are accessible to children, and there is often little evidence of children's views influencing outcomes (Sinclair 2004; Stafford, Laybourn, Hill, & Walker, 2003). Beyond consultation, children and young people across the world engage with decision makers in person by presenting at public conferences, giving evidence at committee hearings, meeting policymakers and politicians directly, and organizing events to share their views or present research findings (Lansdown, 2011). Methods for direct and indirect engagement between children and young people and public decision makers are diverse and offer potentially different advantages and disadvantages for all those involved.

Direct contact between rights holders and duty bearers is only one of a number of ways in which children and young people's participation in public decision-making may occur. However, it is a process that has been endorsed explicitly by the Committee (UN, 2003, para. 12), which has suggested that:

> It is important that Governments develop a direct relationship with children, not simply one mediated through non-governmental organizations (NGOs) or human rights institutions. In the early years of the Convention, NGOs had played a notable role in pioneering participatory approaches with children, but it is in the interests of both Governments and children to have appropriate direct contact.

This chapter explores the experience of direct participation of children and young people in public decision-making from the perspective of adult duty bearers, NGO staff members who facilitate it, and young people themselves.[1] The chapter is based on evidence collected in two studies conducted in Northern Ireland, one of which explored barriers to government delivery for children and the other effective advocacy for children's rights. A core aspect of both studies was the experience and impact of children and young people's participation.

---

1. The term "young people" is used in this chapter in reference to respondents (aged 14–25) involved in the "Advancing Children's Rights" research. These respondents discussed their experiences of participation in advocacy projects as children and young people (defined by the CRC as under 18). Duty bearers discussed their experiences of children and young people's participation, so both terms are used in reference to data from the NICCY study.

Drawing on this empirical evidence, the chapter focuses on the value and impact of direct face-to-face meetings between children and adult duty bearers. It begins by recounting the experiences of the different stakeholders before examining some of the challenges that emerge for children and young people in being themselves and representing others in such processes ("being the face") and for adult duty bearers, who are navigating what for many is a unique form of public engagement ("keeping up face"). It concludes by reflecting on what is achieved through this particular form of engagement ("facing the issues") and identifying ways in which the type of direct contact might be implemented to enhance its value in terms of rights-based participation.

METHODS AND METHODOLOGY

The chapter draws on two studies: the first explored the key barriers to effective government delivery for children and young people more generally, and the second used children's rights-based research methods to explore young people's views of engaging with public decision-making. Children and young people's participation is increasingly common in the UK (e.g., Tisdall, Davis, Prout, & Hill, 2006), and Northern Ireland's relatively small population and high proportion of policymakers means that most NGOs advocating for children's rights have experience facilitating face-to-face engagement. These conditions offered a valuable opportunity to explore public decision-making processes from the lens of duty bearers, rights holders, and the NGOs that supported and facilitated this engagement. The studies engaged a diverse range of stakeholders across government departments and issues facing children and young people in Northern Ireland. The research focused primarily on young people's (aged 14–20) engagement with policymakers, with some examples from adult respondents of engagement with children (aged 8–12). Our arguments in this chapter are therefore related to the conditions and potential for older children's direct participation in public decision-making. However, we suggest that the broad principles explored here provide insights into the challenges and opportunities for securing meaningful participation more generally.

The first study, which was carried out for the Northern Ireland Commissioner for Children and Young People (NICCY), explored key structural barriers to government delivery for children and young people in Northern Ireland. NICCY's primary role, as defined in the Commissioner for Children and Young People (Northern Ireland) Order 2003, is to safeguard and promote the rights and best interests of children and young persons. This legislation (2003) also details NICCY's duties, which include keeping under review the adequacy and effectiveness of law and practice relating to the rights and welfare of children and young persons, and providing advice to government in relation to the same. In the exercise of his or her functions, including research and investigations, the

Commissioner is required to have regard to any relevant provisions of the CRC. The research (Byrne & Lundy, 2011, 2013) was carried out in 2011 and had three key strands. First, the project team developed a set of qualitative indicators specific to the implementation of the CRC in policy to provide an overall frame for the project. The second stage of the project consisted of a review of key government strategies, policies, and action plans of relevance to children and young people in Northern Ireland, using the developed indicators as benchmarks. Finally, sixteen semistructured interviews were carried out with representatives from voluntary agencies, statutory agencies, government departments (including policymakers), and politicians (members of the Northern Ireland Assembly).

The second study, "Advancing Children's Rights in Ireland, North and South," was a two-year strategic evaluation of a program of work funded by the Atlantic Philanthropies in relation to children's rights advocacy. The research was conducted by parallel research teams at Queen's University Belfast and University College Cork in 2013–2014. This chapter considers the research conducted with six NGOs in Northern Ireland in 2013. Semistructured interviews and focus groups were conducted with directors and staff of the six NGOs and with young people associated with four of these projects, including young people in care, young people in conflict with the law or with experience of the criminal justice system, and young people not in employment, education, or training. NGOs involved in this research used a variety of methods to engage decision makers in their advocacy work. For example, young people were involved in consultation processes, facilitated by NGO staff and external decision makers, and some acted as representatives on statutory advisory boards. Many young people involved with the research had attended conferences and events to present their views and experiences and those of their peers. One group had presented the findings of a youth-led research project to a public audience, politicians, and government officials at the local parliament.

The "Advancing Children's Rights" study included young people as respondents, and as such, researchers worked with co-researchers to ensure that young people, who had experience of children's rights advocacy, informed the questions, methods, and analysis used. Lundy and McEvoy (2012) argue that the key elements of CRC Article 12—enabling children to express their views and giving due weight to those views in all matters affecting them—should be extended beyond individual research participants to the research process generally. The way researchers view children and childhood has direct implications for how they conduct research (Kellett, Robinson, & Burr 2004), and one way to use a children's rights-based approach to research is to involve children and young people as co-researchers. As Lundy and McEvoy (2012, pp. 129–130) note:

> . . . when children are viewed as rights-holders they are not just recognized as able to but also as entitled to be engaged in this process, with a concomitant duty on the

adults working with them to ensure that their right to express their views and influence their own lives is respected.

The research team in the "Advancing Children's Rights" study established a Young Person's Advisory Group (YPAG; Lundy & McEvoy, 2009) with an existing group of young people associated with an NGO that was not involved in the research cohort. YPAG members were invited to participate as co-researchers with particular expertise as young people involved with advocating for children's rights. Reflecting the membership of the group and their availability to attend the sessions, the YPAG consisted of seven young people (aged 18–20, six female and one male). All members had been involved in children's rights advocacy for three to four years. The YPAG advised the researchers on the content and order of the focus group structure to be used with young people. Meetings were arranged with the support of the group's participation worker, and they took place at the organization's offices or other venues that met the young people's availability. When determining the location of the YPAG meetings, the researchers worked with the participation worker to ensure the venue would be comfortable and appropriate to allow the young people to express their views freely.

FACE TO FACE

While the Committee has emphasized that participation must be "direct" (UN, 2003), this does not mean that the contact has to be in person or indeed *in situ*. It does mean that the state actors are seeking children's views actively (as opposed to being the passive recipients of NGO lobbying). In the research for NICCY, duty bearers identified a range of approaches to participation that they had considered to be useful, many of which had occurred remotely. In fact, in most cases, the contact with children and young people had been indirect. In such cases, significant value was placed on the expertise of others (usually NGOs) to conduct consultations on their behalf. A typical comment in this respect was: "We're not the experts in participation, they are." This response may reflect a common attitude among some adults that they do not have the skills to speak to young people and that it is best left to the experts. This view reflects research from many jurisdictions that a significant barrier to effective participation is adults' attitudes to children and young people as too difficult to consult meaningfully (e.g., Lansdown, 2011).

The "Advancing Children's Rights" research involved young people whose participation in public decision-making was facilitated by NGOs. A common method of participation was consultation exercises with NGO staff, who then presented children and young people's views via written consultation responses, meetings with government officials, or oral evidence to parliamentary committees. Other methods of indirect engagement included creating and performing drama representations of research findings and preparing videos to communicate young people's views. One group explained that, typically, they discussed their experiences and views of an issue with a dedicated participation worker, whose role was to ensure these views informed the NGO's formal communication with decision makers. Policy workers often considered *their* direct engagement with individuals or groups of children and young people as a more appropriate, and sometimes more meaningful, strategy for including children and young people's views in decision-making processes:

> ... [youth group] would get involved in consultation events. So it's directly enabling those young people to have their voices heard on issues impacting on their lives. Not only on their lives but also on the lives of other children and young people. (NGO representative)

Policy officers campaigning on behalf of children's rights felt their direct engagement with children and young people was critical to their capacity to advocate properly:

> ... we need to check things with them to see if we're getting it right and they're in some ways a validation mechanism that are necessary to make sure we have the true picture and we're presenting that true picture. (NGO representative)
>
> I often think that I know what they think, and I know what they would say, but I'm always wrong about that. You do a consultation with [youth group] and it is an incredible eye-opener, and there are times that they say things to me that not only did I not think of but I couldn't have put it as well actually. (NGO representative)

Adults facilitating young people's participation often view "the involvement of children in adult forums as disempowering unless the way of operating is modified significantly" (Bessell, 2009, 311). Traditional methods of engagement in public decision-making have been designed for adult participants, and these formats can marginalize children and young people further from decision-making through subtle or overt practices. NGO workers in this study explained that young people's direct attendance at meetings with duty bearers was not always considered appropriate, strategic, or in line with the best interests of the child as required by Article 3 of the CRC. Indirect engagement, such as NGOs representing young people's views in written consultation responses or in *their* professional engagement with decision makers, was considered useful and important in many instances. Indeed, indirect participation may be the most appropriate rights-based method of including the views of children and young people who are not confident or interested in speaking publicly or with adults in positions of power. Without presuming that these challenges cannot be overcome, such groups may include very young children, children with mental health issues, children who speak nonmajority languages, or those with additional communication needs. When determining the value and appropriateness of children and young people's direct engagement, NGO representatives balanced logistical barriers, such as children and young people being in school or employment when government officials and politicians usually meet, the desire to advocate successfully for change, and consideration of whether participation was in the best interests of the child or young person.

Nonetheless, it was apparent in our studies that, when it did occur, direct human engagement, where rights holders encounter duty bearers in face-to-face meetings, was one approach to nonmediated contact that was appreciated highly by young people and adults alike. Particularly for children and young people who were confident and/or well supported by trusted adults, this created an opportunity to express their views directly to duty bearers. Decision makers who met with children directly spoke about the positive value of these types of encounters. For example, one public official said:

> I mean, it was complicated stuff, pure policy stuff, but it wasn't like a game or an exercise that we did in a facilitated way, it was a proper meeting. I think there should be a little bit more of that done. (Government representative)

In particular, it was seen as way of getting to the crux of the issues:

> In the past year, for example, I can think of conversations I've had with children and young people and they weren't like [consultation events]. They were proper business meetings where we sat down and talked very seriously about their situations and in those meetings I got to hear probably some of the most salient pieces of information about policy-making that I needed to . . . (Government representative)

Public engagement events were also seen by young people as useful opportunities to express their views directly to decision makers:

> I wasn't afraid to tell him what I thought and that was a good thing because when do I ever meet the Education Minister?! (Young person)

Some young people argued that decision makers "listened better because it was a young person saying it" than they would to an adult representative. One young person explained that what struck her most about engaging directly with a decision maker was that "it was us being able to ask about decisions that were being made about us." The immediacy and opportunity for interaction were identified as positive consequences of direct meetings:

> . . . to have the Education Minister there as well was brilliant and to get his immediate feedback—just the presentation and then he was on the spot. . . (Young person)

Graham and Fitzgerald (2010, p. 354) suggest the value of a dialogical approach is in "its productive potential." Face-to-face engagement created an opportunity for young people to put pressure on decision makers for a response. This was considered an unusual advantage compared to what many perceived as long delays and avoidance of their questions or concerns in other forms of engagement.

The adults' and young people's accounts were endorsed by staff in the NGOs that brought children and young people to meet officials or politicians. For instance, in their observations of the impact of direct meetings for the duty bearers involved, they emphasized that it gave the government officials a different but realistic insight into what the issues were for children:

> I think what they would say is it's a bit of a reality check to a large degree . . . these guys [civil servants] are so detached at times from the reality of a child's life. It gives them a new perspective. (NGO representative)
>
> . . . it was a bit more reality of what a child's life is like . . . realizing that three young people standing on a street corner does not equate to a riot . . . So I think it is about a different perspective. (NGO representative)

It wasn't just the different perspective, however. It was that hearing it this way seemed to result in a shift in understanding of the issues:

> As soon as they hear it from young people, somehow it's different. (NGO representative)
>
> The penny drops. This works. (NGO representative)

From an advocacy perspective, direct engagement was an opportunity to engage decision makers' perceptions of the lived experiences of their policies. NGO staff believed that with children and young people in the room, duty bearers seemed to understand the issues and significance in real terms in a way that did not occur through indirect methods.

FACELESS NO MORE?

A potential advantage of face-to-face meetings is the fact that they are more personal: Both duty bearers and rights holders are no longer "faceless" entities. The children and young people involved in these meetings will be able to put a human face to the name or official position. As one young person noted, "there was nothing he [government minister] could do to ignore you" during a public event, especially "if you were running that event." One of the perceived problems with large consultations, particularly online, is that there may be no sense that there is a real person at the end of the information collection process who will actually be listening. While there are ways of overcoming this remoteness, even online

(Lundy & McEvoy, 2009), the person-to-person contact addresses the perceived remoteness of the decision maker from the rights holder. As one young person pointed out:

> This is a person making decisions about me every day of his life but I've never spoken to him. So I think that was what I liked the best, getting to speak to the people that are making the decisions because it never happens really.

From a psychological perspective there are various positive features about face-to-face meetings that are lost in forms of indirect contact. These include the fact that they allow participants to engage in and observe verbal and nonverbal behavior such as hand gestures and facial expressions that are not captured otherwise (e.g., Goffman, 2005). These, along with the opportunity for humor and the chance to find out more about the individuals involved, may build a sense of trust, and that connection may translate into a greater personal commitment beyond the meeting itself (e.g., Bos, Gergle, Olson, & Olson, 2001).

Relationship building is recognized as key to the effective participation of children in decision-making (Graham & Fitzgerald, 2010). This was recognized by NGO staff members who emphasized the importance of building relationships over time:

> Whereas if you can actually create a relationship … You know, it's putting the public servants into a space where there's a physical space or metaphorical space where they're challenged to think differently and realize, "Oh yeah, that's the impact we're having by doing this."

The impact of human contact may be amplified by the fact that young people are communicating their problems to other humans who have taken on some sort of official responsibility for addressing them. The emotional impact can be increased when the young people have experienced significant life challenges. It is one thing to read that a certain percentage of children in state institutions have been abused and another to hear a child give a direct account of how the system has failed him or her. This point was made regularly by the NGOs working for children and young people. Their observations included the following:

> I know when you sit in a room with a group of people, and they talk about locking up kids. But then when you start talking about the child down the road, and what he or she has experienced in their life, you will hear those adults who two minutes earlier were saying "lock them up because they put a bit of graffiti on my gate-post" will say "God love them. Is it any wonder that they ended up the way they did?" You know, they didn't have this, they never had shoes on their feet—you know, all those sorts of

things. So that's what we have to do, is to humanize. To help them see the child, not the issues. (NGO representative)

And these people went back into the department, and the human bit of them—like, "I am a mother, and I couldn't have this for my son." (NGO representative)

NGO staff routinely spoke about the "humanizing" effect of direct contact. It is therefore interesting that, when asked why direct contact was valuable, neither adult duty bearers nor children identified the psychological impact of meeting and conversing *per se*. While the motivations or perceived benefits were different, the value attributed to direct interaction was readily apparent. However, this is not to suggest that it is entirely unproblematic and that direct meetings are always effective and/or appropriate. Issues arise for both rights holders and duty bearers, and these are explored below.

BEING THE FACE

Many young people involved in the study felt their role in public decision-making was to "be the face" of children and young people, either in general or of a particular group such as young people in care or in conflict with the law. By sharing their experiences, or representing those of their peers, young people felt that they were exposing adults in positions of power to the effect of their policymaking. One young woman explained that as a representative on a regional advisory group, she and others informed decision-making by responding from their lived experiences:

Because we have such a wide experience here … we would know what the situation that they have there so we would be able to have a view on it and how to put it forward in the best way, instead of, like, going to a 12-year-old and going, "Right, come on, tell us what the problems are."

Young people considered sharing experiences, such as what it was like "when you were arrested by cops … about how you were in jail or foster homes … what it was like for you as you were growing up in children's homes," as an opportunity to explain to adults the effects of their decisions. Often, young people participated by expressing their own views and experiences of the criminal justice system, education, living in care, or living as a young person not in employment, education, or training. Sometimes groups conducted formal or informal surveys with other young people to represent a wider group within their communities or regionally. One young person explained that it was precisely because her group experienced relative privilege and security that they were motivated to campaign for changes for those with more barriers to expressing their views:

. . . everybody here has—appears to have a very good education and they're able to talk about issues. But the reason we're here is because there are people that can't, and we're meant to be here to, like, represent—we're young people but we don't exactly know what situation they're in, but because we're young we should be able to try and empathize with how they'd feel … we're here to sort of work for the people that don't have the facilities to do it for themselves, because if everybody knew how to do it then we wouldn't be here.

Whether young people were contributing perspectives from their own experiences or those of other young people in a similar situation, many explained their role engaging with decision makers as "to try and help make changes" within a system.

Many young people were motivated to participate in public decision-making processes because they had felt disempowered as individuals to change their own personal circumstances. For example, some young people who had left the care system felt that those living in care currently would have less power and opportunity to make a change in their own situations:

. . . all the wee kiddies that are in the care system now, poor wee souls, need help. So we're helping them . . .

Most young people believed police officers, judges, or social workers were less likely to listen to a single child's or young person's concerns. At an individual level, they described experiences of power imbalances that made it too difficult for a young person to effect change in his or her personal circumstances in the care system, in conflict with the law, or as a person not in employment, education, or training. One young person described the different power dynamic he felt when speaking to a judge as a representative of his and other young people's experiences in court compared to standing before a court as an individual:

See, when I was talking to the judge [representing young people's views about how judges should engage young people in court], you could tell he was taking it into consideration. Obviously he doesn't think about it when he's in court, like, but when you were mentioning to him, he was thinking about it—do you know what I mean?

By "being the face" of young people in these situations, those involved in public decision-making often felt they could make a difference for others, but this was not guaranteed. Despite feeling his views were listened to more effectively during a direct meeting, this young person still felt that the judge would be unlikely to take these views into consideration when he returned to court. His statement revealed the longstanding effect of feeling discounted and ignored by adult decision makers, which many young people were working to overcome through their involvement in public decision-making processes.

Although young people articulated many advantages to representing their views and those of others in face-to-face situations with decision makers, direct engagement exposed participants to a variety of challenges and additional vulnerabilities. Challenges included being unfamiliar with the language and format of meetings, feeling that they did not have the proper clothing, and feeling unprepared for difficult questions. For example:

> **YP 1:** Remember that [conference]? That was fucking nerve-racking. We had to stand up in front of, like, 300 people—
> **YP 2:** And we had to stand and answer all these questions. I felt like people were judging me the way I looked because they were all like very smart . . . because they were all dressed like really smart. We were told we could just come dressed as, like, whatever way we wanted to dress and then they were all . . . I felt as if somebody was looking at me because I'd worn tracksuit bottoms and really and I was like, "Oh God."

Young people's commitment to "making a change" by sharing their views and experiences with decision makers meant most were willing to face these challenges. However, pressures were confronted often with support from NGOs. Staff members helped to prepare young people for the types of questions that would be asked in public meetings, for example at parliamentary committee hearings, or sent supportive messages:

> . . . she [participation worker] texted me on both of the days that I was in it to make sure that I had arrived okay and like texted me at the end to see how it went . . . even though she wasn't there, she was just making sure that I was okay in that day. (Young person)

Sometimes support was described as encouragement from a particular youth worker who respected their capacities and interests as young people or offered logistical advice and support to participate. Other times, the ethos of an organization and multiple opportunities to gain confidence in safe environments helped children and young people to prepare for public engagement. This institutional support made young people feel respected, listened to, and encouraged to share their views. This was seen by many as critical to their initial and ongoing engagement with decision makers (see also Shier, Hernández Méndez, Centeno, Arrólinga, & González, 2014).

BEING RESPECTED AND TAKEN SERIOUSLY

Perspectives on preferred methods for engagement differed among those involved in the research, yet the strong desire to be taken seriously and listened to by adults when they shared their views and experiences was consistent throughout. In direct meetings with decision makers, young people felt that they were able to tell immediately whether adults were taking them seriously. Physical and social indicators of being listened to, such as when adults kept eye contact, asked relevant follow-up questions, and subsequently took action (or explained why action was not possible at that time), were identified by young people as vital in the process of engagement:

> I don't know, he just seemed like a—he maintained eye contact, know what I mean? And he always, he seemed like he was listening.

Some young people felt it was more difficult to know whether their views were being considered when they participated in larger public events:

> Wherever we were speaking [at conferences] they would sit up and they'd listen, but it's whether they were takin' anything in, I don't know.
> They show their face but you don't know whether they're actually listening.

Some respondents reflected on experiences presenting at conferences, and they felt their views were taken seriously only when attendees asked questions or approached them afterward. When this occurred, young people felt they had made an impact on the adults' understanding of their situation:

> I knew they'd listened to what I was saying because they were asking me questions. . .

Adults' engagement in face-to-face conversations with young people who had presented provided an opportunity for young people to assess whether their views were being taken seriously. Equally, there was significant resentment and criticism of those who, some young people believed, did not take the time to acknowledge their contribution:

> . . . there's maybe only one or two people from each group that come up and speak to us . . . just saying, like, "Well, if we were to do this, how would you feel about that?" and maybe we'd turn around and say, "Yes, that might work," or, "No, that won't work for us for such and such a reason." That's when I really felt as if it was important, but not all the time. Half the time it was just, "Right, in and out, see you later." Done. "Thanks for your time."

These perceptions revealed the challenges associated with larger public engagement events for adults, specifically the importance of respectful engagement and demonstrating to young people who put themselves forward to participate that their views have been taken seriously.

Without follow-up action on the part of the decision-makers, however, young people described becoming frustrated and cynical about further face-to-face engagement. Although they felt the immediate response of adults was a crucial indicator of whether they were being respected and taken seriously, many felt that the outcome of their participation was as important as the process. For those young people who had been involved in advocacy projects for many years, the most important indicator of meaningful participation was whether the decision makers had taken action. Many young people had worked to overcome barriers to public engagement, by building confidence and gaining experience expressing their views in front of audiences or in adult-centered situations. As such, they were disappointed when they felt decision makers had not acted in response. Comments from three young people demonstrated these common concerns:

> "It got boring, being asked the same questions over and over again."
>
> "Monotonous, repeating your answer, and repetitive."
>
> "Why should anyone ask you that so often?"

Many felt decision makers' actions following their meetings revealed how seriously young people's views were considered. Since young people's motivation to engage in public decision-making was based on a desire to "make a change" or "make a difference," it is important to ensure that their direct engagement is with an adult who has the authority to make this change possible. Who this person is will depend on the issue under review, but an important lesson from young people's reflections on their engagement is the cynicism that can develop when they are asked to repeat their experiences to multiple adults or do not feel that the person with whom they are sharing their experiences will effect change as a result.

KEEPING FACE

The requirement for public consultation in public decision-making has brought with it particular responsibilities for duty bearers as the move from faceless policy-making to face-to-face engagement, and ultimately to "keeping face," takes hold. While direct contact between duty bearers and rights holders generally has been commended for promoting civic engagement, for enhancing the legitimacy of government decisions, and for its potential to contribute to more effective policy outcomes (e.g., Michels & De Graaf, 2010), this is not a streamlined or problem-free process. The obligation to consult was acknowledged by duty bearers in the NICCY study as one that is now "routine and by law," yet its practical implications bring with it a range of challenges for those upon whom the obligation to engage falls. The resulting need for a wide-ranging set of skills to facilitate face-to-face engagement can at times be to the detriment of children and young people as policymakers come to grips with new forms of governance. For example:

> In my experience we understand consultation and the need to consult, [but] I think we've missed consultation with children and young people's groups and have factored them in a secondary manner. (Government representative)

It was clear from the studies that while this still lagged behind levels of adult engagement, engaging directly with children and young people was something that had been gaining increasing momentum. However, what was deemed to be "appropriate" engagement was something that was clearly evolving as the complexities, challenges, and shortcomings of "keeping face" became apparent:

> We have done two or three major public consultations on my areas whilst I've been working here. With the first one we did . . . we produced a full public consultation on that and we had a big document for the public to digest and gave twelve weeks for the public to respond on it. We didn't produce a children and young people's version. We held sessions and actively sought young people's views but we didn't produce a children and young people's version, which was an omission. We did do that in subsequent consultations of a slightly smaller scale but we did learn the lesson to produce children's versions of the documents. We learned from that and got it better the next time. (Government representative)

The benefits of initial face-to-face interaction were widely espoused by all duty bearers in the NICCY study, yet focus was also beginning to shift to more comprehensive ways of "keeping face" through, for example, producing child-friendly materials to accompany and/or supplement direct contact. This was not always perfect, with NGOs noting that "you can critique those, whether they were as useful as they could have been." The need to build the capacity and skills of young people to participate in policymaking processes is acknowledged (see Tisdall, 2008; Tisdall, Davis, & Gallagher, 2008), not least given the knowledge capital that duty bearers often bring with them to policy processes. Duty bearers highlighted how, in engaging with children and young people, they had to take account of a range of factors:

> I think it's making sure you know how to engage, which is why I would use the professionals. There are of course all the child protection issues and so on to make sure as one has to be careful in the participation of young people that you're not abusing it by putting too much of a burden on the same young people all the time. Making sure you have got the hard-to-reach young people . . . it's very important to remember to go back to the children and young people and tell them if things are being changed and if not, why not.

Duty bearers suggested that this was not necessarily something they had the required skills to do, or could do on their own, and discussed how they had to draw on a range of support mechanisms in their attempt to take children and young people's experiences into account in policy processes. Policymakers highlighted, for example, the services of the Participation Network, a government-funded, NGO-managed project that supports government departments, local government, and public bodies to engage with children and young people. The role of NICCY was also highlighted as an important source of support. Thus, the extent to which duty bearers possess, or perceive themselves as possessing, the relevant skills can be a key challenge in the process of "keeping face."

It is not uncommon for broad rules of participation to be laid down in guidance relating to the requirement for public engagement—for example, the length of time a policy consultation period should last, whom duty bearers should consult with, and so on (e.g., Cabinet Office, 2008, 2013). Similarly, the Equality Commission for Northern Ireland (2008) produced guidance for public authorities on consulting and involving children and young people, called "Let's Talk, Let's Listen," which set out examples of best practice and practical solutions to engaging with children and young people. Other rules may be "assumed"—that is, they are not explicitly set out but nevertheless become taken for granted or widely accepted as "the way to do things." Such rules can make the act of "keeping face" problematic in the context of children and young people, particularly when they are not recognized as such. For example, one NGO noted:

> [Government department] were doing a consultation . . . and they wanted young people to engage with them and they'd set up a meeting for . . . I think it was for four o'clock on a particular day in the spring . . . And I wrote back to them in an email and said, "Look, that's not really practical for us because a lot of them are only getting out of schools at that stage and we have to get them together and get them out to you. Would you mind having them in a bit later?" . . . And I think that attitude is very widespread, you know, and adults don't want to be inconvenienced by having to meet young people in the evening . . . (NGO representative)

Other concerns were raised with respect to the length of consultation periods and the implications this had for face-to-face engagement. At times, children and young people's views were not sought until close to a deadline for consultation, which raised issues on the extent to which direct engagement in this context could be understood as meaningful. On other occasions, not enough time had been factored in to allow for capacity building with children and young people prior to direct engagement taking place.

The extent to which the views of children and young people were given due weight in subsequent policies, as a direct result of any engagement, was unclear. Duty bearers recognized that this was a difficult process and that face-to-face engagement did not always result in any change or follow-up. While there was a general perception that children's views were helpful, duty bearers had difficulty eliciting examples of concrete impact:

> In my area policy development has only gone so far, so to credit the views of children and young people delivering any impact might be difficult, but no particular perspective has won out . . . I have difficulty there but it's not to say that the views of children and young people haven't informed policy development, far from it, it's been hugely helpful. (Government representative)

There were a number of reasons provided by duty bearers for the apparent lack of substantive impact, most of which were beyond the control of the duty bearer who had engaged directly with children and young people. The ability to translate views into policy actions could be compounded by the complexity of the political system and ongoing policy debates. For example:

> [NICCY] produced the report on Transfer 2010[2] that reported children's perspectives on it in a very useful manner and they concluded that it really represented a need for the politicians to sort it out. Now that hasn't yet happened. I don't think that represents a denial of the usefulness of the NICCY report any more than it represents anyone else's desire for the situation to be sorted out . . . In that particular instance it did enable the minister to address, for instance, that she did try and broker some sort of compromises. So the report was very consciously listened to by our department. (Government representative)

The stumbling block here was the different viewpoints on academic selection between the main political parties in Northern Ireland. As such, politics and other external factors can be the primary determinants of policy and need to be considered when assessing the ability of a duty bearer to "keep face."

Other relevant structural factors that impinged on the outcomes of direct contact included the number of government departments involved in a particular policy or strategy. In cases where responsibility for policy implementation fell across a number of departments, it was particularly difficult to ascertain whether or not, and, if so, to what extent, children and young people's views informed subsequent practices:

> Well, because so many departments feed into the action plan, a summary was drawn up and passed out to all the different departments, so I can't really say how other departments have taken [children and young people's views] on board.

Duty bearers acknowledged that on some occasions "the Government will say 'sorry, you know, this is the policy of the Government,' and will decide to set aside arguments put forward in consultation." Thus, while face-to-face engagement has become increasingly common, the longer-term process of "keeping face" can be complicated by a range of pertinent issues, some of which are intrinsic to the process of direct interaction while others reflect the external structural and cultural complexities of the society in which children and young people live.

2. This was a consultation on Northern Ireland's controversial academic selection policy for children who are transferring to secondary education at age 11–12 (also known as the "eleven plus" because of the age at which it takes place).

FACING THE ISSUES

The Committee (2009, para. 134) articulates nine "basic requirements for the implementation of the right of the child to be heard" in its general comment on Article 12. Participative processes must be transparent and informative, voluntary, respectful, relevant, child-friendly, inclusive, supported by training, safe and sensitive to risk, and accountable. Face-to-face engagement does not occur in isolation from other participative processes, and many of the Committee's requirements inform broader conditions that contribute to rights-based participation. Experiences and perspectives of direct participation discussed in this chapter provide a lens through which these requirements can be examined. Based on these findings, the following is a summary of the specific challenges and opportunities for duty bearers when seeking to meet these requirements through face-to-face engagement:

Transparent and informative: Face-to-face engagement must include the "right" people (both children and young people and decision makers) in the room, and policymakers should ensure that the people who engage directly with children and young people have the scope either to make decisions based on the views and perspectives they hear from this engagement or that they can explain clearly to the children and young people how their involvement is likely to effect change. Children and young people were frustrated and disappointed by sharing their views and experiences with adults who were unable to take action and, conversely, enthusiastic about meeting those who were responsible for making decisions that affect them. The Committee recommends that children should be told at the outset of a process of engagement what influence they can make and subsequently what influence they have in fact had (CRC, 2009). Adults, including NGO staff members, facilitating young people's direct engagement with decision makers should also be clear about the expected outcome of the children and young people's involvement to inform them of the scope of their potential influence.

Voluntary: Face-to-face engagement must take into consideration the many and multiple forms of potential coercion children and young people might feel when asked to express their views with public decision makers. Due to the strategic advantages of direct engagement for adults seeking policy change, the need to ensure that involvement is voluntary and informed is particularly important. Practically, children and young people should be assured that they would be able to opt out of the engagement at any stage of their involvement with no adverse consequences to them or their families. For example, young people in this study managed their direct engagement by remaining silent or leaving the room when they were uncomfortable, and these forms of resistance to the pressures they perceived in that situation must be supported. The challenges associated with ensuring that participation is voluntary will vary according to the individual circumstances of the child, including his or her evolving capacities, and he or she has the right to adult guidance in making an informed decision about whether to be involved (CRC, Article 5).

Respectful: Face-to-face engagement must acknowledge the full potential and entitlement of children and young people to contribute to decision-making processes as individuals and/or representatives of a wider group. Children and young people discussed feeling acutely aware of adults' perception of them in direct engagement, which either enhanced or diminished their interest in further participation. Conditions should be put in place to ensure that all individuals feel their views and contributions have been acknowledged, valued, and taken seriously by others in the room. Decision makers engaged in such processes should be aware of the significance young people place on acknowledgment of their contributions and follow-up actions. During face-to-face engagement, it is possible to demonstrate this respect through simple conversational indicators such as eye contact, relevant questions, or follow-up comments. Provided that these conditions are met, face-to-face engagement creates opportunities to "humanize" the relationship between rights holders and duty bearers.

Relevant: Face-to-face engagement must acknowledge the time children and young people commit to engaging with decision makers by seeking children and young people's views on issues that are relevant to their lives. Space and time should be created for children and young people's views to be expressed fully, and decision makers involved should be willing to listen to the issues that children and young people raise as important from their perspectives. This does not preclude seeking views on issues children and young people may not identify as relevant themselves, but conditions should be set in place to offer meaningful opportunities to children and young people to engage with issues they feel are important. Provided that these conditions are met, face-to-face engagement creates opportunities for children and young people to discuss issues that matter to them and highlight additional concerns or interests that decision makers may not have identified as important.

Child-friendly: Face-to-face engagement must employ appropriate methods, settings, and circumstances to ensure the child is able, and supported, to freely express his or her views. Practical steps duty bearers can take can include presenting themselves in a less formal manner, such as wearing casual clothing rather than suits and ties, sitting with children and young people rather than standing in front of a group, and using language that is familiar to the children and young people involved. Further, decision makers should be prepared to engage with children and young people at a time that fits appropriately into their lives and circumstances, such as after school or weekends, and for a duration that is appropriate for the individuals involved. The conditions needed to meet this requirement will vary depending on the children or young people involved and should therefore reflect the ages, ability, circumstances, and interests of those involved.

Inclusive: Face-to-face engagement must be in accordance with the CRC's principle of nondiscrimination (Article 2), which requires that duty bearers monitor participation in a disaggregated manner and develop appropriate methods of outreach and communication with children, young people, and their parents. When read alongside the Committee's other requirements, this requirement may present prohibitive challenges to duty bearers as they begin to develop systems for face-to-face engagement. Decision makers should therefore ensure inclusive participation through other available methods, such as surveys or indirect consultation, until they can engage meaningfully with all children and young people.

Supported by training: Face-to-face engagement must recognize the individual support and training needs of each child and young person who engages directly with public decision-makers. Given the traditional marginalization of children and young people in adult decision-making processes, duty bearers should ensure that all children and young people have access to appropriate support before, during, and after their engagement. In these studies, NGO groups developed longer-term relationships with children and young people, which helped build their confidence and supported the potential for direct engagement. Each child and young person will have varying levels of confidence and capacity to engage directly with decision-makers, but if conditions are in place to meet the other basic requirements for participation, this requirement should not be too burdensome to satisfy.

Safe and sensitive to risk: Face-to-face engagement must not place the child at risk for any form of harm, including exposure to violence or exploitation. Given the direct engagement between adults in positions of power and the participating child or young person, specific consideration of child protection measures will need to be in place to ensure this requirement is met. These conditions will vary according to individual circumstances.

Accountable: Face-to-face engagement must ensure duty bearers are in a position to follow up on issues raised by children and young people in these situations, which may enhance the accountability of participative processes. It is important to recognize that policymakers experience constraints, including wider political agendas and procedural barriers, in their capacity to make decisions, and these constraints should be properly acknowledged and communicated throughout the process of engagement. However, the potential for accountability to children and young people may be strengthened when personal connections and relationships are established, provided decision makers agree to take action in response.

CONCLUSION

Children and young people's participation is critical to the realization of their rights. A plethora of methods are employed by policymakers, NGOs facilitating such engagement, and children and young people themselves to ensure their views are included in public decision-making. The studies discussed here suggest that face-to-face engagement between rights holders and duty bearers holds a distinctive place among participative methods. From an advocacy perspective, young people and NGOs argued that decision makers were more likely to listen to, and to act on the basis of, children and young people's views when communicated directly. For policymakers, hearing views directly from children and young people brought a human element to the decisions they were making. Young people felt they were able to assess better whether they were being respected and their views were being taken seriously when they engaged in face-to-face interactions. Drawing on studies conducted with a range of stakeholders in Northern Ireland, this chapter argues that face-to-face engagement can be a particularly useful form of ensuring that children and young people have the opportunity to express their views and that those views are given due weight.

Distinctive features of face-to-face engagement include the opportunity for dialogue and conversation between rights holders and duty bearers. For adult duty bearers the main advantages appeared to be the opportunity to get to focus on the issues by conversing with those affected. Those who interacted directly with children and young people felt they understood the lived experience of their decisions more fully. For young people it was the sense that they were being taken seriously and that change might be more likely to occur. Young people described considerable institutional support provided by NGOs with whom they worked in order to build the confidence to engage directly with decision makers. With proper support to participate, however, young people appreciated the rare opportunity to share their experiences with and to ask direct questions of adults who made decisions that affected them. For the former, the key advantage was getting to the heart of the issue; for the latter, it was getting to the source of the solution. We argue these distinctive features present particular challenges and opportunities within the context of four key requirements for implementation of the right to be heard: that participation must be transparent and informative, respectful, relevant, and accountable.

We suggest that the Committee's basic requirements for participation, discussed above, are not all equally relevant to every participative process, nor are they equally relevant across groups of children and young people, time, or issues to be considered. We argue that these requirements matter differently in different situations and that some matter more during face-to-face participation—when rights holders and duty bearers are in a room together. This involves the "humanizing" element of face-to-face engagement described by adults, children, and young people. As Graham and Fitzgerald (2010, p. 354) note, dialogue has "productive potential" to build understanding between participants in conversations about what matters to those involved. They argue that participation includes both "the child's capacity to participate and the adult's capacity to acknowledge, reassess and reposition existing understandings such that the conversation opens up a new space for transformation and change" (Graham & Fitzgerald, 2010, p. 355). Unlike written consultation responses, where topics and questions are often driven by policymakers' concerns, face-to-face engagement may provide more flexibility for children and young people to focus on what matters to them. Such engagements offer an opportunity for children and young people to learn more about the processes, and constraints, of decision-making. Conversely, when adults do not listen, are dismissive of children and young people's views, use inaccessible language, or do not engage responsively with relevant questions or follow-up actions, these experiences are likely to frustrate or dishearten participants. NGOs in both studies emphasized the significance of building relationships with duty bearers and noted that when policymakers met individuals and groups of children and young people about whom they were responsible for making decisions, they were more likely to follow up with meaningful actions in response to the views expressed during these direct interactions.

This is not to say that direct participation is straightforward or without challenges. Respondents in these studies focused primarily on the value of "proper business meetings," where young people had the opportunity to share their experiences with policymakers. Although this format was appropriate for many of the young people we interviewed, such situations are not always appropriate or possible—for example, additional considerations and support would be needed to engage very young children or children with additional needs in such meetings. Moreover, when children and young people felt they had not been treated respectfully, or that their views had not been taken seriously, this reinforced feelings of powerlessness and marginalization. In one example, young people who did not speak the language a minister was using felt excluded from the discussion and frustrated by what they felt was a dismissal of their perspectives. It will not be appropriate for children and young people to be asked to participate directly when decision makers are not in a position to ensure that their engagement will be transparent, respectful, relevant, and accountable. Indirect methods of including children and young people's views in public decision-making may be most appropriate in these circumstances, especially to comply with governments' obligations to respect the principle of nondiscrimination and ensure that the best interests of the child are a primary consideration. However, the obligation is on duty bearers to ensure that *all* children and young people are encouraged to express their views freely and that those views are given due weight. Given the advantages of face-to-face engagement, duty bearers should work to expand and improve opportunities for direct participation.

Simultaneously, these studies demonstrated that meaningful, effective face-to-face engagement does not demand extensive capacity building of either rights holders or duty bearers. Those involved in this research represented diverse groups, including classically "hard-to-reach" or marginalized young people. Young people acknowledged, along with NGO staff, the often-extensive processes of building confidence to speak publicly. They also expressed a deeply felt sense of the support they gained from working with NGOs who treated them with respect. However, when they articulated priorities for meaningful participation in public decision-making, these were that processes should be respectful and that their views should be taken seriously by decision makers. The simplicity of these basic elements of meaningful participation suggest that policymakers' concerns about "letting the experts do it" are misplaced. Young people, even those with complex needs and from marginalized backgrounds, refuted the idea that exceptional methods were necessary for direct engagement. Decision makers suggested that they gained the most from hearing directly from children and young people who were willing to share their experiences—often of quite difficult circumstances—or help them understand how others felt. Although decision makers may require training, education, or support about how to ensure that the conditions of engagement satisfy the Committee's basic requirements, especially until these conditions become routine, we suggest that at times they could draw on an existing set of respectful interpersonal skills. Both young people's priorities and policymakers' perceptions of when participation was most effective demonstrated the centrality of human dignity to participative processes. Face-to-face participation requires, as a baseline, a commitment to respect the inherent dignity of all those involved. This demands reasonable support and conditions in place for children and young people to express their views fully, safely, and freely (Lundy, 2007) and for adults' engagement to be transparent, respectful, relevant, and accountable. We argue that, in most instances, there is no need to overcomplicate such engagement; indeed, to do so may mitigate the very advantages brought about by the "humanizing" effect of having children, young people, and decision makers in the same room discussing issues of mutual concern or interest, albeit from different perspectives. Face-to-face contact can be a uniquely powerful means for decision makers to confront (in the truest sense of the word) the issues faced by children and young people.

REFERENCES

Bessell, S. (2009). Children's participation in decision-making in the Philippines: Understanding the attitudes of policy-makers and service providers. *Childhood, 16*(3), 299–316.

Bos, N., Gergle, D., Olson, J. S., & Olson, G. M. (2001). Being there versus seeing there: Trust via video. In *CHI '01 Extended abstracts on human factors in computing systems* (pp. 291–292). New York: ACM.

Byrne, B., & Lundy, L. (2011). *Barriers to effective government delivery for children in Northern Ireland.* Belfast: Northern Ireland Commissioner for Children and Young People.

Byrne, B., & Lundy, L. (2013). Reconciling children's rights and children's policy. *Children and Society*, published on Early View ahead of print, DOI:10.1111/chso.12045.

Cabinet Office (2008). *UK Code of Practice on Consultation.* Available at http://www.berr.gov.uk/files/file47158.pdf

Cabinet Office (2013). *Consultation Principles.* Available at: https://www.gov.uk/government/publications/consultation-principles-guidance

Commissioner for Children and Young People (Northern Ireland) Order 2003, No. 439 (N.I. 11).

Equality Commission for Northern Ireland (2008). *Let's talk, let's listen: Guidance for public authorities on consulting and involving children and young people.* Belfast: Author.

Freeman, M. (2000). The future of children's rights. *Children and Society, 14*(4), 277–293.

Goffman, E. (2005). *Interaction ritual: Essays in face-to-face behavior.* New Brunswick, NJ: Transaction Publishers.

Graham, A., & Fitzgerald, R. M. (2010). Progressing children's participation: Exploring the potential of a dialogical turn. *Childhood, 17*(3), 343–359.

Hill, M., Davis, J., Prout, A., & Tisdall, K. (2004). Moving the participation agenda forward. *Children & Society, 18*(2), 77–96.

Kellett, M., Robinson, C., & Burr, R. (2004). Images of childhood. In S. Fraser, V. Lewis, S. Ding, M. Kellett, & C. Robinson (Eds.), *Doing research with children and young people* (pp. 27–42). London: Sage.

Lansdown, G. (2011). *Every child's right to be heard: a resource guide on the UN Committee on the Rights of the Child General Comment No. 12.* UNICEF and Save the Children.

Lundy, L. (2007). Voice is not enough: Conceptualising Article 12 of the United Nations Convention on the Rights of the Child. *British Educational Research Journal, 33*(6), 927–942.

Lundy, L., & McEvoy, L. (2009). Developing outcomes for educational services: a children's rights-based approach. *Effective Education, 1*(1), 43–60.

Lundy, L., & McEvoy, L. (2012). Children's rights and research processes: Assisting children to (in)formed views. *Childhood, 19*(1), 129–144.

Lundy, L., & Stalford, H. (2013). *Children's rights and participation: background paper for Eurochild.* Eurochild.

Michels, A., & De Graaf, L. (2010). Examining citizen participation: local participatory policy making and democracy. *Local Government Studies, 36*(4), 477–491.

Shier, H., Hernández Méndez, M., Centeno, M., Arrólinga, I., & González, M. (2014). How children and young people influence policy-makers: lessons from Nicaragua. *Children & Society, 28*(1), 1–14.

Sinclair, R. (2004). Participation in practice: making it meaningful, effective and sustainable. *Children & Society, 18*(2), 106–118.

Stafford, A., Laybourn, A., Hill, M., & Walker, M. (2003). "Having a say": children and young people talk about consultation. *Children & Society, 17*(1), 361–373.

Tisdall, E. K. M., & Davis, J. (2004). Making a difference? Bringing children's and young people's views into policy-making. *Children & Society, 18*(2), 131–142.

Tisdall, E. K. M., Davis, J. M., Prout, A., & Hill, M. (Eds.) (2006). *Children, young people and social inclusion: Participation for what?* Bristol: The Policy Press.

Tisdall, K. (2008). Is the honeymoon over? Children and young people's participation in public decision-making. *International Journal of Children's Rights, 16*(3), 419–429.

Tisdall, K., Davis, J., & Gallagher, M. (2008). Reflecting on children and young people's participation in the UK. *International Journal of Children's Rights, 16*(3), 342–354.

United Nations Committee on the Rights of the Child (2003). *General Comment No. 5—General measures of implementation of the Convention on the Rights of the Child* (Articles 4, 42, and 44, para. 6).

United Nations Committee on the Rights of the Child (2009). *General Comment No. 12—The right of the child to be heard.*

United Nations General Assembly (1989). *Convention on the Rights of the Child,* 20 November 1989, United Nations.

CHAPTER 16

Addressing the Challenges of Children and Young People's Participation

Considering Time and Space

E. KAY M. TISDALL

INTRODUCTION

The United Nations Convention on the Rights of the Child provides a platform for children and young people's[1] participation worldwide. Article 12 has been a rallying cry to promote children and young people's human rights to be involved in decisions affecting them. While Article 12 itself does not use the word "participation," the United Nations Committee's description captures the hopes for children and young people's participation:

> . . . ongoing processes, which include information-sharing and dialogue between children and adults based on mutual respect, and in which children can learn how their views and those of adults are taken into account and shape the outcome of such processes. (2009, para. 3)

Yet, as children and young people's participation has gained hold in policy and practice rhetoric in many countries and contexts (e.g., see Percy-Smith &

1. This article generally uses the phrase "children and young people"; this is typically what young people prefer to be called in the UK. Broadly, "children and young people" refers to children up to the age of 18, following the definition in the United Nations Convention on the Rights of the Child.

Thomas, 2010; Tisdall, Butler, & Gadda, 2014), its translation into reality has led to dilemmas and challenges in practice. A very similar list of challenges can be generated across countries (e.g., Hinton, 2008; Lansdown, 2011; Percy-Smith & Thomas, 2010; Thomas, 2007):

1. **Tokenism**. Children and young people may be consulted but their views have no discernible impact on decisions. The policy process often leaves insufficient time to involve children and young people meaningfully.
2. **Lack of feedback**. Children and young people are asked to participate but they do not know what has happened with their contributions.
3. **Who is included or excluded.** Some children and young people risk being "over-consulted," frequently asked for their views, and become frustrated at the lack of subsequent action. Other children and young people are never reached by participation activities. Some children and young people are only invited to participate on certain topics: for example, disabled children and young people have expressed frustration at only being consulted about issues around their disability.

    The children and young people consulted are often presumed to be speaking on behalf of their peers, although they are not supported to be representative in this way.
3. **Consultation but not dialogue.** Children and young people are frequently consulted in one-off activities but are not involved over time in on-going, respectful dialogue.
4. **Adult processes and structures exclude children and young people.** Children and young people's participation is frequently not integrated into how policy decisions are made, implemented and evaluated. It is seen as a specialist activity and not a mainstream one. As a result, children and young people's participation risks being side-lined, if their advice and recommendations run counter to views of other, more powerful, groups.
5. **Lack of sustainability.** Funding for children and young people's participation is frequently short-term. As a result, supporting staff may move on, the groups dissipate and the participative process stops. (Barnardo's Scotland, Children in Scotland, and the Centre for Research on Families and Relationships, 2011, p. 1)

For those who advocate for, and seek to support, meaningful, sustainable, and effective participation by children and young people, what might the solutions be, the new avenues to consider, the theoretical ideas that might assist?

To address such questions, a collaborative program of research and exchange has been undertaken through the Centre for Research on Families and Relationships (CRFR) at the University of Edinburgh to formulate, refine, and test ideas. This includes national and international networks, such as the seminar series (2002–2004) "Challenging Social Inclusion: Perspectives for and from Children and Young People" and the cross-country seminar (2005–2006) "Theorising Children's Participation: International and Interdisciplinary Perspectives," which led to the international academic network (2008–2011) "Theorising Children's Participation: Learning Across Countries and Across disciplines," working with academic, practitioner, and young collaborators from Brazil, India, South Africa, and the UK. The program involved a number of empirical research projects, including a three-year examination of school councils in Scotland ("Having a Say at School" [HASAS]). Most recently, a project ("Children and Young People's Participation: From Fashion Accessory to Part of the Fabric") supported CRFR to work with nongovernmental organization (NGO) partners to facilitate improved mechanisms to involve children and young people in national policymaking in Scotland. While not wanting unhelpfully to separate out children and young people's participation in decision-making about them as individuals, this collaborative program—and thus this chapter—concentrates on their involvement in *collective* decision-making.

Within the field of children and young people's participation, discussions have often relied on very influential typologies—such as Hart's ladder (1992), Treseder's subsequent circle (1997), and Shier's stepwise progression (2001). These have been very useful to challenge policy and practice; they tend to emphasize the lack of children and young people's participation and thus refresh those involved to advocate for more. Indeed, there has been substantial change in many parts of the world, including Scotland and the UK more generally, with a proliferation of participation activities (see, for example, special issues of *Children, Youth and Environments* (2006 and 2007); Hinton, 2008; Tisdall, Davis, Hill, & Prout, 2006). With this growth, these typologies have been insufficient to address the challenges in children and young people's participation described above and thus to assist moving such participation forward (for discussion see Tisdall, 2012). More recently, a number of committed participation advocates have sought theoretical resources that can assist children and young people's participation. For example, Mannion (2007) covers a range of potential theoretical perspectives, from "generationing" to actor network theory, that could acknowledge participation's relational aspects. Thomas (2012) explores Honneth's theory of recognition. Cockburn has an ongoing interest in citizenship, rights, and interdependence (e.g., 2013).

A provocative theoretical area is development studies, which has a longer history than the children and young people's field of advocating for—and looking critically at—participation.[2] Development studies and work embraced the concept of participation in the 1960s and 1970s, inspired by its radical roots in social movements (Leal, 2010). By the 1980s, participation had become an essential "ingredient" in the development industry. Community participation could

---

2. This discussion of participation in development studies draws on the chapter by Teamey and Hinton (2014), which emerged from the "Theorising Children's Participation" network.

ensure that beneficiaries' views were listened to and cultural differences better understood. Chambers and colleagues (e.g., Chambers, 1983) are particularly well known for having developed "bottom-up" approaches of engaging with people in local communities, especially with those who risked being excluded from more formal consultations and research. Development manuals enshrined such methods and an industry grew up around them. Conceptually, participation became linked to improving services and governance, recognizing that the state had to be able to respond and to be responsive, strengthening both government and governance (e.g., Gaventa, 2004).

Throughout its history in development, participation and its associated activities have been criticized. Participation can be coopted to enable those with power to maintain the status quo—through quelling political opposition or coopting the marginalized into mainstream processes. Emphasizing self-help and local participation in developing services can be doubly advantageous by diverting demands on the state to local initiatives while increasing support for the current regime (Vengroff, 1974). Cornwall (2008), writing over thirty years later, notes that such supposed empowerment can instead frustrate citizens who feel the state has not fulfilled its obligations, thus leading to resistance rather than support. Debates have emerged about the "evangelical" proliferation of participative methodology (see Gaventa, 2004). Critics highlight examples of poor-quality data collection, described as extractive rather than empowering (e.g., Cooke & Kothari, 2001). Too many activities concentrate on engaging people and too few on ensuring accountability and impact (Hart, 2008). Cooke and Kothari (2001, pp. 8–9) put forward a harsh critique, which can equally be asked of activities beyond the "majority world":[3]

> The tyranny of decision-making and control: Do participatory facilitators override existing legitimate decision-making processes?
>
> The tyranny of the group: Do group dynamics lead to participatory decisions that reinforce the interests of the already powerful?
>
> The tyranny of method: Have participatory methods driven out others which have advantages participation cannot provide?

These questions, and the other critiques above, illuminate why some of the challenges for children and young people's participation continue despite the growing political rhetoric of support and the increase in activities.

---

3. The terms majority world and minority world refer to what has traditionally been known as the Third World and the First World or more recently as the Global South and the Global North. This terminology acknowledges that the majority, in terms of population, poverty, land mass, and lifestyles, is located in the former, in Africa, Asia, and Latin America, and thus seeks to shift the balance of our worldviews that frequently privilege Western and Northern populations and issues (Punch, 2003).

This chapter draws on this history of discussing participation, in development studies, to apply to the "minority world" context of Scotland. It explores certain requirements developed by Cornwall and colleagues for inclusive "participatory sphere institutions," with a particular emphasis on space-time. With these theoretical resources, the chapter goes on to examine the empirical and experiential findings of HASAS on school councils, and "From Fashion Accessory to Part of the Fabric" on involving children and young people in national policymaking in Scotland. It concludes by considering the opportunities for change, by applying new ways of looking at current trends on children and young people's participation in Scotland and potentially elsewhere.

THE SPACES OF PARTICIPATION

Cornwall and Coelho (2007, p. 1) write about the "participatory sphere." This sphere contains "hybrid new democratic spaces" at the interface between the state and society; these spaces are also often intermediary, ways for negotiation, information, and exchange. Cornwall and Coelho's book explores some of the gaps between "normative expectations and empirical realities" (2007, p. 5) for such spaces. Bringing together the lessons from the case studies in their book, Cornwall and Coelho (2007) develop five requirements for participatory sphere institutions to be inclusive and effect change:

1. People need more than invitations to participate: they need to recognize themselves as citizens, rather than beneficiaries or clients.
2. Representative claims must be considered critically and mechanisms to be representative must be in place.
3. Structures are not enough. The motives of those who participate—including state actors—can be competing and are in constant negotiation.
4. Three factors are essential for change: involvement by a "wide spectrum of popular movements and civil associations, committed bureaucrats and inclusive institutional designs" (p. 9).
5. Participation is a process over time and must be situated alongside other political institutions, within their own social, cultural, and historical contexts.

Cornwall and Coelho (2007) use the word "spaces" in their book title—*Spaces for Change?*—and the word "spaces' can be found frequently in other works by Cornwall on participation (e.g., Cornwall, 2008; Cornwall & Gaventa, 2000). She makes distinctions between the invited spaces of participation and the ones formed by people themselves. Invited spaces are created by the powerful—the policymakers and the decision makers—and others are invited in. These are contrasted to spaces "that people create for themselves" (Cornwall, 2008, p. 275), where people come together with fewer differences of status and power, usually because they have something in common.

While less obvious then her use of "spaces," threaded through the discussions of participation spaces is attention to time. Cornwall (2008), for example, sharply criticizes the influential participation typologies (e.g., Arnstein's ladder of participation, the basis for Hart's ladder for children and young people's participation) for producing static depictions of participatory activities. In their normative judgments about "good" and "bad" participation, these typologies fail to consider change across projects and processes. A project might be at a particular step on the ladder (e.g., low down, at informing) at a particular time, which may open up possibilities to be at a higher ladder step later (e.g., high up, at partnership). Consideration of time is also given at other points in her writings. For example, she writes of "participation fatigue" as people become disenchanted by invitations to participate because nothing has resulted from their previous participation. She advocates recognizing those not included in participation, either because they are deliberately not invited or because people self-exclude. She particularly here mentions the timing and duration of participatory activities, which may discount those with caring or work responsibilities.

Cornwall herself (e.g., 2004a, 2004b) makes references to certain key theorists and ideas of human geography. Human geography has an extensive theoretical history of theorizing and debating space and time. Fundamentally, these rich theoretical discussions critique a notion of space as a "neutral container, a blank canvas which is filled by human activity, something outwith human activity" (Hubbard & Kitchin, 2004, p. 4). Instead, human geographers perceive space as a social rather than merely a physical phenomenon, with reciprocal influences between people and spaces. As Gallagher (2006, p. 161) writes, "At its simplest, the term `social space' can be seen as a way of recognising that space is produced by people (rather than pre-existing), and that spaces in turn shape people (rather than being inert or neutral)." Massey (1999) explicitly brings in a temporal dimension to human geography, critiquing the philosophical association of stasis with spatial and change with time. Instead, space and time are inseparable, and "the spatial is integral to the production of history, and thus to the possibility of politics, just as the temporal is to geography" (Massey, 1994, p. 269). Spaces, therefore, are not static; time, mobility, and change work constitutively with them; spaces and time are relational, creating and composed of human and material relationships.

This chapter takes forward Cornwall and Coelho's requirements for inclusive participatory sphere institutions to evaluate and critique practices of children and young people's participation. Within this generality, the chapter specifically considers space-time to further illuminate and challenge practices.

THE TWO PROJECTS

"Having a Say at School" was a three-year partnership project that was conducted between 2007 and 2009 by Children in Scotland (the national umbrella organization for the children's sector across Scotland) and CRFR at the University of Edinburgh. The project aimed to explore systematically the predominant structural form of children and young people's participation in Scottish schools: school councils.

School councils (also called pupil councils) have no statutory definition in Scotland. The official Welsh website on school councils provides one common understanding of the term:

> A school council is a representative group of pupils elected by their peers to represent their views and raise issues with the senior managers and governors of their school. The school council can also take forward initiatives and projects on behalf of their peers, and be involved in strategic planning and processes such as the School Development Plan, governing body meetings and staff appointments.[4]

HASAS undertook surveys of all thirty-two Scottish local education authorities,[5] a postal school survey of all secondary schools and a representative sample of primary schools[6] (separate questionnaires were sent to the adult adviser/head teachers and to the school council at each school), and case studies of six illustrative schools. These case studies involved focus groups with pupil council members at the start and end of the academic year, a survey of pupil council members, staff interviews, and documentary analysis. Of these six case studies, two were followed in more depth, with the added methods of observation of school council meetings throughout the year and a survey of students who were not members of the pupil council. Ethical considerations, particularly in terms of informed and ongoing consent, confidentiality, and anonymity, were of high importance. A range of stakeholders, including children and young people, advised the project at key points and assisted with developing and piloting field instruments. Further information about the research design, including details on methods, ethics, statistical and qualitative analysis, and findings, can be found at the project website.[7]

"Children and Young People's Participation: From Fashion Accessory to Part of the Fabric" took place from 2011 to 2012 (referred to below as the Participation Initiative). This initiative was also a partnership between CRFR at the University of Edinburgh and Children in Scotland, with the addition of a third partner, Barnardo's Scotland. Barnardo's is a leading children's charity in Scotland, with particular commitment to and expertise on involving children

---

4. http://www.pupilvoicewales.org.uk/english/grown-ups/get-involved/the-school-council/ (accessed Sept. 13, 2013).

5. Local education authorities are part of local councils. They have the legal duty to provide schooling to children in their areas. There are thirty-two local councils across Scotland.

6. In Scotland, primary schools cover the year levels of P1 and P7, which broadly equate to the ages of 5 to 11. Secondary schools contain the year levels of S1 to S6, which broadly equate to the ages of 12 to 18.

7. http://www.havingasayatschool.org.uk/documents/HASASTechnicalReport.pdf (accessed Sept. 13, 2013).

and young people. The initiative was a knowledge exchange partnership, based on a process of action-learning.

The initiative used findings on children and young people's participation to assist organizations to support such participation in national policymaking. It did this by exploring sustainable ways of working with members of the Scotland's Children's Sector Forum, the policy network for the children's sector in Scotland.[8] The initiative undertook three types of knowledge exchange activities: a national Think Tank event, wider discussions and project team reflections; a program developed and run by Barnardo's Scotland to support organizations to involve children and young people; and dissemination of accessible briefings, conference presentations, and published articles. The work was evaluated with a series of interviews, surveys, and group meetings with those involved and certain policy and decision makers. Ethical protocols were developed for working with children and young people directly and indirectly through the initiative, as well as with other people and organizations. Further information about this initiative, and its outputs, can be found at the CRFR website.[9]

Below experiences and findings are brought together, with considerations particularly of space-time, before relating these to the requirements for inclusive participatory sphere institutions.

INCLUSIVE PARTICIPATORY SPHERE INSTITUTIONS? CONSIDERATIONS OF SPACE-TIME

Institutional Space-Time

Schools in Scotland are set in circumscribed locations and now often have protective walls and limited entrances to oversee who comes in and who leaves. Children and young people from ages 5 to 16 are expected to be in school[10] during school hours, unless they are home-schooled. Generally schools in Scotland are tightly timed, frequently with bells or other signals to prepare for or instigate changes of mode, location, or people. Delays and tardiness are frowned upon, with children and young people at risk of being penalized if they are late or elsewhere than the school required. Teaching staff are often concerned about time in their workday—how to fit in curriculum requirements with the everyday experiences in the classroom and how to manage their workloads (e.g., see Scottish Government, 2011).

8. http://www.childreninscotland.org.uk/html/to-ScotlandsChildrensSectorForum. htm (accessed Oct. 2, 2013).
9. http://www.crfr.ac.uk/projects/completed-projects/ (accessed Sept. 13, 2013).
10. Compulsory schooling ends at age 16, although children and young people frequently continue in education past this age.

As nonmandatory activities, school councils need to fit into institutional space-time and pressures. When school councils should meet, how often they should meet, and for how long they should meet are thus not always straightforward to answer. The school survey revealed that the most common pattern across Scotland was for school councils to meet once a month. This applied to about one-third (34%) of schools. Just under one-fifth (19%) of schools councils met fortnightly. Approximately one in seven school councils (14%) met only once each school term. The remaining one-third (33%) of school councils nationwide reported no set schedule and met on an irregular basis. The great majority of school councils (61%) met during lesson times, while one in five (20%) met during break or lunch times. Scottish secondary schools were more likely to hold school council meetings during breaks or lunchtimes compared to Scottish primary schools (30% of secondary versus 19% of primary schools).

Wyness (2005) notes the problems of scheduling school councils, finding in his study that operating school councils during breaks signaled a lack of institutional commitment to the councils. Instead, the important place of school councils should be underlined by having them meet within class time, as a worthwhile commitment for those involved. Timing, thus, has symbolic and institutional value. Two of the six case-study schools make particular efforts to be inclusive in their scheduling. In one small school with many visiting specialists, the head teacher varied the day of school council meetings so that no council member missed one subject more than other members. The adult adviser in another school consulted the pupil council members on suitable dates and compared their individual schedules when setting meeting times.

When involving children and young people in national policymaking, institutional space-time is also critical—and often exclusionary. Policy activities are frequently scheduled during school hours. For example, if children and young people were to give oral evidence to a parliamentary committee, they would have to reschedule their activities. Policy-strategy meetings between leading statutory organizations and NGOs tend to be held during the day. While it may be convenient for policymakers to produce policies for consultation over holiday times, this proves particularly problematic for children and young people. The consultation over the Children and Young People (Scotland) Bill, for example, was from July to September 2012; school holidays in Scotland start at the end of June and last until the end of August, so children and young people could not easily be contacted during that time.

In the Participation Initiative, the Barnardo's program gave the adults involved the space-time to come together. This was highly regarded by those involved, but the larger impact on the organization, past the program activities, was difficult to achieve. As others have noted (e.g., Johnson, 2011), organizational systems can be very hard to shift, replicating some of the same barriers as in policymaking.

Having Enough Time

A complaint invariably made by participation workers (i.e., those facilitating participation activities) and sometimes by the participating children and young people is the lack of time given to involving children and young people meaningfully on a particular policy issue. Lack of time can be exclusionary for certain groups, such as disabled children and young people, whose communication methods require substantial amounts of time. Consultation time periods, the time between the policymakers issuing a document and when members of the public are invited to respond, are described as much too short to identify and engage children and young people, to work with them meaningfully, and then to feed the views back to the policymakers.

When children and young people are reacting to policy developments, the institutional time constraints are often problematic. Voice against Violence, a group of eight young experts on domestic abuse, worked to the key policymakers' timeline for the National Domestic Abuse Delivery Plan for Children and Young People (2008–2011).[11] They found this timeline could push out their own agendas, as the group needed to shift their attention when they had opportunities to meet with influential policymakers in the Scottish Government or local government. But when Voice against Violence was involved in forms of peer research, the timing of activities suited the young people rather than continuously needing to fit into (adults') institutional timings. These research activities were set up for defined time periods and, at the end, the young people produced their findings and waited for the institutional—the policymakers'—responses. While timing was still recognized as tight, the young people did not describe it as exclusionary. They were able to organize and put forward their findings and recommendations.

Inadequate time to operate the school council was a strong and recurrent theme across Scottish schools (see also Cotmore, 2004; Wyse, 2001). In the school survey, "Not enough time to talk at meetings about all the issues" was identified as an obstacle by 55 percent of both school councils and school staff. Observations in the case-study schools often demonstrated the meetings' tight schedules. In all six case-study schools, the school council meetings had a similar format. They started with reading the previous meeting's minutes, followed by discussing the agenda or points raised by pupil council members. These introductory processes frequently took a great deal of time, with collective discussion or decision-making "squeezed out."

Space-timing tensions continued beyond the school council meetings themselves. The school survey found that 38 percent of school councils and 46 percent of school staff selected the answer "Lack of time to collect other pupils' views" as a

---

11. Voice against Violence (http://www.voiceagainstviolence.org.uk/) is a project of the Scottish Government and is located at CRFR.

problem for their school council. In most case-study schools, a strong representative model was promoted: Members of the pupil council were elected from their class to represent their class members' views. In seeking to fulfill this representative function, concern was equally expressed about sessions taking place before school council meetings (so that pupil council members could solicit the ideas, problems, and priorities of those they represented) and sessions after each school council meeting (so they could share what was discussed, decided, and done). These sessions varied markedly in quality and quantity, not only between schools but also within the same school. The processes varied greatly from class to class depending on individual teachers' preferences and priorities. In one school, these consultation and feedback sessions took place in the personal and social education classes, which were led by the same teacher. With this teacher's support, the time dedicated to these sessions were commented on positively by pupil council members. In other schools, pupil council members reported that they were not given enough time to speak to their classes. While all the case-study school councils sought to communicate with their fellow pupils, 70 percent of the pupils not currently on a school council wanted more information from their council representatives. The lack of space-time for such communication was an expressed weakness of the school councils.

Adult advisers are key to the success—or not—of most school councils (see also Maithes & Deuchar, 2006). The school survey showed that 68 percent of schools in Scotland had one staff member working with the school council, usually a senior teacher or head teacher. Adult advisers were pivotal organizationally to the school councils, from organizing elections, to setting up meetings and agendas, to liaising with school management structures. Adult advisers typically had to fit in these responsibilities within very busy teaching days, so lack of time was an issue for them.

Spaces and Time for Change?

On the surface, the purpose of involving children and young people in policy-making was clear within the Participation Initiative: Children and young people's participation should have an impact on policy decisions. In practice, other purposes may well support or run counter to this. For example, government consultations can provide a funding stream for individuals and organizations; it can be astute, when there is a political rhetoric of involving children and young people and potential media attention, to be seen to do so (see Tisdall & Davis, 2004). These later purposes emphasize the process, rather than the impacts, of involving children and young people.

The purpose of school councils is not necessarily clear or consensual. As discussed in more detail in Tisdall (2012), a range of purposes apply to children and young people's participation generally:

1. To uphold children's rights and to fulfill legal responsibilities
2. To improve services and decision-making, particularly in relation to consumer and service user involvement
3. For democratic education, to familiarize and inculcate children and young people into the ways of democracy
4. To improve children and young people's well-being and development.

In the research, the first of these was rarely referred to and was seldom influential.[12] Of more significance was consumer and service user involvement. In the school survey, school councillors stated that representing their fellow pupils, and making their school better, were the most important things that school councils should do. Further, some local authorities used school councils as a consultation network, and case-study schools showed how pupil councils were regularly used as consultation fora for school staff's ideas.

Adult advisers were worried about school councils being "whinging" forums, and research observations of school councils found that some were dominated by pupil council members passing on complaints. As a complaints mechanism, school councils potentially provide the space-time to raise but not always to resolve such complaints, nor to ensure action was taken elsewhere. The school survey, for example, showed that a wide range of issues were discussed in school councils—but this range shrunk when it came to decisions being made, and even fewer decisions were implemented (a common finding across school council research—see Wyness, 2005; Wyse, 2001). More positively, certain school councils took pride in their achievements (e.g., improvements in playgrounds and school gardens). At its most positive, the consumer and service user discourse lead to personal problems being recognized as public ones, resulting in collective responses and responsibility.

The two purposes of democratic education and children's well-being and development were the dominant ones. School councils were predominantly seen as vehicles by which children and young people could practice formal democratic practices in terms of representation and meetings. Members would gain skills and confidence. The school council research confirms findings elsewhere that children and young people value participatory processes, when they are undertaken well, and the skills and positive feelings that result (Davies, Williams, & Yamashita, with Man-Hing, 2006). There can be, however, an emphasis on process and not actual influence on decisions. The head teacher in School A neatly captured this:

> . . . I think the process in itself is worthwhile. Whereas for them [the school council]
> it's probably the outcomes; it's in their mind. But if we can get them some of their

12. This may be an outdated finding, with the recent influence and growth of the Rights Respecting Schools program supported by UNICEF UK.

outcomes and allow them to take part in the process at the same time, I think that's a reasonable trade-off.

School councils in the research were more concerned about outcomes (what actions they would take and goals they would accomplish), while adults involved were more focused on processes within, and the symbolic value of, school councils. This led to frustration for some school council members.

Most school councils start anew each year, with fresh selection or elections. While this increases the number of students who have the chance to serve as a member,[13] the case-study schools showed how this renewal led to a lack of continuity from the previous year's council. For example, in the case-study schools, explicit, robust handover processes did not exist between one year's council and the next. When asked about the achievements of last year's school council, the current year's council members had great trouble identifying any specific achievements. Current members had no structured mechanism to learn from, or shadow, the previous year's members. Similarly, should an adult adviser leave or take on another role, how councils functioned could change substantially. Success, therefore, was highly individualized due to a lack of connections over time, rather than being structurally supported and continuous.

In participation projects, the organization of participation space-times worked in at least three different ways for children and young people's groups. One way was to bring together children and young people, drawing typically from networks or services, in regard to a particular policy issue. A typical example would be the Children's Parliament, which was commissioned by the Scottish Government to produce generally available consultative materials, and then itself consult with a range of groups across Scotland, for the Children and Young People (Scotland) Bill consultation.[14] This way of working is often a reactive response, particularly in terms of government funding (despite NGOs' pleas to plan such activities long in advance) (Tisdall & Davis, 2004). A second way is to establish time-boundaried groups, like the Scottish Borders Youth Commission on Bullying,[15] with the time tied to a particular remit to investigate an issue and make recommendations. This was a proactive commitment by the policymakers to give a set amount of resources (e.g., time, space, money, advice) to children and young people, and the time for setting up and establishing the group was accepted before proceeding on to their focused work. A third way is to have "standing groups" of children and young people who can be called upon

13. From a representative sample of secondary school pupils in Scotland (aged 11–16), one third of respondents been a pupil council member at some point in their schooling (Tisdall, with Milne & Iliasov, 2007).

14. See http://www.childrensparliament.org.uk/children-and-young-people-bill.html (accessed Oct. 2, 2013).

15. This followed a co-production model. Twelve youth commissioners were appointed (aged 14–24 years). From July 2011 to March 2012, they gathered evidence through

to respond to particular issues. The most prominent in Scotland is the Scottish Youth Parliament,[16] which brings together elected representatives aged 14 to 25. It provides regular briefings and responses to policy, has various set interactions with policymakers, and has well-developed systems to consult with children and young people more widely through face-to-face and social media methods.

In each way of organizing a participation space-time, examples can be found of having impact on policies. For example, one can track how children and young people's views, with considerable support of the children's sector, did eventually influence additional support needs policy (Tisdall & Davis, 2004) or provision for young people leaving care (Regulation of Care (Scotland) Act 2001). This is a reactive response to policy. The time-boundaried group has shown demonstrable "celebratory" successes. For example, the recommendations of Voice against Violence led to a ministerial announcement of funding for children's support workers (Houghton, 2013). Standing groups notably have the capacity to react to a range of issues with relative speed and efficiency. A caveat would be that school councils in our research—an ideal standing group from a policymaker's perspective—can be frustrated by being constantly asked to react to consultations, feeling that time for their own issues is limited.

Even if children and young people's views were being taken seriously by the decision makers, the institutional processes can seem lengthy to children and young people. Often, if changes are made, they are made well after such changes will have an impact on the children and young people involved. The institutional processes can mean that going back to the children and young people to let them know how their views were weighed and the results can fall into two categories. First, the feedback is timely, in terms of meeting children and young people's time spans, but superficial: The children and young people are thanked, headline findings are shared, but decisions are still in process. Second, the feedback is given after decisions are made, but the time has been so long that the children and young people may not be easily contacted to receive it (e.g., they have moved schools, services, or locations) and/or the length of time is frustrating. In neither case does feedback satisfy the children and young people involved.

Participation spaces for children and young people are regularly separated out from adults' participation spaces (see Morrow, 2005; Percy-Smith, 2010; Tisdall, 2008). School councils are not councils of the whole school, in Scotland, involving the range of school stakeholders from teachers, to support staff, to parents and pupils. They consist solely of pupils. Positively, this can give children and

---

interviews, focus groups, surveys, observation, and secondary sources. They analyzed this evidence and presented thirty-three recommendations. The Council accepted the recommendations and proceeded to develop its policy on bullying. This development was overseen by an implementation board including education staff, local politicians, parents, and children and young people (Robb, 2012; Scottish Borders Youth Commission on Bullying, 2012).

16. See http://www.syp.org.uk/about-syp-W21page-94- (accessed Oct. 2, 2013).

young people their own spaces and time, ensure that their views are not over-ridden by adults, and encourage ways of communicating, sharing, and deciding that suit the children and young people (Cornwall, 2008). They can be places of resistance, laboratories of self-interest, or empowerment spaces (Kesby, 2007). Negatively, children and young people are removed from the space-times where decisions are made. Some power over decisions may be given or taken by school councils: They regularly undertook fundraising efforts, and decisions were common about playground equipment. But a host of other decisions were not within their remit, from toilets to teaching to the curriculum; these were decided elsewhere. Unlike in some other countries (see Dürr, 2005), school councils in Scotland have no right of membership in school governance and were not included, in our research, on school management teams. Similarly, many partici-pation activities are exclusive to children and young people, with adults present as facilitators but not participants themselves. With their views formed, children and young people may well then go and present their views in various ways (writ-ten, oral, using audiovisual or other media) to adult decision makers.

Exceptions to this segregation both illuminate the typical absence of adult–child space-times and the potential repercussions of this absence. For example, the Youth Commission on Alcohol[17] recruited an advisory group, with members from the Scottish Government, media, business, education, health services, police, and NGOs. The contact with the advisory group proved pivotal, accord-ing to one of the youth commissioners:

> This face-to-face exposure helped us to not only gain an insight into the key issues, but also to interact throughout the process with greater confidence so that we could maximise the opportunities presented to us. (Paul, 2011)

The contact, reported Paul, was not only in advisory group meetings but also in one-to-one visits and discussions between youth commissioners and advisory group members. In another example, young people from Who Cares? Scotland (a national NGO providing a range of advocacy, advice, and support services across Scotland for children and young people with experience of care) engaged with the Education and Culture Committee of the Scottish Parliament over time as the Committee undertook its inquiry into taking children into state care. In itself, this inquiry has resulted in recommendations rather than action, but Who Cares? Scotland was able to leverage the political commitment of the Committee to gain further amendments to the Children and Young People (Scotland) Act 2014 for young people leaving care. What both these examples show is that by

17. The Youth Commission on Alcohol was funded by the Scottish Government and sup-ported by Young Scot, an NGO. Sixteen young people were recruited onto the Commission through an open recruitment process. Running over a year, the Youth Commission under-took consultations, surveys, investigations, and study visits.

bringing people together in time and spaces, children, young people, and adults built up relationships that were meaningful on both sides—and had an impact on decisions.

Invited Spaces

Most school councils and policy participation activities are "invited spaces." Schools are where most children and young people spend many of their daytime hours—but the school councils themselves tend to be for the selected, representational few. The average number of council members per council was thirteen in the school survey. Although there were exceptions, most councils were deliberately balanced, by school staff, by age and gender. The perceived "fairness" of elections was statistically correlated with the perceived "effectiveness" of a school council in the school survey—irrespective of a school council having accomplished a great deal. When pupils were surveyed who were not currently on their school council, fairness in selecting members was central to their perception of the council.

What constituted "fairness" was explored in the case-study schools. In five of the six schools, the adult advisers considered the selection process fair because every pupil who expressed a desire or who was nominated to be on the school council had the chance to be elected. Advisors also cited diversity (e.g., age, gender, academic standing) as additional evidence of a fair election. Still, both advisers and council members expressed reservations about procedural fairness. For instance, there were low levels or no competition for some council seats. Some members shared the following: They felt they had been elected with little effort (e.g., because of being popular); they had been asked by a teacher to become a candidate; and the actual election mechanics were flawed (e.g., lack of secret ballots or half the class was not present). Only in one case-study school did all the council members view the selection process as fair because they felt all had a chance to be nominated and elected.

The power of invitation and the potential exclusion of a representative structure, are brought out in a related, representative survey of secondary school pupils across Scotland (Tisdall, with Milne & Iliasov, 2007). Pupils who were not currently council members were asked why they were not on the council. The replies included the following: No one had asked them to be a member; they were put off by having to be elected; the teacher had not picked them as a candidate; or they did not know how to become a member. These findings underline that processes of nomination and election have layers of invitation and selection, inclusion and exclusion, that can underlie a seemingly "open" and fair representational process. Not everyone feels invited to be a representative, leading to problems with the legitimacy and symbolic value of school councils.

The Scottish Youth Parliament seeks to be a representative body of young people in a conventional democratic way. However, it lacks the infrastructure of an electoral roll and other institutions, so it relies on networks and marketing to encourage young people to vote for their representatives. Further, the Youth Parliament is for those aged 14 and up; younger children have no equivalent body. Other participation activities and projects engage with groups of children and young people on a variety of bases, often recruiting children and young people from their various services and related organizations. Thus, these activities themselves are either "invited spaces" or—something not considered by Cornwall and Coelho (2007)—captive or at least contained spaces (e.g., children who are in residential homes or receiving services).

The Drama of Impact

At certain spectacular space-times, impact was dramatically indicated by public and policymaker attention. These examples of success were related or observed when a key decision maker agreed with a recommendation from children and young people. In the participation projects, both the Youth Commission on Alcohol and Voice against Violence reported such successes. This involved a government minister unexpectedly (from the young people's perspectives) and publicly announcing an initiative that directly fulfilled a particular recommendation. The Minister linked the announcement to the young people's contributions. The young people were euphoric about the sudden and very public announcements. In the school council research, one school council had set up a campaign that gained national prominence. While little action was in fact forthcoming nationally, the localized attention in the school led to a consistent description of the effectiveness of that year's school council.

These dramatic moments generated a widespread view, by the children, young people, and adults involved, that the children and young people's participation had been meaningful and effective. In none of these examples, however, was there sustainable and sustained engagement over space-time. In all three cases, the groups of children and young people disaggregated (when we contacted the school council the subsequent year, it had different members and was not viewed as particularly effective by adults or members). The "drama" may be inspiring to many, but it does not encompass the plethora of decision-making that might be relevant. While we are just ending a decade in Scotland where children and young people's participation has been promoted, participation risks being a policy "fad" and a public "performance." Once no longer as novel and innovative, it could become marginalized and unsupported.

SPACE-TIME AND PARTICIPATORY INSTITUTIONS

How, then, do these findings match up with Cornwall and Coelho's five requirements for participation-sphere institutions to be inclusive and effect change?

1. People need more than invitations to participate: they need to recognize themselves as citizens rather than beneficiaries or clients.

When we consider the participation activities described here, children and young people are generally not in any of Cornwall and Coelho's cited roles: They are not beneficiaries, clients, or citizens. Children and young people may want to be decision makers at times, in the school councils, but usually are very aware that they are not. Children and young people tend to be mostly "consultees" in school councils and participation activities more generally, with all the weaknesses of that category in terms of lack of influence on setting the agenda as well as the eventual decisions. Children and young people appear to be the most effective in the role of peer researchers or peer experts, in the currently popular co-production model (for a critical discussion, see Tisdall, 2013).

2. Representative claims must be considered critically, and mechanisms to be representative must be in place.

Adults have considerable concerns about who is invited into participation spaces and who is not. If adults do not want to listen to children and young people's views, the criticism of being "unrepresentative" will frequently be given—although it is often unclear about whether the criticism is about being statistically unrepresentative of the population of children or young people or unrepresentative in a democratic sense. Participation activities generally, and school councils in particular, are frequently criticized for only including certain children and young people. School councils are criticized for comprising only the "articulate elite." Although we explicitly sought to investigate this in the research, evidence was not found (HASAS, and Tisdall with Milne & Iliasov, 2007). School staff explicitly sought to encourage diversity, by encouraging certain people to nominate themselves, by requiring classes to elect a girl and a boy, or through other selection processes. Funded consultation exercises frequently set out requirements to consult a range of children and young people, by location, minority and ethnic backgrounds, and other characteristics.

School councils in the case-study schools spent a great deal of time trying to be representative democratically. This was difficult to achieve across the space-time available. The research suggests ways that certain processes could be improved. But the findings raise questions whether the efforts to be representative, in this very traditional democratic way, are worthwhile. The attempt to replicate formal meeting structures, with minutes, agendas, chairs, and committee roles, can effectively train those participating pupil councillors to organize, participate in, or indeed lead such meetings in the future. But, in terms of children and young people having an impact on their school, other ways of involving a wider range of children and young people may be more effective (see Whitty & Wisby, 2007).

Ironically, the school councils observed followed a traditional model of democracy rather than the "deliberative turn" associated with the rise of the participatory sphere.

School councils could draw on methods used in the wider participation activities—from the Scottish Parliament's use of social media to engage with young people across Scotland, or the arts-based activities facilitated by organizations like the Children's Parliament, or the focused co-production model of the Youth Commission on Alcohol. While these methods may be worth considering, these activities all lack the foundation in everyday spaces for most children and young people (Percy-Smith, 2010). Children and young people are extracted out of their communities to participate, raising ongoing issues of sustainability and representativeness.

3. Structures are not enough. The motives of those who participate—including state actors—can be competing and are in constant negotiation.
4. Three factors are essential for change: involvement by a "wide spectrum of popular movements and civil associations, committed bureaucrats and inclusive institutional designs" (p. 9).

Cornwall and Coelho argue that structures are not enough. This is evident in the school council research—even though at least 90 percent of schools in Scotland have a council, many are not considered effective in terms of either process or outcomes. But structural changes could be made for school councils that would enhance their potential effectiveness—such as making them less reliant on individuals and more structurally robust in terms of continuity, adult support, and links into decision-making. Most other participatory activities lack sustainable structural support at all, particularly as budgets are contracting. Children and young people's participation has been highly reliant on NGOs for both funding and to carry out such participation, and as such organizations are squeezed themselves, funding and support may well diminish. In response to Cornwall and Coelho, structures are not enough, but some structures are beneficial for sustainability and effectiveness.

The ideas of space-time, as generated by human geographers, show the relational aspects of participation. When participation seemed to have an impact on decisions, space-time combined in two ways. First, there was a sequential model: The government supports creation of the project, the young people carry out the project, and then the young people re-enter the governance space to present their findings. Second, there was a more co-terminous model, where children, young people, and adults come into relationship with each other and meaningful dialogue seems to occur.

5. Participation is a process over time and must be situated alongside other political institutions, within their own social, cultural, and historical contexts.

The findings underline and amplify Cornwall and Coelho's last requirement. Time emerged as critical throughout both projects—the lack of time, the time of day, and institutional timings and their fit or not with the everyday lives of children and young people. A spatial lens underlines the tendency to separate out participation activities from children and young people—which has some advantages of potentially making them child-friendly, cohesive, and generative—but divides them from spaces of governance and government (and thus from decision-making).

This analysis suggests possibilities for children and young people's participation. The enthusiasm about co-production needs to be evaluated robustly for its strengths and weaknesses. School councils could be developed more creatively, as well as complementary or alternative participation activities in schools. Stronger structural support would benefit school councils and other participatory activities, with more continuity and less reliance on individuals. Consideration should be given to greater linkages and more joint spaces-times between adults and children to avoid the "ghettoization" of children and young people's participation. The relational aspects of participation must be factored in because it is through effective relationships, either sequentially or co-terminously, that participation appears to have an impact on decision-making.

CONCLUSION

The experiences in Scotland, both of school councils and of participatory activities more generally, are not yet ones of consistent celebration. The list of barriers continues to be relevant and endlessly repeated in forums that seek to promote children and young people's participation. There continue to be dramatic successes, which are powerful for those involved and inspirational to others.

It is capturing this potential for inspiration, for cultural change, that is perhaps the most promising. This potential was expressed at the Think Tank in the Participation Initiative, with an articulation of current strengths (Barnardo's Scotland, Children in Scotland, and CRFR, 2011):

- **Government commitment**. It is now expected that children and young people will be involved in the decision-making, and children and young people themselves increasingly expect it.
- **Enthusiasm of the converted.** An ever-growing number of practitioners, managers and policy-makers are committed to children and young people's participation and ensure it is central to their work.
- **Creative, inclusive and productive approaches**. Children, young people and those supporting their participation have developed effective ways of working together.
- **Use of technology**. This allows for inclusive, larger-scale consultations.

As more and more children and young people, and thus their parents and communities, are exposed to ideas of children's rights in their schools or policy discourses, the more possibilities there are for generational shifts. As more and more of those involved in organizations and government institutions articulate the barriers to participation, the more potential there is for barriers to be lifted, taken down, and moved. As experiences of participation accumulate, people may be more open to flexible, inclusive, and meaningful space-times of participation—recognizing that participation is not static but involves relationships over time and spaces.

ACKNOWLEDGMENTS

I would like to thank the generous contributions of children and young people, professionals, and policymakers throughout the studies referred to in this chapter. I want to emphasize the collaborative nature of these studies, with the above and with numerous academic colleagues. The chapter in particular makes reference to collaborative projects funded by the Big Lottery Fund, the British Academy, Economic and Social Research Council (R451265206, RES-189-25-0174, RES-451-26-0685), the European Research Council, the Leverhulme Trust, and the Royal Society of Edinburgh.

REFERENCES

Barnardo's Scotland, Children in Scotland, and the Centre for Research on Families and Relationships (2011). *Children and young people's participation in policy-making.* Edinburgh: CRFR. Accessed November 4, 2013, at http://www.crfr.ac.uk/reports/Participation%20briefing.pdf

Chambers, R. (1983). *Rural development: putting the last first.* Essex: Longmans.

Cockburn, T. (2012). *Rethinking children's citizenship.* Basingstoke: Palgrave.

Cooke, B., & Kothari, U. (Eds.) *Participation: the new tyranny?* London: Zed Books.

Cornwall, A. (2004a). Introduction: new democratic spaces? The politics and dynamics of institutionalised participation. *IDS Bulletin—New Democratic Spaces, 35*(2), 1–10.

Cornwall, A. (2004b). Spaces for transformation? Reflections on issues of power and difference in participation in development. In S. Hickey & G. Mohan (Eds.), *Participation from tyranny to transformation* (pp. 75–91). London: Zed Books.

Cornwall, A. (2008). Unpacking "participation." *Community Development Journal, 43*(3), 269–283.

Cornwall, A., & Coelho, V. S. (2007). Spaces for change. In A. Cornwall & V. S. Coelho (Eds.), *Spaces for change?* (pp. 1–29). London: Zed Books.

Cornwall, A., & Gaventa, J. (2000). From users and choosers to makers and shapers: repositioning participation in social policy. *IDS Bulletin, 31*(4), 50–62.

Cotmore, R. (2004). Organisational competence: The study of a school council in action. *Children & Society, 18*(1), 53–65.

Davies, L., Williams, C., & Yamashita, H., with Man-Hing, K. (2006). *Impact and outcomes: taking up the challenge of pupil participation.* London: Carnegie Foundation. Accessed May 31, 2010, at http://www.participationforschools.org.uk

Dürr, K. (2005). *The school: A democratic learning community.* Strasbourg: Council of Europe. Accessed October 25, 2013, at http://www.edchreturkey-eu.coe.int/Source/Resources/Pack/School_democraticlearning_community_EN.pdf

Gallagher, M. (2006). Spaces of participation and inclusion? In E. K. M. Tisdall, J. M. Davis, M. Hill, & A. Prout (Eds.), *Children, young people and social inclusion: participation for what?* (pp. 159–178). Bristol: Policy Press.

Gaventa, J. (2004). Participatory development or participatory democracy? Linking participatory approaches to policy and governance. *Participatory Learning and Action, 50,* 150–155.

Hart, J. (2008). Children's participation and international development: attending to the political. *International Journal of Children's Rights, 16,* 407–418.

Hart, R. (1992). *Children's participation: the theory and practice of involving young citizens in community development and environmental care.* London: Earthscan.

Hinton, R. (2008). Children and good governance. *International Journal of Children's Rights, 16*(3), 285–300.

Houghton, C. (2013). *Voice against Violence: young people's experiences of domestic abuse policy-making in Scotland.* PhD thesis, University of Warwick.

Hubbard, P., & Kitchin, R. (2004). Introduction to key thinkers. In P. Hubbard & R. Kitchin (Eds.), *Key thinkers on space and place* (pp. 1–15). London: Sage.

Johnson, V. (2011). Conditions for change for children and young people's participation in evaluation: change-scape. *Child Indicators Research, 4*(4), 577–596.

Kesby, M. (2007). Spatialising participatory approaches. *Environment and Planning A, 39,* 2813–2831.

Lansdown, G. (2011). *A framework for monitoring and evaluating children's participation.* Accessed November 4, 2013, at http://resourcecentre.savethechildren.se/content/library/documents/framework-monitoring-and-evaluating-childrens-participation-preparatory-dr

Leal, P. A. (2010). Participation: the ascendancy of a buzzword in the neo-liberal era. In A. Cornwall & D. Eade (Eds.), *Deconstructing development discourse: buzzwords and fuzzwords* (pp. 89–100). London: Oxfam.

Maithes, H., & Deuchar, R. (2006). We don't learn democracy, we live it! Consulting the pupil voice in Scottish schools. *Education, Citizenship and Social Justice, 1*(3), 249–266.

Mannion, G. (2007). Going spatial, going relational: why "listening to children" and children's participation needs reframing. *Discourse: Studies in the Cultural Politics of Education, 28*(3), 405–420.

Massey, D. (1994). *Space, place and gender.* Cambridge: Polity Press.

Massey, D. (1999). Space-time, "science" and the relationship between physical geography and human geography. *Transactions of the Institute of British Geographers, 24,* 261–276.

Morrow, V. (2005). Social capital, community cohesion and participation in England: A space for children and young people? *Journal of Social Sciences* (Special Issue 9), 57–69.

Paul, T. (2011). *Youth Commission on Alcohol. Briefing 1. Children and young people's participation in policy-making.* Accessed November 3, 2012, at http://www.crfr.ac.uk/reports/Participation%20briefing.pdf

Percy-Smith, B. (2010). Councils, consultations and community. *Children's Geographies, 8*(2), 107–122.

Percy-Smith, B., & Thomas, N. (Eds.). (2010). *A handbook of children and young people's participation: perspectives from theory and practice.* Abingdon: Routledge.

Punch, S. (2003). Childhoods in the majority world: miniature adults or tribal children? *Sociology,* 37(2), 277–295.

Robb, S. (2012). Public policy making. *Exploring new pathways: Children in Scotland supplement.* Accessed November 7, 2013, at http://www.crfr.ac.uk/reports/CISAUG.pdf

Scottish Borders Youth Commission on Bullying (2012). *Recommendations.* Melrose: Scottish Borders Council. Accessed November 7, 2013, at http://www.scotborders.gov.uk/downloads/file/3474/scottish_borders_youth_commission_on_bullying

Scottish Government (2011). *Advancing professionalism in Scottish teaching: Report of the Review of Teacher Employment in Scotland.* Accessed October 2, 2013, at http://www.scotland.gov.uk/Resource/Doc/920/0120902.pdf

Shier, H. (2001). Pathways to participation: openings, opportunities and obligations. *Children & Society,* 15(2), 107–117.

Teamey, K., & Hinton, R. (2014). Reflections on Participation and its Link with Transformative Processes. In E. K. M. Tisdall, A. M. Gadda, and U. M. Butler (Eds.), *Children and young people's participation and its transformative potential learning from across Countries* (pp. 22–43). Basingstoke: Palgrave.

Thomas, N. (2007). Towards a theory of children's participation. *International Journal of Children's Rights,* 15, 1–20.

Thomas, N. (2012). Love, rights and solidarity: studying children's participation using Honneth's theory of recognition. *Childhood,* 19(4), 453–466.

Tisdall, E. K. M. (2008). Is the honeymoon over? *International Journal of Children's Rights,* 16(3), 419–429.

Tisdall, E. K. M. (2012). Taking forward children and young people's participation. In M. Hill, G. Head, A. Lockyer, B. Reid, & R. Taylor (Eds.), *Children's services: working together* (pp. 151–162). Harlow: Pearson.

Tisdall, E. K. M. (2013). The transformation of participation? Exploring the potential of "transformative participation" for theory and practice around children and young people's participation. *Global Studies of Childhood,* 3(2), 183–193.

Tisdall, E. K. M., Gadda, A. M., & Butler, U. M., eds. (2014). *Children and young people's participation and its transformative potential learning from across Countries.* Basingstoke: Palgrave.

Tisdall, E. K. M., Davis, J. M., Hill, M., & Prout, A. (Eds.) (2006). *Children, young people and social inclusion: participation for what?* Bristol: Policy Press.

Tisdall, E. K. M., with Milne, S., & Iliasov, A. (2007). *School councils and pupil participation in Scottish secondary schools.* Glasgow: Scottish Consumer Council.

Tisdall, K., & Davis, J. (2004). Making a difference? Bringing children's and young people's views into policy-making. *Children & Society,* 18(2), 131–142.

Treseder, P. (1997). *Empowering children and young people training manual: promoting involvement in decision-making.* London: Save the Children, UK.

United Nations Committee on the Rights of the Child (2009). *General Comment No. 12 The right of children to be heard.* Accessed November 7, 2013, at http://www2.ohchr.org/english/bodies/crc/docs/AdvanceVersions/CRC-C-GC-12.doc

Vengroff, R. (1974). Popular participation in administration of rural development: the case of Botswana. *Human Organization,* 33(3), 303–309.

Whitty, G., & Wisby, E. (2007). *Real decision making? School councils in action.* Accessed February 18, 2008, at http://www.dfes.gov.uk/rsgateway/DB/RRP/u014805/index.shtml

Wyness, M. (2005). Regulating participation. *Journal of Social Sciences,* 9, 7–8.

Wyse, D. (2001). Felt tip pens and school councils. *Children & Society,* 15, 209–218.

CHAPTER 17

Child Participation in Monitoring the United Nations Convention on the Rights of the Child[1]

TARA M. COLLINS

I think it's good to be involved in this reporting proc ess so it's not just adults and staff because sometimes they are out of touch with the way young people are.

(child [Europe], January 20–21, 2014)

INTRODUCTION

In accordance with Article 44, states parties to the United Nations Convention on the Rights of the Child (CRC) (UN, 1989) regularly report to the United Nations Committee on the Rights of the Child (UN Committee).[1] Such reports can provide valuable insight about progress in child rights implementation, but efforts to accomplish this objective can vary.

Due to international legal recognition and universal relevance, the CRC provides a vision and reflects a standard to be respected in all efforts involving children (Collins, 2007). A relevant measure of its significance is whether CRC monitoring reflects and respects the child's right to participate. While the role and support for child participation are well established in the current literature, participation is not yet widely or practically understood in relation to monitoring. Consequently, this chapter addresses the question of why children should

1. Earlier versions presented at annual conference of Interdisciplinary Research Laboratory on the Rights of the Child (IRLRC), University of Ottawa, November 18, 2009; and submitted to UN Committee on the Rights of the Child, for General Day of Discussion on "The Right of the Child to be Heard," September 10, 2006.

participate and what experiences some children and their advocates have had in national and international CRC monitoring.

In ascertaining the situation of children's rights, monitors generally inadequately consider child participation. International child rights law not only establishes standards for children but should also influence all processes related to children, including monitoring (Collins, 2007). Moreover, without children's engagement, the monitoring process and results will reflect a limited picture with restricted impact (Collins, 2007). Research shows that children are contributing to monitoring in various countries and to the UN Committee's monitoring, but preparations and processes must improve. It is particularly important considering that the Optional Protocol to the CRC on a communications procedure to facilitate individual and collective complaints (UN, 2011) is now in force, facilitating the submission of complaints from children and their supporters in states parties about alleged rights violations to this UN Committee.

This chapter considers the right and contributions of children, regardless of age, to participate in monitoring, whether led by adults or children or intergenerational efforts. While child rights monitoring is commonly assumed to be exclusively defined by the CRC reporting procedure, numerous other procedures and avenues exist at international, regional, national, and local levels (Collins, 2007). Nevertheless, this chapter focuses on the monitoring relationship between the CRC, the primary international binding instrument for child rights, and child participation. Accordingly, discussion emphasizes the UN Committee and national-level efforts. This chapter refers to "children," "youth," and "young person/people" interchangeably to refer to those under 18 years of age, in accordance with the CRC's definition in Article 1.

Two research processes inform this analysis. First, doctoral research undertaken at the University of London from 2001 to 2005 included questionnaires and interviews with fifteen key international actors, five focus groups involving fifty children, and forty-three interviews with adults in three countries (Canada, United Kingdom, and South Africa). To protect their privacy, children's contributions are identified only by hometown and the child's first initial.[2] The North East London Health Authority Research Ethics Sub-Committee approved the children's focus group in London for Queen Mary, University of London (there was no college- or university-level ethics board at that time). Second, a literature review and a small-scale qualitative study incorporate recent developments. Fourteen interviews were conducted from August 2013 until January 2014 with four children and ten adults with international and national monitoring experiences. Children involved ranged from 13 to 18 years of age at the time of their monitoring/reporting engagement. For confidentiality, personal and country names are deleted. Interviewees are categorized by organization type, geographic

2. If the same first initial recurs in a session, the first letter of the child's chosen pseudonym is added.

region, and interview date. Contributions represent perspectives from six different countries, representing high- and low-income groups according to the World Bank (2014), in four regions around the world (Americas, Oceania, Europe, and Asia) as well as international-level actors. No government or UN Committee members were involved. The Ryerson University Research Ethics Board approved the recent interview process.[3]

Child involvement in this research was not representative but was essential for the following reasons: participation is a right; better understanding of children's knowledge and more effective action and responses are advanced; proper measurement of the effectiveness of adults' efforts is facilitated; and it empowers children (Save the Children, 2000). When incorporated into research, children's understandings "both complement and reinforce" studies about them (Mayall, 2000, p. 134). Moreover, children's exclusion is described as "a flaw which severely (even fatally) undermines the validity of the perspectives and insights gained" from research (Masson, 2000, p. 34).

The chapter first explores monitoring before describing child participation in relation to monitoring. Some recent experiences of children and advocates with CRC monitoring are explored. Then, best practices and recommendations are identified before concluding.

WHAT IS MONITORING?

Monitoring of international human rights, including children's rights, should illuminate the status of rights in order to advance their full enjoyment (Collins, 2008a). Monitoring involves three main functions: research or collection of information about rights in a given context; the assessment of this data to ascertain the extent of implementation; and reporting results (Collins 2007, 2008a). Monitoring is important for several reasons, including the following (Collins, 2007, 2008b): accountability of international and national actors for their efforts and results; identification of difficulties to allow improvements; potential development of responsive measures and decision-making; creation of competition within and between states to improve progress; and the mobilization of shame for poor efforts or results. Further, the results should allow for informed action for and with children and others to raise public awareness and urge action, including corrective responses or further support. Monitoring also legitimizes and justifies attention and concerns about rights.

To be effective, monitoring must be an ongoing process to improve the implementation of child rights (Collins, 2007). Monitoring is important because, as Tomaševski (2001) pointed out, implementation does not necessarily lead to child

---

3. Ryerson University Research Ethics Board, REB 2013-169: Child Participation in International Monitoring of Children's Rights, approved June 17, 2013.

rights progress. Monitoring should allow understanding of the success or ineffectiveness of measures and may be intergenerational or adult- or child-led efforts. It includes various formal and informal evaluation activities about children and childhood by actors at the international, regional, national, and local levels. This chapter focuses on formal monitoring because the CRC requires states parties to report every five years (after the initial report) to the UN Committee. (The UN Committee meets three times a year for four weeks: three weeks for the formal session and one week for the presession working group to prepare for the next session.) In accordance with CRC Article 45(a), various actors monitor the national situation and then contribute to international CRC monitoring, including such national child rights coalitions[4] as Ireland's Children's Rights Alliance. The Non-Governmental Organization (NGO) Group for the Convention on the Rights of the Child, now known as Child Rights Connect (2014), coordinates the involvement of civil society in UN reporting.

WHAT IS CHILD PARTICIPATION IN MONITORING?

Child participation in monitoring is necessary since CRC Article 12 establishes the child's right to participate and calls for the establishment of mechanisms to promote and support participation (Santos Pais, 1997). As a CRC general principle,[5] child participation is fundamentally important "not only a right in itself, but should also be considered in the interpretation and implementation of all other rights" (UN Committee, 2009, p. 5). This right is advanced through other CRC provisions, including the freedoms of expression, association, and access to information.

Many interpretations of participation exist, along with various criteria to assess it (Roche, 2000). In general, child participation

> has evolved and is now widely used to describe ongoing processes, which include information-sharing and dialogue between children and adults based on mutual respect, and in which children can learn how their views and those of adults are taken into account and shape the outcome of such processes. (UN Committee, 2009, p. 5)

There are several important objectives. Participation allows respect for human rights; and "listening to children is central to recognizing and respecting their worth as human beings" (Roberts, 2000, p. 229). While participation should

---

4. See, for example, the International Save the Children Alliance Working Group on the CRC (1996).

5. The other general principles are nondiscrimination (a. 2), life and development (a. 6), and best interests (a. 3).

not be romanticized (Ennew, 1998), it can contribute to the development of participants' capacities and support mutual learning of the subjects and others in processes. Participation also makes children visible outside traditional private spheres of the family and institutions, including schools.

Consequently, the role of, and support for child participation are well established in the literature. Views can be expressed in many ways, including through emotions and drawing, and young children and children with disabilities can express views (Lansdown, 2005). Efforts to identify a minimum age for child participation are unsubstantiated in international law (Collins, 2007). For instance, CRC Article 12(1) does not address freedom of expression in terms of age, but rather in terms of ability. Further, the Hague Convention on Abduction (Hague Conference, 1980) does not specify a minimum age for consideration of children's objections regarding return to a parent (Van Bueren, 1993). Research shows that children assume close-knit interests with others and a participatory approach to issues (Stevens, in Berman, 1997). Children often express their attitudes and judgments about society and the world around them (Berman, 1997). Child participation is well advanced.

Nonetheless, some dissent exists. For example, Hafen and Hafen (1996) misconstrue participation and child rights as irresponsible "autonomy."[6] Yet the CRC is clear about recognizing children's relationships with others, identifying family/caregivers in the Preamble and in Articles 5 and 18(1) in order to realize child rights. Thus, participation is more complex than most critics understand. It is important to recognize that participation does not require children to have more influence or authority but requires consideration of their views along with others.

OBSTACLES TO PARTICIPATION

Although an essential CRC principle, child participation in monitoring has not yet been widely explored in the literature, except brief academic publications and limited nongovernmental work.[7] Flekkøy (1993) is an early advocate for the monitoring structure to be "a voice for children" (Flekkøy, 1996, p. 59). Two practical NGO guides now support child participation in CRC monitoring and reporting (Dimmock, 2011a, 2011b). World Vision has experience in CRC reporting and supporting child-led reports in Lebanon for the Universal Period Review (World Vision, 2010).

The CRC does not explicitly provide for child participation in monitoring, and the UN Committee currently lacks appropriate guidelines to support child participation. The UN Committee (2009, p. 29)

6. See further Collins (2013).
7. These examples include Flekkøy (1996), p. 59; Flekkøy's acknowledgment in European Union (2009); Save the Children (2000); and Miller (n.d.).

welcomes written reports and additional oral information submitted by child organizations and children's representatives in the monitoring process ... and encourages
States parties and NGOs to support children to present their views to the Committee.

The UN Committee chair (as she then was) confirmed "great importance" placed
on children's participation (Lee, 2011, p. vii). Doek (2009, p. 778) describes that
child participation "can be found in the reports of States Parties, NGOs and UN
agencies submitted to the CRC Committee over the past 20 years."

While child participation in international activities is important and increasing, effectiveness is difficult in practice. The logistics and resources (time, technical, and financial) involved can be significant. Challenges for Committee
reporting include "difficulties include getting visas (children often don't have
birth certificates, let alone passports), ensuring children are prepared for the
experience and confident to brief the Committee or Governments. Risk of
flight (children taking off to be economic migrants)" (international NGO actor,
November 11, 2013).

There is no official average of child involvement, but in 2012, less than ten children were involved in the CRC reporting process in Geneva (NGO representative
[Europe], August 21, 2013). Generally only two or three children represent their
organization due to prohibitively expensive travel costs (international organization
[IO] official [Europe], November 15, 2013). Their focus is the presession working
group where opportunity exists to influence the formal review (IO official [Europe],
November 15, 2013), with "[v]ery few [children] or none" for the subsequent formal
session, "especially now that it's webcast" (NGO representative [Europe], August
21, 2013). The Committee has been meeting with children since 1999 and this participation is increasing (IO official [Europe], November 15, 2013).

The UN's adoption of the aforementioned third OP to the CRC redresses a
major procedural gap. While communications are time-consuming and reactive to (rather than preventing) alleged violations (Van Bueren, 1998), the CRC
had been the only major UN human rights instrument lacking this right to petition, reflecting lack of international respect of the child's right to participate.
This important procedure can redress individual cases, reveal patterns of injustice, and support interpretation of international standards (Van Boven, 2002).
Now that the OP is in force, additional resources are needed to provide adequate
child-friendly support for successful operation and to respect child rights. The
UN Committee (2013) adopted OP rules of procedure, but necessary guidance
is lacking on how to support children with the exception of Rule 15(3), which
requires "an appropriate and accessible format, adapted, to the extent possible, to
the age and maturity of the child" for clear or additional communications with the
author(s) and/or alleged victim(s). These rules inadequately consider what this
may mean other than requiring attention to the child's best interests. Moreover,
the UN Committee has not yet provided guidelines for meeting with children, but
they are planned for the future (IO official [Europe], November 15, 2013).

Children are often largely invisible in monitoring of their rights (Collins, 2007). As Boyden explains, invisibility may occur for various reasons, including institutionalization, migration, fear, or monitoring procedures focusing on the household rather than individuals (Black, 1994). Obstacles may include limited awareness of monitoring, adult restrictions, and different interpretations of or criteria to assess participation that, for instance, exclude children from "participatory" exercises (Roche, 2000). Children's different abilities also are challenging: "Because children are constantly changing, and because our cultural expectations, theories, and research data change, adults frequently under- or overestimate children's abilities and knowledge" (Garbarino, Stott, & Faculty of the Erikson Institute, 1990, p. 10). Adults' prejudices and misperceptions of children and their roles and capabilities must be challenged. Such undervaluing of their abilities is largely restricted to their right to participate and be heard, but not in terms of meeting the demand for work and sexual exploitation.

Conventional approaches generally consider monitoring to be an "adult" concern or pursuit and do not provide roles for children because attitudes and established practices do not support child participation. Some perceive children as "incapable" or "uninterested" in monitoring.[8] Consequently, much monitoring inadequately illuminates the situation of the child and his or her rights (Collins, 2007). Flekkøy (1993, p. 61) affirms that children's capacities "have clearly been under-estimated." Extensive child development research shows competence is largely contextualized, and thus the best approach "is to assume competence in some degree, and to ask at every age: what support can be provided to enable children to participate to the best of their ability?" (Children's Participation in Community Settings, 2000, p. 12).

The CRC affirms "child-oriented freedom of expression," which demands reform "from what children cannot do to what children can do, and to which decisions and parts of decisions children may make" (Van Bueren, 1998, p. 742). States parties must remove restrictions and provide significant support to children to express themselves (Van Bueren, 1998). The most appropriate form of participation, as Chawla (2001, p. 9) explains, "varies with circumstances, including culture, age, gender, setting, political conditions, available resources, and participants' goals." While not all children will be interested, it is important that they have the opportunity to decide. Children should be respected as rational human beings and, as Alderson and Goodwin note, "their experiences must be seen as profound sources of knowledge" (quoted by Van Bueren, 1998, p. 137). Qvortrup (1997) argues that children should speak for themselves about their situation individually and aggregately.

Children's rights demand participation in monitoring. It is in the child's best interests, as per CRC Article 3, to involve him or her in monitoring. For example,

---

8. For example, an academic challenged the author in April 2009 about the veracity of children's contributions (provided on the next page), believing children to be incapable of such understanding.

child impact assessments by decision makers to respect their best interests (i.e., Hammarberg, 2001) include children's opportunity to express opinions to gauge the actual effect of decision-making (Sylwander, 2001). Since CRC Articles 42 and 12 require children to know about their rights, and state that children have the right to express their opinions, it is consistent to consider how children interpret and evaluate their rights, which in turn enhances both children's and adults' understanding of those rights.

Children consulted in focus groups identified several reasons for such participation (Collins 2007, p. 9; 2008b, pp. 6–7):

> To find out if children understand their rights; to find out children's views and beliefs; to find out if there is any problem in their groups and areas; to monitor the children's health and well-being—VV (12-year-old girl), M (12-year-old boy), and G (17-year-old boy), Cape Town

> To get accurate information from the parties involved and to have proof that directives [of the CRC] are being followed. If those involved are saying something, in this case the children, they might have a different opinion. That is why monitoring is important, to show that they do think otherwise than what they are being told. To get many diverse opinions.—TA & RJ (13-year-old boys), Ottawa

Their contributions describe many benefits (Collins, 2007, 2008b). First, the monitoring process can determine whether and how children comprehend their rights. Second, children's knowledge and views about their rights and their status, which may differ from those of adults, become available. Third, the information may illuminate new emerging issues. Fourth, their involvement supports a comprehensive picture, not simply an adult perspective. As rights bearers, children need data both to challenge the situation and to recognize beneficial measures. Lastly, if children themselves inform others about their rights, the message will likely be more powerful to decision makers and will receive an appropriate response.

Although some Canadian focus group participants (13-year-olds TA and RJ, and 15-year-old RL) expressed reservations about engaging children in "Third World countries" who must focus on survival, 15-year-old L that believes rights awareness remains an obstacle to monitoring (Collins, 2007, p. 300). Yet participatory monitoring is not simply a "developed world" proposal. Organizations from various countries, including Yemen (Children's Parliament, 2008), Thailand (ECPAT International, 2011), and Peru (*Acción por los Niños*, n.d.), and interviewees from around the world all support child participation.

The CRC requires all efforts related to children, including monitoring, to respect child rights. While states have been the traditional international legal actors, participation has expanded to include IOs, business, NGOs, and individuals (Higgins, 1994). Moreover, "[U]niversal respect for, and observance of, human rights" is an international goal as per UN (1945) Charter Article 55(c). While the CRC's monitoring provisions in Articles 43 through 45 do not require children's participation, the guiding principle of Article 12 should support monitoring since CRC Article 4 requires "all appropriate . . . measures" for implementation. Further, this approach may elaborate the Committee's function enunciated in CRC Article 45(d) to "make suggestions and general recommendations" about monitoring.

In summary, child participation must be an integral part of monitoring in order to include the child's knowledge, perspective, and priorities, which may differ from those of adults. Such engagement supports respect of rights and improves the monitoring process and results, which should have improved accuracy and relevance. Thus, children from various contexts and populations should have the opportunity to participate in monitoring with dedicated and consistent attention to improve efforts over time.

PARTICIPATION EXPERIENCES

While there is much theoretical support for participation, the practice of monitoring children's rights demands analysis. Research for this chapter has found that children almost always participate in monitoring through NGOs (NGO representative [Switzerland], August 21, 2013) because governments generally conduct restricted efforts without public participation or child involvement (Woll, 2000). Some states parties may include nongovernment representatives on their delegation to report to the UN Committee. For example, Thailand in February 2012 and Egypt have included children (IO official [Europe], November 15, 2013). But government delegations generally do not include children.

Government inclusion of two children on one delegation, for example, brought complications due to their "very scripted" responses and questionable accuracy of government translation (NGO representative [Switzerland], August 21, 2013). Indeed, such involvement should not implicate their responsibility for state measures or inaction (David, in Collins, 2007, p. 16). Consequently, clarification of various roles and responsibilities in monitoring is needed.

Two main distinctions in the monitoring experience are discerned from the research. One approach involved children in some jurisdictions in report development, conducting research through interviews and questionnaires, analyzing the data, and report writing (young person, January 22, 2014; young person, January 20–21, 2014; and NGO representatives [Americas], November 8, 2013). While demanding work, child interviewees identified that they learned valuable lessons about rights and developed skills (Europe, January 22, 2014; Europe, January 20–21, 2014). One European organization supported two separate participatory avenues to assist efforts of younger and older children (not-for-profit organization representative [Europe], January 13, 2014). A national coalition established a child forum in 2010 in an Asian country where children created a movie to monitor children's rights and selected their 16-year-old peer to present to national events and the UN Committee (NGO actor [Asia], January 12, 2014). This participatory approach to monitoring has international scope as evidenced in various reports, including Scotland (Article 12, 2008), and Cambodia (Cambodian Children and Young People Movement, 2010). These efforts support children's voices, familiarizing and empowering children with their rights and state obligations (IO official [Europe], November 15, 2013).

Another approach involved consultations or involvement with children through focus groups or questionnaires to provide input to the UN Committee (Oceania, December 16, 2013; Americas, August 25, 2013; NGO actor [Asia], January 12, 2014). For example, one national NGO engaged over 750 young people in an online survey and in-person consultations (NGO representative [Oceania], December 20, 2013). This organization also involved two people under 18 years of age and three people 18 to 24 years of age in Geneva (NGO representative [Oceania], December 20, 2013). One short-term example identified three children between 14 and 18 years and three people between 19 and 25 years of age for Geneva participation following an application form, essay, and interview process (indigenous young adult delegate [Americas], December 20, 2013). Consultations with children are included in numerous reports from around the world, including Bangladesh (Adolescent Development Foundation, 2008), Afghanistan (2009), Germany (Child and Youth Welfare Association, 2010), and Seychelles (Vel, 2011).

The former process of engaging children in monitoring described earlier is time-intensive, while the latter consultation approach usually contributes to reporting. While other research finds that most children were involved in children's rights before reporting in Geneva (Dimmock, 2009), not everyone has this understanding. If participants have limited experience, they seem more likely to have unrealistic expectations. The scope of child engagement is "related to his or her level of understanding" of processes and procedures (international NGO actor, November 11, 2013).

Understanding of participation also varies across countries. For instance, one organization included in its Geneva delegation "a young person" under the age of 35, reflecting that country's definition of youth, due to children's time challenges and inconsistent meeting attendance (NGO representatives [Americas], November 8, 2013). Another country brought people both under and over the age of 18, resulting in a different treatment that, as described later, was difficult for those involved (indigenous young adult delegate [Americas], December 20, 2013). The nature and success of participation often depend on adults' understanding and commitment over time. "[V]ery different standards, expectations and impact" result, according to an IO official (November 15, 2013).

Hence, children's experiences varied in the research: Some felt their contributions were considered by their governments and/or the UN Committee while others did not. One young person felt "listened to and taken seriously" by the Committee, yet she "felt largely ignored by my country" (Oceania, December 16, 2013). Another child also felt "heard and appreciated" by "UN officials and other powerful people" but "felt differently" about government officials: "I didn't feel heard by them; they just wanted to hear their own side of the story" (Americas, August 25, 2013). Another felt that her government officials "are stuck in their own ways" (Europe, January 20–21, 2014). This distinction is largely due to different roles and expectations of participants in CRC monitoring and reflects varying approaches (Collins, 2008a). The CRC reporting process generally involves the following (Collins, 2007): governments interested in defensively protecting their efforts; NGOs critically focusing on lacunae; and the UN Committee attempting to balance varying information as the "monitor of monitors" (Hammarberg, 1993). Thus, greater attention to these roles and realistic expectations should be advanced.

Children often feel that others do not listen to them, but contributing to international processes is empowering. One young person identified that "getting the chance to do something like this makes up for that" (young person [Europe], January 22, 2014). Based on children's perspectives, greater communication is generally needed between children and authorities.

While the Committee can engage children, it must be more encouraging, with clearer expectations. It is beneficial that the Committee has drafted working methods adopted in October 2014 to "provide some guidance to child-led organizations, groups and NGO/international organizations accompanying children" (IO representative, November 15, 2013). (However, it is noted that these working methods inadequately consider the various issues related to formal participation discussed below.) Guidance is urged to support understanding of Committee engagement by both children and adults and to require the Committee to identify how child contributions are valued and inform the development of the UN Committee's concluding observations about the state party (NGO representative [Switzerland], August 21, 2013). Guidelines are necessary to build the Committee's capacity "because while there are child rights experts, they are not necessarily experts in engaging with children in this type of context" (NGO representative [Switzerland], August 21, 2013).

Nevertheless, monitoring participation cannot be defined simply by a Geneva trip; it is a process, requiring significant time and effort (NGO representative [Americas], January 15, 2014; young person [Europe], January 20–21, 2014; and not-for-profit organization representative [Europe], January 13, 2014), which causes some issues. For instance, other demands and changing interests mean that children may inconsistently engage. The "challenges of time management for children, to study, rest, play and [be] active in child forum" exist (NGO actor [Asia], January 12, 2014). Two NGO actors noted: "It's very easy to get them in one session" but difficult to sustain "continuous involvement in a process" (Americas, November 8, 2013). High turnover among participants complicates understanding and requires many introductions to the process and material (Europe, January 20–21, 2014). Participation requires recognition of the changing nature of children's involvement over time (Lansdown, 2014). Moreover, collaborative efforts must improve (NGO representatives [Americas], November 8,

2013). Determination and cooperative support from others (young and older) advance monitoring (young person [Europe], January 20–21, 2014).

Children can be involved in relation to any and all stages of monitoring, namely research, assessment, and reporting. Child involvement in adult research requires conducive conditions encouraging children to take responsibility (Theis, 1998), while child-led research reflects varying circumstances, objectives, and children involved. Excellent examples of child-led research processes exist, but child engagement in monitoring is "still very dependent upon how adults set it up . . . there's such a range of consultation because it comes down to . . . the time, and capacity and the resources that the NGOs are working with the children. And how . . . seriously have those adults actually taken it?" (NGO representative [Switzerland], August 21, 2013). Respectful cooperation requires clear roles and responsibilities. Participants appreciate intergenerational support (young person [Oceania]. December 16, 2013; indigenous young adult delegate [Americas], December 20, 2013). Further, several countries have already emphasized intergenerational working methods to support monitoring, including Moldova (Child Rights Information Centre Moldova, 2008), Bangladesh (National Children Task Force, 2007), Norway (The Ombudsman for Children, 2009), and Albania (United for Child Care and Protection, 2011).

But not every child will want to participate even though it is his or her right. Indeed, the world's influence on a child will affect his or her potential participation (Qvortrup, 2000). For instance, the contributions of girls may differ from boys, so single-sex groups may be useful in some contexts; contributions of older children will often contrast with those of younger children (Johnson, Ivan-Smith, Gordon, Pridmore & Scott, 1998). Children at different stages of maturity can contribute in various ways reflecting their developing mental, physical, emotional, and intellectual states and abilities (Garbarino et al., 1990).

Participation is not just a matter of providing the opportunity, however: children also need support (Van Bueren, 1998). Institutional assistance is recommended for children "to share their ideas and give attention to what they said and considering their ideas into decision-making" (NGO actor [Asia], January 12, 2014). One NGO actor urged the creation and maintenance of children's groups as a "proven" strategy for them "to learn and exercise their right to participate" (Asia, January 12, 2014). Structural, cultural, and other barriers should also be challenged by providing information and so on (McIvor, 2001). Processes should be explained to parents and caregivers to garner support because some believe that "children get nothing" from participation, but this assumption is now "decreasing" (NGO actor [Asia], January 12, 2014). Monitors cannot assume that children will be interested, even if they are informed, due to other responsibilities and pursuits. Interest must be inspired through fun, engaging processes (young person [Europe], January 22, 2014) and incentives (including information campaigns, music, and awards), as children consulted repeatedly emphasized (Collins, 2007). Nonetheless, the child's individual circumstances may mean that participation is not realistic or practical or even may be "exploitative or inappropriate" (Roberts, 2000, p. 225). Thus, the child's right to participate includes both developmental and protectionist elements (Brems, 2002). In sum, participation is both important and complex in monitoring.

IMPACT OF PARTICIPATION

This section considers the impact of child monitoring participation upon several actors and concerns: children, adults, the UN Committee, improved understanding of child rights, and improved national profile of CRC.

Children

Monitoring and reporting experiences in UN and national-level activities have significance for children. National-level involvement provides important opportunities, as two NGO actors remarked: "Quite a few of these young people were astonished" that they were trained to do the survey and that they conducted it (Americas, November 8, 2013). UN Committee reporting was generally positive, supporting learning, the value of hard work (child [Americas], August 25, 2013), and one's CV (child [Europe], January 22, 2014). An adult saw changes in the child who traveled to Geneva and his friends with improved CRC understanding and increased confidence and skills for self-expression and interacting with adults (NGO actor [Asia], January 12, 2014). Consequently, children generally benefit from monitoring participation.

However, guidance and support are needed. As the UN Committee highlights throughout its concluding observations, many children remain unaware of their rights and monitoring. Moreover, "[v]ery little direction was given from the committee on what they wanted to hear [during the children's meeting], or how they wanted to hear it" (indigenous young adult delegate [Americas], December 20, 2013). An international survey of thirty-seven young people involved in Committee processes in 2009 confirmed this lack of clarity (Dimmock, 2009). Despite mostly positive feedback, "children were not really aware or informed of their role in the process and of the impact their participation would have. This Committee is looking . . . to find ways to bridge the gaps" (IO official [Europe], November 15, 2013). Clear information is required.

Adults

Adult interviewees were similarly supportive of child participation but revealed inconsistent experiences. NGO leaders involved children to respect children's rights (NGO representative [Oceania], December 20, 2013; NGO actor [Asia], January 12, 2014; international NGO actor, November 11, 2013). One identified the importance of commitment to the process of participation, not to the outcomes, so that a child can "understand the processes and procedures, which we adults have put in place to improve his or her life" (international NGO actor, November 11, 2013). Accountability was another reason "to ensure organizations and governments are effectively working" (NGO representative [Oceania], December 20, 2013). Despite the cost and logistical challenges, Geneva involvement supported adult appreciation of the value of child participation in monitoring, which is important due to the national

> challenge with culture of not giving children importance . . . So the fact that we can elevate children to a level that they could chime in internationally would perhaps send a message home to adults, [who] manage the issues that affect children . . . it would make a huge difference . . . it would make a big difference for children as well. (NGO representatives [Americas], November 8, 2013)

While the UN Committee's specific children's meetings impressed several adults (NGO representatives [Americas], November 8, 2013; NGO representative [Oceania], December 20, 2013), some children and adults experienced difficulties due to lack of clear guidance as described above. Thus, one recommended that Geneva processes "be more open and receptive . . . I believe that the committee could use training of some sort in how to work more effectively with children and youth" (indigenous young adult delegate [Americas], December 20, 2013). Child engagement can have wide-ranging implications for adults and others.

UN Committee

Child participation influences both the UN Committee members and the Concluding Observations to varying degrees. As one young person affirmed:

> I think the Committee members are more "touched" by the involvement of young people . . . For example, earlier this year I attended an event where one of the Committee members was speaking . . . and although this event was nearly 2 years after our session with the Committee, she (not knowing I was in the audience) mentioned one of my anecdotes to the audience. It was incredible that that had stayed with her for so long and it made me feel as though I had made a genuine impression on the Committee. (Oceania, December 16, 2013)

Another child was pleased that her priorities of climate change and child participation in government policies were included in the UN's Concluding Observations (Americas, August 25, 2013). Some interviewees noted that children's contributions "appeared to have had a profound impact" (NGO representative [Oceania], December 20, 2013) and that Committee members "were more interested in these answers than what the adults had put together in the report" (NGO representatives [Americas], November 8, 2013). But others had negative experiences and concerns, including an indigenous young adult delegate who felt that "we were somewhat ignored, and/or not taken as seriously while we spoke" (Americas, December 20, 2013). Even with positive experiences, challenges included the intimidating physical environment for children and that "not all the questions were asked in plain language or in a child-friendly way" (NGO representative [Oceania], December 20, 2013). Guidance is needed to support child participation in the UN Committee's work.

Improved Understanding of Child Rights

There is strong consensus that child participation improves the monitoring process and results as contributions support understanding of the situation. As one young person explained:

> by having young people have their say, it put a human face to it all, and I think it gave some reality and perspective. . . . I think it's also important to mention the things that aren't reported. For example, . . . I had Indigenous peers who would come to school unfed and having spent the previous evening not in a safe environment . . . without having some young people here, no one really hears those little voices." (Oceania, December 16, 2013)

An NGO actor outlined: "Involving children . . . is an essential way to ensure that the UN Committee have the complete and comprehensive picture about the implementation of UN CRC in each country, even in the world" (Asia, January 12, 2014). This understanding cannot be advanced without children. For instance, one NGO representative acknowledged its earlier error of excluding to "protect" children involved in commercial sexual exploitation; the group now understands that children's participation brings greater awareness and respect of their capabilities and experiences (Americas, January 15, 2014). Participation "ensures that the governments and organizations are correctly reporting on the real experiences of children" (NGO actor [Oceania], December 20, 2013) and improves adults' understanding of children. An IO official confirms that participation "can definitely improve the . . . reporting process and results" to support the Committee's understanding of CRC implementation and how rights can be advanced, and to develop pertinent country-specific recommendations (November 15, 2013).

Indeed, children in focus groups consistently confirmed their interest in monitoring and noted that it requires children's perspectives, which may differ from those of adults (Collins, 2007). Children's research "identified issues that would otherwise not be covered, or would be covered in an adult-centered way . . . The role child and youth participation has is that it provides a perspective a government report cannot" (not-for-profit organization representative [Europe], January 13, 2014). Children's approaches to monitoring may counter the limitations of other efforts. Therefore, for one NGO actor, children and youth are "the main source of the monitoring process" (Asia, January 12, 2014). Consequently, child participation

> can improve the monitoring process because it will identify issues which would other-
> wise be overlooked. In our experience children and young people are very often able
> to identify issues which do not appear on the radar of government until years later. It
> can also be used as a barometer for the effects of government policies, the intentions of
> which are noble but the application of which can be sporadic or in worst cases, coun-
> terproductive." (not-for-profit organization representative [Europe], January 13, 2014)

"[K]ids also provide a sense of urgency about certain things, because they affect them directly" (young person [Americas], August 25, 2013). Child involvement can advance data accuracy, supporting validity (young person [Americas], August 25, 2013), and children "are more likely to express their opinions than to adults sometimes" (Europe, January 20–21, 2014). A not-for-profit organization representative confirmed that child participation "significantly enriches the analysis" (Americas, January 15, 2014). Moreover, the UN Committee can only monitor based on the information it receives (Collins, 2007), highlighting the importance of various perspectives to support comprehension.

With commitment to the process and not the outcome, child participation can support a circular approach to monitoring where "the final result is a researched, reasoned one, rather than predetermined to promote the monitor's particular perspective or concern" (Collins, 2008, p. 162). "It shapes the messaging to better reflect the issues which children are concerned about, rather than the advocacy priorities of the sending/convening organizations. For the listeners, it brings a reality to the concerns they are hearing about" (international NGO actor, November 11, 2013). "If children and young people are not involved, then how do they know how young people feel properly?" (child [Europe], January 20–21, 2014). While children's engagement does not provide a comprehensive description of all CRC articles in a jurisdiction (international NGO actor, November 11, 2013), the monitoring process and results benefit from participation.

Improved National Profile of CRC

Child participation in monitoring also supports stronger national CRC awareness. Results include more effective reporting to the domestic population and enhanced public exposure in media and advocacy; thus, "[c]hild and youth participation is a great advocacy and marketing tool to raise the profile, credibility and awareness of children's rights" (NGO representative [Oceania], December 20, 2013). Another national coalition also confirmed greater public awareness due to the child participation in Geneva (NGO actor [Asia], January 12, 2014). Hence, participation contributes to support CRC progress and implementation.

BEST PRACTICES

Research highlights best practices for child participation, including effective preparation, means, and tools.

Effective Preparation

Children's national-level preparations must improve before reporting to the UN Committee (IO official, November 15, 2013) because the UN Committee is dependent on the national-level preparations (Collins, 2007). For instance, some children have gone to Geneva believing that their participation "could change their personal situation" (NGO representative [Switzerland], August 21, 2013). Children's engagement in local and national monitoring is necessary, but the UN Committee must also prepare by clarifying procedures and expectations.

Personal Testimonies

The UN Committee should inform others about its opposition to personal testimonies in monitoring. Personal testimonies illustrate the realities of certain issues, contexts, or populations. Such experiential perspective has been valued since the first World Congress on the Commercial Sexual Exploitation of Children in Stockholm in 1996, which included representatives from many countries, NGOs, and agencies and yet "so few youth who had experienced sexual exploitation themselves" (Bramly & Tubman, 1998, p. 3). However, the Committee seems to prefer generalizations rather than personal testimonials. For instance, one interviewee was shocked by a UN Committee chair who "quite rudely" cut off his young colleague who was providing "a very personal and heartfelt account of her experiences" of violence against Indigenous women (indigenous young adult delegate [Americas], December 20, 2013). Apparently, the UN Chair wanted "more important information" and not to be "wasting our time with testimonials," which could be shared during the children's meeting; the result was angry and confused young delegates because "In just a few seconds, her experience was disregarded, and ignored" (indigenous young adult delegate [Americas], December 20, 2013).

According to the Committee, testimonies should not be shared during children's meetings, however, because Committee members want children to speak about others they represent and not feel pressured to detail their "personal experience that is usually attached to a whole range of emotions, and risk of re-traumatization" (NGO representative [Switzerland], August 21, 2013). The children's meeting time provides the opportunity for children's recommendations for the state (NGO representative [Switzerland], August 21, 2013). Nevertheless, this approach is contested as "[t]o disregard youth statements when they're right there in front of them seems irresponsible. Their stories should be seen as valid and meaningful" (indigenous young adult delegate [Americas], December 20, 2013). Indeed, monitoring should not only meet the needs of the monitor but should also consider the issues and concerns of children themselves (Alderson, 2000a; Flekkøy, 1996). Before Geneva participation, detailed guidance is clearly needed to inform expectations and preparations for all involved, including Committee members.

Children's Meetings

While specific children's meetings with the UN Committee are generally supported, some concern exists. One interviewee preferred that this meeting not be separated from the main committee (indigenous young adult delegate [Americas], December 20, 2013). But children's meetings are held to "create a space to ensure that children are heard" (NGO representative [Switzerland], August 21, 2013). Nonetheless, these meetings must be carefully managed, because undue influence from adults can adversely affect discussions. For example, adults may theoretically support children's right to participate but may restrict these views in practice to avoid being "disrespectful" and critique one's country in an international environment, which is "like criticizing your family in public" (NGO representative [Switzerland], August 21, 2013). Consequently, both national and international actors have roles to support and not impede open dialogue and "manage those relationships in the interests of the children" (NGO representative [Switzerland], August 21, 2013). Children should "feel free to say what they want to say whether they're prepared, or to answer the questions" without wondering whether it was "the right answer" (NGO representative [Switzerland], August 21, 2013). However, as identified earlier, lack of direction during these meetings poses problems with expectations of children and adults. The strict scheduling of Committee meetings may also restrict genuine dialogue among participants. Thus, efforts are needed to ensure that children feel comfortable and respected during this meeting, which should never be diminished in importance.

Evidence of tensions due to the lack of a specific role for people over 18 in UN Committee processes is unfortunate and avoidable. Young adults included in one country's nongovernmental delegation felt unwelcome since they were over 18 (indigenous young adult delegate [Americas], December 20, 2013). It is reasonable that these older participants may participate in the presession working groups, but they "are not considered children" (IO official [Europe], November 15, 2013). If children participate in monitoring, delays often mean that children become adults by the time their country reports to the UN Committee. Thus, it is critical to manage

> expectations. There's no reason why a person over eighteen shouldn't have been informed or received information to the effect that their opportunities to engage directly with the committee were going to be different from those under eighteen. . . . [T]hey are at different points in their lives. And it's not that they don't have opportunities to engage directly with the committee, but they shouldn't have come with the expectation." (international NGO representative [Switzerland], August 21, 2013)

Hence, preparations must be comprehensive to avoid disappointment.

In addition to coordination, preparations for all involved should advance respect of child participants, maximize successes, and learn lessons from failures or weaknesses.

Means and Tools

Various means and tools exist to support participation, and children should determine how they participate in monitoring; they can redress power imbalances, widen collection methods, and promote data understanding (Alderson, 2000a). Valuable scholarship relating to children's roles in research includes Knowing Children (2009), Punch (2002), and Grover (2004). Numerous successful examples include researchers, reporters, and editors with Headliners in United Kingdom, Y-Press and 8-18 Media and WireTap in the United States;[9] research led by street children in Bangladesh (West, 1998); and child researchers in Zimbabwean informal settlements (McIvor, 2001). The recent release of a toolkit to assess child participation is promising (Lansdown & O'Kane, 2014). Various avenues exist or can be developed in different jurisdictions not only at local but also national and international levels.

Techniques address concerns about adult influence and manipulation (Collins, 2007). For example, child impact assessments and other monitoring efforts compensate for the little political power that children have, directly or indirectly, in society (Hammarberg, 2001). But O'Kane acknowledges the

---

9. See http://www.headliners.org, www.ypress.org www.cplmedia.org, and www.wiretapmag.org (last visited March 14, 2014).

significant challenge of "the disparities in power and status between adults and children" (Morrow & Richards, in O'Kane, 2000, p. 136).

Participatory research can redress ethical difficulties in working with children and enhance the validity and reliability of the research results (Thomas & O'Kane, in O'Kane, 2000). Choosing a method involves (Lewis & Lindsay, 2000) preference, practicality, view of research or ideology, ethical considerations, and the research questions. But "practical considerations and preferences, . . . should not *determine* the method, although they may determine the research focus and hence the questions" (Lewis & Lindsay, 2000, pp. 190–191). Roche proposes that several perspectives about the participation and results be considered to determine the quality and depth of participation (Roche, 2000).

Monitoring tools including indicators, benchmarks, and indices have been developed to evaluate rights, but one's approach influences the selection and usage (Collins, 2007, 2008a). Moreover, these tools inconsistently support participation. The Roeher Institute (2002) identifies the following monitoring problems: children may be excluded for not meeting such measurement criteria as verbal skills; they may be included but if they cannot accomplish the measured outcomes, they will be seen as failures; or children may not be considered if they have disabilities because of the poorer cost–benefit ratios in investments compared to other children. Thus, self-determined tools should be developed to determine the reality of various elements in a person's life and reflect inclusion and participation (Roeher Institute, 2002). Such complications demand that monitoring tools and their results be critically analyzed (Collins, 2008a).

As identified earlier, consulting with children is likely the most common and popular tool of engagement in monitoring due to its simplicity, adult involvement (if not influence or control), cost, and so on (Collins, 2007). Yet consultation is not simple or always successful due to barriers (Alderson, 2000b), including lack of time; lack of confidence or skill in communicating with children, possible language barrier, family dynamics, fear of losing control, anxiety about children's potential problems, and prejudice against engaging young children. Nonetheless, many conferences involve consultations, and various resources exist to support such engagement (including Cockburn, 2001).

Other means support consideration of children as research subjects. Participatory monitoring and evaluation of projects and programs, commonly termed participatory rural appraisal or participatory rapid assessment, may be useful, including visualization (through participants' diagrams and pictures), interviewing, and group work (Estrella & Gaventa, 1998; Woodhead in Save the Children, 2000). For example, young children's perceptions of protection and risk involved group discussions with visual methodologies in postconflict Liberia (Ruiz-Casares, Rousseau, Morlu, & Browne, 2013). Child-to-child methods can also be used to educate, empower, and monitor children by encouraging older children to support younger ones (Otaala, 1998). Such techniques are important in minimizing the use of age as a barrier to the child's ability to participate (Solberg, in O'Kane, 2000, p. 140).

Quantitative research methods, including community surveys or ecological assessments, should be participatory to respond to community needs and situations where participants determine what information to collect and the collection method and timing (Estrella & Gaventa, 1998). Children's elections and opinion polls can also support identification and assessment of children's perspectives, although these generally adult-instigated efforts may be manipulative or tokenistic (UNICEF, 1998).

Other tools include the conversation between the researcher and a child and listening to children (Mayall, 2000). The research conversation has several advantages (Mayall, 2000): Children can control or influence the conversation; adults can learn about children's social worlds and knowledge gathering; and the conversation can demonstrate children's social skills. It could mean that children themselves contribute to revealing the situation of invisible children (Boyden, cited in Black, 1994, p. 27). But Lewis stresses that "the greatest imperative is to engender a listening culture amongst the adults to whom they must direct their voice" (Lewis, 1996, p. 214). Facilitators—whether adult or child—must be skilled in communications, facilitation, and conflict negotiation (O'Kane, 2000).

Communication other than by verbal means, including "play, activities, songs, drawings and stories," can be used with children of varying ages and skills, although some methods require certain conceptual or physical abilities (O'Kane, 2000, pp. 139, 155). With various means of communication, problems in interpretation can occur (Lewis & Lindsay, 2000). Adults must ensure accuracy and not simplify their interpretations of children's rights (Alderson, 2000b).

Observation is a technique common to certain disciplines, but it does not involve direct contributions of children. It may be useful for interpreting the perspectives of very young children, such as those involved in early childhood programming (Gosling with Edwards, 2003). However, its use should be restricted because it can become an excuse to avoid child engagement; even very young children can be consulted or engaged (see Alderson, 2000b, Chapter 4).

In sum, many means and tools exist to support effective child participation. Creative approaches, including technology, should be pursued to elicit views and other data from children about rights. In particular, children themselves should be involved in determining how monitoring participation should be undertaken and assessed regularly over time.

RECOMMENDATIONS

Inspired by the research, the following recommendations to advance child participation in monitoring are interconnected but discussed separately.

UN Guidelines to Support Child Participation

While working methods (UN Committee, 2014) now exist, further explicit UN Committee guidance is needed to advance child participation in CRC reporting. The creation of "a policy and/or a set of guidelines [will] ensure young people are involved and that they understand, and get the level of help they need" (young person [Europe], January 22, 2014). States and civil society organizations should be urged to engage children in preparing reports (NGO representative [Americas], January 15, 2014) as the working methods encourage. But further efforts are required to ensure that child participation is "well coordinated and well facilitated," and that all adults, including Committee members, take it "seriously" (IO official [Europe], November 15, 2013). Further information for adults and children should clarify expectations, support preparations, and guide interactions in Geneva.

It must be remembered that the UN Committee members serve as volunteers with great demands on them in preparation for, and during their meetings. They are expected to critically analyze voluminous readings to monitor each state party. Work is also complicated by Committee membership turnover when terms expire and new members are added; for example, there were eight new members in 2012 and a new chairperson (NGO representative [Switzerland], August 21, 2013). These requirements and realities do not excuse disrespectful behavior but highlight the need for effective, consistent guidance.

The UN Committee should clearly enunciate what it would like from children without influencing what is said (indigenous young adult delegate [Americas], December 20, 2013). Its opposition to personal testimonies must be explicitly identified. The working methods (UN Committee, 2014) have recently acknowledged the role and use of various media to present information, including Internet communications and video, as Funky Dragon has done (2012). Children's expectations must also be informed by the reality that international participation "can influence change in the long term ... [but] might never have an effect on their lives" (NGO representative [Switzerland], August 21, 2013).

Guidelines should address how children's contributions are used in the reporting process. For instance, there may be views that adults may not want to hear, including research and some children highlighting the importance of work, which cannot only be criticized as a violation of children's rights (Bourdillon, Levinson, Myers, & White, 2010; and NGO representative [Switzerland], August 21, 2013). To be respectful, such information should not be disregarded. A moderator should be identified to support respectful and accessible interactions between children and Committee members and avoid issues such as undesired essay reading or problematic time management (indigenous young adult delegate [Americas], December 20, 2013). Guidelines must also task the Committee to provide feedback to children about their engagement and how it was used (NGO representative [Switzerland], August 21, 2013).

It should be recognized that the UN Committee is intimidating for both adults (NGO representatives [Americas], November 8, 2013) and children (NGO representative [Oceania], December 20, 2013). Participation would advance with an accessible, welcoming meeting space and consistent use of child-friendly language (NGO representative [Oceania], December 20, 2013). During children's meetings, questions should be phrased to support understanding, without the use of unfamiliar technical terms (NGO representative [Switzerland], August 21, 2013). The UN Committee's website needs to provide more than "simpler language and pretty colours" about how children can engage with the Committee (NGO representative [Switzerland], August 21, 2013). UN Committee members are encouraged to visit countries "to meet the children and see what is actually happening" (NGO representatives [Americas], November 8, 2013).

Rarely considered in practical monitoring, ethical child participation must be advanced in the guidelines, since ethical processes are required when interacting with human beings in research processes as per Christensen and James (2000) and university ethics boards. Researchers must consider (Alderson, in Roberts, 2000, pp. 229–230): purpose; costs and expected benefits; privacy and confidentiality; selection of participants; funding; information for participants and their caregivers; review of research aims and methods by others; dissemination of results; and overall impact upon children. Issues of voluntary and informed consent and consideration of power dynamics to advance respectful interactions must be included. Several factors exist for valuable data collection (Scott, 2000): questions must be appropriate for the child's experience or knowledge; the child must be willing and able to respond to questions based on his or her experience and knowledge; and the child's motivation to participate must be considered. Valuable guidance is available in the recent release of a compendium for ethical research involving children (Graham, Powell, Taylor, Anderson, & Fitzgerald, 2013).

Risks must be recognized in the guidelines. Safety must be ensured for participants, as several research participants highlighted (NGO actor [Asia], January 12, 2014; and KM, RL, P, and S, in Collins, 2007, p. 294, note 146). The NGO Group developed a template risk assessment for child rights research (Dimmock, 2011a, 41–41). Risks include the dangers of engagement "in political processes in countries where civil society doesn't have much voice, or where it is culturally inappropriate for children to participate" (international NGO actor, November 11, 2013). Thus, organizations "should fully take into account protection concerns of children before and after they are involved" (IO official [Europe], November 15, 2013). One respondent included garnering support from parents/caregivers and youth facilitators because it is "crucial to prepare the adults and community" (NGO actor [Asia], January 12, 2014).

These guidelines can support engagement in the UN reporting process and further monitoring participation in other international, national, and local fora.

Comprehensive Training at the UN and National Levels

In addition to guidelines, training to support monitoring and participation, including effective preparation and collaboration, would be beneficial (indigenous young adult delegate [Americas], December 20, 2013). One NGO actor outlined that training should include the following: support understanding of the issues and context; skills in participation; and "fun and creative" approaches (Asia, January 12, 2014). Various guidelines and tools exist to support children's participation in monitoring, including awareness-raising and research techniques, and could inform training, including the Council of Europe (2004), Miller (n.d.), Orama (2009), and the Canadian Coalition for the Rights of Children (2003).

Improving Child Involvement in Monitoring

Children's participation is "absolutely essential" (not-for-profit organization representative [Europe], January 13, 2014) and should be improved at local, national, and international levels. In essence, participation processes must reflect the nine criteria identified by the UN Committee (2009, and 2014): transparent and informative, voluntary, respectful, relevant, child-friendly, inclusive, supported by training, safe and sensitive to risk, and accountable. Children can engage with NGO or ombudsman activities with institutional support and/or pursuing their priorities supported by such organizations, as Article 12 in the United Kingdom. One child noted the lack of other children in the process, and her conversations during her UN experience revealed "that not a lot of children participate in the UN's decisions. Therein lies the problem" (Americas, August 25, 2013). Another young interviewee recommends increasing the number of children involved because "although I tried to represent the views of lots of young people, it's more genuine if it comes from the horse's mouth (for us there was only two of us)" (Oceania, December 16, 2013). Placing such heavy expectations on one individual may be overwhelming and should be addressed in preparations.

Because participation must be meaningful (NGO representative [Oceania], December 20, 2013), tokenism occurs where children lack a substantive role; this is challenging in practice because "[n]ot all adults and community are ready to accept and take consideration of children's opinion" (NGO actor [Asia], January 12, 2014). Some organizations use children "to further their own objectives rather than [giving them] the platform to speak for themselves" (international NGO actor, November 11, 2013). Children should be monitoring partners, requiring attention to the appropriate accommodations, reflecting their interests and expertise. Adults' understanding of participation in international fora must also be improved because "people just shut off," assuming lack of relevance—or if children "speak too well, then they say they've been told what to say, and if they don't, they say: 'well, that just shows that it's completely useless" (NGO representative [Switzerland], August

21, 2013). Moreover, having unreasonable expectations of children who are pushed into roles similar to those of adults is "disrespectful of their rights," leaving them frightened about failing to meet expectations and lowering their self-esteem (NGO representative [Americas], January 15, 2014). The ideal adult role is as a "facilitator: to guide but not to control unduly, and least of all to extinguish" (Black, 1994, p. 30). Thus, participation is not simply a method but also "part of a process of dialogue, action, analysis and change" (Pretty and others, in O'Kane, 2000, p. 138).

While challenging, representation in monitoring and reporting requires diversity. As an international body, the Committee depends on the information from NGOs and others, and methodology and rationale for participant selection processes are important (IO official [Europe], November 15, 2013). For example, two NGO representatives concluded that they "did not have enough participation" and were challenged by engaging children in protection, the justice system, and younger children (Americas, November 8, 2013). Hence, NGOs are urged to engage marginalized children in monitoring and to provide opportunities to participate in Geneva (IO official [Europe], November 15, 2013). Geographic representation across jurisdictions is also important, including rural and urban children for instance (child [Oceania], December 16, 2013). Representation can be advanced through different technology, including children's audio and visual recordings, as done by the Philippines (NGO representatives [Americas], November 8, 2013) While children's diversity complicates participatory undertakings, it also enhances the exercise's value.

Due to the evolving engagement of children, participation may not necessarily involve the same children over time. Years of delays in the monitoring process can mean that the child could age out of childhood and other changes could occur before Committee proceedings (NGO representative [Switzerland], August 21, 2013). Participation should not be dependent upon a trip to Geneva. Young adults can become valuable mentors to children on delegations or join the NGO adult delegation (NGO representative [Switzerland], August 21, 2013).

Representation is advanced with consistent monitoring, without recreating new processes and structures every five years to meet CRC deadlines, which also maximizes understanding and rights awareness (Collins, 2007). NGO representatives outlined the goal that children regularly identify their concerns in an ongoing survey (Americas, November 8, 2013). Consistent monitoring involving children's meetings "where they get to gather and learn about rights, or they get to have discussion groups on particular topics, that can be really useful just to grow up as informed citizens" (NGO representative [Switzerland], August 21, 2013).

Need for Further Resources

Limited or lack of such resources as financial, human resources, organizational, and technical (Himes, 1992) impedes effective monitoring and child participation

(Collins, 2007). Children need information and support to learn about children's rights and monitoring in order to determine if and how they should proceed. Such investments would support awareness of the CRC and monitoring reports in accordance with the obligations of CRC Articles 42 and 44(6).

A distinction between international support and lack of local support is prevalent (Collins, 2007). Child Rights Connect (2014) provides some funding to some NGOs to participate in UN reporting. Resources remain an issue because children's rights are not yet a priority. NGO representatives confirmed that: "We were excited to have overseas donor's support ... but very little local support" (Americas, November 8, 2013). The Geneva experience lessens the gap between international and national processes.

However, child engagement does not necessarily require Geneva travel. For instance, social media, recordings, and texting will engage more children, and use of an Internet webcam is another possibility. The UN Treaty Body Webcast (n.d.) already livestreams proceedings and maintains an archive, which can ensure state accountability to civil society unable to attend proceedings.

Thus, resources are needed to advance children's rights, to encourage child participation, and to support monitoring.

Improving Awareness

Engagement and support of child participation in monitoring are complicated due to lack of awareness about the CRC and monitoring among children and professionals despite the CRC Article 2 and 44(6) obligation for awareness of the CRC and its reports (youth [Europe], January 20–21, 2014; not-for-profit organization representative [Europe], January 13, 2014). Other actors in society have roles including the national youth council for example (NGO representatives [Americas], November 8, 2013). While much progress has been made, additional effort is required to improve global and local awareness.

Improving Child Participation in the Committee

Children could contribute as UN Committee members because no age-related criteria exist and "children are recognised by the Convention, by virtue of articles 12 and 13, as having a competence in the field of children's rights" (Van Bueren, 1998, p. 389). One child recommends having child representatives from each country (Americas, August 25, 2013) but believes that this idea is far-fetched. Her doubt reveals lack of confidence in adults to appreciate children's rights and capacities. Thus, child membership is a valuable response to advance understanding of children and their rights.

CONCLUSION

The establishment of the UN Committee was an important step forward as the first monitor exclusively dedicated to children's rights.[10] However, child participation inadequately influences monitoring. As 15-year-old L notes, "Because you are doing the monitoring for the benefit of people, so if . . . you don't get their opinion, then what is the use of doing what you are doing?" (Collins, 2007, p. 304). Children's contributions during the research process provided thoughtful, useful suggestions to improve monitoring and to confirm the potential of improved child engagement. Adults may be well meaning, but their monitoring may not reflect the child's right to participate. Complacency with existing efforts is unacceptable, as the child rights challenge must continually be addressed in every jurisdiction and its groups and individuals.

While monitoring is demanding, actors should dedicate greater attention to follow-up to their efforts. Follow-up is important since limited UN and other resources and mechanisms exist to ensure responses (Collins, 2007). Children consistently enunciated in focus groups their expectation of effective action to monitoring results in order to support progress (Collins, 2007). Such follow-up will support the individual child as well as groups and the community (NGO actor [Asia], January 12, 2014). Responses are necessary to justify monitoring efforts and to confirm the role and relevance of child rights (Collins, 2007). Yet, while the UN Committee's Concluding Observations can support advocacy for progress, research indicates difficulty with follow-up to monitoring results due to such issues as lack of resources and political will (NGO representative [Switzerland], August 21, 2013). Children are generally disappointed with inadequate responses by the government to the UN Committee's recommendations (Oceania, December 16, 2013; Americas, August 25, 2013). Hence, preparations must support children's realistic expectations and follow-up must include child participation (UN Committee, 2009; and NGO representative [Switzerland], August 21, 2013).

With the twentieth-fifth anniversary of the CRC in 2014, it is important to consider not only substantive but also procedural issues related to child rights. Despite the third OP's entry into force, inadequate attention to support this OP and overall CRC monitoring remains. With further cooperative work, adults and children will improve their confidence and expertise, leading to greater participation at national and international levels (Alderson, 2000b). In essence, "[a]s long as we give opportunity and trust for children and youth, they can play a significant role" (NGO actor [Asia], January 12, 2014). This is important because their involvement "now will benefit the world in the future" (child [Europe], January 20–21, 2014).

---

10. There is now a committee to monitor the African Children's Charter (Organization of African Unity, 1990).

In conclusion, child participation will benefit the monitoring process and results as well as serve rights because, as George Bernard Shaw (1930) observed: "It's all that the young can do for the old, to shock them and keep them up to date."

ACKNOWLEDGMENTS

Many thanks to the interviewees and focus group participants; this chapter is dedicated to them in appreciation of all their valuable efforts to support children's rights. Thanks also to Rachel Roberts for her excellent research support. This study has been supported by the Research Studentship, Queen Mary, University of London, and funding from the Office of the Dean of the Faculty of Community Services (FCS) and the SRC Travel Grant, FCS, Ryerson University.

REFERENCES

Acción por los Niños (n.d.). Programas. Accessed March 16, 2014, from http://www.accionporlosninos.org.pe/programas.php

Adolescent Development Foundation (2008). *UNCRC Alternative Report to 3rd & 4th Periodic Report from Bangladesh: Looking through adolescent lens.* Chittagong: Author. Accessed March 16, 2014, from http://www.crin.org/docs/Bangladesh_ADF_NGO_Report.pdf

Afghanistan UNCRC Civil Society Coalition (2009). *Every single right for every single child.* NGO Alternative Report on the Implementation of the Convention on the Rights of the Child, Afghanistan. Accessed March 17, 2014, from http://www.crin.org/docs/Afghanistan_ACRCC_NGO_Report.pdf

Alderson, P. (2000a). Children as researchers: the effects of participation rights on research methodology. In P. Christensen & A. James (Eds.), *Research with children: perspectives and practices.* London & New York: Falmer Press.

Alderson P. (2000b). *Young children's rights: exploring beliefs, principles and practice,* London & Philadelphia, PA: Jessica Kingsley.

Article 12 in Scotland (2008). *I witness: The UNCRC in Scotland.* Burnbank, Ogilvie Terrace, Ferryden, Montrose, Angus. Accessed March 17, 2014, from http://www.crin.org/docs/I_%20WITNESS%20_THE_%20UNCRC_%20IN_%20SCOTLAND%20.pdf

Berman, S. (1997). *Children's social consciousness and the development of social responsibility.* Albany: University of New York Press.

Black, M. (1994). *Monitoring the rights of children.* Innocenti Global Seminar Summary Report. Florence: UNICEF International Child Development Centre.

Bourdillon, M., Levinson, D., Myers, W., & White, B. (2010). *Rights and wrongs of child work.* New Brunswick, NJ, & London, Rutgers University Press.

Bramly, L., & Tubman, M. (Eds.). (1998). *Out of the shadows: the Sexually Exploited Youth Project: final report.* Victoria: Save the Children Canada. Accessed February 7, 2014, from http://www3.carleton.ca/landonpearson/vicreport-e.htm

Brems, E. (2002). Children's rights and universality. In J. Willems (Ed.), *Developmental and autonomy rights of children: empowering children, caregivers and communities* (pp. 21–45). Antwerp, Oxford, & New York: Intersentia.

Cambodia Children and Young People Movement for Child Rights (2010). *Cambodian Children's Report: my life, my suggestions.* Phnom Penh: Author. Accessed March 17, 2014, from http://www.crin.org/docs/Cambodia%20%5BChildren's%20 Report%5D_My%20Life . . . My%20Suggestions_CCYMCR.pdf

Canadian Coalition for the Rights of Children (2003). Monitoring children's rights: a toolkit for community-based organizations. Ottawa: Author. Accessed March 16, 2014, from http://www.rightsofchildren.ca/wp-content/uploads/english_toolkit.pdf

Chawla, L. (2001). Evaluating children's participation: seeking areas of consensus. In L. Chawla (Ed.), *PLA notes, October 2001.* London: International Institute for Environment and Development.

Child and Youth Welfare Association (2010). *First Children and Young People's Report on UN Reporting on the Implementation of the UN Convention on the Rights of the Child in Germany: A Report Card for Children's Rights in Germany 2010.* Berlin: AGJ. Accessed March 17, 2014, from http://www2.ohchr.org/english/bodies/crc/docs/ngos/ Germany_National%20Coalition%20for%20the%20Implementation%20of%20 the%20UNCRC%20in%20Germany_CRC%20Children's%20ReportCRCWG65.pdf

Child Rights Connect (2014). What we do. Available at http://www.childrightsconnect. org/index.php/about-us/what-we-do

Child Rights Information Centre Moldova (2008). *Life through children's eyes: children's report on the respect of the Convention on the Rights of the Child in the Republic of Moldova.* Chisinău: Author. Accessed March 16, 2014, at http://www.crin.org/docs/ Moldova_CRIC_NGO_Report.pdf

Children's Parliament (2008). *First Report by the Children's Parliament on The Conditions of Children in Yemen.* Save the Children. Accessed March 16, 2014, at http://mena. savethechildren.se/PageFiles/2867/Children%20parliament%20%20in%20 Yemen%20-%20shadow%20report.pdf

Children's Participation in Community Settings (2001). Conclusions from June 2000 Symposium. In L. Chawla (Ed.), *PLA notes, October 2001.* London: International Institute for Environment and Development.

Christensen, P., & James, A. (Eds.) (2000). *Research with children: perspectives and practices.* London & New York: Falmer Press.

Cockburn, G. (2001). *Meaningful youth participation in international conferences: a case study of the International Conference on War-Affected Children.* Hull, Quebec: Canadian International Development Agency.

Collins, T. M. (2007). *The monitoring of the rights of the child: a child rights-based approach.* Ph.D. thesis (law), defended in 2006, University of London.

Collins, T. M. (2008a). The significance of different approaches to monitoring: a case study of child rights. *International Journal of Human Rights, 12*(2), 159–187.

Collins, T. M. (2008b). Monitoring: more than a report. In T. Collins et al. (Eds.), *Droits de l'enfant: Actes de la Conférence internationale, Ottawa, 2007 [Rights of the Child: Proceedings of the International Conference]* (pp. 1–14). La Collection Bleue, Collins, Grondin, Pinero, Pratte and Roberge (editors), Montreal: Wilson & Lafleur.

Collins, T. M. (2013). International child rights in national constitutions: Good sense or nonsense for Ireland? *Irish Political Studies, 28*(4), 591–619. Available at http://www. tandfonline.com/doi/full/10.1080/07907184.2013.838951.

Council of Europe (2014). *Children, participation, projects: how to make it work!* Strasbourg: Council of Europe. Accessed March 16, 2014, at http://www.coe.int/t/dg3/children/pdf/ChildrenParticipationProjects_en.pdf

David, P., Secretary to the UNCRC (as he then was), Personal communication with author, May, 11, 2001.

Dimmock, S. (2009). *Maximising children's engagement in the reporting process for the Convention on the Rights of the Child: research report.* Geneva: NGO Group for the Convention on the Rights of the Child.

Dimmock, S. (2011a). *Together with children—for children: A guide for non-governmental organizations accompanying children in CRC reporting.* Geneva: NGO Group for the Convention on the Rights of the Child.

Dimmock, S. (2011b). *My pocket guide to CRC reporting—A companion guide for children and adolescents willing to tell the United Nations Committee on the Rights of the Child about how children's rights are respected in their country.* Geneva: NGO Group for the Convention on the Rights of the Child.

Doek, J. (2009). The CRC 20 years: An overview of some of the major achievements and remaining challenges. *Child Abuse & Neglect, 33,* 771–782.

ECPAT International (2011). Alternative Report: Following the initial report from Thailand on the implementation of the Optional Protocol to the CRC on the Sale of Children, Child Prostitution and Child Pornography. Bangkok: Author. Accessed March 16, 2014, at http://www.crin.org/docs/Thailand_ECPAT_OPSC%20 Report.pdf

Ennew, J. (1998). Preface. In V. Johnson, E. Ivan-Smith, G. Gordon, P. Pridmore, & P. Scott. (Eds.), *Stepping forward: children and young people's participation in the development process.* London: Intermediate Technology Publications.

Estrella, M., & Gaventa, J. (1998). *Who counts reality? Participatory monitoring and evaluation: a literature review.* Brighton: Institute of Development Studies at University of Sussex.

European Union, Agency for Fundamental Rights (2009). Developing indicators for the protection, respect and promotion of the rights of the child in the European Union, Summary Report. Accessed March 16, 2014, at http://fra.europa.eu/fraWebsite/attachments/RightsofChild_summary-report_en.pdf

Flekkøy, M. (1993). Monitoring implementation of the UN Convention on the national level. *International Journal of Children's Rights, 1,* 233–236.

Flekkøy, M. (1996). Children's participation and monitoring children's rights. In E. Verhellen (Ed.), *Monitoring children's rights.* The Hague: Martinus Nijhoff Publishers, 57–65.

Funky Dragon (2012). Our rights, our story. Swansea: Author. Accessed March 17, 2014, at http://www.youtube.com/watch?v=GOYm2KNkiS8

Garbarino, J., Stott, F. M., & Faculty of the Erikson Institute (1990). *What children can tell us.* San Francisco: Jossey-Bass Publishers.

Gosling, L., with Edwards, M. (2003). *Toolkits: A practical guide to planning, monitoring, evaluation and impact assessment.* London: Save the Children.

Graham, A., Powell, M., Taylor, N., Anderson, D., & Fitzgerald, R. (2013). *Ethical research involving children.* Florence: UNICEF Office of Research—Innocenti.

Grover, S. (2004). Why won't they listen to us? On giving power and voice to children participating in social research. *Childhood, 11*(1), 81–93.

Hafen, B., & Hafen, J. (1996). Abandoning children to their autonomy: the United Nations Convention on the Rights of the Child. *Harvard International Law Journal, 37,* 449–491.

Hague Conference on International Private Law (1980). *Hague Convention on the Civil Aspects of International Child Abduction*, signed on October 25, 1980.

Hammarberg, T. (1993). The work of the Expert Committee on the Rights of the Child. Consultation on the role of the UN and NGOs in the implementation of the Convention on the Rights of the Child, March 24, 1993, unpublished paper, UNICEF House, New York.

Hammarberg, T. (2001). Preface. In L. Sylwander (Ed.), *Child impact assessments: Swedish experience of child impact analyses as a tool for implementing the UN CRC*, Stockholm: Ministry of Health and Social Affairs & Ministry for Foreign Affairs.

Higgins, R. (1994). *Problems & process: international law and how we use it.* Oxford: Clarendon Press.

Himes, J. (1992). *Implementing the United Nations Convention on the Rights of the Child: resource mobilization and the obligations of the states parties.* Florence: UNICEF International Child Development Centre *Spedale degli Innocenti.*

International Save the Children Alliance Working Group on the Convention on the Rights of the Child (1996). *Monitoring the Convention on the Rights of the Child at the national level: the experiences of some national coalitions.* Stockholm: Save the Children.

Johnson, V., Ivan-Smith, E. Gordon, G., Pridmore, P., & Scott, P. (Eds.). (1998). *Stepping forward: children and young people's participation in the development process.* London: Intermediate Technology Publications.

Knowing Children (2009). *The right to be properly researched: How to do rights-based, scientific research with children, Manuals 1–10.* Bangkok: Black on White Publications.

Lansdown, G. (2005). *The evolving capacities of the child.* Florence: Save the Children Sweden and UNICEF Innocenti. Accessed October 13, 2009, at http://www.unicef-irc.org/publications/pdf/evolving-eng.pdf.

Lansdown, G. (2014). *25 years of the CRC: Learning on child participation.* Presented at "Advancing children's rights," Queens University Belfast, January 27, 2014.

Lansdown, G., & O'Kane, C. (2014). *A toolkit for monitoring and evaluating children's participation.* London: Save the Children UK. Retrieved July 2014 from http://www.savethechildren.org.uk/resources/online-library/toolkit-monitoring-and-evaluating-childrens-participation

Lee, Y. (2011). Preface. In S. Dimmock (Ed.), *Together with children—for children: A guide for non-governmental organizations accompanying children in CRC reporting* (pp. vii–viii). Geneva: NGO Group for the Convention on the Rights of the Child.

Lewis, A., & Lindsay, G. (2000). Emerging issues. In A. Lewis & G. Lindsay (Eds.), *Researching children's perspectives.* Buckingham: Open University Press.

Lewis, J. (1996). Children teaching adults to listen to them. In John (Ed.), *Children in charge*, London & Bristol, PA: Jessica Kingsley.

Masson, J. (2000). Researching children's perspectives: legal issues. In A. Lewis & G. Lindsay (Eds.), *Researching children's perspectives.* Buckingham & Philadelphia: Open University Press.

Mayall, B. (2000). Conversations with children. In P. Christensen & A. James (Eds.), *Research with children: perspectives and practices.* London & New York: Falmer Press.

McIvor, C. (2001). "Do not look down on us": child researchers investigate informal settlements in Zimbabwe. In L. Chawla (Ed.), *PLA notes 42.* London: International Institute for Environment and Development.

Miller, J. (n.d.) *Children as change agents: guidelines for child participation in periodic reporting on the Convention on the Rights of the Child.* Mississauga: World Vision Canada.

National Children Task Force (2007). *I speak about me: alternative report on child rights in Bangladesh.* Save the Children Sweden and Denmark. Accessed March 17, 2014, at http://www.crin.org/docs/Bangladesh_ICHCHEY_NGO_Report.pdf

O'Kane, C. (2000). The development of participatory techniques: facilitating children's views about decisions which affect them. In P. Christensen & A. James (Eds.), *Research with children*. London & New York: Falmer Press.

Ombudsman for Children in Norway (2009). *Supplementary report to the UN Committee on the Rights of the Child*. Oslo: Author. Accessed March 16, 2014, at http://www.crin.org/docs/suplementary-report-to-the-un_english.pdf

Orama, K. (2009). *Child-led organizations on a quest for dialogue*. The Institute of Human Rights. Accessed March 16, 2014, at http://www.crin.org/docs/KristaOmara.pdf

Organization of African Unity (1990). *African Charter on the Rights and Welfare of the Child*, OAU Doc. CAB/LEG/24.9/49. Entered into force November 29, 1999.

Otaala, B. (1998). Children's participation for research and programming in education, health and community development: selected experiences in Africa. In V. Johnson, E. Ivan-Smith, G. Gordon, P. Pridmore, & P. Scott (Eds.), *Stepping forward: children and young people's participation in the development process* (pp. 135–142). London: Intermediate Technology Publications.

Punch, S. (2002). Research with children: the same or different from research with adults? *Childhood*, 9(3), 321–341.

Qvortrup, J. (1997). A voice for children in statistical and social accounting: a plea for children's right to be heard & postscript. In James & Prout (Eds.), *Constructing and reconstructing childhood: contemporary issues in the sociological study of childhood* (2nd ed., pp, 85–106). London & Washington, DC: Falmer Press.

Qvortrup, J. (2000). Macroanalysis of childhood. In P. Christensen & A. James (Eds.), *Research with children: perspectives and practices*. London & New York: Falmer Press.

Roberts, H. (2000). Listening to children and hearing them. In P. Christensen & A. James (Eds.), *Research with children: perspectives & practices*. London & New York: Falmer Press.

Roche, C. (2000). Impact assessment: seeing the wood *and* the trees. *Development in Practice*, 10, 546.

Roeher Institute (2002). *Toward an inclusive approach to monitoring investments and outcomes in child development and learning*. North York: Author.

Ruiz-Casares, M., Rousseau, C., Morlu, J., & Browne, C. (2013). Eliciting children's perspectives of risk and protection in Liberia: how to do it and why does it matter? *Child & Youth Care Forum*, 42, 425–437.

Santos Pais, M. (1997). The Convention on the Rights of the Child. In United Nations. *Manual on human rights reporting*. United Nations (ed.) Geneva: United Nations: 393–504.

Save the Children (2000). *Children and participation: research, monitoring and evaluation with children and young people*. London: Author.

Scott, J. (2000). Children as respondents: the challenge for quantitative methods. In P. Christensen & A. James (Eds.), *Research with children: perspectives and practices*. London & New York: Falmer Press.

Shaw, G. B. (1930). Introduction. In 'Fanny's First Play' from *Misalliance, The Dark Lady of the Sonnets, and Fanny's First Play*, c. 1914. London: Constable and Company.

Sylwander, L. (2001). *Child impact assessments: Swedish experience of child impact analyses as a tool for implementing the UN Convention on the Rights of the Child*. Stockholm: Ministry of Health and Social Affairs & Ministry for Foreign Affairs.

Theis, J. (1998). Participatory research on child labour in Vietnam. In V. Johnson, E. Ivan-Smith, G. Gordon, P. Pridmore, & P. Scott (Eds.), *Stepping forward: children and young people's participation in the development process* (pp. 81–85). London: Intermediate Technology Publications.

Tomaševski, K. (2001). Indicators. In A. Eide et al. (Eds.), *Economic, social and cultural rights: a textbook* (2nd rev. ed.). Dordrecht: Martinus Nijhoff Publishers.

United for Child Care and Protection (BKTF) Albania (2011). *Report on children's rights in Albania to the UN CRC Committee.* Accessed March 16, 2014, at http://www.crin.org/docs/Albania_United%20for%20Child%20Care%20Protection%20Coalition%20Children's%20Report_CRC.doc.pdf

United Nations (1945). *Charter of the United Nations,* adopted June 26, 1945, entered into force October 24, 1945, as amended.

United Nations (1989). *Convention on the Rights of the Child.* Adopted by the General Assembly November 20, 1989, and entered into force September 2, 1990.

United Nations (2011). *Optional Protocol to the Convention on the Rights of the Child on a communications procedure.* Adopted December 19, 2011, and entered into force April 14, 2014.

United Nations Committee on the Rights of the Child (2009). *General Comment No. 12, The right of the child to be heard.* Adopted July 20, 2009.

United Nations Committee on the Rights of the Child (2013). *Rules of procedure under the Optional Protocol to the Convention on the Rights of the Child on a communications procedure.* Adopted April 8, 2013.

United Nations Committee on the Rights of the Child (2014). Working methods for the participation of children in the reporting process of the Committee on the Rights of the Child. Adopted October 16, 2014.

United Nations Treaty Body Webcast (n.d.). Accessed February 3, 2014, at http://www.treatybodywebcast.org/

UNICEF (1998). *Indicators for global monitoring of child rights: Summary Report— International meeting sponsored by UNICEF, 9-12 February 1998, Geneva, Switzerland.* New York: Division of Evaluation, Policy and Planning, UNICEF.

van Boven, T. (2002). Children's rights are human rights; current issues and developments. In Willems (Ed.), *Developmental and autonomy rights of children: empowering children, caregivers and communities.* Antwerpen; Oxford; New York: Intersentia.

Van Bueren, G. (1998). *The international law on the rights of the child.* Dordrecht: Martinus Nijhoff Publishers.

Van Bueren, G., on behalf of the British Institute of Human Rights, & Reunite: National Council for Abducted Children (1993). *The best interests of the child: international co-operation on child abduction.* London: Queen Mary and Westfield College.

Vel, B., et al. (2011). Together we can do better for Children of Seychelles. Seychelles Alternative Report to the United Nations Committee on the Rights of the Child. Accessed March 17, 2014, at http://www.crin.org/docs/Seychelles_CCYN_CRC_Report.pdf

West, A. (1998). Different questions, different ideas: child-led research and other participation. In V. Johnson, E. Ivan-Smith, G. Gordon, P. Pridmore, & P. Scott (Eds.), *Stepping forward: children and young people's participation in the development process.* London: Intermediate Technology Publications.

Woll, L. (2000). Reporting to the UN Committee on the Rights of the Child: A catalyst for domestic debate and policy change? *International Journal of Children's Rights, 8,* 72.

World Bank (2014). Country and lending groups. Accessed February 28, 2014, at http://data.worldbank.org/about/country-classifications

World Vision (2010). Interview_Hassan. Accessed February 7, 2014, at http://www.youtube.com/watch?v=sNPAf4FvvZE.

CHAPTER 18

Children's Participation in Haiti

BENEDETTA FAEDI DURAMY

INTRODUCTION

The adoption of the United Nations Convention on the Rights of the Child (CRC) has essentially unfolded the concept and practice of child participation, to be intended, generally, as children partaking in an activity and, specifically, as children partaking in decision-making processes related to their lives. In particular, CRC Articles 12 and 13 provide that children, who are capable of forming their own opinions, should be granted the right to freely express them and to have them taken into due account according to their age and maturity. Moreover, children's right of freedom of expression should provide them with the opportunity to "seek, receive and impart information and ideas of all kinds, regardless of frontiers, either orally, in writing or in print, in the form of art, or through any other media of their choice."

Such an increased degree of attention toward children's right to participation has led to its international recognition and support. However, the concept as captured by the CRC is very broad and may refer to a wide range of different practices, including children taking part in activities initiated and facilitated by adults; children being consulted by adults during processes affecting the lives of both; children partaking in civic processes; as well as children independently organizing themselves or facilitating decision-making among other parties of the process. Certainly, all these different practices of child participation have different objectives and implications and may take place in different situations and contexts.

For instance, children's right to participation, however it may be intended, can occur both in the private domain, such as in the family and the household, as well as in the public domain, such as at school, in the larger community, and at the government level. Often the current challenge is to ensure that children's right to participate in such different situations is effectively protected by the enforcement system in line with the domestic and international law provisions. Especially in a developing country like Haiti, and in similar contexts in some African and Latin American countries, children's right to participation is often implemented in a limited and sporadic way, despite the ratification of the CRC by relevant governments.

The goal of this chapter is to provide a summary of current knowledge, policy, and practice about children's right to participation in Haiti. The goal is to highlight themes and issues occurring in a very different context from the ones presented in the other chapters of this volume. The right of children to participate can be very different in situations where they are often victims of abuse and violence both in the domestic sphere and in the public domain. Given the limited literature and research on the concept and practice of child participation in Haiti currently available, this chapter's attempt to summarize the areas in which children do or do not partake in decision-making is mainly supported by empirical evidence. The chapter also highlights the different roles that children play in Haitian society as well as the challenges of the few participatory processes and programs currently in place.

The chapter begins by summarizing the empirical research that supports children's right to participation or lack thereof. It then discusses the socioeconomic context in which children live and their participation should take place. Drawing from the data collected, the chapter also describes the few participatory initiatives adopted in various arenas by some organizations. Such analysis will, it is hoped, provide insights for future research and approaches to be employed in the Haitian context.

THE RESEARCH

The findings presented in this chapter draw from a much bigger empirical study conducted in Haiti between early June 2006 and late December 2008. The objective of the study was to explore the incentives, conditions, and decision-making processes that motivated some girls and women who had been victims of rape and other forms of sexual abuse to join the armed groups, becoming their active affiliates and perpetrators of violence themselves. The goal of such investigation was to suggest effective measures to free girls and women from violence, to encourage their participation in effective forms of community reconciliation, and to improve their reintegration and rehabilitation into society.

The study was informed by a longitudinal fieldwork conducted during twelve months in the three Haitian cities mostly affected by armed violence—Port-au-Prince, Cap-Haitien, and Gonaives. In-depth face-to-face interviews, focus group sessions, and participant observation were held with a heterogeneous sample of informants composed of girls and women, who either had been victims of gender-based violence or had been involved with the armed groups. Representatives of international and civil society organizations as well as members of the judicial, enforcement, and institutional systems working on these issues were also interviewed.[1]

Findings related to children's participation or lack thereof in the private sphere and in the various sectors of the Haitian society were also collected but never previously published (Faedi, 2008, 2010; Faedi Duramy, 2014). This chapter discusses these results corroborated by other gray sources, including working documents, reports from organizations, and newspaper articles.

SOCIOECONOMIC CONTEXT

The different ways in which childhood is defined and constructed are fundamentally influenced by the general living conditions of children, meaning the economic, social, and political contexts in which they are situated. This is certainly true in Haiti, which is the poorest country in the Latin American and Caribbean region and the most disadvantaged of the Western Hemisphere (World Bank, April 27, 2006). About 54 percent of the entire Haitian population of nearly 8 million live below the US$1-a-day poverty line and 78 percent live on less than US$2 a day (World Bank, August 15, 2006).

Not surprisingly, child poverty and lack of education are inextricably connected: only 55 percent of children, for the most part boys, between the ages of 6 and 12 are enrolled in school; and many of them decide to drop out before completing their studies (World Bank, April 27, 2006).

Lack of infrastructure and basic services, including potable water, electricity, and sanitation place further strain on the difficult living conditions of the people residing in the slums and foster their discontent. Persistent indigence and high youth unemployment rate in urban communities beget an environment susceptible to civil unrest and gang activity, where children become orphans, homeless, and later recruited by the armed groups. For girls, often, the gangs represent the foreseeable risk of becoming victims of rape, sexual slavery, and forced prostitution. A recent study conducted by the United Nations Stabilization Mission in Haiti and the United Nations Development Programme in Haiti (2006) indeed assessed that the armed groups are primarily composed of children and young adults between the ages of 10 and 25. Girls may also be involved in the gangs, serving both as combatants as well as partners of members, prostitutes, or sex slaves.

---

1. The research included 150 in-depth interviews, ten focus group sessions with victims living in the slum communities of Port-au-Prince, Gonaives, and Cap-Haitien, and participant observation in support groups for victims.

The massive destruction caused by the 7.0-magnitude earthquake that hit Haiti on January 12, 2010, devastating the capital of the country, Port-au-Prince, and other cities and causing hundreds of thousands of deaths and injured, exacerbated the already ardous conditions for children (Faedi Duramy, 2011). Many of them, who survived the natural disaster but lost their families and homes have been living in wretched conditions in displacement camps, facing sexual violence and other forms of abuse and exploitation (Kristof, 2010). Additionally, the heavy seasonal rains combined with the lack of clean water, sanitation, and hygiene in many spontaneous camps facilitated the spread of cholera, which killed thousands of displaced people, including countless children, by the end of 2010 and the beginning of 2011 (Amnesty International, 2010; Roberts, 2011).

CHILD PARTICIPATION IN THE PRIVATE SPHERE

The way in which childhood is perceived in a society determines the way children can participate at home, at school, and in their larger community. In particular, an analysis of Haitian children's condition inside the household is necessary to explain their roles and power or lack thereof when partaking in or succumbing to decisions made by others in relation to their lives. It is indeed within the household that relations between adults and children are firstly defined by power, authority, and conflict dynamics. Cultural beliefs, traditions, poverty, and violence lead to inequity and imbalanced relationships between family members, which often degenerate into patterns of abuse. Living and "sleeping in Haiti is dangerous" (Maternowska, 2006, p. 46) inside poor and cramped shanties, which often include only one or two rooms, shared by adults and children alike and easily accessible to neighbors or strangers.

Representatives of civil society organizations interviewed for this study agreed that, generally, children's first sexual encounter occurs around the age of 5 or 6, often with relatives or neighbors. A psychologist working for a rape victims' rehabilitation center reported that children are also victims of discrimination, neglect, and concealed incest behind closed doors. Although aggregated data on domestic violence in Haiti are not currently available, findings from a random survey of households in Port-au-Prince revealed that, between 2004 and 2006, 35,000 women were sexually assaulted, half of whom were under the age of 18 (Kolbe & Hutson, 2006).

Abuse and sexual assault of children inside the household represent the product of customary norms of repression against the vulnerable and the inferior. A professor at the University of Port-au-Prince reported that within Haitian social hierarchies, women are ranked as second-class citizens and children are "so at the very bottom of the society that they are not even regarded as such." Participants recalled the popular Haitian proverb "*ti moun se riches pòv malèrè*" (children are the wealth of the poor), stressing the purpose of children to promote the economy of the household. They are expected to carry water, prepare food, wash dishes and clothes, help selling in the markets, and run errands for their families. Representatives of the Ministry for the Status of Women interviewed for this study argued that even poverty in Haiti is gendered: Girls are fed less than their brothers, forced to take on domestic chores, provided with less schooling opportunities and access to medical care.

A professor of sociology at the University of Port-au-Prince shared his thoughts on children's role in the private realm:

> Haitian children don't feel that they are entitled to have any opinions regarding their lives. This is because any decisions concerning them is taken by their parents without consulting them. There is no participation of children in the decision-making processes and no consideration of their feelings. If you mention to parents that they should give their children a say, they look at you as if they had no idea of what you are talking about. There is simply no respect for children in this country and no understanding of what . . . [child participation] means.

Another informant reported that "Haitian parents spend any little money they have to buy school uniforms for their children and they care more to straighten and decorate their hair than to listen to them and to provide for their emotional and educational needs." Representatives of a civil society organization working in the field shared that "adults are scared of their children . . . they are threatened to lose their power inside their homes and . . . don't want them to take part in decisions. This was the way they were raised, and this is the way they raise their children . . . it's the only way they know."

In Haiti the patriarchal conception of children as property generates a specific practice of exploitation: *restavék* ("to stay with" in Creole). Around one out of ten children from 10 to 17 years old are currently exploited to provide domestic work away from their own families (UNICEF, 2006). Girls account for over 75 percent of the 300,000 estimated Haitian children, who have been sent away from their indigent families to serve as domestic helpers in richer households. Desperate parents, especially from rural areas, who live at the economic margins of poverty and cannot feed or send to school their numerous offspring resolve to send their children, in exchange of few *gourdes*[2], to wealthier families residing in urban communities.

In exchange of their domestic help, host families promise to feed, educate, and take care of their *restavéks* However, in most cases, these children end up being malnourished, victims of violence and exploitation, and with very limited possibilities to go to school. The parish priest of a Catholic church in Martissent, a poor neighborhood in Port-au-Prince, who is the director of a specific youth program, reported that *restavéks* "are treated like dogs, sometimes even worse

---

2. Haitian currency (one Haitian *gourde* = US.02).

than dogs in Haiti" (Faedi Duramy, 2014). They often sleep on the floor or standing up if they have misbehaved, eat leftovers, and wear old shreds of clothing. He also added that a further problem encountered by his organization is the lack of birth certificates of most *restavéks,* who, therefore, may, more easily, disappear, or be exploited and enslaved.

The initiative run by the Catholic church of Martissent includes educational and vocational programs for *restavéks.* Representatives of the organization approach employing families and try to negotiate with them to limit the children's work inside the household to the mornings and to give the children the opportunity to attend school or job-training courses in the afternoon for free: "It is a long process convincing these families that *restavéks* have same rights as their own children have . . . We try to explain that *restavéks* want to go to school and learn and that they [employing families] should listen to them and include them in the decisions affecting their future." The program leader stressed the importance of educating families, both birth and employing ones, about the right of children to participate in the decisions related to their departure from their original family and to the services they are expected to give once they arrive in the host family. Indeed, the program leader explained that without giving children the chance to understand the reasons behind their family's decision to send them away and the expectations of the host family, they feel abandoned and unloved. This has enormous consequences on their emotional and psychological development. "No matter how rudimentary and poorly a decision is made, it is still a decision about their life, and children should have the right to participate in the process," he concluded.

Children attending the program also shared their views: "I know my mom is poor but I wish she could have given me the choice . . . to find a job near her, or just another family near her . . . I am so far now that I can never go home. I don't have the money to go home. It is sad that I will not see my home ever again." Another said: "I left my house early in the morning and no one told me where I was going . . . I thought I was going to Port-au-Prince to visit my aunt, but instead I was going to work for strangers." Interviews with children revealed how little information they received at the time of the departure, how much they felt that their feelings and opinions were irrelevant during the process, and how little they knew about what the future was holding for them. To be sure, in relative terms, the *restavéks* attending this program still represent a fortunate sample among the many more who are daily victims of abuse, slavery, and sexual violence and whose destination families were not willing to participate in this initiative.

CHILD PARTICIPATION IN THE PUBLIC DOMAIN

At the time this study was conducted, the United Nations estimated that in the shantytowns of Port-au-Prince, where armed violence among rival gangs was prevalent, an estimated 50 percent of girls had been victims of rape, often by more than one perpetrator (United Nations, 2006).[3] Another recent study on factors influencing youth development in Haiti revealed that 46 percent of girls had been victims of sexual violence (33 percent were between 5 and 9 years of age and 43 percent were between 10 and 14) (Justesen & Verner, 2007). A World Bank study also showed that sexual violence is the most prevalent form of violence in Haiti, affecting 35 percent of women over 15 years of age, with a higher incidence in rural areas (41 percent) than in cities (34 percent) (World Bank, April 27, 2006). Finally, data collected for this study from civil society organizations operating in Port-au-Prince found that among the rape victims, 65 percent were girls between the ages of 3 and 18, and 17 percent were between 19 and 25 years of age (Kay Fanm, 2007; SOFA, 2007). Among the rape cases documented, 53 percent were committed by gangs and 29 percent by more than one of their members.

Girls participating in this study lamented the high level of insecurity in their daily life, which prevented them from walking safely to school, to the market, to medical facilities, and to collect water for their families. One of them explained: "I cannot go to school because many girls have been raped on their way . . . I need to cross another neighborhood to reach my school . . . and there are gangs fighting and raping girls." Another added: "I wish I could be a boy, I always wished I could be a boy. Boys can go to school, can walk around without fear . . . and can have guns to defend themselves too." Informants generally stressed the government's responsibility to guarantee their citizens' protection and equal opportunities for their children. "The state should take care of us . . . protect the children in this country . . . you know, [it should] at least care that its children are safe . . . this is the most important thing, otherwise children will become violent . . . and violence will keep spreading." Another informant shared: "Children are worthless here, especially girls once they are raped. No one cares about victims, no one asks for what they need. The state has nothing for us . . . they do nothing to protect us, nothing to help us."

Many of the excerpts collected referred to the rampant armed violence affecting the slum communities of Port-au-Prince, Cap-Haitien, and Gonaives, where gangs, mostly composed of children and youth between 10 and 25 years old, fight against each other and engage in narcotics trafficking, extortion, and kidnapping (United Nations Stabilization Mission, 2006). In search of protection and social status, girls are also recruited into the armed groups both as partners of gang members and as perpetrators, actively taking part in illicit activities and in violent attacks against the local population or rival groups. Informants of this study

---

3. Given the lack of national aggregated data on gender-based violence in Haiti, it is impossible to estimate the number of victims. The only figures currently available are those provided by individual studies conducted by international and local organizations, as reported in this paragraph.

explained that their involvement in armed violence was a direct response to the corruption of the enforcement system and the shortcomings of the state, which failed to protect them and disregarded their requests for justice, education, support, and participation in the fabric of the society.

Among the many organizations included in this research, only a couple of them had, at the time, specific projects aimed at ensuring the participation of children and youth in decisions affecting their lives. Interviews with a program manager of one of the organizations revealed that the goal of the initiative was to build a dialogue with Haitian authorities to guarantee that children and youth can enjoy equal protection and opportunities, including their fundamental rights to education, leading a healthy life, partaking in decisions affecting them, and developing skills to become active citizens in their communities. The project assembled children into various groups and asked them to express their most urgent needs using drawings, paintings, and other artwork.

The program manager reported that one group created a patchwork of pictures cut out from magazines representing forests and abundant nature, which expressed children's concern for the reforestation of Haiti to prevent flooding and landslides, especially in rural areas as well as in the mountains surrounding cities where shantytowns are often located. Other patchworks included photos from fashion, interior design, and wellness magazines suggesting children's need to conform with social models in terms of health, cleanliness, and beauty. Drawings represented people sitting around a banquet table, suggesting their need for food. Others pictured colorful toys, including balls, balloons, drums, and trumpets, expressing their expectation for leisure and fun. Others depicted houses with proper roofs and front doors as well as family members holding their hands, which revealed children's priorities for safe housing and family bonds and connection. A painting showed a teacher instructing students from the blackboard, with many books all around, telling their desire to go to school and receive an education. The need for freedom, safety, and protection was also extensively represented in the depictions of flying birds in the blue sky and people standing in a circle with open arms. Peace and unity for the country were symbolized by a papier-mâché dove and a quilted Haitian flag.

Informants of this study revealed that children's priorities included safe housing and security, food and sanitation, education, health, leisure and toys, peace, and political stability. Some children also showed a strong sense of community and civic engagement. They were concerned about their country in terms of reforestation, cleanliness of the rivers, electricity, decentralization of the state to better manage diversity in needs and resources, agriculture, and construction of modern houses, schools, and roads to ensure proper transportation and communication between the different regions. "Children are sensitive to their environment and social context [...] they want to help and be part of their communities. They are asking to participate in decision-making which will affect their future as citizens," the informant articulated. Unfortunately, though, the

Haitian government and authorities have not been receptive to the important role that children can play in the public domain. "Our society is not ready to talk about child participation. In fact, it's not even ready to include citizens' participation either," the interviewee concluded with dismay.

Other organizations participating in this study run programs designed to provide education and vocational training to children living in the slums, who are affected by armed violence in many ways. None of them, though, was specifically focused on child participation. However, interviews with representatives of these organizations revealed that children were actively involved in the decisions regarding their enrollment in a specific program or training: "These are important decisions for their future, and we try to accommodate their inclinations and preferences as much as we can . . . given the funding and resources we are working with." When asked why so few organizations operating in Haiti focused on the right of children to participate in processes affecting their lives, informants responded that although child participation is a fundamental right, it was not the priority for most initiatives at that point:

> Children here don't even exist . . . don't have birth certificates . . . they are enslaved, abused, exploited, neglected . . . society does not even conceive that they could have a say . . . and we are trying to change that slowly, as much as we can, but it's hard, we have no funding and very little support. Our philosophy, at this stage, is more about doing concrete things for them [children], like education, employment. . .

To be sure, though, by involving children in the decisions related to their enrollment in the specific programs offered, as well as by encouraging them to participate in projects that include teamwork and group activities, these organizations have indirectly implemented important elements of child participation.

DISCUSSION AND CONCLUSION

The preamble of the Haitian Constitution of 1987 provides that one of its objectives is

> to establish a system of government based on fundamental liberties and the respect for human rights, social peace, economic equity, dialogue and participation of all the people in major decisions affecting the national life, through effective decentralization.

In addition to the constitutional commitment to ensure the participation of its population in national development and local governance, the Haitian government also ratified the CRC in 1995, committing to adopt any measures necessary to implement the right of children to participate under Article 12. However, the findings presented above show that, despite this obligation, children in Haiti are currently prevented from taking part effectively in public life and, generally, are not considered as stakeholders who should be consulted in developing programs or policies. Current national legislators mostly see children as a vulnerable group entitled to protection-oriented rights rather than citizens with their own agency. The bias toward protection is reinforced by the social hierarchies constructing adults' perceptions of children and their value.

To be sure, the socioeconomic conditions in which Haitian youth live raise challenges and inevitably constrain the ways in which they can participate. For instance, in such a context, as described by interviews' excerpts above, the right to education depends on children's access to food and transportation as well as on their right to be safe. Therefore, even if some children have the opportunity to take part in some processes affecting their lives, they may be still unable to do so because other basic rights are not met. Moreover, as proven by the findings reported in this chapter, international and national efforts often prioritize addressing basic needs versus funding participation programs. This strategy, however, underestimates the fact that the participation of children in developing specific programs and services for them is likely to result in better outcomes and a more efficient use of resources.

The conceptualization of childhood and the power dynamics in the relationships between children and adults in Haiti have a significant impact on the opportunities for children and youth to participate in the decision-making processes both in their households and in their community. As revealed by the informants of this study, adults define children's roles in the private realm as much as in the public domain and thus control their ability to express their views, to have their input and opinions taken seriously, and to be able to make or to be consulted in the decisions affecting their lives. The status and power disparities between children and adults entail that the former are not considered independent actors and are rarely if ever involved in decision-making. Cultural norms of authority, obedience, and respect prevent children from speaking up and voicing their opinions or concerns. In contrast to such understanding of childhood, however, children contribute in significant ways to their households by taking care of younger siblings and doing domestic chores, fetching water and food, and earning part of the family income. However, these abilities don't seem to be enough to convince adults of their ability to contribute also to the decision-making processes both in private and public domains. Finally, gender bias also creates disparities in the opportunities provided to boys versus girls, confining the latter to the domestic sphere and to very little access to basic rights as well as to participate in the few programs run by organizations.

On the other hand, some informants have acknowledged that adults struggle to understand and support initiatives designed to empower children to participate because they are the first to not being able to participate in the society. Thus, raising awareness among them can lead to concrete positive changes, as suggested by the program run by the Catholic church in Martissent, which convinced host families of *restavéks* to enroll them in the program. As highlighted by the data, international, national, and civil society organizations have mostly focused on children and young people living in the slums, who have already been or are at risk of being victims and/or recruited by violent gangs that engage in narcotics trafficking, kidnapping, and armed confrontations. The work of these organizations, which used participatory methods such as expressive forms, on the one hand, can encourage children and young people to reflect on, portray, and recreate their social reality, and, on the other hand, it can help the society itself to understand children and young people's needs and comprehend how they perceive their communities.

The analysis above has showed that socioeconomic conditions and the interdependence of children's rights in Haiti determine the lack of opportunities for children and young people to participate in their everyday life at home and beyond. Multiple exclusions because of gender, poverty, cultural norms, and inequality should be considered when discussing and designing participatory processes and measures. Moreover, when thinking about opportunities for children to participate, it is important to reflect also on the role of social hierarchies in Haiti. This means that initiatives supporting child participation should consider both the relationship between children and other social actors and the sociopolitical and economic context, which largely influences the other kinds of environments—the home, the local community and the state—in which children live. Thus, in the Haitian context the possibility for children to participate in decisions affecting their life is highly constrained by societal forces, cultural conceptions of childhood, gender bias, and status and power disparities between children and adults. These factors should be taken into consideration when facilitating participatory processes or assessing the ones already in place.

REFERENCES

Amnesty International (2010). *Haiti: after the earthquake, initial mission findings,* 7. Available at http://www.amnesty.org

Cadet, J-R. (1998). *Restavec: from Haitian slave child to middle-class American.* Austin: Texas University Press.

Constitution of Haiti (1987). Preamble. Available at https://www.constituteproject.org/constitution/Haiti_2012.pdf

Faedi, B. (2008). The double weakness of girls: discrimination and sexual violence in Haiti. *Stanford Journal of International Law, 44*(1), 147.

Faedi, B. (2010). From violence against women to women's violence in Haiti. *Columbia Journal of Gender and Law, 19*, 1029–1075.

Faedi Duramy, B. (2011). Women in the aftermath of the 2010 Haitian earthquake. *Emory International Law Review, 25*(3), 1193–1215.

Faedi Duramy, B. (2012). Gender-based violence, help seeking, and criminal justice recourse in Haiti. In T. St. Germain and S. Dewey (Eds.), *Conflict-related sexual violence: international law, local responses* (pp. 103–119). Sterling, VA: Kumarian Press/Stylus.

Faedi Duramy, B. (2014). *Gender and violence in Haiti—women's path from victims to agents.* New Brunswick, NJ: Rutgers University Press.

Justesen, M., & Verner, D. (2007*). Factors impacting youth development in Haiti.* World Bank Policy Research Working Paper 4110. Washington, DC: World Bank.

Kay Fanm (2007). *Violence envers les femmes et les filles—Bilan de l'année 2006 [Violence against women and girls—Assessment of 2006].* Port-au-Prince: Author.

Kolbe, R. A., & Hutson, R. A. (2006). Human rights abuse and other criminal violations in Port-au-Prince, Haiti: a random survey of households. *Lancet, 368,* 864–873.

Kristof, N. D. (2010, Dec. 1). Haiti, nearly a year later. *New York Times.*

Maternowska, M. C. (2006). *Reproducing inequities: poverty and the politics of population in Haiti.* New Brunswick, NJ: Rutgers University Press.

Moses, S. (2008). Children and participation in South Africa: an overview. *International Journal of Children's Rights, 16,* 327–342.

Roberts, M. (2011, March 15). Haiti cholera "far worse than expected," experts fear. *BBC News Health.*

SOFA (2007). *Rapport bilan IV, cas de violence accueillis et accompagnés dans les centres douvanjou de la SOFA de juillet à decembre 2006 [Assessment report IV, cases of violence received and accompanied by the SOFA centers from July to December 2006].* January. Port-au-Prince: Author.

Sommerfelt, T. (2002). *Report to UNICEF, ILO, Save the Children UK, and Save the Children Canada.* Oslo: Fafo Institute for Applied International Studies.

Table de Concertation Nationale sur les Violences specifiques faites aux Femmes et leur Prise en Charge, Rapport De Commission De Collecte De Données, 8, November 2005.

Thomas, N. (2007). Towards a theory of children's participation. *International Journal of Children's Rights, 15,* 199–218.

United Nations Convention on the Rights of the Child, adopted November 20. 1989, G.A. Res. 44/25, U.N. GAOR 44th Sess., Supp. No. 49, U.N. Doc. A/44/49 1989, entered into force September 2, 1990. Available at http://www.ohchr.org/en/professionalinterest/pages/crc.aspx

United Nations General Assembly Security Council (2006, Oct. 26). *Children and armed conflict—report of the Secretary General.* U.N. DOC No. A/61/529-S/2006/826.

United Nations International Children's Emergency Fund (UNICEF). (2006, March). *Child alert: Haiti.*

United Nations Stabilization Mission in Haiti (MINUSTAH) & United Nations Development Programme in Haiti (UNDP) (2006). *The situation of women in the context of armed violence In Haiti.*

World Bank, Haiti (2006, April 27). *Social resilience and state fragility in Haiti, a country social analysis.* Report No. 36069-HT.

World Bank, Republic of Haiti (2006, August 15). *Enhanced heavily indebted poor countries (Hipc) initiative, preliminary document.* Report No. 36917.

CHAPTER 19

Conclusion

From Social Exclusion to Child-Inclusive Policies: Toward an Ecological Model of Child Participation

TALI GAL

INTRODUCTION

The right to participate in decision-making processes is a widely accepted international human right of children today. The United Nations Convention on the Rights of the Child (CRC), with its nearly universal acceptance, has been instrumental in shifting the perception of children from objects of protection to subjects with individual rights. The participation right is arguably the one representing most vividly this shift in the social construction of children because it requires parents, guardians, educators, social workers, and leaders to consider the perspectives of children and assign due weight to their views, even when they assumingly represent the children's best interests. At the same time, the participation right also reflects the relational meaning of rights promoted by the CRC. Rather than dictating their wishes or submitting their views unilaterally, the CRC requires that children be included in a dialogue, a mutual exchange of views, feelings, and thoughts.

Indeed, as the acme of the perception of children as relational right holders, the right of children to participate has created a need to search for new and innovative joint decision-making processes. Accordingly, since the acceptance of the CRC in 1989, the meaning of the participation right and the ways it can be implemented have been deliberated by academics, advocates, service providers, and policymakers. This book aims at contributing to the debate on child participation by putting together a collection of different experiments, programs, and projects that sought to explore the ways children and adults experience child participation. The chapters in this book describe the ways children and youth take part in decision-making processes in education, child protection, family disputes, criminal justice, research, and policymaking. They present actual experiences led by the various authors in Canada, the United States, Scotland, Ireland, Britain, Australia, New Zealand, Israel, and Haiti. They are based on different methodologies, including quantitative, qualitative, action, archival, and theoretical research. They illuminate the difficulties in implementing meaningful child participation as well as its advantages, and they provide thoughtful insights as to possible ways to achieve child-inclusive participatory processes.

This concluding chapter has two goals. The first is to outline the general themes emerging from this rich, diverse, informative collection of chapters. The second is to extend from these emerging themes, as well as from the cumulative knowledge presented in the book as a whole, an ecological model of child participation.

Beginning with the first goal, the paragraphs below outline five broad themes emerging from the various experiences presented in this book: the need for *legislation*; the importance of *promoting participation among professionals*; the challenge of shifting from *token to inclusive participation*; the need for *managing expectations*; and an understanding of participation as *relational*.

THE IMPORTANCE OF LEGISLATION

There is clear evidence that for child participation to become routine, there is a need for specific legislation making it the default option or at a minimum a preferred policy. When the involvement of children is embedded in a legislated children's rights framework, children are more likely to participate regularly. Without such legislation, participatory encounters are more likely to remain marginal (see Chapters 2, 5, 6, 7, 9, 10, 17, and 18). For instance, in Chapter 5, Aisling Parkes' comparison of children's involvement in family courts in Ireland and New Zealand provides a vivid example of the impact of participatory legislation. Lacking a mandatory provision on child participation, adults act as gatekeepers in family courts in Ireland, in contrast with the more structured participatory regime in New Zealand, where judicial interviews are routine. In Chapter 6, Nicholas Bala, Rachel Birnbaum, and Francine Cyr found a similar trend in Canada, where judicial interviews of children are more common in Quebec than in other provinces due to legislation making a judicial interview a right of children in family courts. Naturally, the content of the legislation affects its impact. Concrete guidelines regarding desired legislative provisions appear in the UN General Comment 12 (2009). The significance of the chapters here in this regard lies in their clear overall empirical validation of the importance of legislation regulating child participation.

PROMOTING PARTICIPATION THROUGH THE THREE E'S: EXPERIENCE, EXPOSURE, AND EDUCATION

Legislation, however, is only a first step toward greater use of participatory practices with children. Across various arenas and jurisdictions, adults emerge as key gatekeepers as well as facilitators of children's participation. Adults' perceptions of children as incapable of making decisions (Chapter 11), professionals' disbelief in their own ability to talk with children (Chapter 6), their fear of the emotional burden they themselves might endure (Chapter 7), or their perception of participation as potentially harmful for children (Chapter 11) act as barriers against the use of participatory practices. In school settings, adult advisors to school councils were found to be key to their success as well as their failure (Chapter 16). Chapters 2 and 3, discussing the involvement of children with special needs in school-related decision committees in Israel and Ontario, Canada, demonstrated that without structured participation of children in decision committees, their level of participation depends largely on their parents' support of their involvement. In research, the ability of children to become lead researchers was similarly dependent on academics' willingness to cede power to children and to create participatory environments for them (Chapter 4). The extent to which policymakers perceive themselves as possessing the relevant skills for speaking with children also emerged as a key challenge to participation (Chapter 15). It seems, then, that to mainstream child participation there is a need to address professionals' reluctance to involve children while making decisions affecting their lives. Three key avenues may address professionals' reluctance, and they might be titled the "three E's": Education, Experience, and Exposure. Once they are introduced to one or more of these elements, professional reluctance gradually faded. This was found true for judges (Chapters 5, 6, and 7), social workers and therapists (Chapters 6, 8, and 11), educators (Chapter 2 and 3), and policymakers (Chapters 15, 16, and 17). Education does not necessarily mean formal training, although such training may be effective in many instances. The "action research" conducted by Anne Graham, Robyn Fitzgerald, and Judith Cashmore (Chapter 11) in Australia involving family service professionals illustrates the effectiveness of a joint learning process, as opposed to "coerced teaching," in implementing change among professionals' perceptions about children, childhood, and participation. Chapter 7, by Tamar Morag and Yoa Sorek, describes experimental child participation mechanisms in family courts in Israel and illustrates the value of experience as well as exposure. Child participation rates rose as professionals gained practice and conviction, demonstrating the importance of professionals' experience in recruiting parents, judges, and children themselves to child participation. But beyond the experience of those involved in the pilot project, exposure to the new participatory practice percolated sideways, among colleagues from different courts, and initiated change. Following the pilot project in two jurisdictions, staff members of the social service units in family courts in other parts of Israel voluntarily began to provide children with the opportunity to fulfill their participatory right even before the national regulations entered into force. Similarly, in Canada, once exposed to the positive experience of interviewing children in Quebec, judges in other provinces became more supportive of judicial interviewing of children (see Chapter 6). It seems, then, that initial education followed by hands-on experience may enhance professionals' willingness to engage in participatory practices; broader exposure to such pioneering practices may extend child participation beyond local initiatives to create a culture of child participation.

From Token to Inclusive Participation

Beyond reluctance, resistance is another reaction manifested by professionals who do not embrace a children's rights philosophy. Often perceptions of children as inferior, incapable, and "yet-to-become" full persons coincide with conscientious as well as unconscious fears of ceding power (Chapter 1). When faced with expectations to involve children in decision-making processes, such professionals frequently involve children in "tokenistic" participation, as demonstrated in many of the studies presented in the book. Sharon Bessell in Chapter 8 draws attention to social workers who don't even know the names of the out-of-home children they are formally in contact with. In Chapter 13 Emily Buss, describing youth court practices in the United States, colorfully portrays young offenders being invited to speak in court without having any impact on the outcomes—as if "the judge had invited the young person to sing an aria." Kay Tisdall, in Chapter 16, demonstrates token participation of children in elections for school councils in Scotland, where formal invitations for all children to participate are topped by informal, selective invitations for "preferred" children to run for councils. Mona Paré's study (Chapter 2) revealed that when children attended special education placement meetings in Ontario they were "talked about in the third person," and Eran Uziely (Chapter 3) similarly describes minimal participation of pupils in Israeli special education committees. Both Chapters 15 and 16 present evidence that when children's participation platforms are separated from those of adults, children's participation is more likely to be tokenistic and to lack any impact, whereas joint projects have the potential of being more influential on policy. Another version of child participation that is not grounded in a children's rights framework is instrumentalized participation—emerging when the involvement of children is used as a mechanism to assist decision makers in "hard cases" (Chapter 7) or as an instrument to challenge parents' views (Chapter 2).

Token participation may be more problematic than nonparticipation because the invitation to participate creates expectations that remain unfulfilled (Chapter 17). Children easily detect false invitations and empty statements. In Chapter 15,

Marshall, Byrne and Lundy analyze direct contacts between children and policy-makers in Northern Ireland, illustrating children's highly developed skills to spot such token participation. When they identify tokenism, children feel frustrated, angry, or disappointed (see Chapters 8, 15, and 17). In contrast, when children are met with genuine interest in what they have to say, they feel "important" (Chapter 9) and "influential" (Chapter 15); they are satisfied with the process and feel happy about "having their voice heard" (Chapters 2, 6, 7, 8, 9, 14, and 15). Indicators of genuine interest, according to the children interviewed by Marshall, Byrne, and Lundy in Chapter 15, include eye contact, raising relevant questions, follow-ups, and the presence of an agency representative with actual decision-making power.

The challenge, then, goes beyond structuring participation into decision-making processes. There is a need to encourage a "culture of inclusiveness" (Chapters 8, 9, and 13) in which inclusive participatory encounters with children occur regularly. Legislation may authorize professionals to conduct participatory encounters; the "three E's" approach may address professionals' reluctance; and ongoing enculturation toward inclusive participation may reduce resistance and enhance child-inclusive participation. A child-inclusive process is, arguably, one that regards children as active, equally respected partners in it. It is inspired by the concept of inclusion in the context of children (and adults) with special needs (see Chapter 2). "Inclusion" in that context calls for the promotion of environments that meet the diverse needs of everybody. A child-inclusive process therefore suggests that all participatory mechanisms should be designed according to the specific needs of each child. Although children as young as 3 and 4 are potentially capable of expressing their views, intentions, and difficulties, they rely on a child-inclusive process that uses ways of involving them as partners in the process, in accordance with their specific age, needs, abilities, and wishes. Adults committed to child inclusiveness develop their abilities to listen to children and understand their messages. Furthermore, they are attentive to them and respect their views not only during the process but also before it, while making the decision regarding the form of participation.

What lessons can we learn about ways to make child participation inclusive, meaningful, and genuine? The UN Committee General Comment on child participation (2009) specifies nine basic requirements that offer initial guidance. According to the General Comment, participatory encounters with children must be transparent and informative; voluntary; respectful, relevant; child-friendly; inclusive; supported by training; safe; and accountable. Many of the chapters in the book provide further evidence-based insights as to existing structures that promote significant child participation.

In the public policy sphere, Marshall, Byrne, and Lundy in Chapter 15 identify ways these nine requirements may be implemented in face-to-face encounters with policymakers. Four of these requirements—transparent, respectful, relevant, and accountable—are recognized as crucial. The authors suggest that if policymakers cannot ensure their adherence, they should avoid direct interactions and use indirect consultations instead. The Young People's Advisory Group that was established for their research provides an example of meaningful involvement of youth in research. Extensive efforts were made to make young people feel sufficiently confident to speak freely. The advisory group met in places and at times according to the participants' availability, and the research was designed together with them so that the research questions, methodology, data analysis and interpretation of the data were not adult-oriented. Chapter 4, by Nigel Thomas, describes joint research projects in Wales and similarly identifies some helpful methods of promoting adult–child research partnerships.

In Chapter 16, Tisdall's discussion on time and space in the context of child participation in school leadership as well as in national decision-making provides another perspective toward inclusive participation in public matters, supported by findings in other chapters. First, the *timing* of children's involvement may affect their ability to meaningfully participate: a last-minute consultation might be experienced as pointless (Chapter 15), but too early a consultation might also be futile and theoretical in nature. Second, the *length* of the consultation is a matter of concern. Exceedingly long processes may be difficult for young children or may become irrelevant if they last until children age out of minority (Chapter 17), but rushed meetings also reflect disrespect for the child (Chapters 8 and 13). Lack of adequate time for the various stages of children's participation emerged as a third obstacle in Tisdall's study on school councils: Many pupils pointed to the fact that insufficient time was dedicated for council members to consult their home class before and after school council meetings, preventing the class representatives from actually representing their peers. Inadequate time allocation was similarly identified as problematic for youth involvement in the various stages of research (Chapter 4). Fourth, the meeting's *scheduling* needs to be selected with children's accessibility in mind (Chapters 4 and 15) as well as their other commitments (Chapter 16). Tisdall found that schools differed in their level of willingness to adjust the timing of school council meetings according to children's schedules and other commitments, reflecting different levels of child inclusiveness. And fifth, relating to *continuity,* both Tisdall (Chapter 16) and Marhall, Byrne, and Lundy (Chapter 15) identify "peaks" in children affecting public policy in specific matters, contrasted with sustainable inclusion of children in public policy formation, which is still lacking in Northern Ireland and Scotland. Positive experiences of child participation linked with adults' effort to adjust the length, timing, scheduling, or continuity of decision-making processes appeared in Chapter 9 by Hall, Pennell, and Rikard, which described recurring family meetings with foster children in North Carolina; in Chapter 3 by Uziely, which highlighted the success of reconvened meetings in terms of pupils' ability to actively participate; and in Chapter 8 by Bessell, which identified continuing relationships between Australian out-of-home children and their social workers as enabling genuine participation.

In individual legal procedures, while there are findings supporting the merits of child participation in adversarial processes (Chapters 6, 7, 12, and 13), there are inherent obstacles for meaningful participation in adversarial contexts. Both Parkes (Chapter 5) and Bala, Birnbaum, and Cyr (Chapter 6) identify formal family law proceedings as challenging child participation: To make children feel comfortable expressing their feelings and wishes, encounters should be private and informal; however, such private and informal conversations potentially jeopardize the rights of the litigants, who want to have their representative present and be able to appeal. In juvenile justice, Buss in Chapter 13 highlights the structural incentives for prosecutors and defense attorneys to collaborate, ensuring speedy and smooth processes at the expense of youths' ability to engage meaningfully. By contrast, it seems that nonadversarial fora create natural environments for meaningful child participation. Based on shared decision-making ideology, they facilitate dialogue and nondominated discussion between children and adults. In particular, practices inspired by restorative justice systematize group discussions in which family members play key roles in making decisions. Social, generational, and gender-based disadvantages may be balanced by involving support people and using a strengths-based approach. In line with previous studies, some of the chapters in the book demonstrate the success of restorative practices in involving children in meaningful ways: in North Carolina's child and family team meetings involving foster youth (Chapter 9); in Vermont's family group conferences involving at-risk or offending youths (Chapter 10); and in Hawai'i's reentry circles involving children of incarcerated parents (Chapter 14). Arguably, the success of such restorative practices in involving young participants lies in their ability to adjust according to the children's specific needs, wishes, and capabilities. Their success may also result from their emphasis on the contribution of children's natural support systems, providing approximated, enhanced replications of daily intrafamilial decision-making processes.

Finally, elsewhere (Gal, 2011) I proposed eight heuristics for inclusive child participation. They were drawn from an analysis of the various needs of victimized children, specified in the psychosocial literature, as well as from their internationally recognized rights stipulated by the CRC. In a nutshell, the eight heuristics are as follows:

1. Children should be treated holistically instead of addressing the current problem in isolation.
2. Tailor-made processes should be designed to enable children to participate in the most comfortable setting for them.
3. Children should be treated as partners during the process, acknowledging their irreplaceable role in the discussion.
4. Participation should be considered as a continuum, starting from an informed decision not to participate and ending in full and equal participation.

5. Adults are responsible to "liberate children's voices," to find ways to faithfully decipher children's messages.
6. Adults should "let go" and allow children to take calculated risks while taking the needed precautions to prevent harm.
7. A deliberative, empowering, restorative process should be seen as a goal in itself rather than a mere instrument to reach a decision.
8. When relevant, child representation should provide children with an experience of "empowering advocacy" rather than one of disempowerment.

The chapters in this book provide important empirical validation for these heuristics, extending their relevance beyond child victimization and thus making them more robust: *holism* (Chapters 10 and 11); *tailor-made process* (Chapters 2 and 16); *children as partners* (Chapters 4, 12, and 14), *participation as a continuum* (Chapters 5 and 7), *liberating children's voices* (Chapters 6 and 7), *"let go" approach* (Chapters 3 and 11), *restorative process as a goal* (Chapters 9, 10, and 14), and *empowering advocacy* (Chapters 8, 9, 13, and 15).

Managing Expectations

An important theme emerging from children's testimonies is the need to manage children's expectations of the participatory process beforehand. This is particularly relevant in areas where token participation is likely to occur. But even when professionals are not particularly resistant to meaningful participation, it might be worthwhile to understand what children consider as fruitful participation. Typically, children do not consider making the final decision as their priority; rather, they want adults to listen to them continually and respectfully. This was particularly evident in individual decision-making processes such as in child protection and among at-risk children (Chapters 8, 10, and 13) as well as in family disputes (Chapters 6 and 7). But even modest expectations to simply be heard often prove unrealistic. In Chapter 13 by Buss, the gap between children's expectations to have their day in court and the reality of a rushed assembly line was particularly evident. In Chapter 18 by Faedi Duramy, girls who were sent away as domestic workers expressed disappointment that they were not given an opportunity to suggest alternatives, such as being sent to families who live closer to their own.

However, it is important not to assume that in all matters, children care only about being listened to and being taken seriously. In public matters in particular, children's motivation might come from a desire to actually "make a difference" (Chapters 15, 16, and 17). When children are told their engagement would result in policy change or that it might affect the decision regarding their own situation, they will be disappointed when their involvement fails to achieve this outcome. In Chapter 16, Tisdall's study on pupil councils in Scottish schools identified a gap between pupils' and teachers' expectations. While many pupils were focused on making a difference and achieving outcomes, teachers considered the process as the focal point of the school council, to the point that some explicitly stated that they were willing to trade off some outcomes in order to gain pupils' engagement in the process. Chapter 4 by Thomas more implicitly suggests that while research projects co-managed with children may often be irrelevant for policymakers, children gain from the process itself. It remains to be explored whether young researchers are aware of this gap between their own and the adult researchers' expectations. In Chapter 17, Collins' examination of the involvement of children in monitoring the implementation of the CRC reveals that children are frequently disappointed by the limited effect they actually have compared with their expectations from national and international monitoring proceedings.

Relational Participation

Finally, the one element that emerges as central for children to feel involved, heard, and considered is some form of a relationship with the relevant adults. Children value continued and respectful contact based on personal acquaintance and genuine interest; they react with resentment, disengagement, or indifference to encounters that lack these qualities. Participation for youth means, more than anything, being a part of a dialogue and a community, feeling as if they are involved and they belong. Children and young people want to be able to agree, object, change their mind, and then change it again; they want to be supported and listened to while they contemplate options or express inconsistent views. Children's yearning for meaningful relationships with the adults making decisions affecting their lives, appearing repeatedly in the various chapters, validates the conceptualization of children's rights as relational (Chapter 1). Chapter 8, by Bessell, captures most explicitly children's wishes to have meaningful relationships with adults, and specifically with the social workers who regularly make decisions regarding their out-of-home care. They wanted their social workers to remember their names, their birthdays, their hobbies, and their preferred places for meetings; they hoped to see the same social worker at every scheduled appointment; and they appreciated any expressions of personal interest in them.

The centrality of youth's relationships with their peers was highlighted by Kohm's portrayal in Chapter 12 of teen courts and of their potential to promote youth's self-respect. In Chapter 13 Buss envisions a developmentally sensitive juvenile justice system, highlighting that children learn best how to participate in decision-making processes when they are supported by adults. This support may be achieved either through their natural environment or, when absent, by professionals. She considers problem-solving courts as inspirational for such adult-supported processes because they structure continuing relationships between defendants and judges. In the child protection context, Buss describes the Benchmark Hearing Program at the Cook County Circuit Court Child Protection Division. The judge develops a relationship with the youth (foster children aged 16 and over), aiming to "address the relationship void" experienced by foster children. While such a relationship cannot be as intimate as family or peer relationships, the judge strives to develop it to the maximum extent possible. Buss sees direct dialogue, based on a continuing relationship between juvenile offenders and judges inspired by these examples, as one of the desired goals for reform in the American juvenile justice system.

Another direction for reform is the development of restorative justice–based programs, which consider children's personal relationships as paramount for their resiliency and therefore structure the involvement of family members and friends in the decision-making processes. The emphasis on a relational perspective was evident in the child and family team meetings program for foster youth in North Carolina (Chapter 9); in family group conferences in Vermont for at-risk children (Chapter 10); and in Hawaii's reentry circles with children of incarcerated parents (Chapter 14).

In the public sphere, the findings by Marshall, Byrne, and Lundy in Chapter 15 as well as Tisdall's (Chapter 16) regarding the "humanizing effect" of direct dialogue suggest that only through face-to-face consultations may there be some form of relationships between young people and policymakers that promote youth's ability to influence policy.

The next section builds on these five general emerging themes: the need for *legislation*; the importance of *promoting participation among professionals*; the challenge of shifting from *token to inclusive participation*; the need for *managing expectations*; and an understanding of participation as *relational*. Based on these themes as well as the overall accumulated knowledge of the book's chapters, this section provides a more general perspective of the various factors affecting child participation. To do so in a meaningful way it develops an ecological model that maps the multiple layers of elements affecting child participation (Fig. 19.1).

AN ECOLOGICAL MODEL OF PARTICIPATION

The form, level, and effectiveness of child participation are affected, first and foremost, by the specific circumstances of the case. These include the type of the specific decision—whether it will affect the child only or others as well. Public policy matters differ from individual decisions, among other things, by the number of people affected. Individual decisions about the child's educational setting differ from individual decisions about residency because in the latter other family members are directly affected. The characteristics of the case also refer to the specific forum for participation, be it a court, the school, the family, a social work professional setting, or policymakers. The specific child's characteristics, such as

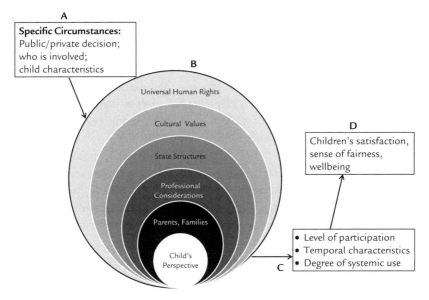

Figure 19.1:
Elements Affecting Child Participation.

age, gender, level of development, and cognitive and emotional qualities, can also be considered as "independent variables" that influence child participation.

Other factors that shape the level, form, and effectiveness of child participation are situated in the various circles around the individual child, beginning with his or her subjective and current perspective: Does the child trust the decision makers or other adults involved in the process? Does the child have strong opinions, feelings, or wishes regarding the decision at hand? Does the child want to have a voice in the process, and to what extent does the child wish to have a sense of control over the process? These factors are amenable according to the ways children are prepared for the process (short-term efforts) and educated (long-term efforts). Trust can be built, opinions and wishes can be actively sought, and a sense of control may be developed through ongoing encouragement and specific preparation. Low self-esteem can be a critical barrier to participation, as children can develop coping mechanisms such as being silent and obedient. Indeed, focusing on children's strengths rather than their vulnerabilities and weaknesses may increase their trust in themselves and enhance their motivation to take an active role in the process.

The immediate circle supporting children and potentially enhancing their participation is that of the parents and family. Parents that regularly involve their children in decisions-making processes provide opportunities for children to develop and practice their participation skills. Parents may also act as their children's advocates, insisting on a participatory process when decisions affecting their children's lives are made. And in cases where the child is invited to participate in a decision-making process outside the family, parents may encourage a reluctant child to appear and take an active role in the process; they may support their child throughout the process and assist them in making their voice heard. By contrast, parents unsupportive of child-participation may discourage, prohibit, or simply fail to assist children when their participation becomes relevant in forums outside the family. To increase parental support toward child participation parents may be educated to assist their children in practicing their participation rights, as suggested by CRC Article 5.

Child participation is also affected by professional considerations. The personal skills of the professionals involved in the decision-making process, their subjective feelings of possessing such skills, and their moral standing regarding child participation all affect the level and effectiveness of children's participation in professionally led decision-making processes. The skills, moral inclinations, and self-confidence of professionals are, in turn, influenced by the availability of appropriate training or sensitization to children's rights and needs, the existence of pilot projects or other hands-on experiences, and time and budgetary limitations. The emerging themes of promoting participation through the three E's and of the need for inclusive participation are particularly relevant in affecting this tier of professionals' variables.

Professionals do not work in a vacuum nor are they influenced solely by their internal organizational training. Their work and ability to involve children in decision-making processes is heavily influenced by state structures. States provide laws, regulations, and guidelines that shape substantive law, procedures, and professional behaviors. As such, they determine whether decision-making processes would be adversarial or deliberative (and restorative) in nature, who may participate in them, and how they will be facilitated. The practice of North Carolina family team meetings is an example of a systemic use of deliberative decision-making processes in the context of child protection. Without a regulatory regime that requires, encourages, or at least enables child-inclusive processes, it is difficult to imagine the systemic use of such practices.

Legal structures as well as on-the-ground practices are influenced, however, by cultural values and norms. There are cultural differences between societies and communities relating to the social status of children of various ages and the roles of extended family and parents in raising them. Communities and societies also differ in their perceptions of childhood and the meanings of responsibility, capability, and rights. Such social constructions affect the inclination of various communities to allow child participation and the level and quality of such participation.

Finally, beyond cultural, jurisdictional, organizational, familial, and individual differences, child participation is affected by universal human rights and principles. Without the CRC, children's participation in decision-making processes would have not penetrated the public discourse nor would have it become a matter of academic research. While there are disparities in the ways children's rights are understood and enforced, child participation is accepted, at least on the declarative level, across the globe.

According to the suggested model, the specific circumstances (A) together with the six tiers of ecological variables (B) affect children's participation in three interrelated parameters (C):

1. The level of participation: Is the decision-making process "adult-centric," where the child is invited to state his or her opinion and then leave (consultation)? Or is it based on genuine dialogue and joint decision making (deliberation)? Or does it enable the child to make the decision (choice)?
2. The temporal elements of participation: Are children involved in decision-making processes in a single event (one-off)? Is there continuity in their involvement (ongoing)? Are they invited to take part irregularly (peaks)? Or is there a recurring child-participation mechanism (regular)?
3. The degree of systemic use: Are participatory mechanisms used as the default option? Are they practiced only in complex cases/simple cases? Do children participate only in exceptional cases? Or is child participation nonexistent in the formal system?

Finally, children's ability to participate regularly, meaningfully, and systemically, in turn, arguably affects their sense of fairness, satisfaction, and well-being (D).

The model as a whole calls for empirical validation, but significant parts of it are based on the findings presented in this book. Ideally, the model will contribute to the theoretical understanding of the multilayered system of variables affecting child participation, as well as to the promotion of meaningful, inclusive, systemic use of participatory decision-making processes with children.

REFERENCES

Gal, T. (2011). *Child victims and restorative justice: a needs–rights model.* New York, NY: Oxford University Press.

UN Committee on the Rights of the Child (2009). *General Comment No. 12, The right of children to be heard.* Accessed November 7, 2013, at http://www2.ohchr.org/english/bodies/crc/docs/AdvanceVersions/CRC-C-GC-12.doc

INDEX